# Simulation in Computer Network Design and Modeling:

## Use and Analysis

Hussein Al-Bahadili
*Petra University, Jordan*

**Information Science**
**REFERENCE**

| | |
|---|---|
| Managing Director: | Lindsay Johnston |
| Senior Editorial Director: | Heather Probst |
| Book Production Manager: | Sean Woznicki |
| Development Manager: | Joel Gamon |
| Development Editor: | Myla Harty |
| Acquisitions Editor: | Erika Gallagher |
| Typesetters: | Chris Shearer |
| Cover Design: | Nick Newcomer, Greg Snader |

Published in the United States of America by
Information Science Reference (an imprint of IGI Global)
701 E. Chocolate Avenue
Hershey PA 17033
Tel: 717-533-8845
Fax: 717-533-8661
E-mail: cust@igi-global.com
Web site: http://www.igi-global.com

Library of Congress Cataloging-in-Publication Data


Library of Congress Cataloging-in-Publication Data
Simulation in computer network design and modeling: use and analysis / Hussein Al-Bahadili, editor.
     p. cm.
  Includes bibliographical references and index.
   ISBN 978-1-4666-0191-8 (hardcover) -- ISBN 978-1-4666-0192-5 (ebook) --
ISBN 978-1-4666-0193-2 (print & perpetual access) 1. Computer networks--
Design and construction. I. Al-Bahadili, Hussein.
  TK5105.7.S563 2012
  004.6'5011--dc23
                                    2011042027


British Cataloguing in Publication Data
A Cataloguing in Publication record for this book is available from the British Library.

*To my wife, daughters, and son with love and appreciation.*

# Editorial Advisory Board

# Table of Contents

**Chapter 24**

*Ali Maqousi, Petra University, Jordan*
*Tatiana Balikhina, Petra University, Jordan*

# Detailed Table of Contents

Chapter 1, "Modeling and Simulation of Game Applications in Ad Hoc Wireless Networks Routing," presents a game theory based routing algorithm, which defines the best route based on the power consumption that each intermediate node will suffer to forward a packet, the price the destination will pay to the source, and the amount of compensation the source will pay to each intermediate node. The chapter also presents a polynomial time algorithm that can give a Nash Equilibrium path and use it to evaluate the performance of the game. The key features of the introduced mechanism are: it uses the first and second price auctions; the auction mechanism insures a fare allocation of the data to the user who values it the most; the second-price sealed-bid auction gives better revenue to the source when compared to the random allocation scheme and the first-price sealed-bid mechanism; the game mechanism combines both source compensation to the intermediate nodes and the power consumption to improve the path reliability between the source and the destination (i.e. the winning bidder); the source payoff will increase once the network density increases; and, finally, the simulation results prove that the introduced auction mechanism dramatically increases the destination's revenue whether he decide to choose the first or second-price auction.

Chapter 2, "Simulating Game Applications in Mobile IPv6 Protocol," proposes a novel game-based green interface/network selection mechanism, which is an extension to the multi-interface fast-handover MIPv6 protocol. It works when the mobile node has more than one wireless interface. The mechanism controls the handover decision process by deciding whether a handover is needed or not and helps the node to choose the right access point at the right time. What's more, the mechanism switches the mobile nodes interfaces "ON" and "OFF" when needed to control the mobile node's energy consumption and improves the handover latency.

## Chapter 3

*Alexander Garcia D., Universidad Autonoma de Occidente, Colombia,*

*Lina Escobar P., Universidad Autonoma de Occidente, Colombia*

*Andres Navarro C., Universidad ICESI, Colombia*

*Fabio G. Guerrero, Universidad del Valle, Colombia*

*Enrique Stevens-Navarro, Universidad Autonoma de San Luis Potosi, Mexico*

Chapter 3, "Evaluation Model for Vertical Handoff Algorithms," begins by introducing the problem of vertical handoff in heterogeneous wireless networks and illustrates the lack of a proper evaluation model to compare the different Vertical Handoff Algorithms (VHAs) that have been proposed in the literature over the last few years. This chapter introduces and describes a novel evaluation model for VHAs. The design of the new evaluation model is based on the multi-criteria evaluation methodology and criticality analysis, which permitted the model to be developed as a software component. The new proposed evaluation model is flexible in terms of the number of evaluation parameters and facilitates the analysis of VHAs by researchers. A specific case study considering some VHAs is presented, analyzed and discussed in detail. The case study is used to compare the proposed evaluation model with another evaluation model (which is named Ordinal Model) for VHAs. The comparison of the new evaluation model with an alternative evaluation model was an important exercise because it gave feedback on both models, to refine them and to propose extensions to their capabilities and features. The obtained results show that both models are valid and effective for the evaluation of the VHAs and each one has his advantages and disadvantages.

## Chapter 4

*Alexander Garcia D., Universidad Autonoma de Occidente, Colombia*

*Andres Navarro C., Universidad ICESI, Colombia*

*Adriana Arteaga A., Universidad ICESI, Colombia*

*Fabio G. Guerrero, Universidad del Valle, Colombia*

*Enrique Stevens-Navarro, Universidad Autonoma de San Luis Potosi, Mexico*

Chapter 4, "Simulation of Vertical Handoff Algorithms for Heterogeneous Wireless Network," discusses the importance of computer simulation is in studying and analyzing communication networks; especially, simulation of Vertical Handoff Algorithms (VHAs) for heterogeneous wireless networks. For VHAs simulation, there are two approaches: using a network simulator or using general purpose programming languages. The objective of this chapter is to present and compare both approaches, by means of two study cases. The first case considers the use of network simulator NCTUns (National Chiao Tung University Network Simulator), while the second case considers the use of MATLAB.

## Chapter 5

*Nurul I. Sarkar, Auckland University of Technology, New Zealand*

*Roger McHaney, Kansas State University, USA*

Chapter 5, "Modeling and Simulation of IEEE 802.11 Wireless LANs: A Case Study of a Network Simulator," demonstrates the increasing popularity of using stochastic discrete event simulation methodology among network researchers worldwide in recent years. This popularity results from the availability of various sophisticated and powerful simulation software packages, and also because of the flexibility in model construction and validation offered by simulation. In this chapter, the authors describe their experience in using the Network Simulator 2 (NS-2), a discrete event simulation package, as an aid to modeling and simulation of the IEEE 802.11 Wireless Local Area Networks (WLANs). The chapter provides an overview of NS-2 focusing on simulation environment, architecture, model development and parameter setting, model validation, output data collection and processing, and simulation execution. The strengths and weaknesses of NS-2 are discussed. The chapter also emphasizes that selecting a good simulator is crucial in modeling and performance analysis of wireless networks.

## Chapter 6

Chapter 6, "OPNET Simulation Setup for Quality of Experience (QoE) Based Network Selection," focuses on developing a simulation setup for QoE based network selection using standard discrete event network simulator, OPNET. It outlines the general development procedures of different components in simulation and details the following important aspects: Long Term Evolution (LTE) network component development, impairment entity development, implementing IPv6 flow management, developing an integrated heterogeneous scenario with LTE and WLAN, implement an example scenario, and generating and analyzing the results.

## Chapter 7

Chapter 7, "Simulation of Multihop Wireless Networks in OMNeT++," presents a brief description of the OMNeT++ network simulator with main emphasis on the InetManet framework. This framework is especially oriented to the simulation of MANET and wireless mesh networks. It offers all the basic models and tools necessary to begin the simulation of this type of networks. Since the source code is offered, the researcher can modify and include their models and they can simulate their own protocols. The InetManet is specifically oriented to the simulation of MANET over IPv4 networks. The flexibility of the code and the oriented based model of OMNeT++ (and its frameworks) allow reusing the wireless model with other types of networks different to IPv4.

## Chapter 8

Chapter 8, "Simulation of a Dynamic-Noise-Dependent Probabilistic Algorithm in MANETs," presents the detail description of a new dynamic probabilistic algorithm in which the retransmission probability of the transmitting node pt is determined as a function of the number of first-hop neighbours (k) and probability of reception (pc), which gives an indication on the network noise-level or packet-loss rate, and therefore, it is referred to as the Dynamic Noise-Dependent Probabilistic (DNDP) algorithm. The DNDP algorithm is implemented using the Mobile Ad Hoc Network (MANET) Simulator (MANSim), which is used to simulate a number of scenarios to evaluate and compare the performance of the algorithm with pure flooding and fixed and dynamic probabilistic algorithms. The simulations results demonstrated that the DNDP algorithm provides an excellent performance in various network conditions, where it almost maintains the same network reachability in noiseless and noisy environments inflicting insignificant increase in number of redundant retransmissions.

## Chapter 9

*Hussein Al-Bahadili, Petra University, Jordan*
*Azmi Halasa, The Arab Academy for Banking and Financial Sciences, Jordan*

Chapter 9, "A Location-Based Power Conservation Scheme for MANETs: A Step towards Green Communications," addresses the issue of energy efficiency in Mobile Ad Hoc Networks (MANETs), where a node consumes most of its power in message communication. In particular, this chapter presents a description and performance evaluation of the new efficient power conservation scheme for message communication, namely, the Location-Based Power Conservation (LBPC) scheme. It is based on the concept of adjusting the transmitting node radio transmission range (R) according to one of the three proposed radius adjustment criteria: farthest, average, and random. So that instead of transmitting with full power to cover-up to its maximum radio transmission range (Rmax), the transmitting node adjust R to less than Rmax, which provides a power conservation depending on the square of the ratio R/Rmax. The performance of the LBPC scheme is evaluated through a number of simulations. A number of scenarios were simulated using the MANET Simulator (MANSim) to calculate the power conservation ratio that can be achieved for two route discovery algorithms, namely, pure flooding and Location-Aided Routing Scheme 1 (LAR-1) algorithms. The simulation results demonstrated that the scheme can provide power conservation ratios between 10 to 50% without adding any extra overheads or complexity to the routing algorithm.

## Chapter 10

*Hussein Al-Bahadili, Petra University, Jordan*
*Abdel Rahman Alzoubaidi, NYIT Amman Campus, Jordan*
*Ali Al-Khalidi, Yanbu University College, Saudi Arabia*

Chapter 10, "Comparing Various Route Discovery Algorithms in Ad Hoc Wireless Networks," compares the performance of various route discovery algorithms in ad hoc wireless networks. The chapter starts with an introduction to the use of simulation in ad hoc wireless networks, and then addresses the process of evaluating route discovery algorithms in such networks. It also provides a description of network simulator used in this chapter, namely, MANSim. It discusses its capabilities, features, and main programming modules. The chapter presents the tutorial steps required to set-up and run a simulation for the pure flooding mechanism. Using the same approach (simulation setup and run), the tutorial progressively approaches the issues of pure flooding mechanism by rallying over the different flooding optimization algorithms: Probabilistic, Location-Aided Routing Scheme 1 (LAR-1), LAR-1-Probabilsitic (LAR-1P), and Optimal Multipoint Relaying (OMPR). The results obtained through the different simulations are analyzed and compared. Based on these results conclusions are drawn, and a number of suggestions and recommendations for future work are pointed-out. This chapter will help practitioners of various kinds (academics, professionals, researchers, and students) grasp a solid understanding for the behavior of ad hoc wireless networks route discovery algorithms and develop an appreciation for flooding optimization mechanisms. It also substantiates the case of experimenting via simulation with such models and shows how the different simulation parameters interplay.

Chapter 11, "Simulation in Amateur Packet Radio Networks," summarizes the results of recent experiments in network simulations by using amateur radio software in a local area network. The author tested main features of those amateur radio programs and their repercussions to the functionality of simulated networks and to the comfort and satisfaction in average network participants. Described tests help practitioners, students and teachers in computer science and communication technologies, in implementing amateur radio within the existing computer networks and in planning and using telecommunication systems – without making any investment in hardware infrastructure.

Chapter 12, "Modeling of TCP Reno with Packet-Loss and Long Delay Cycles," presents a description, derivation, implementation, and comparison of two well-known analytical models, namely, the PFTK and PLLDC models. The first one is a relatively simple model for predicting the performance of the TCP protocol, while the second model is a comprehensive and realistic analytical model. The two models are based on the TCP Reno flavor as it is one of the more popular implementation on the Internet. These two models were implemented in a user-friendly TCP Performance Evaluation Package (TCP-PEP). The TCP-PEP was used to investigate the effect of packet-loss and long delay cycles on the TCP performance measured in terms of sending rate, throughput, and utilization factor. The results obtained from the PFTK and PLLDC models were compared with those obtained from equivalent simulations carried-out on the widely used NS-2 network simulator. The PLLDC model provides more accurate results (closer to the NS-2 results) than the PFTK model.

Chapter 13, "Wireless Identity Management: Multimodal Biometrics and Multilayered IDM," defines digital users in electronic world (e-world) as represented by a set of data called digital identity (ID), which they use, among other functions, for authentication purposes. Within the e-world, it is risky to lose the identity and so security solutions are required to protect IDs. Information security should provide the necessary Identity Management (IDM) process to mitigate that threat. Moreover, efficient protection of the digital identity would encourage users to enter the digital world without worries. The suggested solution depends on three dimensions: management, security solution and security dimensions. The proposed model appears as a multi-layered security approach, since it tries to integrate different security technologies and multimodal biometrics tools and practices, such as wireless management, policies, procedures, guidelines, standards and legislation. The advantages, limitations and requirements of the proposed model are discussed.

Ali H. Al-Bayatti, De Montfort University, UK
Hilal M. Al-Bayatti, Applied Science University, Bahrain

Chapter 14, "Security Management and Simulation of Mobile Ad Hoc Networks (MANET)," provides a detail description of a framework for designing, analyzing, deployment and enforcement of high level security management for Mobile Ad Hoc Networks (MANETs). The framework, which can be used by researchers, academics, security administrators, network designers and post-graduate students, is designed and simulated using the object oriented Network Simulator-2 (NS-2). In this chapter, the authors also provide a full illustration of how to design and implement a secure MANET and maintaining the security essentials using NS-2. Then, they describe the characteristics, applications, design, coding style, advantages/disadvantages, and implementation of the NS-2 simulator. Finally, this chapter provides a description of the future trend NS-3, which is the "eventual replacement" of NS-2.

Hussein Al-Bahadili, Petra University, Jordan
Shakir M. Hussain, Petra University, Jordan
Ghassan F. Issa, Petra University, Jordan
Khaled El-Zayyat, Al-Ahliyya Amman University, Jordan

Chapter 15, "Investigating the Performance of the TSS Scheme in Noisy MANETs," describes the implementation and investigates the performance of the Threshold Secret Sharing (TSS) node authentication scheme in noisy Mobile Ad Hoc Networks (MANETs). A number of simulations are performed using the MANET Simulator (MANSim) to estimate the authentication success ratio for various threshold secret shares, number of nodes, node speeds, and noise-levels. Simulation results demonstrate that, for a certain threshold secret share, presence of noise inflicts a significant reduction in the authentication success ratio, while node mobility inflicts no or insignificant effect. The outcomes of these simulations are so important to facilitate efficient network management.

Ali H. Hadi, Philadelphia University, Jordan
Hussein Al-Bahadili, Petra University, Jordan

Chapter 16, "A Hybrid Port-Knocking Technique for Host Authentication," presents a detail description, implementation, and performance evaluation of a new Port-Knocking (PK) technique, namely the Hybrid PK (HPK) technique, which is developed to avert all types of port attacks and meets all network security requirements. It is referred to as the HPK technique because it combines four well-known security concepts: PK, cryptography, steganography, and mutual authentication. It is implemented as two separate modules, one is installed and run on the client (HPK client), and the other one is installed and run on the server (HPK server), either behind the network firewall or on the firewall itself. The HPK technique can be used for host authentication to make local services invisible from port scanning, provide an extra layer of security that attackers need to penetrate before accessing the resources, act as a stop-gap security measure for services with known unpatched vulnerabilities, and provide a wrapper for a legacy or proprietary services with insufficient integrated security. The main innovative idea in the HPK technique is that it is designed to work in two different modes without pre-adjustment or setting: the interactive and the non-interactive modes. The performance of the HPK technique is evaluated and compared with other PK techniques through simulation.

## Chapter 17

Chapter 17, "The State of the Art and Future Prospective of the Network Security," first discusses the fact that the continuous deployment of network services over the wide range of public and private networks has led to transactions and services that include personal, and sometimes quite sensitive, data. Example of services include: pay-per-view, cable telephony, bill payments by phone, credit card charging, and Internet banking. Such services require significant effort not only to protect the sensitive data involved in the transactions and services, but to ensure integrity and availability of network services as well. The requirement for employing heterogeneous networks and systems becomes increasingly important, and as the view of traditional distributed systems has changed to a network centric view in all types of application networks; therefore, the complexity of these systems has led to significant security flaws and problems. Using existing conventional approaches for security service development over such complex and most often heterogeneous networks and systems are not satisfying and cannot meet users and applications needs; therefore, several approaches have been developed to provide security at various levels and degrees, such as: secure protocols, secure protocol mechanisms, secure services, firewalls, Intrusion Detection Systems (IDS) and later Intrusion Prevention System (IPS), etc. This chapter considers and addresses several aspects of network security, in an effort to provide a publication that summarizes the main current status and the promising and interesting future directions and challenges. This chapter presents the state-of-the-art for the following topics: Internet security, secure services, security in mobile systems and trust, anonymity and privacy.

## Chapter 18

Chapter 18, "Toward Distributed QoS Driven Wireless Messaging Infrastructure," discusses the Telecoms market and it shows that Telecoms market is demanding more services which involve an increased mobile accessibility to the Internet, real time video transmission, real time games, Voice Over IP (VOIP, and business critical transactions such as billing transactions and banking services. Meeting these challenges require the mobile operators to change the way they design their telephony and messaging systems. As the mobile market moves to become more service centric, rather than technology centric, Quality of Service (QoS) has grown to become imperative, since in the Telecoms, innovative services are very often short lived, where the quality aspects of a system and the provided services contribute as key differentiators. Thus, the main focus of this chapter is based around the QoS issues which have lead to the consideration to a distributed messaging model to address the challenges faced in the Telecoms industry.

## Chapter 19

Chapter 19, "A Simulation Model for Large Scale Distributed Systems," presents the design characteristics of the simulation model proposed in MONARC 2, which is a multithreaded, process oriented simulation framework designed for modeling large scale distributed systems, allows the realistic simulation of a wide-range of distributed system technologies, with respect to their specific components and characteristics. The model includes the necessary components to describe various actual distributed system technologies, and provides the mechanisms to describe concurrent network traffic, evaluate different strategies in data replication, and analyze job scheduling procedures. The chapter also provides a background on the use of discrete-event simulators in the design and development of large scale distributed systems due to their efficiency, scalability, and most importantly their core abstractions of process and event map neatly to the components and interactions of modern-day distributed systems allowing designing realistic simulation scenarios. The chapter analyses existing work, outlining the key decision points taken in the design of the MONARC's simulation model.

## Chapter 20

Chapter 20, "Future Approach of Next Generation Cellular Mobile Communications," first, studies and analyzes the performance of existing mobile systems and services, and estimates the future aspects of next generation mobile communications. Second, it proposes and investigates the performance of a new approach that is based on using the abilities of satellite communications as part of the mobile communication systems. Such an approach introduced advanced communication solutions that could be set up anywhere/anytime subject to the existence of satellite coverage. The proposed solution tries to eliminate all boundaries of telecommunications and leads to a universal approach to overcome all technical and managerial issues.

## Chapter 21

Chapter 21, "Evaluation of Simulation Models," reviews and evaluate the performance of simulation models that are concentrating on develop types of discrete event simulation. Different models are discussed but special attention is given to systems that use spatial decomposition. This involves that data may have to be transmitted by mediator tiles to its purpose depending on the decomposition post. For congruent simulation the challenge is to decompose the tool in order to make effective use of the original processor design. This chapter also discusses a number of methodologies and architectural design that have been developed for efficient simulation model decomposition.

## Chapter 22

*Jafar Ababneh, World Islamic Sciences and Education University, Jordan*
*Hussein Abdel-Jaber, World Islamic Sciences and Education University, Jordan*
*Firas Albalas, University of Jadara, Jordan*
*Amjad Daoud, World Islamic Sciences and Education University, Jordan*

Chapter 22, "Analyzing and Evaluating Current Computer Networks Simulation Models," presents the methodologies and techniques used to evaluate and analyze the performance of communication and computer networks routers, such as mathematical analysis, computer simulations techniques, and empirical measurements; identify the workload required for accomplishing a simulation model or mathematical analysis; identify the main metrics used to evaluate, manage and control the performance of the computer networks; present the advantage and disadvantage of these techniques; identify the challenges facing these different methodologies.

## Chapter 23

*Shao Ying Zhu, University of Derby, UK*
*Gerald Schaefer, Loughborough University, UK*

Chapter 23, "Network Simulation Tools for Supporting Teaching in Computer Networks," investigates the use of network simulation tools as an alternative to be employed in computer networking laboratories. Network simulation tools provide students with the opportunity to freely experiment with virtual computer networks and equipment without the expensive costs associated with real networking hardware. The results of the research show that students appreciate the use of network simulators and see them as an effective approach to learning computer networking concepts and gaining the relevant experience. This was also confirmed by the actual performance of students who experienced different levels of exposure to networks simulators during their studies. The authors furthermore investigate the use of interactive, electronically assessed lab sessions, where students get immediate and interactive feedback while they are going through lab exercises. The outcome of the this research shows that this approach not only releases the lecturer from less demanding students to better support weaker students, but that this will also lead to improved student performance and better student retention.

## Chapter 24

*Ali Maqousi, Petra University, Jordan*
*Tatiana Balikhina, Petra University, Jordan*

Chapter 24, "Wire and Wireless Local Area Networks Simulation: OPNET Tutorial," presents a number of tutorials for using OPNET to setup different wire and wireless LANs simulations. These tutorials help network designers, analysts, managers, researchers, etc. to simulate, evaluate, and investigate the performance of more complicated and realistic networks. Moreover, it encourages and helps students to easily perform LANs simulations for better understand to the network performance under different network conditions.

# Preface

In the information technology age and with tremendous advancement in computer and communication technologies, a computer network has become an integral part of our daily life in universities, organizations, schools, factories, and almost everywhere. Furthermore, there has been a remarkable increase in computer networks users, services, and applications. Therefore huge efforts have put forward by researchers, designers, managers, analysts, and professionals to accomplish an optimum cost-effective performance to satisfy users, services, and applications needs.

Computer networks designers use performance evaluation as an integral component of the design effort. The designer relies on the simulation model to provide guidance in choosing among alternative design choices, to detect bottlenecks in network performance, or to support cost-effective analyses. Another important use of simulation is as a tool to help validate an analytical approach to performance evaluation. Computer simulation is widely-used in investigating the performance of existing and proposed computer networks designs, protocols, security algorithms, models, etc.

The application of computer simulation can potentially improve the quality and effectiveness of the network design. It is generally unfeasible to implement a computer network design, protocol, algorithm, or model before valid tests are performed to evaluate their performance. It is clear that testing and evaluating such implementations with real hardware is quite hard, in terms of the manpower, time, cost, and other resources.

The preferred alternative is to model these implementations in a detailed simulator and consequently perform various scenarios to measure their performance for various patterns of realistic computer networks environments (e.g., connection media, node densities, node mobility, transmission range, size of traffic, etc.). The main challenge to simulation is to model the process as close as possible to reality; otherwise it could produce entirely different performance characteristics from the ones discovered during actual use. In addition, the simulation study must be repeatable, unbiased, realistic, statistically sound, and cost-effective. There are a number of computer network simulators that have been developed throughout the years to support computer networks design and modeling. Some of them are of general-purpose use and other dedicated to simulate particular types of computer networks.

*Simulation in Computer Network Design and Modeling: Use and Analysis* is composed of 24 chapters written by highly qualified scholars discussing a wide range of topics; these are: modeling and simulation of game theory in wireless networks routing and mobile IPv6 protocol, evaluation and simulation of Vertical Handoff Algorithms (VHAs), simulation of various network protocols and applications using a variety of network simulators (e.g., OPNET, NS-2, OMNeT++, MANSim), Simulation in amateur packet radio networks, modeling of TCP in wireless network, network security, distributed systems, cellular networks, simulations models, and network simulation as a teaching aid.

Chapter 1, "Modeling and Simulation of Game Applications in Ad Hoc Wireless Networks Routing," presents a game theory based routing algorithm, which defines the best route based on the power consumption that each intermediate node will suffer to forward a packet, the price the destination will pay to the source and the amount of compensation the source will pay to each intermediate node. The chapter also presents a polynomial time algorithm that can give a Nash Equilibrium path and use it to evaluate the performance of the game.

Chapter 2, "Simulating Game Applications in Mobile IPv6 Protocol," proposes a novel game-based green interface/network selection mechanism, which is an extension to the multi-interface fast-handover mobile IPv6 protocol. The mechanism controls the handover decision process by deciding whether a handover is needed or not and helps the node to choose the right access point at the right time. What's more, the mechanism switches the mobile nodes interfaces "ON" and "OFF" when needed to control the mobile node's energy consumption and improves the handover latency.

Chapter 3, "Evaluation Model for Vertical Handoff Algorithms," describes a novel evaluation model for Vertical Handoff Algorithms (VHAs). The design of the new evaluation model is based on the multi-criteria evaluation methodology and criticality analysis, which permitted the model to be developed as a software component. The new proposed evaluation model is flexible in terms of the number of evaluation parameters and facilitates the analysis of VHAs by researchers.

Chapter 4, "Simulation of Vertical Handoff Algorithms for Heterogeneous Wireless Network," discusses the importance of computer simulation is in studying and analyzing communication networks; especially, simulation of Vertical Handoff Algorithms (VHAs) for heterogeneous wireless networks. The chapter also presents and compares using two approaches for VHAs simulations, namely, using network simulator and using a general purpose programming languages by means of two study cases. The first case considers the use of network simulator NCTUns (National Chiao Tung University Network Simulator), while the second case considers the use of MATLAB.

Chapter 5, "Modeling and Simulation of IEEE 802.11 Wireless LANs: A Case Study of a Network Simulator," describes the authors experience in using the Network Simulator 2 (NS-2), a discrete event simulation package, as an aid to modeling and simulation of the IEEE 802.11 Wireless Local Area Networks (WLANs). The chapter provides an overview of NS-2 focusing on simulation environment, architecture, model development and parameter setting, model validation, output data collection and processing, and simulation execution. The strengths and weaknesses of NS-2 are discussed. The chapter also emphasizes that selecting a good simulator is crucial in modeling and performance analysis of wireless networks.

Chapter 6, "OPNET Simulation Setup for Quality of Experience (QoE) Based Network Selection," focuses on developing a simulation setup for QoE based network selection using standard discrete event network simulator, OPNET. It outlines the general development procedures of different components in simulation and details the following important aspects: Long Term Evolution (LTE) network component development, impairment entity development, implementing IPv6 flow management, developing an integrated heterogeneous scenario with LTE and WLAN, implement an example scenario, and generating and analyzing the results.

Chapter 7, "Simulation of Multihop Wireless Networks in OMNeT++," presents a brief description of the OMNeT++ network simulator with main emphasis on the InetManet framework, and how this framework is especially oriented to simulate Mobile Ad Hoc Networks (MANETs) and Wireless Mesh Networks (WMNs).

Chapter 8, "Simulation of a Dynamic-Noise-Dependent Probabilistic Algorithm in MANETs," provides a detail description and performance evaluation of the novel Dynamic Noise-Dependent Probabilistic (DNDP) algorithm for route discovery in noisy Mobile Ad Hoc Networks (MANETs). The performance of the DNDP algorithm is evaluate and compared with pure flooding, fixed and dynamic probabilistic algorithms.

Chapter 9, "A Location-Based Power Conservation Scheme for MANETs: A Step towards Green Communications," addresses the issue of energy efficiency in Mobile Ad Hoc Networks (MANETs), where a node consumes most of its power in message communication. In particular, this chapter presents a description and performance evaluation of the new efficient power conservation scheme for message communication, namely, the Location-Based Power Conservation (LBPC) scheme. The simulation results demonstrated that the scheme can provide power conservation ratios between 10 to 50% without adding any extra overheads or complexity to the routing algorithm.

Chapter 10, "Comparing Various Route Discovery Algorithms in Ad hoc Wireless Networks," compares the performance of various route discovery algorithms in ad hoc wireless networks. The chapter starts with an introduction to the use of simulation in ad hoc wireless networks, and then addresses the process of evaluating route discovery algorithms in such networks. It also provides a description of network simulator used in this chapter, namely, MANSim. It discusses its capabilities, features, and main programming modules. The chapter presents the tutorial steps required to set-up and run a simulation for the pure flooding mechanism. Using the same approach (simulation setup and run), the tutorial progressively approaches the issues of pure flooding mechanism by rallying over the different flooding optimization algorithms: Probabilistic, Location-Aided Routing Scheme 1 (LAR-1), LAR-1-Probabilsitic (LAR-1P), and Optimal Multipoint Relaying (OMPR). The results obtained through the different simulations are analyzed and compared. Based on these results conclusions are drawn, and a number of suggestions and recommendations for future work are pointed-out. This chapter will help practitioners of various kinds (academics, professionals, researchers, and students) grasp a solid understanding for the behavior of ad hoc wireless networks route discovery algorithms and develop an appreciation for flooding optimization mechanisms. It also substantiates the case of experimenting via simulation with such models and shows how the different simulation parameters interplay.

Chapter 11, "Simulation in Amateur Packet Radio Networks," summarizes the results of recent experiments in network simulations by using amateur radio software in a local area network. The author tested main features of those amateur radio programs and their repercussions to the functionality of simulated networks and to the comfort and satisfaction in average network participants. Described tests help practitioners, students and teachers in computer science and communication technologies, in implementing amateur radio within the existing computer networks and in planning and using telecommunication systems – without making any investment in hardware infrastructure.

Chapter 12, "Modeling of TCP Reno with Packet-Loss and Long Delay Cycles," presents a description, derivation, implementation, and comparison of two well-known analytical models, namely, the PFTK and PLLDC models. The first one is a relatively simple model for predicting the performance of the TCP protocol, while the second model is a comprehensive and realistic analytical model. In order to validate the accuracy of the PFTK and PLLDC models, the results obtained from these two models are compared with those obtained from equivalent simulations carried-out on the widely used NS-2 network simulator.

Chapter 13, "Wireless Identity Management: Multimodal Biometrics and Multilayered IDM," proposes a multi-layered security model for authentication purposes within the e-world. It depends on three dimensions: management, security solution and security dimensions; and it tries to integrate different security technologies and multimodal biometrics tools and practices, such as wireless management, policies, procedures, guidelines, standards and legislation. The advantages, limitations and requirements of the proposed model are discussed.

Chapter 14, "Security Management and Simulation of Mobile Ad Hoc Networks (MANET)," provides a detail description of a framework for designing, analyzing, deployment and enforcement of high level security management for Mobile Ad Hoc Networks (MANETs). The framework, which can be used by researchers, academics, security administrators, network designers and post-graduate students, is designed and simulated using the object oriented Network Simulator-2 (NS-2). The chapter also provides a full illustration of how to design and implement a secure MANET and maintaining the security essentials using NS-2. Finally, this chapter provides a description of the future trend NS-3, which is the "eventual replacement" of NS-2.

Chapter 15, "Investigating the Performance of the TSS Scheme in Noisy MANETs," describes the implementation and investigates the performance of the threshold secret sharing (TSS) node authentication scheme in noisy MANETs. A number of simulations are performed using the MANET Simulator (MANSim) to estimate the authentication success ratio for various threshold secret shares, number of nodes, node speeds, and noise-levels. The outcomes of these simulations are so important to facilitate efficient network management.

Chapter 16, "A Hybrid Port-Knocking Technique for Host Authentication," presents a detail description, implementation, and performance evaluation of a new Port-Knocking (PK) technique, namely the Hybrid PK (HPK) technique, which is developed to avert all types of port attacks and meets all network security requirements. It is referred to as the HPK technique because it combines four well-known security concepts: PK, cryptography, steganography, and mutual authentication. The performance of the HPK technique is evaluated and compared with other PK techniques through simulation.

Chapter 17, "The State of the Art and Future Prospective of the Network Security," considers and addresses several aspects of network security, in an effort to provide a publication that summarizes the main current status and the promising and interesting future directions and challenges. In particular, the chapter presents the state-of-the-art in Internet security, secure services, security in mobile systems and trust, and anonymity and privacy.

Chapter 18, "Toward Distributed QoS Driven Wireless Messaging Infrastructure," discusses the Telecoms market and shows that Telecoms market is demanding more services which involve an increased mobile accessibility to the Internet, real time video transmission, real time games, Voice Over IP (VOIP) and business critical transactions such as billing transactions and banking services. As the mobile market moves to become more service centric, rather than technology centric, Quality of Service (QoS) has grown to become imperative. Thus, the main focus of this chapter is based around the QoS issues which have lead to the consideration to a distributed messaging model to address the challenges faced in the Telecoms industry.

Chapter 19, "A Simulation Model for Large Scale Distributed Systems," presents the design characteristics of the simulation model proposed in MONARC 2, which is a multithreaded, process oriented simulation framework designed for modeling large scale distributed systems, allows the realistic simulation of a wide-range of distributed system technologies, with respect to their specific components and characteristics. The model includes the necessary components to describe various actual distributed system technologies, and provides the mechanisms to describe concurrent network traffic, evaluate different strategies in data replication, and analyze job scheduling procedures. The chapter also provides a background on the use of discrete-event simulators in the design and development of large scale distributed systems due to their efficiency, scalability, and most importantly their core abstractions of process and event map neatly to the components and interactions of modern-day distributed systems allowing designing realistic simulation scenarios. The chapter analyses existing work, outlining the key decision points taken in the design of the MONARC's simulation model.

Chapter 20, "Future Approach of Next Generation Cellular Mobile Communications," studies and analyzes the performance of existing mobile systems and services, and estimates the future aspects of next generation mobile communications. It also proposes and investigates the performance of a new approach that is based on using the abilities of satellite communications as part of the mobile communication systems. Such an approach introduced advanced communication solutions that could be set up anywhere/anytime subject to the existence of satellite coverage. The proposed solution tries to eliminate all boundaries of telecommunications and leads to a universal approach to overcome all technical and managerial issues.

Chapter 21, "Evaluation of Simulation Models," reviews and evaluate the performance of simulation models that are concentrating on develop types of discrete event simulation. Different models are discussed but special attention is given to systems that use spatial decomposition. This involves that data may have to be transmitted by mediator tiles to its purpose depending on the decomposition post. For congruent simulation the challenge is to decompose the tool in order to make effective use of the original processor design. This chapter also discusses a number of methodologies and architectural design that have been developed for efficient simulation model decomposition.

Chapter 22, "Analyzing and Evaluating Current Computer Networks Simulation Models," presents the methodologies and techniques used to evaluate and analyze the performance of communication and computer networks routers, such as mathematical analysis, computer simulations techniques, and empirical measurements; identify the workload required for accomplishing a simulation model or mathematical analysis; identify the main metrics used to evaluate, manage and control the performance of the computer networks; present the advantage and disadvantage of these techniques; identify the challenges facing these different methodologies.

Chapter 23, "Network Simulation Tools for Supporting Teaching in Computer Networks," investigates the use of network simulation tools as an alternative to be employed in computer networking laboratories. Network simulation tools provide students with the opportunity to freely experiment with virtual computer networks and equipment without the expensive costs associated with real networking hardware. The outcome of the this research shows that this approach not only releases the lecturer from less demanding students to better support weaker students, but will also lead to improved student performance and better student retention.

Chapter 24, "Wire and Wireless Local Area Networks Simulation: OPNET Tutorial," presents a number of tutorials for using OPNET to setup different wire and wireless LANs simulations. These tutorials help network designers, analysts, managers, researchers, etc to simulate, evaluate, and investigate the performance of more complicated and realistic networks. Moreover, it encourages and helps students to easily perform LANs simulations for better understand to the network performance under different network conditions.

The book concludes with compilation of references, contributors' biographies, and a comprehensive index.

# Acknowledgment

The editor would like to take this opportunity to express his deep appreciation to the IGI Global team for their relentless and significant support and patience. Moreover, the editor would like to thank Ms. Jan Travers, Director of Intellectual Property and Contracts at IGI Global for her encouragement and patience. Likewise, the editor would like to extend his deep appreciation to the Development Division at IGI Global, namely, Mr. Joel A. Gamon, Development Editor, Editorial Content Department, and Ms. Myla Harty, Editorial Assistant, Development Division.

During his work on editing this book, the editor has moved from the Arab Academy for Banking and Financial Sciences to Petra University in Jordan. In this regard, the editor would like to express his recognition of his respective organizations and colleges for their moral support and encouragement that have proved to be indispensible. In the same token, the editor conveys his thanks to the Editorial Advisory Board and reviewers for their relentless work and for their constant demand for perfection.

The editor is heartily thankful to the distinguish chapters' authors for submitting such excellent and valuable chapters and for their tremendous support, cooperation, and patience throughout the development process.

More importantly, the editor would like to extend his heartfelt appreciation and indebtedness to his wife, daughters, and son for their support and patience.

*Hussein Al-Bahadili*
*Petra University, Jordan*

# Chapter 1
# Modelling and Simulation of Game Applications in Ad Hoc Wireless Networks Routing

**Omar Raoof**
*Brunel University, UK*

**Hamed Al-Raweshidy**
*Brunel University, UK*

## ABSTRACT

*This chapter presents a game theory based routing algorithm that defines the best route based on the power consumption that each intermediate node will suffer to forward a packet, the price the destination will pay to the source, and the amount of compensation the source will pay to each intermediate node. The chapter also presents a polynomial time algorithm that can give a Nash Equilibrium path and use it to evaluate the performance of the game. The key features of the introduced mechanism are: it uses the first and second price auctions; the auction mechanism insures a fare allocation of the data to the user who values it the most; the second-price sealed-bid auction gives better revenue to the source when compared to the random allocation scheme and the first-price sealed-bid mechanism; the game mechanism combines both source compensation to the intermediate nodes and the power consumption to improve the path reliability between the source and the destination (i.e. the winning bidder); the source payoff will increase once the network density increases; and, finally, the simulation results prove that the introduced auction mechanism dramatically increases the destination's revenue whether the first or second-price auction is chosen.*

## INTRODUCTION

A wireless ad hoc network is characterized by a distributed, dynamic, self-organizing architecture. In such a network, each node is capable of independently adapting its operation based on the

current environment according to predetermined algorithms and protocols. In multi-hop wireless ad hoc networks, networking services are provided by the nodes themselves. Generally, the nodes must make a mutual contribution to packet forwarding in order to ensure an operable network. If the network is under the control of a single authority,

DOI: 10.4018/978-1-4666-0191-8.ch001

as is the case for military networks and rescue operations, the nodes cooperate for the critical purpose of the network. However, if each node is its own authority, cooperation between the nodes cannot be taken for granted; on the contrary, it is reasonable to assume that each node has the goal to maximize its own benefits by enjoying network services and at the same time minimizing its contribution.

In this chapter, we investigate the case where a group of wireless nodes in an ad hoc network are interested in some information within server node. In order to get such information, the nodes will compete between each other, using auction theory, to grant the access to these data. The node that appreciates the offered data more, will value it more, and win the bid. The chapter discusses the first and second price auctions (Parrsch & Robert, 2003; Menezes & Monteiro, 2004; Krishna, 2009). Generally, the mechanisms works as follows; the destination will pay some money to the source and the source will try it is best to compensate the intermediate nodes in order to insure the reliability of the end-to-end route. The intermediate nodes will decide whether to participate on this route or not depending on the price the source will pay and on how much energy is needed to forward the packets to the next hop. We will see that there are two kinds of sources, cooperative and selfish source. Where the first will accept any positive payoffs and will do it's best to cooperate with the destination to insure the reliability of the route. On the other hand the selfish course will try to maximize its own profit without taking care of choosing the most reliable path.

## AUCTION THEORY: A BRIEF HISTORY

Economists consider auctions as one of oldest surviving classes of economic institutions (Milgrom, 1985). One of the earliest reports of an auction was from interpreting the biblical account

of the sale of Joseph (the great son of Abraham) into slavery as being an auction sale (Cassady, 1967). Another report was by the Greek historian Herodotus, who described the sale of women to be wives in Babylonia around the fifth century B.C. (Shubik, 2004; Krishna, 2002) these auctions use to begin with the woman the auctioneer considered the most beautiful and progressed to the least. In fact, at that time, it was considered illegal to allow a daughter to be sold outside of the auction method. During the closing years of the Roman Empire; the auction of plundered booty was common, following military victory, Roman soldiers would often drive a spear into the ground around which the spoils of war were left, to be auctioned off. Later slaves, often captured as the "spoils of war," were auctioned in the forum under the sign of the spear, with the proceeds of sale going towards the war effort (Shubik, 2004).

Moreover, the personal belongings of deceased Buddhist monks were sold at auction as early as the seventh century A.D. in China. In some parts of England during the seventeenth and eighteenth centuries auction by candle was used for the sale of goods and leaseholds. This auction began by lighting a candle after which bids were offered in ascending order until the candle spluttered out. The high bid at the time the candle extinguished itself won the auction (Patten, 1970). During the end of the 18th century, French started auctioning art, soon after the French Revolution, daily in taverns (which was used to be considered as a place of business and social activities) and coffeehouses, during these auctions, catalogues used to be printed to show available items. Which lead us to mention the oldest auction house in the world, known as "Stockholm Auction House," it was established in Sweden in 1674 (Varoli, 2010; Stockholm Auction House, 2010).

As impressive as the historical facts of auctions is the remarkable range of situations in which they are currently used in our day-to-day life. There are auctions for livestock, auctions for rare and unusual items like diamonds, work of arts and other collectibles. Reports from recent can be seen in the United States in the 1980's, where every week, the U.S. treasury sells billions of dollars of bills and notes using a sealed-bid auction. The Department of the Interior sells mineral rights on federally-owned properties at auction. Furthermore, many examples can be seen throughout the public and private sectors, purchasing agents solicit delivery-price offers of products ranging from office supplies to specialized mining equipment; sellers auction antiques and artwork, flowers and livestock, publishing rights and timber rights, stamps and wine and many other market transactions (Milgrom, 1985).

From the academic point of view, (Vickrey, 1961; Laffont & Maskin, 1980) can be considered as one of the influential contributions of auction theory; it was followed by a large amount of literature, which examined the behaviour of competitive bidders in auctions. (McAfee & McMillan, 1987a, 1987b, 1992) define an auction to be a market institution with an explicit set of rules determining resource allocation and prices on the basis of bids from the market participants. Consequently, the auctioned good is to be sold with a price resulted from direct competition of the potential buyers, who know exactly their individual willingness to pay better than the seller. Finally, the development of the internet, however, has led to a significant increase in the use of auctions as sellers can seek for bids via the internet (such as the bidding system in eBay (Houser & Wooders, 2001; Resnick & Zeckhauser, 2002) from a wide range of buyers in a much wider range of commodities than was previously practical (Shubik, 2004).

It is important to mention that for several reason this work is restricted to the discussion of a single object auctions. On one hand, in order to analyze such auctions, it might get rather difficult if multiple objects are to be allocated. On the other hand, the results derived for single unit auctions definitely give a good understanding over the effects auction rules and behavioural assumptions have on the bidding behaviour.

Generally speaking, there are four standard auctions that are discussed in the literature. These standards are; the ascending-bid auction (known as the English auction), the descending-bid auction (known as the Dutch auction), first-price auction and the second-price auction (known as Vickery auction). All of these auctions apart from Vickery auction are used in business transactions, while Vickery auctions is rarely used but it has some theoretically appealing properties. These mechanisms assigns the highest bidder to be a winner, however, they can be classified basically by two main factors. Firstly the bidders can submit open or sealed bids; secondly the price may be determined by the highest or the second highest bid.

The *ascending-bid auction* is the most common auction form. In this type of auctions, the price is successively raised until only one bidder remains. This can be done either by the auctioneer, announcing prices, or by the bidders calling for higher bids themselves. Thus, the remaining bidder receives the object paying only the second highest bid. A very important feature of this auction is that each bidder knows the current highest bid at any point in time.

The *descending-bid auction* is the converse of the ascending-bid auction. The seller begins by announcing a price that exceeds the willingness to pay of every bidder (i.e., a very high price). Then he lowers the price until one bidder accepts the actual offer. This bidder pays the price at which he claimed the object.

In the *first-price sealed-bid auction* bidders submit sealed bids and the highest bidder gets the object for the price he bid. In the *second-price sealed-bid auction*, however, the highest bidder is awarded the item and pays the second highest bid.

## PROPOSED AUCTION MECHANISM

In order to reflect user *i*'s valuation about the data information in the server, a simple valuation function is proposed:

$$I = C_i \times v_i \qquad (1)$$

Where $I$ is the importance of the data information offered by the source node; which is assumed to be known to all destinations and its set by each destination randomly according to the need of each individual node. $C_i$ is the normalized channel capacity, which can be expressed as the tightest upper bond on the amount of information that can be reliably transmitted over a communication channel, and $vi$ is user $i$'s valuation to the data offered by the source about his strategic situation defined in percentage. Shannon Channel capacity is defined as:

$$C_i = B \log_2(1 + \frac{f_i p}{N \circ}) \qquad (2)$$

where $fi$ is the channel coefficient between user $i$'s transmitter and receiver; $B$ is the channel bandwidth in $Hz$; $p$ is the amount power that the source need to transmit the data to the next hop, and $N \circ$ is the mean channel noise power (The mean noise power in the receiver $N$ is given by $N = kT \circ B$ $[W]$. Where is the Blotzmann's Constant $= 1.38 \times 10^{-23} JK^{-1}$ and $T \circ$ is the system temperature, which is generally assumed to be $290K$). Then each user valuation can derived from (2) and expressed as:

$$v_i = \frac{I}{B \times \log_2(1 + \frac{f_i p}{N \circ})} \qquad (3)$$

The valuation of the data information can be interpreted that user $i$ uses the importance of the data (already know to all users) as a ruler to set his bid in the auction. This valuation measures the destination (if he wins the auction) capabilities to bid more for the offered data keeping in mind the capacity of his channel. We can see that when the channel condition is good (according to equation

2), the user will be more willing to increase his bid for the offered data. As a result, a higher bid would be expected from him and vice versa.

We must mention that the auction mechanism is designed in such a way that $v_i$ does not represent the real price that a destination node has to pay during the auction. Simply it is an interpretation of the strategic situation that a node is facing. In fact $v_i$ reflects the relationship between the node valuation and the channel condition. Additionally, since the channel coefficient $f$ is a constant random variable with a known distribution to each user, the distribution of the valuation $v_i$ is also known (according to their relationship shown in [2]), which means that; $v_i$ lies in the interval $[v_{min}, v_{max}]$.

We defined *Bid* as the bid space in the auction, $\{bid_0, bid_1, bid_2, ..., bid_n\}$, which represent the set of possible bids submitted to the source. We can simply assign $bid_0$ to zero without loss of generality, as it represent the null bid. Accordingly, $bid_1$ is the lowest acceptable bid, and $bid_n$ is the highest bid. The bid increment between two adjacent bids is taken to be the same in the typical case. In the event of ties (*i.e.* two bidders offer the same final price), the object would be allocated randomly to one of the tied bidders.

To find the winner of the first-price sealed-bid auction, a theoretical model is defined based on the work of Harry J. Parrsch and Jacques Robert (2003). The probability of detecting a bid $bid_i$ is denoted as $\pi$, the probability of not participating in the named auction will be denoted as $\pi_0$. Then the vector $\pi$, which equals to $(\pi_0, \pi_1, \pi_2, ..., \pi_n)$, and it is denoted as probability distribution over *Bid*, where $\sum_{i=0}^{n} \pi_i = 1$. Now we introduce the cumulative distribution function, which is used to find out whether a user $i$ will bid with $bid_i$ or less, $\Pi_i = \sum_{j=0}^{i} \pi_i$, all of them are collected in the vector $\Pi$, which equals to $(\pi_0, \Pi_1, ..., \Pi_{k-1}, 1)$.

Then, any rational potential bidder with a known valuation of $v_i$ faces a decision problem of maximizing his expected profit from winning the auction; i.e.

$$\max_{<b_i \in Bid>} (v_i - bid_i)\Pr(winning \mid bid_i) \qquad (4)$$

The equilibrium probability of winning for a particular bid $bid_i$ is denoted as $\vartheta_i$, and these probabilities are collected in $\vartheta,(\vartheta_0,\vartheta_1,\vartheta_2,...,\vartheta_n)$. Using $\pi$, the elements of the vector $\vartheta$ can be calculated. We can easily find that $\vartheta_0$ is know to be zero, as if any bidder submitted a null bid to the source, he is not going to win. We can calculate the remaining elements of $\vartheta$ as it can be directly verifying that the following constitute a symmetric, Bayes-Nash equilibrium of the auction game:

$$\vartheta_i = \frac{(\Pi_i)^n (\Pi_{i-1})^n}{n(\Pi_i - \Pi_{i-1})} \; \forall i = 0,1,2,...,n \qquad (5)$$

Throughout this chapter, we will use the notation of Bayes-Nash equilibrium as defined in (Krishna 2009), there approach is to transform a game of incomplete information into one of imperfect information, and any buyer who has incomplete information about other buyers' values is treated as if he were uncertain about their types.

From equation (5), we can see that the numerator is the probability that the highest bid is exactly equal to $bid_i$ while the denominator is the expected number of user how are going to submit the same bid (i.e. $bid_i$). For any user in the game, the best response will be to submit a bid which satisfies the following inequality;

$$(v_i - bid_i)\vartheta_i \geq (v_j - bid_j)\vartheta_j \,\forall j \neq i$$

The above inequality shows that user $i$'s profit is weakly beat any other user $j$'s profit. The above inequality is the discrete analogue to the equilibrium first-order condition for expected-profit maximization in the continuous-variation model (Parrsch & Robert, 2003), which takes the form of the following ordinary differential equation in the strategy function $\delta(v_i)$;

$$\delta'(v_i) + \delta(v_i)\frac{(n-1)f(v_i)}{F(v_i)}$$
$$= v_i \frac{(n-1)f(v_i)}{F(v_i)} \qquad (6)$$

Where $f(v_i)$ and $F(v_i)$ are the probability density and cumulative distribution function of each bidder valuation respectively. We assume that they are common knowledge to bidders along with $n$, the number of bidders in the system. The reserve price is denoted by $r$, (In many instance, sellers reserve the right not to sell the object if the price determined in the auction is lower than some threshold amount (Menezes & Monteiro, 2004; Krishna, 2009), say $r > 0$), and the above differential equation has the following solution;

$$\delta(v_i) = v_i - \frac{\int_r^{v_i} F(u)^{n-1} du}{F(v_i)^{n-1}} \qquad (7)$$

In order to get to equation (5-7), we simply multiply both sides of equation (6) by $\frac{F(v_i)}{(n-1)f(v_i)}$. This will lead us to;

$$\frac{F(v_i)}{(n-1)f(v_i)}\delta'(v_i) + \delta(v_i) = v_i,$$

which can be easily arranged to;

$$\delta(v_i) = v_i - \delta'(v_i)\frac{F(v_i)}{(n-1)f(v_i)},$$

and based on the fact that

$$\frac{d}{dv}F(v)^{(n-1)-} = (n-1)f(v),$$

it can be easily shown that the solution is straight forward and lead us to equation (7).

In the case of the first-price sealed-bid auction, the bidder $i$ will submit a bid of $b_i = \delta(v_i)$ in equilibrium and he will pay a proportional price to his bid if he wins. On the other hand, for the second-price sealed-bid auction, a user $i$ will submit his valuation truthfully. This is because the price a user has to pay if he wins the auction is not the winning bid but the second highest one. Therefore, there is nothing to drive a user to bid higher or lower than his true valuation to the data offered by the server. In this case, $b_i = v_i$, shown in equation (3), and the payment process is the same as in the first-price auction.

## MODELLING OF TRADITIONAL ROUTING TECHNIQUES

One of the recent application of game theory to ad hoc routing (Zaikiuddin, et al., 2005; Felegyhazi, et al., 2007; Yuan & Yu, 2008; Yang & Chen, 2008; Abaii, et al., 2008; Abuzanat, et al., 2008; Zhu & Lui, 2005; Jianwei, et al., 2008; Coucheney, et al., 2009; Dutta, 2001) focuses on the analysis of the effectiveness of three ad hoc routing techniques, namely link state routing, distance vector routing and multicast routing (reverse path forwarding), in the event of frequent route changes. The objective of the analysis is to compare and contrast the techniques in an ad hoc setting. These techniques are evaluated in terms of:

1.  **Soundness:** whether routers have a correct view of the network to make the correct routing decisions under frequent network changes;
2.  **Convergence:** length of time taken by the routers to have a correct view of the network topology as nodes move; and
3.  **Network overhead:** amount of data exchanged among routers to achieve convergence.

Routing is modelled as a zero sum game between the two players; the set of routers and the network itself. In a zero-sum game (Das, et al., 2003; Urpi, et al., 2003) the utility function of one player (minimizing player's utility) is the negative of the other's (maximizing player's utility). The game has equilibrium when the *(min,max)* value of any player's payoff is equal to its *(max,min)* value. In a zero sum game, the *(max,min)* value is defined as the maximum value that the maximizing player can get under the assumption that the minimizing player's objective is to minimize the payoff to the maximizing player. *In other words*, the *(max,min)* value represents the maximum among the lowest possible payoffs that the maximizing player can get; this is also called the *safe* or *secure payoff*.

In the routing game, the payoff to each player (i.e. wireless nodes) consists of two cost components, one being the amount of network overhead and the other varying with the performance metric under consideration. For example, for evaluating soundness the cost to the routers is "0" if all routers have a correct view of the topology when the game ends and "1" if any one router does not. The objective of the routers is to minimize the cost function. The action for the routers involved is to send routing control messages as dictated by the routing technique and update their routing information, and for the network to change the state of existing links from up to down and vice versa. The game is solved to determine the *(min,max)* value of the cost function. It serves to compare the different routing techniques in terms of the amount of routing control traffic required to achieve convergence and the soundness of the routing protocol to network changes. One of the main conclusions reached in the comparative analysis was that reverse path forwarding requires less control traffic to achieve convergence, against traditional link state routing.

Another issue related to routing involves studying the effect of selfish nodes on the forwarding operation, as to be discussed in the following sections.

## SELFISH BEHAVIOUR IN FORWARDING PACKETS

The establishment of multi-hop routes in ad hoc networks relies on nodes' forwarding packets for one another. However, a selfish node, in order to conserve its limited energy resources, could decide not to participate in the forwarding process by switching off its interface. If all nodes decide to alter their behaviour in this way, acting selfishly, this may lead to the collapse of the network. The works of (Felegyhazi, et al., 2006; Michiardi & Molva, 2005; Srinivasan, et al., 2003; Felegyhazi, et al., 2004; Altman, et al., 2004; Axelrod, 1984) develop game theoretic models for analysing selfishness in forwarding packets. Under general energy-constraint assumptions, the equilibrium solution for the single-stage game results in none of the nodes' cooperating to forward packets. A typical game theoretic model that leads to such equilibrium is parameterized in this section.

Now, let us consider strategy

$$\overline{s} = \{\overline{s}_1, \overline{s}_2, \overline{s}_3, ..., \overline{s}_n\}$$

and let $\sigma = \{k \in N \mid \overline{s}_k = 1\}$.

The utility of any node $k \in \sigma$ is given by:

$$u_k(\overline{s}) = (\mid \sigma \mid -1) - \overline{s}_k = \sigma - 2 \qquad (8)$$

Let us consider that node $k$ unilaterally deviates to a strategy of not participating. The utility of node $k$ is given by:

$$u_k(s'_k, \overline{s}_{-k}) = \mid \sigma \mid -1 \qquad (9)$$

Since $u_k(s'_k, \overline{s}_{-k}) > u_k(\overline{s})$, strategy $s$ can only be a Nash equilibrium when $\sigma = \varphi$. Generally, in wireless games, $N$ is the number of wireless nodes in the network, $S_k$ is the actions set for node $k$ in the network; $S_k = \{0,1\}$.

$$s_k = \begin{cases} 0, \text{when the node action is not participate} \\ 1, \text{when the node action is participate} \end{cases}$$

$S$ is the joint action set; $S = X_{k \in N} S_k$. $s = \{s_1, s_2, ...., s_n\}; s \in S, \alpha_k(s)$ is the benefit accrued when other nodes participate; $(\alpha_k(s) = \sum_{i=1, i \neq k}^{n} s_k) \cdot \beta_k$ is the energy consumption of the node when it participate; $(\beta_k = -s_k)$. $u_k(s)$ is the utility function for each node; $(u_k(s) = \alpha_k(s) + \beta_k(s))$.

However, in practical scenarios, ad hoc networks involve multiple interactions among nodes/players with a need for nodes to participate. In order to account for such interactions, the basic game is extended to a repeated game model. Different repeated game mechanisms such as tit-for-tat (DaSilva & Srivastava, 2004) and generous tit-for-tat are investigated in (Michiaradi & Molva, 2005; Abuzanat, et al., 2008; Altman, et al., 2004) to determine conditions for a desirable Nash Equilibrium – one in which all nodes would forward packets for one another leading to a high network-wide social welfare. The tit-for-tat based mechanisms provide an intrinsic incentive scheme where a node is served by its peers based on its past behavioural history. As a result a node tends to behave in a socially beneficial manner in order to receive any benefit in the later stages.

The work in (Lee, et al., 2008; Kannan, et al., 2003) extends this concept of exploiting the intrinsic 'fear' among nodes of being punished in the later stages of the game by deriving the conditions under which a grim-trigger strategy is a Nash equilibrium in a game where nodes are asked to voluntarily provide services for others (examples of these include peer-to-peer networks and distributed clusters, as well as ad hoc networks). A node following the grim trigger strategy in a repeated game is characterized by a behaviour wherein it continues to cooperate with other nodes until a single defection by any of its peers, following which it ceases to cooperate for all subsequent stages. The sustainability of the equilibrium for this strategy depends on the number of nodes in the network and the exogenous beliefs that the nodes have regarding the possible repetitions of the game. The authors conclude that the greater the number of nodes in the network the higher the chances of achieving a desirable equilibrium, even if the likelihood that the game will be repeated is low. These games are different from those analysed in (Michiaradi & Molva, 2005; Axelrod, 1984) as the decisions of the nodes are not based on an external incentive scheme such as reputation.

Other functions related to the network layer or to the management plane, such as service discovery and policy-based network management, are also amenable to a game-theoretic analysis. There is scarce literature on those issues, with the notable exception of (McAfee & McMillan, 1987b), which studies management in a sensor network.

The algorithm represented in this chapter is mainly focusing on keeping the defined path stable, where all the participating nodes are faithful to forward the packets to the next hop all the time is really important in this case. Game theory defines such a point as Nash Equilibrium. Adding some suitable modifications to the well know Dijkstra algorithm, a polynomial-time solution to find the Nash Equilibrium is shown in the following sections. We also present simulations to evaluate the reliability of the obtained route as a function of the destination and source offered payments, the source to intermediate nodes payments, power consumption and degree of source-destination cooperation for different network parameter settings.

Finally, we have to mention that these investigations are motivated by the works of Kannan, Sarangi and Iyengar on reliable query routing (Kannan, et al., 2004a, 2004b, 2002; Kuznetsov & Fetisov, 2008). To the knowledge of the authors, they are the first to formulate a game where the node utilities show a tension between path reliability and link costs, and they have considered different interesting variants of this problem. A key difference in this work is that we explicitly allow the null strategy in which nodes may choose not to forward packets to any next-hop neighbour. This allows us to provide a polynomial time algorithm for obtaining an efficient Nash equilibrium path. Another key difference in our work is that we consider the notion of destination and source payments and the amount of consumed power in each intermediate node when participating in any defined path and incorporate them into the utility functions. Every intermediate node will have the right to decide whether to participate in a route or not, based on the amount of energy the node has by the time the request is received from the source. The nodes will not argue with any request if it has more than %50 of its battery life, it will take into account the source compensation when it has less than %50 and will not participate in any route if it has less than %30 of energy. Finally, we used auction theory to decide the winner of the data information offered by the source.

## PRICE AND POWER-BASED ROUTING ALGORITHM

In this section, we define the destination driven pricing and power saving routing problem formally. A wireless network is modelled as non-cooperative game *Game(N,L)* where $N$ denotes all the nodes in the network and $L$ represents the link set. Each node $n_i$ in $N$ is associated with a reliability parameter $R_i$; $(0 \leq R_i \leq 1)$. $R_i$ indicates the node availability and stability – the probability that it can forward a packet sent to it. Each link $l = (n_i, n_j) \in L$ has a link cost parameter $C_{i,j}$, which represent the communication set up cost between two end nodes. Each link $l = (n_i, n_j) \in L$ has a link power consumption parameter $P_{i,j}$, which represent the power consumed by node $i$ when it communicate with node $j$ (i.e. node $i$ forwards a packet to node $j$).

There are three kinds of nodes in the network: destination node (*dst*) (i.e. the winner of the auction), source node (*scr*) (i.e. the server node, which offers the data information) and other intermediate nodes $n_i$ (where $n_i \in N/\{dst, scr\}$) that are candidates for participating in a route between the source and the destination. We assume that both destination node and source node always have node reliability (While the destination does play a role in offering the payment $G$ ($G$ must be more than or equal to the source reserved price $G \geq r$), this is a constant that only affects the utility for the source). The destination node offers to the source a payment amount $G_d$ for the source node, which is equal to $v_i$ defined in equation (3) (i.e. $G_d = v_i$). The source in turn offers a payment $G_s$ (for each successfully delivered packet) that will be given to any intermediate node if it participates in the routing path.

Similarly, we are assuming that each node in the network, which will participate in any defined path, will lose some of its power $P_f$ when forwarding any packets to the neighbours. To formulate the core game, we now give the definition of the triplet $(I, (s_i)_{i \in I}, (u_i)_{i \in I})$ where $I$ is the set of players; $S_i$ is the set of available actions with $S_i$ be the non-empty set of actions for player $i$; and $u_i$ is the set of payoff functions. In this game, we define $I = N\setminus\{dst\}$ which means that all nodes except the destination are players (While the destination does play a role in offering the payment $G_d$, this is a constant that only affects the utility for the source). In an $n$ nodes network (including source and destination nodes), for each node $n_i \in N\setminus\{dst\}$, its strategy is an $n$-tuple $Si = (s_{i,1}, s_{i,2}, \ldots s_{i,n})$ where:

$$S_{i,j} = \begin{cases} 1, & \text{if node } n_j \text{ is } n_i\text{'s next hope in path} \\ 0, & \text{otherwise} \end{cases}$$

(10)

We have to mention that $n_i \in N\{dst\}$ and $n_j \in N$. Each strategy tuple has at most one 1. That is, $\forall n_i, \sum_{j=1}^{n} s_{i,j} \leq 1$.

If node $n_i$'s strategy tuple contains all zeros, node $n_i$ does not participate on packet forwarding in the game. A system strategy profile $(S_i)_{i \in I}$ is a profile which contains all players' strategies in the network. Given this strategy profile, there is either no path from the source to the destination, or else, there is exactly one path *Path* (since each node can point to only next-hop). Without loss of generality, let's denote *Path* = $(src, n_1, n_2, \ldots, n_h, dst)$. Here $h$ denotes the number of hops between the source node and the destination node (not inclusive). The utility function for each player is defined as follows:

For the source node:

$$u_{src} = \begin{cases} 0, & \text{if no path exists} \\ (G_d - h.G_s - P_{tr})\Pi_{n_i \in P} R_i - C_{src,n1}, & \text{otherwise} \end{cases}$$

(11)

The utility of the source node equals to the difference between the expected income of the source and the link set up cost from the source node to the first next hop routing node. The expected income of the source is the destination payment minus the source pay to all the intermediate nodes minus the power lost to transmit packets to the next hop times the probability that the packet is successfully delivered.

For each other node $n_i$:

$$u_{node} = \begin{cases} 0, & \text{if no path exists or } n_i \notin P \\ G_s \prod_{n_{i+1}}^{n_h} R_i - C_{n_i, n_{i+1}} - P_f, & \text{otherwise} \end{cases}$$

(12)

$n_i$ is the $i_{th}$ node in the path if the named node is going to participates in the defined path. The utility of each intermediate routing node equals to the expected payment it obtains from the source node times the ongoing route reliability minus the transmission cost per packet to its next hop neighbour minus the power lost to forward the packets to the next hop.

We have to mention that the cost is made proportional to the square of the distance between two nodes if they are in each other's transmission range and how much power is consumed. If the two nodes are out of each other's transmission range, the link cost between these two nodes is set to be infinity. The mathematical representation is as follows:

$$C_{i,j} = \begin{cases} P_f . \varepsilon . d(i,j)^2, & if\, d(i,j) \leq \partial \\ \infty, & otherwise \end{cases} \qquad (13)$$

where $d(i,j)$ is the distance between node $n_i$ and node $n_j$; and $\partial$ is the transmission range of the wireless nodes. In the simulation settings, $\varepsilon$ is set to 0.1 (we also did extensive simulations for different $\varepsilon$ values, similar curve trends are observed).

The link reliability can be represented in the form;

$$R_{i,j}(t) = \frac{\sum_{i,j} P_{kts^f_{i,j}}(t)}{\sum_{i,j} P_{kts^g_{i,j}}(t) \sum_{i,j} P_{kts^r_{i,j}}(t)} \qquad (14)$$

The link reliability between two nodes (i.e. *i and j*) is defined as the ratio of the number of packets forwarded to the total number of received and generated packets the two nodes at time *t*.

If the node does not participate in the routing, it gains (and loses) nothing. We now develop an algorithm to obtain an efficient Nash equilibrium for this game. We have to mention that both values of $G$ and $P$ must be normalized in order to get the normalized value of the utility for each node. The following two equations shows how the more the source pays to the intermediate nodes the more the nodes participate in forwarding packets to its neighbours, and the more power and cost the node have to consume in order to forward the source packets the less the node will be willing to contribute in the path

$$nf_{G_{s,i}} = \frac{i}{e^{\frac{\alpha_i}{G_{s,i}}}}, nfc_{ni,ni+1} = \frac{1}{e^{\frac{C_{ni,ni+1}}{\gamma_i}}}$$

and $nf_{P_{f,i}} = \frac{1}{e^{\frac{P_{f_i}}{\beta_i}}}$,

where, $\alpha_i \geq 0$, $\gamma_i \geq 0$, $\beta_i \geq 0$. The exponential functions have been used to increase the sensitivity of the functions to the respective parameters they are related to. Finally, they are inversed in order to bound the functions to a value between zero and one.

## IMPROVEMENT SCHEMES FOR AUCTION AND ROUTING ALGORITHMS

The auction mechanism mentioned earlier, is repeated every time the offered data have been successfully delivered to the destination node, the winner of the auction. We are assuming that the source has different types of data that he offers to other nodes, the reservation price will change according to the data the source is offering for sale. We also considered the case of *winner retreat*, by which the winner is not interested anymore in the offered data (*for example*; link failure, the node run out of power, etc.). In such a case, a *counter* with a random value is introduced in the server to check whether the winner node is still interested in the offered data or not. Once the source finishes sending the data to the winner, it should wait for an acknowledgement that the data been received and starts a new auction for another pair of data, and that's when the *counter* value is set. If there is no acknowledgement been received when counter=0, the source send a message to the winner node to confirm the receiving of the data. If no reply been received after this message, the source will assume that the node is no longer in the network and starts a new auction.

From the routing point of view, our goal is to develop an algorithm for computing an efficient Nash equilibrium path that provides maximum reliability while ensuring that all nodes obtain non-negative payoffs (We should note that in our model even any shortest-hop path that ensures non-negative payoffs to all nodes are in Nash equilibrium). The algorithm we present could be potentially modified to provide such a shortest-hop Nash equilibrium path; however, our interest is in finding an efficient equilibrium path that also provides maximum reliability. This allows us to characterize the performance of the most efficient equilibrium path that can be obtained under different prices). The link between non-negative payoffs and the equilibrium path is given by the following simple lemma.

*Lemma 1: If a path exists and it is a Nash Equilibrium, every node on the path must have non-negative payoff.*

The proof for this lemma is straightforward. According to the payoff function, a node would rather choose not to participate in routing (with payoff 0) if joining the routing makes its payoff negative. However, we must note that it is not necessary for all the paths with non-negative payoff to be Nash equilibrium. We will term such a path a PPP (Positive Payoff Path). We will correspondingly term a path with all routing nodes having non-positive payoff an NPP (Negative Payoff Path).

To find a PPP, we first simplify the problem to a more concise representation. According to the definition, we need that for each intermediate routing node $n_i$, its utility $u_{ni} \geq 0$. This implies

$$\prod_{k=1}^{n} R_k \geq \frac{C_{i,i+1}}{G_s} \quad (15)$$

In order to convert the product to summation, we take the logarithm of both sides and get:

$$\sum_{k=i}^{n} \log R_k \geq \log \frac{C_{i,i+1}}{G_s} \quad (16)$$

Notice that $0 \leq R_k \leq 1$; we take the inverse of each $R_k$ to make each term in the summation positive. The original formula now transforms to;

$$\sum_{k=i}^{n} \log \frac{1}{R_k} \leq \log \frac{G_s}{C_{i,i+1}} \quad (17)$$

For each $n_i$. Replacing $\log \frac{1}{R_k}$ by $r_k$ (when $r_k \geq 0$) and replacing $\log \frac{G_s}{C_{i,i+1}}$ by $C_{i,i+1}$, we formulate the problem of finding a PPP in the original graph to an equal problem of finding an NPP in a transformed network graph, where each node has a positive value $r_k$ and each edge is assigned a value $C_{i,j}$, according to the following transformed utility functions $\tilde{u}$. For the intermediate node,

$$\tilde{U}_{n_1} = C_{i,i+1} - \sum_{k=i}^{n} r_k \quad (18)$$

For the source node, we get

$$\sum_{k=i}^{n} \log \frac{1}{R_k} \leq \log \frac{G_s - h_p}{C_{scr,n1}} \quad (19)$$

Replacing $\log \frac{1}{R_k}$ by $r_k$ and replacing $\log \frac{G_s - h_p}{C_{scr,n1}}$ by $C_{scr,nbr}$, we will have

$$\tilde{u}_{n_{ser}} = C_{scr,nbr} - \sum_{k=i}^{n} r_k \quad (20)$$

With these log-transformed formulae, in the following, we will first find an NPP of smallest $\sum r_k$ from each neighbour of source node. Then, if the source node is selfish, it picks up a feasible path provided by neighbours that gives it smallest $C_{scr,nbr} - \sum r_k$ or else if cooperative with the destination, it picks the path with the smallest $\sum r_k$. In either case, the source only participates

*Table 1. Modified Dijkstra algorithm to fir the defined auction-game scheme*

---

**Finding an NPP with Minimum** $\sum r_k$ in Transformed Network Game

1) Initialization:
Set $FS = \{dst\}$
All other nodes labeled as $(-,\infty,-)$, $L(dst) = 0$

2) while $src \notin FS$ && $N(FS) \neq 0$
 • for each $n_i \in N(FS)$
– while ( $\exists n_k \in FS$ such that $(ni,n_k) \in E$)
  $\_L(n_i) = min\ (L(n_i))$,
  $min\ n_j \in FS$ && $(n_i,n_j) \in E(L(n_j)+r_j))$ let $n_j$ be the corresponding next hop node
✓ if $\tilde{u}_{n_1} - c_{i,j} \geq 0$ : delete edge $(n_i,n_j)$.
   ✓ else: update the label triplet to $(n_j,L(n_i),L(n_i)-c_{i,j})$;
   add $n_i$ to $FS$;
   break
  – end while
 • end for
end while

---

in routing if its own original expected utility will be positive.

A polynomial time algorithm modified from *Dijkstra's algorithm* can be applied to find the NPP with the smallest $\sum r_k$ from each neighbour of the source to the destination. The pseudo code for the algorithm is given below. Note that the original source does not participate in this algorithm, so we denote the neighbour in question as *src* in the algorithm. In brief, the algorithm starts labelling nodes from the destination, applying *Dijkstra's algorithm*, with adding negative utility checking step. In the algorithm, each node has a label which is a tuple $(from,L(ni),\tilde{u}ni)$. The first item in the tuple indicates from which node the label comes (i.e., the next hop of current node starting from source). The second term in the tuple records the summation of $r_k$, which is analogous to the length in *Dijkstra's algorithm*. The third term tracks the current $\tilde{u}$ value. This algorithm is applied in turn for each neighbour of the source before the source picks one of these neighbours to form the path, as described above. Since the *r* value is related to nodes instead of the

links, we need a definition of neighbourhood set for vertices in a given game $G(N,L)$.

*Theorem: The path found by the algorithm is a Nash equilibrium path in the PPP finding problem.*

Proof (by contradiction): Assume that the algorithm returns a path $Path = (i_1,n_2,...,n_i,n_{i+1},n_j,...n_N)$ which is not a Nash equilibrium. Without loss of generality, suppose only one node $n_i$ wants to switch his next hop from $n_{i+1}$ to $n_j$, where $j > i+1$.

Path $\tilde{P}ath = (n_0,n_1,...,n_i,n_j,...,n_n)$ is also a PPP, since the payoff of the nodes before $n_j$ increases by the increase of path reliability (remember $0 \leq R_k \leq 1$) and the payoff after (including $n_j$) keep unchanged. Thus path $\tilde{P}ath$ is one of the feasible paths. Since the path abandoned some intermediate nodes, the path reliability of $\tilde{P}ath$ is larger than Path. This would imply that the algorithm should return path $\tilde{P}ath$ instead of Path, which contradicts the assumption. By construction, the node has no incentive to switch its next hop to a node that is not on the returned path since those nodes do not pick any next-hop neighbour.

*Figure 1. Example of an auction scenario*

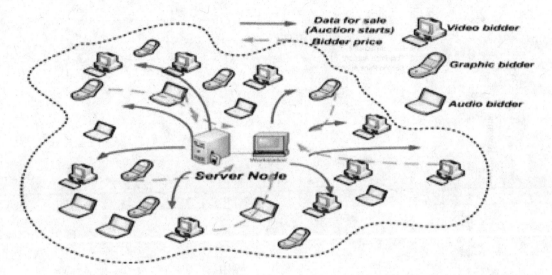

As we mentioned before, the algorithm runs to obtain a positive payoff path to destination from each neighbour of the source node. If the source node is selfish, among all the feasible paths reported from its set of neighbours, it will pick the one that gives its maximum profit according to the source's utility function. If the source node is cooperative, it will pick the path, which gives the highest path reliability (see Table 1)

## SIMULATION RESULTS

This section shows the introduced auction mechanism and the improvement scheme added to it in the previous section, along with the dynamic routing algorithm in ad hoc networks. We used a fixed $450 \times 450$ square meters area as our simulation area and 35 intermediate nodes within the network. The node's transmission range is set to 60 meters. The node reliability is uniformly chosen at random in interval [0.1, 1]. Furthermore, we assumed that the packets length is 1000 bytes, and the bandwidth of the channel to be 1 MHz, all nodes to use *250mW* transmitting power. The importance of the data is defined in each user, for simplicity, each user will choose the importance

of the data at random from the interval [1, 95]. The importance of the data information offered by the source is measured in percentage, the user need will change whenever a new auction is announced by the source.

We first compare our model with similar model with a game-based model only, which is similar to the ones introduced in (Kannan, et al., 2002, 2004a, 2004b; Kuznetsov & Fetisov, 2008), where the source will assign the data to the first buyer without waiting for any other offers and pays all intermediate nodes the same amount of compensation. We will also compare this model with the model introduced by this work, where we combined Auction and Game theory's, using two auction mechanisms; first-price and second price sealed auctions.

Figure 1 shows a very simple example of an auction scenario. Where the source node announces the auction and waits for the users' bids.

Figure 2 shows the source revenue when the number of users competing between each other is low, where the auction only starts when there are two users or more competing with each other. If there is only one user interested in the offered data, then it's up to the source to accept his offer when it's more than the reserved price. The rev-

*Figure 2. Source revenue with few competitors*

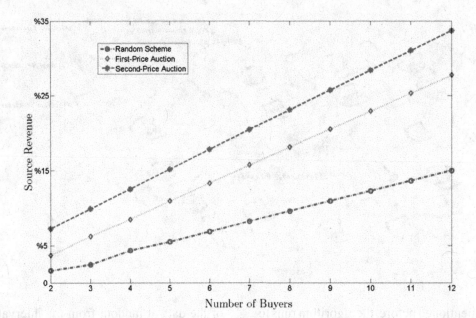

enue is measured on how much the source will gain more than the reserved price.

From Figures 2 and 3, it is clearly shown that when the number of competitors increase the source revenue will increase dramatically. The second-price sealed-auction gives better revenue to the seller as it force the buyers to offer their true valuation of the offered good. This might not be so obvious in the first-price sealed-auction, as the bidder is trying to maximize their own profit from winning by lowering the bid below its true valuation. However, in equilibrium, as every bidder adopts the same strategy, the bidder with the highest valuation still stands out. Compared with the game-based random allocation scheme, introduced in (Kannan, et al., 2002, 2004a, 2004b; Kuznetsov & Fetisov, 2008). Where the source is sells the data to the first node that offers a price any price and pays in advance for all the intermediate nodes and waits for their response whether to participate or not (all intermediate nodes will receive the source payment, which is why the source revenue will go down when the number of intermediate nodes rise). We can observe that

the auction-based schemes are significantly better in terms of improving the seller's revenue and improving the system efficiency.

Figure 4 illustrates the path reliability versus source pay for intermediate nodes when fixing $G_d$ to 300% of the reserved price (a sufficient large amount). From this figure, we can see that the density of the deployments increases, the maximum reachable path reliability increases. This result is expected; when the source pays more to intermediate nodes, the expected path reliability increase too. We notice in both cases that when $G_s$ exceeds some threshold point; the path reliability will remain almost constant. We must mention that the source payment to the intermediate nodes is measured in percentage, of how much the source is ready to offer the network of his revenue.

Figure 5 plots the source gain versus the source pay to the intermediate nodes with fixed number of nodes (25 nodes) and the area size. Recall that from the source utility function in section 7, source utilities in most cases are dominated by the term of $(G - h.G_s)\Pi_{n_i \in Path} R_i$ Increasing $G_s$ can lead to

*Figure 3. Source revenue with large number of competitors*

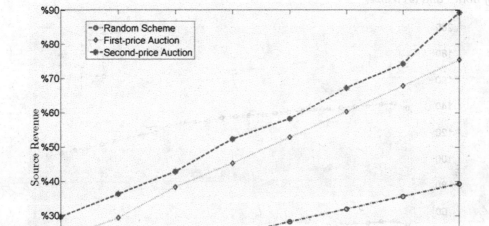

*Figure 4. Path reliability versus source pay to each routing node when changing number of nodes in a fixed area*

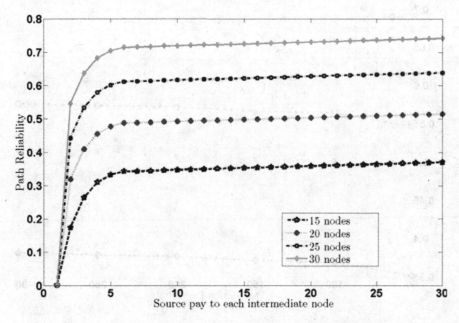

*Figure 5. Source gain versus source pay to each routing node for different destination pay, when fixing number of nodes and area size*

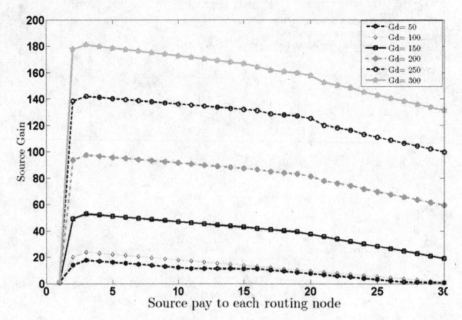

*Figure 6. Behaviour of selfish source node effect on the path reliability*

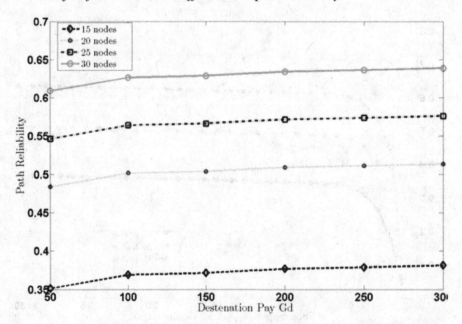

*Figure 7. Behaviour of cooperative source node effect on the path reliability*

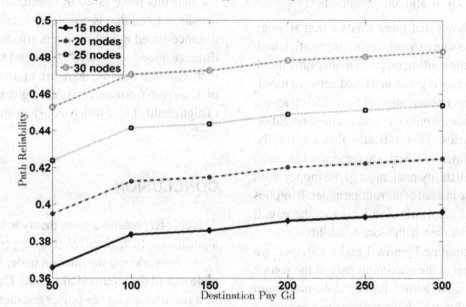

*Figure 8. Cumulative distribution function for the existence of Nash Equilibrium path when increasing source pay to each routing node*

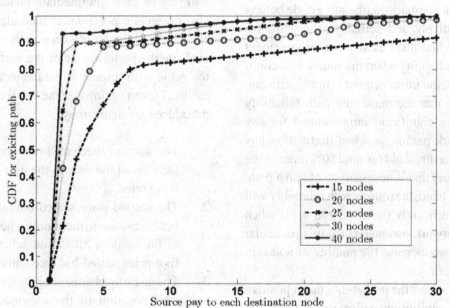

decreasing of $h$ and increment of $\Pi_{n_i \in Path} R_i$. Figure 4 shows that there exists a best strategy point for the source to maximize its payoff, which is at the same routing price no matter how much destination pay is given in a fixed network topology. The other observation of Figure 5 is that; the portion of source gain increases as the destination pays increases. This indicates that even if the destination increase the pay to the source to request a certain reliability path, most of the money goes to the source instead of the routing nodes. It implies that even if the destination increases the pay, it will not get a path with more reliability.

If we examine Figures 4 and 5 together, we will find that at the maximum gain of the source node, the path reliability is close to the maximum path reliability which the network can reach.

This gives us an important insight: selfish behaviour of source node in such system will not hurt system performance much. Figures 6 and 7 show a comparison of source node behaving cooperatively and selfishly. These figures demonstrate that there exist some improvement to the path reliability when the source acts cooperatively, but the improvement is not significant. We also see that the maximum path reliability will not have significant improvement for any fixed network parameter when destination pay exceeds some threshold (around 50% more of the reserved price) that is necessary to obtain a path. On the other hand, the routing path reliability will increase significantly (from 0.39 to 0.74) when changing network parameters (in this particular simulation, we increase the number of nodes in the fixed area).

Figure 8 shows the probability that a positive payoff Nash equilibrium path exists as a function of the price offered by the source. For each case, we see that the curve increases to a point where it is close to one. This shows the existence of critical threshold prices (independent of the exact configuration) that ensure the existence of a Nash Equilibrium path with high probability. We also see that this price threshold decreases with the density, a trend that is concrete visualized in the distance-based model, which is affected by node distance more seriously. This trend is because with growing density, there are more choices to pick the path from, and there are a greater number of high quality links, which incur low transmission cost.

## CONCLUSION

This chapter presents a game theory based routing algorithm, which involves three types of nodes in the network: the destination node, the source node and all the intermediate nodes. Defining the best route based on the power consumption that each intermediate node will suffer to forward a packet, the price the destination will pay to the source and the amount of compensation the source will pay to each intermediate node. The paper also presents a polynomial time algorithm that can give a *Nash Equilibrium* path and use it to evaluate the performance of the performance of the game with respect to parameters mentioned earlier. We can summarize the key findings of the introduced mechanism by;

1.  The auction mechanism insures a fare allocation of the data to the user who values it the most.
2.  The second-price sealed-bid auction gives better revenue to the source when compared to the random allocation scheme and the first-price sealed-bid mechanism.
3.  The game mechanism combines both source compensation to the intermediate nodes and the power consumption to improve the path reliability between the source and the destination (i.e. the winning bidder).
4.  The source payoff will increase once the network density increases (i.e. the number of intermediate nodes increases). This is because the routing paths become cheaper

and more reliable and even if the source is acting selfishly, the path reliability will not be downgraded significantly.

Finally, the simulation results prove that the introduced auction mechanism dramatically increases the seller's revenue whether he decide to choose the first or second-price auction. Moreover, the results briefly evaluate the reliability of predefined route with respect to the data prices and source and destination cooperation for different network settings.

## REFERENCES

Abaii, M., Yajian, L., & Tafazolli, R. (2008). An efficient resource allocation strategy for future wireless cellular systems. *IEEE Transactions on Wireless Communications*, 7(8), 2940–2949. doi:10.1109/TWC.2008.060161

Abuzanat, H., Trouillet, B., & Toguyeni, A. (2008). Routing fairness model for QoS optimization in wireless network. In *Proceedings of the 2ⁿᵈ International Conference on Sensor Technologies and Applications (SENSORCOMM 2008),* (pp. 776-781). Cap Esterel, France: IEEE Press.

Altman, E., Kherani, A. A., Michiardi, P., & Molva, R. (2004). *Non-cooperative forwarding in ad hoc networks (Report 5116)*. Sophia-Antipolis, France: INRIA.

Axelrod, R. (1984). *The evolution of cooperation*. New York, NY: Basic Books.

Cassady, R. (1967). *Auction and auctioneering*. Berkeley, CA: University of California Press.

Coucheney, P., Touati, C., & Gaujal, B. (2009). Selection of efficient pure strategies in allocation games. In *Proceedings of the International Conference on Game Theory for Networks (GameNets 2009),* (pp. 658-666). Istanbul, Turkey: IEEE Press.

Das, A., Neishaboori, A., & Kesidis, G. (2009). Wireless mesh networking games. *In Proceedings of the International Conference on Game Theory for Networks (GameNets 2009),* (pp. 565-574). Istanbul, Turkey: IEEE Press.

DaSilva, A., & Srivastava, V. (2004). *Node participation in peer-to-peer and ad hoc networks: A game theoretic formulation*. Paper presented at the Workshop on Games and Emergent Behaviour in Distributed Computing. Birmingham, UK.

Dutta, P. K. (2001). *Strategies and games: Theory and practice*. Boston, MA: MIT Press.

Felegyhazi, M., Buttyan, L., & Hubaux, J. P. (2004). Equilibrium analysis of packet forwarding strategies in wireless ad hoc networks – The dynamic case. In *Proceeding of the 2ⁿᵈ Workshop on Modelling and Optimization in Mobile, Ad Hoc and Wireless Networks (WiOpt 2004)*. Cambridge, UK: IEEE Press.

Felegyhazi, M., Buttyan, L., & Hubaux, J. P. (2006). Nash equilibria of packet forwarding strategies in wireless ad hoc networks. *IEEE Transactions on Mobile Computing*, 5(5), 463–476. doi:10.1109/TMC.2006.68

Felegyhazi, M., Cagalj, M., Bidokhti, S., & Hubaux, J. (2007). Non-cooperative multi-radio channel allocation in wireless networks. In *Proceedings of the 26ᵗʰ IEEE International Conference on Computer Communications (INFOCOM 2007),* (pp.1442-1450). Anchorage, AK: IEEE Press.

Houser, D., & Wooders, J. (2001). *Reputation in auctions: Theory and evidence from eBay (working paper)*. Phoenix, AZ: University of Arizona.

Jianwei, H., Zhu, H., Mung, C., & Poor, H. V. (2008). Auction-based resource allocation for cooperative communications. *IEEE Journal on Selected Areas in Communications*, 26(7), 1226–1237. doi:10.1109/JSAC.2008.080919

Kannan, R., Sarangi, S., & Iyengar, S. S. (2002). A simple model for reliable query reporting in sensor networks. In *Proceedings of the 5th International Conference on Information Fusion*, (pp. 754-759). Annapolis, MD: ACM Press.

Kannan, R., Sarangi, S., & Iyengar, S. S. (2004). Game-theoretic models for reliable path-length and energy-constrained routing with data aggregation in wireless sensor networks. *IEEE Journal on Selected Areas in Communications, 22*(6), 1141–1150. doi:10.1109/JSAC.2004.830937

Kannan, R., Sarangi, S., & Iyengar, S. S. (2004). Sensor-centric energy constrained reliable query routing for wireless sensor networks. *Journal of Parallel and Distributed Computing, 64*, 839–852. doi:10.1016/j.jpdc.2004.03.010

Kannan, R., Sarangi, S., Iyengar, S. S., & Ray, L. (2003). Sensor centric quality of routing in sensor networks. In *Proceeding of the 22nd Annual Joint Conference of the IEEE Computer and Communications (INFOCOM 2003)*, (vol 2), (pp. 693-701). San Francisco, CA: IEEE Press.

Krishna, V. (2002). *Auction theory*. San Diego, CA: Elsevier.

Krishna, V. (2009). *Auction theory* (2nd ed.). London, UK: Elsevier.

Kuznetsov, N. A., & Fetisov, V. N. (2008). Enhanced-robustness Dijkstra algorithm for control of routing in the IP-networks. *Automation and Remote Control, 69*(2), 247–251. doi:10.1134/S0005117908020069

Laffont, J., & Maskin, E. (1980). Optimal reservation prices in the Vickrey auction. *Economics Letters, 6*, 309–313. doi:10.1016/0165-1765(80)90002-6

Lee, J. F., Liao, W., & Chen, M. C. (2008). An incentive-based fairness mechanism for multi-hop wireless backhaul networks with selfish nodes. *IEEE Transactions on Wireless Communications, 7*(2), 697–704. doi:10.1109/TWC.2008.060631

McAfee, R., & McMillan, J. (1987a). Auctions and bidding. *Journal of Economic Literature, 25*, 699–738.

McAfee, R., & McMillan, J. (1987b). Auctions with a stochastic number of bidders. *Journal of Economic Theory, 43*, 1–19. doi:10.1016/0022-0531(87)90113-X

McAfee, R., & McMillan, J. (1992). Bidding rings. *The American Economic Review, 82*, 579–599.

Menezes, F. M., & Monteiro, P. K. (2004). *An introduction to auction theory*. Oxford, UK: Oxford University Press.

Michiardi, P., & Molva, R. (2005). Analysis of coalition formation and cooperation strategies in mobile ad hoc networks. *Journal of Ad Hoc Networks, 3*(2), 193–219. doi:10.1016/j.adhoc.2004.07.006

Milgrom, P. R. (1985). A theory of auction and competitive bidding. *Journal of Econometrics, 50*(5), 1089–1122.

Parrsch, H. J., & Robert, J. (2003). *Testing equilibrium behaivour at first-price, sealed-bid auctions with discrete bid increments (working paper)*. Montreal, CA: CIRANO. Retrieved from http://econpapers.repec.org/paper/circirwor/2003s-32.htm.

Patten, R. W. (1970). *Tatworth candle auction*. London, UK: Taylor & Francis.

Resnick, P., & Zeckhauser, R. (2002). Trust among strangers in Internet transactions: Empirical analysis of eBay's reputation system. In Baye, M. R. (Ed.), *The Economics of the Internet and E-Commerce: Advances in Applied Microeconomics (Vol. 11)*. Amsterdam, The Netherlands: Elsevier Science. doi:10.1016/S0278-0984(02)11030-3

Shubik, M. (2004). *The theory of money and financial institutions (Vol. 1)*. Cambridge, MA: MIT Press.

Srinivasan, V., Nuggehalli, P., Chiasserini, C. F., & Rao, R. R. (2003). Cooperation in wireless ad hoc networks. In *Proceeding of the 22ⁿᵈ Annual Joint Conference of the IEEE Computer and Communications (INFOCOM 2003)*, (vol 2), (pp. 808-817). San Francisco, CA: IEEE Press.

Stockholm Auction House. (2011). *About the company*. Retrieved 5 March 2010 from http://www.auktionsverket.se/historike.htm.

Urpi, A., Bonuccelli, M., & Giordano, S. (2003). Modeling cooperation in mobile ad hoc networks: A formal description of selfishness. In *Proceeding of the 1ˢᵗ Workshop on Modeling and Optimization in Mobile, Ad Hoc and Wireless Networks (WiOpt 2003)*. Sophia-Antipolis, France: IEEE Press.

Varoli, J. (2007). Swedish auction house to sell 8 million Euros of Russian art. *Bloomberg News*. Retrieved 3 March 2010 from http://www.bloomberg.com/apps/news?pid=20601088&sid=aGlwT7.MHwzw&refer=muse.

Vickrey, W. (1961). Counter speculation, auctions, and competitive sealed tenders. *The Journal of Finance, 16*, 8–37. doi:10.2307/2977633

Yang, D., & Chen, M. (2008). Efficient resource allocation for wireless multicast. *IEEE Transactions on Mobile Computing, 7*(4), 387–400. doi:10.1109/TMC.2007.70739

Yuan, J., & Yu, W. (2008). Joint source coding, routing and power allocation in wireless sensor networks. *IEEE Transactions on Communications, 56*(6), 886–896. doi:10.1109/TCOMM.2008.060237

Zaikiuddin, I., Hawkins, T., & Moffat, N. (2005). Towards a game-theoretic understanding of ad hoc routing. *Electronic Notes in Theoretical Computer Science, 119*(1), 67–92. doi:10.1016/j.entcs.2004.07.009

Zhu, H., & Liu, K. J. R. (2005). Noncooperative power-control game and throughput game over wireless networks. *IEEE Transactions on Communications, 53*(10), 1625–1629. doi:10.1109/TCOMM.2005.857136

## KEY TERMS AND DEFINITIONS

**Auction Theory:** Is a glossary of Game Theory terms, which deals with how people act in auction situations and researches the properties of auctions.

**First-Price Sealed-Bid Auction:** One type of auctions, bidders submit sealed bids and the highest bidder gets the object for the price she/he bid.

**Game Theory:** Game theory is the mathematical study of the ways in which strategic interactions among agents (i.e. players) produce outcomes with respect to the preferences (i.e. utilities) of those agents, where the outcomes in question might have been intended by none of the agents.

**Resource Allocation:** Sometimes called resource management and is used to assign all available resources between all participants in a fair, economic way.

**Second-Price Sealed-Bid Auction:** One type of auctions, the highest bidder is awarded the item and pays the second highest bid.

**Wireless Ad-Hoc Networks:** Is a decentralized wireless network, where each node participates in routing by forwarding data for other nodes, and so the determination of which nodes forward data is made dynamically based on the network connectivity.

# Chapter 2
# Simulating Game Applications in Mobile IPv6 Protocol

**Omar Raoof**
*Brunel University, UK*

**Hamed Al-Raweshidy**
*Brunel University, UK*

## ABSTRACT

*This chapter proposes a novel game-based green interface/network selection mechanism that is an extension to the multi-interface fast-handover mobile IPv6 protocol and works when the mobile node has more than one wireless interface. The mechanism controls the handover decision process by deciding whether a handover is needed or not and helps the node to choose the right access point at the right time. Additionally, the mechanism switches the mobile nodes interfaces "ON" and "OFF" when needed to control the mobile node's energy consumption and improves the handover latency.*

## INTRODUCTION

In recent years, we have seen an increasing demand from end-users to access network resources from anywhere and at any time from all kinds of devices. Mobile computing has become an important area of computer networking and is expected to play a fundamental role in the ubiquitous access of Internet resources in the future. A greater degree of connectivity is almost becoming mandatory in today's business world. In addition, mobility

of end-users is placing further requirements on network systems and protocols to provide uninterrupted services.

Mobile IP (MIP) is an open standard, defined by the Internet Engineering Task Force (IETF) (RFC, 2002) that allows users to keep the same IP address, stay connected, and maintain ongoing applications while roaming between IP networks. MIP is scalable for the Internet because it is based on IP—any media that can support IP can support MIP (Cisco, 2001). Roaming is a general term in wireless communications that means the ability of Mobile Node (MN) to extend connectivity in

DOI: 10.4018/978-1-4666-0191-8.ch002

a location that is different from its home location where the service was registered. MIP provides efficient, scalable mechanisms for roaming within the Internet (Ernst, 2006; Clincy & Mudiraj, 2007). Moreover, the use of MIP, allow MN's to randomly change their point of attachment and maintain ongoing communication with their destinations without changing their IP addresses.

Mobile network protocols such as Mobile IPv4 (MIPv4) have emerged as one of the promising solutions capable of providing uninterrupted connectivity. It allows the users to travel beyond their home network while still maintain their own home IP address. Similarly, Mobile IPv6 (MIPv6) is the protocol that deals with the mobility for the IPv6 nodes. This protocol allows an IPv6 node to be mobile, and randomly change its location on the IPv6 Internet while still maintaining its existing connections (Clincy & Mudiraj, 2007). The following sections include brief definitions of some of the most important terms used within this chapter.

## RECENT DEVELOPMENT TO MIPV6 PROTOCOL

## Background

Nowadays, wireless technologies are widely used in IPv6 communications (Johnson, et al., 2004). In addition to sharp increase of mobile terminals, various kinds of wireless technologies are available for MNs. Therefore, many mobile nodes begin to have multiple wireless interfaces and every user wants to use them simultaneously to reinforce connectivity to the Internet. Selection of the most efficient and suitable access network to meet a specific application's Quality-of-Service (QoS) requirements has thus recently become a significant topic, the actual focus of which is maximizing the QoS experienced by the user. The main concept is that users will rely on intelligent network selection decision strategies to aid them

in optimal network selection. Fast-Handover Mobile IPv6 (FMIPv6) (Koodli, 2005) already offers some rudimentary handover features. For instance, a MN may send a binding update to its Present Access Router (PAR). This causes the PAR to redirect packets towards the new Care-of-Address (CoA) of the MN.

In the present context, while the MN moves around a certain area, it keeps checking the around Access Routers (ARs), once it receives that there is an AR around it, it will start the handover procedure between the PAR and the New Access Router (NAR). Yet, there is no way for the user and/or the application to force the MN not to make the handover in order to stay with the AR that offers a better service. On the other hand, game theory (Rasmusen, 2006) is a set of tools developed to model interactions between agents with conflicting interests, and is thus well suited to address some problems in communications systems, which might be related to interface and/or network selection mechanisms. Game theory skills can be easily adapted for use in radio resource management mechanisms in a heterogeneous environment. Accordingly, the following sections present a mechanism for combining interface and/or network selection mechanisms and game theory. In such a way that the user and/or the application will have the ability to dynamically control which network to access while moving around different AP's.

## Recent Extensions to MIPv6

Recently, various kinds of wireless technologies are available for the MNs. MIPv6 (Cisco, 2001) describes the protocol operations for a MN to maintain connectivity to the Internet during its handover from one AR to another. As mentioned earlier that the solution of keeping ongoing connectivity on the move is by using several interfaces and use them simultaneously. However, the basic MIPv6 protocol (Johnson, et al., 2004) cannot support the simultaneous usage of multiple interfaces, because

MIPv6 does not allow a MN to register multiple CoA's corresponding to multiple attachments of several interfaces. The reason why everybody is looking to add multiple wireless technologies to a MN is clearly, that they can be used for various purposes. For example, an interface can be used as backup to recover from possible loss of Internet connectivity of another interface. Moreover, two or more interfaces can be used simultaneously to increase the aggregate bandwidth, or load sharing of different applications.

Lately, the multiple CoA registration protocol (Wakikawa, et al., 2009) extends MIPv6 protocol with an option called "Binding Unique Identifier (BID) sub option" to associate multiple CoA's with one home address. Although the MIPv6 protocol describes a procedure to maintain connectivity to the Internet during handover, the involved handover latency may degrade the quality of the Internet applications, which are delay-sensitive or throughput-sensitive. However, in the case of MIPv6 using multiple CoA registration, packet tunnelling to a NAR during handover of one interface can incur performance degradation due to severe packet reordering when multiple interfaces are simultaneously used for load sharing. This is because the partial traffic flow destined to the interface involved in handover is suspended during the handover process and later tunnelled to NAR, but the MN may receive continuously the other partial traffic flow through another interfaces not involving handover. That could incur severe reordering if the handover procedure is delayed or unstable by ping-pong effects, the repeated handoffs between two access points caused by rapid fluctuations in the received signal strengths from both access points. In case the traffic is a TCP flow, this reordering severely degrades the throughput performance by turning on the TCP congestion control. This could also affect real-time applications.

As a result, the Fast Handover MIPv6 (FMIPv6) protocol (Koodli, 2005) has been proposed to reduce the handover latency. Generally,

FMIPv6 tries to reduce the movement detection latency and the new CoA configuration latency by processing the handover signalling in advance. The basic idea behind the FMIPv6 is that the PAR forwards the arriving packets designated to the MN to the NAR by setting up a tunnel to the NAR in order to prevent packet losses incurred by handover latency during handover procedure. For the same reason, it is necessary for the multiple interface MIPv6 protocol to adopt a fast handover procedure to enhance its handover performance by reducing handover latency and packet losses.

The FMIPv6 protocol works as follows; essentially the handover procedure starts when a MN sends an RtSolPr (router solicitation for proxy, which is a message from the MN to the PAR requesting information for a potential handover) message to its AR through a handover-interface to resolve one or more Access Point (AP) identifiers to subnet-specific information. In response, the AR sends a PrRtAdv (proxy router advertisement, which is a message from the PAR to the MN that provides information about neighbouring link facilitating expedited movement detection [Koodli, 2001]) message containing one or more access point ID and information. The MN may send an RtSolPr as a response to some link-specific event (a "trigger") or after performing router discovery. However, prior to sending RtSolPr, the MN should have discovered available APs by link-specific methods such as AP scanning procedure in IEEE 802.11 wireless LAN.

The RtSolPr and PrRtAdv messages do not establish any state at the AR (Koodli, 2005). The exact details about the packet format are out of the scope of this chapter. However, more details about them can be found (Johmson, et al., 2004). With the information provided in the PrRtAdv message, the MN formulates a prospective NCoA (New CoA) and sends an FBU (Fast Binding Update) message. For a single interface FMIPv6, the main purpose of the FBU is to inform PAR of binding PCoA (Previous CoA) to NCoA, so that arriving packets can be tunnelled to the new location of the MN. The PAR will send FBAck (Fast Binding Acknowledgment) message to the MN and NAR to initiate the handover mechanism. The MN disconnects from the PAR and sends FNA (fast neighbour advertisement) message to the NAR in order to start the communication and that will reduce the handover latency. Figure 1 shows the handover procedure for the FMIPv6 protocol.

Park et al (2008) proposed a multi-interface fast handover MIPv6 (MFMIPv6) protocol as an extension to the FMIPv6 that can mitigate the reordering problem during handover when MN's have multiple wireless interfaces and multiple CoA registrations. This procedure can indicate a specific tunnelling destination except the NAR, for example, one of the other interfaces (or CoAs) in the same MN. One of the main advantages of the MFMIPv6 protocol is that the throughput of a TCP flow would increase by avoiding the unnecessary congestion control. Moreover, the named mechanism can improve the handover signalling performance because data traffic is redirected to another interface during handover signalling. After the successful handover of the

corresponding interface, the redirected traffic flow is restored to be directed to the NAR and finally to the original interface. In general, the MFMIPv6 Protocol works very similar to the FMIPv6. However, instead of forwarding the packets to the NAR during the handover process, the packets are forwarded to the other interface of the same MN.

For a multi-interface FMIPv6, tunnelling packets to NCoA may degrade traffic performance by severe reordering as mentioned before. In the propose extension, the FBU message not only carries the NCoA but also a "tunnel destination" mobility option which could be another CoA that is registered for other interface of the same MN. This message is called as "Multi-Interface FBU (MFBU) message" to distinguish it from the FBU message of the basic FMIPv6 protocol, as shown in Figures 2 and 3.

More details about each field of these two messages in (Koodli, 2005; Rasmusen, 2006; Wakikawa, et al., 2009). However, the tunnel destination option should be included as a mobility option in the MFBU message in order to inform the PAR of the tunnel destination address to re-

*Figure 1. Handover procedure in FMIPv6 protocol*

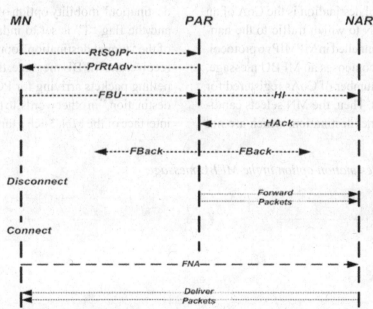

*Figure 2. FBU message*

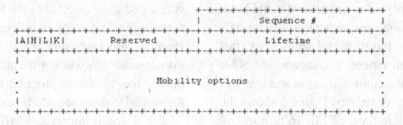

*Figure 3. MFBU message*

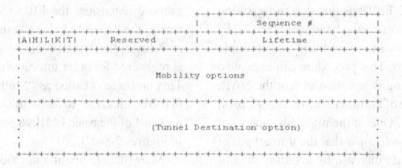

direct traffic toward the handover interface of the MN to other interface CoA. This option is valid only in MFBU message. The format of the tunnel destination option is shown in Figure 4.

Where the type filed is to be determined by IANA (Internet assigned number authority). The length filed represents the length of an IPv6 address and the tunnel destination is the CoA of an interface of the MN to which traffic to the handover interface is tunnelled in MFMIPv6 protocol.

When the MN composes an MFBU message, it first checks the number of CoAs registered for multiple interfaces. Then, the MN selects candidate CoAs for tunnel destination, which are not being involved in handover. Among them, the MN checks each interface whether or not it has appropriate characteristics for the traffic to be tunnelled. The MN also examines the available bandwidth of candidate interfaces whether they can accommodate the traffic. Finally, the CoA of the selected interface is inserted into the "tunnel destination" mobility option of the FBU message and the flag "T" is set to indicate the existence of the "tunnel destination" option. After the PAR receives the MFBU message, the PAR begins tunnelling packets arriving for PCoA to the "tunnel destination," in other words, to the CoA of the other interface of the MN. Such a tunnel remains active

*Figure 4. Tunnel destination option in the MFBU message*

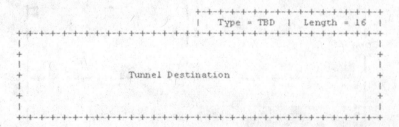

until the MN completes the registration of a new CoA with its Home Agent or correspondents. After that, the HI (Handover Initiate), HAck (Handover Acknowledge), FBAck, and FNA (Fast Network Attachment) messages are used in the protocol as the same way in the basic FMIPv6 protocol (Koodli, 2005). The overall handover procedure of MFMIPv6 is illustrated below in Figure 5.

After the successful handover of the corresponding interface, the redirected traffic flow is restored to direct to the NAR and finally to the original interface. In this protocol, a mobility option that indicates a tunnel destination point for the coming traffic flow to a PAR. The ARs should recognize the tunnel destination option and redirect the traffic flow to another AR that is connected to another active interface of the same MN. There are no special requirements for a home agent to behave differently with respect to the basic FMIPv6 procedure.

In a handover scenario, the second interface of the MN (IF2) is about to begin handing over from one AR to another. The first interface (IF1) is attached to PAR and remains stable. If the MN runs the original FMIPv6, the NAR begins buffer-

ing the traffic to the MN when it receives the FBU message and tunnelling to the NAR starts after exchanging the HI and HAck messages. During this fast handover procedure, half of the traffic is continuously transferred to the MN through the first interface (IF1). This process MAY cause severe packet reordering if the handover delay is large or traffic load is heavy. For example, it is assumed that the characteristics of the two paths such as delay and bandwidth between the HA and two interfaces of the MN are similar, and the HA divides the traffic alternatively to IF1 and IF2 as shown in Table 1 (Park, et al., 2008):

Then, the MN can receive in-order packets when the MN is not involved in any handover. However, when IF2 starts handing over from one AR to another and the MN runs the original fast handover procedure, the order of packet arrivals may become as follows if the MN's handover events occur as:

1, 2, 3, 4, 5, 7, 9, 11, 6, 8, 10, 12, 13, 14, 15

Then, because it is assumed that the traffic is a TCP flow, the above reordering issues three dupli-

*Figure 5. Handover procedure in MFMIPv6 protocol*

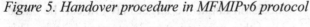
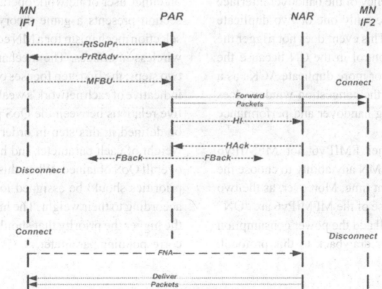

*Table 1. Ha divides he traffic to IF1 and IF2*

| IF1 (CoA1): | 1 | | 3 | | 5 | | 7 | | 9 | | 11 | | 13 | | 15... |
|---|---|---|---|---|---|---|---|---|---|---|---|---|---|---|---|
| IF2 (CoA2): | | 2 | | 4 | | 6 | | 8 | | 10 | | 12 | | 14... | |
| | | | | | | \|< Handover instant | | | | | | | | | |
| | | | | | | (FBU or MFBU message arrival to PAR) | | | | | | | | | |
| | | | | | | | FNA message arrival to NAR >\| | | | | | | | |

cate ACK's when the MN receives packet number 11. The Corresponding Node (CN) receives these three duplicate ACKs, takes this event as a packet loss and starts a congestion control procedure. Therefore, the CN reduces its sending rate, which causes performance degradation. In contrast, when the MN runs the MFMIPv6, the traffic toward IF2 is redirected to CoA1 of IF1 when the PAR receives the MFBU message that includes "tunnel destination" option equal to CoA1. Then, the order of packet arrivals may become as follows if the MN's handover events occur:

1, 2, 3, 4, 5, 7, 9, 6, 11, 8, 13, 10, 15, 12, 14

In this scenario, although the packet reordering could occur, three duplicate ACKs do not occur frequently because the CoA1 is not involved in the handover process at this moment and stable. Even if the handover latency of the handover interface becomes very large, only one or two duplicate ACKs may occur. This event does not trigger the TCP congestion control in the CN because the TCP regards three or more duplicate ACKs as a packet loss. Thus, the congestion window does not decrease during handover and performance is not degraded.

However, neither FMIPv6 nor MFMIPv6 protocols offer the MN any ability to choose the right AR at the right time. Moreover, as the two interfaces in the case of the MFMIPv6 are "ON" all the time that will add the power consumption problem as another drawback to this protocol.

Furthermore, both protocols uses only static factors to decide whether the handover is needed or not and both suffer from the ping-pong effect.

## GAME-BASED DYNAMIC NETWORK SELECTION MECHANISM

Admission control schemes are the decision making part of networks with the objective of providing services to users with guaranteed QoS in order to reduce the network congestion and call dropping probability and achieve as much resource utilization as possible (MacKenzie & deSilva, 2006). When several radio technologies may at the same time attend the user services demand, a decision is necessary to select the most suitable radio access technology on a per user basis. The decision about the target network can be based on either user or network/operator criteria. This section presents a game theory based network selection mechanism for a MN equipped with two wireless interfaces. The mechanism consists of two steps; the first step focuses on finding factors indicative of each network's weak points. Qualitative relations between the QoS parameters must be defined in this step in order to calculate the weight of each parameter and how it affects the overall QoS obtained. When this step is finished, priorities should be assigned to each parameter according to their weight. The higher a weight is, the higher the priority that should be given to the corresponding parameter.

The second step investigates all available networks in order to find the optimal choice. A questionnaire filled by the users of the networks might give a great understanding of the weight of each QoS parameter mentioned earlier. To estimate how each parameter fails to satisfy the system specifications, the ratio

$$\frac{\Delta x}{x} = \frac{|x - x_\mu|}{x}$$

is used to determine how much worse the network's performance as compared to the desired one. Where $(x)$ is a set of values, which considered as optimal, and $(x_\mu)$ is the measurement mean value of each QoS parameter, $(x_\mu)$ is always assumed to be worse than $(x)$ (i.e., $x_\mu < x$ or $x_\mu > x$ for the values considered to be larger or smaller than the better respectively). With this ratio, the mechanism manages to assign each parameter a weight proportional to the extent at which it fails to satisfy the specifications. Moving forward to find the optimal solution where matrices are used to synthesize all problem-deciding factors. With the matrix form, the elements are compared in each level of the hierarchy in order to provide a degree of preferences of one parameter against the other, as shown in Figure 6.

More specifically, depending on the factors from each interface under comparison, the following cases exist:

1. $W_{i,j} = 1$, when a factor is compared to itself.
2. $W_{i,j} > 1$, then factor $i$ is assumed to be more important than factor $j$.
3. $W_{i,j} < 1$, then it's the opposite, when factor $j$ is more important than $i$.

Relative weights generated after a repetitive process with which the decision elements participate in the configuration of the final objective of the mechanism.

The mechanism consists of two main parts, network discovery and network analysis. In the Network Discover model, all available networks are identified and priorities are assigned to them. This process is divided into two parts: Firstly, the networks are added to the candidate list if the Received Signal Strength (RSS) is higher than its threshold value and its mobility threshold is greater than the velocity of MN. We assume that $N = \{n_1, n_2, _3, ..., n_k\}$ is the set of available network

*Figure 6. Matrix format of the game mechanism*

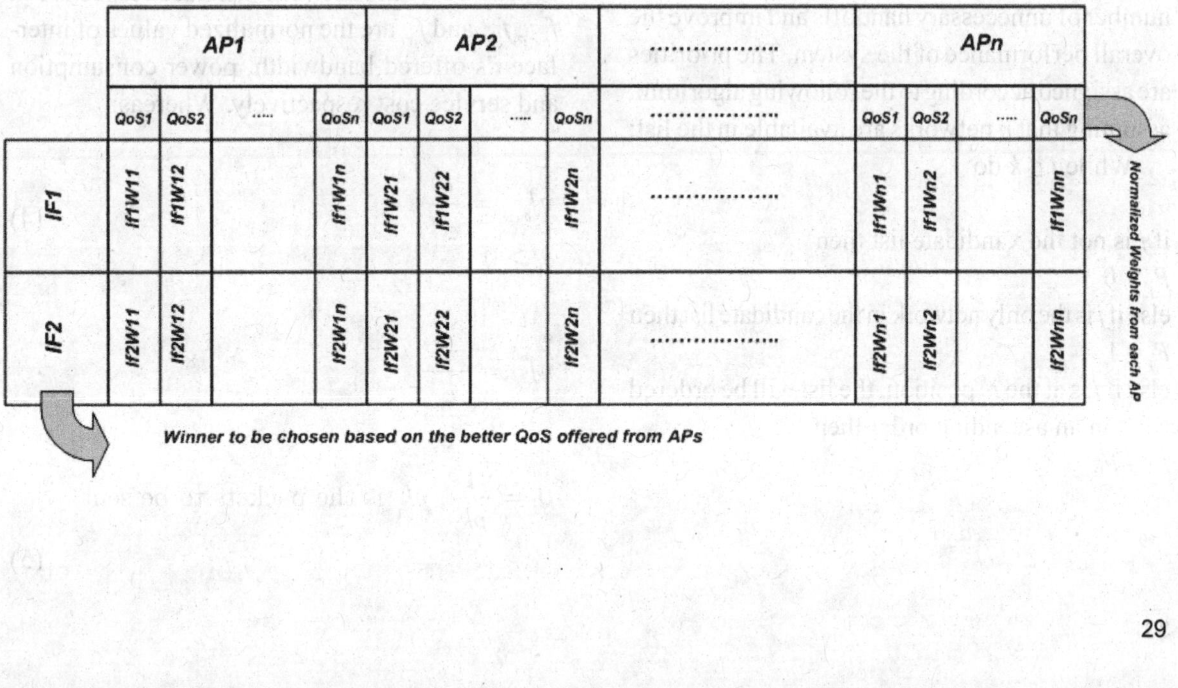

| | | AP1 | | ..... | | AP2 | | | ..... | .................... | | APn | | | |
|---|---|---|---|---|---|---|---|---|---|---|---|---|---|---|---|
| | | QoS1 | QoS2 | ..... | QoSn | QoS1 | QoS2 | ..... | QoSn | .................... | | QoS1 | QoS2 | ..... | QoSn |
| IF1 | | If1W11 | If1W12 | | If1W1n | If1W21 | If1W22 | | If1W2n | ................. | | If1Wn1 | If1Wn2 | | If1Wnn |
| IF2 | | If2W11 | If2W12 | | If2W1n | If2W21 | If2W22 | | If2W2n | ................. | | If2Wn1 | If2Wn2 | | If2Wnn |

*Normalized Weights from each AP*

**Winner to be chosen based on the better QoS offered from APs**

interfaces in our MN. $RssT = \{rt_1, rt_2, rt_3, ..., rt_k\}$ is the set of threshold values of RSS of respective networks. The set of values of difference between the RSS and its threshold value is represented by $RssDiff = \{rd_1, rd_1, ..., rd_k\}$. The set of eligible candidate networks into which the handoff can take place is represented by CN.

$$P = \left\{0, \frac{1}{k}, \frac{2}{k}, ..., \frac{j}{k}, ..., 1\right\}$$

is the set of priorities of the $j^{th}$ network, and $j = 1, 2, ..., k$. The network AP and MN is observed for the RSS and mobility respectively at the specified time intervals and the decisions are taken as the algorithm below to select the candidate networks, assuming that MN is currently in network $n_i$:

If $RSS_i < rt_i$ then for all $n_j$ where $j \neq i$.
If ($RSS_j > rt_i$ and $m_j < mt_i$) then
$\{CN\} = \{CN\} \cup \{n_j\}$
$RssDiff_j = RSS_j - dr_j$

Then, the network with the highest $RssDiff$ will be assigned with a higher priority. This is because a higher $RssDiff$ means the MN is nearer to the AP of the named network and hence the MN can stay in that cell for longer before looking to handoff to another network. This will reduce the number of unnecessary handoffs and improve the overall performance of the system. The priorities are assigned according to the following algorithm, assuming that $n$ networks are available in the list:
While $j \leq k$ do

if $j$ is not the xandidate list then
$P_j = 0$
else if $j$ is the only network in the candidate list then
$P_j = 1$
else if $j$ is at the $i^{th}$ position, the list will be ordered in an ascending order then
$P_j = i/k$

Secondly, the Network Analysis model is based on a static score function $SC$, which is a function of the offered bandwidth by the network ($BW_n$), interface energy consumption ($P_n$) and service charge ($C_n$).

$$SC_n = f(BW_n, P_n, C_n) \tag{1}$$

Where, SCn is the static score function of network $n$. Normalization is needed to ensure that the sum of the values in different units is meaningful. If there are $k$ factors to be considered in the score function, the score function of the interface $i$ will be a sum of $k$ weighted factors.

$$SC_i = \sum_{j=1}^{k} w_i nf_i$$
$$0 < SC_i < 1, \tag{2}$$
$$\sum_{j=1}^{k} w_i$$

In the equation, $w_i$ represents the weight of factor $j$ of interface $i$, and $nf_i$ is the normalized score value of factor $j$ for interface $i$. For our model:

$$SC_i = w_{bw}f_{bw,i} + w_cf_{c,i} + w_pf_{p,i} \tag{3}$$

Where $w_{bw}$, $w_c$, and $w_p$ are the weight factors of the offered bandwidth, service cost, and the power consumed by the network interface respectively. $f_{bw,i}$, $f_{c,i}$, and $f_{p,i}$ are the normalized values of interface $i$'s offered bandwidth, power consumption and service cost respectively. Whereas:

$$nf_{bw,i} = \frac{e^{\delta_i}}{e^{bw_i}} \tag{4}$$
$$\delta_i \geq 0$$

$$nf_{c,i} = \frac{1}{\frac{c_i}{e^{\beta_i}}}$$

$$\beta_i = \frac{1}{pk_i}, pk_i \text{ is the packets to be sent}$$

$$\tag{5}$$

$$nf_{p,i} = \frac{1}{\frac{p_i}{e^{\gamma_i}}} \tag{6}$$

$$\gamma_i = \frac{1}{t_i}, \; t_i = \text{time in hours}$$

The coefficients $\delta_i$, $\beta_i$, and $\gamma_i$ are defined same way as in chapter three. The exponential functions used to increase the sensitivity of the functions to the respective parameters they are related to. Finally, they are inversed in order to bind the functions to a value between zero and one. It can be observed from these equations that high bandwidth value contributes proportionately to the SC function, whereas cost and power consumption contribute inversely to SC. This is because, an interface with a better bandwidth is a better choice to the MN, while an interface costing more or consuming more power is a poor choice to the MN.

Given that the two interfaces are wireless, thus all requested services are of equal priority, therefore are characterized by similar requirements, we aim to distribute a set of requests to a number of access networks so that all of them gain the maximum payoff. The information needed in order to deduce the user preferences and thus the optimal distribution of service requests involves two parameters: network efficiency and network status. Network efficiency is taken into consideration based on the static and dynamic factors mentioned earlier to decide whether the handover is needed or not. A normalized value of each element of the mentioned factors is to be considered in order to get an overall weight factor to represent each individual AP. On the other hand, the second parameter, network status, that affects user preferences, is involved taking into account information such as the static and dynamic factors needed to decide the handoff process. Therefore, network preferences are roughly reflected by the following equation:

Net Preferences (NP) = Net Efficiency (NE) x Net Capacity (NC) $\tag{7}$

NE will be calculated the same way the cost function been calculated, as in Equation (1), so NE can be represented as:

$$NE = SC \times RSS_N \tag{8}$$

Where $RSS_N$ is the normalized value of the RSS:

$$RSS_N = \frac{e^\varepsilon}{e^{RSS}} \tag{9}$$

$$\varepsilon \geq 0$$

However, NC should indicate the network's current capability to fulfil the request's requirements and therefore should include both the network's available bandwidth, as well as the service's required bandwidth. This will lead us to the following fact:

$$NC = \frac{\text{Available } BW}{\text{Required } BW} \tag{10}$$

Then, combining the two equations will give us:

$$NP = SC \times RSS_N \times \frac{BW_{av}}{BW_{req}} \tag{11}$$

The proposed game can be represented as $G = \{N, A, S_i, U_i\}$. Where $N = \{1, 2,..., n\}$ is the number of players in the game, in this case AP's. The number of actions is represented by $A = \{1, 2,..., n\}$. $S_i$ denotes the set of strategies for each player, *i.e.*, all possible choices of a specific request from set $A$. Finally, $U_{ij}$ denotes the payoff assigned to the MN by selecting player $i$ after choosing resource $j$. This payoff can be modeled as described in Equation (11). The game is played in rounds, in each round of the game the MN decide which request will maximize its own payoff and then select it. Another aspect that needs to be clarified is the one where more than one network provides the same services. In this case, we randomly let the network with the highest payoff handle the service and move on to the next round of the game, without removing a second request. In the case of multiple Nash equilibriums, for simplicity reasons, we will assume that the MN will choose the first one, since it possesses chronological priority. The proposed game is also a non-zero sum game.

The proposed extension to the MFMIPv6 is shown below in Figure 7, and works as follows: as the MN receives the PrRtAdv messages from the PAR as it moves around, the game controller will be responsible of extracting the QoS parameters of them. The network interface receives all the packets at the node channel from other nodes or access points. Each transmitted packets is stamped by the interface with the meta-data related to the transmitting interface (The Network Simulator NS-2, 2011).

*Figure 7. Using game mechanism to choose the best AP*

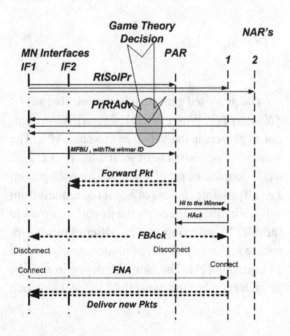

The meta-data in the packet header includes information such as transmitting power, wavelength, available QoS, security authentication etc., of the transmitted packets. The Game Controller is to be inserted at the network interface in the MN. The game controller extracts the packet header in the same way used in the propagation model, where the meta-data in the packet header is used by the propagation model to determine if the packet has the minimum power to be received and/or captured and/or detected. When the MN sends and receives the RtSolPr and PrRtAdv messages, the game controller will know the source of each PrRtAdv message and extract the QoS information from it and by using the mechanism mentioned earlier. The MN will decide which AR is the best to go with. The MN will send the address of the NAR to the PAR by the MFBU message.

Similar to the MFMIPv6 (Park, et al., 2008), the game decision is based on the information obtained from the PrRtAdv message. Then, using the MFBU message, the winner (i.e., the access point that offers the best services) ID will be sent to the PAR in order to forward the packet to it, as shown in Figure 8. During the game, the MN might face different cases. If there were two or more AP's offering the same services to the MN (i.e., multiple-Nash equilibrium case), the MN will not face any problem in choosing any one of them at that point. On the other hand, if one of the AP's managed to improve the offered QoS to the MN, the MN will switch to it, where it is impossible to improve the utility of one player without harming the others. However, the last point that we need to look at will be the energy consumption in the MN as the two interfaces are 'ON' all the time to insure getting the full advantage of the MFMIPv6 protocol. In order to solve such an issue, we used the scheme shown in Figure 8.

Received Signal Strength "ON" Threshold ($RSS_{ONT}$) point; with this method, one of the interfaces will be turned OFF until the RSS from the AP reaches a certain point "$RSS_{ONT}$" which

*Figure 8. Handover decision points*

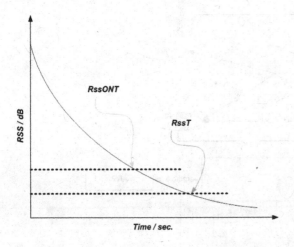

means that the MN is moving away from the AP and reaching the boundaries of its coverage, as shown in Figure 9. Once the MN reaches the named point, the game mechanism will work as explained earlier saving more energy to the MN by keeping the other interface "OFF" most of the time. However, the drawback of the RSS$_{ONT}$ point model will be the chance that the MN might lose to handoff to a better network within the coverage of the bigger network. To solve this problem, the first interface will trigger the second interface once it receives any advertisement messages from the around APs. The game mechanism will work to check whether a handover is needed or not, if so, the game process will proceed, if not, the second interface will be turned "OFF" and wait for either the RSS$_{ONT}$ point or forced by the other interface.

Finally, the previous additions to the MFMIPv6 protocol leads to our proposed Game-Based Multi-Interface Fast-Handover MIPv6 (GMFMIPv6). By adding game theory to the MFMIPv6 the MN will choose the "best" AP at the right time, making the handover decision more accurate and save the MN more energy.

To this end, in order to evaluate the performance of the proposed mechanism, we implement a similar design of the MFMIPv6 simulator introduced in (Park, et al., 2008) using NS-2 (The Network

Simulator NS-2, 2011) and its extension Mobie-Wan (MOTOROLA Labs and INRIA PLANETE Team, 2002). One more wireless interface was added and one channel, the game controller was added between the network interfaces (NetIF0 and NetIF1 shown in Figure 9), which will decide which AR to go with.

## SIMULATION SCENARIO AND RESULTS

The network topology for our simulation is shown in Figure 10, five 802.11b APs are assumed to cover the simulation area of (440 x 440 *m*) with different characteristics. At the beginning of the simulation, the MN is assumed to be settled within the coverage area of AP number one. Throughout the simulation time, which is set to be 24 minutes, the MN is assumed to have a data of 50000 packets to transmit. The MN is assumed to cross all coverage areas several times and it will never stop in one position with an average speed of 1 m/sec. Table 2 shows our scenario assumptions starting with the service cost, available bandwidth, delay and power consumption of each AP in the network. The MN battery is assumed to have 10000 Joule of energy.

Simulation results compare the number of successfully received packets, the number of dropped packets, the overall end-to-end delay and the MN power consumption using three different protocols namely MIPv6, MFMIPv6 and GM-FMIPv6.

Figures 11 and 12 compare the number of acknowledgements of every successfully delivered packet and the number of dropped packets over the simulation time using four different protocols. Both MFMIPv6 and GMFMIPv6 show the same number of acknowledgments received and the same number of dropped packets over the simulation time. The two protocols show a much better performance as compared to both MIPv6 and FMIPv6, as both GMFMIPv6 and MFMIPv6

*Figure 9. Multiple-interfaces mobile node*

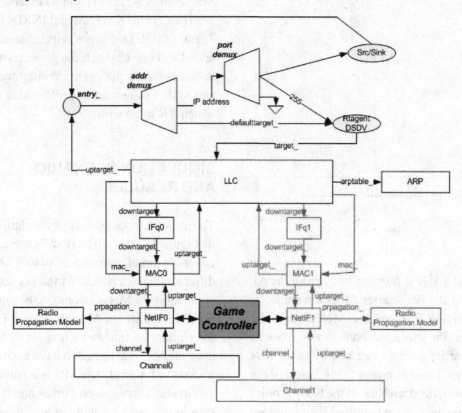

*Figure 10. Simulation scenario*

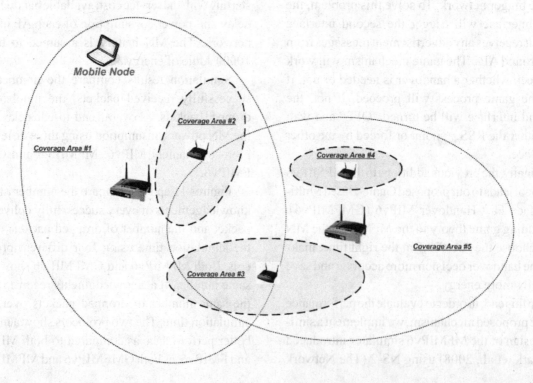

*Table 2. Simulation statistics*

| AP | QoS parameters | | | | |
|----|------------------------|--------------------|--------------|-----------------------------------------------|---------------------------------------------|
|    | Service Cost (£/h) | Bandwidth (Mbps) | Delay (μsec) | Power consumption per every transmitted bit | Power consumption per every received bit |
| #1 | Free | 4.5 | 12 | 320 mW | 300 mW |
| #2 | Free | 4 | 16 | 250 mW | 230 mW |
| #3 | Free | 4 | 16 | 250 mW | 230 mW |
| #4 | 1.5 | 8 | 4 | 200 mW | 170 mW |
| #5 | Free | 5 | 11 | 320 mW | 300 mW |

use two interfaces to pack up the communication link as compared to other protocols.

Figure 13 shows the total number of handovers the MN forced during the simulation time when using the four protocols one at a time. It can be easily observed that GMFMIPv6 protocol shows a sharp decrease in the number of handoffs as compared to the other three protocols and this is because of the game-controller introduced in the previous section. Since the MN is using GM-FMIPv6 protocol, it has the ability to decide whether switching to another AP will achieve a better QoS or not. By reducing the number of handovers, the communication link will not be

disturbed, thus a better end-to-end quality. Moreover, reducing the number of handovers will reduce the need to switch the other interface "ON," accordingly, saving more energy.

Figure 14 shows the end-to-end delay of the four protocols; GMFMIPv6 shows the lowest end-to-end delay as compared to the other protocols. This is because of its ability to decide whether a handoff is needed or not and the fact that the MN is using two interfaces to pack up its communication. FMIPv6 shows a better response when compared with MIPv6 protocol, as the MN tries to reduce the movement detection latency and the new CoA configuration latency by pro-

*Figure 11. Number of received ACKs*

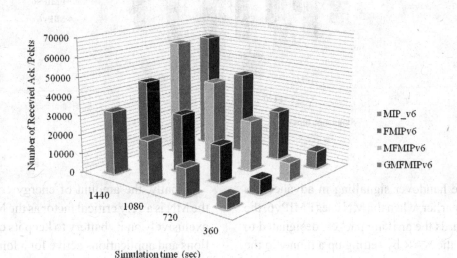

*Figure 12. Number of dropped packets*

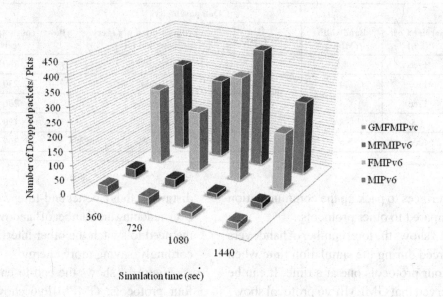

*Figure 13. Overall number of handovers*

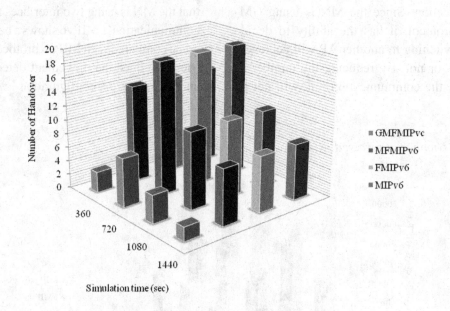

cessing the handover signalling in advance. As explained earlier, when the MN uses FMIPv6, the PAR forwards the arriving packets designated to the MN to the NAR by setting up a tunnel to the NAR in order to prevent packet losses incurred by handover latency during handover procedure.

Finally, the amount of energy consumed by the MN is a very critical factor as the MN depends exclusively on its battery to keep its communications and applications active for a longer time. In order to test the protocol ability to consume less energy, a modification has been done to the En-

*Figure 14. End-to-end delay over the simulation time*

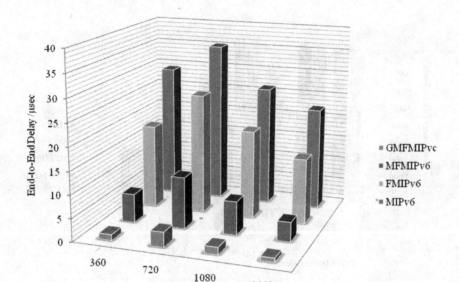

ergyModel Class in NS-2 (The Network Simulator NS-2, 2011) to calculate the amount of energy consumed per every transmitted and received bit through the MN interfaces.

```
class EnergyModel: public TclObject {
public:
. EnergyModel(double energy)
  { energy_ = energy; }
  inline double energy() { return
  energy_; }
  inline void setenergy(double e)
  {energy_ = e;}
  virtual void DecrTxEnergy(double
  txtime, double P_tx) {
    energy_ = ((P_tx/8) * txtime);
  }
  virtual void DecrRcvEnergy(double
  rcvtime, double P_rcv) {
    energy_ -= ((P_rcv/8) * rcvtime);
  }
```

```
protected:
  double energy_;
};
```

Where, energy_ is the single class variable and represents the level of energy in the MN at any given time. The constructor EnergyModel(energy) requires the initial_energy to be passed along as a parameter. The other class methods are used to decrease the energy level of the node for every bit transmitted (DecrTxEnergy(txtime, P_tx)) and every bit received (DecrRcvEnergy(rcvtime, P_rcv)) by the MN. Moreover, P_tx and P_rcv are the transmitting and receiving power respectively, required by the MN's interface. At the beginning of simulation, energy_ is set to initialEnergy_ (set to be 10000 joule), which is then decremented for every transmission and reception of packets at the MN. When the energy level at the node goes down to zero, no more packets can be received or transmitted by the node, i.e., the node is dead.

*Figure 15. Energy consumption in the mobile node*

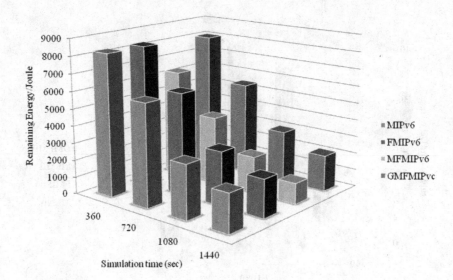

Figure 15 shows the amount of energy left in the MN battery during the simulation time. Both MIPv6 and FMIPv6 show more energy left in the battery when compared to the MFMIPv6 protocol, this is because the MFMIPv6 protocol uses two interfaces and keeping them 'ON' during the entire simulation time to achieve a better communication. However, the GMFMIPv6 protocol shows almost similar results as compared to the MIPv6 and FMIPv6 and a much better results as compared to the MFMIPv6. This is again because of its ability to use one interface at a time and use the other interface only when a handoff is needed.

Although, the amount of energy consumed by the GMFMIPv6 protocol is slightly more as compared to the MIPv6 and FMIPv6 protocols, it can be easily deduce the magnificent advantage throughout the fact that the MN is using tow interfaces at the same time. Thus, reducing the number of dropped packets all the way through the communication time. The other advantage of this protocol is by reducing the number of unnecessary handoffs (i.e., eliminating the problems of the ping-pong effects), thus reducing the end-

to-end delay and improving the QoS throughout the entire communication time.

## CONCLUSION

This chapter presents a novel methodology for combining Game Theory and wireless network selection mechanisms in multiple-interfaces MIPv6 wireless portable devices. What's more, it presents an extension to the MFMIPv6, by which the MN can decide whether to make the handover or not when it have multiple CoA's and/or multiple wireless interfaces. The proposed mechanism can indicate the best access point to choose during the handover procedure by sending the "winner" destination address (i.e., the NAR address) to the PAR using the FBU message. Moreover, the mechanism switches the mobile nodes interfaces "ON" and "OFF" when needed to control the mobile node's energy consumption and improves the handover latency.

# REFERENCES

Chowdhury, P. K., Atiquzzaman, M., & Ivancic, W. (2006). SINEMO: An IP-diversity based approach for netwrok mobility in space. In *Proceedings of the 2nd IEEE International Conference on Space Mission Challenges for Information Technology (SMC-IT 2006)*, (pp. 109–115). Pasadena, CA: IEEE Press.

Cisco. (2001). *Introduction to mobile IP*. Retieved March 14, 2010 from http://www.cisco.com/en/US/docs/ios/solutions_docs/mobile_ip/mobil_ip.html.

Clincy, V. A., & Mudiraj, P. (2007). The future leading mobility protocol: Mobile IPv4 or Mobile IPv6? *Journal of Computing Sciences in Colleges*, *22*(6), 197–203.

Ernst, T. (2006). *The information technology era of the vehicular industry. ACM SIGCOMM Computer Communication Review* (2nd ed.). New York, NY: ACM Press.

Ernst, T. (2007). *Network mobility support goals and requirements (RFC 4886)*. Retrieved March 18, 2011, from http://www.rfc-archive.org/getrfc.php?rfc=4886.

Ernst, T., & Lach, H. Y. (2007). *Network mobility support terminology (RFC 4885)*. Retrieved 18 May 2011 from http://www.isi.edu/in-notes/rfc4885.txt.

Johnson, D., Prekins, C., & Arkko, J. (2004). *Mobility support in IPv6 (RFC 3775)*. Retrieved March 18, 2010 from http://www.ietf.org/rfc/rfc3775.txt.

Koodli, R. (2005). *Fast handovers for mobile IPv6 (RFC 4068)*. Retrieved March 21, 2010 from http://www.ietf.org/rfc/rfc4068.txt.

MacKenzie, A. B., & deSilva, L. A. (2006). *Game theory for wireless engineering*. New York, NY: Morgan & Claypool.

Motorola Labs & INRIA PLANETE Team. (2002). *MobiWan: NS-2.1b6 extensions to study mobility in wide-area IPv6 networks*. Retrieved May 18, 2010 from http://www.inrialpes.fr/planete/mobiwan/.

Park, M. K., Lee, J. Y., Kim, B. C., & Kim, D. Y. (2008). Design of fast handover mechanism for multiple interfaces mobile IPv6. In *Proceedings of IEEE International Symposium on Wireless Prevasive Computing*, (pp. 697-701). IEEE Press.

Rasmusen, E. (2006). *Games and information: An introduction to game theory* (4th ed.). Oxford, UK: Blackwell Publishers.

The Network Simulator NS-2. (2011). *Website*. Retrieved May 18, 2011 from http://www.isi.edu/nsnam/ns.

Wakikawa, R., Ernst, T., & Nagami, K. (2009). *Multiple care-of addresses registration (RFC 5648)*. Retrieved May, 5, 2010 from http://tools.ietf.org/html/rfc5648.

# KEY TERMS AND DEFINITIONS

**Fast Mobile IPv6:** This protocol is an extension to the Mobile IPv6 protocol, which enables the mobile node to quickly detect that it has moved from one service provider to another. This protocol is described in more details in RFC 4068.

**Game Theory:** Game theory is the mathematical study of the ways in which strategic interactions among agents (i.e., players) produce outcomes with respect to the preferences (i.e. utilities) of those agents, where the outcomes in question might have been intended by none of the agents.

**Mobile IPv4:** Mobile IPv4 is a standard communication protocol aims to allowing mobile users and devices to communicate on the move while maintaining a permanent IP address. This protocol is described in RFC 3344 and 4721.

**Mobile IPv6:** Mobile IPv6 is the implementation of the IP mobility for the next generation of the Internet Protocol, this protocol is described in RFC 3775.

**Multi-Interface Fast Mobile IPv6:** This protocol is another extension to the Mobile IPv6 protocol, which implements the fast mobile IPv6 protocol and use the advantage of the extra interface in the mobile node in order to reduce the handover latency during the node's movement.

# Chapter 3
# Evaluation Model for Vertical Handoff Algorithms

**Alexander Garcia D.**
*Universidad Autonoma de Occidente, Colombia*

**Lina Escobar P.**
*Universidad Autonoma de Occidente, Colombia*

**Andres Navarro C.**
*Universidad ICESI, Colombia*

**Fabio G. Guerrero**
*Universidad del Valle, Colombia*

**Enrique Stevens-Navarro**
*Universidad Autonoma de San Luis Potosi, Mexico*

## ABSTRACT

*This chapter begins by introducing the problem of vertical handoff in heterogeneous wireless networks and illustrates the lack of a proper evaluation model to compare the different Vertical Handoff Algorithms (VHAs) that have been proposed in the literature over the last few years. In the following sections, a novel evaluation model for VHAs is introduced and described. The design of the new evaluation model is based on the multi-criteria evaluation methodology and criticality analysis, which permitted the model to be developed as a software component. The new proposed evaluation model is flexible in terms of the number of evaluation parameters and facilitates the analysis of VHAs by researchers. A specific case study considering some VHAs is presented, analyzed, and discussed in detail. The case study is used to compare the proposed evaluation model with another evaluation model (Ordinal Model) for VHAs. The comparison of the new evaluation model with an alternative evaluation model was an important exercise because it gave feedback on both models, enabling the authors to refine them and to propose extensions to their capabilities and features. The obtained results show that both models are valid and effective for the evaluation of the VHAs and each one has his advantages and disadvantages.*

DOI: 10.4018/978-1-4666-0191-8.ch003

## INTRODUCTION

The next generation wireless networking (4G) is focused on achieving interoperability between different network technologies in a seamless manner, as well as on facilitating the user's mobility through a permanent wireless connection anywhere and at anytime (Hui & Yeung, 2003).

Currently, some of the smartphones in the market are equipped with multiple network interface cards which are able to connect to different wireless networks. However this advance poses an interesting challenge as is the handoff between heterogeneous wireless networks in a seamless way. This important mobility process is known as the vertical handoff (Nasser et al., 2006). In the last few years, plenty of research efforts (Yan, Sekercioglu, & Narayanan, 2010) have been focused in this important and challenging mobility process in heterogeneous wireless systems.

Different Vertical Handoff Algorithms (VHAs) have been proposed in the literature (Kassar, Kervella, & Pujolle, 2008; Garcia & Jimenez, 2008; Hong, Kang, & Kim, 2005). However, there is no consensus on how to evaluate the performance of different VHAs in the research community. Although some models have been proposed for evaluation of the VHAs, this issue has created interesting challenges because the VHAs have become more sophisticated and therefore evaluation models must be consider a variety of parameters. We have proposed a new evaluation model for VHAs that have been designed based on specific concepts taken from multi-criteria evaluation and operational reliability. The proposed evaluation model allows the analysis of VHAs using measured values of some defined parameters, which can be obtained from simulating VHAs on a network simulation tool.

This chapter is organized as follows. In Section 2 the background and related work on vertical handoff evaluation is presented. In Section 3 the proposed evaluation model and the concepts that were used to generate it are explained. Section 4 describes the evaluation process of handoff algorithms In Section 5 a case study of performance evaluation of VHAs using the new evaluation model is presented, and a comparison between the novel model and an alternative evaluation model is presented. Finally, conclusions are given in last section.

## BACKGROUND

### Vertical Handoff

A vertical handoff is the process of changing the mobile connection between access points that support different wireless technologies (i.e. heterogeneous networks). Alternatively, in a horizontal handoff the connection just moves from one base station to another within the same access network. The vertical handoff process consists of three phases (Stevens-Navarro & Wong, 2006): network discovery, handoff decision and handoff execution. In the first phase, the Mobile Terminal (MT) discovers its available neighboring networks. In the decision phase, the MT determines whether it has to redirect its connection based on comparing the decision factors offered by the available networks and required by the mobile user, which is based on the information gathered in the first phase. The last phase is responsible for the establishment and release of the connections according to the vertical handoff decision.

The vertical handoff issue between heterogeneous networks has been much studied by a number of researchers and several solutions have been proposed (Garcia & Jimenez, 2008; Hong, Kang, & Kim, 2005; Kassar, Kervella, & Pujolle, 2008; Lee, et al., 2009; Nasser, et al., 2006; Yan, Sekercioglu, & Narayanan, 2010). However, there is still a lack of a proper evaluation model to compare the vast of VHAs in the literature.

## Evaluation of Vertical Handoff Algorithms

Various recent works show interest in the evaluation of VHAs; however some of them do not evaluate the whole algorithm and study only the decision of network technology phase, which is considered to be the main component in the handoff process (Lassoued, et al, 2008; Stevens-Navarro & Wong, 2006; Zahran & Liang, 2005).

Based on the different proposed VHAs, some studies have focused on defining which of these solutions may be optimal for the network selection process. Consequently, there are studies that use different evaluation methodologies to accomplish this purpose.

### Analytic Hierarchy Process (AHP)

Within the multi-criteria decision analysis is the method called the Analytic Hierarchy Process, AHP (Saaty, 1980), which allows the construction of a hierarchical model that represents the problem and initially proposes alternatives, and then deduces which are the best alternatives to make an optimal decision.

Stevens-Navarro and Wong (2006) compared the performance of four VHAs, namely MEW (Multiplicative Exponent Weighting), SAW (Simple Additive Weighting), TOPSIS (Technique for Order Preference by Similarity to Ideal Solution), and GRA (Grey Relational Analysis). They used the AHP method to determinate the relative importance or weights of each parameter to evaluate, using the fundamental 1-9 AHP scale to answer a sequence of comparisons between paired parameters. Four traffic classes were considered: conversational, streaming, interactive and background. Each traffic class was associated with four different QoS parameters: available bandwidth, end-to-end delay, jitter and Bit Error Rate (BER).

One of the advantages of the AHP method over other methods of multi-criteria decision is that it provides a solid mathematical basis that allows the analysis of any problem and measures quantitative and qualitative criteria by a common scale. However, it requires the participation of different people to generate a consensus and the introduction of a new alternative can change decision maker preference structure or introduce inconsistencies.

### Fuzzy Logic

Lassoued et al. (2008) proposed a performance evaluation of five VHAs: SAW, TOPSIS, GRA, MEW and UA (Ubique's Algorithm). They used the concept of fuzzy logic to build their own valuation scale and compare the different parameters used in the handoff process. They also used the AHP to determine the importance weights of the parameters: available bandwidth, BER, average delay, security level for access network and monetary costs associated with two classes of traffic: conversational and streaming.

For some time, fuzzy logic has become object of interest to provide support for multi-criteria decision problems, and one of the reasons is that fuzzy logic can be applied when certain parts of the problem are unknown and cannot be reliably measured. However, there is no theoretical guarantee that a fuzzy system is stable and definition of the measurements is not always easy and requires extensive testing.

### Use of Simulation Tools in the Analysis

Zhu and McNair (2006) consider that the handoff can be predicted according to the user's movement. Therefore a basic requirement is to simulate the movement of the mobile node in the access network and deduce the QoS parameters from these movements (user's location), such as network traffic, BER and packet transmission delay. Then these parameters become the inputs of the VHA that is used to define the most appropriate network interface. The user's mobility is modeled and simulated using MATLAB.

Likewise, Syuhada, Mahamod, and Firuz (2008) used MATLAB to develop the simulation model and to evaluate the handoff process between WLAN and cellular networks using two algorithms:

- The first is based on the algorithm developed by Zahran, Liang, and Saleh (2006) with a few modifications. This algorithm uses averaged RSS (Received Signal Strength) and lifetime estimation as the criteria to start vertical handoff.
- The second is based on the conventional algorithm which uses the average signal strength as the criteria to start the handoff process.

In this research, the performance of the handoff algorithms was evaluated according to few analyses. The analyses were based on the number of handoffs and handoff delay.

In the other hand, Lassoued et al. (2008) proposed an evaluation methodology (named Ubique middleware) that considers three key factors to decide network connection change, such as applications, user and operator. Additionally, they used the CanuMobiSim simulator (Stepanov et al., 2003) to generate realistic mobility patterns, which is one of the factors taking great importance as a critical element in the new VHA.

The main advantage of using simulation tools for this purpose is that we can simulate the evaluation of VHAs models and determine their benefits, advantages and disadvantages, facilitating the implementation and analysis of increasingly more complex communication systems. However, an appropriated software tool is required to simulate scenarios and sufficient computing resources to carry out the simulation tests.

## Solutions Based on Mathematical and Statistical Models

Mäkelä (2008) presents a framework for performance evaluation of a variety of algorithms for different types of network. The core of this framework is the ability to define a realistic scenario for the evaluation of performance using mathematical analysis and computer simulation. This scenario identifies the wireless network type and topology, defines the location of wireless connection points and specifies a path for the mobile terminal when it experiences a handoff.

Mäkelä (2008) classifies wireless networks into three categories according to their topology and wireless service application: traditional cellular phone, heterogeneous wireless data and rate adaptive wireless data networks. For each wireless network category a performance evaluation scenario is defined, and Monte Carlo simulations, Monte Carlo calculations and direct mathematical analysis are used to analyze the effects of different handoff decision algorithms.

Suciu, Guillouard, and Bonnin (2006) proposed and developed a comprehensive methodology for evaluating and comparing the inter-technologies handoff algorithms. They proposed the definition of a common metric, namely the Standard Deviation from Optimum Interface, based on the well-known standard deviation (i.e. that calculates the deviation from an average value) for the evaluation of VHAs. This optimal interface is actually an ideal interface.

Suciu, Guillouard, and Bonnin (2006) define the standard deviation from optimum for a particular decision parameter (e.g. bandwidth), but they state that the same procedure can be used with all decision parameters involved in a vertical handoff decision algorithm. This proposal combines statistical concepts with the computing capacity to automate calculations for analyzing the handoff process. However, this method can be too complex for more than one criterion (i.e. multivariable optimization problem).

In general, mathematical and statistical models help to predict optimal solutions and they are easier to understand than other analytical models. Although it is possible to gain experience at a lower cost and more rapidly since these models include formulas and complex algorithms that use a lot of computer resources to perform the analysis.

## A NEW MODEL FOR EVALUATION OF VERTICAL HANDOFF ALGORITHMS

Some of the evaluation models that were previously described have been designed to evaluate specific parameters and are not easily adapted to other scenarios. Moreover, a few of the models are very complicated to apply in performance evaluation of VHAs because they are not very flexible in the ability to define the parameters to evaluate.

In order to generate a new evaluation model for VHAs, that is flexible and facilitates the evaluation process for researchers, concepts and models such as multi-criteria evaluation methodologies and the maintenance of equipments or systems were assessed.

### Underlying Concepts to Generate the New Evaluation Model of the VHAs

### The Criticality Concept

Criticality Analysis (CA) is a methodology used to establish a hierarchy or priorities of processes, systems and machines, creating a structure that facilitates effective decision making, directing the effort and resources into areas where it is most needed and/or required to improve operational reli-

ability, based on the current situation (Reliability and Risk Management [R2M], 2010).

The term "critical" and the definition of criticality can have different interpretations and depend on the objectives that are being prioritized. The criticality analysis generates a weighted list from the most critical to least critical of the whole set to be analyzed and differentiates into three classification zones: high, medium and low criticality. After these are identified it is much easier to design a strategy for studies or projects that improve operational reliability, starting the applications on the set of processes that are part of the high criticality zone.

The criteria for criticality analysis are mainly associated with safety, production, operation costs, failure rate and repair time. These criteria are related through a mathematical equation that generates a score for each item evaluated. It is common to find studies that use a criticality matrix in which the important criteria are located and for each zone is defined concepts that allow measuring the degree of impact on operational reliability if a machine fails during their service.

### Multi-Criteria Evaluation

Multi-Criteria Evaluation (MCE) is an effective technique used in multidimensional decisions and evaluation models within the field of decision making (Proctor & Drechsler, 2003). Its main objective is to help the decision makers to evaluate, prioritize and select or reject objects, based on an evaluation by scores and according to several criteria (Colson & Bruyn, 1989).

Almost all MCE techniques consist of some stages, and usually the first stage consists in designing a matrix with defined criteria. The next stage is the addition of the scores to the criteria, with the use of specific aggregation procedures (any MCE technique), taking into account the expressed preference of decision makers in terms of weights assigned to different criteria. This procedure or technique allows the decision maker to compare the different alternatives based on the assigned weights.

The central problem of the EMC is:

- To select the best alternative(s);
- To accept the good alternatives and reject those that are bad; and
- To generate a ranking of the considered alternatives (from best to worst).

It is important to note that the MCE does not allow the possibility of finding an optimal solution.

## Structuring the Evaluation Model

The design of the new model is based on multi-criteria evaluation methodology (Colson & Bruyn, 1989) which is usually used to evaluate alternatives when several criteria exist and also uses the concept of criticality analysis (R2M, 2010) which is taken from the operational reliability strategies.

The main objective of the new evaluation model, which we called EMoVHA (Evaluation Model of Vertical Handoff Algorithms), is to evaluate the performance of VHAs from a number of defined parameters. The evaluation model for VHAs is defined by the following seven steps:

1. Define the evaluation parameters.
2. Define the valuation of performance levels.
3. Define the evaluation matrix.
4. Calculate the weight for each evaluation parameter.
5. Obtain the values of the criticality matrix.
6. Calculate the criticality index for each algorithm.
7. Comparing the algorithms according to their criticality index.

## Define the Evaluation Parameters

The evaluation parameters are indicators that significantly affect the performance of VHAs. These parameters allow the evaluation of each algorithm according to their assigned weights and that reflects the relevance (priority) of each evaluation parameter.

The new model for evaluation of VHAs allows the use of two types of parameter: benefit parameters (the higher is its value, the better its performance) such as bandwidth and cost parameters (the smaller its value, the better its performance) such as delay, jitter and the economical cost of the network connection, among others.

The number of parameters that can be defined for the evaluation model is flexible, but for its validation and for developing as a software component this value has been bound in a range from 3 (minimum) to 5 (maximum). However this is not a shortcoming of the new model design, actually this limitation is related to the constraints of the API which are used for generating the outcomes of the evaluation model in a graphical mode.

## Define the Valuation of Performance Levels

Table 1 is used to evaluate each of the VHAs. It has identified ten ranges rated from 1 to 10. These levels are required in order to minimize subjective assessments and use specific indicators that will easily evaluate the algorithms.

Table 1 is designed to evaluate cost parameters, so when a benefit parameter is analyzed, the inverse of the result obtained in the simulation tests should be calculated and this value will be added to the evaluation matrix.

*Table 1. Valuation of the performance evaluation levels*

| Qualitative evaluation | Quantitative evaluation | Measurement scale |
|---|---|---|
| Bad | 1 | x > 90%<br>of the total sum |
| Very low | 2 | 80% < x ≤ 90%<br>of the total sum |
| Moderately low | 3 | 70% < x ≤ 80%<br>of the total sum |
| Low | 4 | 60% < x ≤ 70%<br>of the total sum |
| Very acceptable | 5 | 50% < x ≤ 60%<br>of the total sum |
| Moderately acceptable | 6 | 40% < x ≤ 50%<br>of the total sum |
| Acceptable | 7 | 30% < x ≤ 40%<br>of the total sum |
| Moderately good | 8 | 20% < x ≤ 30%<br>of the total sum |
| Very good | 9 | 10% < x ≤ 20%<br>of the total sum |
| Excellent | 10 | x ≤ 10%<br>of the total sum |

## Define the Evaluation Matrix

The evaluation matrix is a decision matrix that summarizes the evaluation of each algorithm (rows) under each parameter (columns). Each position of the matrix must be filled with the results obtained from the simulation of the VHA in a previous phase.

If there are several simulation results for each evaluation parameter the following procedure must be applied: assuming data are normally distributed we use the criterion of two times the standard deviation from the average to ensure a large percentage of the data are around the average. The data outside of this range will be ignored and treated as erroneous. Then the average of the new set of data must be calculated and this value will be entered into the evaluation matrix.

## Calculate the Weight for Each Evaluation Parameter

After completing the evaluation matrix it is necessary to determine the weight of each parameter in the final evaluation, i.e. the relative importance given to each parameter in the global set of evaluation parameters.

Since the performance measures of these parameters are in different units, a method that normalizes the matrix $D$ and turns it into $\overline{D}$, so that $d_{ij} \in [0,1]$ was proposed. In this way the magnitude of the attributes is controlled, and also it prevents some attributes being able to dominate others due to their units.

## Obtain the Values of the Criticality Matrix

The evaluation parameters of each algorithm should be analyzed according to the defined valuation scale that is shown in Table 1. For this purpose we add the elements of each column of the evaluation matrix (parameter), and then every element of the column is divided by this result and multiplied by 100. The value obtained represents the variable x in Table 1 (third column).

## Calculate the Criticality Index for Each Algorithm

The criticality level of the algorithms can be represented by the criticality index, $I_c$, applying (1):

$$I_C = 100 \frac{\sum_{i=1}^{n}(n_i p_i)}{q \sum_{i=1}^{n} p_i} \qquad (1)$$

Where:

n = number of parameters
$p_i$ = weight of each parameter
$n_i$ = assigned valuation level to each parameter
q = maximum valuation level of all parameters.

The value of the criticality index allows prioritizing or ordering the evaluated algorithms. The algorithm with the highest score will be considered to be the algorithm with the best performance.

## Comparing the Algorithms According to Their Criticality Index

Two types of evaluation are possible; the first is based on the criticality index and the second o on the valuation of a specific parameter. In the first type the algorithms are ordered according to their criticality index. While in the second type each algorithm is analyzed according to the measure of a particular parameter.

## VERTICAL HANDOFF ALGORITHMS EVALUATION PROCESS

Figure 1 illustrates the evaluation process, which has three phases: the simulation of the VHA (previous phase), the execution of the evaluation model and the generation of results in a simple format (graphics and files) for its analysis.

The evaluation process using the proposed model can be summarized as follows. In the previous phase the selected VHAs are simulated using a network simulation tool or a special programming language. Simulated VHA (e.g. in MATLAB) generate a series of results which constitute the evaluation parameters and the input to the novel evaluation model and these can be developed as a software component developed in Java, C++ or any other programming language. The results of the evaluation process can be analyzed by the graphs generated from the data recorded in an output file so that researchers can analyze the results of the evaluation of selected VHAs.

*Figure 1. The general scheme of the evaluation process of VHA*

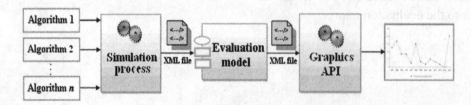

The development of the new evaluation model as a software application automates the evaluation process of the VHAs and helps the researchers to analyze the performance of the selected algorithms in a simple way.

## CASE STUDY

In this section we present the results of the performance evaluation of some of the VHAs considering two different evaluation models: an Ordinal Model based on the work of Martinez-Morales, Pineda-Rico and Stevens-Navarro (2010) and our proposed evaluation model. In our study we consider the following VHAs: SAW (Simple Additive Weighting) (Zhang, 2004), TOPSIS (Technique for Order Preference by Similarity to Ideal Solution) (Zhang, 2004), MEW (Multiplicative Exponent Weighting) (Stevens-Navarro & Wong, 2006), ELECTRE (Elimination and Choice Translating Priority) (Bari & Leung, 2007) and VIKOR (Gallardo-Medina, Pineda-Rico & Stevens-Navarro, 2009). The VHAs are simulated following a discrete-event simulation approach in the numerical computing environment of MATLAB (MATLAB, 2010) and are tested in a scenario of heterogeneous wireless networks.

We consider a scenario integrated by three different types of wireless network such as WLAN, UMTS and WiMAX, and there are two networks of each type for a total of six candidate networks for vertical handoff. The networks are labeled as follows: networks 1 and 2 correspond to networks UMTS1 and UMTS2 respectively, networks 3 and 4 correspond to networks WLAN1 and WLAN 2 respectively, and networks 5 and 6 correspond to networks WiMAX1 and WiMAX2 respectively. Five different decision parameters are considered in this study. The decision parameters are: available bandwidth in Mbps, packet delay in ms, packet jitter in ms, packet loss in per each 106 packets and cost per byte. The ranges of the values of the parameters or decision criteria are shown in Table 2.

The values of the importance weights used to model different services or traffic class considered in this study are allocated as follows: case 1 - packet delay and jitter have 70% (i.e., 35% each) of importance and the rest is equally distributed among the other parameters, this case is suitable for voice connections; case 2 - the available bandwidth has 40% of importance and the rest is equally distributed among the other parameters, this case is suitable for data connections.

This study considers 50 vertical handoff decision points. In each vertical handoff decision point (i.e. the point where the VHA executes the handoff decision) the values of the parameters may be the same, increase or decrease within the range shown in Table 2. In order to vary the values of the decision criteria a discrete-event simulation is conducted in MATLAB (MATLAB, 2010) where a discrete-time Markov chain is used to model the evolution in time of each decision parameter. The transition probabilities for an increment or decrement are 0.4, while the probability of being in the same value is 0.2. Each vertical handoff decision point is the result of an average of 10 simulations.

*Table 2. The range of the values of the networks' parameters*

| Parameters | UMTS1 | UMTS2 | WLAN1 | WLAN2 | WiMAX1 | WiMAX2 |
|---|---|---|---|---|---|---|
| Bandwidth (Mbps) | 0.1 - 2 | 0.1 - 2 | 1 - 11 | 1 - 54 | 1 - 60 | 1 - 60 |
| Delay (ms) | 25 - 50 | 25 - 50 | 100 - 150 | 100 - 150 | 60 - 100 | 60 - 100 |
| Jitter (ms) | 5 - 10 | 5 - 10 | 10 - 20 | 10 - 20 | 3 - 10 | 3 - 10 |
| PER (per $10^6$) | 20 - 80 | 20 - 80 | 20 - 80 | 20 - 80 | 20 - 80 | 20 - 80 |
| Cost (price) | 0.6 | 0.8 | 0.1 | 0.5 | 0.5 | 0.4 |

## Simulation Results

Figures 2 and 3 show the packet delay and packet jitter achieved by each of the handoff decision methods in case 1. The simulation results in Figure 2 indicate that VIKOR is able to obtain the lowest values of delay compared to the rest of VHAs. In fact Figure 2 clearly shows that VIKOR in most of its vertical handoff decisions achieves values of delay lower than 50% of the values of delay achieved by the rest of the VHAs. On the other hand, Figure 3 shows that handoff decision methods MEW and ELECTRE are able to obtain a value of jitter slightly lower than the rest of the VHAs considered in the comparison.

Figure 4 shows the available bandwidth obtained from each of the handoff decision methods in case 2. The simulation results indicate that TOPSIS is able to obtain the highest values of available bandwidth compared to the rest of the VHAs. Note also that the values of available bandwidth from SAW and ELECTRE are close to the values achieved by TOPSIS. Figure 4 also shows that the lowest values of available bandwidth are from VIKOR and MEW.

## VHAs Evaluation with the Ordinal Model

The Ordinal Model allows the comparison of VHAs via computer simulations and performance analysis. The model is partly based on the work described in Martinez-Morales, Pineda-Rico and Stevens-Navarro (2010). From the simulation results the average of the real (i.e. effective) values achieved by the VHAs is used to rank them. For example, in case of a cost parameter such as delay, the VHA with the lowest value is the first followed by the VHA with the closest increasing value of delay. On the other hand, in the case of a benefit parameter such as bandwidth, the VHA with the highest value is the first followed by the VHA with the closest decreasing value of bandwidth.

The Ordinal Model for evaluation of VHAs is defined by the following six steps:

1. Define the evaluation parameters.
2. Define the evaluation matrix.
3. Obtain the average of the simulation results of each parameter.

*Figure 2. Values of delay achieved by the VHAs in case 1*

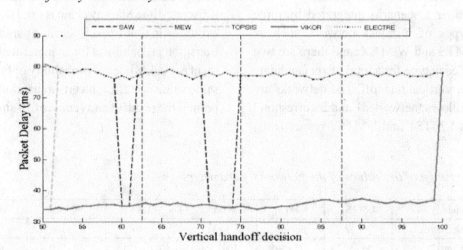

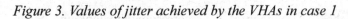

*Figure 3. Values of jitter achieved by the VHAs in case 1*

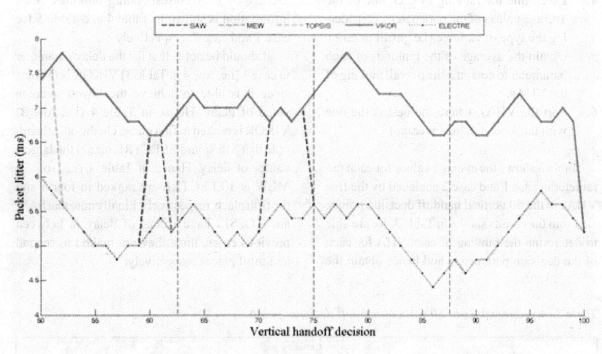

*Figure 4. Values of available bandwidth achieved by VHAs in case 2*

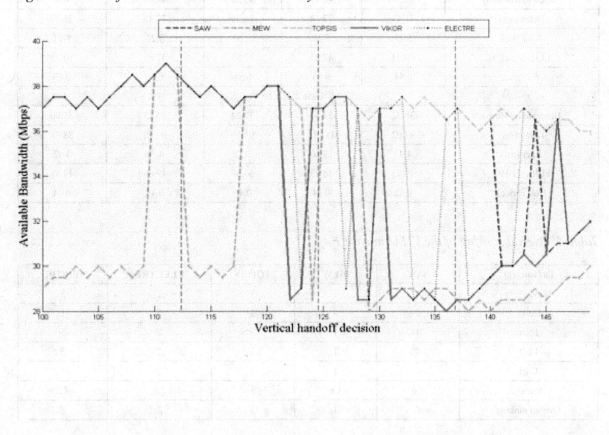

4. Determine the ranking of each one of the average values of the parameters, considering the type of variable (i.e. profit or cost).
5. Obtain the average of the rankings of each parameter to compute the overall ranking of the VHAs.
6. Sort the VHAs, where the best is the one with the lowest value (average).

Table 3 shows the average values for each parameter in case 1 and case 2 achieved by the five VHAs in the 50 vertical handoff decision points.

From the results shown in Table 3, we are able to determine the ranking of each VHA for each of the decision parameters and hence obtain the average of their corresponding rankings. Such information is shown in Table 4 and Table 5 for case 1 and case 2, respectively.

It should be noted that for the delay parameter in case 1 (i.e. row 4 in Table 3) VIKOR is the best since it is able to achieve the lowest average value of delay. Hence in Table 4 (i.e. row 3) VIKOR is ranked in first place. On the other hand, note that MEW and ELECTRE obtain the largest values of delay. Hence in Table 4 (i.e. row 3) MEW and ELECTRE are ranked in fourth and the fifth place, respectively. Finally note that SAW and TOPSIS have values of delay in between previous cases, thus, they are ranked in second and third places respectively.

*Table 3. Average values in 50 vertical handoff decision points*

| Case 1 | | | | | |
|---|---|---|---|---|---|
| **Parameters** | **SAW** | **MEW** | **TOPSIS** | **ELECTRE** | **VIKOR** |
| Bandwidth (Mbps) | 35.56 | 40.93 | 40.20 | 40.93 | 1.78 |
| Delay (ms) | 71.49 | 77.48 | 76.56 | 77.48 | 36.43 |
| Jitter (ms) | 5.43 | 5.23 | 5.26 | 5.23 | 7.01 |
| PER (per $10^6$) | 48.24 | 47.85 | 47.89 | 47.85 | 50.75 |
| Cost (price) | 0.54 | 0.50 | 0.51 | 0.50 | 0.79 |
| Case 2 | | | | | |
| Bandwidth (Mbps) | 36.32 | 31.37 | 37.22 | 35.23 | 34.00 |
| Delay (ms) | 92.02 | 111.86 | 94.16 | 90.68 | 88.78 |
| Jitter (ms) | 4.93 | 13.60 | 5.32 | 4.74 | 4.42 |
| PER (per $10^6$) | 49.92 | 48.03 | 50.07 | 49.60 | 49.33 |
| Cost (price) | 0.42 | 0.14 | 0.40 | 0.43 | 0.44 |

*Table 4. Overall ranking of the VHAs in case 1*

| Parameters | SAW | MEW | TOPSIS | ELECTRE | VIKOR |
|---|---|---|---|---|---|
| Bandwidth | 4 | 1 | 3 | 2 | 5 |
| Delay | 2 | 4 | 3 | 5 | 1 |
| Jitter | 4 | 1 | 3 | 2 | 5 |
| PER | 4 | 1 | 3 | 2 | 5 |
| Cost | 4 | 1 | 3 | 2 | 5 |
| Average | 3.6 | 1.6 | 3 | 2.6 | 4.2 |
| Overall ranking | 4 | 1 | 3 | 2 | 5 |

*Table 5. Overall ranking of the VHAs in case 2*

| Parameters | SAW | MEW | TOPSIS | ELECTRE | VIKOR |
|---|---|---|---|---|---|
| Bandwidth | 2 | 5 | 1 | 3 | 4 |
| Delay | 3 | 5 | 4 | 2 | 1 |
| Jitter | 3 | 5 | 4 | 2 | 1 |
| PER | 4 | 1 | 5 | 3 | 2 |
| Cost | 3 | 1 | 2 | 4 | 5 |
| Average | 3 | 3.4 | 3.2 | 2.8 | 2.6 |
| Overall ranking | 3 | 5 | 4 | 2 | 1 |

For the jitter parameter in case 1 (i.e. row 5 in Table 3) the best VHAs are MEW and ELECTRE since they have the lowest values of jitter while VIKOR is the worst since it has the highest value of jitter. Finally note that SAW and TOPSIS have values of delay in between previous cases, thus, they are ranked in fourth and third places respectively.

Based on the results from the evaluation in case 1 and according to the overall ranking in Table 4, the Ordinal Model concludes that MEW obtained the lowest grade (calculated from the average of the ordinal position in each parameter) which represents the best performance. VIKOR obtained the highest grade which represents the worst performance.

Note that in case 2 for the available bandwidth parameter (i.e. row 9 in Table 3) TOPSIS is the best since it is able to achieve the highest value of available bandwidth while MEW is the worst. SAW, ELECTRE and VIKOR have closer values of available bandwidth and they are ranked by the Ordinal Model in second, third and fourth places, respectively.

Based on the results from the evaluation in case 2 and according to the overall ranking in Table 5, the Ordinal Model concludes that VIKOR obtained the lowest grade (calculated from the average of the ordinal position in each parameter) which represents the best performance. MEW obtained the highest grade which represents the worst performance.

## VHAs Evaluation with the New Proposed Model

A software component called the *Evaluation Engine* was developed. This component has the logic of the new evaluation model and it is used to analyze the VHAs in an automated way. The simulation results of the evaluation parameters that were obtained by simulating VHAs in MATLAB are entered to the Evaluation Engine through an XML file, which is a standard format.

Figure 5 shows the evaluation results generated by the Evaluation Engine for case 1.

SAW, MEW, TOPSIS and ELECTRE have the highest score (see last column of the table in Figure 5), this means they have a "good performance." VIKOR has the lowest score and for this reason is considered as the algorithm with the "worst performance."

If we evaluate the algorithms with respect to the delay parameter we can say that VIKOR is the "best" of all because it has the highest value (see the third column of the table in Figure 5). The measure of this parameter is within the level of performance "Very good" (see Table 1) and therefore it has a valuation of 9, while the rest of the algorithms have a valuation of 8 given that their measures are within the level of performance "Moderately good."

The opposite occurs with the jitter parameter (see the fourth column of the table in Figure 5) where SAW, MEW, TOPSIS and ELECTRE have

*Figure 5. Evaluation results generated by the evaluation engine for case 1*

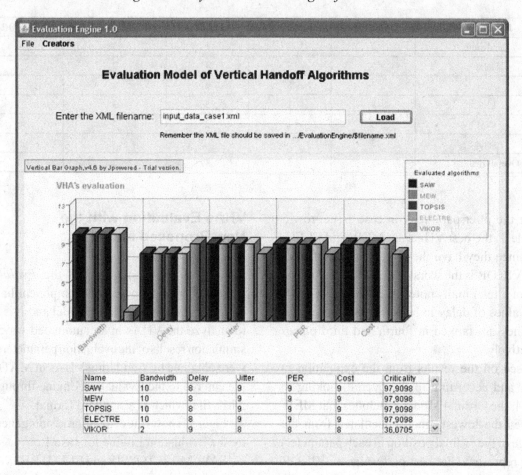

the highest valuation. The measures of these algorithms for this parameter are within the level of performance "Very good" and therefore they have a valuation of 9, while VIKOR has a valuation of 8 because its measure is within the level of performance "Moderately good."

Figure 6 shows the evaluation results generated by the Evaluation Engine for case 2.

SAW, TOPSIS and ELECTRE have the highest score (see last column of the table in Figure 6), this means they have a good performance. Otherwise, MEW and VIKOR have the lowest scores however; the score of the VIKOR is slightly higher compared with the score of MEW,

which is considered the algorithm with the worst performance.

If we evaluate the algorithms with respect to the bandwidth parameter (see the second column of the table in Figure 6) we can say that SAW, TOPSIS and ELECTRE are the "best" because they have the highest rating. The measures of these algorithms for the bandwidth parameter are within the level of performance "Very good" and therefore they have a valuation of 9, while VIKOR and MEW have a valuation of 8 given that their measures are within the level of performance "Moderately good."

*Figure 6. Evaluation results generated by the evaluation engine for case 2*

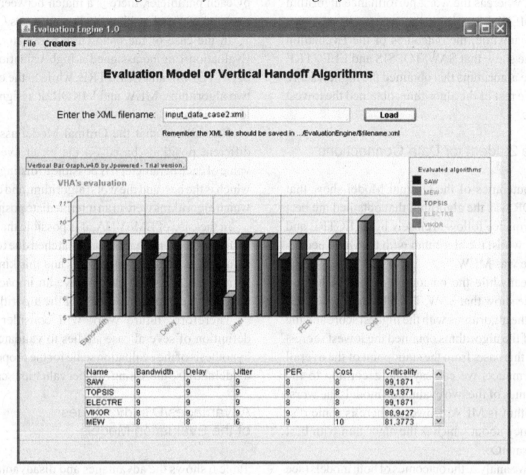

## Comparison of the Two Evaluation Models

This section presents the comparison of the evaluation results obtained by the Ordinal Model and the new proposed evaluation model.

### Case 1: Ideal for Voice Connections

When the Ordinal Model was used for evaluation of the selected VHAs, the MEW algorithm was the one that obtained the best performance and VIKOR was the algorithm with the worst performance.

The tests with the Evaluation Engine show that SAW, MEW, TOPSIS and ELECTRE algorithms obtained the highest score, while VIKOR obtained the lowest score. Therefore, from the standpoint of the overall performance (i.e. considering all the parameters) we can say that, according to the two evaluation models, MEW appears as the best algorithm and VIKOR as the worst algorithm for case 1.

If the evaluation results of the models are analyzed by parameter (see the rows of the Table 4 for the Ordinal Model and the table of the Figure 5 for the Evaluation Engine) the outcomes show that there is a match between the best and worst algorithm for all the evaluation parameters.

For example, in the case of delay parameter the outcomes of the Ordinal Model show that VIKOR is the algorithm that obtained the best performance followed closely by ELECTRE and

SAW; whereas the worst performance algorithm was MEW.

Meanwhile, the outcomes of the Evaluation Engine show that SAW, TOPSIS and ELECTRE are the algorithms that obtained the highest score and the rest of the algorithms obtained the lowest scores.

## Case 2: Ideal for Data Connections

The outcomes of the Ordinal Model show that VIKOR was the algorithm that obtained the best performance followed closely by ELECTRE and SAW, whilst the algorithm with the worst performance was MEW.

Meanwhile the outcomes of the Evaluation Engine show that SAW, TOPSIS and ELECTRE were the algorithms with the highest score and the rest of the algorithms obtained the lowest scores.

In this case, from the standpoint of the overall performance, we can say that according to the outcomes of the two evaluation models the worst algorithm is MEW. However there is some discrepancy about which is the algorithm with best performance.

If we analyze the outcomes of both models (see the rows of the Table 5 for the Ordinal Model and the table in the Figure 6 for the Evaluation Engine)

by each parameter, there is a match between the best and worst algorithm in all parameters.

In the case of the bandwidth parameter, the Evaluation Engine assigned a high valuation to SAW, TOPSIS and ELECTRE, while to the other two algorithms, MEW and VIKOR, it assigned a lower valuation.

Considering that the Ordinal Model assigns different positions based on the exact average value of each parameter it is possible to distinguish which is the best and the worst algorithm, and even which algorithms were in an intermediate position.

In the case of EMoVHA, it is possible that the valuations of some parameters matched due to the valuation scale used for analysis and this kind of "draw" can (in some cases) have an impact on the overall evaluation process of the algorithms.

Therefore, future work will consider the definition of several case studies to validate the hypothesis of the evaluation scale for the proposed model and also the testing of other valuation scales.

## Advantages/Disadvantages of the Evaluation Models

Table 6 shows the advantages and disadvantages of each evaluation model.

*Table 6. Advantages/disadvantages of the evaluation model*

| Evaluation models | Advantages | Disadvantages |
|---|---|---|
| Ordinal Model | • The design of the evaluation model allows calculation of the performance of VHAs based on parameters, whose amounts can be defined by the researcher.<br>• The use of exact average values of performance of each decision parameter allows the researcher to clearly distinguish the performance of each algorithm. | • In its current state the model lacks the implementation of software that allows automated calculations.<br>• In its current state the model lacks an interface (GUI) for the presentation of results. |
| EMoVHA | • Evaluates the VHAs using a software component, the inputs of which are the values of the evaluation parameters that are obtained from the simulation of the algorithms using simulation tools.<br>• Generate the results in a graphic mode and using a table with the evaluation of VHAs so researchers can analyze the evaluation results in a simple way. | • The number of evaluation parameters for the evaluation of the VHAs is defined in a specific range (3 to 5 parameters) due to the constraint of the software component.<br>• Using the valuation scale of 10 levels can in some cases generate "ties" between algorithms. |

One of the main advantages of the Ordinal Model is that its methodology does not set a maximum number of VHAs to evaluate, nor a maximum number to use in the evaluation process. In the case of EMoVHA, the number of algorithms is limited to a maximum of 5 algorithms and the number of evaluation parameters is defined in a specific range (minimum 3, maximum 5 parameters). Actually, this is a constraint of the implementation through software and not a limitation of the design of the evaluation model, therefore can not be considered as a disadvantage of the model.

Based on the above discussions, we cannot say that either evaluation model is better than the other, both models are valid and effective for the evaluation of the VHAs and each one has his advantages and disadvantages.

## CONCLUSION

The interest in vertical handoff has generated a vast number of VHAs. Some of them are pure theoretical solutions but others have already been implemented as prototypes. Given this number of VHAs of different complexity, researchers have begun to generate some evaluation models to analyze their performance and efficiency, or simply to compare the algorithms.

The problem of performance evaluation of VHAs has therefore become an interesting challenge given the amount of proposed algorithms and the need for an objective assessment of these solutions. However, some of the proposed evaluation models have been designed to evaluate specific parameters and are not easily adapted to other scenarios. Also a few of the existing evaluation models are not very flexible in terms of the evaluation parameters and some of them are very complex to apply.

The new proposed evaluation model is flexible in terms of the number of evaluation parameters and facilitates the analysis of VHAs by researchers.

The design of the new evaluation model is based on the multi-criteria evaluation methodology and criticality analysis, which permitted the model to be developed as a software component.

The proposed evaluation model is available on the web as a software tool (EMoVHA web site - http://turing.uao.edu.co:8080/modelovho/interfaces/home.jsp) and as a standalone software component available for download. Therefore researchers can use it for an automated evaluation of the VHAs.

The comparison of the new evaluation model with the other existing model (which is named Ordinal Model) was an important exercise because it gave feedback on both models, to refine them and to propose extensions to their capabilities and features.

## FUTURE RESEARCH DIRECTIONS

Future work will consider the definition of several case studies to validate the hypothesis about the evaluation scale for the new evaluation model and also to test the other valuation scales.

Another approach is to integrate both evaluation models in a web application, so the user can expand the possibilities for evaluating VHAs using both evaluation models and then can compare the outcomes for enhanced analysis.

## REFERENCES

Bari, F., & Leung, V. (2007). Application of ELECTRE to network selection in a heterogeneous wireless network environment. In *Proceedings of IEEE Wireless Communications and Networking Conference (WCNC 2007),* (pp. 3810-3815). IEEE Press.

Colson, G., & Bruyn, C. (1989). Models and methods in multiple objectives decision making. *Mathematical and Computer Modelling, 12,* 1201–1211. doi:10.1016/0895-7177(89)90362-2

Gallardo-Medina, R., Pineda-Rico, U., & Stevens-Navarro, E. (2009). VIKOR method for vertical handoff decision in beyond 3G wireless networks. In *Proceedings of IEEE International Conference in Automatic Control, Computing Science and Electronic Engineering (CCE 2009)*, (pp. 1-5). IEEE Press.

Garcia, A., & Jimenez, O. (2008). *Software prototype for network re-selection in heterogeneous wireless environments*. Paper presented at IEEE Communications Colombian Congress. Bogata, Colombia.

Hong, C., Kang, T., & Kim, S. (2005). An effective vertical handoff scheme supporting multiple applications in ubiquitous computing environment. In *Proceedings of the Second International Conference on Embedded Software and Systems*, (pp. 407-440). IEEE Press.

Hui, S. K., & Yeung, K. H. (2003). Challenges in the migration to 4G mobile systems. *IEEE Communications Magazine, 41*(12), 54–59. doi:10.1109/MCOM.2003.1252799

Kassar, M., Kervella, B., & Pujolle, G. (2008). An overview of vertical handover decision strategies in heterogeneous wireless networks. *Computer Communications, 31*(10), 2607–2620. doi:10.1016/j.comcom.2008.01.044

Lassoued, I., Bonnin, J., Hamouda, Z., & Belghith, A. (2008). A methodology for evaluation vertical handoff decision mechanisms. In *Proceedings of the International Conference on Networking*, (pp.377-384). IEEE Press.

Lee, S., Sriram, K., Kim, K., Kim, Y., & Golmie, N. (2009). Vertical handoff decision algorithms for providing optimized performance in heterogeneous wireless networks. *IEEE Transactions on Vehicular Technology, 58*(2), 865–881. doi:10.1109/TVT.2008.925301

Mäkelä, J. (2008). *Effects of handoff algorithms on the performance of multimedia wireless networks*. Academic dissertation. Oulu, Finland: University of Oulu.

Martinez-Morales, J. D., Pineda-Rico, U., & Stevens-Navarro, E. (2010). Performance comparison between MADM algorithms for vertical handoff in 4G networks. In *Proceedings of IEEE International Conference In Automatic Control, Computing Science and Electronic Engineering (CCE 2010)*, (pp. 309-314). IEEE Press.

Mathworks. (2010). *MATLAB and Simulink for technical computing*. Retrieved 28 June 2010 from http://www.mathworks.com.

Nasser, N., Hasswa, A., & Hassanein, H. (2006). Handoffs in fourth generation heterogeneous networks. *IEEE Communications Magazine, 44*(10), 96–103. doi:10.1109/MCOM.2006.1710420

Proctor, W., & Drechsler, M. (2003). *Deliberative multi-criteria evaluation: A case study of recreation and tourism options in Victoria, Australia*. Paper presented at European Society for Ecological Economics, Frontiers 2 Conference. Tenerife, Canary Islands.

Reliarisk. (2010). *Reliability and risk management: Criticality analysis*. Retrieved 20 March 2010 from http://www.reliarisk.com.

Saaty, T. (1980). *The analytic hierarchy process*. New York, NY: McGraw-Hill.

Stepanov, I., Hahner, J., Becker, C., Tian, J., & Rothermel, K. (2003). A meta-model and framework for user mobility in mobile networks. In *Proceedings of IEEE International Conference*, (pp. 231-238). IEEE Press.

Stevens-Navarro, E., & Wong, V. (2006). Comparison between vertical handoff decision algorithms for heterogeneous wireless networks. In *Proceedings of the IEEE Vehicular Technology Conference*, (pp. 947-951). IEEE Press.

Suciu, L., Guillouard, K., & Bonnin, J. (2006). A methodology for assessing the vertical handover algorithms in heterogeneous wireless network. In *Proceedings of the Workshop on Broadband Wireless Access for Ubiquitous Networking*, (p. 196). ACM Press.

Syuhada, M., Mahamod, I., & Firuz, W. (2008). *Performance evaluation of vertical handoff in fourth generation (4G) networks model.* Paper presented at the 6th National Conference on Telecommunication Technologies and IEEE 2008 2nd Malaysia Conference on Photonics. Putrajaya, Malaysia.

Yan, X., Sekercioglu, Y., & Narayanan, S. (2010). A survey of vertical handover decision algorithms in fourth generation heterogeneous wireless networks. *Computer Networks: The International Journal of Computer and Telecommunications Networking, 54*(11), 1848–1863.

Zahran, A., & Liang, B. (2005). Performance evaluation framework for vertical handoff algorithms in heterogeneous networks. In *Proceedings of the IEEE International Conference on Communications,* (pp. 173-178). IEEE Press.

Zahran, A., Liang, B., & Saleh, A. (2006). Signal threshold adaptation for vertical handoff in heterogeneous wireless network. *Mobile Networks and Applications, 11*(4), 625–640. doi:10.1007/s11036-006-7326-7

Zhang, W. (2004). Handover decision using fuzzy MADM in heterogeneous networks. In *Proceedings of IEEE Wireless Communications and Networking Conference (WCNC 2004),* (pp. 653-658). IEEE Press.

Zhu, F., & McNair, J. (2006). Multiservice vertical handoff decision algorithms. *URASIP Journal on Wireless Communications and Networking, 2,* 52–64.

## ADDITIONAL READING

Balasubramaniam, S., & Indulska, J. (2004). Vertical handover supporting pervasive computing in future wireless networks. *Computer Communications, 27*(8), 708–719. doi:10.1016/j.comcom.2003.10.010

Bonnin, J., Hamouda, B., Lassoued, I., & Belghith, A. (2008). Middleware for multi-interfaces management through profiles handling. In *Proceedings of Mobilware 2008* (p. 8). IEEE Press. doi:10.4108/ICST.MOBILWARE2008.2899

Chakravorty, R., Banerjee, S., Rodriguez, P., & Chesterfield, J. (2004). Performance optimizations for wireless wide-area networks: Comparative study and experimental evaluation. In *Proceedings of the International Conference on Mobile Computing and Networking,* (pp. 159-173). IEEE Press.

Chakravorty, R., Vidales, P., Subramanian, K., Pratt, I., & Crowcroft, J. (2004). Performance issues with vertical handovers – Experiences from GPRS cellular and WLAN hot-spots integration. In *Proceedings of the Second IEEE Annual Conference on Pervasive Computing and Communications,* (pp.155-164). IEEE Press.

Chalmers, D., & Sloman, M. (1999). A survey of quality of service in mobile computing environments. *IEEE Communications Tutorials and Surveys.* Retrieved from http://pubs.doc.ic.ac.uk/Mobile-QoS-survey/Mobile-QoS-survey.pdf.

Durantini, A., & Petracca, M. (2008). Performance comparison of vertical handover strategies for PSDR heterogeneous networks. *IEEE Wireless Communications, 15*(3), 54–59. doi:10.1109/MWC.2008.4547523

Eng, H. O., & Khan, J. Y. (2010). On optimal network selection in a dynamic multi-RAT environment. *IEEE Communications Letters, 14*(3), 217–219. doi:10.1109/LCOMM.2010.03.092378

Guo, Q., Zhu, J., & Xu, X. (2005). An adaptive multi-criteria vertical handoff decision algorithm for radio heterogeneous networks. In *Proceedings of IEEE International Communications Conference (ICC 2005),* (pp. 2769-2773). IEEE Press.

Hou, J., & O'Brien, D. C. (2006). Vertical handover-decision-making algorithm using fuzzy logic for the integrated Radio-and-OW system. *IEEE Transactions on Wireless Communications, 5*(1), 176–185. doi:10.1109/TWC.2006.1576541

Lampropoulos, G., Salkintzis, A., & Passas, N. (2008). Media-independent handover for seamless service provision in heterogeneous networks. *IEEE Communications Magazine, 46*(1), 64–71. doi:10.1109/MCOM.2008.4427232

Liu, M., Li, Z., Guo, X., & Lach, H. (2006). *Design and evaluation of vertical handoff decision algorithm in heterogeneous wireless networks.* Paper presented at the 14th IEEE International Conference on Networks. Chengdu, China.

McNair, J., & Zhu, F. (2004). Vertical handoffs in fourth-generation multinetwork environments. *IEEE Wireless Communications, 11*, 8–15. doi:10.1109/MWC.2004.1308935

Murthy, M., & Phiri, F. (2005). Performance analysis of downward handoff latency in a WLAN/GPRS interworking system. *Journal of Computer Science, 1*(1), 24–27. doi:10.3844/jcssp.2005.24.27

Ormond, O., Murphy, J., & Muntean, G. (2006). Utility-based intelligent network selection in beyond 3G systems. In *Proceedings of IEEE International Communications Conference (ICC 2006)*, (pp. 1831-1836). IEEE Press.

Park, S., Yu, J., & Ihm, J. (2007). A performance evaluation of vertical handoff scheme between mobile-WiMax and cellular networks. In *Proceedings of 16th International Conference on Computer Communications and Network*, (pp. 894-899). IEEE Press.

Pollini, G. (1996). Trends in handover design. *IEEE Communications Magazine, 34*(3), 82–90. doi:10.1109/35.486807

Sgora, A., & Vergados, D. (2009). Handoff prioritization and decision schemes in wireless cellular networks: A survey. *IEEE Communications Tutorials and Surveys, 11*(4).

Song, Q., & Jamalipour, A. (2005). Network selection in an integrated wireless LAN and UMTS environment using mathematical modeling and computing techniques. *IEEE Wireless Communications, 12*(3), 42–48. doi:10.1109/MWC.2005.1452853

Stemm, M., & Katz, H. (1998). Vertical handoffs in wireless overlay networks. *ACM Mobile Networks and Applications, 3*, 335–350. doi:10.1023/A:1019197320544

Stevens-Navarro, E., Lin, Y., & Wong, V. (2008). An MDP-based vertical handoff decision algorithm for heterogeneous wireless networks. *IEEE Transactions on Vehicular Technology, 57*(2), 1243–1254. doi:10.1109/TVT.2007.907072

Stevens-Navarro, E., Pineda-Rico, U., & Acosta-Elias, J. (2008). Vertical handover in beyond third generation (B3G) wireless networks. *International Journal of Future Generation Communication and Networking, 1*(1), 51–58.

SuKyoung, L., Sriram, K., Kyungsoon, K., Yoon Hyuk, K., & Golmie, N. (2009). Vertical handoff decision algorithms for providing optimized performance in heterogeneous wireless networks. *IEEE Transactions on Vehicular Technology, 58*(2), 865–881. doi:10.1109/TVT.2008.925301

Vanem, E., Svaet, S., & Paint, F. (2003). Effects of multiple access alternatives in heterogeneous wireless environments. *IEEE Wireless Communications and Networking, 3*, 1696–1700.

Wang, H., Katz, R., & Giese, J. (1999). Policy-enabled handoffs across heterogeneous wireless networks. In *Proceedings of Second IEEE Workshop on Mobile Computing Systems and Applications*, (pp. 51-60). IEEE Press.

Zhang, J., Stevens-Navarro, E., Wong, V., Chan, H., & Leung, V. (2008). Protocols and decision processes for vertical handovers. In Zhang, Y., Yang, L., & Ma, J. (Eds.), *Unlicensed Mobile Access Technology: Protocols, Architectures, Security, Standards and Applications* (pp. 123–145). Boca Raton, FL: Taylor & Francis Group. doi:10.1201/9781420055382.pt2

## KEY TERMS AND DEFINITIONS

**Criticality Analysis:** Methodology to establish a hierarchy or priorities of processes, systems and machines, creating a structure that facilitates effective decision making, directing the effort and resources to areas where it is most required and/or needed to improve operational reliability based on the current situation.

**Criticality Index:** Represents the criticality level of the vertical handoff algorithms which are evaluated. The value of this index allows prioritizing or ordering the algorithms.

**Criticality Matrix:** Is a matrix used to analyze the evaluation parameters of each algorithm according to a defined valuation scale.

**Multi-Criteria Evaluation:** Is an effective technique used in multidimensional decision and evaluation models within the field of decision making. The main objective of which is to help the decision makers to evaluate, prioritize, and select or reject objects based on an evaluation by scores and according to several criteria.

**Multiple Attribute Decision Making (MADM):** Is a decision making methodology, which deals with the problem of choosing an alternative from a set of alternatives which are characterized in terms of their attributes.

**Vertical Handoff:** Is the process of changing the mobile connection between access points supporting different wireless technologies (i.e. heterogeneous networks).

**Vertical Handoff Algorithm:** The set of rules and/or mathematical procedures for performing the vertical handoff decision.

# Chapter 4
# Simulation of Vertical Handoff Algorithms for Heterogeneous Wireless Networks

**Alexander Garcia D.**
*Universidad Autonoma de Occidente, Colombia*

**Andres Navarro C.**
*Universidad ICESI, Colombia*

**Adriana Arteaga A.**
*Universidad ICESI, Colombia*

**Fabio G. Guerrero**
*Universidad del Valle, Colombia*

**Enrique Stevens-Navarro**
*Universidad Autonoma de San Luis Potosi, Mexico*

## ABSTRACT

*Computer simulation is an important tool for the study and analysis of communication networks. In the case of simulation of Vertical Handoff Algorithms (VHAs) for heterogeneous wireless networks there are two approaches: using a network simulator or using general purpose programming languages. The objective of this chapter is to present and compare both approaches, by means of two study cases. The first case considers the use of network simulator NCTUns (National Chiao Tung University Network Simulator), while the second case considers the use of MATLAB.*

## INTRODUCTION

Computer simulation is a very important tool for the study and analysis of communication networks (Pawlikowski, Jeong, & Lee, 2002). Network simulators are tools that allow researchers in the telecommunications field to create virtual environments where they can design, configure, implement, and analyze different types of networks. Thus, research efforts can be focused on the study itself rather than in the implementation (i.e., in terms of time and cost) of the infrastructure for the test.

Currently, there are plenty of network simulators for communication networks (Kash, Ward, &

DOI: 10.4018/978-1-4666-0191-8.ch004

Andrusenko, 2009; Rahman, Pakštas, & Wang, 2009). However, most of them have been developed for very specific objectives (e.g., just to test a single network component or protocol). There are several simulation tools that can be extended by users to incorporate new models, protocols, network components, or features. On the other hand, there is another approach to simulate communication networks, which relies on the use of general purpose programming languages and/or programs for numerical computations.

The objective of this chapter is to present and compare, by means of two study cases, both approaches to simulate communication networks. We focus on simulation of Vertical Handoff Algorithms (VHAs) for heterogeneous wireless networks. The first case study considers the use of the network simulator NCTUns, while the second study uses the programming language and interactive environment MATLAB.

This chapter is organized as follows. In Section 2, we explain what is a vertical handoff algorithm. Section 3 gives the background and related work on VHA simulation. Section 4 presents a case study of vertical handoff simulation with NCTUns, while in Section 5 there is another case study, using MATLAB. Section 6 gives an analysis of these simulation tools. Finally, some conclusions are given in the last section.

## VERTICAL HANDOFF ALGORITHMS (VHAS)

The envisioned environment of heterogeneous wireless networks is expected to integrate multiple communication networks over a common IP (Internet Protocol) platform, such as Wireless Local Area Networks (WLAN), Universal Mobile Telecommunications System (UMTS) networks, CDMA 2000 networks, Wireless Metropolitan Area Networks (WMAN), etc., allowing the best connectivity to applications anywhere at anytime. In this scenario, mobile users will switch between different wireless networks to satisfy their communication needs.

A vertical handoff is the process of changing connections among heterogeneous wireless networks (Nasser, Hasswa, & Hassanein, 2006; Kassar, Kervella, & Pujolle, 2008). It can be divided into three phases: network discovery, handoff decision, and handoff execution. In the first phase, the mobile terminal discovers its available neighboring networks. In the decision phase, the mobile terminal determines whether or not it has to redirect its current connection based on comparing the decision factors offered by the discovered networks, e.g., available bandwidth, latency, packet error rate, monetary cost, battery consumption, mobility speed, and network coverage. The last phase is responsible for establishing the connection according to the vertical handoff decision.

In the last few years, several VHAs have been proposed in the research literature, some of them consider the three phases while others restrict their attention to a specific phase. In the same way, different authors have chosen different simulation tools to study, evaluate, and compare their proposed VHAs. In the following section, we present a brief literature review of several simulation approaches that have been used to study VHAs for heterogeneous wireless networks.

## SIMULATION OF VHAS AND SIMULATION APPROACHES

Usually, a computer network simulator presents wired and wireless networking and, in its basic software release, horizontal handoff (handoff between access points of the same technology) is suitable for wireless networks including WiMAX, GPRS, 802.11a, 802.11b in ad hoc and infrastructure mode. Some network simulators do not have the functionality of vertical handoff, but the user can manipulate the tool to include it.

Altwelib, Ashibani, and Shatwan (2007) proposed a novel layer 2 VHA for UMTS and WLAN networks; Jo and Cho (2008) proposed a VHA considering signaling information from layers 2 and 3 for CDMA2000 and Mobile WiMAX networks. Both proposals were implemented and evaluated using network simulator ns-2.

Melia, Vidal, De la Oliva, Soto, Corujo, and Aguiar (2006) studied the mobility management problem with Mobile IP protocol and IEEE 802.21 standard in 3G cellular and WLAN networks, and Abdelatif, Kalebaila and Chan (2007) studied the mobility management problem considering only IEEE 802.21 standard in CDMA2000, WLAN and WiMAX networks. Both proposals were implemented and evaluated using network simulator OMNeT++.

Stevens-Navarro and Wong (2006) implemented and evaluated several VHAs based on Multiple Attribute Decision Making (MADM) methods in UMTS and WLAN networks. Gallardo-Medina, Pineda-Rico and Stevens-Navarro (2009) proposed a VHA based on the VIKOR method for UMTS, WLAN and WiMAX networks. Results in these proposals were obtained by simulations in MATLAB.

Garcia, Escobar, Navarro, Arteaga, Guerrero, and Salazar (2010) implemented and evaluated three VHAs with different degrees of complexity to the decision phase in WiMAX, GPRS and WLAN networks. Algorithms were implemented using simulator NCTUns.

As shown above, some authors obtained their results about VHAs using network simulators such as ns-2, OMNet++ or NCTUns, while others used general purpose programming languages such as MATLAB.

## CASE STUDY: SIMULATION OF VHAS USING NCTUNS

This section describes some VHAs implementations using the network simulator National Chiao Tung University Network Simulator (NCTUns) for heterogeneous wireless networks. Three VHAs are implemented and several performance results are shown.

## NCTUns

NCTUns is an open source tool developed by National Chiao Tung University for communication networks simulation. It allows simulating networking device behavior such as switches, routers, mobile nodes, links, and the execution of some application programs on these devices. NCTUns offers models for several network technologies, such as wired networks, 802.11a and 802.11b networks, ad hoc networks, WiMAX, GPRS, satellite, and vehicular networks. This is an important feature because it allows bringing together the most representative wireless technologies at present and the user can simulate the wireless technology change. Also, NCTUns directly uses the real TCP/IP protocol stack in the Linux kernel to run simulations and generate more realistic and faithful results.

"Supernode" is a new and powerful NCTUns feature. With it, a user can group and merge multiple mobile nodes with different types of wireless interfaces to form a multi-interface mobile node. The applications running on it can easily switch the interface to continue sending or receiving data, a key functionality for vertical handoff. So far, the free NCTUns version does not support vertical handoff, therefore it is necessary include some components within the tool to simulate it.

The tool also has emulation functionality, allowing exchange traffic between a simulation scenario and a real external device to the simulation, such as a PC or a router. This is used to test the performance of a real device under the changing traffic conditions generated in the simulation.

## Methods to Add New Components to NCTUns

NCTUns is built of modules and each is responsible for a process of simulation. The most used components are the traffic generators that are responsible for sending and receiving traffic in the simulation scenario, so they are designed in pairs: a source and a receiver. There are special generators for TCP and UDP traffic, and several traffic parameters can be configured, including the package size.

Each layer of the TCP/IP stack has its own components and these are grouped into modules. All network device are made with elements from different modules and in the case of technologies such as GPRS, WiMAX or Intelligent Transportation Systems (ITS), some higher-level components have their behavior defined in a single component.

A very important feature is that NCTUns has its own Linux kernel to execute any system call and a scheduler to organize the execution of simulation tasks. NCTUns is able to run any script written in a low level language such as Perl or C, so most of the components are written in C and its code can be modified according to the developer's needs.

There are two ways to add new components to NCTUns. The first is writing a low-level language script and placing it in the module that contains the elements of the corresponding layer. The developer manual explains briefly how to do it, but you have to design the connectors between the added element and the upper and lower layers, making this a highly complex method. The second option is to design a script written at a

low-level but not use it as an element of a layer of the TCP/IP but as a high-level component, as traffic generators. In this way, communication between components is done through sockets and takes advantage of the fact that the kernel can perform system calls directly.

## Selected VHAs

VHAs have been object of study for different research groups, including the main universities and companies around the world. Nevertheless the investigations always have been oriented to improve the performance of algorithms by achieving a decrease in delay, processing, and unnecessary vertical handoffs. Several VHAs were reviewed to design a simulation scheme and use them like study cases, but finally three VHA were selected, taking into account their complexity levels.

## VHA Based on User Preferences

The algorithm proposed by Garcia and Jimenez (2008) involves a cost function designed to test the decision phase of a VHA, omitting multiple handoffs, giving an extra credit to the actual network and taking into account simple input parameters, as a first approach to the algorithm's complexity. Parameters are bandwidth (bit rate), battery consumption, monetary connection cost, and mobility speed, multiplied by the weight chosen by the user for each parameter. Unnecessary handoff processes are avoided with a dwell timer once a first attempt to transfer the communication to a new network is done. This timer is activated after making the first decision, and the dwell timer is 5 seconds. The extra credit to the evaluated network is managed by a hysteresis margin, which intends to avoid the ping-pong effect. The numeric measurements for these two values depend on the mobility speed being developed by the simulation, and the received power threshold given by the actual access point or base station.

The power consumption of the interfaces is given by an approximation to power consumption with respect to the distance between the node and Base Station (BS) or Access Point (AP). Weights for parameters are between 0 and 1; the user assigns the highest value to the parameter which is considered to be the determinant in the network selection process. Experience suggests taking values of 0.7 for bandwidth weight, 0.1 for monetary connection cost weight, and 0.2 for mobility weight (the highest value is given to the bandwidth parameter as it is a sensitive variable for handoff performance).

Equation (1) represents the cost function, $f_i$. For each network i, $B_i$ is bandwidth, $C_i$ is monetary cost and V is the velocity of movement of mobile node; $W_b$, $W_c$ and $W_v$ are weights for bandwidth, monetary cost and velocity, respectively.

$$f_i = W_b \ln \frac{1}{B_i} + W_c \ln C_i + W_v \ln \frac{1}{V} \qquad (1)$$

The network with the lowest value of the cost function is selected.

## VHA Based on Application Requirements

This algorithm, proposed by Hong, Kang and Kim (2005), is based on the application requirements running on the mobile node and that must be covered by the conditions of some of the available networks. The parameters considered for this decision are: bandwidth, latency and percentage packet loss rate. The proposed algorithm is divided into three components:

- **Application Manager:** runs on the mobile node and analyzes the application requirements. These requirements specify, for each application, the ideal ($AUf_n$) and acceptable ($ALf_n$) values for each parameter and determine what are the critical values of the parameters to be covered with the network conditions, that is, the highest bandwidth, the lowest latency and the lowest packet loss rate and respective acceptable values. This is the abstracted multi-application profile, and in this case the bandwidth selected by the algorithm does not satisfy this need for all applications, so they do not run simultaneously.

- **Network Manager:** runs on the network and is responsible for determining which network meets the requirements of the abstracted multi-application profile. Furthermore, this component indicates to the mobile node the network to run the applications.

- **Network Layer:** is responsible for taking measurements of the parameters in the available networks (bandwidth, latency and percentage packet loss rate) all the time, so the network manager compares them with the abstracted multi-application profile requirements.

The algorithm uses the dwell timer concept to perform several evaluations on a network to determine if its conditions are stable and so avoid unnecessary network changes that are caused by momentary changes in the networks. Each evaluation generates normalized factors that are calculated as follow:

For network parameters that offer better performance with greater values, such as bandwidth, use the following expression, UR is the largest value of the parameter, UL is the least, m corresponds to the network and n is the parameter:

$$f_{m,n} = \begin{cases} -1, & \frac{UR_{m,n} + LR_{m,n}}{2} < ALf_n \\ 0, & ALf_n \leq \frac{UR_{m,n} + LR_{m,n}}{2} \leq AUf_n \\ 1, & \frac{UR_{m,n} + LR_{m,n}}{2} > AUf_n \end{cases}$$

$$(2)$$

For those network parameters that offer better performance with lower values, such as latency and packet loss rate, use the following expression, where UR is the largest value of the parameter, UL is the least, m corresponds to the network and n is the parameter:

$$
f_{m,n} = \begin{cases} -1, & \dfrac{UR_{m,n} + LR_{m,n}}{2} > ALf_n \\[2mm] 0, & ALf_n \geq \dfrac{UR_{m,n} + LR_{m,n}}{2} \geq AUf_n \\[2mm] 1, & \dfrac{UR_{m,n} + LR_{m,n}}{2} < AUf_n \end{cases}
$$

(3)

After all evaluations, average normalized factors are estimated and the handoff decision is taken: If the evaluated network has more than one average normalized factor greater than 0, then the network is chosen. Otherwise, the node remains connected to the current network.

## VHA Based on Load Balancing and Power Consumption

The algorithm proposed by Lee, Sriram, Kim, Kim, and Golmie (2009) is mainly focused on decisions to connect a group of nodes to the available networks, seeking low battery consumption, load balancing between access points of different networks, or both. A master node establishes a logical communication with each mobile node in the network using Media Independent Handover Function (MIHF) (Yang, Choi, Choi, Park, & Kim, 2006), where each of these send information regarding its current battery consumption rate to each access node and the current bandwidth to each node access. This information is stored in a matrix by the master node and this is used in a cost function to evaluate all the possible combinations between nodes and their connections. It gets a threshold to indicate the optimum configuration consumption, determined by battery or load balancing.

Equation (4) defines the total charge for access node (AP or BS), which performs a summation of traffic represented by each mobile node MN on n-th node i, by applying (4) on all nodes access, you get a vector of size N + M, where N refers to the amount of AP and M refers to the amount of BS.

$$
\rho_i = \sum_{U_j \in V_a} e_{ij}
$$

(4)

where:

$e_{ij}$ = Connection rate of the j-th mobile node with respect to the i-th node access
$\rho_i$ = Total charge of the i-th-node access.

Equation (5) gives the lifetime of the battery of the MN with respect to the i-th connecting node. Applying (5) to all the MN with respect to all AP or BS, we have a matrix of size (N + M) x K.

$$
l_{ij} = x_{ij} * \frac{\rho_j}{\rho_{ij}}
$$

(5)

where:

$\rho_i$ = Energy consumption rate of the j-th MN necessary to maintain links with the i-th access node (BS or AP).
$\rho_{ij}$ = Amount of node battery in the first connection to AP or BS.
$x_{ij}$ = A binary variable which gets a value equal to 1 if the i-th MN exceeds the threshold of connection to the j-th access node (AP and/or BS), otherwise x assumes a value of zero.

If the objective of the algorithm is to save on battery consumption, it is sufficient to minimize the array generated by (5), which is defined as lt(X). To include load balancing for all access nodes, (6) and (7) are included.

$$\text{Opt - F:Min } F = \text{Min}_{\forall X \in} X \sum_{1 < i < N+M} w(i) \left( \frac{\rho_i + \gamma_i(X)}{z_i} \right)^p \tag{6}$$

Subject to

$$\rho_i + \gamma_i(X) \leq z_i \quad for \quad 1 \leq i \leq N+M \tag{7}$$

If the objective of the algorithm is both load balancing and to save on battery consumption, it is necessary to minimize (8):

$$G(X,\alpha,\beta) = \alpha \sum_{u_j \in U} lt_{ij}(X) - \beta \sum_{1 < i < N+M} w(i) \left( \frac{\rho_i + \gamma_i(X)}{z_i} \right)^2 \tag{8}$$

Subject to

$$\text{Opt} - \text{G:Max} \quad G(X,\alpha,\beta) \tag{9}$$

## General Scheme of VHA Simulation

As mentioned, the vertical handoff process can be divided into three phases: network discovery, handoff decision, and handoff execution. In the first phase, it is necessary to collect data to evaluate handoff possibilities between heterogeneous networks. These data depend on the parameters evaluated by each algorithm: node position, bandwidth, network latency, network packet loss, battery consumption, etc. Once all the information needed for the process is gathered, the decision is taken and if the node has to change the network connection, the vertical handoff is executed; otherwise, data gathering is done again.

From this, we designed a scheme of simulation to follow in implementing the three algorithms chosen (Figure 1). As the three algorithms evaluate the available networks based on network parameters, the first step is to collect the parameters involved in each algorithm (node position, bandwidth, delay, network latency, power consumption). Each algorithm has a mechanism to choose the best network, but the execution phase is the same for all algorithms because the chosen network connections have to be opened and the current network connections should be closed.

Algorithms were studied according to the proposed scheme, identifying which part of the algorithm corresponds to one or more scheme components. After further study of NCTUns and contrasting the methods for adding new components to the tool with the selected algorithms, we decided that the most convenient way to implement them would be to design high-level scripts handled as TCP traffic generators, and other components for extracting the parameters needed to assess the available networks. The scripts were written in C and Perl because almost all NCTUns components are written in C, and using another language like PERL, we could then evaluate the tool's functionality to run scripts written in different languages. VHA based on user preferences and VHA based on load balancing and power consumption was implemented with C, and VHA based on application requirements, with PERL.

*Figure 1. General scheme for VHA simulation in NCTUns*

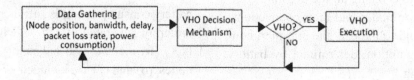

## VHA Implementation

This section explains which components were designed to implement the selected algorithms and the modifications made to some tool components.

## Implementation of VHA Based on User Preferences

This algorithm is designed to make vertical handoff between two networks and acts as follows: it takes the IP addresses of both mobile device interfaces and calculates the distance between the device current position and the static AP and BSs positions. With this, it calculates the received power and the available bandwidth for each wireless interface. This information is put into the cost function along with the mobility speed (fixed value of 10 meters per second) and cost of connection (based on WiFi, WiMAX or GPRS operators per kilobyte billing system). If the decision indicates that the handoff should be executed, the algorithm waits for the dwell timer to confirm the network conditions before doing the handoff. If these are confirmed, the traffic is sent to the selected network.

This algorithm requires the following components: one that is responsible for knowing the position of the mobile device throughout the simulation, another to run the cost function, Equation (1), and select the best network, and another to close and open connections after the decision.

For the node position, it is necessary to determine what type of mobile node is used in the simulation. When using the ITS network, the component modified is CarAgent.c that knows the position of the car at all times, so that the most useful thing to do is to add some code to write the position in a file, and it is read by the algorithm. If the mobile node used is a laptop, the modified component is Magnet.c, in the same way.

The script that evaluates the networks is VHO.c that calculates the cost function for the networks tested. For this, it reads the file with the node position and calculates the received power using the Okumura-Hata model or the COST 321 model, depending on the technologies; the network with lower cost function is the best. Reception.c is the script responsible for controlling the handoff, closing the connection to the current network and opening new connections to the network chosen. To synchronize the communication in the algorithm, we define specific ports where the socket will be opened for each technology.

To test the algorithm we designed two simple stages. The first is made up of a WiFi/GPRS network and uses an ITS. The car is a multi-interface node, which moves across the road network, depending on the distance between the mobile node and an AP or a BS (Figure 2).

The second scenario consists of WiFi/WiMAX Mobile, but the multi-interface node could not be used because the WiMAX Mobile horizontal handoff is not well implemented in this node. For this reason, there are a WiFi node WiFi and a WiMAX Mobile node moving in the same direction and the same speed as if these were a single node (Figure 3).

Mobile nodes must run the script reception.c and a network node (in this case the sending node) executes the script vho.c, taking into account the following parameters: IP WiFi interface, IP WiMAX interface, bandwidth weight, monetary cost weight, power consumption weight, number of APs and number of BSs.

## Implementation of VHA Based on Application Requirements

The algorithm is included in the tool using three scripts written in PERL that are responsible for generating the abstracted multi-application profile, take measures of packet loss rate and delay, and evaluate network conditions with respect to the profile. The traffic generators are stcp and rtcp, but these were copied to modify certain parameters and measure the bandwidth of the network. For the execution of applications the mobile node use

*Figure 2. Topology with WiFi/GPRS networks*

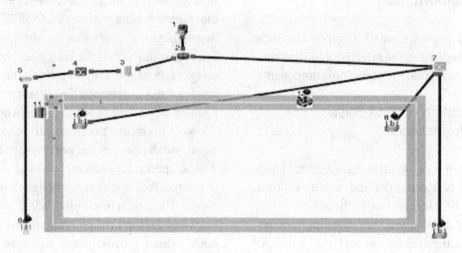

*Figure 3. Topology with WiFi/WiMAX mobile networks*

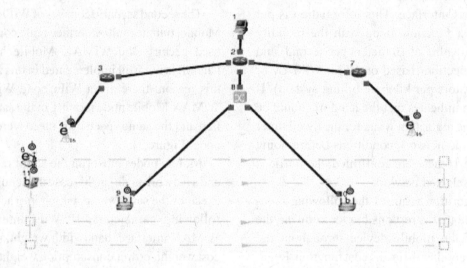

the original generators, but with a different name for their manipulation using system calls.

The algorithm is tested for WiFi/WiMAX Mobile networks and Figure 4 shows the topology with these networks. We tried to test it in WiFi/GPRS networks, but the measurement bandwidth is faster than assembly speed GPRS traffic. Measurements of bandwidth, latency and packet loss rate in networks involves traffic generation and in the user interface is not possible to differentiate the traffic that produces these measurements from that which implements the applications. For

this reason, we use two fixed nodes to receive the application traffic generated by the mobile node: one receives the traffic sent by the WiMAX Mobile node and the other receives that from the application's WiFi node.

## Implementation of VHA Based on Load Balancing and Power Consumption

This algorithm focuses on taking a connection decision for a nodes group, so we designed two scripts in C and communication between the nodes

*Figure 4. Topology with WiFi/WiMAX mobile networks*

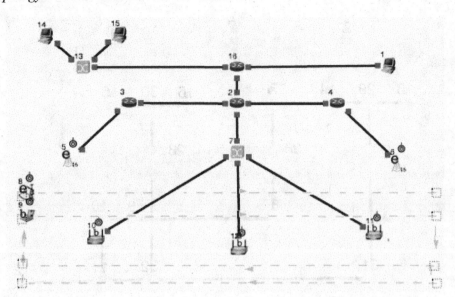

and the node that takes the handoff decision is made through the evaluation engine. Client.c is a script running on all mobile nodes and it sends the values of power consumption and available bandwidth to the evaluation engine. These values are accessed using a NCTUns API, sending to the simulation engine and reading for the master node. The algorithm suggests that sending this information is done by MIHF messages, but NCTUns don't have the necessary modules for communication between the layers of the protocol stack mobile nodes. For this reason, sending the variables of power consumption and load on the access nodes is done through sockets between each mobile node, the simulation engine and the master node. After sending data, the mobile node waits until the master node indicates whether there is a topology change: if there is, then the node changes the network that is connected, otherwise it expects to forward node variables to the master node.

The algorithm is tested on a scenario with WiFi/GPRS networks and ITS technology used to displace the mobile node following the road

shown in Figure 5. As the algorithm is focused on a group decision, every time the algorithm evaluates the available networks and determines the most appropriate topology, some nodes are connected to WiFi and others to GPRS.

## VHAs Simulation and Results

To simulate the three vertical handoff algorithms, seven new components were designed (two scripts written in C for VHA based on user preferences, three scripts written in PERL for VHA based on application requirements, and two scripts written in C for VHA based on load balancing and power consumption). Three NCTUns components were modified: rtcp.c to know the bandwidth of a connection, and Magnet.c and CarAgent.c, to know the mobile nodes' position throughout the simulation. Figures 2, 3, 4 and 5 were used to collect the measurements of three parameters to analyze the performance of vertical handoff algorithms: handoff delay, number of handoffs avoided, and computational complexity.

*Figure 5. Topology with WiFi/GPRS networks*

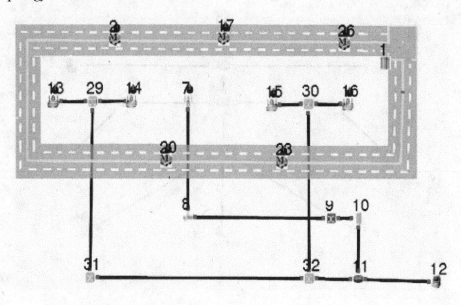

## Handoff Delay

Handoff delay is equal to the time spent by the algorithm in network evaluation and decision. The decision may cause a handoff or not, triggering other processes that change the measured time. So, we only measured the evaluation and decision process.

Table 1 shows the handoff delays for the algorithms. "Pref." is the algorithm based on user preference, "Appls." is the algorithm based on application requirements, and "Opt." is the algorithm based on load balancing and power consumption. These results were calculated with the algorithms implemented in WiFi/GPRS and WiFi/WiMAX Mobile networks. In some cases, the algorithm was not designed to run on the specific scenario, and is marked with N/A.

The algorithm based on user preferences run on WiFi/GPRS and WiFi/WiMAX Mobile networks has a handoff delay of 5000 milliseconds, corresponding to the dwell timer between the two evaluations that the algorithm runs before executing the handoff; mathematical processing included in the evaluation and decision runs very quickly, so that time is insignificant. The algorithm

based on application requirements run on WiFi/ WiMAX Mobile and four evaluations are executed with a dwell timer at 3 seconds, so the minimum delay is 9000 milliseconds. The additional milliseconds correspond to file manipulation processes performed by the implementation of the algorithm to extract the network parameters. If the dwell timer is not used, the handoff delay is less than 1 microsecond for the first algorithm and 386 milliseconds for the second.

VHA based on load balancing and power consumption focuses on making decisions oriented at the network, because it takes into account all the variables delivered by both the mobile nodes and access nodes. Nevertheless, the delay is generated by the mathematical and matrix processes and it increases in a non-linear way because the algorithm executes the cost function, that evaluates all possible combinations of logic connection, and it chooses a network topology, so, this algorithm is efficient only for networks of medium complexity. With this, we can see that the handoff delay is associated with mechanisms that guarantee network stability and evaluation and decision process run very quickly, taking into account that simulations are done in computers with fast processors.

*Table 1. Handoff delay for the three algorithms*

| # Samples | Handoff Delay(ms) WiFi/GPRS networks | | | Handoff Delay (ms) WiFi/WiMAX Mobile networks | | |
|---|---|---|---|---|---|---|
| | Pref. | Appls. | Opt. | Pref. | Appls. | Opt. |
| 1 | 5000 | N/A | 246 | 5000 | 9370 | N/A |
| 2 | 5000 | N/A | 309 | 5000 | 9737 | N/A |
| 3 | 5000 | N/A | 217 | 5000 | 9289 | N/A |
| 4 | 5000 | N/A | 202 | 5000 | 9330 | N/A |
| 5 | 5000 | N/A | 239 | 5000 | 9296 | N/A |
| 6 | 5000 | N/A | 495 | 5000 | 9240 | N/A |
| 7 | 5000 | N/A | 151 | 5000 | 9078 | N/A |
| 8 | 5000 | N/A | 282 | 5000 | 9720 | N/A |
| 9 | 5000 | N/A | 255 | 5000 | 9340 | N/A |
| 10 | 5000 | N/A | 237 | 5000 | 9258 | N/A |
| 11 | 5000 | N/A | 295 | 5000 | 9801 | N/A |
| 12 | 5000 | N/A | 192 | 5000 | 9250 | N/A |
| 13 | 5000 | N/A | 252 | 5000 | 9273 | N/A |
| 14 | 5000 | N/A | 196 | 5000 | 9320 | N/A |
| 15 | 5000 | N/A | 291 | 5000 | 9195 | N/A |

## Number of Avoided Handoffs

The number of avoided handoffs is the number of handoff that the algorithm avoids by using a mechanism such as the dwell timer to ensure network stability. To measure this parameter we simulate the two first algorithms with and without the dwell timer and count the handoffs in each case. The difference between these is the number of handoffs that the algorithm avoids. This parameter is associated with network conditions and how often the available networks are evaluated. Results are shown in Figure 6.

The algorithm based on application requirements using a dwell timer executes twice the number of handoffs as the algorithm without a dwell timer, because the networks are evaluated several times before deciding and there should be some time between them to ensure that the network maintains its conditions. If the network does not maintain good conditions, the handoff does not execute and the algorithm evaluates the available networks while the node is still connected to the current network. When the algorithm does not use a dwell timer, the evaluation of the network is faster, without ensuring that the network is stable, so the mobile node executes a handoff to a network because its conditions were good at the time, but in the next evaluation the algorithm decides to execute a handoff to the previous network. Without the dwell timer, the amount of times the algorithm evaluates networks during also increases because networks are evaluated more frequently. The expected increase for this reason is not double, yet several of the handoffs that occur are unnecessary.

By the nature of the decision function of the algorithm based on load balancing and power consumption (8), the maximum value obtained after performing all possible connection topologies is a value that dependends on all mobile nodes in the networks. This implies that if one of these changes abruptly, e.g., the node is moving at high speed, the decision function will change slowly, avoiding some unnecessary handoffs.

*Figure 6. Number of handovers: WiFi/WiMAX mobile networks*

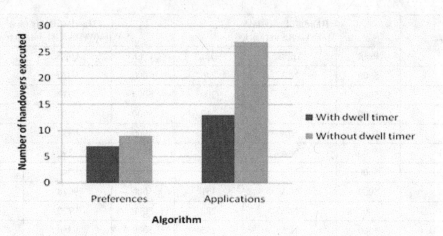

## Computational Complexity

The computational complexity is defined using the concept of algorithmic complexity order (Goldschlager, 1986), in which each code's line has an order depending on the task performed: allocation, cycles, decisions, etc. The computational complexity of the three algorithms is O(n) because almost all the procedures performed are simple math and writing files, these process have complexity order O(1). Evaluation processes and decision are in a cycle, so the order of complexity is O(n).

## Additional Parameters

The simulation attempted to measure two additional parameters: packet loss rate (PER) and power consumption of the mobile device during handoff execution. In the three scenarios the type of handoff which was executed was a hard handoff (i.e. the mobile device is completely disconnected from the current network and opens a new connection to the new network). For this reason, the PER is 100% because during the handoff the IP address and packet source port change. To avoid this, it is necessary to design additional NCTUns modules to be responsible for mapping packets

between the two IP addresses, so these can control the amount of packets sent during the handoff and not all packets will be lost.

In order to measure the power consumed by the mobile node during handoff execution, the Linux command "top" was used. This command lets you know how much CPU time is being consumed by a process, and with this we then know the power consumed by the execution of the algorithm component that corresponds to the mobile node. However, this command shows that the simulation process "nctunsse," which includes the execution of the scripts of the algorithm and traffic generators, consumes approximately 90% of the processor cycles but it is not possible determine how much of this percentage corresponds to the scripts executed at the mobile node. Therefore, this value cannot be determined from the simulation algorithms.

## CASE STUDY: SIMULATION OF VHAS USING MATLAB

This section describes the implementation of VHAs using MATLAB for heterogeneous networks. A couple of VHAs are implemented and several performance results are shown.

## MATLAB

MATLAB (MATrix LABoratory) is a high-level computing language and interactive environment for algorithm development, data visualization, data analysis and high performance numeric computation (MATLAB, 2010). The MATLAB environment can be used in a wide range of applications, including signal and image processing, communications, control design, test and measurement, financial modeling and analysis, and computational biology. MATLAB also has several collections of special-purpose functions, available separately (i.e., named tool-boxes) that are able to extend the environment to solve particular classes of problems in these application areas. The code generated in MATLAB can be integrated with other languages and applications such as C/C++, Fortran, Java and Microsoft spreadsheet Excel.

The MATLAB programming language is based on vector and matrix operations that are fundamental to any kind of engineering and scientific problems and applications. Thus, it enables fast development and execution. One of the main advantages of using the MATLAB programming language is that the programming and developing of algorithms is faster than with traditional programming languages. The reason is that there is no requirement of performing low-level administrative tasks, such as declaring variables, specifying data types, and allocating memory. Furthermore, MATLAB provides all the features of a traditional programming language, including arithmetic operators, flow control, data structures, data types, object-oriented programming, and debugging features.

MATLAB also contains a lot of mathematical, statistical, and engineering functions to support all common engineering and science operations. It includes general purpose functions for performing mathematical operations and analyzing data such as: matrix manipulation and linear algebra, polynomials and interpolation, Fourier analysis and filtering, data analysis and statistics, optimi-

zation and numerical integration, ordinary and partial differential equations, among others. All these functions make MATLAB a very flexible and robust simulation tool to implement and evaluate any type of VHA for heterogeneous wireless networks.

## Discrete-Event Simulation Approach

According to Banks et al. (2010), a system simulated following a discrete-event approach is a system model in which the state variables of interest only change at a discrete set of points in time. In particular, we are interested in the simulation of a dynamic model that represents a system that changes over time. Also, we are going to follow the approach that a model is an approximation of a physical situation and it attempts to explain the behavior of a complex system using a set of simple and simplified rules (Leon-Garcia, 1994). Thus, in this case, we consider that the parameters of the heterogeneous networks such as bandwidth, delay, jitter, etc. change their value after a certain period of time even though in real wireless networks several of these parameters change continuously: we are going to restrict our attention to the point in time when the VHAs have to take the handoff decision.

In order to vary the values of the decision parameters for the VHAs, we use a discrete-time Markov chain to model the time evolution of each parameter. The transition probabilities for an increment or decrement are $p_c$, while the probability of remaining in the same value is $p_s$. Thus, the corresponding set of discrete-time Markov chains modeling the heterogeneous wireless system can be seen in Figure 7.

## VHAS Based on MADM Methods

Multiple Attribute Decision Making (MADM) methods consider problems which involve making preference decisions over available alternatives characterized by multiple and usually conflict-

*Figure 7. Simplified discrete-event system model of heterogeneous wireless networks for performance evaluation of VHAs*

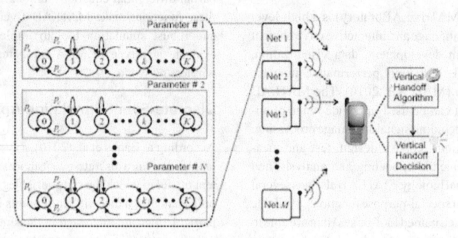

ing attributes (Yoon, 1995). MADM is a branch of the field Multiple Criteria Decision Making (MCDM). MADM problems are diverse, but all share the following common characteristics: the presence of alternatives to select, multiple attributes describing the alternatives in different units of measurement, and a set of weights representing the relative importance among attributes.

Let $M$ be the set of alternatives and $N$ be the set of parameters or attributes in a MADM problem. Such a decision problem can be concisely expressed in a matrix format, where the columns indicate attributes and the rows list alternatives. A typical element of the matrix $x$-$ij$ indicates the performance rating of the $i$-th alternative with respect to the $j$-th attribute. Thus, a MADM problem with $|M|$ alternatives and each with $|N|$ parameters is given by a decision matrix of dimensions $|M|X|N|$.

When the vertical handoff decision is formulated as a MADM problem, the alternatives to select are the candidate wireless networks and the attributes are the parameters describing the network. MADM methods use scoring techniques to rank alternatives. An index or score is calculated by taking into account the contributions from each parameter. Before the calculation of the index, the parameters must be normalized in

order to deal with different type of units (e.g., bps, sec, price, etc.)

Additionally, a set of importance weights $w_j$ have to be defined for the calculation of the ranking for each parameter $j$. The value of such weights should represent the different levels of importance of a parameter for the decision maker. The set of importance weights has to satisfy the constraint:

$$\sum_{j=1}^{|N|} w_j = 1 \qquad (10)$$

In the case of the vertical handoff decision, the importance weights should represent the QoS requirements of the connection as well as the user's preferences. For example, in a voice connection the importance weights of packet delay and packet jitter be higher than those of the available bandwidth of the network. It is also important to note the difference between a benefit parameter and a cost parameter. For a benefit parameter, larger is better, for example, the parameter bandwidth in a data connection where 1 Mbps is better than 256 Kbps. For a cost parameter, the lower the better, for example, the parameter packet delay in a voice connection where 80 ms is better than 400 ms.

Several MADM methods have been proposed in the literature for vertical handoff, methods such as SAW (Simple Additive Weighting) (Zhang, 2004), TOPSIS (Technique for Order Preference by Similarity to Ideal Solution) (Zhang, 2004), MEW (Multiplicative Exponent Weighting) (Stevens-Navarro & Wong, 2006), ELECTRE (Elimination and Choice Translating Priority) (Bari & Leung, 2007), and VIKOR (Gallardo-Medina, Pineda-Rico, & Stevens-Navarro, 2009). There has been considerable research in developing and modifying MADM methods for vertical handoff.

For the scope of the present chapter and in order to show an example of simulation of VHAs followings the approach of discrete-event simulation with MATLAB, we implement three VHAs based on MADM methods: SAW (Simple Additive Weighting) (Zhang, 2004), TOPSIS (Technique for Order Preference by Similarity to Ideal Solution) (Zhang, 2004), and VIKOR (Gallardo-Medina, Pineda-Rico, & Stevens-Navarro, 2009). For more complete and detailed simulation studies of VHAs, please refer to (Kassar, Kervella & Pujolle, 2008), (Martinez-Morales, Pineda-Rico, & Stevens-Navarro, 2010), and the references therein.

## Scenario Proposed for VHAs and Simulation Results

This section compares the performance of the MADM methods SAW, TOPSIS and VIKOR for vertical handoff in heterogeneous wireless networks (Gallardo-Medina, Pineda-Rico, & Stevens-Navarro, 2009). Let us consider a wireless system consisting of $|M|$=6 candidate networks and each network with $|N|$=6 parameters. The scenario consists of two 3G cellular networks (UMTS1 and UMTS2), two WLANs (WLAN1 and WLAN2), and two WMANs (WiMAX1 and WiMAX2). For the vertical handoff decision, six parameters are considered: available bandwidth, total bandwidth, packet delay, packet jitter, packet loss, and cost per byte.

A discrete event simulation model is implemented in MATLAB to represent the evolution in time of the values of the decision parameters of the $|M|$ candidate networks. Thus, we have a sequence of $|M|X|N|$ matrices and each represents a vertical handoff decision point. During the simulation, the values of the decision parameters randomly vary according to the ranges shown in Table 2 and following the simplified discrete-event model shown in Figure 7. The transition probabilities in the discrete-time Markov chains for an increment or decrement are $p_c = 0.4$ while the probability of remaining with the same value is $p_s = 0.2$.

The users are assumed to be moving within the overlapped coverage area of the wireless system. Thus, we analyze the values of the networks and networks selected by the three decision algorithms in 10 vertical handoff decision points. We consider two set of importance weights in (10): for case 1 all parameters have the same

*Table 2. Range of values of the networks parameters in simulation*

| Parameters | UMTS 1 | UMTS 2 | WLAN 1 | WLAN 2 | WiMAX 1 | WiMAX 2 |
|---|---|---|---|---|---|---|
| Available bandwidth (Mbps) | 0.1 - 2 | 0.1 - 2 | 1 - 11 | 1 - 54 | 1 - 60 | 1 - 60 |
| Total bandwidth (Mbps) | 2 | 2 | 11 | 54 | 60 | 60 |
| Delay (ms) | 25 - 50 | 25 - 50 | 100 - 150 | 100 - 150 | 60 - 100 | 60 - 100 |
| Jitter (ms) | 5 - 10 | 5 - 10 | 10 - 20 | 10 - 20 | 3 - 10 | 3 - 10 |
| PER (per $10^6$) | 20 - 80 | 20 - 80 | 20 - 80 | 20 - 80 | 20 - 80 | 20 - 80 |
| Cost (price) | 0.6 | 0.8 | 0.1 | 0.05 | 0.5 | 0.4 |

weight, this is the baseline case; and for case 2, packet delay and packet jitter have 50% of the importance and the rest is equally distributed among the other parameters. This case is suitable for voice connections.

Figures 8 and 9 show the networks selected by the three vertical handoff decision algorithms in case 1 and case 2, respectively. The three algorithms select wireless networks WiMAX1 and WiMAX2 (i.e., networks 5 and 6, respectively) most of the time. Note in Table 2 that those networks offer acceptable values for the parameters. On the other hand, SAW is the only scheme that in some points selects other networks such as UMTS1 and WLAN2 (i.e., networks 1 and 4, respectively). Finally, although VIKOR is able to provide a set of networks as solution, here we assume that the network with the lowest score is the best option for vertical handoff.

Figure 10 shows the values of packet jitter in ms provided by the networks selected by the three vertical handoff decision algorithms in case 2. Note that 60% of the time VIKOR selects the networks with the lowest values of packet jitter. Figure 11 shows the values of available bandwidth

in Mbps provided by the networks selected by the three vertical handoff decision algorithms in case 2. Note that 60% of the time VIKOR is able to select wireless networks offering the highest values of available bandwidth. The results indicate that the behavior of TOPSIS and VIKOR is similar. Thus, both VHAs tend to select the same network for vertical handoff very often.

## ANALYSIS AND RESULTS

This section presents a comparison analysis among the two approaches in terms of applicability, the flexibility to modify and incorporate new models and features, accuracy of the results, maturity of the simulation tool, ease of learning to use the tool, documentation and support, efficiency, user interface and portability, among others features. Table 3 shows a comparison between NCTUns and MATLAB.

One of the most important advantages of NCTUns is that it has implemented the most common network technologies (wired networks, 802.11a, 802.11b, WiMAX, GPRS, etc.) and its

*Figure 8. Network selected for vertical handoff in case 1*

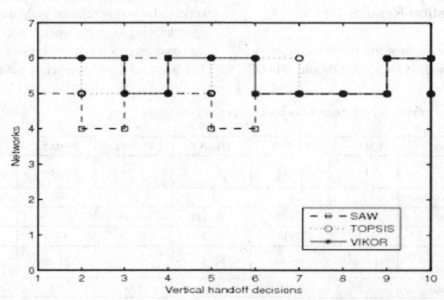

*Figure 9. Network selected for vertical handoff in case 2*

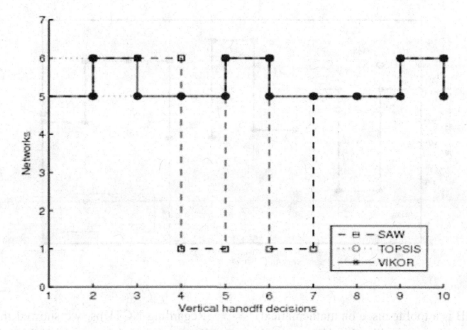

*Figure 10. Values of packet jitter in ms provided by the selected networks*

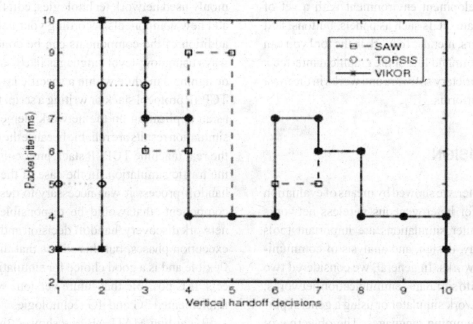

operation is well controlled by the simulation engine because is has its own kernel and interacts with the operating system. Additionally you can modify the existing modules because all components' code is available and can be recompiled easily, and you can also add new components

using low-level languages like C and PERL. The graphical interface is easy to use and the simulation results are reliable because the simulation engine uses the real machine TCP/IP protocol stack in order to send traffic simulation.

*Figure 11. Values of available bandwidth in Mbps by the selected networks*

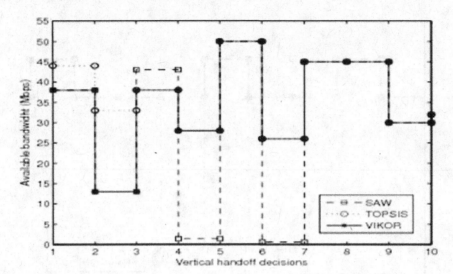

MATLAB is a tool focused on mathematical modeling using languages like C and Fortran and includes a complete Graphical User Interface (GUI) development environment with a set of tools to create GUIs such as panels, buttons, text fields, sliders, menus. To work in the tool you can used the command line or the graphical interface. This is proprietary software and works in the most popular platforms.

## CONCLUSION

In this chapter, we showed by means of evaluation of VHAs for heterogeneous wireless networks why computer simulations are important tools for the study, design, and analysis of communications networks. In general, we considered two approaches to simulate communication networks: using a network simulator or using a general purpose programming languages. The objective of the chapter was to present and compare by means of two cases studies both approaches to simulate VHAs. The first case was the use of the network simulator NCTUns, while the second case was the use of MATLAB.

Regarding NCTUns, we showed that it is a well constructed simulation tool that allows you to create simulation scenarios with the most commonly used network technologies, edit them and add new components according your needs. The addition of the components can be done in two ways using low-level languages like C or PERL: designing a module within a specific layer of the TCP/IP protocol stack or writing a script that runs as an application on the network elements. The simulation results are reliable because the tool uses the real machine TCP/IP stack protocols to send the traffic simulation. In the case of the vertical handoff process it was necessary to design new components that would be responsible for the network discovery, handoff decision and handoff execution phases, but this shows that the tool is flexible and is a good choice for simulation projects. It is possible that future versions will have implemented 3G and 4G technologies.

Regarding MATLAB, we showed that using a general purpose programming language offers several advantages such as: lots of built-in math functions and specialized toolboxes, re-use of C or Fortran code, faster computing, etc. However, since there are no specific modules for wireless

*Table 3. NCTUns/MATLAB characteristics*

| NCTUns | MATLAB |
|---|---|
| • Feature: Flexibility to modify and incorporate new models and features | |
| • NCTUns allows adding new components and modifying existing processes involved in modeling different scenarios and network technologies.<br>• Mechanisms for adding new components:<br>  ○ Modules: Understanding deeply the architecture of the tool.<br>  ○ High-level scripts: Knowing a low level language and protocol for communication between sockets. | • Includes a complete high-level programming language with several built-in mathematical functions and specialized toolboxes.<br>• It also allows object oriented programming and interfacing of C or Fortran source code to MATLAB.<br>• However, the flexibility to create new models depends on the skills of the programmer. |
| • Feature: Accuracy of the results | |
| • Uses the TCP/IP protocol stack operating system during the simulation, so the traffic delivery across the stage is real and the measured parameters are reliable. | • MATLAB is very accurate and widely accepted in the scientific community for numerical computations.<br>• MATLAB can solve computing problems faster than other programming languages (C, C++, Fortran). |
| • Feature: Maturity of the simulation tool | |
| • NCTUns has implemented several network technologies: Wired networks, 802.11a and 802.11b networks, ad hoc networks, WiMAX, GPRS, satellite and vehicular networks.<br>• It has its own kernel, so that communication with the operating system is efficient and the tool controls the simulation process.<br>• The tool still has some components that do not work properly: Multi-interface nodes and the horizontal handoff to run this node. | • MATLAB has more than 7 version and more than 14 releases with several periodic service packs to add functions and correct reported bugs. The first version was released in 1984.<br>• However, since MATLAB is a general purpose computing environments, it lacks specific implementations of network protocols and technologies |
| • Feature: User interface | |
| • Interface has four modes: Draw topology, Edit property, Run simulation and Play back.<br>• Stage design is done by dragging components.<br>• Presentation of simulation results shows completely the exchange of traffic between the stage components and the movement of mobile nodes. | • It has a console-mode to type/execute commands, but also has an editor to create and debug more complex programs.<br>• Provides a wide variety of techniques to display and analyze the simulation results graphically (2D and 3D plots).<br>• Includes a complete graphical user interface (GUI) development environment with a set of tools to create GUIs such as panels, buttons, text fields, sliders, menus. |
| • Feature: Easy of learning to use the tool, documentation and support | |
| • There is a user manual and a developer manual.<br>• Both manuals have examples to help in learning to operate the tool. Additionally, as the stage is designed by dragging components, is very intuitive.<br>• Has an active forum to post questions that are answered primarily by the tool developers. | • The MATLAB distribution includes complete documentation with lots of examples and demos. |
| • Feature: Portability | |
| • Open tool that works in Fedora | • MATLAB is proprietary software and requires licenses. MathWorks has MATLAB versions for current 32-Bit and 64-Bit Windows, Mac, and Linux platforms. |

networks and protocols, the simulation model has to be simplified to consider only the more relevant aspects and characteristics of the real system. Thus, in this case the heterogeneous wireless system had to be modeled as a set of discrete Markov chains and we could focus only on the specific decision part of the evaluated VHAs.

Both tools allow the study of telecommunications processes in two different and complementary ways: in MATLAB, a process can be modeled mathematically and all the analysis focuses on observing their behavior depending on changes in the controlled variable, while NCTUns simulation takes into account the relationship between different network technology components. For this reason, MATLAB can be used to design and optimize a process and NCTuns to test it in context with different characteristics.

## REFERENCES

Abdelatif, M., Kalebaila, G., & Chan, H. (2007). A joint IEEE802.21 and cross layer model. *The International Journal of Computer and Telecommunications Networking, 51*(17), 4849–4866.

Altwelib, H., Ashibani, M., & Shatwan, F. (2007). *Performance evaluation of an integrated vertical handover model for next generation mobile networks using virtual MAC addresses*. Paper presented at the Southern Africa Telecommunication Networks and Applications Conference (SATNAC). Johannesburg, South Africa.

Banks, J., Carson, J. II, Nelson, B., & Nicol, D. (2010). *Discrete-event system simulation* (5th ed.). New York, NY: Prentice Hall.

Gallardo-Medina, J., Pineda-Rico, U., & Stevens-Navarro, E. (2009). VIKOR method for vertical handoff decision in beyond 3G wireless networks. In *Proceedings of IEEE International Conference on Electrical Engineering, Computing Science and Automatic Control (CCE 2009)*. IEEE Press.

García, A., Escobar, L., Navarro, A., Arteaga, A., Guerrero, F., & Salazar, C. (2010). *Simulation of vertical handover algorithms with NCTUns*. Paper presented at 2010 Summer Simulation Multiconference. Ottawa, Canada.

Hong, C., Kang, T., & Kim, S. (2005). An effective vertical handoff scheme supporting multiple applications in ubiquitous computing environment. In *Proceedings of the Second International Conference on Embedded Software and Systems,* (pp. 407–440). IEEE Press.

Jo, J., & Cho, J. (2008). A cross-layer optimized vertical handover schemes between mobile WiMAX and 3G networks. *KSII Transactions on Internet and Information Systems, 2*(4), 64–69. doi:10.3837/tiis.2008.04.001

Kash, W., Ward, J., & Andrusenko, J. (2009). Wireless network modeling and simulation tools for designers and developers. *IEEE Communications Magazine, 47*(3), 120–127. doi:10.1109/MCOM.2009.4804397

Kassar, M., Kervella, B., & Pujolle, G. (2008). An overview of vertical handover decision strategies in heterogeneous wireless networks. *Computer Communications, 31,* 2607–2620. doi:10.1016/j.comcom.2008.01.044

Lee, S., Sriram, K., Kim, K., Kim, Y., & Golmie, N. (2009). Vertical handoff decision algorithms for providing optimized performance in heterogeneous wireless networks. *IEEE Transactions on Vehicular Technology, 58*(2), 5164–5169.

Leon-Garcia, A. (1994). *Probability and random processes for electrical engineering* (2nd ed.). Oxford, UK: Addison-Wesley.

Mathworks. (2010). *MATLAB and Simulink for technical computing*. Retrieved 28 June 2010 from http://www.mathworks.com.

Melia, T., Vidal, A., De la Oliva, A., Soto, I., Corujo, D., & Aguiar, R. (2006). *Toward IP converged heterogeneous mobility: A network controlled approach*. Paper presented at the Seventh International Conference on Networking on Mobile Data Management. Nara, Japan.

Nasser, N., Hasswa, A., & Hassanein, H. (2006). Handoffs in fourth generation heterogeneous networks. *IEEE Communications Magazine, 44*(10), 96–103. doi:10.1109/MCOM.2006.1710420

NSL. (2010). *NCTUns network simulator and emulator*. Retrieved 20 June 2010 from http://nsl.csie.nctu.edu.tw/nctuns.

Pawlikowski, K., Jeong, J., & Lee, R. (2002). On credibility of simulation studies of telecommunication networks. *IEEE Communications Magazine, 40*(1), 132–139. doi:10.1109/35.978060

Rahman, M., Pakštas, A., & Zhigang, F. (2009). Network modelling and simulation tools. *Simulation Modelling Practice and Theory, 17*(6), 1011–1031. doi:10.1016/j.simpat.2009.02.005

Stevens-Navarro, E., & Wong, V. (2006). Comparison between vertical handoff decision algorithms for heterogeneous wireless networks. In: *IEEE Vehicular Technology Conference: Vol. 2* pp. 947–951.

Wang, S., Chou, C., & Lin, C. (2007). The design and implementation of the NCTUns network simulation engine. *Simulation Modelling Practice and Theory, 15*, 57–81. doi:10.1016/j.simpat.2006.09.013

Wang, S., Chou, C., Lin, C., & Huang, C. (2008). *The GUI user manual for the NCTUns 5.0 network simulator and emulator.* Retrieved from http://nsl10.csie.nctu.edu.tw/support/documentation/GUIManualNCTUns5.0.pdf.

Wang, S., Chou, C., Lin, C., & Huang, C. (2008). *The protocol developer manual for the NCTUns 5.0 network simulator and emulator.* Retrieved from http://nsl10.csie.nctu.edu.tw/support/documentation/DeveloperManual.pdf.

Yang, O., Choi, S., Choi, J., Park, J., & Kim, H. (2006). A handover framework for seamless service support between wired and wireless networks. *International Conference on Advanced Communication Technology (ICACT 2006)*, (Vol. 3), (pp. 1791-1796). IEEE Press.

Zhang, W. (2004). Handover decision using fuzzy MADM in heterogeneous networks. In *Proceedings of IEEE Wireless Communications and Networking Conference (WCNC 2004)*, (Vol. 2), (pp. 653–658). IEEE Press.

## ADDITIONAL READING

Balasubramaniam, S., & Indulska, J. (2004). Vertical handover supporting pervasive computing in future wireless networks. *Computer Communications, 27*, 708–719. doi:10.1016/j.comcom.2003.10.010

Durantini, A., & Petracca, M. (2008). Performance comparison of vertical handover strategies for PSDR heterogeneous networks. *IEEE Wireless Communications, 15*, 54–59. doi:10.1109/MWC.2008.4547523

Guo, Q., Zhu, J., & Xu, X. (2005). An adaptive multi-criteria vertical handoff decision algorithm for radio heterogeneous networks. In *Proceedings of IEEE International Communications Conference (ICC 2005)*, (Vol. 4), (pp. 2769–2773). IEEE Press.

Ong, E., & Khan, J. (2010). On optimal network selection in a dynamic multi-RAT environment. *IEEE Communications Letters, 14*, 217–219. doi:10.1109/LCOMM.2010.03.092378

Sgora, A., & Vergados, D. (2009). Handoff prioritization and decision schemes in wireless cellular networks: A survey. *IEEE Communications Tutorials and Surveys, 11*, 57–77. doi:10.1109/SURV.2009.090405

Song, Q., & Jamalipour, A. (2005). Network selection in an integrated wireless LAN and UMTS environment using mathematical modeling and computing techniques. *IEEE Wireless Communications, 12*, 42–48. doi:10.1109/MWC.2005.1452853

Stevens-Navarro, E., Lin, Y., & Wong, V. (2008). An MDP-based vertical handoff decision algorithm for heterogeneous wireless networks. *IEEE Transactions on Vehicular Technology, 57*, 1243–1254. doi:10.1109/TVT.2007.907072

Stevens-Navarro, E., Pineda-Rico, U., & Acosta-Elias, J. (2008). Vertical handover in beyond third generation (B3G) wireless networks. *International Journal of Future Generation Communication and Networking*, *1*, 51–58.

SuKyoung, L., Sriram, K., Kyungsoon, K., Hyuk, K., & Golmie, N. (2009). Vertical handoff decision algorithms for providing optimized performance in heterogeneous wireless networks. *IEEE Transactions on Vehicular Technology*, *58*, 865–881. doi:10.1109/TVT.2008.925301

## KEY TERMS AND DEFINITIONS

**Discrete-Event Simulation:** Simulation approach in which the state variables of interest in the system only change at a discrete set of points in time.

**Heterogeneous Wireless Networks:** Envisioned wireless system integrated by different radio access technologies (e.g., 3G cellular, WLANs, WMANs, etc.)

**MATLAB:** It is a high-level computing language and interactive environment for algorithm development, data visualization, data analysis and high performance numeric computation. Its name is given by Matrix Laboratory.

**Multi-Interface Node:** Mobile node with multiple wireless interfaces. The node can use any of the interfaces to communicate, always be found in the coverage area of the respective network.

**NCTUns:** Simulator and emulator for heterogeneous wireless networks created by National Chiao Tung University Network Simulator.

**Vertical Handoff:** Process responsible for changing the network to a mobile device must be connected when moving between coverage areas of heterogeneous networks.

**Vertical Handoff Algorithm:** Set of rules and/or mathematical procedures in charge of performing the handoff decision.

# Chapter 5
# Modeling and Simulation of IEEE 802.11 Wireless LANs:
## A Case Study of a Network Simulator

**Nurul I. Sarkar**
*Auckland University of Technology, New Zealand*

**Roger McHaney**
*Kansas State University, USA*

## ABSTRACT

*Stochastic discrete event simulation methodology is becoming increasingly popular among network researchers worldwide in recent years. This popularity results from the availability of various sophisticated and powerful simulation software packages, and also because of the flexibility in model construction and validation offered by simulation. In this chapter, the authors describe their experience in using the network simulator 2 (ns-2), a discrete event simulation package, as an aid to modeling and simulation of the IEEE 802.11 Wireless Local Area Networks (WLANs). This chapter provides an overview of ns-2 focusing on simulation environment, architecture, model development and parameter setting, model validation, output data collection and processing, and simulation execution. The strengths and weaknesses of ns-2 are discussed. This chapter also emphasizes that selecting a good simulator is crucial in modeling and performance analysis of wireless networks.*

## INTRODUCTION

The use of discrete event simulation packages as an aid to modeling and performance evaluation of WLANs has grown in recent years (Bianchi, 2000; Chen, Jian, & Lo, 2002; Das, Castaneda, & Yan, 2000; Fantacci, Pecorella, & Habib, 2004;

Tickoo & Sikdar, 2003). This popularity is due to the availability of sophisticated simulation software packages and low cost powerful personal computers (PCs), but also because of the flexibility in rapid model construction and validation offered by simulation.

A detailed discussion of simulation methodology, in general, can be found in numerous literature (Carson, 2004; Law & Kelton, 2000).

DOI: 10.4018/978-1-4666-0191-8.ch005

More specifically, Pawlikowski (1990) in a comprehensive survey of problems and solutions suited for steady-state simulation highlighted the relevance of simulation technique for modeling and performance evaluation of telecommunication networks. This view of simulation and modeling is frequently supported in the wireless communication and networking literature (Hassan & Jain, 2004; Holloway, 2003; Nicopolitidis, Obaidat, Papadimitriou, & Pomportsis, 2003; Sarkar & Pawlikowski, 2002).

A typical WLAN can easily be simulated and its performance evaluated by a network software package (i.e., simulator). It is important for researchers to choose a simulator which is easy to use; more flexible in model development, modification and validation; and incorporates appropriate analysis of simulation output data, pseudo-random number generators, and statistical accuracy of the simulation results (i.e., desired relative precision of errors and confidence interval). These aspects of credible simulation studies are recommended by leading network simulation researchers (Law & Kelton, 2000; Pawlikowski, Jeong, & Lee, 2002; Schmeiser, 2004).

While various simulators exist for building a variety of WLAN models, we briefly describe two popular network simulators namely, ns-2 (Fall & Varadhan, 2011) and OPNET Modeler (www.opnet.com). The ns-2 simulator is one of the most commonly used simulators today and is very popular with researchers, including CS and EE students worldwide. The ns-2 is open-source software and provides an environment for rapid model construction and simulation output data collection.

OPNET, developed by OPNET technologies, is another popular commercial software package commonly used by researchers and practitioners for modeling and performance evaluation of telecommunication networks. It has a robust and flexible wireless node model which consists of process models of the different layers of the network protocol stack. As ns-2, OPNET is an object-oriented simulation package. However, unlike ns-2, it is totally menu-driven with an easy-to-use Graphical User Interface (GUI) for rapid model construction, data collection and other simulation tasks. It is often of interest to study a proposed or existing wireless network to gain insight into its expected behavior. However, since experimentation with the live network is disruptive and not very cost effective, a model is required for this purpose.

This chapter emphasizes that selecting a good network simulator is crucial in modeling and performance analysis of wireless communication networks. Both the ns-2 and OPNET offer flexibility in model construction and validation, and incorporates appropriate analysis of simulation output data, pseudo-random number generators, and statistical accuracy of the simulation results. Without an underlying framework for the model, a valid, verifiable model become much more difficult to develop, particularly in the time-constrained environments found in many wireless application areas.

The remainder of this chapter is organized as follows. We first provide an overview of ns-2 simulator and then describe our experiences in using ns-2 as an aid to modeling and performance evaluation of IEEE 802.11 WLANs. The strengths and weaknesses of ns-2 are discussed, and a brief conclusion ends the chapter.

## THE NS-2 SIMULATOR

### Environment

Ns-2 is an object-oriented discrete-event network simulator originally developed at Lawrence Berkeley Laboratory at the University of California, Berkeley, as part of the Virtual InterNetwork Testbed (VINT) project. Berkeley released the initial code that made wireless network simulation possible in ns-2. The Monarch project at Carnegie Mellon University has extended the ns-2 with support for node mobility, a realistic physical layer model and an implementation of the IEEE 802.11b Distributed Coordination Function (DCF) Medium Access Control (MAC) protocol (CMU Monarch Project, 2011).

Ns-2 is an open source simulation package which has improved significantly over time through various contributions made by network researchers worldwide. It has three substantial changes from ns version 1: (1) the more complex objects in ns v1 have been decomposed into simpler components for greater flexibility and composability; (2) the configuration interface is now an object oriented version of Tcl (OTcl); and (3) the interface code to the OTcl interpreter is separate from the main simulator (Fall & Varadhan, 2011). This section provides an overview of ns-2 focusing on environment, architecture, model construction and parameter setting, model validation, simulation execution, and output data analysis.

## Architecture

Ns-2 is written in C++ and uses OTcl as a command and configuration interface. The OTcl scripts are used to set up simulation scenarios in the simulator. The main benefit of using OTcl scripts is that there is no need to recompile the simulator between different simulation scenarios. This feature is particularly useful (in terms of saving

recompilation time) to study the impact of various influencing factors on the network performance.

Figure 1 shows the architecture of ns-2 illustrating the interaction between a user written program and ns-2 library components. The event scheduler is one of the main components of ns-2. An event in ns-2 is a packet ID that is unique for a packet with scheduled time and the pointer to an object that handles the event. The event scheduler keeps track of simulation time and fires all events in the event queue scheduled for the current time by invoking appropriate network components or objects.

The ns-2 simulator is written in C++ and uses OTcl as a command and configuration interface. The OTcl scripts are used to set up simulation scenarios in the simulator. One of the main benefits of OTcl scripts is that there is no need to recompile the simulator between different simulation scenarios. This feature is particularly useful (in terms of saving recompilation time) to study the impact of various influencing factors on the network performance. By using OTcl scripts, one can easily set up network topologies, specific protocols, link bandwidths, traffic sources and applications to be simulated (these behaviors are already defined in the compiled hierarchy) and the form of the output required.

The ns-2 has a rich library of network and protocol objects called ns objects. These objects

*Figure 1. An overview of ns-2 architecture*

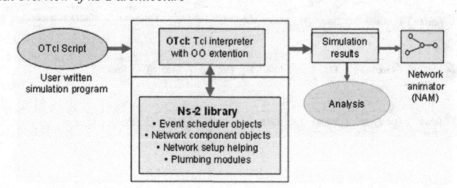

include nodes, classifiers, links, queues, etc. All objects are derived from a class called NsObject, which is the base for all classes. There are two class hierarchies: the compiled C++ hierarchy and the interpreted OTcl, with one to one correspondence between them. However, the compiled C++ hierarchy provides a greater efficiency in simulation runs in terms of faster execution times. This is particularly useful for detailed analysis of network protocol's behavior.

In ns-2, the timing of events is determined by a scheduler. The scheduler keeps track of simulation time and fires all events in the event queue scheduled for the current time. The influence of network traffic load distribution on network performance is an important observation that interests many researchers. For this task, a variety of traffic generators is needed for automatic traffic creation according to a desired pattern and load. The ns-2 supports several traffic generators, e.g., Exponential ON-OFF, Pareto ON-OFF, and Constant Bit Rate (CBR). More information about the capabilities of ns-2 can be found in the ns manual (Fall & Varadhan, 2011).

## Model Construction and Parameter Setting

A network model in ns-2 is constructed by interconnecting several objects, such as nodes, queues, links, and classifiers. The ns-2 objects are built from a hierarchical C++ class structure as illustrated in Figure 2.

Table 1 lists frequently used ns-2 commands and objects for network simulation. More details about ns-2 objects and commands can be found in the ns-2 user manual (Fall & Varadhan, 2011). A user can easily set up and run a simulation by writing an OTcl script using the available simulator objects in the OTcl library. In the script, one defines the network topology, routing algorithm, protocols and applications, initiates the scheduler by instructing traffic sources when to start and stop sending packets, length of the simulation runs, and the form of the output required.

*Figure 2. A partial tree of ns-2 class hierarchy*

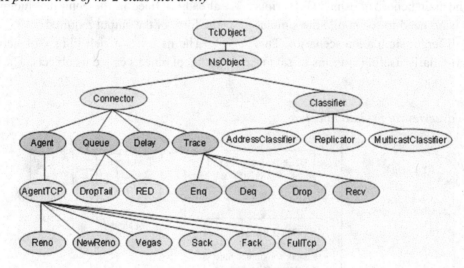

*Table 1. Frequently used ns-2 commands and objects*

| Ns-2 command | Object | Description |
|---|---|---|
| set n0 [$ns node] | node | Create a node called n0 on the network. |
| $ns duplex-link $n0 $n1 6Mb 5ms DropTail | link | Create a duplex link with a drop-tail queue from node n0 to n1 with a capacity of 6 Mbps and a propagation delay of 5 ms. |
| set udp [new Agent/UDP] | UDP agent | Setup a UDP connection |
| set tcp [new Agent/TCP/Newreno] | TCP agent | Setup a TCP connection |
| set ftp [new Application/FTP]<br>$ftp attach-agent $tcp | Application | Setup a FTP application over TCP connection |
| set cbr [new Application/Traffic/CBR] | Traffic generator | Create a constant bit rate (CBR) traffic generator |
| set e [new Application/Traffic/exponential] | Traffic generator | Create an exponential on-off traffic generator |
| set p [new Application/Traffic/Pareto] | Traffic generator | Create a Pareto on-off traffic generator |

## Model Validation

A main concern in wireless network simulations or any simulation efforts is to ensure a model is credible and represents reality. If this can't be guaranteed, the model has no real value and can't be used to answer desired questions (McHaney, 1991; Sargent, 2004). The ns-2 models described in this chapter are no exception and were subjected to rigorous validation.

Validation is the process of determining the real-world system being studied is accurately represented by the simulation model. Not only does this process provide assurance that the conceptual approach is correct, it establishes an acceptable level of confidence in the conclusions drawn from running the simulation and provides an insight into the true operating characteristics of the modeled system (McHaney, 2009). As with any form of simulation, a simulator plays an important role in building a credible model for the system under study. Therefore, it is important for researchers to use the right simulator which offers flexibility in model construction and validation along with appropriate analysis of simulation output data, and statistical accuracy of the simulation results. More details about building credible simulation models can be found in (Law & Kelton, 2000; Pawlikowski, et al., 2002).

The simulation models were validated using one or more of the following methods: (1) we ran the same simulation experiment several times and found that ns-2 produced repeatable results ensuring the credibility of the final results of our simulation studies; (2) results obtained from ns-2 are compared and validated with empirical measurements using wireless laptops and access points for WLANs; (3) we compared our results with that of published results (both academic and industry white papers) by other researchers and found a good match ensuring the credibility of our simulation studies; and (4) discussion with experienced colleagues and researchers in the areas of network simulation.

## Output Data Collection and Processing

When a simulation experiment is finished, ns-2 produces one or more output data files (e.g., trace file "out.tr" and network animator "out.nam") that contained detailed simulation output data. The trace file (out.tr) records each packet as it arrives at a node, departs a node, or is dropped at a link or queue. The trace file is useful for debugging or verification of the simulation program, but it is very difficult to obtain a specific performance metric directly from this file. We have written a perl script for output data processing and to obtain the desired performance metrics, such as delay, throughput, fairness and packet drop ratio, from a trace file.

An example of a trace file containing simulation output data for five trace entries is shown in Table 2. The first column shows the type of operation performed on the packet: enqueue (represented by +), dequeue (-), receive (r) and drop (d). The second column shows the time at which the event occurs. The source and destination nodes are shown in columns 3 and 4, respectively. The packet type, IP packet size, flags, and IP flow identifier are shown in columns 5 to 8, respectively. The source and destination IP addresses (in the form of "node.port") are shown in columns 9 and 10, respectively. The packet sequence number and unique packet identifier are shown in columns 11 and 12, respectively.

The out.nam can be used as an input to a network animator (NAM) tool for graphical simulation display. More details about NAM can be found at http://www.isi.edu/nsnam/nam/.

## Simulation Execution

After a network model is constructed and various simulation parameters and performance measures are set, the next step is to execute a simulation. To achieve this in ns-2, an object of class Simulator needs to be created first as follows: set ns [new Simulator]. The simulation can then be executed by the following command: $ns run.

## CASE STUDY

We have been using ns-2 for several years and our experiences are generally favorable. The ns-2 provides an excellent environment for easy simulation model development and performance evaluation of wireless communication networks. Figure 3 shows a simple framework in which we develop and execute various simulation models under ns-2 to study the performance of the IEEE 802.11 WLAN. In addition to modeling wireless network protocols, ns-2 also supports various propagation modeling.

Our current research focuses on developing a framework for estimating as well as improving the capacity of WLANs by integrating wireless network protocols and propagation modeling (Sarkar, 2004). We believe that our work contributes substantial extensions to ns-2 and provides insights into the simulator.

One of the main issues in network simulation is the statistical accuracy of simulation results. A model must be validated and used in a 'valid experiment,' which requires suitable sources of 'randomness' as well as appropriate means of analyzing simulation output data.

Fortunately, ns-2 simulator takes care of simulation output-data analysis and statistical accuracy of simulation results. Therefore, researchers can focus on developing and validating simulation models for various performance measures without worrying about controlling the simulation itself e.g., length of simulation runs (to get steady-state

*Table 2. An example of a trace output showing first five trace entries*

| + | 1.94375 | 0 | 2 | tcp | 1000 | ------- | 0 | 0.0 | 3.1 | 235 | 610 |
|---|---------|---|---|-----|------|---------|---|-----|-----|-----|-----|
| - | 1.94375 | 0 | 2 | tcp | 1000 | ------- | 0 | 0.0 | 3.1 | 235 | 610 |
| r | 1.94471 | 2 | 1 | tcp | 1000 | ------- | 1 | 3.0 | 1.0 | 195 | 600 |
| r | 1.94566 | 2 | 0 | ack | 40 | ------- | 2 | 3.2 | 0.1 | 84 | 602 |
| d | 1.94609 | 2 | 3 | tcp | 1000 | ------- | 0 | 0.0 | 3.1 | 235 | 610 |

*Figure 3. A framework for developing and executing simulation models under ns-2*

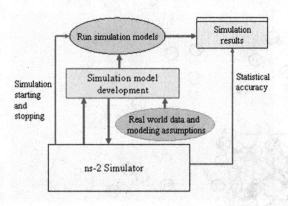

analysis), number of independent simulation runs, and use of appropriate random number generators.

## Simulation Scenarios

In this section we present two simulation scenarios based on the ns-2, namely, IEEE 802.11 ad hoc and infrastructure networks. Figure 4 illustrates the basic concept of a simulated ad hoc wireless network with 50 mobile stations. These stations communicate without any infrastructure or centralized control.

Figure 4 shows the simulated infrastructure-based wireless LAN with 50 mobile stations and one wireless access point (AP) linked to wired backbone with 50 fixed stations. In the infrastructure network, data traffic travels from mobile stations to wired stations via the AP. Both Figures 4 and 5 are captured from animation output using ns-2's Network Animator (NAM) utility (ISI, 2010).

*Figure 4. Simulation scenario of the IEEE 802.11 ad hoc network with 50 mobile stations (176x176 m grid)*

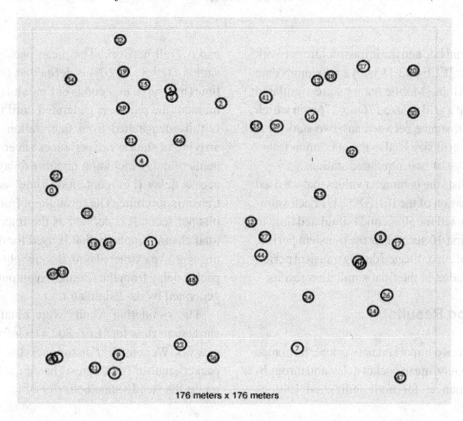

*Figure 5. Simulation scenario of IEEE 802.11 infrastructure network with 50 mobile stations, one AP and 50 fixed stations (176x176 m grid)*

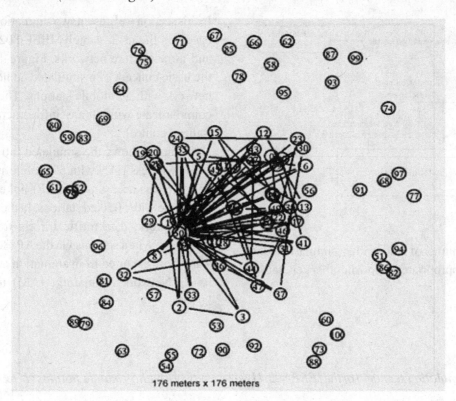

176 meters x 176 meters

Both the ad hoc and the infrastructure network are based on IEEE 802.11 with a maximum data rate of 11 Mbps. Mobile stations are simulated by setting up a grid of size 176m x 176m in which the longest distance between any two stations is 250m. This grid size is also the maximum transmission range of two simulated stations.

Table 3 lists the parameter values that we used in the simulation of the IEEE 802.11. Each simulation run lasted for 50 seconds simulated time in which the first 10 seconds is the transient period. The observations collected during transient period are not included in the final simulation results.

## Simulation Results

We consider two important network performance metrics, namely, mean packet delay and throughput performance, for both individual stations and overall network. The mean packet delay at station $i$ ($i = 1, 2,..., N$) is defined as the average time (measured in seconds or time slots) from the moment the packet is generated until the packet is fully dispatched from that station. A packet arriving at station $i$ experiences several components of delay including queuing delay, channel access delay (i.e., contention time) and packet transmission time. The throughput (measured in bits per second) is defined as the fraction of the total channel capacity that is used for data transmission. We extracted both throughput and mean packet delay from the simulation output trace file generated by ns-2 simulator.

The simulation results were obtained from simulation runs for IEEE 802.11b infrastructure network. We consider Poisson packet arrivals and a packet length of 1,500 bytes. The simulation results report the steady-state behavior of the network.

*Table 3. Simulation parameters*

| Parameter | Value |
|---|---|
| Data rate | 11 Mbps |
| Basic rate | 2 Mbps |
| Wireless cards | 802.11b |
| Slot duration | 20 µs |
| SIFS | 10 µs |
| DIFS | 50 µs |
| MAC header | 30 bytes |
| CRC | 4 bytes |
| PHY header | 96 µs |
| Packet/Traffic type | UDP |
| Application | CBR |
| RTS-CTS | Off |
| PHY modulation | DSSS |
| Propagation model | Two ray ground |
| CWmin | 31 |
| CWmax | 1023 |
| Simulation time | 50 minutes |

The effect of increasing the number of active users on network throughput and mean packet delay performance of the IEEE 802.11b infrastructure network under various offered loads are shown in Figure 6 and 7, respectively. These results were validated through radio propagation measurements from wireless laptops and access points for 802.11b (Sarkar & Sowerby, 2006; Siringoringo & Sarkar, 2009). A good match between ns-2 simulation and real measurement results for N = 2 to 4 stations validates the simulation model.

## STRENGTHS AND WEAKNESSES OF NS-2

Although the use of ns-2 as a network modeling and simulation tool has many advantages over other competing options, the simulation package has some limitations. The relative strengths and weaknesses of ns-2 are discussed next.

*Figure 6. Offered load versus network throughput of IEEE 802.11b infrastructure network*

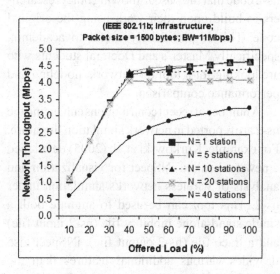

*Figure 7. Offered load versus packet delay of IEEE 802.11b infrastructure network*

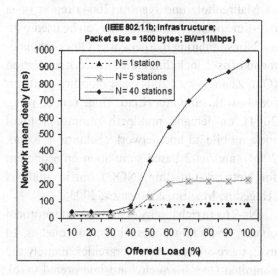

## Strengths

Ns-2 is available for download on a variety of operating systems at no cost, including Red Hat Linux, FreeBSD, and MS Windows. Another strength of ns-2 is that many network researchers are contributing towards further extension of ns-2 since it is an open source software package (ISI,

2011). Authors of research papers often publish ns-2 code that they used, allowing other researchers to build upon their work using the original code. This is particularly useful to academia, specifically Master's and Doctoral students who are looking for a tool for network modeling and performance comparison.

A number of recent contributions enhancing the ns-2 are reported in network simulation literature. For example, Kurkowski et al. (2005) developed a new tool called iNSpect for visualization and analysis of wireless networks simulation under ns-2. This tool can be used to animate both a single stand-alone mobility file (ns-2 input file) and a trace file (ns-2 output file). iNSpect also provides various additional features than the ns-2's NAM, including analysis and validation of mobility models, debugging ns-2 scripts, and optimization of network protocol performance.

Mahrenholz and Ivanov (2004) report on a real-time network emulator that can be used with ns-2 for simulating live networks. Other enhancements of ns-2, including GPRS network simulation (Qiu, Zhang, & J., 2004), ant mobility platform for network simulator (Liao, Ting, Yen, & Yang, 2004), on-demand multipath routing protocol for a mobile ad hoc network (Sakurai & Katto, 2004), and ns-2 based simulation environment for Network-On-Chip (NOC) traffic analysis (Hegedus, Maggio, & Kocarev, 2005).

Ns-2 has a rich library of network and protocol objects, including nodes, links, and queues. In ns-2, there are two class hierarchies, namely the compiled C++ hierarchy and interpreted OTcl, with one to one correspondence between them. The compiled C++ hierarchy provides a greater efficiency in simulation runs in terms of faster simulation execution, which is particularly useful for detailed analysis of network protocol's behavior.

Ns-2 is a multi-protocol simulator that supports a wide range of network protocols, including unicast and multicast routing algorithms, network and transport layer protocols, TCP congestion control,

router queuing policies, reservation and integrated services, and application layer protocols such as HTTP (Fall & Varadhan, 2011). In addition, ns-2 incorporates a range of link-layer protocols and scheduling algorithms, including wireless and mobile networks (Breslau, et al., 2000). Ns-2's in-built Network Animation (NAM) tool allows graphical display of links, packet flows, network node position and movement which is very useful for debugging and testing network models.

While various network simulators exist for simulation and modeling of link-layer protocols, very few of them can support a realistic physical layer modeling. Ns-2, however, supports three radio propagation models: free-space, two-ray ground, and shadowing, for wireless channel modeling (Dricot & De Doncker, 2004; Fall & Varadhan, 2011).

The influence of traffic load distribution on network performance is an important observation that interests many network researchers. For this task, a variety of traffic generators is needed for automatic traffic creation according to a desired pattern and load. The ns-2 supports several traffic generators including Poisson, Pareto, Exponential, CBR, and Hyperexponential.

In stochastic discrete-event simulation, the Pseudorandom Number Generators (PRNGs) are used in generating various random variables, including traffic generators, random movement of wireless nodes, and link error models. Therefore, it is important for network researchers to select a network simulator that has a good PRNG. However, Ns-2 (versions 2.1b9 and later) implements a combined Multiple Recursive Generator (MRG32k3a) proposed by L'Ecuyer (2001), which is one of the well established generators that has been tested thoroughly for its robustness. This generator replaces the previous implementation of PRNG, which was a rather weak generator based on the minimal standard multiplicative linear congruential generator of Park and Miller (Park & Miller, 1988). More details about PRNGs and their strengths and weaknesses can be found in computer simulation and modelling literature (Hechenleitner & Entacher, 2002; L'Ecuyer, 2001; L'Ecuyer, Richard, Chen, & Kelton, 2001; Law & Kelton, 2000; Matsumoto & Nishimura, 1999; Park & Miller, 1988; Pawlikowski, et al., 2002).

The implementation of MRG32k3a in ns-2 provides $1.8 \times 1019$ independent streams of random numbers, each of which consists of $2.3 \times 1015$ sub-streams, and each sub-stream has a period (i.e., the number of random numbers before overlap) of $7.6 \times 1022$ with a total period for the entire generator is $3.1 \times 1057$. With these features of PRNG, ns-2 can produce acceptable (un-biased) simulation results, and consequently users of ns-2 do not need to worry about the credibility of their simulation results as long as they use valid simulation models. The source code for ns-2 PRNG can be found in the ns-2 package under tools/rng.h and tools/rng. cc (Fall & Varadhan, 2011).

## Weaknesses

In spite of possessing strengths, ns-2 has several limitations. Firstly, it does not provide any support for creating sophisticated graphical presentations of simulation output data. The raw data must be processed using scripting languages such as 'awk' or 'perl' to produce data in a suitable format for tools like Xgraph or Gnuplot (Fall & Varadhan, 2011; Sarkar & McHaney, 2006).

Another disadvantage of ns-2 is that it is not a user-friendly package because of its text-based interface, and many student researchers point out that ns-2 has a steep learning curve. A tutorial contributed by Marc Greis (2011) and the continuing evolution of ns documentation have improved the situation, but ns-2's split-programming model remains a barrier to many developers.

Although ns-2 supports various radio propagation and error models, the software neither supports Bit-Error Rate (BER) nor Signal-to-Noise-and-Interference Ratio (SNIR), which are important parameters that need to be considered when simulating real-world wireless network scenarios. In addition, ns-2 does not support simulation of co-channel interference, which is one of the major limitations of ns-2's wireless network simulation engine. These limitations of ns-2 are also highlighted by leading network researchers (Hegedus, et al., 2005; Wellens, Petrova, Riihijarvi, & Mahonen, 2005).

In summary, it is quite difficult to implement a new channel access protocol in ns-2. A sound knowledge and understanding of both the high-level programming and operating systems is required in implementing a new protocol under ns-2. We experienced similar difficulty in implementing the BUMA protocol in ns-2 (Sarkar & Sowerby, 2005).

## CONCLUSION AND FUTURE WORK

Stochastic discrete event simulation methodology has become popular as a network modeling and performance analysis tool. In this chapter we described the use of a network simulator, ns-2 and wireless networking issues addressed by simulation. The models built under ns-2 simulator were validated using empirical measurements from wireless laptops and access points for an IEEE 802.11b WLAN. A good match between ns-2 simulation results and empirical measurements were reported. The chapter provides a general discussion on techniques for building valid and credible models, and on the strengths and weaknesses of simulation methodology. Although our case study focused on the use of ns-2 for modeling and performance evaluation of IEEE 802.11 wireless LANs, this case study can be used in other fields, such as management, and engineering.

In summary, we want to stress the importance of using a good simulator for modeling and performance analysis of wireless communication networks. The ns-2 offers more flexibility in model construction and validation, and incorporates appropriate analysis of simulation output data, pseudo-random number generators, and statistical accuracy of the simulation results. Without these features, a simulation model would be useless since it will produce invalid results. As Kleinjen (1979) pointed out that "*…instead of an expensive simulation model, a toss of the coin had better be used.*"

There are several interesting research problems in the emerging area of network simulation and modeling. Some of these research issues include use and misuse of simulation according to a survey of recent IEEE publications. We are currently addressing some of these research problems, and research results will be presented in future articles.

## ACKNOWLEDGMENT

The first author was supported in part by the AUT University's School of Computing and Mathematical Sciences Contestable Research Grant. An earlier version of the chapter appears as: Sarkar, N. I, & McHaney, R. Modeling and Simulation of IEEE 802.11 WLANs: A Case Study of a Network Simulator, *Proceedings of the 2006 Information Resources Management Association International Conference, May 21-24, Washington DC, USA.*

## REFERENCES

Bianchi, G. (2000). Performance analysis of the IEEE 802.11 distributed coordination function. *IEEE Journal on Selected Areas in Communications*, *18*(3), 535–547. doi:10.1109/49.840210

Breslau, L., Estrin, D., Fall, K., Floyd, S., Heimann, J., & Helmy, A. (2000). Advances in network simulation. *Computer*, *33*(5), 59–67. doi:10.1109/2.841785

Carson, J. S., II. (2004). Introduction to modeling and simulation. In *Proceedings of 2004 Winter Simulation Conference*, (pp. 1283-1289). IEEE Press.

Chen, W.-T., Jian, B.-B., & Lo, S.-C. (2002). An adaptive retransmission scheme with QoS support for the IEEE802.11 MAC enhancement. In *Proceedings of the 55th IEEE Vehicular Technology Conference*, (pp. 70-74). IEEE Press.

CMU Monarch Project. (2011). *Webpage*. Retrieved January 5, 2011 from http://www.monarch.cs.cmu.edu.

Das, S. R., Castaneda, R., & Yan, J. (2000). Simulation-based performance evaluation of routing protocols for mobile ad hoc networks. *Mobile Networks and Applications*, *5*(1), 179–189. doi:10.1023/A:1019108612308

Dricot, J.-M., & De Doncker, P. (2004). High-accuracy physical layer model for wireless network simulations in ns-2. In *Proceedings of 2004 International Workshop on Wireless Ad-Hoc Networks*, (pp. 249-253). IEEE Press.

Fall, K., & Varadhan, K. (2011). The ns manual. *The VINT Project*. Retrieved January 5, 2011 from http://www.isi.edu/nsnam/ns/doc/.

Fantacci, R., Pecorella, T., & Habib, I. (2004). Proposal and performance evaluation of an efficient multiple-access protocol for LEO satellite packet networks. *IEEE Journal on Selected Areas in Communications*, *22*(3), 538–545. doi:10.1109/JSAC.2004.823437

Greis, M. (2011). *Ns-2 tutorial*. Retrieved January 5, 2011 from http://www.isi.edu/nsnam/ns/tutorial/index.html.

Hassan, M., & Jain, R. (Eds.). (2004). *High performance TCP/IP networking - Concepts, issues, and solutions*. New York: Pearson Prentice Hall.

Hechenleitner, B., & Entacher, K. (2002). On shortcomings of the ns-2 random number generator. In Znati, T., & McDonald, B. (Eds.), *Communication Networks and Distributed Systems Modeling and Simulation* (pp. 71–77). New York: The Society for Modeling and Simulation International.

Hegedus, A., Maggio, G. M., & Kocarev, L. (2005). A ns-2 simulator utilizing chaotic maps for network-on-chip traffic analysis. In *Proceedings of the IEEE International Conference on Circuits and Systems (ISCAS 2005)*, (pp. 3375-3378). IEEE Press.

Holloway, D. (2003). *Wireless networking: A guide to wireless networking and deployment*. Retrieved September 25, 2003 from http://www. hill.com/archive/pub/papers/2003/01/paper.pdf.

ISI. (2010). *Network animator*. Retrieved June 5, 2010 from http://www.isi.edu/nsnam/nam/.

ISI. (2011). *ns-2 contributed code*. Retrieved January 5, 2011 from www.isi.edu/nsnam/ns/ns-contributed.html.

Kleijnen, J. P. C. (1979). The role of statistical methodology in simulation. In Zeigler, B. P. (Ed.), *Methodology in Systems Modelling and Simulation. North Holland*. The Netherlands: Academic Press. doi:10.1145/1102786.1102793

Kurkowski, S., Camp, T., Mushell, N., & Colagrosso, M. (2005). A visualization and analysis tool for ns-2 wireless simulations: iNSpect. In *Proceedings of the 13th IEEE International Symposium on Modeling, Analysis, and Simulation of Computer and Telecommunication Systems*, (pp. 503-506). IEEE Press.

L'Ecuyer, P. (2001). Software for uniform random number generation: Distinguishing the good and the bad. In *Proceedings of the 2001 Winter Simulation Conference*, (pp. 95-105). Arlington, VA: IEEE Press.

L'Ecuyer, P., Richard, S., Chen, E. J., & Kelton, W. D. (2001). An object-oriented random number package with many long streams and substreams. *Operations Research, 1*(1).

Law, A. M., & Kelton, W. D. (2000). *Simulation modelling and analysis* (3rd ed.). New York: McGraw-Hill.

Liao, H.-C., Ting, Y.-W., Yen, S.-H., & Yang, C.-C. (2004). Ant mobility model platform for network simulator. In *Proceedings of the International Conference on Information Technology: Coding and Computing (ITCC 2004)*, (pp. 380-384). IEEE Press.

Mahrenholz, D., & Ivanov, S. (2004). Real-time network emulation with ns-2. In *Proceedings of the Eighth IEEE International Symposium on Distributed Simulation and Real-time Applications (DS-RT 2004)*, (pp. 29-36). IEEE Press.

Matsumoto, M., & Nishimura, T. (1999). Mersenne twister: A 623-dimentionally equidistributed uniform pseudorandom number generator. *ACM Transactions on Modeling and Computer Simulation, 7*(1), 3–30.

McHaney, R. (1991). *Computer simulation: A practical perspective*. San Diego, CA: Academic Press.

McHaney, R. (2009). *Understanding computer simulation*. Frederiksberg, Denmark: Ventus Publishing APS. Retrieved December 20, 2010 from http://bookboon.com/us/textbooks/it/understanding.

Nicopolitidis, P., Obaidat, M. S., Papadimitriou, G. I., & Pomportsis, A. S. (Eds.). (2003). *Wireless networks*. New York: John Wiley & Sons, Ltd.

Park, S. K., & Miller, R. W. (1988). Random number generators: Good ones are hard to find. *Communications of the ACM, 31*(10), 1192–1201. doi:10.1145/63039.63042

Pawlikowski, K. (1990). Steady-state simulation of queuing processes: A survey of problems and solutions. *ACM Computing Surveys, 1*(2), 123–170. doi:10.1145/78919.78921

Pawlikowski, K., Jeong, H.-D. J., & Lee, J.-S. R. (2002). On credibility of simulation studies of telecommunication networks. *IEEE Communications Magazine, 40*(1), 132–139. doi:10.1109/35.978060

Qiu, Q., Zhang, D., & J., M. (2004). GPRS network simulation in ns-2. In *Proceedings of the 10th Asia-Pacific Conference on Communications and 5th International Symposium on Multi-Dimentional Mobile Communications*, (pp. 700-704). APCC Press.

Sakurai, Y., & Katto, J. (2004). AODV multipath extension using source route lists with optimized route establishment. In *Proceedings of the 2004 International Workshop on Wireless Ad-Hoc Networks*, (pp. 63-67). IEEE Press.

Sargent, R. G. (2004). Validation and verification of simulation models. In *Proceedings of the 2004 Winter Simulation Conference*, (pp. 17-28). IEEE Press.

Sarkar, N., & Pawlikowski, K. (2002). A delay-throughput performance improvement to the pi-persistent protocol. *Pakistan Journal of Applied Sciences, 2*(3), 390–399.

Sarkar, N. I. (2010). *Capacity estimation of wireless LANs*. Retrieved March 15, 2010 from http://elena.aut.ac.nz/homepages/staff/Nurul-Sarkar/capacity/.

Sarkar, N. I., & McHaney, R. (2006). Modeling and simulation of IEEE 802.11 WLANs: A case study of a network simulator. In *Proceedings of the 2006 Information Resources Management Association International Conference*, (pp. 715-718). Washington, DC: IEEE Press.

Sarkar, N. I., & Sowerby, K. W. (2005). Buffer unit multiple access (BUMA) protocol: an enhancement to IEEE 802.11b DCF. In *Proceedings of the IEEE Global Telecommunications Conference (GLOBECOM 2005)*, (pp. 2584-2588). St. Louis, MO: IEEE Press.

Sarkar, N. I., & Sowerby, K. W. (2006). Wi-Fi performance measurements in the crowded office environment: A case study. In *Proceedings of the 10th IEEE International Conference on Communication Technology (ICCT 2006)*, (pp. 37-40). Guilin, China: IEEE Press.

Schmeiser, B. (2004). Simulation output analysis: A tutorial based on one research thread. In *Proceedings of the 2004 Winter Simulation Conference*, (pp. 162-170). IEEE Press.

Siringoringo, W., & Sarkar, N. I. (2009). Teaching and learning Wi-Fi networking fundamentals using limited resources. In Gutierrez, J. (Ed.), *Selected Readings on Telecommunications and Networking* (pp. 22–40). Hershey, PA: IGI Global. doi:10.4018/9781605660943.ch003

Tickoo, O., & Sikdar, B. (2003). On the impact of IEEE 802.11 MAC on traffic characteristics. *IEEE Journal on Selected Areas in Communications, 21*(2), 189–203. doi:10.1109/JSAC.2002.807346

Wellens, M., Petrova, M., Riihijarvi, J., & Mahonen, P. (2005). Building a better wireless mousetrap: Need for more realism in simulations. In *Proceedings of the Second Annual Conference on Wireless On-Demand Network Systems and Services (WONS 2005)*, (pp. 150-157). IEEE Press.

## KEY TERMS AND DEFINITIONS

**Access Point (AP):** A device which acts as a bridge between wireless LANs and a wired backbone network. An AP coordinates communication among the mobile stations.

**Ad-Hoc Network:** A class of wireless LAN where nodes communicate without wireless access points. A wireless network operating in ad-hoc mode is also called an Independent Basic Service Set (IBSS).

**IEEE 802.11:** A family of wireless LAN standards.

**Infrastructure Network:** A class of wireless network in which mobile stations are connected to the wired backbone network through wireless access points.

**Ns-2:** An open source discrete event network simulation package.

**OPNET:** A commercial network simulation package which is available to many educational institutions under OPNET academic program worldwide.

**Simulator:** A software package used for modeling and simulation tasks.

# Chapter 6
# OPNET Simulation Setup for QoE Based Network Selection

**Umar Toseef**
*University of Bremen, Germany*

**Manzoor Ahmed Khan**
*Technical University of Berlin, Germany*

## ABSTRACT

*In its most generic sense, the user-centric view in telecommunications considers that the users are free from subscription to any one network operator and can instead dynamically choose the most suitable transport infrastructure from the available network providers for their terminal and application requirements. In this approach, the decision of interface selection is delegated to the mobile terminal enabling end users to exploit the best available characteristics of different network technologies and network providers, with the objective of increased satisfaction. In order to more accurately express the user satisfaction in telecommunications, a more subjective and application-specific measure, namely, the Quality-of-Experience (QoE) is introduced. QoE is the core requirement in future wireless networks and provisions. It is a framework that optimizes the global system of networks and users in terms of efficient resource utilization and meeting user preferences (guaranteeing certain Quality-of-Service [QoS] requirements). A number of solution frameworks to address the mentioned problems using different theoretical approaches are proposed in the research literature. Such scholarly approaches need to be evaluated using simulation platforms (e.g., OPNET, NS2, OMNET++, etc.). This chapter focuses on developing the simulation using a standard discrete event network simulator, OPNET. It outlines the general development procedures of different components in simulation and details the following important aspects: Long Term Evolution (LTE) network component development, impairment entity development, implementing IPv6 flow management, developing an integrated heterogeneous scenario with LTE and WLAN, implementing an example scenario, and generating and analyzing the results.*

DOI: 10.4018/978-1-4666-0191-8.ch006

# INTRODUCTION

The business models of telecommunication operators have traditionally been based on the concept of the so called closed garden: they operate strictly in closed infrastructures and base their revenue-generating models on their capacity to retain a set of customers and effectively establish technological and economical barriers to prevent or discourage users from being able to utilize services and resources offered by other operators. After the initial monopoly like era, an increasing number of (real and virtual) network operators have been observed on the market in many countries. Users benefit from the resulting competition by having much wider spectrum choices for more competitive prices. On the other hand, current practices in telecommunication business still tie the users to a single operator even though the number of players in the market has been growing. The users tend to manually combine their subscriptions to multiple operators in order to take simultaneous advantage of their different offers that are suited for a variety of services. For example, a user might hold two SIM cards/phones from two distinct operators, one of which provides a fixed rate national calling plan while the other provides low cost, high quality international calling with pay-as-you-go option. Extending this example to a case where there are a large number of operators with a multitude of service options and offers in future all-IP telecommunication networks, manual handling of such multi-operator service combinations is clearly tedious and impractical for the users.

In its most generic sense, the user-centric view in telecommunications considers that the users are free from subscription to any one network operator and can instead dynamically choose the most suitable transport infrastructure from the available network providers for their terminal and application requirements. In this approach, the decision of interface selection is delegated to the mobile terminal enabling end users to exploit the best available characteristics of different network technologies and network providers, with the objective of increased satisfaction. The generic term satisfaction can be interpreted in different ways, where a natural interpretation would be obtaining a high Quality-of-Service (QoS) for the lowest price. In order to more accurately express the user satisfaction in telecommunications, the term QoS has been extended to include more subjective and also application specific measures beyond traditional technical parameters, giving rise to the Quality-of-Experience (QoE) concept.

These facts dictate that QoE is the core requirement in the future wireless networks and provisions a framework that optimizes the global system of networks and users in terms of efficient resource utilization and meeting user preferences (guaranteeing certain QoS requirements). A number of solution frameworks to address the mentioned problems using different theoretical approaches are proposed in the research literature. Such scholarly approaches need to be evaluated using simulation platforms, e.g., OPNET, NS2, OMNET++, etc. It is expected that the simulation settings are driven by the objective of problem that has to be analyzed; therefore simulation proves to be a very helpful tool in evaluating the proposed approaches in terms of their efficiency, gain, loss, etc.

Given the facts discussed in the preceding paragraphs, this chapter focuses on developing the simulation using standard discrete event network simulator, namely, OPNET (OPNET, 2011). It outlines the general development procedures of different components in simulation and details the following important aspects:

- Long Term Evolution (LTE) network component development.
- Impairment entity development.
- Implementing IPv6 flow management.
- Developing an integrated heterogeneous scenario with LTE and WLAN (OPNET standard model).
- Implement an example scenario.
- Generating and analyzing the results.

## BACKGROUND

Motivated by the arguments in introduction section, this chapter focuses on explaining the potential of integrating 3GPP (3rd Generation Partnership Project) and non-3GPP networks. We assume that readers have a general overview of the 3GPP and non-3GPP standard. Owing to expected widespread deployment of LTE in near future, this section illustrates over the pre-requisite knowledge about the LTE, 3GPP and non-3GPP network integration architecture design, protocols and their functionalities.

### Background on Long Term Evolution (LTE)

#### Expectations from LTE

In contrast to the circuit-switched model of previous cellular systems, LTE is designed to support only packet-switched services. It aims at providing seamless Internet Protocol (IP) connectivity between User Equipment (UE) and the Packet Data Network (PDN), without any disruption to the end users' applications during mobility. LTE is the result work by the 3GPP project, a collaborative group of international standards organizations and mobile-technology companies. 3GPP had defined a set of high level requirements for LTE, which are detailed as:

- **Increased spectral efficiency and capacity.** LTE is expected to deliver five to ten times greater capacity than the most advanced current 3G networks, e.g., it enables cellular networks to support up to 10 times higher data rate and more users than existing HSPA networks.
- **Lower cost per bit.** Increased spectral efficiency combined with the operational benefits of an all-IP network will reduce the cost per bit compared to 3G solutions.

- **Flexible operational frequency.** LTE must have flexibility to operate in wide number of frequency bands.
- **Simplified architecture.** LTE should utilize open interfaces, offer a simplified architecture, and should have reasonable power requirements at the mobile terminal.
- **Improved QoE.** One of the benefits LTE/SAE (system architecture evolution) will bring a reduction in latency time, which will enhance the behavior of time-sensitive applications, such as VoIP, thus improving the user experience. For instance, the latency time, expressed as the time for a 32-byte ping, is expected to reach 20ms (compared with 120ms for a typical 3G network).

### LTE/SAE Architecture Overview

We now briefly define the main logical components of the LTE/SAE architecture. These logical components are broadly categorized into: (1) Radio access through the E-UTRAN – it contains the evolved base station (eNodeB) and (2) Non-radio aspects – This comes under the term SAE or the core network and also called as Evolved Packet Core (EPC), which comprises of Packet Data Network (P-GW), Serving Gateway (S-GW), Mobility Management Entity (MME), etc. The entire system is called Evolved Packet System (EPS), i.e., LTE + SAE = EPS.

EPS provides bearer path of a certain QoS. It should be noted that multiple bearers can be established for a user in order to provide different QoS streams or connectivity to different PDNs. For instance, a user might be engaged in a voice (VoIP) call while at the same time performing Web browsing or FTP download. A VoIP bearer would provide the necessary QoS for the voice call, while a best-effort bearer would be suitable for the Web browsing or FTP session. However, the control of multimedia applications is provided by the IP Multimedia Subsystem (IMS), which is considered as an entity outside the EPS.

As can be viewed in the Figure 1, that each of the LTE network elements is interconnected via interfaces that are standardized in order to allow multi-vendor interoperability. These standardized interfaces provide the network operators with the possibility to source different network elements from different vendors.

## LTE Architecture Functional Entities

### Evolved nodeb (eNodeB or eNB)

It is the key element in E-UTRAN network. It hosts the Physical (PHY), Medium Access Control (MAC), Radio Link Controller (RLC), and Packet Data Convergence Protocol (PDCP) layers. eNB provides the radio interface and is responsible for radio resource management of LTE including radio bearer control, radio admission control, scheduling of Uplink (UL) and Downlink (DL) radio resources for individual UEs. It also supports IP header compression and encryption of user plan data. eNB connects to the transport network (EPC) through S1 and X2 interfaces at one side of the network; on the other side, it connects with users through Uu interface. These are defined as:

- **X2 interface:** This interface is responsible for connecting eNBs and carrying out the handover procedures.
- **S1 interface:** This interface is responsible for connecting eNB with EPC. Its functionality is further split into control and user plans.

In addition this entity is also responsible for: (1) enforcement of negotiated UL QoS, (2) cell information broadcast, (3) ciphering/deciphering of user and control plan data, (4) compression/decompression of UL/DL user plane packet headers, (5) selection of MME at UE attachment when no routing to an MME can be determined from the information provided by the UE, (6) routing of user plane data towards serving gateway, (7) scheduling and retransmission of paging messages (originated from the MME), and (8) scheduling and retransmission of broadcast messages (originated from MME and Operation and Maintenance [O&M]).

LTE integrates the radio controller function into the eNB. This allows tight interaction between the different protocol layers of the Radio Access Network (RAN), thus reducing latency and improving efficiency. Such distributed control eliminates the need for a high-availability, processing-intensive controller, which in turn has the potential to reduce costs and avoid "single points of failure." Furthermore, as LTE does not support soft handover there is no need for a centralized data-combining function in the network. One consequence of the lack of a centralized controller node is that, as the UE moves, the network must transfer all information related to the UE, that is, the UE context, together with any buffered data, from one eNB to another. Mechanisms are therefore needed to avoid data loss during handover.

### Serving Gateway (S-GW)

This entity performs several functions for both GTP (GPRS based Tunneling Protocol) based and PMIP (Proxy Mobile IP) based network architectures. The S-GW terminates the interfaces towards E-UTRAN; every UE that attaches to EPS is associated with a single S-GW. It acts as a local mobility anchor point in the case of inter-eNB handovers and mobility anchor for inter-3GPP mobility. Once a UE is associated with any S-GW, it handles the forwarding of end-user data packets and also acts as a local anchor point when required for inter-eNB handover. During the handover from LTE to other 3GPP access technologies, the S-GW terminates the S4 interface and provides a connection for transfer of user traffic from 2G/3G network system and the PDN-GW. When a UE is in idle state, the S-GW terminates the downlink path for data, if new packets arrive, the S-GW triggers paging towards the UE. As part of this, the

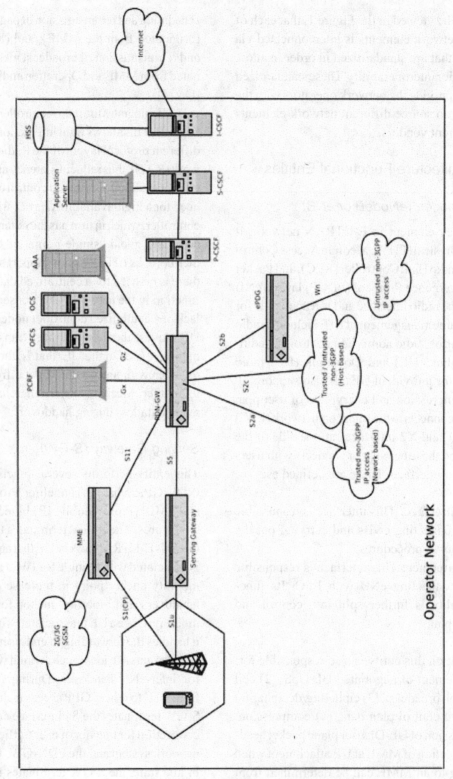

*Figure 1. The basic architectural view of LTE/SAE architecture*

S-GW manages and stores information relevant to UE; for example parameters of IP bearer service of internal network routing information. S-GW is also responsible for: (1) managing and storing UE contexts, e.g., parameters of the IP bearer service, network internal routing information, and (2) performing replication of user traffic in case of lawful interception.

### Mobility Management Entity (MME)

This entity terminates Non-Access Startum (NAS) signaling. From the core-network perspective, MME is the main controlling entity for LTE access network. It is responsible for selecting S-GW and UE during the initial attachment and at the time of intra-LTE handover that involves core network node relation. It also tracks and carries out paging procedures for UE during the idle mode. This entity activates and deactivates the barrier on behalf of UE, and authenticates the end-users through interaction with HSS entity. MME also checks the authorization of the UE to camp on the service provider's Public Land Mobile Network (PLMN), enforces UE roaming restrictions, and provides the control plane function for mobility between LTE and 3G access networks with the S3 interface terminating at the MME from the SGSN.

### Packet Data Network Gateway (PDN-GW)

This entity provides the connectivity to the UE to external packet data networks by being the point of exit and entry of traffic for the UE. A UE may have simultaneous connectivity with more than one PDN-GW for accessing multiple PDNs. The PDN-GW performs: (1) policy enforcement, (2) packet filtering for each user, (3) charging support, (4) lawful interception, (5) packet screening, and (6) the job of an anchor for mobility between 3GPP and non-3GPP technologies such as WiMAX and 3GPP2.

## LTE Protocol Layers

This section outlines the radio protocol architecture of E-UTRAN. In the user plane an IP packet for a UE is encapsulated in an EPC-specific protocol and tunneled between the P-GW and the eNB for transmission to the UE. Different tunneling protocols are used across different interfaces. A 3GPP-specific tunneling protocol called the GTP is used over the core network interfaces, S1 and S5/S8. The E-UTRAN protocol stack is shown Figure 2, where broader views of the E-UTRAN protocol stack and main functionalities of EPC entities is presented. The E-UTRAN protocol includes PDCP, RLC, MAC and PHY.

### Packet Data Convergence Protocol (PDCP)

PDCP protocol layers exists both in UE and eNB, it is the part of LTE air interface control and user planes. Its functions in the user plane include: (1) decryption, (2) Robust Header Compression (ROHC) and header decompression, (3) sequence numbering, and (4) duplicate removal. PDCP functions in the control plane include: (4) decryption, (2) integrity protection, (3) sequence numbering,

*Figure 2. Protocol stack of EPS highlighting the main functionalities of EPC*

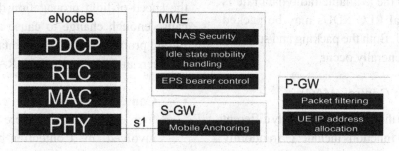

and (4) duplicate removal. There is one PDCP instance per radio bearer. The radio bearer is similar to a logical channel for user control data.

## Radio Resource Control (RRC)

RRC layer in the eNB: (1) makes handover decisions based on neighbor cell measurements sent by the UE, (2) pages for the UEs over the air, (3) broadcasts system information, (4) controls UE measurement reporting such as the periodicity of Channel Quality Information (CQI) reports, (5) allocates cell-level temporary identifiers to active UEs, (6) executes the transfer of UE context from source eNB to the target eNB during handover, and (7) does the integrity protection of RRC message.

## Radio Link Control (RLC)

RLC is symmetrical for the UL and DL. RLC layer is used to format and transport traffic between the UE and the eNB. RLC provides three different reliability modes for data transport: (1) Acknowledgement-Mode (AM), (2) Unacknowledged Mode (UM), or (3) transparent mode. The UM mode is suitable for the transport of Real Time (RT) services because such services are delay sensitive and cannot wait for retransmissions. The AM mode, on the other hand, is appropriate for NRT services.

The UL process concatenates the SDUs into transport blocks; such a process is called concatenation process. The RLC PDU size is chosen based on the transport block size for the radio bearer. If the RLC SDU is large, or the available radio data rate is low, the RLC SDU may be split into several RLC PDUs. However, if the RLC SDU is small, or the available radio data rate is high, then several RLC SDUs may be packed into a single PDU. Both the packing and splitting processes may generally occur.

## Medium Access Control (MAC)

MAC functions in the UL are significantly different than that of DL. U functions include: (1) randomly

accessing the channel, (2) scheduling, (3) building headers, and (4) selecting the transport format.

By selection of the transport format, it is meant, to figure out, how to pack the information in, and what modulation and coding are available and configure the PHY appropriately to be ready to transmit. This dictates that MAC determines the capacity of a transport block based on the transport format. It should be noted that, the UL Shared Channel (UL-SCH) is the primary transport channel and format variables are modulation and coding, which determine data rate. In this connection, the Common Control Channel (CCCH), Dedicated Control Channel (DCCH) and Dedicated Traffic Channel (DTCH) are all mapped to the UL-SCH and all MAC transmissions on the UL-SCH must be scheduled by the Random Access Channel (RACH) procedure.

When the UE is not connected, no transmit slots are ever scheduled. The RACH provides a means for disconnected devices to transmit. Transmitting on the UL-SCH requires a resource allocation from the eNB, and time alignment to be current. Otherwise the RACH procedure is required.

The RACH procedure is used in four cases: (1) initial access from disconnected state (RRC_IDLE) or radio failure, (2) handover requiring random access procedure, (3) DL or UL data arrival during RRC_CONNECTED after UL PHY has lost synchronization (possibly due to power save operation), and (4) UL data arrival when are no dedicated scheduling request (PUCCH) channels available.

Timing is also critical because the UE can move different distances from the base station, and LTE requires microsecond-level precision; the speed-of-light propagation delay alone can cause enough change to cause a collision or a timing problem if it is not maintained.

There are two forms of the RACH procedure:

- **Contention-based:** This can apply to all four events above. There are four steps involved in Contention-based Random

Access, in the first step a random access preamble is sent on a special set of physical layer resources, which are a group of subcarriers allocated for this purpose and uses a CDMA like coding, Zadoff-Chu sequence to allow simultaneous transmissions to be decoded. In the second step a random access response is sent on Physical Downlink Control Channel (PDCCH) within a time window of a few TTI. For initial access, conveys at least RA-preamble identifier, timing alignment information, initial UL grant, and assignment of temporary C-RNTI. One or more UEs may be addressed in one response. In the third step the transmission is scheduled using HARQ and RLC transparent mode on UL-SCH, and the UE identifier is conveyed. The final optional step of conflict resolution is used by eNB to end the RACH procedure.

- **Non-contention based:** This applies to only handover and DL data arrival. There exists no chance of a preamble collision because the code is pre-assigned a 6-bit preamble code by the eNB and the UE transmits the assigned preamble. The random access response in the case is similar to the one explained for contention-based approach. The difference is whether or not there is a possibility for failure using an overlapping RACH preamble.

## LTE Protocol Operation

### MAC Scheduling

The eNB allocates physical layer resources for the Uplink and Downlink Shared Channels (UL-SCH and DL-SCH). Resources are composed of Physical Resource Blocks (PRB) and Modulation Coding Scheme (MCS). The MCS determines the bit rate, and thus the capacity, of PRBs. Allocations may be valid for one or more TTIs; each TTI interval is one sub-frame (1 ms).

In most cases, scheduling is fully dynamic, which is suitable for bursty, infrequent and bandwidth consuming data transmissions (e.g., Web surfing, video streaming, emails) it is less suited for real time streaming applications such as voice calls. Here, data is sent in short bursts while at regular intervals. If the data rate of the stream is very low, as is the case for voice calls, the overhead of the scheduling messages is very high as only little data is sent for each scheduling message.

The solution for this is semi-persistent scheduling. Instead of scheduling each uplink or downlink transmission, a transmission pattern is defined instead of single opportunities. This significantly reduces the scheduling assignment overhead. Semi-persistent scheduling reduces control channel signaling. If every allocation was individually signaled, the overhead would be unacceptable. In an application such as voice over IP, for example, a downlink frame occur every 10 to 20 milliseconds. If each downlink frame were signaled individually, it would cause a lot of traffic on the control channel and the control channel would need a lot more bandwidth than necessary. Semi-persistent scheduling lets you set up an ongoing allocation that persists until it is changed. Semi-persistent schedules can be configured for both uplink and downlink.

The LTE physical channel, PDCCH, which is responsible for conveying the UE specific information. It carries the Cell Radio Network Temporary Identifier (C-RNTI), which is the dynamic UE identifier. The C-RNTI indicates that an upcoming downlink resource has been de-multiplexed by the MAC and passed on to higher layers and is now scheduled for this UE. Semi-persistent scheduling periodicity is configured by RRC. Whether scheduling is dynamic or semi-persistent is indicated by using different scrambling codes for the C-RNTI on PDCCH. The PDCCH is a very low-bandwidth channel; it does not carry a lot of information compared to the downlink shared channel.

## QoS Architecture

LTE architecture supports "hard QoS," with end-to-end quality of service and Guaranteed Bit Rate (GBR) for radio bearers. Just as Ethernet and the internet have different types of QoS, for example, various levels of QoS can be applied to LTE traffic for different applications. Because the LTE MAC is fully scheduled, QoS is a natural fit. EPS bearers provide one-to-one correspondence with RLC radio bearers and provide support for Traffic Flow Templates (TFT). There are four types of EPS bearers: (1) GBR bearer – resources permanently allocated by admission control, (2) non-GBR bearer – no admission control, (3) dedicated bearer – associated with specific TFT (GBR or non-GBR), and (4) default bearer – non GBR, "catch-all" for unassigned traffic.

## Handover Management

Handover is an important function that maintains seamless connectivity when transitioning from one base station to another. There are two types of handover: intra-RAT, which is within one radio access technology (i.e., LTE-to-LTE from one eNodeB to another), and inter-RAT between radio access technologies. Inter-RAT could be between LTE and GSM or 3G WCDMA, 3GPP2, WiMAX or even wireless LAN. These non-LTE handovers are being defined for the LTE standard. These involve higher layers and often different radio modems, but call continuity is guaranteed with up to 100 milliseconds of disruption when a call is transferred using techniques such as mobile IP or operations in software layers above the modem stack. Handover occurs in the active state; it is controlled by the network (the eNB). The network uses measurements from the UE and its own knowledge of the network topology to determine when to handover a UE, and to which eNB. Cell re-selection occurs in the idle state; it is controlled by the UE.

## Handover Measurement

In single radio architecture, it is challenging to monitor other networks while the receiver is active, because they are on different frequencies. The radio can only receive on one channel at a time. The radio needs to listen to other frequencies to determine if a better base station (eNB) is available. In the active state, the eNB provides measurement gaps in the scheduling of the UE where no downlink or uplink scheduling occurs. Ultimately the network makes the decision, but the gap provides the UE sufficient time to change frequency, make a measurement, and switch back to the active channel. This can normally occur in a few TTIs. This has to be coordinated with the DRX, which also causes the system to shut off the radio for periods of time to save power.

## Integration of Operator Technologies

It is widely accepted that the 4G networks will purely be IP based, and will be characterized by the independent drives, such as users, network operators, and service providers etc. Given the user-centric vision, the mobility management turns out to be a crucial issue for the operators. Owing to the maturity of current communication paradigm, it is needless to highlight the importance heterogeneous wireless technologies and their co-existence to extend service to end-consumers. When it comes to heterogeneous wireless technologies, one can discern various prevailing standards in the current communication market, such as 3GPP, non-3GPP, 3GPP2 etc. Both 3GPP and non-3GPP are of core importance; however the difference is dictated by the preference of incumbent and the new entrants, for example an incumbent operator with its infrastructure in place is comfortable with 3GPP technologies, whereas the non-3GPP technologies are the technologies of choice for new entrants. Now that the market is framed to accept both the 3GPP and non-3GPP technologies, this provisions that end-consumers should be enabled to make efficient use of the services extended through both the technologies. Intuitively the objective function of operators will include the profit maximization through integration of 3GPP and non-3GPP technologies. Good news is that 3GPP has come up with standards for such integration; Figure 3 represents such integration architecture.

Given the integration solution, incumbent operators might prefer to hold the market by deploying the non-3GPP technologies. In this case although the operators are better off by providing diversified interfaces to the end-consumers, they are faced with crucial mobility management issues. Thanks to 3GPP, who address these issues and provide mobility management solutions for

different use cases. Let us now have a bird's eye view over the solutions; basically non-3GPP technologies can be integrated with 3GPP technologies through one of the three interfaces (S2a, S2b, S2c) provided by EPC / SAE. The description of the each interface is as follows:

- **S2a:** It provides the integration path between the trusted non-3GPP IP networks and 3GPP networks. In this case the mobility is handled by the network based mobility solution, e.g., Proxy MIPv6.
- **S2b:** It provides the integration path between the un-trusted non-3GPP IP networks and 3GPP networks. In this case the mobility is handled by the network based mobility solution.

*Figure 3. 3GPP standard for integration of 3GPP and non-3GPP technologies*

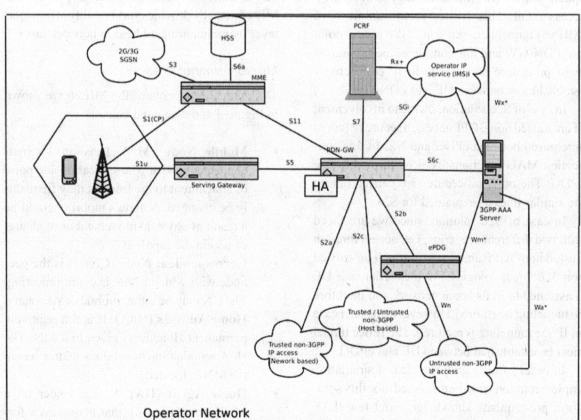

- **S2c:** It provides the integration path between both trusted and un-trusted non-3GPP IP networks and 3GPP networks. In this case the mobility is handled by the host based mobility solution, e.g., dual stack MIPv6.

The detail of procedures for each interface solution is given below.

In case of S2a solution, after L2 attachment with non-3GPP access point, the AAA authentication procedure is performed. Upon the successful authorization and authentication, L3/IP attachment procedures are triggered. In this case the non-3GPP access point takes the role of MAG and sends proxy binding update message to PDN-GW. PDN-GW updates its address to 3GPP AAA server followed by proxy binding update procedures, which results in IP address allocation for UE. The UE IP address is then sent within proxy binding update acknowledgement message to non-3GPP access point. This creates proxy mobile IPv6 (MIPv6) tunnel between non-3GPP access point and PDN-GW and this completes the L3 attachment procedure and results in IP connectivity establishment between UE and PDN-GW.

In case of S2b solution, owing to involvement of un-trusted non-3GPP access, a secure IP tunnel is required between ePDG and UE. In this connection MAG functionality is performed by the ePDG. The other procedures are carried out on the similar lines as explained for S2a.

In case of S2c solution, since we are faced with two different scenarios, i.e., access through trusted non-3GPP and access through un-trusted non-3GPP technologies. For the earlier case UE is assumed to in its home network and therefore no tunneling is required. However in the later case an IPSec tunneling is required. The IPSec tunnel must be established between UE and ePDG.

In order to fully grab the idea of simulation implementation with the discussed mobility solutions, pre-requisite knowledge about few IETF Requests for Comments (RFCs) and drafts is required, which is detailed as below:

## MIPv6 Overview

MIPv6 allows a node to maintain its existing connection on network layer while it is changing its location and possibly the link it is connected to. In this case, the MN needs to change its link to get a new topologically correct IPv6 address to stay connected with Internet. But as soon as IP address of the MN changes all of the connections that were initiated with previous IP address will terminate ungracefully and MN will not be reachable with that previous IP address. However with the help of MIPv6, MN can maintain its existing connection while it is changing its location and the IP address. MIPv6 accomplishes this by assigning a particular IPv6 address to the node that is used to initiate all of the communications with that MN and through which MN is always reachable. MIPv6 actually provides survivability at transport layer by maintaining address at network layer.

### MIPv6 Terminologies

The main components of the MIPv6 are shown in Figure 4 and discussed below:

- **Mobile Node (MN).** It is an Internet-connected device whose location and point of attachment to the Internet may frequently be changed. A node's mobility could be a result of physical movement or of changes within the topology.
- **Correspondent Node (CN).** It is the peer node with which a MN is communicating. The CN may be either mobile or stationary.
- **Home Address (HoA).** It is the relatively permanent IP address given to a MN. The HoA remains unchanged no matter where the MN is located.
- **Home Agent (HA).** It is a router on a MN's home network that maintains infor-

*Figure 4. MIPv6 components*

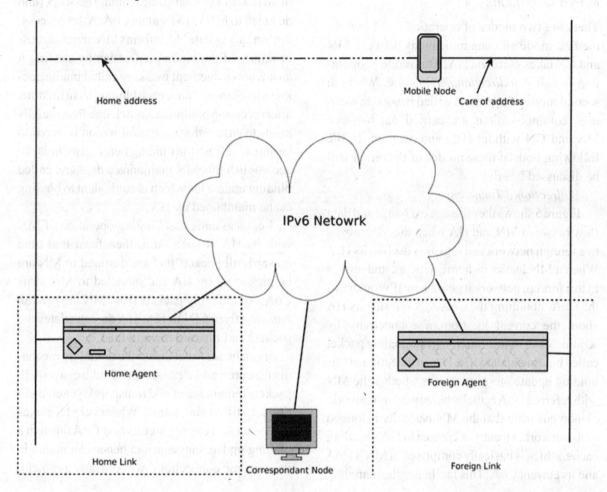

mation about the device's current location, as identified in its care-of-address.

- **Home Network.** The home network is where a MN has its permanent IP address (HoA)
- **Foreign Network.** It is any network other than the home network to which a MN may be connected.
- **Care-of Address (CoA).** A CoA is a temporary IP address for a MN that enables message delivery when the device is connecting from somewhere other than its home network.

- **Binding.** It is the association of the HoA of a MN with a CoA for that MN, along with the remaining lifetime of that association.
- **Binding Cache.** It is a database that is maintained both at HA and at CN consisted of binding information of MN with which they are communicating.
- **Binding Update List.** It is a database that is maintained at MN about all bindings that it has sent to its home agent and CNs. This database helps MN to keep track of the lifetime of all bindings so that they can be refreshed before they get expired.

## MIPv6 Operations

There are two modes of operation of MIPv6. In the first mode all communications between MN and CN takes place via HA. This mode of operation is called *bidirectional tunneling*. While in second mode of operation called *route optimization*, communications are carried out between MN and CN without HA's intervention. In the following both of these modes of operation will be discussed briefly.

### Bidirectional Tunneling

Figure 5 shows the message exchange and data flow between MN and HA when the MN moves to a foreign network and registers itself to its HA. When a MN leaves its home network and moves in to a foreign network it gets a new IPv6 address, the CoA, obtaining the CoA MN informs its HA about the current location of connectivity by sending its CoA information in a signaling packet called binding update. The HA on reception of this binding update message checks whether the MN with referred HoA actually belongs to its network. . Upon ensuring that the MN basically belonged to its network, an entry is created in HA's binding cache, which is basically comprised of MN's HoA and its current CoA. This facilitates the tunneling of all the packets that come to home network (and destined to MN) to MN at its CoA. After processing binding update HA informs MN about success or failure of the binding operation by sending it an acknowledgement message called binding acknowledgement. Since each binding has a lifetime, after receiving binding acknowledgement the MN needs to ensure that such information is stored to be able to refresh the binding before it expires. To accomplish this MN maintains a database called binding update list which is equivalent to binding cache maintained by HA.

Let us assume that binding operation of MN with its HA is successful, then from that time onwards all packets that are destined to MN are be picked up by HA and tunneled to MN at its CoA. All the reply packets from MN are *reverse tunneled* from MN to HA. HA de-capsulates the packets and forward them to the CN.

It can be seen that due to the tunneling mechanism source and destination IP addresses of IP packets remain intact and transport layer connection can still be maintained. Whenever MN makes a movement it can register its new CoA through a binding update message and hence can maintain its existing connections without any problem.

*Figure 5. Exchange of packets while MN is in foreign network*

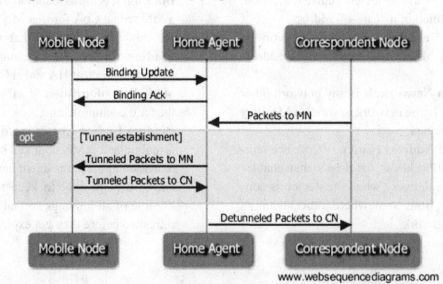

www.websequencediagrams.com

Moreover MN is always reachable through its HoA irrespective of the actual attachment point of MN to the Internet.

*Route Optimization*

It is obvious from Figure 5 that routing packets through HA adds additional delays in communication between MN and CN. Amongst the intuitive drawbacks of bidirectional tunneling are: (1) the introduction of single point of failure in network, and (2) higher bandwidth demands than is actually needed for direct communication between MN and CN. All this suggests is that it should be possible that MN and CN can communicate without HA's intervention. Although it is not possible to keep HA completely out of the scene but a direct communication between MN and CN is possible if HA informs CN about the current CoA of MN. Once CN and MN are reachable for each other they can decide for direct communication without HA's involvement.

When a MN receives a tunneled packet from HA it may decide for route optimization by sending a binding update message, similar to one that is sent to HA, to the CN. This binding update informs the CN about the current CoA of the MN. CN maintains a database similar to HA's binding cache and puts an entry for this MN's CoA corresponding to its HoA. After processing binding update CN informs MN about the status of this binding by sending binding acknowledgement. If binding is successful then CN can communicate directly by sending packets to MN's CoA. The process of establishing the direct communication is called the Return Routability Procedure (RRP).

## MCoA Support in MIPv6 and NEMO

MIPv6 helps users to stay always connected but what should be the behavior of a MN that can connect to multiple available network interfaces. According to MIPv6 RFC 3775 (Johnson, et al., 2004), a user is not allowed to use multiple active network connections simultaneously. However there is an extension RFC 5648 (Wakikawa, et al., 2009), that deals with how mobility protocols can be modified to allow mobile devices using multiple connections simultaneously. This task is referred as Multiple Care-of Addresses (MCoAs) registration in MIPv6 terminology.

In MCoA registration all available CoAs of MN can be registered to the HA/CN. It improves MN's connectivity with its HA/CN. It is because with single CoA registration if MN loses accidentally its connectivity to the Internet before registering another CoA, it will be unreachable for HA/CN. However, with multiple CoAs registration if one of the connections is lost, MN will still be reachable at other CoAs. In addition many other advantages of MCoAs may be found in the evolving wireless communication and current research literature, e.g., optimizing cost, bandwidth utilization, load balancing, QoS assurance, and flow management etc.

## MCoA Registration Operation

MCoA registration extension proposes a new identification number called Binding Unique Identification (BID) number for each binding cache entry to accommodate multiple binding registrations. A unique BID number is assigned to each network interface or CoA bound to a single HA. MN sends this BID number in each binding update message for receiver to distinguish between bindings corresponding to same HA. In other words HoA is used to identify a MN while BID number is used to identify multiple bindings (i.e., network interfaces) registered by the MN.

In order to transport BID and related information between MN, HA and CN, an extension to mobility option header is proposed. This mobility option is called BID, which is included in a binding update, binding acknowledgement and binding refresh request messages. Figure 6 shows the structure of BID mobility option.

It should be noted that HA/CN can use any of the registered CoA to communicate with the MN.

*Figure 6. The BID mobility option*

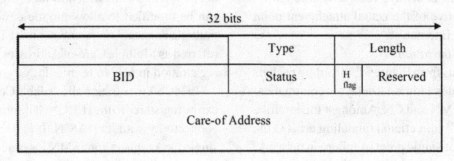

- **Type:** Type value for BID is 35.
- **Length:** It is 8 bit unsigned integer number to indicate length of this option.
- **BID:** It is a 16-bit unsigned integer field to assign a unique identifier to this binding.
- **Status:** It is 8 bit unsigned integer field to indicate success or failure of the binding operation for the particular CoA in the option
- **H flag:** This flag indicates that the MN registers multiple bindings to the HA while it is attached to the home link. This flag is valid only for a Binding Update sent to the HA.

Figure 7 shows a scenario where a MN has connections with two foreign networks and performs the MCoA registration with its HA. In Figure 7 MN acquires two CoAs at its two interfaces because it is connected to two different foreign networks. However it is also possible for a node to acquire MCoAs over one interface connected to a single physical network. An example of latter case is a network where multiple prefixes are announced on the link to which MN is attached. In this case several global addresses will be configured on this interface of MN for each of the announced prefixes. When it comes to concept, there is no difference in above two cases, as the difference is only in the number of physical interfaces. However BID number is used just to identify the binding. To simplify the situation BID numbers can be assigned to CoA instead of physical network interfaces.

- **Binding registration:** When a MN leaves its home network and is connected to the Internet through foreign networks, it should decide whether it wants to register MCoA with its HA or only the primary CoA. If MN wants to proceed with MCoA registration it assigns a BID number to each of its CoAs. MN now generates a BID mobility option for each binding to attach it to binding update message. Each BID with corresponding lifetime and CoA is stored in Binding Update List (BUL) of MN so that it can be refreshed before getting expired.
- **Processing binding update:** When the HA receives a binding update with BID mobility option included, it verifies the binding HoA by Duplicate Address Detection (DAD) (Moore 2006). If the verification succeeds and BID mobility option fields carries acceptable values, HA registers a binding with the specified BID as a MN's binding and sends a binding acknowledgement to MN. The binding acknowledgement also contains BID mobility option as indication to MN that HA is MCoAs capable.
- **Receiving binding acknowledgement:** If the binding acknowledgement received by MN does not contain any BID mobility option then it is an indication that HA is not MCoA registration capable. In this case only one CoA registration is possible with HA. However if the replied binding

*Figure 7. MCoA registration*

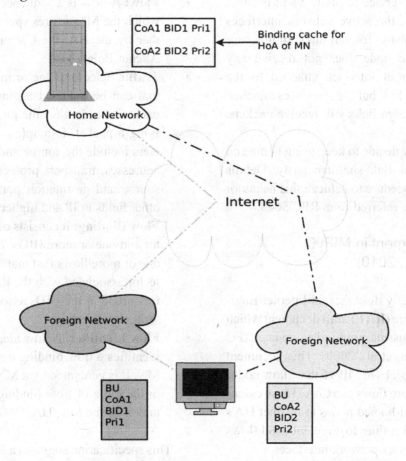

acknowledgement contains BID mobility option, MN checks the status field to know about the status of sent binding request. If status indicates the success code then it means that binding operation at HA was successful. Otherwise MN would check the error code in status field to figure out the reason of rejection of binding.

- **Sending binding refresh request:** If HA feels that a certain binding is going to expire soon, it may send a binding refresh request to MN. This binding refresh request contains BID mobility option with corresponding BID number to tell MN which binding needs to be refreshed.

- **Receiving binding refresh request:** When a MN receives a binding refresh request with BID mobility option, it should update the respective binding. The node may include multiple BID mobility options if there are multiple bindings that need to be refreshed.

- **Removing binding:** If a MN wants to delete a particular binding(s) from its HA and CN, the MN sends a Binding Update with lifetime set to zero and includes a BID mobility option(s) with the BID(s) it wants to de-register.

- **Returning Home:** When a MN returns home:
  ○ It may deregister all of its binding with that home agent. OR
  ○ It may disable its interface attached to home link and send deregistration for

that interface to home agent through one of the active network interfaces attached to foreign links. In this case mobile node does not receive any packet at interface attached to the home link but the interfaces attached to foreign links still receive packets. OR

◦ It may decide to keep using home and visited link simultaneously. Details of procedure to achieve this behavior can be referred from RFC 5648.

## Flow Management in MIPv6 (Tsirtsis, et al., 2010)

This section briefly discusses an Internet Engineering Task Force (IETF) draft document which is an under discussion proposal to update RFC 5648 (Wakikawa, et al., 2009). This document introduces extensions to MIPv6 that allow nodes to bind one or more flows to a CoA. These extensions allow multi-homed nodes to instruct HA's and other MIPv6 entities to direct inbound flows to specific addresses/network interfaces.

As discussed in previous section that in RFC 5648 MIPv6 and NEMO Basic Support are extended to allow the binding of more than one CoA to a HoA. This specification further extends MIPv6, DSMIPv6, and NEMO Basic Support to allow it to specify policies associated with each binding. A policy can contain a request for special treatment of a particular IPv4 or IPv6 flow, which is viewed as a group of packets matching a traffic selector. Hence, this specification allows a MN/mobile router to bind a particular flow to a CoA without affecting other flows using the same HoA. The MN/mobile router assembles the flow binding requests based on local policies, link characteristics and the types of applications running at the time. Such policies are outside the scope of this chapter.

We now briefly define the involved terminologies in flow management as follows:

- **Flow:** A flow is a sequence of packets for which the MN desires special handling either by the HA, the CN or the (Mobility Anchor Point) MAP.

- **Traffic Selector:** One or more parameters that can be matched against fields in the packet's headers for the purpose of classifying a packet. Examples of such parameters include the source and destination IP addresses, transport protocol number, the source and destination port numbers and other fields in IP and higher layer headers.

- **Flow Binding:** It consists of a traffic selector and one or more BIDs. IP packets from one or more flows that match the traffic selector associated with the flow binding are forwarded to the BIDs associated with the same flow binding.

- **Flow Identifier:** A flow identifier uniquely identifies a flow binding associated with a MN. It is generated by a MN and is cached in the table of flow binding entries maintained by the MN, HA, CN or MAP.

This specification suggests a slight modification in BID mobility option defined in RFC 5648. With suggested modification BID mobility option is shown in Figure 8. It can be noticed that only change is introducing a BID-PRI field. This is a 7-bit unsigned integer which reflects relative priority of this BID with other registered BIDs.

In order to install flow management related policies, this specification introduces a new mobility option as shown in Figure 9.

FID field is 16 bit unsigned integer number which is a unique identifier for this flow binding.

FID-PRI is 16 bit unsigned integer number which indicates relative priority of this flow binding. This number must be unique in the sense that two flow bindings must not have same FID-PRI value.

Status is 8 bit unsigned integer field to indicate success or failure of the flow binding operation for the particular flow in the option.

*Figure 8. The BID mobility option*

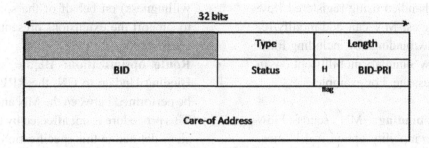

*Figure 9. The flow identification mobility option*

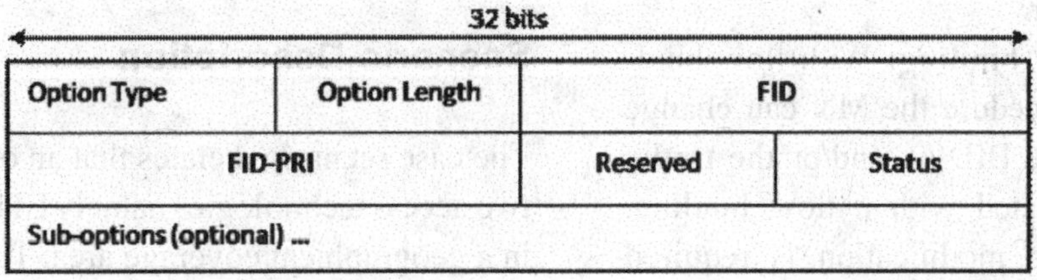

Sub-options It can be included in this flow identification mobility option, if necessary. This specification defines four sub-options which are listed below along with brief description.

- **Binding Reference Sub-Option:** This sub-option associates the flow described in a flow identification mobility option with one or more registered CoAs. BIDs of intended CoAs are included in this sub-option.
- **Traffic Selector Sub-Option:** This sub-option includes the parameters used to match packets for a specific flow binding. The traffic selector defined in accompanying specification (Tsirtsis et al 2011) is mandatory to implement. According to Tsirtsis et al (2011) a traffic selector can be formed using one or more of following parameters. Moreover these parameters can be mentioned either as a single value or as a range of values.
  - Source address
  - Destination address

  - IPSEC SPI - Security Parameter Index
  - IPv6 Flow label
  - Source port
  - Destination port
  - Traffic Class
  - First IPv6 next header value
- **Pad1/PadN:** These sub-options may be included in order to full fill any alignment requirements.

In addition to above mobility option another new mobility option "Flow Summary Mobility Option" is also introduced. The purpose of this mobility option is to refresh the status of already registered flow bindings. This mobility option carries FIDs of all flow bindings whose status has to be refreshed.

## Protocol Operation

All nodes which implement this specification maintain an ordered list of CoAs according to their BID-PRI. The CoA with the highest priority is considered as default CoA for all packets which cannot be handled using registered flow management policies. MN can add/modify/refresh or delete flow bindings by including Flow Identification/Flow Summary mobility options in binding update message. For example:

- **New flow binding:** MN sends Flow Identification mobility option in BU message with a unique FID which is associated with one of already registered CoA of MN. A Flow Binding must have exactly one Traffic Selector.

- **Updating flow binding:** With flow binding update procedure the MN can change the priority, the BID(s), and/or the traffic selector associated with a flow binding. However if no modification is required traffic selector and binding reference sub option may be omitted.

- **Refreshing flow binding:** MN must refresh all of its flow bindings in every binding update message even if it does not want to change any of their parameters. Flow bindings can be refreshed by sending flow summary option.

- **Removing flow binding:** Removal of flow binding entries is performed implicitly by omission of a given FID from a binding update.

- **Returning home:** If the MN performs an (Johnson, et al., 2004) style deregistration, all of its bindings, including flow bindings are deleted. If the MN, however, performs an (Wakikawa, et al., 2009) style home registration, then the home link is associated with a specific BID and so it is treated as any other link associated with a given BID.

- **Binding acknowledgement:** A binding acknowledgement message in response to in response to a Binding Update with flow identification mobility option must include flow identification option. Otherwise it

would be an indication of inability (or unwillingness) on behalf of the source node to support the extensions presented in this specification.

- **Route optimization:** Before sending a Binding Update to CN, the RRP needs to be performed between the MN and the CN. This procedure is not affected by the extensions defined in this specification.

## SIMULATION IMPLEMENTATION

### Scenario Description

The case scenario dictates that an operator owns two access technologies namely LTE and WLAN in a geographical coverage area. The operator is enabled to extend heterogeneous services to the users via both the access technologies. A user may be connected to the application server for an application via both the access network interfaces simultaneously, or on two different interfaces for two different applications. Owing to the wireless medium in the access network, users experience quality degradation. The user (in case of simultaneous interfaces connectivity per application) may switch the interfaces during the life-time of the call, similarly user applications (in case of one application per interface) may be switched between the two interfaces, these switching over decisions are driven by different factors, which may include change in user-preferences, user-context, application requirements etc. Although the scope of the scenario is limited to a single operator, which does not explicitly analyze the inter-operator handover, the scenario is flexible enough to infer the effects of handovers among network operators for simultaneous interface utilization. The simulation setup focuses on the solution considering the integration of host based access with trusted 3GPP network.

Assume that Alice has contractual agreement for heterogeneous services (video and FTP) with operator-A, the operator-A has deployed LTE and WLAN access technologies, which are connected to the common core network of the operator. Although mobile Alice is under the overlapping coverage of both LTE and WLAN access technologies. Alice at different time instances use two simultaneous interfaces for both video and FTP applications, however the preferences over the interface usage is dynamic and depends on her mood, time of the day, service charges or service quality. She has the option to use one interface per application, or multiple interfaces per application meaning thereby both the applications run simultaneously on both the interfaces.

## An Overview of OPNET Simulator

OPNET is an event driven simulation, where an event is a request for a particular activity to occur at a certain time. Time, in the simulation, advances when an event occurs. The OPNET simulation maintains a single global event list, and all the objects access a shared simulation time clock. Events are scheduled on the list in time order. Upon completion of the event it is removed from the list. The event turns into an interrupt when it reaches the head of the event list and is delivered by the Simulation Kernel to the designated module. Data associated with the event can be obtained by the module when the interrupt occurs. OPNET comprises of:

1. **Subnets:** A sub network abstracts network components specified within it into a single object and represent identical constructs in an actual network.
2. **Links:** Link objects model physical layer effects between nodes, such as delays, noise, etc.
3. **Nodes:** These are basic building blocks of node models. A node model is comprised of processors, queues, transceivers and generators.

4. **Processor:** These are the primary general purpose building blocks of node models, and are fully programmable.
5. **Queues:** They offer all the functionality of processors, and can also buffer and manage a collection of data packets.

Each object has associated attributes, which can be configured to depict the object behavior. Attributes may be dynamically changeable during simulation. Different attribute values allow objects of the same type to behave differently. An attribute value can be promoted, which means that attribute value is assigned at the higher hierarchical level.

Communication protocols, algorithms, queuing disciplines, traffic generators, statistics collection mechanism are all described in the process models of OPNET. The simulation termination is dictated by factors including; 1) the event list is emptied, 2) simulation attribute duration expires, 3) a process calls for termination using the kernel process, and iv) any fatal error occurs. For more details the readers are encouraged to read the OPNET tutorial (OPNET, 2011).

## OPNET Simulation Implementation of the Scenario

The basic reference architecture shown in Figure 10 is implemented using OPNET simulator environment.

As can be viewed in Figure 10 that two access networks namely LTE and WLAN are connected to a common core network of the operator as per 3GPP recommendations for integration of 3GPP and non-3GPP access technologies (Guardini, et al., 2007). To have greater control of environment in terms of analysis, impairment entities are placed in the transport networks of each access technology. These entities introduce the controlled IP level impairments, e.g., packet delays, packet delay variations, and packet loss rate etc., hence providing more control for experimentation. Further detail about this entity is provided later

*Figure 10. Reference simulation scenario*

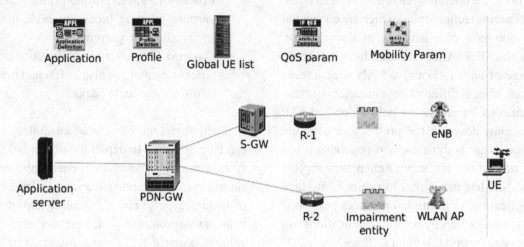

in this chapter. User terminal is multi-interface device, and capable of simultaneously connecting to multiple access technologies.

In order to simulate the reference scenario presented in Figure 10, the following entities are implemented:

1. User Equipment(UE)
2. e-Node-B (eNB)
3. Serving Gateway (S-GW)
4. Packet Data Network Gateway (PDN-GW)
5. Impairment Entity (IE)

Whereas the following entities are used in the simulation from OPNET standard node model library:

1. Wireless LAN access point, (wlan_ethernet_slip4_adv)
2. Application server, (Ethernet_server_adv)
3. Ethernet link (1000BaseX_int),
4. Routers (ethernet8_router),
5. Mobility model (Mobility Config)

## UE Node Model Implementation

The scenario provisions multi-interface terminal, which enables users to be associated with both WLAN and LTE. Figure 11 shows the protocol stack for development of such a UE node, it further indicates the respective protocols of each interface, e.g., PDCP, RLC, MAC, and PHY layers for LTE interface, and LLC, MAC, PHY for WLAN interface. This dictates that implementing these protocol functionalities is necessary to have the required UE node. All the LTE protocols are implemented following 3GPP specifications. The transmission between the UE and eNB entities is modeled on the following lines:

- To better understand the procedure in the uplink, let us assume that UE receives the grant for transmission in the uplink from eNB MAC scheduler. Upon reception of the grant UE MAC scheduler computes the "effective
- [1] SINR" value and consults the AWGN Block Error Rate (BLER) curves to determine feasible Modulation Coding Scheme

*Figure 11. Protocol stack in UE node model*

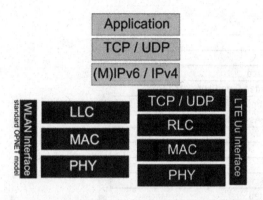

(MCS) for the target Bit Error Rate (BER). As soon as the MCS value is known, 3GPP tables (3GPP, 2010) are consulted to figure out the Transport Block Size (TBS), now that TBS is known the MAC layer requests a RLC PDU of corresponding to TBS size. RLC then creates a PDU of required size by concatenating[2] or segmenting PDCP PDUs. RLC PDUs are the handed over to MAC layer and subsequently to PHY layer for further transmission to eNB. It should be noted here that PHY layer modeling is not included in the scope of this implementation, and its scope is only to tele-port the frames received from MAC to PHY layer of eNB.

- On downlink, the data received on the physical layer is forwarded to MAC, which upon reception of the data processes the frame headers and forwards the frames to RLC layer. RLC then de-capsulates PDUs and performs the re-assembly (in case of segmented PDCP PDUs) and re-ordering to ensure the in-sequence delivery of downlink data to PDCP layer. PDCP further de-capsulates the received PDUs and forward packets to IP layer.

The transmission between UE and WLAN access point is handled by the WLAN standards modeled in OPNET inherent model libraries,

and readers are encouraged to refer the OPNET documentation for details, however for a reference the snap-shot of WLAN model attributes is given in Figure 12.

In addition to LTE and WLAN related protocol stacks shown in Figure 13, one can notice the presence of another process model called flow_manager.

As evident from the figure that data from/to both the interfaces converge to the flow_manager, this highlights the importance of the process model and provisions the detailed functionality of it. The flow_manager entity in Figure 13 takes care of splitting and managing the flow according to defined policies or any scholarly proposed algorithm. Upon implementation of algorithm in this entity, flow splitting, flow blocking, and flow steering can be performed as per requirements, and behavior/efficiency of the system may be analyzed. Figure 14 represents the process model view of the flow_manager process model entity.

Now that reader is familiar with the necessary knowledge about the protocol stack functionalities and UE basic correlation with eNB, it is the time to introduce the flow chart view[3] of these functionalities, which are followed for UE node model implementation.

A UE either receives data from eNB (downlink), or send data to eNB (uplink).

1.  In the downlink, the packets received from either interfaces (LTE or WLAN) at flow_manager process model, and are simply relayed to IP layer. At IP layer the packets are de-capsulated and further forwarded to upper layers until they reach the application layer. This is illustrated by the Figure 15.
2.  In the uplink, the packets are received from the application layer, processed in the UDP/TCP layer and forwarded to IP layer. Since the IP layer implements MIPv6, therefore, the received IP packets tunneled to HA address using IPv6 encapsulation mechanism.

*Figure 12. Snap shot of WLAN model attribute in OPNET*

| Attribute | Value |
|---|---|
| ⊟ Wireless LAN Parameters | (...) |
| —BSS Identifier | 111 |
| —Access Point Functionality | Disabled |
| —Physical Characteristics | Extended Rate PHY (802.11g) |
| —Data Rate (bps) | 54 Mbps |
| ⊞ Channel Settings | Auto Assigned |
| —Transmit Power (W) | 1.0 |
| —Packet Reception-Power Thre... | -95 |
| —Rts Threshold (bytes) | None |
| —Fragmentation Threshold (byt.. | None |
| —CTS-to-self Option | Enabled |
| —Short Retry Limit | 7 |
| —Long Retry Limit | 4 |
| —AP Beacon Interval (secs) | 0.02 |
| —Max Receive Lifetime (secs) | 0.5 |
| —Buffer Size (bits) | 1024000 |
| —Roaming Capability | Enabled |
| —Large Packet Processing | Drop |
| ⊞ PCF Parameters | Disabled |
| ⊞ HCF Parameters | Not Supported |

As can be seen from the Figure 13 the IP packet leaving the IP process model enters the flow_manager process model entity, where the packet filtering takes place (as explained earlier). The flow_manager process model decides over interface selection for forwarding the packets to either LTE or WLAN access networks.

◦ In case packets are to be forwarded to WLAN interface, the availability of WLAN network is checked. Packets are forwarded to WLAN only if the WLAN network is available, else they are forwarded to LTE network.

◦ In case packet are to be forwarded to LTE network, on the similar lines as for WLAN, the availability of LTE network is checked and packets are forwarded to LTE only if it is avail-

able, otherwise they are forwarded to WLAN.

Intuitively, when none of the networks is available, the packets are dropped. This process is illustrated in flow chart given in Figure 16.

*Note: The behavior of network selection in situations, when the preferred network is unavailable may be modified, e.g., if the preferred network interface is unavailable, then the packets may be dropped instead selecting the alternate access network.*

It's worth mentioning how the UE maintains network availability information. The network availability update process is carried out by periodically updating UE's context information. However to keep things simple, here UE measures its distance from either of the access point / eNB. Technology availability flag is set or reset based on its distance measurements from the eNB or

*Figure 13. Layered hierarchy of UE node model*

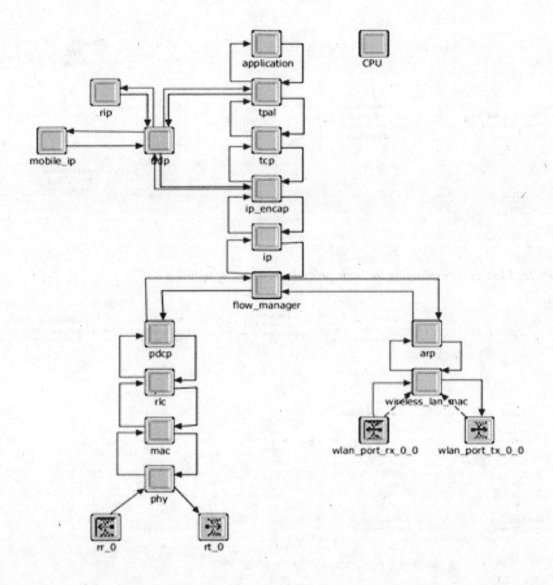

*Figure 14. Process model view of flow management entity*

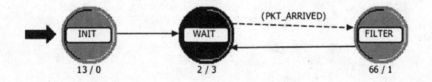

*Figure 15. Flow chart explaining the node procedure in case of downlink data*

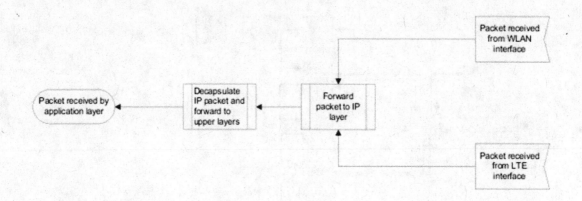

*Figure 16. Flow chart explaining the node procedure in case of uplink data*

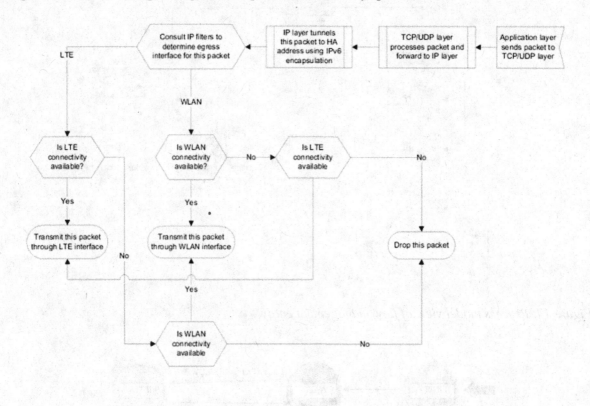

access point and the configured network coverage. This process is illustrated in Figure 17.

## eNB Node-Model Implementation

As per 3GPP specifications, eNB has at least two user-plane interfaces, namely, Uu and S1 interfaces; Uu interface is responsible for providing the radio access to UEs and S1 interface transports the data to/from Serving Gateway (S-GW) via transport network. Figure 18 shows the eNB node model respective protocol layers. The details of interface functionalities are as follows:

1. **Uu interface:** This interface includes the following four protocol entities:

   ◦ **PDCP:** The simplified version of user plan protocol layer of PDCP is implemented as per 3GPP specifications (3GPP, 2008a; 3GPP, 2008b). PDCP is mainly responsible for: (1) maintains the list of active bearers, (2) allocates the buffer space for each bearer of the active bearer list,

   (3) identifies the bearer associated with the incoming packet and buffers them in to their respective queues, (4) carries out the buffer management following buffer management techniques, such as RED, WRED, or simple tail-drop etc., and (5) performs the encapsulation and de-capsulation of PDCP PDUs.

   ◦ **RLC:** This protocol layer performs in exact similar fashion as explained in UE node model implementation, therefore, the details are left away here.

   ◦ **MAC:** This protocol layer encampuses the resource scheduling functionalities. Air interface resources are scheduled amongst the users in both uplink and downlink by the MAC schedulers. Owing to the fact that OFDM technology is used in LTE, the scheduler effectively distributes the radio resources in both time and frequency domains. The smallest

*Figure 17. Flow chart explaining the node distance time update process*

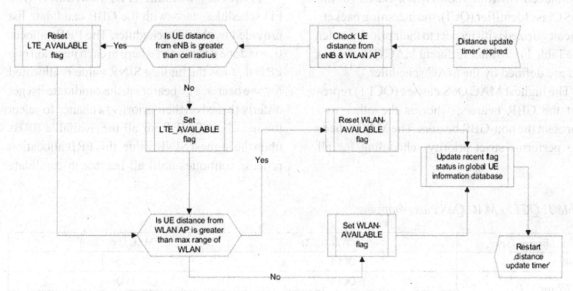

*Figure 18. Layered hierarchy and protocol stack of eNB node-model*

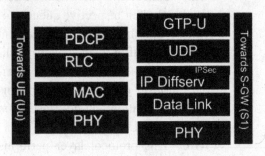

scheduling resources unit is called Physical Resource Block (PRB). LTE MAC scheduling is carried out by schedulers at two different stages; these schedulers are known as Time Domain (TD) and Frequency Domain (FD).

The TD scheduler is used to differentiate and prioritize the users according to their QoS characteristics/requirements, whereas the FD scheduler is responsible for assigning the radio resource among the users selected by TD scheduler. The MAC scheduler considers two main types of QoS bearers: Guaranteed Bit Rate (GBR) and Non-Guaranteed Bit Rate (non-GBR). Based on the QoS Class Identifier (QCI), the incoming packets are categorized with respect to their priority order (see Table 1) into three different MAC QoS classes that are defined by the MAC scheduler.

The highest MAC QoS classes (QCI 1) represent the GBR bearers, whereas the other two represent the non-GBR bearers. The MAC scheduler performs strict priority scheduling for all

GBR bearers (i.e., served first) and then scheduling of the non-GBR bearers.

**Time-Domain (TD) Scheduler:** The TD scheduler creates two candidate lists (one for GBR and the other for non-GBR). The GBR candidate list is created by adding all bearers in MAC-QoS1 As for the non-GBR bearer list, the TD scheduler adds the entire non-GBR MAC-QoS class bearers into the candidate list and then prioritizes them based on their priority factor. The priority factor is calculated as follows:

$$P_f = MQoS \,/\, R_{occur}$$
$$P_f = MQoS_{weight} \,/\, R_{avg}$$

Where $P_{f0}$ is the priority factor at iteration 0, $QoS_{weight}$ is the weight of the MAC QoS class, and $R_{avg}$ is the averaged data rate of that bearer from the past. $R_{avg}$ can be calculated as follows:

$$R_{avg}(n) := \alpha R_{avg}(n-1) + (1-\alpha)R_{inst}$$

Where $R_{avg}(n)$ is the averaged bearer data rate at the $n_{th}$ TTI, $\alpha$ is the smoothing factor, and $R_{inst}$ is the instantaneous bearer data rate at $n_{th}$ TTI.

**Frequency-Domain (FD) Scheduler:** The FD scheduler starts with the GBR candidate list provided by the TD scheduler. The PRBs allocation is done iteratively, where in each iteration one PRB that has the highest SINR value is allocated for one bearer. The bearers in the candidate list get orderly (based on their priority) a chance to select the next best PRB from all the available PRBs upon the highest SINR value, this PRB allocation process continues until all bearers in candidate

*Table 1. QCI to MAC QoS class mapping*

| Bearer Type | Service type (QCI) | MAC QoS Class |
|---|---|---|
| GBR | QCI 1 | M-QoS1 |
| Non-GBR | QCI 8 | M-QoS2 |
|  | QCI 9 | M-QoS3 |

list get one PRB. At the end of each iteration the achieved data rate of each bearer is calculated and checked if sufficient data is available in the bearer buffer to be served or if the sufficient guaranteed rate is achieved for that particular bearer. In case, one of the above conditions is satisfied, the bearer is removed from the candidate list and scheduled. Otherwise, the bearer is kept in the candidate list for the next iteration. The data rate for each bearer is calculated through the allocated PRB's SINRs, where the effective SINR value of all the allocated PRB(s) can be calculated by using the Effective Exponential SINR Mapping (EESM) Blankenship et al 2004). Then it is compared against the target SINR value that is calculated from the Additive White Gaussian Noise (AWGN) Block Error Rate (BLER) curves (by setting a target BLER value to 10%). If the effective SINR is lower than the target one, then the Modulation and Coding Scheme (MCS) is lowered, and the effective SINR is recalculated. Otherwise, using the 3GPP tables defined in (Valentin 2006), the Transport Block Size (TBS) is determined and it represents the data rate of the bearer for this TTI. Once all GBR bearers are scheduled, the FD scheduler starts scheduling the non-GBR bearers. The FD scheduler picks the highest N non-GBR bearers from the non-GBR candidate list to be served this TTI. N is a configurable parameter mostly set to 10. The same iterative procedure used in the GBR scheduling is also used here with one exception: after each iteration the non-GBR bearers are re-prioritized using the newly calculated priority factor as given below:

$$P_{fj} = (P_{fj} - 1)TBS_j$$

Where $P_{fj}$ is the priority factor at the *jth* iteration, $TBS_j$ is the transport block size at the *jth* iteration. The reason why the re-prioritization of the non-GBR bearers is done between the iterations is mainly to provide more chances to the

non-GBR bearer who has better channel conditions compared to others to select its best PRBs first.

**Channel Modeling:** The channel model includes the well known factors: path loss, slow fading and fast fading. By using the link budget the different Signal to Interference plus Noise Ratio (SINR) per each Physical Resource Block (PRB) is calculated for each connection. This represents the user channel conditions that differ between the different PRBs due to the frequency and time selectivity. The path loss is calculated as follows:

$$L = 128.1 + 37.6 Log_{10}(d)$$

The slow fading is typically modeled using a log normal distribution with zero mean and a variance, but the time correlation between the slow fading values needs to be considered. For such a model, consider a moving mobile user starting at an initial point P where the slow fading value is to be randomly generated using the log-normal distribution equal to S (0). The shadowing at points which are at distance $\delta$, $2\delta$, $3\delta$ away from P, can be determined according to (3GPP, 2010) as follows:

$$S(n\delta) = e^{-\frac{\delta}{Xc}} S((n-1)\delta) + V_i$$

Where $V_i$ are independent and identically distributed normal random variables with zero mean, and a variance $\sigma_2^2 = \sigma^2[1 - e(-2\delta / Xc)]$ in dB. $Xc$ is the de-correlation distance. As for the fast fading, the implementation of the ChSim (Valentin, 2006) is used to model the Doppler spread for the time selectivity and the delay spread for frequency selectivity.

- **PHY:** The modeling of PHY layer is out of the scope of implementation setup, therefore it is only responsible for tele-porting the frames received from MAC layer to UE physical layer.

- **S1 interface:** This interface includes the following protocol entities:
- **GTP:** The simplified version of user plan protocol layer of GTPv1 is implemented as per 3GPP specifications (3GPP, 2008a; 3GPP, 2008b). GTP creates the transport tunnel over the UDP protocol between eNB and S-GW. On the uplink, the IP packets from PDCP process model are encapsulated in GTP packet format, which are further handed over to UDP. At UDP layer the GTP packet is taken as the payload of the UDP datagram, which is then forwarded to IP layer. IP packets are then forwarded over the transport network to the S-GW. On the downlink, GTP receives the GTP encapsulated packets from UDP layer. After processing the GTP headers, the de-capsulated IP packets are forwarded to PDCP layer.
- **UDP:** The simulation includes standard OPNET model that forwards datagrams to GTP layer with a specified port number.
- **IP:** The simulation includes standard OPNET model that transmit IPv4 and IPv6 formatted packets.
- L2, and L1 layers are standard OPNET model that perform the Ethernet MAC and PHY related functions.

An important point here to notice is the block highlighting the eTPS node. eTPS is the node where diffServ model can be implemented, which may further include traffic differentiation and scheduling in the IP layer as well as shaping functionalities at the Ethernet layer in the uplink. The eTPS scheduler is specific to uplink and addresses the potential bottleneck in last mile link.

## Serving Gateway (S-GW) Node Model Implementation

S-GW is a logical entity. Figure 19 depicts the user plane transport protocols and Figure 20 represents the S-GW node model view. S-GW has two interfaces, namely, S1, that connects the S-GW to eNB, whereas on the other interface, S5 connects S-GW to PDN-GW. S5 interface is used in non-roaming scenarios, where the S-GW is located in the home network. S-GW provides on both sides peer to peer transport protocol, i.e., GTP, UDP, IP, and Ethernet, which are located towards the transport network. It should also be noted that the S-GW serves as a termination point for two GTP tunnels; one from eNB and the other from PDN-GW.

S-GW is mainly responsible for creation, deletion, modification, change of bearers for individual users connected to EPS, these functions are performed on a per PDN connection for each UE. The S-GW provides the local anchor functionality for a single terminal for all of its bearers and manages them towards PDN-GW.

In addition to the functionalities discussed in the previous paragraph, S-GW also takes care of routing uplink traffic from eNB to the PDN-GW, and downlink traffic from PDN-GW to eNB using the GTP tunnels. The traffic routing procedure details are presented in Figure 21, which says that the source IP address is checked after GTP packet decapsulation, if the source address is that of eNB, the S-GW assumes that the packet has to

*Figure 19. Protocol stack in S-GW model*

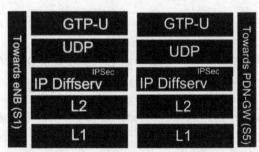

be GTP encapsulated and forwarded to PDN-GW and vice versa.

## Packet Data Network Gateway (PDN-GW) Implementation

PDN-GW is a logical entity; Figure 22 depicts the user plane transport protocols of PDN-GW. It is a central entity for connecting the external IP networks through SGi[4] interface, all 3GPP networks through S5[5] and non-3GPP networks through interface S2c[6], within the scope of this implementation, the trusted non-3GPP network

with host-based mobility solution is considered. As evident from the Figure 23 that other than the mentioned three interfaces, there exists a fourth interface, which is basically assumed to be associated with the home link of UE. As the UE is always associated with either eNB or WLAN and is never associated with its home link, therefore it can be assumed that UE is always in foreign network.

The details of PDN-GW functionalities are given earlier in this chapter. In order to understand the functionalities of PDN, let us consider a scenario, where a UE is mobile and its current point

*Figure 20. Service gate-way node model view*

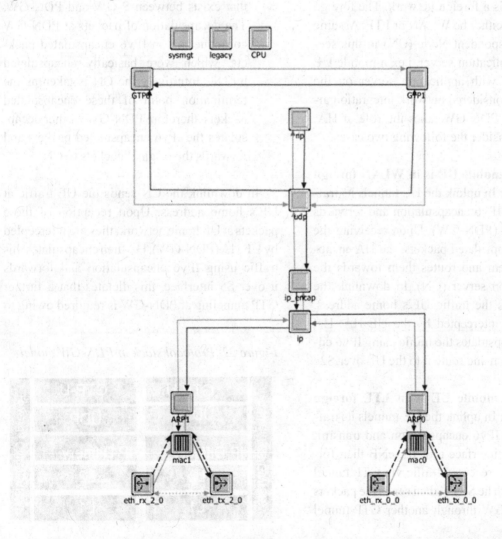

*Figure 21. Flow chart explaining the gate-way node model functionalities*

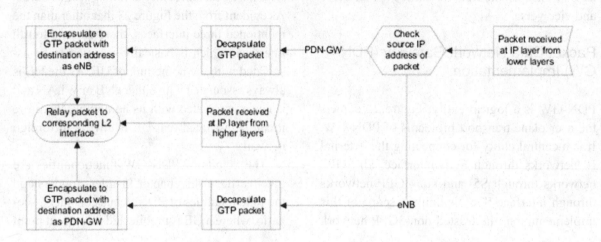

of attachment is a foreign network. The foreign networks may either be WLAN or LTE. Assume that the Correspondent Node (CN) in this scenario is an application server, i.e., a mobile UE communicates with application server on the move. In the considered network integration architecture, the PDN-GW takes the role of HA. Let us now consider the following two cases:

- **When a mobile UE is in WLAN foreign network:** In uplink the UE tunnels its traffic using IPv6 encapsulation and forwards to its HA (PDN-GW). Upon receiving the IPv6 encapsulated packets, the HA encapsulate them and routes them towards the application server (CN). In downlink the CN sends the traffic UE's home address, which is intercepted by the UE HA. HA then encapsulates the traffic using IPv6 encapsulation and route it to the UE over S2c interface.
- **When a mobile UE is in LTE foreign network:** In uplink the UE tunnels its traffic using IPv6 encapsulation and transmit it via Uu interface to eNB. eNB then forwards UE received traffic via GTP tunnel to S-GW. The S-GW then sends the packets to PDN-GW through another GTP tunnel

that exists between S-GW and PDN-GW. The decapsulation of packets at PDN-GW consequences in IPv6 encapsulated packets, which were basically encapsulated by UE. Intuitively the CN is taken as the termination point of these encapsulated packets, therefore PDN-GW further decapsulates the IPv6 encapsulated packets and forwards the original packets to CN.

In downlink the CN sends the UE traffic at UE's home address. Upon reception of these packets at UE home network, they are intercepted by UE HA (PDN-GW), HA then encapsulates this traffic using IPv6 encapsulation and forwards it over S5 interface, this dictates that a further GTP tunneling at PDN-GW is required owing to

*Figure 22. Protocol stack in PDN-GW model*

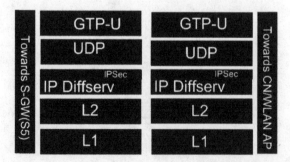

*Figure 23. Layered hierarchy of PDN-GW node-model*

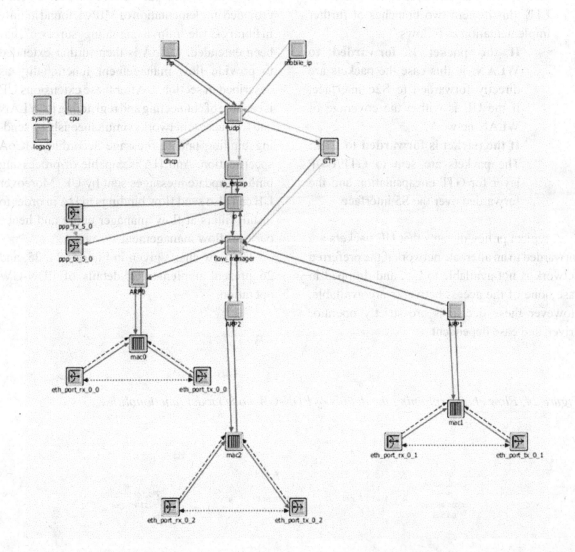

the fact that there exists a GTP tunnel between PDN-GW and S-GW. S-GW now decapsulates the received packets and in order to send these packets over another GTP tunnel between S-GW and eNB, S-GW encapsulates the packets using GTP tunneling protocol. Upon reception at eNB, the packets are decapsulated, which result in IPv6 encapsulated packets. These IPv6 encapsulated packets are then transmitted over the Uu interface to UE, where the decapsulated and forwarded to application layer.

** **When packets are forwarded to FM entity:** The flow_manager process model acts a relay to the IP process model in the uplink, whereas in the downlink it applies the filter rules over the traffic, e.g., upon reception of the packets at the flow_manager process model from the IP layer, then the flow-splitting algorithm(s) are executed and the decision over further forwarding the packets to either WLAN or LTE is taken, otherwise the packets are relayed to corresponding L2 interface. Intuitively the consequence of flow splitting algorithm is either WLAN or LTE, this discern two branches of further implementation as follows:

○ **If the packet is forwarded to WLAN:** in this case the packets are directly forwarded to S2c interface, if the UE is within the coverage of WLAN network.

○ **If the packet is forwarded to LTE:** The packets are sent to GTP/UDP layer for GTP encapsulation and the forwarded over the S5 interface.

A typical policy dictates that UE packets are forwarded to an alternate network if the preferred network is not available to UE, and dropped in case none of the access networks are available. However these decisions are strictly operator driven and case dependent.

In order to provide MCoA support OPNET provided implementation of MIPv6, found mainly in library C file "mipv6_signaling_sup.ex.c", has been extended. MCoA is then further extended to provide flow management functionality as described in section 2. After these extensions UE is capable of connecting and registering its WLAN and LTE access networks simultaneously by sending binding update message according MCoA specification. And HA is capable of processing binding update messages sent by UE. Moreover UE can also send flow bindings to HA in order to install filters at flow_manager entity and hence perform flow management.

The flow charts given in Figures 24, 25, and 26 present implemented details of PDN-GW operation.

*Figure 24. Flow chart explaining the details of PDN-GW node model functionalities*

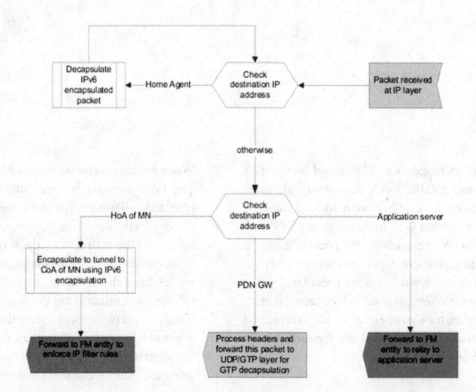

### Impairment Entity Implementation

In order to model the behavior of IP impairments in the LTE/WLAN transport network, and impairment injecting entity is simulated using OPNET simulator. This entity can impose certain packet delays, packet delay variation as well packet losses according to pre-defined impairment profiles on all packets flowing through the transport link. For generating packet delays and delay variations the probability distribution functions and associated parameters (e.g., standard deviation, mean etc.) need to be given as input for impairment injecting entity. For generating packet losses, a single packet loss ratio is specified. Packet losses introduced in IP packet stream are uniformly distributed.

Figure 27 presents the node model view of the impairment entity.

The crux of the procedure is highlighted in the flow chart given in Figure 28.

### Results of the Scenario Run on Implemented Simulation Setup

The scenario developed in "Scenario description" is analyzed on the implemented simulation setup. The implemented simulation can be useful in various research directions including mobility management (vertical/horizontal handovers, handover delays, packet loss etc.), load balancing (effects of congestion on the transport network, routing traffic on alternate paths etc.), efficiency introduced by traffic splitting, user-centric network selection etc.

*Figure 25. Flow chart explaining the details of PDN-GW node model functionalities*

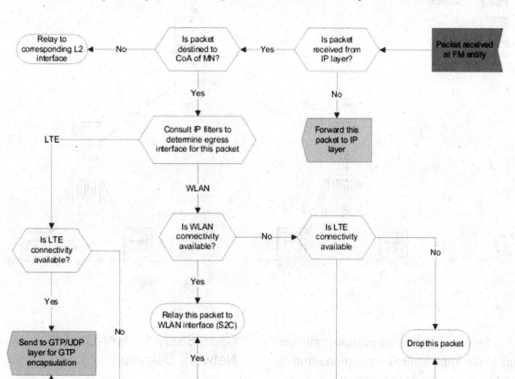

*Figure 26. Flow chart explaining the details of PDN-GW node model functionalities*

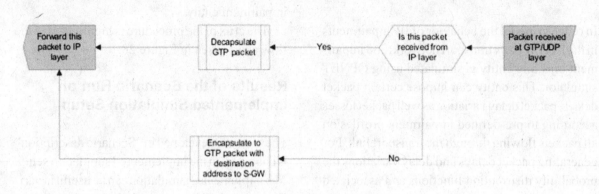

*Figure 27. The node model view of impairment entity*

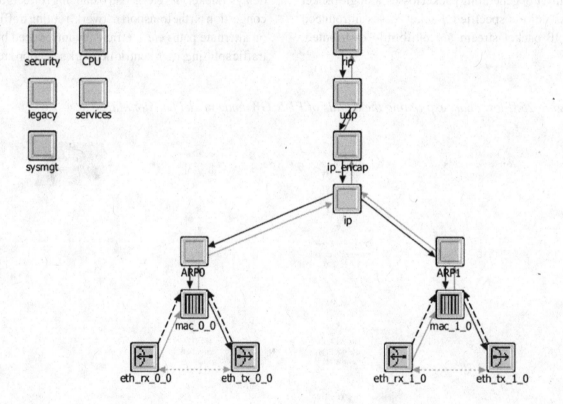

However for very minute modification or attribute settings in the implemented simulation setup are needed to analyze the desired scenario.

## Case Study 1: User-Centric Network Selection

As a first case study we analyze a simple user-centric network selection scenario in the context of scenario described in section-3.1. The simu-

*Figure 28. Flow chart presenting the details of impairment entity node model*

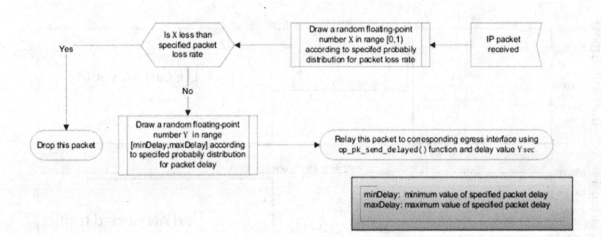

lation settings for this simple scenario say, that Alice aggregated request for both services is 600 kbps where 300 kbps are counted for video service and 300 kbps are counted for FTP. Maximum bandwidth available to FTP connection is controlled by performing shaping at IP layer of UE (not discussed in this chapter). Homogeneous quantity of traffic demands has been considered for the sake of simplicity.

At the start of simulation UE has only LTE interface available. UE attaches to LTE network, gets an IP address which is actually a CoA. Afterwards it registers its first CoA with Home Agent (HA). A moment after this operation UE detects WLAN hotspot coverage. UE attaches to the WLAN network and obtains another IP address which is its second CoA. Thanks to MCoA implementation, this allows UE to register its second CoA with Home Agent. After successful completion of this operation UE has two network access interfaces available however LTE is configured as default interface by sending a flow binding update.

At first time instance (at 300 sec in results shown in Figure 29), Alice starts two services simultaneously. Data streams of both services reach UE through LTE because it is the default interface. However just a moment later due to cheaper

WLAN access availability UE prefers shifting the FTP traffic to WLAN. This triggers a flow binding update message carrying a filter rule which is received and installed at flow manager entity inside home agent. The result of this operation is visible in Figure 29 where 300k bps of data traffic is steered towards WLAN. And therefore FTP data stream takes its path to UE through WLAN while Video is still being forwarded through the default LTE network.

Few moments later around busy hour calls the 3GPP connection, i.e., LTE is least preferred by Alice and all the traffic is transferred to WLAN. This decision of Alice again triggers the transmission of a flow binding message by UE. This flow binding update message carries a new filter rule which overrides previous filter rule. According to new filter rule WLAN shall be considered as default interface for all user traffic. After installing this filter rule now flow manager entity steers both FTP and Video traffic to WLAN interface. This effect is visible at simulation time instance 600 sec.

Although very simple scenarios run on the simulation, the objective is to evaluate the correct functionalities implementation of simulator. As can be seen that the results advocate that flow

*Figure 29. Simulation result of flow splitting for scenario in "scenario description"*

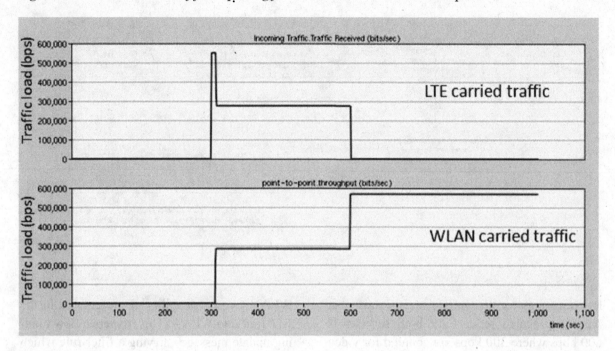

splitting functionality, handover functionality, and simultaneous connectivity functionality are accurately implemented. Flipping this scenario by activating the network-based mobility solution will provide excellent evaluation platform for operator resource allocation problems.

## Case Study 2: Effect of Transport Network Impairments on User QoE

In this case study we will analyze the effects of IP transport network impairments on user QoE by our simulation environment. Impairments are introduced using IP impairment entity and the results obtained from OPNET simulator are used to evaluate VoIP call quality. OPNET has built-in functionality for VoIP call quality evaluation using modified E-model (Cole & Rosenbluth, 2001). We have analyzed mean opinion score (MOS) (Recommendation P.800 1996) values of uncompressed voice codec G.711 (ITU-T, 1988) against different values of packet loss and packet delay. G.711 was chosen because it is lossless codec and

therefore it can be considered as a benchmark for other lossy codec like G.729A (ITU-T, 2007), GSM EFR (EST, 2005), …, etc. which are mostly used in IP networks to save network bandwidth.

In order to make the scenario simple only one user is considered in LTE system that is making a voice call using G.711 codec with data rate 96kbps. There is no user in WLAN network and user handover from LTE to WLAN network is disabled. LTE Transport network and Uu interface has sufficient bandwidth to carry this call and hence there is no congestion at any point in the system. Therefore it can be safely assumed that major component of VoIP packet end-to-end delay and loss will come from impairment entity.

Figure 30 shows interface for setting attributes values of impairment entity. The impairment entity influence both downlink (IF0) and uplink (IF1) traffic. Impairment packet delay can be defined as either a constant value or probability distribution. Moreover a probability distribution can also be truncated or time shifted using "Max packet delay," "Min packet delay" and "Time

*Figure 30. Interface for setting attributes values of impairment entity*

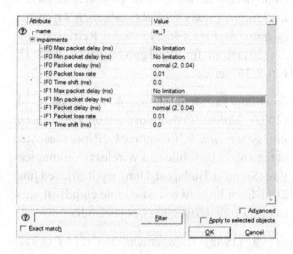

shift" values. However packet loss rate is defined as a probability of packet loss following uniform distribution.

In current scenario packet loss rate is changed from 0% to 3% and packet impairment delay is changed from 0 ms to 300 ms. Packet impairment delay follows normal distribution. Other parameters to modify packet impairment delay distribu-

tion like "Max packet delay," "Min packet delay" and "Time shift" remain unaffected.

User profile has been configured in a way that he makes VoIP call of length 90 sec and time between end of a call and start of next call is negative exponentially distributed with mean 10 s. Simulation is run for 3000 sec of simulation time and repeated for 3 different seed values. Average value of MOS from each scenario with a particular packet impairment delay and packet loss rate value is collected. Afterwards another mean MOS value is obtained by taking average of MOS values for three simulations run with different seed values. Figure 31 is the final figure of average MOS values against packet impairment delay and Packet Loss Rate (PLR).

## CONCLUSION

This chapter extensively details the simulation setup that may be used an evaluation framework for broad range of future wireless communication scholarly approaches. It also gives the detailed back ground knowledge on the provisioned stan-

*Figure 31. MOS values of G.711 codec for different packet impairment delay and packet loss rate values*

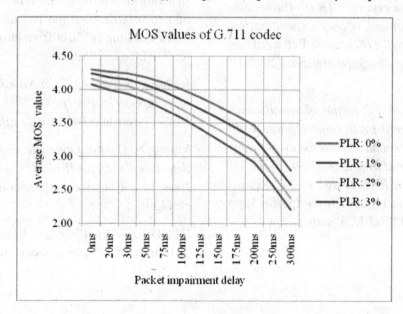

dards and approaches, thus facilitating readers with basic knowledge and guiding them to evaluate their ideas on a well know network simulation framework.

## REFERENCES

Blankenship, Y. W., Sartori, P. J., Classon, B. K., Desai, V., & Baum, K. L. (2004). Link error prediction methods for multicarrier systems. In *Proceedings of the IEEE 60th Vehicular Technology Conference (VTC 2004)*, (vol 6), (pp. 4175-4179). Los Angeles, CA: IEEE Press.

Cole, R. G., & Rosenbluth, J. (2001). Voice over IP performance monitoring. *Journal of ACM SIGCOMM Computer Communications Review*, *31*(2), 9–24. doi:10.1145/505666.505669

ETS. (2005). *European telecommunications standards institute ETS 300 726 v6.0.1:2005: Digital cellular telecommunications system (Phase 2+) (GSM): Enhanced full rate (EFR) speech transcoding: GSM 06.60 version 5.2.1*. Retrieved June, 14, 2011 from http://zmailer.org/p/mea/ham/GSM/.

3GPP. (2008a). *3GPP technical specification services and system aspects: Evolved universal terrestrial radio access (E-UTRA) - Packet data convergence protocol (PDCP) specification: 3GPP TS 36.323 v8.2.1 (Release 8)*. Retrieved June 14, 2011, from ftp://ftp.3gpp.org/specs/2008-12/Rel-8/36_series/.

3GPP. (2008b). *3GPP technical specification services and system aspects: General packet radio services (GPRS) enhancements for evolved universal terrestrial radio access network (EUTRAN) specification: 3GPP TS 23.401 v8.2.0 (Release 8)*. Retrieved June 14, 2011 from ftp://ftp.3gpp.org/specs/2008-12/Rel-8/23_series/.

3GPP. (2010). *3GPP technical specification group radio access network: Evolved universal terrestrial radio access (E-UTRA) - Physical layer procedures: 3GPP TS 36.213 v9.3.0*. Retrieved June 14, 2011 from ftp://ftp.3gpp.org/specs/2008-12/Rel-8/36_series/.

Guardini, L., Demaria, E., & La Monaca, M. (2007). *Mobile IPv6 deployment opportunities in next generation 3GPP networks*. Paper presented at the 16th IST Mobile and Wireless Communications Summit. Budapest, Hungary. Retrieved June 2011 from http://www.ist-enable.eu/pdf/ist_mobile_summit_07/session3-paper2.pdf.

ITU-T. (1988). *Recommendation ITU-T G.711: Pulse code modulation (PCM) of voice frequencies: Approved in November 1988*. Retrieved June 14, 2011 from http://www.itu.int/rec/T-REC-G.711-198811-I/en.

ITU-T. (1996). *Recommendation P.800: METHODS for subjective determination of transmission quality: APPROVED in August 1996*. Retrieved June 14, 2011 from http://www.itu.int/rec/T-REC-P.800-199608-I/en.

ITU-T. (2007). *Recommendation ITU-T G.729A: Coding of speech at 8 kbit/s using conjugate-structure algebraic-code-excited linear prediction (CS-ACELP): Approved in January 2007*. Retrieved June 14, 2011 from http://www.itu.int/rec/T-REC-G.729/en.

Johnson, D., Perkins, C., & Arkko, J. (2004). *Mobility support in IPv6 (RFC 3775)*. Retrieved June 14, 2011 from http://www.ietf.org/rfc/rfc3775.txt.

Moore, N. (2006). *Optimistic duplicate address detection (DAD) for IPv6 (RFC 4429)*. Retrieved June 14, 2011 from http://tools.ietf.org/html/rfc4429.

OPNET. (2011). *Webpage*. Retrieved June 14, 2011 from http://www.opnet.com.

Tsirtsis, G., Giaretta, G., Soliman, H., & Montavont, N. (2011). *Traffic selectors for flow bindings (RFC 6088)*. Retrieved June 14, 2011 from http://www.faqs.org/rfcs/rfc6088.html.

Tsirtsis, G., Soliman, H., Montavont, N., Giaretta, G., Montavont, N., & Kuladinithi, K. (2010). *Flow bindings in mobile IPv6 and NEMO basic support (RFC 6089)*. Retrieved June 14, 2011 from http://tools.ietf.org/id/draft-ietf-mext-flow-binding-09.html.

Valentin, S. (2006). *ChSim: A wireless channel simulator for OMNeT++*. Paper presented at the TKN TU Berlin Simulation Workshop. Berlin, Germany. Retrieved June 14, 2011 from http://www.cs.uni-paderborn.de/en/research-group/research-group-computer-networks/publications/talks-without-proceeding.html.

Wakikawa, R., Devarapalli, V., Tsirtsis, G., Ernst, T., & Nagami, K. (2009). *Multiple care-of addresses registration (RFC 5648)*. Retrieved June 14, 2011 from http://www.faqs.org/rfcs/rfc5648.html.

## ENDNOTES

[1] Effective SINR value of all allocated PRBs is calculated using effective exponential SINR mapping (Blankenship et al 2004).

[2] Concatenation is carried out in situations, where the data from multiple PDCP PDUs are packed into one RLC PUD, whereas on the contrary segmentation process bifurcates the bigger PDCP PDU into smaller size that fits RLC PDU size.

[3] Flow chart view focuses on the functionalities above L2; however the details of lower layers are already given in the start of this section.

[4] SGi interface is based on the standard OSI protocol stack

[5] S5 interface utilizes the GTP protocol over UDP / IP

[6] S2c interface implements IP over Ethernet

# Chapter 7
# Simulation of Multihop Wireless Networks in OMNeT++

**Alfonso Ariza**
*Universidad de Málaga, Spain*

**Alicia Triviño**
*Universidad de Málaga, Spain*

## ABSTRACT

*In this chapter, the authors present a brief description of the OMNeT++ network simulator with the main emphasis on the InetManet framework. This framework is especially oriented to the simulation of MANET and wireless mesh networks. It offers all the basic models and tools necessary to begin the simulation of this type of network. Since the source code is offered, the researcher can modify and include their models and they can simulate their own protocols. The InetManet is specifically oriented to the simulation of MANET over IPv4 networks. The flexibility of the code and the oriented based model of OMNeT++ (and its frameworks) allow reusing the wireless model with other types of networks.*

## INTRODUCTION

The inclusion of accurate models (propagation, mobility, traffic, etc) has enabled that simulation results are similar to those expected in a real scenario. Due to this similarity, simulation tools have become a helpful mechanism to evaluate new communication protocols. Moreover this evaluation is achieved at a reduced cost since the acquisition of expensive equipment for the

testing is avoided. As this software allows testing conditions to be maintained constant, simulation tools are a fundamental instrument in the research field of telematics where different solutions are evaluated.

Today, several simulator tools (open source and proprietary) are available. Especially in the European Universities, the simulation tool OMNeT++ (Varga, 2010a) has experienced an increasing popularity in the networking area. This Chapter intends to provide a comprehensive overview on how this simulation tool should be used to study

DOI: 10.4018/978-1-4666-0191-8.ch007

multihop wireless networks. In order to accomplish this task, some theoretical concepts related to wireless systems are also explained. With this explanation, we aim at easing the selection of models when the simulation tool is used.

This Chapter starts by describing the main characteristic of the OMNeT++ simulator. Then the analysis of the main frameworks that support the simulation of multihop wireless networks is presented. A more detailed description of the frameworks is presented in Section 4. Section 5 describes the steps to be done in a typical simulation of a multihop wireless network. Finally, some main conclusions are draws and presented in the conclusions section.

## THE OMNET++ SIMULATION TOOL

OMNeT++ (Varga, 2010a) provides a discrete-event simulation framework. Thus, the operation of a network is modeled as the chronological sequence of events. In this sense, only one type of event is considered in this simulator: the message event. For instance, a timer is implemented as a message that a module sends to itself when the timer expires. The use of just one type of message improves the simulator efficiency.

Concerning its architecture, OMNeT++ differentiates the libraries related to simulation (the core libraries) to the libraries containing the models. Models are coded in C++ so they can be easily extended. It is just necessary to know which model we should work with. Section 4 describes some of the most important models already included in OMNeT++.

A basic functionality in OMNeT++ is the use of the NED (Network Description) language (Varga, 2010a). This language possesses a syntax very similar to Java. Its main goal consists of joining several modules (which are coded in C++) so the functionality that they offer can be extended. In order to illustrate how NED works, here we present a simple example on the definition of a wireless network.

We can see in the code two areas: one concerning the specification of the parameters and another one related to the modules that are going to support the complex model. In particular, this scenario is composed of fixed hosts and mobile hosts. There is a channel in the medium and the configurator module is included in order to cope with the address configuration of the nodes. All these modules need to be configured. This is done in the configuration file omnetpp.ini.

The Integrated Development Environment allows the representation of the scenario defined in NED. For instance, the scenario specified in Figure 1 is shown in Figure 2 when the number of mobile hosts and the number of fixed hosts are set to 10 to 1 respectively.

## EXTENDING OMNET ++ FUNCTIONALITY: OMNET ++ FRAMEWORKS

Models which may be applied in similar domains are grouped into frameworks in OMNeT++. The already implemented frameworks in conjunction with the core library enable the simulation of complex systems. The most important frameworks concerning the simulation of multihop wireless networks are:

- **INET** (Varga, 2010b). It is oriented to modeling TCP/UDP/IP networks. Concerning IP implementation, it provides the model to simulate IPv4 and IPv6. 802.11-based technologies, Ethernet and PPP are also incorporated into this framework. One fork of this framework is InetManet which is intended to the modeling of multihop ad hoc networks. In this sense, InetManet provides models for multihop routing protocols, new wireless propagation models, mobility models and even obstacle models.

*Figure 1. Example of the definition of a wireless network in NED language*

```
//
network Net80211_aodv
{
    parameters:
        int numHosts;
        int numFixHosts;
        double playgroundSizeX;
        double playgroundSizeY;
    submodules:
        fixhost[numFixHosts]: FixManetRoutingHost {
            parameters:
                @display("i=device/pocketpc_s;r=,,#707070");
        }
        host[numHosts]: MobileManetRoutingHost {
            parameters:
                @display("i=device/pocketpc_s;r=,,#707070");
        }
        channelcontrol: ChannelControlExtended {
            parameters:
                playgroundSizeX = playgroundSizeX;
                playgroundSizeY = playgroundSizeY;
                @display("p=60,50;i=misc/sun");
        }
        configurator: FlatNetworkConfigurator {
            parameters:
                networkAddress = "145.236.0.0";
                netmask = "255.255.0.0";
                @display("p=140,50;i=block/cogwheel_s");
        }
    connections allowunconnected:
}
```

- **Mixim** (Koepke, 2010). It focuses on the simulation of mobile and fixed wireless networks (wireless sensor networks, body area networks, ad-hoc networks, vehicular networks, etc.). It offers detailed models of radio and link layers. In this sense, the framework includes wave propagation, interference estimation, radio transceiver power consumption and wireless MAC protocols (e.g. Zigbee). In contrast, the implementation of upper layers (networking or transport) is very simple. However, wireless networks not based on IP routing can be accurately studied with this simulator.

## INETMANET FRAMEWORK: SIMULATING 802.11-BASED MULTI-HOP NETWORKS

The InetManet framework evolves from the INET framework. It incorporates new modules that are especially necessary for wireless and multihop communications. Most modules implement models which can be grouped into the following categories:

### Propagation Models

The propagation model determines the signal strength received by a node according to its dis-

*Figure 2. Graphical representation of example of Figure 1*

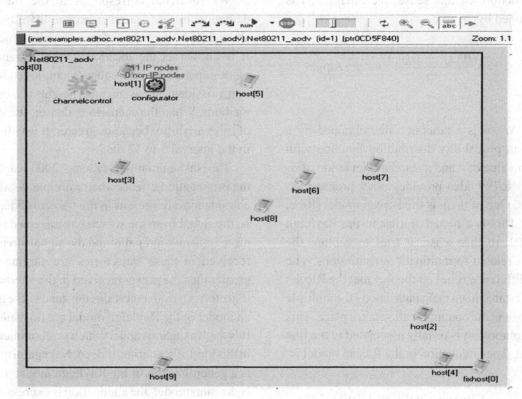

tance to the source (Rappaport, 2001) (Saunders & Aragón-Zavala, 2007). The radio module of the receptor uses this model so it can be considered as a node characteristic. This could lead to scenarios where different nodes where supported by different propagation models. In this sense, asymmetric links are easily implemented in OMNeT++.

The propagation model is specified in the configuration file. By default, this parameter is set to Free Space. In this model, the signal loss is related to the distance as follows:

$$free\,space = \left(\frac{c}{4 * \pi * d * f}\right)^2$$

Where $d$ represents the distance between the source and the receptor, $f$ the utilized frequency and $c$ is the light speed. Thus, the signal strength of the received packet ($P_r$) is:

$$P_r = P_t * free\,space$$

where $P_t$ is the power of the transmission in the source.

Although the Free space model does not model realistic propagation conditions, it is quite useful because of its simplicity. In fact, it is recommended to use it in the initial tests as it is easy to derive if two nodes are interfering each other. In this kind of models (geometric models), two nodes are connected when the distance between them does not exceed a parameter often known as the transmission range.

The Rayleigh propagation models tries to model the fading related to multipath transmissions. Multipath transmissions often occur when obstacles are present in the scenario. Under these circumstances, the signal strength in a transmission can suffer from random fadings which can be modeled by a Rayleigh probability distribution function. In this sense, the attenuation is determined by:

$$Rayleigh = \frac{N(0,1)^2 + N(0,1)^2}{2} * free\,space$$

where $N(\lambda,\sigma)$ is a random value obtained by a Gaussian probability distribution function with a mean value of $\lambda$ and a standard deviation of $\sigma$.

OMNeT++ also provides other propagation models. One of them is the Ricean model (Rice, 1948). This is a model similar to the Rayleigh proposal. In this sense, it tries to capture the fadings related to multipath transmissions. The main difference relies on the fact that the Ricean model establishes a main path among the multiple paths where the communication takes place. This main component is usually associated to the line of sight. The attenuation in the Ricean model is:

$$Ricean = \frac{\left(N(0,1) + \sqrt{2K}\right)^2 + N\left(0,1\right)^2}{2\,(K+1)}$$
$$* free\,space$$

where $K$ (the Ricean constant) models the relevance of the main component (related to the other paths). This parameter can be easily configured in OMNeT++. By default, its value is 8 dB which leads to $K = 6.3095$.

On the other hand, the lognormal propagation model captures the effects of multiple reflections and diffractions between the transmitter and the receptor. In this case, the attenuation (in dBs) is computed as:

$$attenuation(dB) = 20\log_{10}(d_0)$$
$$+20\log_{10}\left(f(Hz)\right)$$
$$-147.55 + 20\log_{10}\left(d/d_o\right)$$
$$+N(0, sigma)$$

Where *sigma* corresponds to the standard deviation in the Gaussian probability function and $d_0$ is the reference distance (usually 1 meter). It is known as the location variability and its value depends on the frequency employed in the transmissions, on the antennas heights and on the medium. When the scenario is denser, the value of this variability becomes greater. It usually fits in the interval 5 to 12 dB.

The Nakagami model (Zhang, 2003) captures the propagation effects when multiple dominant components are present in the transmission, that is, the signal from the source has traversed two o more transmission paths and the signal strengths received in these trajectories are similar (and greater than the power received in the alternative trajectories). Under these circumstances, the Ricean model or the Rayleigh model are not suitable. It is the Nakagami model which is recommended in this kind of scenarios. Indeed, Nakagami model is a generalization of the Rayleigh model. In the Nakagami model, the attenuation is expressed as:

$$Nakagami = \Gamma\left(m, \frac{free\,space\,/\,1000}{m}\right) * 1000$$

Where $m$ is the parameter of the Nakagami-m probability distribution function. In order to use this distribution, an estimation of the $m$ parameter is required. This estimation is carried out from the empirical data. Anyway, there are some methods that estimate this parameter in the literature (Saunders & Aragón-Zavala, 2007).

The two-ray propagation model is quite used in the simulation experiments. This model assumes that the transmitted signal traverse two different trajectories on its way to the receptor: one related to the line of sight and one happening when the signal is reflected from the ground. Figure 3 shows the two trajectorie considered in this model.

In order to apply this model, the anntena heights should overpass 50 meters. It is important to re-

*Figure 3. Illustration of the two-ray propagation model*

mark that there should be a minimum distance between the two antennas in order to correctly apply this model. When the antennas are very closed, the Fresnell zones do not provoke the reflection of the wave on the ground. The critical distance from which this effect does not occur is computed as:

$$Critical\,distance = \frac{4 * h_t * h_r}{\lambda}$$

Where $h_t$ is the height of the transmitter antenna, $h_r$ is the height of the receptor antenna and $\lambda$ is the wave length used in the transmission. When this distance is exceeded and has a value $d$, the attenuation is expressed as:

$$two\,ray = \left(\frac{h_t * h_r}{d^2}\right)^2$$

The propagation models affect the connectivity between nodes. Two nodes are said to be connected when the strength of the signal emitted from one of them reaches the other node with a power greater than a predetermined threshold (usually related to the sensitivity of the receptor). The zone in which this condition holds for a transmitter is known as the coverage area. The coverage area of a node is mainly affected by three basic parameters. Firstly, the propagation model determines the attenuation that a signal suffers. On the other hand, the power used by the emitter also impacts on the received signal strength. Finally, the sensitivity of the receptor is related to the required minimum signal

strength. The propagation model, the power of the transmissions and the sensitivity of the receptors are parameters easily configured in OMNeT++. In the file omnetpp.ini, we set these parameters in Figure 4.

Thus, the radius of the coverage area (*radius*) is derived from the propagation attenuation which is specific for each propagation model. This parameter is computed as:

Propogation attenuation(dB) = Power emission(dBm) – Sensitivity(dBm)

For instance, for the Free Space model, the radio is computed as:

$$20 \log_{10}\left(\frac{4 * \pi * radius * f}{c}\right)$$
$$= Power\,emision\,(dBm) - Sensitivity\,(dBm)$$

So:

$$radius = e^{\frac{Power\,emision(dBm) - Sensitivity(dBm) + 20\,\log_{10}\left(\frac{c}{4*\pi*f}\right)}{20}}$$

The obtained radius is measured in meters while the light speed is in m/s and the frequency in Hz.

## Interference Computation

Interference models and propagation models play an important role in the simulation of wireless systems. The code related to the interferences

*Figure 4. Setting of the transmission parameters*

```
**.wlan.radio.transmitterPower=2.0mW
**.wlan.radio.sensitivity=-90dBm
*.channelcontrol.carrierFrequency = 2.4GHz
*.channelcontrol.pMax = 2.0mW
*.channelcontrol.sat = -110dBm // Thermal noise
*.channelcontrol.alpha = 2
```

computation can be found in the classes GenericRadioModel, AbstractRadioExtended and AbstractRadio. The latter two classes are similar but AbstractRadioExtended allows the use of multiple radio interfaces which is not included in AbstractRadio. In constrast, AbstractRadio is more efficient so its utilization is recommended when just one interface per radio is going to be employed.

Concerning the computing in OMNeT ++, interferences are derived from the information contained in the packets. In particular, when a source emits a packet in the radio medium, this packet is sent to all the nodes that are inside the source's coverage area (the so-called neighboring nodes). In this emission, the packet is encapsulated in a special packet known as AirFrame. The special packet contains additional information such as the source's coordinates, the power transmission, the used channel and the frequency selected for the transmission. Based on the propagation model and on these additional data, the receptors are able to compute the signal strength of the received packet.

Once the packet is received, the receptor determines the time the packet has arrived and when the reception is about to end (by means of the packet length and the transmission rate). If the received packet has a signal strength greater than a configurable threshold and the node is neither transmitting nor receiving any other packet, the receptor creates a list with the interfering packets. Packets overheard by the node along the reception will be included in the created list. When the reception has ended, the signal strength of all the interfering packets are summed up leading to the interference estimation. If the interference exceeds a predetermined threshold, the simulator assumes that a collision has occurred and the upper layers are notified about this eventuality. On the other hand, when the signal to noise (noise and interference) ratio is high, the binary error rate is computed. Figure 5 depicts how this process works.

As we can see, this model considers the effect of all the packets transmitted along the reception in order to estimate the interferences. It is said to be an additive model. However, the model is not completely precise. Figure 6 illustrates the procedure to compute the interference in OMNeT++. In the case depicted in a), packet A and packet B are being sent while the target packet is received. However, their emissions do not overlap. In this case, the simulator will consider the interference as the sum of the signal strength of packet A at the receptor and the signal strength of packet B at the receptor. This is a valid assumption. In contrast, in case b), part of the transmission of packet A coincides with part of the transmission of packet B ($t_{collision}$). However, this coincidence is not taken into account by the interference computation in OMNeT++.

On the other hand, the error binary rate is based on the minimum noise strength obtained during the packet reception. In this sense, the percentage of time that this noise is present (related to the reception time) is not considered. By this assumption, a worst-case analysis is performed as the noise is thought to affect along the complete reception (see Figure 7).

The module in charge of transmitting the packets to the neighboring nodes is ChannelCon-

*Figure 5. Flowchart with the actions performed with a new wireless packet received by a node*

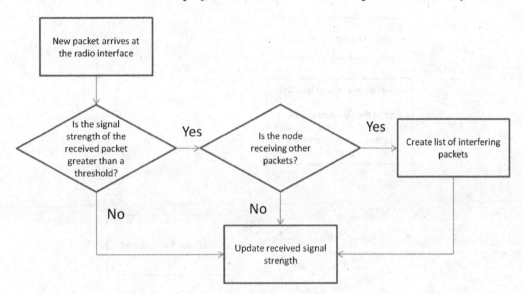

*Figure 6. Illustrative example with the additive interference model used by InetManet and INET frameworks*

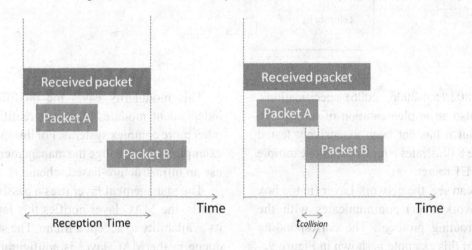

trol (if multiple interfaces are implemented in the nodes, the responsible module is ChannelControlExtended). This module determines which nodes are the neighbors of a determined sender and up to which distance communications interferes others nodes. For a scenario, only one module ChannelControl (or ChannelControlExtended for multiple interfaces) is necessary. This is independent of the number of network nodes.

The implementation considers that the channels are orthogonal, that is, different channels do not interference among them. This orthogonality is also assumed when the transmitter uses a frequency quite different from that employed by the receptor. This condition is configurable in the simulator tool.

## Link Layer Protocols

The wireless link layer models available in OMNeT++ are derived from the 802.11 (IEEE Standard 802.11-2007, 2007) and 802.15.4 (IEEE

*Figure 7. Flowchart with the actions performed once the reception of a wireless packet has ended*

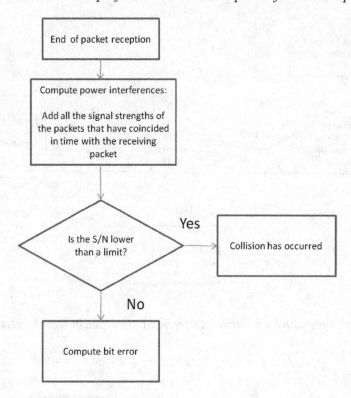

Standard 802.15.4-2006, 2006) specifications. There is also an implementation of the 802.16 protocol but it has not been extensively tested yet. Figure 8 illustrates a representative example of a MANET router.

As we can see, the network Layer (in the box titled networkLayer) communicates with the MANET routing protocol. The corresponding NED file of this example is shown in Figure 9.

In order to change the link layer, it is just necessary to modify the referenced model in "wlan:". In this example, the IEEE 802.11g is selected as the link layer so we configure the ned file with "wlan: Ieee80211gNicAdhoc". In case we need a 802.15.4 link layer, we would replace this line by "wlan: Ieee802154csmaNic".

INET framework and InetManet separate the radio layer, the management layer and the MAC functionalities. This separation is depicted in Figure 10 for a IEEE 802.11g model (named Ieee80211gNicAdHoc).

This modularity eases the modification of independent modules and their reutilization in other more complex systems. For instance, in this example we can change the management layer to use an infrastructure-based scheme.

The management layer uses a passive queue, that is, the MAC layer notifies this layer about its availability to accept a frame. The size of the queue in the MAC layer is configurable in the configuration file.

Concerning the radio layer, it can be in four states: receiving, transmitting, idle and sleeping. The radio layer notifies the MAC layer any change on its state by means of an event-based system which is similar to the signal notification defined in the POSIX standard (IEEE Standard 1003.1™-2008, 2008).

The current implementation of the IEEE 802.11 in InetManet allows the use of precomputed tables to estimate the binary error rate. Their use is not mandatory and basic models to estimate this error

*Figure 8. Graphical representation of a MANET wireless node*

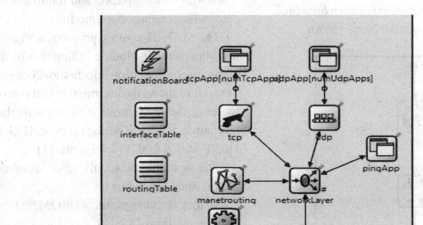

*Figure 9. Description of the MANET wireless node in NED language*

```
            globalARP = true;
            @display("p=248,247;i=block/fork;q=queue");
        gates:
            ifIn[1];
            ifOut[1];
    }
    manetrouting: ManetRouting {
        parameters:
            @display("p=153,247;i=block/network2");
    }
    //the name of radio interface must have "vlan"; valid examples vlan
    wlan: Ieee80211gNicAdhoc { // Nic80211 also works, it uses MF's 802.
        parameters:
            @display("p=248,349;q=queue;i=block/ifcard");
    }
    //      vlan: Nic80211;
    //          display: "p=248,349;q=queue;i=block/ifcard";
    mobility: NullMobility {
        parameters:
            //      x = x;
            //      y = y;
            @display("p=149,307;i=block/cogwheel");
    }
    connections allowunconnected:
```

are also available in OMNeT++. The appropriate model depends on the modulation used in the transmission. Concerning the standards, OMNeT++ provides the models for 802.11a, 802.11b and 802.11g. Additionally, 802.11e is also available in conjunction with one of the previous schemes.

An alternative implementation of the link layer for multihop wireless networks relies on 802.15.4.

*Figure 10. Graphical representation of an 802.11g interface where the separation between the MAC, management, and radio models are shown*

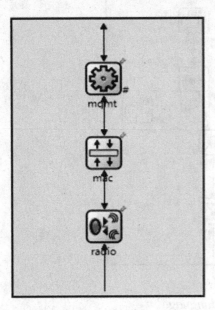

This scheme tries to reduce the consumption in the nodes so it is focused on wireless sensor networks.

## Mobile Routing Protocols

When working with multihop wireless networks, MANET (Mobile Ad hoc NETwork) routing protocols are usually employed. Most of these routing protocols are defined in their standards as modules that use the UDP transport layer (Chakeres & Perkins, 2010; Perkins, Belding-Royer, & Das, 2003; Clausen & Jacquet, 2003). However, InetManet has a peculiar implementation of the MANET routing protocol as they are directly connected to the IP network layer module. Nevertheless, the MANET protocols encapsulate packets into a UDP datagram to ensure that the simulation is realistic in terms of overhead. The main difference is that the identifier of the UDP protocol type in the IP header is set to 254. Using this setting, the IP layer knows that the packet is a MANET routing packet and it initiates the corresponding management module.

The MANET routing protocol is triggered by the Management Module in function of the omnetpp.ini configuration information. For instance, next figure shows the information that is necessary to set in the configuration file to start the DSR (Dynamic Source Routing) protocol) (Johnson, Hu, & Maltz, 2007) (see Figure 11).

The available protocols up to October 2010 are presented in Table 1.

To include these protocols in OMNeT++, their implementations in other simulators were taken into account. In the column named "Code source," we indicate the affiliation of the researchers which implemented the protocol for these other simulators. At the University of Málaga (Spain), Dr. Alfonso Ariza was in charge of adapting them to OMNeT++ and modifying them.

Once the protocol is defined in the configuration file (omnetpp.ini), it is necessary to specify their parameters. The parameters to configure depend on the routing protocol.

With these parameters, the manager module (implemented in the class ManetManager) starts and initializes the MANET routing protocol. Moreover, it can also clear the routing tables from the information set in the startup phase by the autoconfiguration modules. The autoconfiguration modules allow assigning address automatically and they also set a basic configuration in the routing table as like the default route. Although this task is really useful to automatically configure every node, its use is not suitable for wireless networks where the routing protocol should be in charge of completing the routing information. The management module can also automatically assign the IP address. To set this option, the AUTOASSIGN_ADDRESS parameter should be activated in the configuration file and the range for the IP addresses is specified by the AUTOASSIGN_ADDRESS_BASE parameter.

*Figure 11. Selection of the active MANET routing protocol in the omnetpp.ini file*

```
**.manetrouting.manetmanager.routingProtocol="DSR"
```

*Table 1. List of MANET routing protocols and the option that must be selected in the configuration file*

| Option | Protocol | Code source |
|--------|----------|-------------|
| DSR | DSR | Upsala University |
| AODV | AODV | Upsala University |
| DSDV | DSDV | |
| OLSR | OLSR | University of Murcia |
| OLSR_ETX | OLSR with ETX implementation | |
| DYMO | DYMO | University of Murcia |
| DYMOFAU | DYMO | University of Erlangen-Nürnberg |

All the MANET routing protocols implementation, except the DSR protocol, are derived from the ManetRoutingBase class. This class provides common functionalities to the different routing protocols such as encapsulation of the protocol packets in UDP packets or the possibility of using triggering functions (in this case the function will be executed when the timer expires). The ManetRoutingBase timer management uses a list of events which is independent of the list of events in the simulator. This reduces the number of events queued in the simulator event list and improves its efficiency. The improvement is achieved by means of much shorter lists (it creates one per protocol and per node) which reduces the complexity of the insertion and extraction of events in/from the lists. Moreover, this class offers methods that allow the routing protocols to modify their IP routing tables and to access to wireless interfaces data. This additional functionality simplifies the code of the protocols. Other functionality offered by this class is acting as the interface to process the signals that the MANET routing protocol may receive. In Table 2 the signals that the routing protocol can receive are shown and the method

that will be triggered when these signals are received is included in the column named Method.

Another feature which can be accessed through this class is the position of the node in the simulation area. This functionality emulates a GPS device and it allows the implementation of protocols based on the node location.

Next list summarizes the main functionalities offered by the link layer class:

- Timer triggering functions
- Position of node in the simulation area (similar to a GPS based device).
- Access to the ICMP protocol.
- Access to the IP routing table
- Access to the interface table. It is also possible to access to the information interfaces.
- Signal processing
- "Only wireless" interface table.
- UDP Encapsulation
- A transparent interface that allows that the same code may be executed using the IP layer, or directly, in the link layer without the network layer.

*Table 2. List of the signals received by the routing modules*

| Signal | Method | Description |
|---|---|---|
| NF_LINK_PROMISCUOUS | **processPromiscuous()** | Send all packets received in this node to the routing module |
| NF_LINK_FULL_PROMISCUOUS | **processFullPromiscuous()** | Send all packets listening in this node (even the packets that have destination to other nodes) to the routing module |
| NF_LINK_BREAK | **processLinkBreak()** | Notify the routing module that the transmission of a packet has failed |

Finally, the MANET routing protocols (except DSR) uses the class Uint128. This class offers a multi type address container which allows that the same code may work with IPv4, IPv6 or 40 bits MAC address indistinctly. This eases reusing the code as most part of the code can work, without changes, with IPv4, IPv6 or directly in the link layer in a similar way to the 802.11s standard (IEEE Draft Standard 802.11S, 2009).

## Mobility Models

The mobility module is in charge of managing the position of the nodes in the simulation area. This module supports a great variety of mobility models as the Random WayPoint (Broch, Maltz, Johnson, Hu, & Jetcheva, 1998) and the Constant Speed model. The supported mobility patterns can be found in the directory src/mobility.

The parameters of the model must be defined in the configuration file. Figure 12 shows how the Random WayPoint mobility model may be configured. The speed of the nodes, the pause time (waitTime) and the updateInterval are speci-

fied. In this case the selected speed is modeled as a uniform distribution between 20 m/s and 50 m/s and a pause time is randomly obtained by an exponential distribution whose mean value is 10 s.

It could happen that the available models are not appropriate for the scenario to study. Under these circumstances, it is convenient to describe the mobility pattern. To do so, there are two models that capture the mobility traces specified in a file. The first one is the BonnMotionMobility tool (University of Bonn, 2010) which uses the trace format defined in the Bonn Motion tool by the University of Bonn. The second option is the Ns2MotionMobility pattern which can work with traces following the format used in NS-2 (Fall & Varadhan, 2010).

## Battery Model

When analyzing portable devices, a model for their battery becomes necessary. The InetManet framework implements a simple model in the module InetSimpleBattery. This module can be

*Figure 12. Configuration of the random way point mobility model in the omnetpp.ini file*

```
**.host*.mobilityType = "RandomWPMobility"
**.host*.mobility.speed = uniform(20mps,50mps)
**.host*.mobility.waitTime = exponential(10s)
**.host*.mobility.updateInterval = 100ms
```

accessed by other modules so they can know the consumption that the node is making.

By default, every radio module registers itself in the battery module whenever the battery model is present in the configuration. In this registration, the radio module informs about the consumption in the four states that it manages (receiving, transmitting, idle, sleep). Whenever the radio module changes its state, the battery model modifies the way it computes the consumption.

Additionally, any module with any number of consumption states can registers in the battery module. However, it should inform about its state and about the change on the state to the battery module. This functionality could allow the computation of the battery consumption of the sensor CPU.

Figure 13 shows how the previous scenario is completed with a battery module.

## HOW TO RUN A WIRELESS-BASED SIMULATION IN OMNET++

So far, we have described the modules contained in the InetManet framework in OMNeT++. In this Section, we will focus on how the modules should be used and how their parameters can be configured. In the directories examples/adhoc, examples/wireless y examples/wpan we can find some examples that can be used as a starting point to generate our scenarios.

We will now describe the phases involved in the simulation of wireless networks in OMNeT++.

### Phase 1: What to Do Before Starting

The first step consists of establishing the simulation scenario. In this sense, it is necessary to define the simulation area. To do so, we should consider

*Figure 13. Graphical representation of a wireless router with the battery model included*

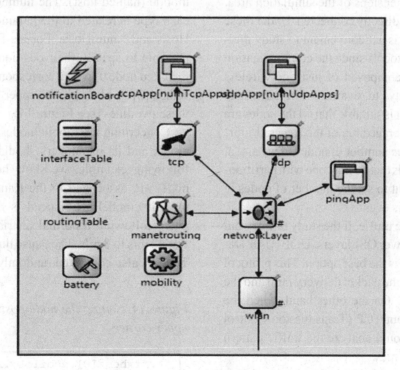

which scenario we want to emulate. The simulation area to model an office, a campus, a city or a PAN (Personal Area Network) is very different.

Then we should determine the mobility of the nodes. We should answer to the following questions. Are there fixed nodes in the scenario? Are there mobile nodes? If so, which mobility model is more convenient? Which parameters for the mobility model should be set? The work in (Kurkowski, 2006) analyses the parameters to set for the mobility model in order to obtain realistic results. On the other hand, synthetic models are also useful to compare protocols under stress conditions.

The propagation model, the MAC implementation and the transmission rates need to be defined in the scenario to simulate. For instance, a wireless sensor network should not be evaluated defining the MAC layer as 802.11 or 802.16.

On the other hand, the transmission range also impacts on the results. If this parameter is similar to the dimensions of the simulation area, the nodes may be directly connected. Under these circumstances, it is not convenient to study multihop routing protocols since the communication paths would be composed of just one wireless link. Alternatively, to evaluate infrastructure-based networks, it is suitable that all the nodes are placed in the coverage area of the Access Point.

Concerning the number of nodes, if we aim at studying protocols that do not cope with partitioning, it is important to set the number of nodes in order to avoid this event.

Relating to the traffic, if the study to carry out focuses on the lower OSI layers, UDP (User Datagram Protocol) is the best option. This protocol allows obtaining the packet delivery ratio and the end-to-end delay. On the other hand, when the evaluation is about TCP (Transmission Control Protocol), we should analyze the traffic pattern and the session times.

Finally, we should also decide the simulation time. A straight-forward answer would be: the longer, the better. However, a limit should be defined according to the goals of the simulation. For instance, if the simulation analyzes a VoIP (Voice over IP) network, the simulation time should excess ten or more times the mean time of a call. Simulation time should also permit obtaining results statistically representative.

## Phase 2: The Scenario is Defined, What is Next

Once we have determined the simulation parameters, we need to set them in the simulation tool. To do so, we need to modify the file omnetpp.ini. An example of this file for multihop wireless networks can be found in InetManet/examples/adhoc/net80211_aodv.

The parameters *.playgroundSizeX and *.playgroundSizeY are used to define the dimensions of the simulation area.

This example works with two types of nodes: fixed (named fixhost in the simulation file) and mobile (named host). The number of nodes for each type is related to the parameters *.numFixHosts and *.numHosts. For the fixed hosts, it is possible to specify their position. For instance, the fixed node 0 (which corresponds to the object fixhost[0]) is placed in the upper left corner with these two lines (see Figure 14).

Concerning the mobile nodes, their mobility model and its parameters should be set. In the following example, we show how the mobile nodes are associated to the Random WayPoint mobility model. The speed is randomly computed following a normal distribution function from 2 m/s to 8 m/s. The pause time (called wait-Time) is also computed randomly by means of a

*Figure 14. Setting the node position to the left-upper corner*

```
**.fixhost[0].mobility.x=0

**.fixhost[0].mobility.y=0
```

normal distribution from 2 seconds to 100 seconds. The parameter upadteInterval concerns the period of update, that is, how often the simulator tool updates the position of the nodes and it notifies about the changes to other modules (see Figure 15).

Relating to the propagation model, the transmission power and the radio sensitivity are set with the following code lines (see Figure 16).

The simulation time is set by the *sim-time-limit* parameter.

Since the simulation is based on random processes, it is recommended to repeat the simulation several times. Once run, the variance on the results should be studied. If the variance is too high, more simulations should be taken into account. In this context, the book (Montgomery, 2006, 2009) provides a deep understanding about how to carry out experiments with reliable results.

## Phase 3: What to do After the Simulation has been Run

Once the simulations have been run, it is time to process the results. OMNeT++ provides two methods to store the results: by means of vector files and scalar files.

Vector files store some metrics along the simulation and their corresponding temporary references. The main problem of this option relies on the fact that vector files can achieve a great size. On the other hand, scalar files store the value of these metrics just at the end of the simulation. These values are usually sufficient for the study being done.

A very helpful software tool to analyze the results is the OMNeT++ R package (Varga, 2010c). This packet allows processing the results files with the R tool (Gentleman & Ihaka, 2010), that includes advanced statistic analysis programs.

## CONCLUSION

This chapter provides a deep understanding about how OMNeT++ should be used to simulate multihop wireless networks. In particular, we have described the available models to emulate a wireless network. We have also analyzed the methodology to define the simulation parameters and how to process the results obtained in OMNeT++.

*Figure 15. Setting the mobility model for the nodes*

```
**.host*.mobilityType = "inet.mobility.RandomWPMobility"
**.host*.mobility.waitTime = truncnormal(2s, 100s)
**.host*.mobility.speed = truncnormal(2mps, 8mps)
**.host*.mobility.updateInterval = 100ms
```

*Figure 16. Parameters that determine the maximum transmission distance*

```
**.wlan.radio.transmitterPower
**.wlan.radio.sensitivity
```

# REFERENCES

Broch, J., Maltz, D., Johnson, D., Hu, Y.-C., & Jetcheva, J. (1998). *A performance comparison of multi-hop wireless ad hoc network routing protocols*. Paper presented at the ACM International Conference on Mobile Computing and Networking (Mobi-Com 1998). Dallas, TX.

Chakeres, I., & Perkins, C. (2010). Dynamic MANET on-demand (DYMO) routing. *IETF Internet Draft*. Retrieved from http://www.ietf.org.

Clausen, T., & Jacquet, T. (2003). Optimized link state routing protocol (OLSR). *IETF RFC 3626*. Retrieved from http://www.ietf.org.

Fall, K., & Varadhan, K. (Eds.). (2010). *The network simulator ns-2: Documentation*. Retrieved from http://www.isi.edu/nsnam/ns/ns-documentation.html.

Gentleman, R., & Ihaka, R. (2010). *R-project*. Retrieved from http://www.r-project.org.

IEEE Draft Standard 802.11S. (2009). *Telecommunications and information exchange between systems-local and metropolitan area networks: Specific requirements-Part 11: Wireless LAN medium access control (MAC) and physical layer (PHY) specifications-Amendment 10: Mesh networking*. New York: IEEE Press.

IEEE Standard 1003.1-2008. (2008). *Portable operating system interface (POSIX)*. New York: IEEE Press.

IEEE Standard 802.11-2007. (2007). *Telecommunications and information exchange between systems-local and metropolitan area networks: Specific requirements - Part 11: Wireless LAN medium access control (MAC) and physical layer (PHY) specifications*. New York: IEEE Press.

IEEE Standard 802.15.4-2006. (2006). *Telecommunications and information exchange between systems- local and metropolitan area networks: Specific requirements part 15.4: Wireless medium access control (MAC) and physical layer (PHY) specifications for low-rate wireless Personal area networks (WPANs)*. New York: IEEE Press.

Johnson, D., Hu, Y., & Maltz, D. (2007). *The dynamic source routing protocol (DSR) for mobile ad hoc networks for IPv4 (RFC 4728)*. Retrieved from http://www.ietf.org.

Kurkowski, S. (2006). *Credible mobile ad hoc network simulation-based studies*. PhD Dissertation. Boulder, CO: Colorado School of Mines.

MiXiM Project. (2010). *Website*. Retrieved from http://mixim.sourceforge.net.

Montgomery, D. C. (2006). *Applied statistics and probability for engineers* (4th ed.). New York: John Wiley.

Montgomery, D. C. (2009). *Design and analysis of experiments* (7th ed.). New York: John Wiley.

Perkins, C., Belding-Royer, E., & Das, S. (2003). *Ad hoc on-demand distance vector (AODV) routing, (RFC 3561)*. Retrieved from http://www.ietf.org.

Rappaport, T. (2001). *Wireless communications: Principles and practice* (2nd ed.). Upper Saddle River, NJ: Prentice Hall.

Rice, S. O. (1948). Mathematical analysis of a sine wave plus random noise. *The Bell System Technical Journal*, *27*(1), 109–157.

Saunders, S., & Aragón-Zavala, A. (2007). *Antennas and propagation for wireless communication systems* (2nd ed.). Chichester, UK: John Wiley.

University of Bonn. (2010). *BonnMotion: A mobility scenario generation and analysis tool*. Retrieved from http://net.cs.uni-bonn.de/wg/cs/applications/bonnmotion.

Varga, A. (2010a). *OMNeT++ user manual*. Retrieved May 2011 from http://www.omnetpp.org/doc/omnetpp41/manual/usman.html.

Varga, A. (2010b). *INET-framework*. Retrieved from http://inet.omnetpp.org.

Varga, A. (2010c). *Omnetpp R package*. Retrieved from http://github.com/omnetpp/omnetpp-result-files/wiki/Tutorial-for-the-omnetpp-r-package.

Zhang, Q. T. (2003). A generic correlated Nakagami fading model for wireless communications. *IEEE Transactions on Communications, 51*(11), 1745–1748. doi:10.1109/TCOMM.2003.819216

## KEY TERMS AND DEFINITIONS

**Battery Model:** Consumption model for a node. The battery model tries to model the energy consumption of the different components of a node and how much time the node can work with a battery of a nominal capacity.

**Discrete Event Simulator:** A simulator where the operation of the system is represented as a chronological list of events. Each even occurs at an instant of time and it marks a change in the state of the system. A characteristic of this type of simulator is that the timer of the system is increased in the interval that there is between two consecutive events.

**INETManet:** Framework belonging to OMNeT++ which implements the source code related to MANETs.

**Interference Model:** Mathematical algorithm used to compute the Signal to Noise received by a node.

**Mobile Ad Hoc Network (MANET):** Wireless communication network in which nodes can move and the nodes can work like routers and hosts interchangeably. This communication paradigm allows the communication between nodes that are outside direct range.

**Mobility Model:** Pattern that determines how the nodes move around the landscape. These patterns can be synthetic or can be based in captured traces. In the case of synthetic patterns the model can reproduce similar behavior observed in real objects. In this case the pattern is realistic. Otherwise, it is an unrealistic model. The unrealistic model are usually more simple to implement and more stressful for the network so that they are useful to test the network under the worst conditions.

**Omnet++:** Object-oriented Modular discrete event Network Simulation framework. Discrete event simulator written in C++. It is multiplatform and oriented to the simulation of packet communication networks.

**Propagation Model:** Mathematical algorithm used to compute the strength of a signal radiated with a predeterminated power (which depends on the distance to the destination).

**Routing Protocol:** Communication protocol that has the objective of finding a path between groups of nodes. There are multiple classification criteria. The most common criteria of classification are: depending of the size of this groups, the protocols can be classified unicast (one-to-one), multicast (one-to-many or many-to-many) and anycast (one to any in a group); depending on how the information are processed, the protocols can be classified in link state or vector state; depending where the routing decision is taken, it can be centralized or distributed; and depending how the protocol reacts, the protocols can be classified in reactive (the route are searched on demand) or proactive (the protocol are searching the routes even if the route is not used).

**Wireless Medium Access Control (MAC):** Link layer protocol used directly upper the physical layer and designed with the intention of optimizing the transference of data with a specific physical media. The MAC protocol has a direct influence in the consumption and in the performance due to the close collaboration with the physical layer.

# Chapter 8
# Simulation of a Dynamic-Noise-Dependent Probabilistic Algorithm in MANETs

**Hussein Al-Bahadili**
*Petra University, Jordan*

**Alia Sabri**
*Applied Science University, Jordan*

## ABSTRACT

*In the current dynamic probabilistic algorithm, the retransmission probability ($p_t$) has always been formulated as a linear/non-linear function of a single variable, namely, the number of first-hop neighbors (k), and therefore denoted as $p_t(k)$. The performance of the probabilistic algorithm has severely suffered in the presence of noise due to the reduction in the probability of reception ($p_c$) of route request packets by receiving nodes. This chapter presents a detailed description of a new dynamic probabilistic algorithm in which $p_t$ is determined as a function of k and $p_c$, and therefore, it is referred to as the Dynamic Noise-Dependent Probabilistic (DNDP) algorithm. The DNDP algorithm is implemented using the Mobile Ad Hoc Network (MANET) Simulator (MANSim), which is used to simulate a number of scenarios to evaluate and compare the performance of the algorithm with pure flooding and fixed and dynamic probabilistic algorithms. The simulation's results demonstrated that the DNDP algorithm provides an excellent performance in various network conditions, where it almost maintains the same network reach-ability in noiseless and noisy environments, with the noisy environments inflicting an insignificant increase in the number of redundant retransmissions.*

## INTRODUCTION

A Mobile Ad Hoc Network (MANET) is defined as a collection of low-power wireless mobile nodes forming a temporary network without the aid of any established infrastructure or central-

ized administration (Toh, 2002). A data packet in a MANET is forwarded to other mobile nodes within the network through a reliable and an efficient route established by routing protocols (Sasson et al 2003). The most widely used routing protocols in MANETs are known as dynamic routing protocols, such as: Ad Hoc On-Demand Distance Vector Routing (AODV) (Perkins &

DOI: 10.4018/978-1-4666-0191-8.ch008

Royer, 1999), Dynamic Source Routing (DSR) (Johnson & Maltz, 1995), Zone Routing Protocol (ZRP) (Joa-Ng & Lu, 1999), and Location-Aided Routing (LAR) (Boleng & Camp, 2004, Ko & Vaidya, 2000).

Dynamic routing protocols consist of two major phases, these are: (1) route discovery in which a route between source and destination nodes is established for the first time, and (2) route maintenance in which the route is maintained; and if it is broken for any reason, then the source node either finds other known route on its routing table or initiates new route discovery procedure (Royer & Toh, 1999, Rajaraman, 2002). It has been recognized that the cost of information exchange during route discovery is higher than the cost of point-to-point data forwarding after the route is established (Rahman, et al., 2004).

Broadcasting is a fundamental communication primitive for route discovery in MANETs. One of the earliest broadcast mechanisms proposed in the literature is pure flooding, which is also called simple or blind flooding (Bani-Yassin, et al., 2006). Although it is simple and reliable, pure flooding is costly where it costs $n$ transmissions in a network of $n$ reachable nodes. In addition, pure flooding in wireless networks results in serious redundancy, contention, and collisions in the network; such a scenario has often been referred to as the Broadcast Storm Problem (BSP) (Tseng, et al., 2002).

To eliminate the effects of the BSP during route discovery in MANETs, a variety of flooding optimization techniques have been developed to reduce the number of retransmission. As the number of retransmissions required for broadcasting is decreased, the bandwidth is saved and contention, collision, and node power consumption are reduced, and this will improve the overall network performance. Examples of flooding optimization algorithms: probabilistic broadcast (Al-Bahadili, 2010, Al-Bahadili & Kaabneh, 2010, Bani-Yassin, et al., 2006), LAR (Ko & Vaidya, 2000), Multi-point Relaying (MPR) (Al-Bahadili & Jaradat,

2010; Qayyum, et al., 2002), counter-based and distance-based (Tseng, et al., 2002), cluster-based (Bettstetter, 2004), etc.

This chapter concerns with the probabilistic broadcast algorithm. In this algorithm, each intermediate node (any node on the network except the source and the destination) is assigned a certain retransmission probability ($p_t$). There are two approaches that can be used to set a satisfactory $p_t$ for intermediate nodes within the network, namely, static and dynamic approaches. In the former approach, a pre-determined $p_t$ is set for each node on the networks, while for the later, each node on the network locally and dynamically calculates its $p_t$ according to the number of first-hop neighboring nodes ($k$) and therefore $p_t$ is expressed as: $p_t = f(k)$, where $f(k)$ is a linear/non-linear function of $k$.

In reality, communication channels in MANETs are unreliable due to many types of impairments, such as: signal attenuation, free space loss, noise, atmospheric absorption, etc. In addition, in MANETs, error in reception may occur due to rapidly changing topologies that are caused by nodes movement. All of these impairments and changing topologies may cause an error in reception and are represented by a generic name, noise (Al-Bahadili & Jaradat, 2007). The effect of noise in MANET can be simulated through introducing a probability factor that is the probability of reception ($p_c$), and then the effect of noise can be determined randomly by generating a random number $\xi$ ($0 \leq \xi < 1$). If $\xi \leq p_c$, then the packets is successfully delivered to the receiving node, otherwise, unsuccessful delivery occurs and the packet is lost.

It has been proved in the literature that the performance of probabilistic route discovery algorithm is severely suffered in presence of noise (Al-Bahadili & Kaabneh, 2010). Due to the fact that presence of noise increases packet-loss rate in the network or in other words it decreases $p_c$ of a RREQ packet by neighboring nodes and consequently the destination node. In order to enhance the performance of the dynamic probabilistic route discovery algorithm in noisy MANETs, we believe it is necessary to accommodate the inevitable presence of noise in MANET's environment.

In this chapter, we provide a detail description of a dynamic probabilistic route discovery algorithm in which $p_t$ is calculated locally considering both $k$ and $p_c$, i.e., $p_t=f(k, p_c)$; and the algorithm is referred to as the dynamic noise-dependent probabilistic (DNDP) algorithm (Al-Bahadili & Sabri, 2011, Al-Bahadili, et al., 2011). The proposed algorithm is implemented on the MANET simulator (MANSim) (Al-Bahadili, 2010). The performance of the proposed algorithm is evaluated through a number of simulations. The outcomes of these simulations demonstrated that the DNDP algorithm presents higher network reachability than the current dynamic noise-independent probabilistic algorithm at a reasonable increase in the number of retransmissions for a wide range of $p_c$'s or noise-levels.

## PREVIOUS WORK

In this section we present a review of some of the most recent and related work on probabilistic flooding in both noiseless and noisy MANETs. Probabilistic algorithm was used for ad hoc route discovery by Haas et al (2002), and they called it a Gossip-Based Ad Hoc Route Discovery (GOSSIP1) approach. They used a predefined $p_t$ to decide whether or not an intermediate node forwards the RREQ packets. GOSSIP1 has a slight problem with initial conditions. If the source has relatively few neighbors, there is a chance that none of them will gossip, and the gossip will die. Similar conclusions were also explored by Ni et al 1999. To make sure this does not happen, Haas et al proposed a modified protocol, in which they gossip with $p_t=1$ for the first $h$ hops before continuing to gossip with $p_t<1$. Their results showed that they can save up to 35% message overhead compared to pure flooding. Furthermore, adding gossiping to a protocol such AODV and ZRP not only gives improvements in the number of messages sent, but also results in improved network performance in terms of end-to-end latency and throughput.

Tseng et al (2002) investigated the performance of the probabilistic flooding for various network densities in noise-free environment. They presented results for three network parameters, namely, reachability, saved rebroadcast, and average latency, as a function of $p_t$ and network density.

Sasson et al (2003) explored the phase transition phenomenon observed in percolation theory and random graphs as a basis for defining probabilistic flooding algorithms. They also suggested exploring algorithms in which nodes would dynamically adjust their $p_t$ based on local topology information. Because in their work they made the assumption that all nodes possess the same transmission range, they suggested another potential area for study which is to modify $p_t$ of the transmitting according to its radio transmission range.

Kim et al (2004) introduced a dynamic probabilistic broadcasting approach with coverage area and neighbors confirmation for MANETs. Their scheme combines probabilistic approach with the area-based approach. A mobile host can dynamically adjust $p_t$ according to its additional coverage in its neighborhood. The additional coverage is estimated by the distance from the sender. The simulation results showed this approach generates fewer rebroadcasts than pure flooding approach. It also incurs lower broadcast collision without sacrificing high reachability.

Scott & Yasinsac (2004) presented a dynamic probabilistic solution that is appropriate to solving broadcast storm problems in dense mobile networks, also referred to as gossip protocol. The approach can prevent broadcast storms during flooding in dense networks and can enhance comprehensive delivery in sparse networks.

Bani-Yassein et al (2006) proposed a dynamic probabilistic flooding algorithm in MANETs to improve network reachability and saved rebroadcast. The algorithm determines $p_t$ by considering the network density and node movement. This is done based on locally available information and without requiring any assistance of distance measurements or exact location determination devices. The algorithm controls the frequency of rebroadcasts and thus might save network resources without affecting delivery ratios.

Viswanath & Obraczka (2005) developed an analytical model to study the performance of plain and probabilistic flooding in terms of its reliability and reachability in delivering packets. They provided simulation results to validate the model. The preliminary simulation results indicated that probabilistic flooding can provide similar reliability and reachability guarantees as plain flooding at a lower overhead.

Zhang & Agrawal (2005) proposed a probabilistic approach that dynamically adjusts $p_t$ as per the node distribution and node movement. The approach combines between probabilistic and counter-based approaches. They evaluated the performance of their approach by comparing it with the AODV protocol (which is based on simple flooding) as well as a fixed probabilistic approach. Simulation results showed that the approach performs better than both simple flooding and fixed probabilistic schemes.

Bani Yassein et al (2007) combined probabilistic and knowledge based approaches on the AODV protocol to enhance the performance of existing protocol by reducing the communication overhead incurred during the route discovery process. The simulation results revealed that equipping AODV with fixed and adjusted probabilistic flooding helps to reduce the overhead of the route discovery process whilst maintaining comparable performance levels in terms of saved rebroadcasts and reachability as achieved by conventional AODV. Moreover, the results indicated that the adjusted probabilistic technique results in better performance compared to the fixed one for both of these metrics.

Abdulai et al (2006) analyzed the performance of AODV protocol over a range of possible $p_t$. Their studies focused on the route discovery part of the routing algorithm, they modified the AODV routing protocol implementation to incorporate $p_t$; the RREQ packets are forwarded in accordance with a predetermined $p_t$. Results obtained showed that setting efficient $p_t$ has a significant effect on the general performance of the protocol. The results also revealed that the optimal $p_t$ for efficient performance is affected by the prevailing network conditions such as traffic load, node density, and node mobility. During their study they observed that the optimal $p_t$ is around 0.5 in the presence of dense network conditions and around 0.6 for sparse network conditions.

Abdulai et al. (2007) proposed two probabilistic methods for on-demand route discovery, that is simple to implement and can significantly reduce the overhead involved in the dissemination of RREQs. The two probabilistic methods are: the Adjusted Probabilistic (AP) and the Enhanced Adjusted Probabilistic (EAP) which address the broadcast storm problem in the existing OADV routing protocols.

Hanash et al. (2009) proposed a dynamic probabilistic broadcast approach that can efficiently reduce broadcast redundancy in MANETs. The algorithm dynamically calculates $p_t$ according to $k$. They compared their approach against simple flooding approach, fixed probabilistic approach, and adjusted probabilistic flooding by implementing them in a modified version of the AODV protocol using the GloMoSim network simulator. The simulation results showed that broadcast redundancy can be significantly reduced through their approach while keeping the reachability high. It also demonstrates lower broadcast latency than all the existing approaches presented.

Khan et al. (2008) proposed a coverage-based dynamically adjusted probabilistic forwarding scheme and compared its performance with simple flooding and fixed probabilistic schemes. The proposed scheme keeps up the reachability of pure flooding while maintaining the simplicity of probability based schemes.

Barret et al. (2005) introduced probabilistic routing protocols for sensor networks, in which an intermediate sensor decides to forward a message with $p_t$ that depends on various parameters, such as the distance of the sensor to the destination, the distance of the source sensor to the destination, or the number of hops a packet has already traveled. They proposed two protocol variants of this family and compared the new methods to other probabilistic and deterministic protocols, namely constant-probability gossiping, uncontrolled flooding, random wandering, shortest path routing, and a load-spreading shortest-path protocol. The results showed that the multi-path protocols are less sensitive to misinformation, and suggest that in the presence of noisy data, a limited flooding strategy will actually perform better and use fewer resources than an attempted single-path routing strategy, with the parametric probabilistic sensor network routing protocols outperforming other protocols. The results also suggested that protocols using network information perform better than protocols that do not, even in the presence of strong noise.

Al-Bahadili & Jaradat (2007) investigated the effect of noise-level on the performance of the probabilistic algorithm in MANETs. They investigated the effect of node density, node average speed, radio transmission range, $p_t$, and $p_c$ on number of retransmissions, duplicate reception, average hop count, and reachability. Their results showed that the performance of the network is severely suffered as $p_c$ increases, i.e. the noise-level increases.

## WIRELESS NETWORK ENVIRONMENTS

Depending on presence of noise, MANET environment can be categorized into two types; these are (Al-Bahadili & Jaradat, 2007, Al-Bahadili & Kaabneh, 2010):

1.  Noiseless (error-free) environment. It represents an ideal network environment, in which all data transmitted by a source node is assumed to be successfully and correctly received by a destination node. It can be characterized by the following axioms or assumptions:
    ◦   The world is flat
    ◦   All radios have equal range, and their transmission range is circular
    ◦   Communication link symmetry
    ◦   Perfect link
    ◦   Signal strength is a simple function of distance

The above assumptions are still part of many MANET'S simulation studies, despite the increasing awareness of the need to represent more realistic noisy features.

2.  Noisy (error-prone) environment. It represents a realistic network environment, in which the received signal will differ from the transmitted signal, due to various transmission impairments, such as:
    ◦   Wireless signal attenuation ($p_{att}$)
    ◦   Free space loss ($p_{free}$)
    ◦   Thermal noise ($p_{therm}$)
    ◦   Atmospheric absorption ($p_{atm}$)
    ◦   Multipath effect ($p_{mult}$)
    ◦   Refraction ($p_{ref}$)

All of these impairments are represented by a generic name, noise. The environment is called noisy environment. For modeling and simulation purposes, the noisy environment can be described by introducing a probability function, which referred to as the probability of reception ($p_c$). It defined as the probability that a wireless transmitted data is survived being lost and successfully delivered to a destination node despite the presence of all or any of the above impairments. Thus, $p_c$ can be calculated as:

$$p_c = p_{att} \cdot p_{free} \cdot p_{therm} \cdot p_{atm} \cdot p_{mult} \cdot p_{ref} \cdots\cdots \qquad (1)$$

## ROUTE DISCOVERY IN MANET

This section introduces the concept of route discovery. To initiate a route discovery process, the source node transmits a Route Request (RREQ) packet as a single local broadcast packet, which is received by (approximately) all nodes currently within the radio transmission range of the source node. Each RREQ packet identifies the source (initiator) and the destination (target) of the route discovery, and also contains a unique request sequence number or identification number (ID), determined by the source of the request. Each RREQ also contains a record listing the addresses of intermediate nodes through which this particular copy of the RREQ packet has been forwarded. This route record is initialized to an empty list by the source of the route discovery. In addition, the header of the RREQ packet contains information on the lifetime of the request. This is expressed in terms of the maximum number of intermediate nodes (hop-count) that are allowed to forward the data packet from the source node to the destination node.

During the route discovery phase, each intermediate node reduces the hop-count by 1. If at a particular intermediate node, the hop-count approaches 0 before the RREQ reaches its destination, an error is detected and this is considered as an unsuccessful route discovery process. Then, this last node sends back a unicast Route Error (RERR) packet to the source. Upon receiving it, the source node initiates a new RREQ with different sequence number. If the destination node is located and successfully receives the RREQ, the destination node sends back a unicast Route Reply (RREP) packet to the source node; otherwise, if the destination node is not located, then this is considered as an unsuccessful route discovery

process and the source node should initiate a new RREQ with different sequence number. The RREP packet usually follows the same route followed by the first RREQ that has reached the destination, but in reverse order (Royer & Toh 1999).

## PURE FLOODING

Pure flooding (also known as simple or blind flooding) is a fundamental communication primitive for route discovery in DRPs in MANETs. In pure flooding, each node apart from the source and the destination rebroadcasts the RREQ to its neighbors upon receiving it for the first time. In this algorithm, nodes are allowed to rebroadcast the same packet only once (packets are identified through their sequence number). Figure 1 outlines this pure flooding broadcast algorithm (Bani-Yassein, et al., 2006).

It can be easily observed in pure flooding that the RREQ would reach every node that is reachable on the network, and some measures may be needed to damp long lived packets. One such measure is to have a hop counter contained in the header of each packet, which is decremented at each hop, with the packet being discarded when the counter reaches zero. Ideally, the hop counter should be initialized with an adequate value representing the length of the path from source to destination. If the sender does not know how many hops the path is, it can initialize the counter to the worst case, namely, the maximum hop-count.

The main advantages of pure flooding are its simplicity and reliability. At the same time pure flooding suffers from serious redundancy, contention, and collisions; such a scenario has often been referred to as the Broadcast Storm Problem (BSP) (Tseng, et al., 2002). Thus, effective and efficient broadcasting protocols are always required to limit the probability of collisions and contention by limiting the number of retransmissions in the network.

*Figure 1. Pure flooding algorithm*

> On receiving a RREQ packet at node $i$, do the following:
> **If** Ret($i$)=0 **Then** // Ret($i$) is a flag that indicates whether node $i$ have or haven't transmitted the RREQ packet before.
>     Retransmit packet // The node has not retransmit the request before Ret($i$)=0.
>     Ret($i$)=1 // Update the node retransmission index Ret($i$) by equating it to 1.
> **End if**

## PROBABILISTIC FLOODING ALGORITHM

Probabilistic algorithm is widely-used for flooding optimization during route discovery in MANETs. It aims at reducing number of retransmissions, in an attempt to alleviate the effects of the BSP in MANETs (Al-Bahadili, 2010; Al-Bahadili & Kaabneh, 2010; Bani-Yassin, et al., 2006). In this scheme, when receiving a RREQ packet, a node retransmits the packet with a certain $p_t$ and with probability $(1-p_t)$ it discards the packet. A node is allowed to retransmit a given RREQ packet only once, i.e., if a node receives a packet, it checks to see if it has retransmitted it before, if so then it just discards it, otherwise it performs its probabilistic retransmission check. Nodes usually can identify the RREQ packet through its sequence number. The source node $p_t$ is always set to 1, to enable the source node to initialize the RREQ. While, $p_t$ for intermediate nodes (all nodes except the source) is determined using a static or dynamic approach.

There are two approaches that can be used to set a satisfactory $p_t$ for intermediate nodes within a noiseless wireless environment. These are:

1. Static approach in which a pre-determined $p_t$ ($P_t$) ($0 \leq P_t \leq 1$) is set for each node on the networks.
2. Dynamic approach in which each node on the network locally calculates its $p_t$ using certain probability distribution function of one or more independent variables.

Figure 2 outlines the probabilistic broadcast algorithm.

## DETERMINATION OF DYNAMIC RETRANSMISSION PROBABILITY

### Determination of Dynamic $p_t$ in Noiseless Environment

In a dynamic probabilistic algorithm, $p_t$ is usually calculated as a function of the number of first-hop neighbors ($k$), and it is referred to as $p_t(k)$. Many functions have been developed for calculating $p_t(k)$ (Al-Bahadili, 2010; Bani-Yassin, et al., 2006; Hass, et al., 2002; Kim, et al., 2004; Sasson, et al., 2003; Scott & Yasinsac, 2004; Zhang & Agrawal, 2005).

In this work, the function for $p_t(k)$ presented in Al-Bahadili (2010) is considered. This is because it demonstrated an excellent performance in comparison with other distribution functions in various network conditions, which is calculated as:

$$p_t = \begin{cases} p_{\max} & for\ k \leq N_1 \\ p_1 - \dfrac{k - N_1}{N_2 - N_1}(p_1 - p_2) & for\ N_1 < k < N_2 \\ p_{\min} & for\ k \geq N_2 \end{cases}$$

(2)

Where $p_t(k)$ is the node retransmission probability; $k$ is the number of first-hop neighbor for the transmitting node; $p_{min}$ is the minimum $p_t$ that could be assigned for a node; $p_{max}$ is the maximum $p_t$ that could be assigned for a node; $N_1$ is the number of nodes at or below which $p_t$ is equal to $p_{max}$; $N_2$ is the number of nodes at or above which $p_t$ is equal to $p_{min}$, $p_1$ and $p_2$ are the $p_t$s assigned to intermediate nodes surrounded by $k=N_1+1$ and $k=N_2-1$ nodes, respectively, $p_1$ and $p_2$ should lie

*Figure 2. The probabilistic broadcast algorithm*

**If** (IRange=1) **Then** {The receiving node is within the transmission range of the sender, in a noiseless
                environment this guarantees request reception by the receiver. IRange=0 means the receiver
                is not within the transmission range of the sender}
  **If** (IRet(i)=0) **Then** {The node has not retransmitted the request before (IRet(i)=0)}
    $\xi_1$=rnd() {$\xi_1$ some random number between 0 and 1}
    $p_t$=function_$p_t$()
    **If** ($\xi_1 <= p_t$) **Then**
      Retransmit RREQ
      IRet(i)=1 {Update the node retransmission index IRet(i) by equating it to 1}
    **End if**
  **End if**
**End if**
**Function_$p_t$()** {Determining $p_t$}
  **If** (IProb="Static") **Then** {IProb is an integer indicates the approach to be used for determining $p_t$ whether it is
                static or dynamic}
    $p_t$=constant value
  **Else** (IProb="Dynamic")
    $p_t$=$f(k)$
**End If**

between $p_{max}$ and $p_{min}$ (i.e., $p_{max} \geq p_{1/2} \geq p_{min}$), and also $p_1 \geq p_2$. Figure 3 shows the variation of $p_t$ with $k$. In general, selection of satisfactory distribution in the interval [$N_1$+1, $N_2$-1] and the values of $p_{max}$, $p_{min}$, $p_1$, $p_2$, $N_1$, and $N_2$ depend on a number of factors and need to be carefully considered for every network condition.

The reasons for selecting three rages can be explained as follows:

*Figure 3. Retransmission probability as a function of k*

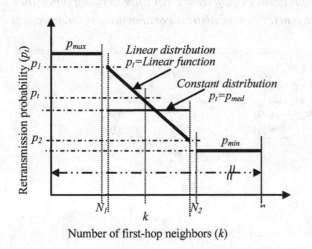

Number of first-hop neighbors ($k$)

1. Low node density neighborhood ($k \leq N_1$). In this case, $p_t$ of the intermediate node is set to $p_{max}$ to increase the probability of forwarding the RREQ packet across this low density neighborhood to ensure high reachability. Due to the small number of neighboring nodes this may incur an insignificant increase in the number of retransmissions.

2. Medium node density neighborhood ($N_1 < k < N_2$). In this case, $p_t$ of the intermediate node is either a constant value or calculated using a linear function of $k$. In a linear relation, for example, $p_t$ can be assumed to decrease linearly from $p_1$ to $p_2$ with increasing $k$. This looks very acceptable, because as $k$ increases, some of the intermediate nodes may fail retransmitting the RREQ packets, but still some will succeed, so that the chance of forwarding the RREQ packets remains high incorporating insignificant reduction in network reachability.

3. High node density neighborhood ($k \geq N_2$). In this case, $p_t$ of the intermediate node is set to $p_{min}$ to reduce the probability of forwarding the RREQ packet. But, due to the high node

density some nodes will success in forwarding the RREQ packet. Thus, the number of retransmissions is reduced incurring lower broadcast collision without sacrificing high reachability.

## Effect of Noise

It has been proved in the literature that the performance of probabilistic flooding, in particular, the network reachability is significantly affected in presence of noise, which is so common and unavoidable in MANET environment (Al-Bahadili, 2010). This section shows how a noise negatively affects the performance of probabilistic algorithms. This can be explained with the help of Figure 4 as follows: Assume that nodes A and G are the source and destination nodes, and nodes B and C are intermediate nodes. Node G can be reached through nodes B and C. Figure 4a shows the RREQ packet dissemination from node A to G using pure flooding in noiseless environment, in which node G receives the RREQ packet twice through nodes B and C. However, it will send only one RREP through node B or C depending on which one forward the RREQ first.

On the other hand for the same network topology, if probabilistic flooding is used, there are three possibilities, these are: (1) both B and C, (2) either B or C, and (3) neither B nor C will retransmit the RREQ packet. Assume that only node B succeeds to retransmit the RREQ packet. For the same topology in noisy environment, assume that node A be unsuccessful in delivering the RREQ packet to node B (due to presence of noise) and be successful in delivering the RREQ packet to node C. Thus, the RREQ packet will not be delivered to node G, and node G appears as unreachable. This is because node B has no packet to retransmit and node C prohibits from retransmission by the probabilistic algorithm.

According to the above discussion, in order to enhance the performance of the dynamic probabilistic route discovery algorithm in noisy MANETs, we believe it is important to re-adjust $p_t$ in such a way to compensate for the negative effect of noise, and $p_t$ is expressed as:

$$p_t = p_t(k, p_c) \tag{3}$$

## Determination of the Dynamic $p_t$ in Noisy Environment

In order to calculate $p_t(k, p_c)$, we assume it consists of two terms, one represents $p_t$ as in noiseless environment, which is determined as a function of $k$

*Figure 4. Pure and probabilistic algorithms in various network conditions: (a) Pure flooding algorithm, (b) Probabilistic algorithm in noiseless environment, and (c) Probabilistic algorithm in noisy environment*

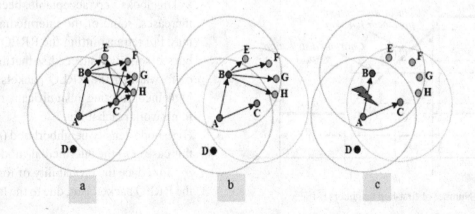

$(p_t(k))$, and the second represents $p_t$ due to noise, which is determined as a function of $p_c$ $(p_t(p_c))$. The second term is added as a compensation for the effect of noise. Thus, $p_t(k, p_c)$ can be mathematically expressed as (Al-Bahadili & Sabri, 2011):

$$p_t(k, p_c) = p_t(k) + p_t(p_c) \qquad (4)$$

It can be seen from Equation 4 that in order to calculate $p_t(k, p_c)$, we need to calculate $p_t(k)$ and $p_t(p_c)$. $p_t(k)$ can be calculated using Equation 2, and next we discuss the calculation of $p_t(p_c)$. The following main constraints should be considered when calculating $p_t(p_c)$:

1.   The value of $p_t(p_c)$ should be $\geq 0$ and $\leq 1 - p_t(k)$, so that $p_t(k, p_c)$ will always be $\leq 1$.
2.   The value of $p_t(k, p_c)$ lies between $p_t(k)$ and $p_{t,pcmin}$, which is a pre-adjusted maximum allowable $p_t$ at a certain minimum value of $p_c$ $(p_{c,min})$.
3.   The value of $p_{t,pcmin}$ should be $\leq 1$ and $\geq p_t(k)$.

Considering the above constraints, $p_t(p_c)$ can be calculated as:

$$p_t(p_c) = \alpha \, (p_{t,pcmin} - p_t(k)) \qquad (5)$$

Where $\alpha$ is called the noise-correction factor, which is a function of $p_c$, and has a value that lies between 0 and 1. Substituting Equation 5 into Equation 4 yields:

$$p_t(k, p_c) = p_t(k) + \alpha \, (p_{t,pcmin} - p_t(k)) \qquad (6)$$

The value of $\alpha$ can be calculated using the following equation (Al-Bahadili & Sabri, 2010):

$$\alpha = \frac{1 - p_c}{1 - p_{c,min}} \qquad (7)$$

Now, substituting Equation 7 into Equation 6 yields the following equation for $p_t(k, p_c)$:

$$p_t(k, p_c) = p_t(k) + \frac{1 - p_c}{1 - p_{c,min}}(p_{t,pc\min} - p_t(k))$$

$$(8)$$

Where $p_t(k, p_c)$ is the dynamic noise-dependent $p_t$; $p_t(k)$ is the dynamic $p_t$ as given in Equation 2; $p_{t,pcmin}$ is the maximum allowable $p_t$ in presence of noise, $p_c$ is the probability of reception; and $p_{c,min}$ is the minimum probability of reception.

In a noiseless environment $p_c=1$, $\alpha=0$ and consequently $p_t(k, p_c)=p_t(k)$, i.e., $p_t$ is a function of $k$ only. In a noisy environment, when $p_c=p_{c,min}$, then $\alpha=1$ and $p_t(k, p_c)=p_{t,pcmin}$. If $p_c$ is any value between $p_{c,min}$ and 1, then $p_t(k, p_c)$ varies between $p_t(k)$ and $p_{t,pcmin}$ depending on $p_c$. According to the above discussion, $p_t(k, p_c)$ always lies between $p_t(k)$ and $p_{t,pcmin}$ as shown in Figure 5.

It can be seen from Equation 6 that $p_t$ depends on a number of factors; these are:

1.   The distribution function used for the calculation of $p_t(k)$
2.   Number of the first-hop neighbors for the transmitting node ($k$).
3.   Probability of reception ($p_c$)
4.   The maximum allowable $p_t$ in presence of noise ($p_{t,pcmin}$)

## THE DNDP ALGORITHM

The description of DNDP algorithm is straightforward (Al-Bahadili & Sabri, 2011). It is simply, when the receiving node is within the radio transmission range of the transmitting node, a flag *IRange* is assigned to 1 otherwise it is set to 0. For *IRange*=1 a random test is performed to decide whether the request is successfully delivered to the receiver or being lost due to error. The

*Figure 5. Variation of $p_t(k, p_c)$ with k (constant $p_{t,pcmin}$)*

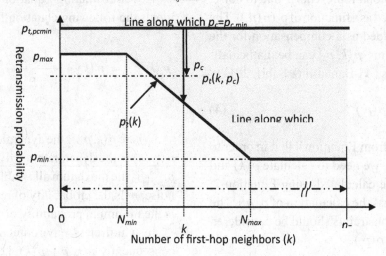

random test is performed as follows: a random number $\xi_1$ ($0 \leq \xi_1 < 1$) is generated and compared with $p_c$, if $\xi_1$ is $\leq p_c$, then successful delivery occurs; otherwise, the request is not successfully delivered or being lost. The value of $p_c$ is either predetermined or instantly computed using a certain probability distribution function. In this work the value of $p_c$ is set to a fixed value. Each time a node $i$ successfully receives a request an index *IRec(i)* is incremented by 1. The value of *IRec(i)* gives an indication about how many times the request packet has been received by the first-hop neighboring nodes and can be used to compute the network parameters such as the Reachability (RCH) and Average Duplicate Reception (ADR).

In conventional probabilistic algorithm, when receiving a RREQ packet each node is allowed to rebroadcast the received packet only once. So that a node retransmission index *IRet(i)* is defined and initially set to 0, i.e., the node has not retransmitted the RREQ packet yet. *IRet(i)* is set to 1 soon after a node $i$ retransmits a received RREQ. *IRet(i)* is used to calculate other network parameters, such as the number of retransmission (RET).

To calculate the node *IRet(i)*, another random number $\xi_2$ ($0 \leq \xi_2 < 1$) is generated and compared with $p_t$ of the node $i$. If $\xi_2$ is $\leq p_t$, then successful retransmission occurs and *IRet(i)* is set 1; other-

wise, the request is not retransmitted and *IRet(i)* is remained unchanged. Figure 6 outlines the DNDP algorithm.

## Enhancing the DNDP Algorithm

In Equation 8, $p_{t,pcmin}$ is assumed to be a constant value, and as it can be seen in Figure 5 that the computed $p_t$ is increased considerably with decreasing $p_c$. This may result in a significant increase in the number of retransmission, especially at high $k$. In order to alleviate the impact of the significant increase in $p_t$ and to provide adjustable measure to control that increase, the following solution can be introduced. The solution, which is discussed in detail in (Al-Bahadili, et al., 2011), is simply based on using a $k$-dependent distribution for calculating $p_{t,pcmin}$, i.e., $p_{t,pcmin}$ can be set as a function of $k$ ($p_{t,pcmin}(k)$) as shown in Figure 7. This distribution can be discrete similar to $p_t(k)$ or continuous distribution, such as linear, parabolic, exponential, etc. Thus, Equation 8 can be re-written as:

$$p_t(k, p_c) = p_t(k) + \frac{1 - p_c}{1 - p_{c,min}}(p_{t,pc\min}(k) - p_t(k)) \tag{9}$$

*Figure 6. The DNDP algorithm*

```
If  (IRange=1) Then {The receiving node is within the transmission range of the sender, in a noiseless
                     environment this guarantees request reception by the receiver, while in a noisy
                     environment a random test must be performed to find out whether a successful
                     delivery occurs or not. IRange=0 means the receiver is not within the transmission
                     range of the sender}
    ξ₁=rnd() {ξ₁ some random number between 0 and 1}
    If (ξ₁<=pc) Then {Reception random test}
        IRec(i)++ {Update the node reception index IRec(i)}
        If (IRet(i)=0) Then {The node has not retransmitted the request before (IRet(i) = 0)}
            ξ₂=rnd() {ξ₂ some random number between 0 and 1}
            pₜ=function_pₜ()
            If (ξ₂<=pₜ) Then
                Retransmit RREQ
                IRet(i)=1 {Update the node retransmission index IRet(i) by equating it to 1}
            End if
        End if
    End if
End if
Function_pₜ() {Determining pₜ}
    If (IProb="Static") Then {IProb is an integer indicates the approach to be used for determining pₜ whether it
                             is static or dynamic}
        pₜ=constant value
    Else (IProb="Dynamic")
        pₜ=f(k,pc)
    End If
```

Mathematical representation of the linear, parabolic, and exponential distributions of $p_{t,pcmin}(k)$ can be given as follows:

**Linear distribution:**

$$p_{t,pc\min}(k) = p_{t,pc\min 1} + \frac{p_{t,pc\min 2} - p_{t,pc\min 1}}{n-1} k$$

(10)

**Parabolic distribution:**

$$p_{t,pc\min}(k) = p_{t,pc\min 1} + \frac{p_{t,pc\min 2} - p_{t,pc\min 1}}{(n-1)^2} k^2$$

(11)

**Exponential distribution:**

$$p_{t,pc\min}(k) = p_{t,pc\min 1} + \frac{p_{t,pc\min 2} - p_{t,pc\min 1}}{1 - e^{-\beta(n-1)}} (1 - e^{-\beta k})$$

(12)

where $p_{t,pcmin1}$ is the maximum allowable $p_t$ in presence of noise and at $k=0$.

$p_{t,pcmin2}$ is the maximum allowable $p_t$ in presence of noise and at $k=n-1$.

$\beta$ is a constant ($\beta \leq 1$).

It can be deduced from Figure 7 that due to the reduced size of the shaded area when compared with Figure 5, $p_t(k, p_c)$ can be tuned in a controlled way by choosing a proper distribution for $p_{t,pcmin}(k)$ for the sake of achieving optimum performance in terms of network reachability and number of redundant retransmissions.

## RESULTS AND DISCUSSIONS

The DNDP algorithm is implemented on the MA-NET simulator, MANSim, (Al-Bahadili, 2010), which is used to perform a number of simulations

*Figure 7. Variation of $p_t(k, p_c)$ with $k$ ($p_{t,pcmin}(k)$)*

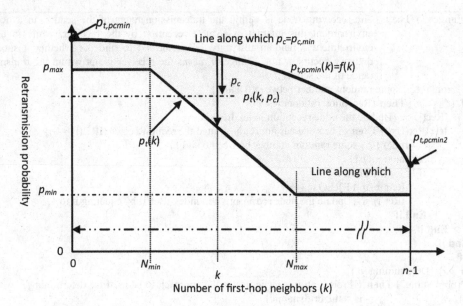

to evaluate and compare the performance of the algorithm in a noisy MANET's environment. A number of network performance measures can be calculated using MANSim, such as: network Reachability (RCH), number of Retransmission (RET), Average Duplicate Reception (ADR), Average Hop Count (AHP), Saved Rebroadcast (SRB), and Disconnectivity (DIS). These parameters are recommended by the Internet Engineering Task Force (IETF) group to judge the performance of the flooding optimization algorithms. Definition of these parameters can be found in (Al-Bahadili & Jaradat, 2010).

In this chapter, we presents results for two parameters only, these are: RCH and RET. RCH is defined as the average number of reachable nodes by any node on the network normalized to $n$ (number of nodes on the network); or the probability by which a RREQ packet successfully delivered from source to destination node. RET is defined as the average number of retransmissions normalized to $n$.

## Scenario #1: The DNDP Algorithm with Constant $p_{t,pcmin}$

In this scenario, we investigate the performance of the DNDP algorithm with constant $p_{t,pcmin}$. The input parameters for this scenario are listed in Table 1. The simulation results obtained using the DNDP algorithm are compared with those obtained by using the following flooding optimization algorithms:

1.  Pure flooding ($p_t = 1$)
2.  Dynamic probabilistic algorithm, in which the values of $p_{max}$, $p_{min}$, $p_1$, $p_2$, $N_1$, and $N_2$ in Equation (2) are taken to be 0.8, 0.5, 0.8, 0.5, 4, and 20, respectively. For this simulation, the average $p_c$ is 0.744.

The simulations results are plotted in Figures 8 and 9.

The main outcomes of Scenario #1 can be summarized:

*   For pure and noise-independent dynamic probabilistic algorithms, RCH decreases

*Table 1. Input parameters*

| Parameters | Values |
|---|---|
| Geometrical model | Random node distribution |
| Network area | 600x600 m |
| Number of nodes ($n$) | 100 nodes. |
| Transmission radius ($R$) | 100 m |
| Average node speed ($u$) | 5 m/sec |
| Probability of reception ($p_c$) | From 0.5 to 1.0 in step of 0.1 |
| Simulation time ($T_{sim}$) | 1200 sec |
| Pause time ($\tau$) | $\tau=0.75*(R/u)=15$ sec |
| Size of mobility loop ($nIntv$) | 80 |

as $p_c$ decreases (i.e., noise-level increases). This is as a consequence of: (1) High packet-loss introduced by the high noise-level, and (2) No measure is taken by the existing probabilistic algorithms to accommodate the negative effect of the noise-level or to replace the high packet-loss.

- The proposed DNDP algorithm presents an excellent performance in terms of increasing RCH in presence of noise by effectively adjusting (increasing/decreasing) $p_t$ based on both $k$ and $p_c$. The results obtained demonstrated that the DNDP algorithm provides the highest RCH for various network noise-level, when compared with noise-independent dynamic probabilistic algorithm.

- It can be seen from Figure 8 that the DNDP algorithm almost produces the same RCH. However, enhancing RCH is paid by increasing RET as shown Figure 9.

Since the main objective of using flooding optimization during route discovery is to achieve a cost-effective RCH, which means achieving the highest possible reachability at a lowest possible number of retransmission. The simulation results demonstrate that the DNDP algorithm provides better performance as it can achieve better cost-

effective reachability than other probabilistic route discovery algorithms.

Figure 8 shows that the probabilistic and DNDP algorithms provide the same performance in noise-less environments ($p_c=1$). But, in terms of network reachability, the DNDP algorithm overwhelms the performance of the other probabilistic algorithms in noisy environment. For example, for $p_c=0.5$, the DNDP algorithm achieves a reachability of 75.2% the same as pure flooding 75.2%, while for the same environment, the fixed and dynamic probabilistic approach achieves 41.8% and 32.7%

*Figure 8. Variation of RCH with $p_c$ for various algorithms*

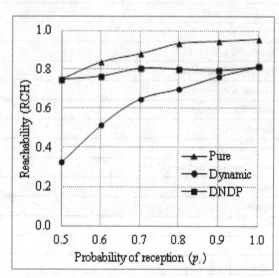

171

*Figure 9. Variation of RET with $p_c$ for various algorithms*

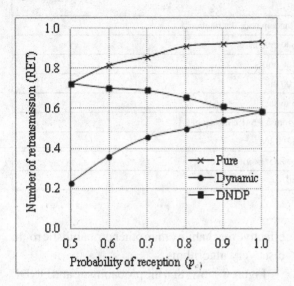

respectively. But, the fixed and dynamic probabilistic approach achieves this reachability at a cost of RET 29.7% and 22.9% compared with RET 92.5% and 93.3% for the DNDP and pure flooding algorithms.

The DNDP algorithm provides an excellent performance as it can achieve an excellent cost-effective reachability, for various network noise levels, as compared to pure flooding algorithm. For example, when $p_c=1$, the DNDP algorithm costs a RET of 58.6% compared with RET= 93.6% in pure flooding algorithm, whereas the achieved reachability is 81.6% and 95.7% respectively.

## Scenario #2: The DNDP Algorithm with $k$-Dependent $p_{t,pcmin}$

In the second scenario, we investigate the effect of $p_{t,pcmin}(k)$ on the performance of the DNDP algorithm through a number of simulations using MANSim. Also, in this scenario, the performance of the enhanced DNDP algorithm ($k$-dependent $p_{t,pcmin}(k)$) is compared against the performance of pure flooding, fixed and dynamic probabilistic algorithms, and the DNDP algorithm with fixed $p_{t,pcmin}$. The input parameters for these simulations are given in Table 2.

Figure 10 shows the variation of the $p_t$ of the intermediate nodes with $k$. The simulations results

*Table 2. Input parameters*

| Parameters | Values |
|---|---|
| Geometrical model | Random node distribution |
| Network area | 600x600 m |
| Number of nodes ($n$) | 100 nodes. |
| Transmission radius ($R$) | 100 m |
| Average node speed ($u$) | 5 m/sec |
| Probability of reception ($p_c$) | From 0.5 to 1.0 in step of 0.1 |
| Simulation time ($T_{sim}$) | 1200 sec |
| Pause time ($\tau$) | $\tau = 0.75*(R/u) = 15$ sec |
| Size of the mobility loop ($nIntv$) | $nIntv = T_{sim}/\tau = 80$ |
| Fixed: $p_t$ | 0.744 |
| Dynamic: $p_{min}, p_{max}, N_{min}, N_{max}, p_1, p_2$ | 0.5, 0.8, 4, 15, 0.5, 0.8 |
| Fixed: $p_{t,pcmin}$ | 1 |
| Linear: $p_{t,pcmin}(k)$ | $p_{t,pcmin1}=1$ and $p_{t,pcmin2}=0.5$ |
| Parabolic: $p_{t,pcmin}$ | $p_{t,pcmin1}=1$ and $p_{t,pcmin2}=0.5$ |
| Exponential: $p_{t,pcmin}$ | $p_{t,pcmin1}=1$ and $p_{t,pcmin2}=0.5, \beta=1$ |

*Figure 10. Variation of $p_{t,pcmin}(k)$ with k*

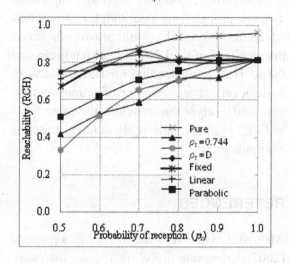

*Figure 11. Variation of RCH with $p_c$ for various algorithms*

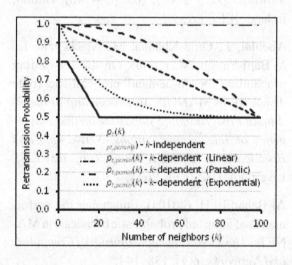

*Figure 12. Variation of RET with $p_c$ for various algorithms*

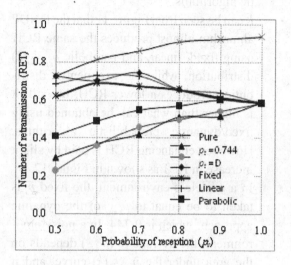

*Figure 13. Variation of $p_{t,avg}$ with $p_c$ for various algorithms*

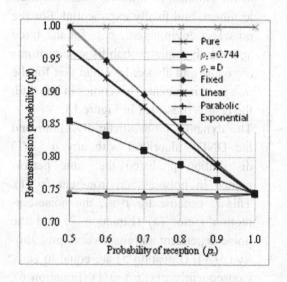

are presented in Figures 11 to 13. The main outcomes of this scenario can be summarized as follows:

- For pure and fixed/dynamic probabilistic algorithms, RCH decreases as noise-level increases, due to the high packet-loss introduced by the high noise-level; and no measure is taken by the existing probabilistic algorithms to accommodate the negative effect of increasing noise-level.

- The DNDP algorithm with any of the suggested distribution functions for $p_{t,pcmin}(k)$ presents a better performance in terms of increasing RCH in presence of noise by effectively adjusting $p_t$ based on both $k$ and $p_c$. The results obtained demonstrated that the algorithm provides the highest RCH for various network noise-level, when compared with fixed/dynamic probabilistic algorithms.

- It can be seen from Figure 11 that the DNDP algorithm almost produces the same RCH using fixed, linear, and parabolic $p_{t,pcmin}(k)$ distribution, while the exponential distribution produces a lower RCH, but still it is higher than what can be obtained using fixed/dynamic probabilistic algorithms. However, enhancing RCH is paid by slight increase in RET as shown in Figure 12.

- In a noiseless environment, the fixed $p_t$ is taken to be equal to $p_{t,avg}$ of the dynamic approach, which is 0.744. In a noisy environment, the average $p_t$ ($p_{t,avg}$) depends on the area under the $p_{t,pcmin}(k)$ curve, and it can be seen in Figure 5 that the area under the curve can be arranged from the largest to the smallest as follows: fixed, parabolic, linear, and finally exponential. For the noiseless environment, $p_{t,avg}$ for the fixed and the dynamic probabilistic algorithms are equal and always less than that for the noisy environment. This comes in line with the results presented in Figure 13.

- The dynamic probabilistic algorithm and the DNDP algorithm with any $p_{t,pcmin}(k)$ distribution produced the same performance in noiseless environment ($p_c$=1). This is because for $p_c$=1, the noise-correction factor ($\alpha$) (Equation 7) and the noise-dependent retransmission probability ($p_t(p_c)$) (Equation 5) are equal to zero. Consequently $p_t(k, p_c)=p_t(k)$ (Equation 6), which means all algorithms use the same distribution for $p_t$ ($p_t=p_t(k)$).

## CONCLUSION

The main conclusion of this work is that the DNDP algorithm demonstrated better cost-effective performance than the current dynamic probabilistic algorithm in noisy environment. The DNDP al-

gorithm provides a higher RCH as compared to dynamic probabilistic algorithm for various network noise-levels. The results also demonstrated that the RCH of the DNDP algorithm is close to the RCH of pure flooding for various network noise levels at less number of retransmission. The DNDP algorithm provides the same RCH and RET as the dynamic $p_t$ algorithm in noiseless environment ($p_c$=1).

## REFERENCES

Abdulai, J., Ould-Khaoua, M., & Mackenzie, L. (2007). Improving probabilistic route discovery in mobile ad hoc networks. In *Proceeding of the 32ⁿᵈ IEEE Conference on Local Computer Networks (LCN 2007)*, (pp. 739-746). Dublin, Ireland: IEEE Press.

Abdulai, J., Ould-Khaoua, M., Mackenzie, L., & Bani-Yassin, M. (2006). On the forwarding probability for on-demand probabilistic route discovery in MANETs. In *Proceeding of the 7ᵗʰ Annual Postgraduate Symposium on the Convergence of Telecommunications, Networking and Broadcasting (PGNET 2006)*, (pp. 120-125). Liverpool, UK: IEEE Press.

Al-Bahadili, H. (2010a). Enhancing the performance of adjusted probabilistic broadcast in MANETs. *The Mediterranean Journal of Computers and Networks*, 6(4), 138–144.

Al-Bahadili, H. (2010b). On the use of discrete-event simulation in computer networks analysis and design. In Abu-Taieh, E. M. O., & El-Sheikh, A. A. (Eds.), *Handbook of Research on Discrete-Event Simulation Environments: Technologies and Applications* (pp. 414–442). Hershey, PA: IGI Global. doi:10.4018/978-1-60566-774-4.ch019

Al-Bahadili, H., Issa, G., & Sabri, A. (2011). Enhancing the performance of the DNDP algorithm. *The International Journal of Wireless and Mobile Networks*, 3(2), 113–124. doi:10.5121/ijwmn.2011.3210

Al-Bahadili, H., & Jaradat, R. (2010). Performance evaluation of an OMPR algorithm for route discovery in noisy MANETs. *The International Journal of Computer Networks and Communications, 2*(1), 85–96.

Al-Bahadili, H., & Jaradat, Y. (2007). Development and performance analysis of a probabilistic flooding in noisy mobile ad hoc networks. In *Proceedings of the 1ˢᵗ International Conference on Digital Communications and Computer Applications (DCCA 2007)*, (pp. 1306-1316). Irbid, Jordan: IEEE Press.

Al-Bahadili, H., & Kaabneh, K. (2010). Analyzing the performance of probabilistic algorithm in noisy MANETs. *International Journal of Wireless & Mobile Networks, 2*(3), 83–95. doi:10.5121/ijwmn.2010.2306

Al-Bahadili, H., & Sabri, A. (2011). A novel dynamic noise-dependent probabilistic algorithm for route discovery in MANETs. *International Journal of Business Data Communications and Networking, 7*(1), 52–67. doi:10.4018/jbdcn.2011010103

Bani-Yassein, M., & Ould-Khaoua, M. (2007). Applications of probabilistic flooding in MANETs. *International Journal of Ubiquitous Computing and Communication, 1*(1), 1–5.

Bani-Yassein, M., Ould-Khaoua, M., Mackenzie, L., & Papanastasiou, S. (2006). Performance analysis of adjusted probabilistic broadcasting in mobile ad hoc networks. *International Journal of Wireless Information Networks, 13*(2), 127–140. doi:10.1007/s10776-006-0027-0

Barrett, C., Eidenbenz, S., Kroc, L., Marathe, M., & Smith, J. (2005). Parametric probabilistic routing in sensor networks. *Journal of Mobile Networks and Applications, 10*(4), 529–544. doi:10.1007/s11036-005-1565-x

Bettstetter, C. (2004). The cluster density of a distributed clustering algorithm in ad hoc networks. In *Proceedings of 2004 IEEE International Conference on Communications (ICC 2004)*, (vol 7), (pp. 4336-4340). Paris, France: IEEE Press.

Boleng, J., & Camp, T. (2004). Adaptive location-aided mobile ad hoc network routing. *Proceedings of the 23ʳᵈ IEEE International Performance, Computing, and Communications Conference (IPCCC)*, (pp. 423-432). Phoenix, AZ: IEEE Press.

Haas, Z. J., Halpern, J. Y., & Li, L. (2006). Gossip-based ad hoc routing. *IEEE/ACM Transactions on Networking, 14*(3), 479–491. doi:10.1109/TNET.2006.876186

Hanash, A., Siddique, A., Awan, I., & Woodward, M. (2009). Performance evaluation of dynamic probabilistic broadcasting for flooding in mobile ad hoc networks. *Journal of Simulation Modeling Practice and Theory, 17*(2), 364–375. doi:10.1016/j.simpat.2008.09.012

Joa-Ng, M., & Lu, I. (1999). A peer-to-peer zone-based two-level link state routing for mobile ad hoc networks. *IEEE Journal on Selected Areas in Communications, 17*(8), 1415–1425. doi:10.1109/49.779923

Johnson, D., & Maltz, D. (1996). Dynamic source routing in ad hoc wireless networks. In Imielinski, T., & Korth, H. (Eds.), *Mobile Computing* (pp. 153–181). Berlin, Germany: Kluwer Academic Publishers. doi:10.1007/978-0-585-29603-6_5

Khan, I., Javaid, A., & Qian, H. (2008). Coverage-based dynamically adjusted probabilistic forwarding for wireless mobile ad hoc networks. In S. Giordano, W. Jia, P. M. Ruiz, S. Olariu, & G. Xing (Eds.), *Proceedings of the 1st ACM International Workshop on Heterogeneous Sensor and Actor Networks (HeterSanet 2008)*, (pp. 81-88). Hong Kong, China: ACM Press.

Kim, J. S., Zhang, Q., & Agrawal, D. P. (2004). Probabilistic broadcasting based on coverage area and neighbor confirmation in mobile ad hoc networks. In *Proceedings of the IEEE Global Telecommunications Conference Workshops (GlobeCom 2004)*, (pp. 96–101). Dallas, TX: IEEE Press.

Ko, Y., & Vaidya, N. (2000). Location-aided routing (LAR) in mobile ad hoc networks. *Journal of Wireless Networks, 6*(4), 307–321. doi:10.1023/A:1019106118419

Ni, S., Tseng, Y., Chen, Y., & Sheu, J. (1999). The broadcast storm problem in a mobile ad hoc network. *Journal of ACM/Springer. Wireless Networks, 8*(2), 153–167.

Perkins, C., & Royer, E. (1999). Ad-hoc on demand distance vector routing. In *Proceedings of the 2nd IEEE Workshop on Mobile Computing Systems and Applications (WMCSA)*, (pp. 90-100). New Orleans, LA: IEEE Press.

Qayyum, A., Viennot, L., & Laouiti, A. (2002). Multipoint relaying for flooding broadcast messages in mobile wireless networks. In *Proceedings of the 35th Hawaii International Conference on System Sciences (HICSS 2002)*, (pp. 3866-3875). Hawaii, HI: IEEE Press.

Rahman, A., Olesinski, W., & Gburzynski, P. (2004). Controlled flooding in wireless ad hoc networks. In *Proceedings of IEEE International Workshop on Wireless Ad Hoc Networks (IWWAN 2004)*. Oulu, Finland: IEEE Press.

Rajaraman, R. (2002). Topology control and routing in ad hoc networks. *ACM Special Interest Group on Algorithms and Computation Theory (SIGACT). News, 33*(2), 60–73.

Royer, E., & Toh, C. (1999). A review of current routing protocols for ad hoc mobile wireless networks. *IEEE Personal Communication Magazine, 6*(2), 46-55.

Sasson, Y., Cavin, D., & Schiper, A. (2003). Probabilistic broadcast for flooding in wireless mobile ad hoc networks. In *Proceedings of IEEE Wireless Communications and Networking (WCNC 2003)*, (Vol 2), (pp. 1124-1130). New Orleans, LA: IEEE Press.

Scott, D., & Yasinsac, A. (2004). Dynamic probabilistic retransmission in ad hoc networks. In H. R. Arabnia, L. T. Yang, & C. H. Yeh (Eds.), *Proceeding of the International Conference on Wireless Networks (ICWN 2004)*, (vol 1), (pp. 158-164). Las Vegas, NV: CSREA Press.

Toh, C. (2002). *Ad hoc mobile wireless networks: Protocols and systems*. New York: Prentice-Hall.

Tseng, T., Ni, S., Chen, Y., & Sheu, J. (2002). The broadcast storm problem in a mobile ad hoc network. *Journal of Wireless Networks, 8*(2), 153–167. doi:10.1023/A:1013763825347

Viswanath, K., & Obraczka, K. (2005). Modeling the performance of flooding in wireless multi-hop ad hoc networks. *Journal of Computer Communications, 29*(8), 949–956. doi:10.1016/j.comcom.2005.06.015

Zhang, Q., & Agrawal, D. P. (2005). Dynamic probabilistic broadcasting in MANETs. *Journal of Parallel and Distributed Computing, 65*(2), 220–233. doi:10.1016/j.jpdc.2004.09.006

## KEY TERMS AND DEFINITIONS

**DNDP Algorithm:** The DNDP (dynamic noise-dependent probabilistic) algorithm is a route discovery algorithm, in which the retransmission probability of the transmitting node is calculated locally by the node itself considering both the number of first-hop neighbors and the noise-level (expressed in terms of probability of reception of transmitted route request packet).

**Flooding Optimization Algorithms:** Algorithms which are developed to reduce the number of redundant retransmissions. As the number of retransmissions required for broadcasting is decreased, the bandwidth is saved and contention, collision, and node power consumption are reduced, and this will improve the overall network performance.

**MANET:** A MANET (mobile ad hoc network) is defined as a collection of low-power wireless mobile nodes forming a temporary wireless network without the aid of any established infrastructure or centralized administration.

**MANSim (MANET Simulator):** It is an academic, research-level computer network simulator, which can be used to evaluate, analyze, and compare the performance of a number of flooding optimization algorithms in ideal and realistic MANET environments. It is written in C++ programming language, and consists of four main modules: network, mobility, computational, and algorithm modules.

**Probabilistic Algorithm:** It is a widely-used flooding optimization algorithm during route discovery in MANETs, which aims at reducing number of retransmissions probabilistically. In this algorithm, when receiving a RREQ packet, a node retransmits the packet with a certain retransmission probability, otherwise it discards the packet.

**Route Discovery:** The first phase of the dynamic routing process, in which a route between source and destination nodes is established for the first time.

**Routing Protocol:** A routing protocol is a set of rules used by routers to determine the most appropriate paths into which they should forward packets towards their intended destinations.

# Chapter 9
# A Location–Based Power Conservation Scheme for MANETs:
## A Step towards Green Communications

**Hussein Al-Bahadili**
*Petra University, Jordan*

**Azmi Halasa**
*The Arab Academy for Banking and Financial Sciences, Jordan*

## ABSTRACT

*In a Mobile Ad Hoc Network (MANET), a mobile node consumes its power in message communication, message processing, and other operation missions. The amount of power a mobile node consumes for communication is the highest and the dominant as compared to what a node consumes for other tasks. The power consumed in communication is proportional to the square of the nodes' radio transmission range (R); therefore, minimizing R contributes to a significant reduction in power consumption and consequently increases node battery-power lifetime. This chapter presents a description and performance evaluation of a new efficient power conservation scheme, namely, the Location-Based Power Conservation (LBPC) scheme. It is based on the concept of reducing R by utilizing locally available nodes' location information to adjust R according to one of the three proposed radius adjustment criteria: farthest, average, and random. So that instead of transmitting with full power to cover up to its maximum radio transmission range ($R_{max}$), the transmitting node adjusts R to less than $R_{max}$, which provides a power conservation factor equivalent to $(R/R_{max})^2$.*

DOI: 10.4018/978-1-4666-0191-8.ch009

## INTRODUCTION

Information and communications technology (ICT) usage is growing at almost exponential rate worldwide contributing to a significant increase in power consumption to operate the different components of this technology. In particular, network expansion and mounting figures of mobile network users have recently highlighted the importance of energy management solutions for existing and emerging network technologies. Radio network normally shares a huge amount of the total electricity usage; therefore the power consumption of each node is coming under intense scrutiny and the mobile wireless network industry is striving to improve the energy efficiency of the next generation of mobile nodes.

Wireless technology specialists have focused technological developments primarily on meeting the demands of the consumer for increased bandwidth. However, the recent dramatic increase in energy costs and greater awareness of their impact on the environment (global warming) is shedding new urgency on improving power efficiency in communications leading to the emergent of new type of communication, namely green communications. Green communications or green networking aims to help reduce power consumption and consequently reduce carbon emission by the ICT industry (Mobile Group, 2008).

In this work, we concern with the development of a power conservation scheme for wireless mobile nodes in Mobile Ad Hoc Networks (MANETs) as a step towards green communications. A wireless mobile node in a MANET consumes its limited battery power in two missions: processing and communication. The amount of power consumed for transmitting one-bit is much higher than the power consumed for one-bit processing (Zarifzadeh, et al., 2008). Therefore, in order to increase the life-time of a node, it is so vital to minimize communication power consumption. From radio communications theory, it is well approved that the power consumption in message passing is directly proportional to the square of radio transmission range. Thus, reducing the radio transmission range can significantly reduce the node power consumption and increase its lifetime on one hand and help with providing green communication on the other hand.

The node consumes its power during communication to exchange data, route discovery messages, or control messages. The cost of information exchange (in terms of power consumption, overhead, and delay) during route discovery is higher than the cost of point-to-point data forwarding or control messages exchange (Al-Bahadili, 2010a). Therefore, minimizing the power consumed for route establishment is a vital requirement to extend the lifetime of the battery-powered nodes, and can be considered as a step towards green communications.

This chapter describes a new power conservation scheme, in which each transmitting node utilizes the location information available on its first-hop neighbors to adjust its radio transmission range. Therefore, it is referred to as the Location-Based Power Conservation (LBPC) scheme (Halasa, 2010; Kaabneh, et al., 2009). In this scheme, for example, each node can obtain its location information using a built-in GPS, and then exchange this location information with its first hop neighbors, so that each node is aware of the location of its first-hop neighbors (Ko & Vaidya, 2000), or a node estimates the distances from its first-hop neighbors through gossiping. Gossiping approach includes a lot of instability and inaccuracy that may degrade the overall performance of network (Kohvakka, et al., 2006).

The LBPC scheme adjusts the radio transmission rage ($R$) of the transmitting node using one of the following criteria: (1) the farthest first-hop neighbor criterion, (2) the average distance of the first-hop neighbors criterion, and (3) a random distance between the nearest and farthest first-hop neighbors criterion. In order to compare and evaluate the performance of the LBPC scheme in MANET's environment, a scenario is simulated using the MANET simulator (MANSim) (Al-Bahadili, 2010b). The scenario estimates and compares the power conservation factor ($P_c$) achieved by the LBPC scheme when used in conjunction with pure flooding, dynamic probabilistic, and LAR-1 algorithms for route discovery in MANETs. In this scenario, $P_c$ is estimated and compared for two radius adjustment criteria: the farthest and the average. Furthermore, the affects of the radius adjustment criteria on two network parameters are also estimated and compared, namely, the network Reachability (RCH) and the number of Retransmissions (RET).

## BACKGROUND

In a MANET that uses a Location-Aided Routing (LAR) algorithm, each node is already aware of the location of other nodes within the network. Therefore, this scheme can be implemented in such networks with absolutely no extra overheads of any sort. In a network that uses other routing algorithms, and in order to minimize communication overheads, nodes can be configured to exchange its location with their first-hop neighbors only.

### Wireless Communication Power Consumption Model

Wireless communication power depends on two factors: the transmission range and data transmission rate. For a node transmitting a bit-stream at a rate of $b$ bps over a distance $R$ m, the minimal transmitter power consumption $E_t$, for free-space radio communication, is given by (Zarifzadeh, et al., 2008; Pan, et al., 2003):

$$E_t(b, R) = (\alpha_1 + \alpha_2 R^2) \cdot b \qquad (1)$$

Where $\alpha_1$ is the power consumed in the transmitter electronic circuit for message processing, which is the distance-independent power consumption term, and $\alpha_2$ is the power consumed in

message passing, which is the distance-dependent power consumption term. The above equation is applicable even with a more complicated model (e.g., including multi-path fading and geographical shadowing effects), as long as the distance related power consumption can be isolated empirically.

For a node to receive a bit-stream at a rate of $b$ bps from other node, the power consumed in the receiver circuit is given by:

$$E_r(b) = \beta \cdot b \qquad (2)$$

Thus, the total power consumed by a node to bypass and forward a bit-stream at a rate $b$ bps over a distance $R$ m, is given by:

$$E_t(b, R) = [(\alpha_1 + \alpha_2 R^2) + \beta] \cdot b \qquad (3)$$

In a MANET of $n$ nodes, a route discovery process may involve $s$ transmissions and $m$ receptions. Thus, the power consumed in message passing and processing ($E_f$) is expressed as:

$$E_f = s \cdot E_t(b, R) + m \cdot E_r(b) \qquad (4)$$

Substituting Equations 1 and 2 into Equation 4 yields:

$$E_f = s \cdot (\alpha_1 + \alpha_2 R^2) \cdot b + m \cdot \beta \cdot b \qquad (5)$$

It is clear from the above equation that the total power consumption during route discovery depends on four parameters, these are:

1. Number of retransmissions ($s$)
2. Number of receptions ($m$)
3. Data transmission rate ($b$)
4. Transmission distance ($R$)

However, due to the fact that the power consumption in message processing is very small as compared to the power consumption in message passing, then Equation 5 can be simplified to:

$$E_f = \alpha_2 \, s \, b \, R^2 \qquad (6)$$

Therefore, optimizing $R$ and $s$ can contribute significantly to reduce the power consumption in wireless nodes.

## Estimating the Locations of First-Hop Neighbors

In this scheme, it is assumed that the location-information of all first-hop nodes is available to each node. Such information is typically available in the Location-Aided Routing (LAR) algorithms (Ko & Vaidy, 2000; Boleng & Camp, 2004), where each node on the network is always aware of the location of all other nodes on the network. But in other routing algorithms, the location information of first-hop nods is not available. To solve this problem we suggest two techniques, namely, using GPS and the power difference.

## Using GPS to Estimate First-Hop Node Location

Each node is assumed to be equipped with GPS to estimate its coordinates at any time, but the problem here is how to exchange the coordinates with other nodes on the network. To solve this problem, a little adjustment can be made on the standard Hello messages used by the protocols that are usually exchanged between the nodes. The new Hello message will be called E-Hello message and it will be the same as the original Hello message with the location coordination appended to its payload. The E-Hello message will work as follows:

1.  Each node will send E-Hallo massage that contains its coordinates with one-hop lifetime.
2.  All first-hop neighbor nodes will receive the E-Hello massages send by their neighbors.
3.  Each node will built a table containing the neighbor nodes and their locations and it is called the neighbors table.

4.  Any node whose receives the E-Hello message will update its neighbors table as follows:
    a.  If the sending node is not in the table, add it with its location.
    b.  If the sending node is already in the table, then updates its location information if there is a change.

## Using Power Difference to Estimate First-Hop Node Locations

In line-of-sight free space, power decreases per the inverse square law, so by knowing the current transmitter signal power, any node can determine its distance from the transmitting node by utilizing the difference between the received signal power and the current transmitter signal power. The current transmitter signal power can be exchanged through, let's say, the standard Hello message of the protocol. The received signal power can be determined by the receiving node. Then, the difference between the two signal powers and the distance separating the two nodes can be calculated using standard equation from communication theory.

There are also many other techniques to determine the distances of first-hop neighbor using time calculations or power calculations but discussing these techniques is beyond the scope of this work and can be found in related literature (Kohvakka, et al., 2006).

## LITERATURE REVIEW

This section presents a literature review that summarizes some of the most recent and related work on power conservation in wireless data communication networks, regardless of their technologies and protocols, but all share the same important feature of having limited energy resources. The review is presented in chronological order. For references published in the same year, they presented alphabetically according the last name of their first author.

B. Alawieh et al. (2009) studied analytically the benefits of transmission power control on throughput and energy consumption in a uniformly distributed power-aware ad hoc network where nodes are equipped with directional antennas. They also investigated the effect of collision on the energy consumption and proposed an energy consumption model that utilizes all aspects of energy wastage.

Xu et al. (2009) reduced energy consumption by exploiting multi-rate diversity in 802.11 wireless networks. They observed that probabilistic rate combination in transmission can significantly reduce power consumption, so they formulate the energy efficient rate combination as a non-convex optimization problem. To mitigate this problem, they proposed a joint Consecutive Packet Transmission (CPT) and Contention Window Adaptation (CWA) mechanism. Simulation results showed that the probabilistic rate combination can greatly save battery power, even up to 700 times compared with standard 802.11a/h protocol, which is the most important concerns in wireless networks because wireless clients usually have limited battery power capabilities.

Bari et al. (2008) proposed an efficient power conservation solution based on a Genetic Algorithm (GA) for scheduling the data gathering of relay nodes, which can significantly extend the lifetime of a relay node network. For smaller networks, where the global optimum can be determined, their GA based approach is always able to find the optimal solution. Furthermore, their algorithm can easily handle large networks, where it leads to significant improvements compared to traditional routing schemes.

Chiganmi et al. (2008) presented a novel approach for network wide broadcast called Inside-Out Power (INOP) adaptive approach. INOP is a novel variable power broadcast approach that uses local (two-hop neighborhood) information for determining the transmission power level at each transmitting node. They also proposed two alternative methods to cover the nodes that are not covered by the transmission of the source or a retransmitting node. Simulation results showed that, compared to other approaches; INOP achieves better results in terms of energy efficiency, and competes with and exceeds other approaches in terms of a number of other performance metrics including traffic overhead, coverage, and convergence time.

Huang et al. (2008) suggested a Self-Configuring Power-Saving (SCPS) protocol for wireless one-hop ad hoc networks. According to IEEE 802.11 WLAN standard, a station may enter a special Power-Saving (PS) mode. SCPS allows all stations in the PS mode to adjust their wakeup schedules whenever a station enters or exits the PS mode. The adjustment can balance the number of wakeup stations in each beacon interval so that the contention for transmission medium and the collisions in transmission will be ameliorated, which resulted in more efficient energy usage. Simulation has been done which showed that SCPS successfully balances the number of stations that wake up in each beacon interval, increases the sleep ratio, and reduces the collision probability. The combined effect reduces total energy consumption.

Namboodiri et al. (2008) presented algorithms that take into account a model of non-uniform gain with the objectives of minimizing the total power and maximum power to keep the network connected. They considered two cases: one where the antenna orientation is assumed given and another where the antenna orientation needs to be derived as well. Simulation results demonstrated that significant reductions were shown in the maximum as well as total power required to keep the network connected for the second case, thus demonstrating the benefits of using antenna orientation as parameter in topology construction.

Sridhar and Ephremides (2008) considered the problem of optimally controlling transmission power in a time-slotted wireless broadcast network. Fixed-length packets and Additive White Gaussian Noise (AWGN) channels are considered, and a simple Automatic Repetition Request (ARQ) scheme (send-and-wait) is used for error control. Packets are retransmitted until a minimum Quality-of-Service (QoS) requirement is met for each packet. Transmission powers were chosen from a finite set depending on the number of nodes that have received the packet successfully. Their goal was to minimize the total energy expended for each successful packet transmission. The system was studied when the transmitter chooses between two distinct powers, and the results were then extended to multiple powers. They observed that the optimal policy is always of the separation type. They also studied the effect of varying the QoS requirement on the energy and service time.

Zarifzadeh et al. (2008) redefined the problem of Topology Control (TC) regarding both transmission range and traffic load parameters. They mathematically formulated a mixed integer linear programming problem to find optimal solutions. Then, they introduced polynomial-time heuristic algorithms to practically solve the problem. During construction of network topology, they deliberately took into account the impact of the employed routing method on load of individual nodes. They formulated a problem, called Min-Max Load Sensitive Topology Control (MLSTC), for multihop wireless ad hoc networks. They showed the advantages of their proposed algorithms through experimental results, and they showed the superiority of the MLSTC approach over former TC schemes.

Wang and Kulkarni (2008) presented a simple local protocol, namely, *pCover*, which provides partial (but high) coverage in sensor networks. Through this protocol, they demonstrated that it is feasible to maintain a high coverage (~90%) while significantly increasing coverage duration when compared with protocols that provide full coverage. They showed that they are able to maintain 94% coverage for a duration that is 2.3–7 times the duration for which existing protocols maintain

full coverage. Through simulations, they showed that the protocol provides load balancing, i.e., the desired level of coverage is maintained (almost) until the point where all sensors deplete their batteries. They also showed that *pCover* handles failure of sensors, different coverage areas, different node densities, and different topologies, and can be used for dynamically changing the level of coverage.

Arora and Krunz (2007) proposed a power-controlled MAC protocol for directional antennas that allows dynamic adjustment of the transmission power for both data and Clear-To-Send (CTS) packets to optimize energy consumption. Simulation results demonstrated that the combined gain from concurrent transmissions using directional antennas and power control results in significant improvement in network throughput and considerable reduction in energy consumption.

Berenbrink et al. (2007) studied broadcasting and gossiping (probabilistic) algorithms in random and general ad hoc networks to minimize broadcasting and gossiping time, and energy consumption, which was measured in terms of the total number of messages (or transmissions) sent.

Powell et al. (2007) proposed a centralized algorithm to compute the optimal parameters of the probabilistic data propagation algorithm, and proved that these parameters maximize the lifespan of the network even when it is not possible to achieve energy balance.

Blumenthal et al. (2006) proved that the autonomous localization of nodes in WSNs is essential to minimize the complex self-organization task and consequently enhancing network lifetime. A method to measure the distance using the minimal transmission power between a transmitting node and a receiving node was proposed. They showed that the determined distance was very precise and has a low variance.

Ingelrest et al. (2006) investigated the problem of minimum energy broadcasting in ad hoc networks where nodes have capability to adjust their transmission range. They considered the minimum energy broadcasting problem, where nodes adjust their transmission power so that each node receives the packet and the total energy consumed by all nodes is minimized.

Karayiannis and Nadella (2006) expanded the versatility of entropy-constrained routing algorithms by making them capable of discovering routes based on multiple performance metrics. They found out that the second performance metric employed for route discovery relied on the power availability in the nodes of the network. Their proposed routing approach was evaluated in terms of the amount of power consumption associated with the routing of packets over an ad hoc mobile network in a variety of operating conditions.

Kohvakka et al. (2006) presented an energy-efficient neighbor discovery protocol targeted at synchronized low duty-cycle MAC schemes such as IEEE 802.15.4 and S-MAC. The protocol is validated by performance analysis and experimental measurements with physical WSN prototypes. Experimental results showed that the protocol can reduce node energy consumption up to 80% at 1-3 m/sec node mobility.

Oikonomou and Stavrakakis (2006) developed two topology-unaware MAC protocols, in which the scheduling time slots are allocated irrespectively of the underline topology, and derived their energy consumption. Using their protocol, they observed through simulation that when the system throughput is maximized, the power consumed is close to the minimum.

Dai et al. (2005) discussed five algorithms for routing tree construction that take advantage of directional antenna, e.g., Reverse-Cone-Pairwise (RCP), Simple-Linear (SL), Linear-Insertion (LI), Linear-Insertion-Pairwise (LIP), and a traditional approximation algorithm for the Travelling Salesman Problem (TSP). Their performances are compared through a simulation study to provide guidelines for tradeoffs under different network situations. These algorithms were also compared with two existing algorithms in terms of their energy efficiency.

Zheng and Kravets (2005) proposed an extensible on-demand power management framework for ad hoc networks that adapts to traffic load. Nodes maintain soft-state timers that determine power management transitions. Simulation results for their scheme with the Dynamic Source Routing (DSR) protocol showed that a reduction in energy consumption near 50% when compared to a network without power management under both long-lived Cluster-Based Routing (CBR) traffic and on–off traffic loads, with comparable throughput and latency. Preliminary results also showed that it outperforms existing routing backbone election approaches.

Son et al. (2004) proposed variable power link quality control techniques to enhance the performance of data delivery in WSNs. Packet based link quality control scheme is proposed to convert unreliable asymmetric and weak links to reliable wireless links with consistent link quality. A blacklisting approach was incorporated together to handle remaining unreliable links at adjusted transmission power level and link-based and packet-based blacklisting approaches were introduced. The proposed transmission power control with blacklisting scheme provides energy-efficient link quality control with minimal channel interference, and generates new network topologies with more consistent and reliable wireless links.

Gelenbe and Lent (2004) proposed a new energy efficient algorithm to find and maintain routes in MANETs. In particular, they introduced a dynamic discovery of paths that offer equilibrium between low-delay routes and an efficient use of network resources that extends the working lifetime of the network.

Younis et al. (2003) proposed an approach for energy-aware management of sensor networks that maximizes the lifetime of the sensors while achieving acceptable performance for sensed data delivery. The approach is to dynamically set routes and arbitrate medium access in order to minimize energy consumption and maximize sensor life. Simulation results showed that an order of magnitude enhancement in the time to network partitioning, 11% enhancement in network lifetime predictability, and 14% enhancement in average energy consumed per packet.

In addition to many individual researches, there are a number of international projects which have been launched for purpose of minimizing power consumption in low-power wireless devices. The efforts towards reducing power consumption are focused on design of energy efficient hardware and software. The US Department of Energy's Lawrence Berkley National Laboratory is working alongside industrial partners to develop energy efficient solutions for networks (Berkeley Lab, 2007). Energy efficient mesh control for WSNs project [Wat 09] aims to design a software layer that can be used for managing the topology and the dynamics in ad hoc wireless sensor networks in an energy efficient way. The results from this project will be applied directly to a product in the area of environmental monitoring and control.

The Energy efficient Internet Project (University of South Florida, 2009) at the University of South Florida addressed energy efficiency of the Internet by focusing on the edge devices. This project also addressed the direct energy use of high speed links connecting the edge devices. The project aimed at minimization of energy consumption in wireless communication networks with high demand for reliability is working on developing algorithms that allow for a network to be highly reliable with minimal energy consumption (Dutch Research Database, 2007).

There are several projects under the umbrella of the seventh framework programs (FP7) projects for example: End-to-End Efficiency (E3) project (E3 Project, 2009), carrier grade mesh networks (CARMEN) (CAMERON, 2008) and enhanced, ubiquitous, and dependable broadband access using mesh networks (EU-MESH) (EU-MESH, 2008), which mostly focus on efficiency of communication networks. However, these projects do not specifically focus on energy and spectrum efficiency of communication networks.

## THE LBPC SCHEME

This section presents a detail description of the LBPC scheme (Halasa, 2010; Kaabneh, et al., 2009). In this scheme, instead of transmitting with maximum power to cover up to its maximum radio transmission range ($R_{max}$), the transmitting node utilizes the location-information available on its first-hop neighbors to adjust its transmission power to cover up to a certain radio transmission range ($R$) according to one of the following radius adjustment criteria (modes):

*Farthest radius adjustment criterion.* In this mode, the transmitting node adjusts it radio transmission range to cover up to the farthest first-hop neighbor, i.e., set $R=R_{far}$, where $R_{far}$ is the distance between the transmitting node and the furthest first-hop neighbor. It can be expressed mathematically as:

$$R_{far} = \max(R_1, R_2, \ldots, R_k) \tag{7}$$

Where $k$ is the number of first-hop neighbors.

*Average radius adjustment criterion.* In this mode, the transmitting node adjusts it radio transmission range to cover up to the average distance of its first-hop neighbors, i.e., set $R=R_{avg} \pm \sigma$, where $R_{avg}$ is the average radius and $\sigma$ is the associated standard deviation. It can be expressed as follows:

$$R_{avg} = \frac{\sum_{i=1}^{k} R_i}{k} \tag{8}$$

$$\sigma = \sqrt{\left[ \frac{\sum_{i=1}^{k} R_i^2}{k} - \left( \frac{\sum_{i=1}^{k} R_i}{k} \right)^2 \right] / k} \tag{9}$$

In this work, we neglected $\sigma$ and set $R=R_{avg}$.

3. *Random radius adjustment criterion.* In this mode, the transmitting node adjusts it radio transmission range to cover up to a random distance between the nearest and furthest of its first-hop neighbors, i.e., $R=R_{ran}$, where $R_{ran}$ is the distance between the transmitting node and a random distance between the nearest and furthest of its first-hop neighbors. It is calculated as follows:

Calculate the distance to the nearest first-hope neighbor $(R_{near})$

$$R_{near} = min(R_1, R_2, ..., R_k) \qquad (10)$$

Calculate the distance to the farthest first-hope neighbor $(R_{far})$

$$R_{far} = max(R_1, R_2, ..., R_k) \qquad (11)$$

Calculate $R_{ran}$ as follows:

$$R_{ran} = R_{near} + \xi (R_{far} - R_{near}) \qquad (12)$$

Where $\xi$ is a random number between 0 and 1 $(0 \le \xi < 1)$.

The transmitting node adjusts its radio transmission range to conserve its energy which leads to total power conservation in MANET. It is clear from the above definition that there will be no extra cost or effect on the network routing algorithms, or any other protocols used, simply the node locally adjusts and controlled its radio transmission range.

In the farthest radius adjustment criterion, the node covers all of its first hop-neighbors as it does if it transmits with its maximum radio transmission range $(R_{max})$ as it is illustrated in Figure 1a. In the other two criteria, it only covers up to some extended radius; therefore, some of its first-hop neighbors that are covered with $R_{max}$ will not be reached. This degrades the network reachability as some nodes may be disconnected or not reachable in the first place as shown in Figures 1b and 1c.

The processing overheads (processing power and delay) due to the storing, retrieving, and calculating the radio transmission range is insignificant in comparison to the processing and storing capacities of the current mobile nodes. The processing overheads depend on the number of first-hop neighbors. Furthermore, to reduce processing overheads, the node does not need to calculate the radio transmission range for each transmission or session, but it can be performed depending mainly on the nodes mobility. For example, for low average nodes speed MANET, the duration for updating the radio transmission range can be increases as only few nodes would

*Figure 1. Radius adjustment criteria*

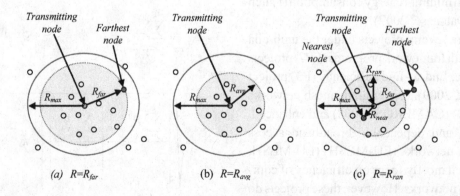

(a) $R=R_{far}$     (b) $R=R_{avg}$     (c) $R=R_{ran}$

change their locations or the change in nodes location is not that significant. While for high average nodes speed MANET, this may need to be done frequently to quickly update the nodes location and adjust the radio transmission range accordingly.

So that instead of transmitting with full power to cover up to its maximum radio transmission range ($R_{max}$), the transmitting node adjust its radio transmission range to less than that, which provides a power conservation depending on the square of the ratio $R/R_{max}$.

## The Power Conservation Ratio ($P_c$)

In order to evaluate the performance of the LBPC scheme, the power conservation ratio ($P_c$) is calculated, which is defined as the fraction of energy conserved, and it can be calculated as:

$$P_c = \left( \frac{E_f(n \rightarrow \bar{n}, r \rightarrow R_{max}) - E_f(n \rightarrow \hat{n}, r \rightarrow R)}{E_f(n \rightarrow \bar{n}, r \rightarrow R_{max})} \right) \times 100 \tag{13}$$

$$P_c = \left( 1 - \frac{\hat{n}R^2}{\bar{n}R_{max}^2} \right) \times 100 \tag{14}$$

Where $\hat{n}$ and $\bar{n}$ are the number of retransmissions with and without implementing the power conservation scheme. $R$ and $R_{max}$ are the adjusted and maximum radio transmission range. It is clear from Equation (14) that if the farthest radius adjustment criterion is used, then the power conservation ratio is only the square of the ratio of $R$ to $R_{max}$. For the other two criteria, it is always expected to have $\hat{n} < \bar{n}$, which in turns provide higher power conservation.

## Implementation of the LBPC Scheme on MANSim

In its current design MANSim (Al-Bahadili, 2010b) can only handle fixed radio transmission range, where all nodes on the network transmit with equal fixed radio transmission range. Therefore, in order to implement the LBPC scheme on MANSim, nodes should be allowed to calculate and adjust its radio transmissions range according to one of the radius adjustment criteria described above, so that another attributes should be named to accommodate the radio transmission range of the node. This is implemented as follows.

For each time interval, each node on the network calculates the distance ($r$) to all other nodes; all nodes for which $r$ is less than or equal to $R_{max}$ are considered as first-hop neighbors. Let us say, the node has $k$ first-hop neighbors. Then, depending on the radius adjustment criteria, the node adjusts its radio transmission range. For example, for the farthest radius adjustment criteria, the node calculates $R_{far}$, and set $R=R_{far}$, while for the average radius adjustment criterion, the node calculates $R_{avg}$ and set $R=R_{avg}$.

The node's estimated radio transmission range will be used until the beginning of the next time interval, because each time interval the nodes are allowed to move, i.e., changing their location (position on the network), which leads to topology change. This procedure is repeated for each time interval. Any node that has no neighbors ($k=0$) is prohibited from transmission for power saving. Thus, the node power conservation ($P_c(i)$) is calculated as $P_c(i)=1-(R/(R_{max})^2$. For each time interval ($j$), the average power conservation for this time interval ($P_{c,avg}(j)$) is calculated and stored. It is obtained by summing $P_c(i)$ for all transmitting nodes during interval *i* divided by the number of nodes (*m*). When the simulation time expires, then average of $P_{c,avg}(j)$ (for *j*=1 to *nIntv*) is calculated (*nIntv* is the number of time intervals). The calculation of $P_c$ can be expressed mathematically as:

$$P_c = \frac{\sum_{j=1}^{nIntv}\sum_{i=1}^{m}(1-\frac{R_i^2}{R_{max}^2})}{m \cdot nIntv} \qquad (15)$$

Figure 2 outlines the main steps for calculating the radio transmission range and number of first-hop neighbors for the LBPC scheme. These calculations are performed each time interval. Furthermore, having *k* and $p_t$ for each node *i* and for each time interval *j*, the average value $k_{avg}$ can be calculated.

## SIMULATION RESULTS AND DISCUSSION

In order to compare and evaluate the performance of the LBPC scheme in MANET's environment, a scenario is simulated using the MANET simulator (MANSim) (Al-Bahadili, 2010b). The scenario estimates and compares $P_c$ achieved by the LBPC scheme when used in conjunction with pure flooding (Bani-Yassein, et al., 2007), dynamic probabilistic (Al-Bahadili, 2010a), and LAR-1 (Ko & Vaidya, 2000) algorithms for route discovery

in MANETs. In this scenario, $P_c$ is estimated and compared for two radius adjustment criteria: the farthest radius adjustment criterion ($R=R_{far}$) and the average radius adjustment criterion ($R=R_{avg}$). Furthermore, the affects of the radius adjustment criteria on two network parameters are also estimated and compared, namely, the network Reachability (RCH) and the number of Retransmissions (RET) (Al-Bahadili & Jaradat, 2010).

RCH is defined as the average number of reachable nodes by any node normalized to the total number of nodes on the network (*n*). It also can be interrupted as the probability of successfully delivering a RREQ message from source to destination nodes anywhere on the network. RET is defined as the average number of retransmissions normalized to *n*.

The network environment for the scenario can be described as follows: The wireless mobile nodes are assumed to be randomly distributed in a fixed-size area of 600x600 m. One condition is enforced in this random distribution and implemented on MANSim geometrical module that is initially each node should have at least one first-hop neighbor. All nodes are allowed to move with the same average speed (*u*) of 2 m/sec (7.2 Km/hr). The nodes can move in all directions with equal probability (way-point model), but not allowed to leave the network area, and every node travelled outside the network area is forced back using the MANSim reduced-weight approach. The maximum radio transmission range ($R_{max}$) of the nodes is fixed at 100 m.

*Figure 2. Calculation of R and k*

```
Do for all nodes (node i=1 to n)
{
    Do for all nodes (node j=1 to n except i≠j)
    {
        Calculate the distance r between nodes i and j
        Identify and count the number of the first-hop neighbors for each node i, for which r≤Rmax
    }
    Calculate the radio transmission range for a node i (Ri) depending on the radius adjustment criterion
        (Rfar, Ravg, Rran)
    Set the number of first-hop neighbors for node i (ki)
}
Calculate the average values for each time interval j (kavg,ji)
```

The simulation time ($T_{sim}$) is taken to be 1800 sec (30 min). The nodes are set to periodically update and exchange their locations with their first-hop neighbors. In MANSim, the duration of the period also refers to as pause time ($\tau$), which is calculated as: $\tau=0.75 \times R_{max}/u$. For this scenario, for example, $\tau$=37.5 sec. Thus, for $T_{sim}$=1800 sec and $\tau$=37.5 sec, the size of the mobility run (nMobs) in MANSim is 48. This means the calculations are averaged after the nodes changed their locations 48 times, which contribute to satisfactory statistical uncertainties in the computed parameters.

For the dynamic probabilistic approach, the retransmission probability ($p_t$) is calculated as a function of the number of first-hop neighbors using the probability distribution function described in (Al-Bahadili 2101a). For the network environment described above the estimated average $p_t$ is 0.743 and the average number of first-hop neighbors is 6.799 nodes, for the maximum and the farthest radius adjustment criteria, while for the average radius adjustment criteria the values of average

$p_t$ and average $k$ are 0.743 and 6.799. However, $p_t$ of ~0.75 is quite reasonable for probabilistic algorithm. The input parameters for this scenario are summarized in Table 1.

The simulation results obtained from this scenario are given in Table 2 and also plotted in Figures 3, 4 and 5.

The main points that can be concluded from this scenario are summarized as follows:

- The LBPC scheme can be easily implemented on any route discovery algorithm in MANETs to provide significant power conservation.
- As it can be seen in Table 2 and Figure 3 that for a certain network setup, the $P_c$ changes from one route discovery algorithm to another, and it depends on the radius adjustment criterion.
- $P_c$ for average radius adjustment criterion is higher than what can be achieved by the farthest. For example, for pure flood-

*Table 1. Input parameters*

| Parameters | Values |
|---|---|
| Geometrical model | Random node distribution |
| Network area | 600x600 m |
| Number of nodes ($n$) | 100 nodes |
| Transmission radius ($R_{max}$) | 100 m |
| Average node speed ($u$) | 2 m/sec |
| Simulation time ($T_{sim}$) | 1800 sec. |
| Pause time ($\tau$) | $\tau = (0.75 \times R_{max})/u = 37.5$ |
| Number of mobility run (nMobs) | 48 |

*Table 2. Simulation results*

| Algorithm | RCH | | | RET | | | $P_c$ (%) | |
|---|---|---|---|---|---|---|---|---|
| | $R_{max}$ | $R_{far}$ | $R_{avg}$ | $R_{max}$ | $R_{far}$ | $R_{avg}$ | $R_{far}$ | $R_{avg}$ |
| Pure | 0.952 | 0.952 | 0.330 | 0.931 | 0.931 | 0.314 | 16.20 | 59.11 |
| Probabilistic | 0.799 | 0.799 | 0.125 | 0.574 | 0.574 | 0.086 | 16.49 | 60.40 |
| LAR-1 | 0.615 | 0.615 | 0.199 | 0.121 | 0.121 | 0.051 | 28.90 | 64.49 |

*Figure 3. Comparison of $P_c$ for pure, probabilistic, and LAR-1 algorithms*

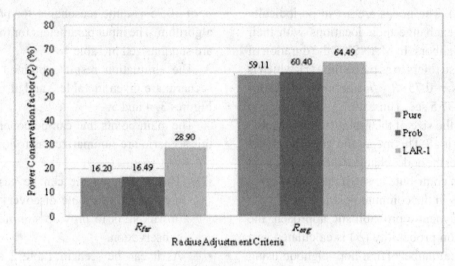

*Figure 4. Comparison of RCH for pure, probabilistic, and LAR-1 algorithms*

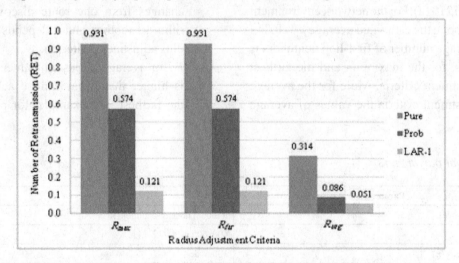

*Figure 5. Comparison of RET for pure, probabilistic, and LAR-1 algorithms*

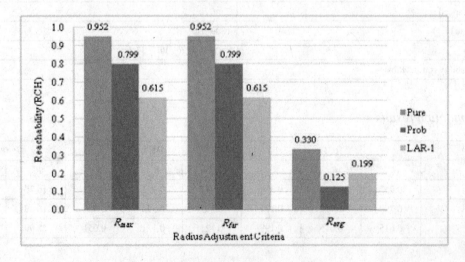

ing, which is considered as a high power consumption algorithm due to the high retransmission rate (RET=0.931), the power conservation ratios are 16.20% for the farthest criterion and 59.11% for the average criterion. However, the $P_c$ achieved by the average radius adjustment criterion is penalized by the significant reduction in RCH, which is reduced from 0.953 to 0.330. This is a significant drawback as RCH is an important performance measure that should be kept as high as possible, or as close as possible to 1.

- The $P_c$ achieved by the LBPC scheme utilizing the farthest radius adjustment criterion comes at no cost, where both RCH and RET are the same for maximum radius adjustment criterion. This is because the number of nodes involved in bypassing the Route Request (RREQ) packet during the route discovery phase is remained unchanged. This means that the LBPC scheme can save a significant power ratio without losing reachability.

- Although, Table 2 shows that $P_c$'s are nearly equal for pure and probabilistic algorithms for both farthest and average criteria, but in fact the total power consumed by the probabilistic is higher, because RET is less for probabilistic than pure because the total node's power consumption is directly proportional to the total number of transmissions.

- One other important point that can be realized, which is the performance of the LAR-1 combined with the LBPC scheme is better than the probabilistic algorithm, when the average radius adjustment criterion is used, as it can provide higher $P_c$ (64.49% compared to 60.50%), higher RCH (0.199 compared to 0.125), and less RET (0.051 compared to 0.086). This is because the nodes involved in computing the average radio transmission range

for each transmitting node are only those who are neighbors and located with the requested zone. Not like in the probabilistic algorithm where all neighboring nodes considered in calculating the average radio transmission range, which means more nodes considered and the possibility of having closer nodes increases. Of course involvement of closer nodes reduces the average transmission range, which consequently reduces the possibility of reaching the destination node, increases the number of hop count, and increases the number of retransmission.

## CONCLUSION

This chapter presented a description and evaluation of new efficient power conservation scheme for wireless mobile node in MANETs, namely, the Location-Based Power Conservation (LBPC) scheme. It is based on the concept of reducing the radio transmission range of the transmitting node by utilizing locally available nodes' location information to adjust R according to one of the three proposed radius adjustment criteria: farthest, average, and random. So that instead of transmitting with full power to cover up to its maximum radio transmission range ($R_{max}$), the transmitting node adjust R to less than $R_{max}$, which provides a power conservation factor equivalent to $(R/R_{max})^2$.

The LBPC scheme can be easily implemented with any route discovery algorithm in MANETs to provide significant power conservation. The amount of power conservation depends on the route discovery algorithm, and for each route discovery algorithm it depends on the selected radius adjustment criterion. The amount of power conservation for average radius adjustment criterion is higher than what can be achieved by the farthest. However, the achievement of the average criterion is penalized by the significant reduction in RCH. This is a significant drawback as RCH is an important performance measure that should be kept as high as possible, or as close as possible to 1. On the other hand, the amount of power conservation achieved by the LBPC scheme utilizing the farthest radius adjustment criterion comes at no cost, where both RCH and RET are the same for maximum radius adjustment criterion.

## RECOMMENDATIONS FOR FUTURE WORK

The main recommendations for future work are:

1. Implement, evaluate, and compare the performance of the LBPC scheme on other route discovery algorithms, such as the Multipoint Relaying (MPR) algorithms, other LAR algorithms, etc.
2. In order to overcome the main drawback of the average radius adjustment criterion, develop a new radius adjustment criterion based on a weighted-average value instead of the equal weight average radius adjustment criterion. In which, the farthest nodes assign a higher weight than the closer nodes to estimate a reasonable average radio transmission range that provides adequate network performance measures.
3. Investigate the performance of the LBPC scheme with random radius adjustment criterion and various distribution functions for randomly calculating the radio transmission range of the transmitting node in the range between the nearest and farthest first-hop neighbors.
4. Evaluate the performance of the LBPC scheme in terms of its effect on the load, throughput, and delay.
5. Evaluate the performance of the LBPC scheme in terms of actual power consumption measured in Watts or the lifetime of the mobile node.

## REFERENCES

E3 Project. (2009). *Website*. Retrieved from http://cordis.europa.eu/fetch?CALLER=FP7_PROJ_EN&ACTION=D&DOC=1& CAT=PROJ&QUERY=011b322313b1:7666:291412e1& RCN=85443.

Al-Bahadili, H. (2010a). Enhancing the performance of adjusted probabilistic broadcast in MANETs. *The Mediterranean Journal of Computers and Networks*, 6(4), 138–144.

Al-Bahadili, H. (2010b). On the use of discrete-event simulation in computer networks analysis and design. In Abu-Taieh, E. M. O., & El-Sheikh, A. A. (Eds.), *Handbook of Research on Discrete-Event Simulation Environments: Technologies and Applications* (pp. 414–442). Hershey, PA: IGI Global. doi:10.4018/978-1-60566-774-4.ch019

Al-Bahadili, H., & Jaradat, R. (2010). Performance evaluation of an OMPR algorithm for route discovery in noisy MANETs. *The International Journal of Computer Networks and Communications*, 2(1), 85–96.

Al-Bahadili, H., & Kaabneh, K. (2010). Analyzing the performance of probabilistic algorithm in noisy MANETs. *International Journal of Wireless & Mobile Networks*, 2(3), 83–95. doi:10.5121/ijwmn.2010.2306

Alawieh, B., Assi, C., & Mouftah, H. (2009). Power-aware ad hoc networks with directional antennas. *Journal of Ad Hoc Networks*, 7(3), 486–499. doi:10.1016/j.adhoc.2008.05.004

Arora, A., & Krunz, M. (2007). Power-controlled medium access for ad hoc networks with directional antennas. *Journal of Ad Hoc Networks*, 5(2), 145–161. doi:10.1016/j.adhoc.2005.10.001

Bani-Yassein, M., & Ould-Khaoua, M. (2007). Applications of probabilistic flooding in MANETs. *International Journal of Ubiquitous Computing and Communication*, 1(1), 1–5.

Bari, A., Wazed, S., Jaekel, A., & Bandyopadhyay, S. (2008). A genetic algorithm based approach for energy efficient routing in two-tiered sensor networks. *Journal of Ad Hoc Networks*, 7(4), 665–676. doi:10.1016/j.adhoc.2008.04.003

Berenbrink, P., Cooper, C., & Hu, Z. (2007). Energy efficient randomized communication in unknown ad hoc networks. In *Proceedings of 19th ACM Symposium on Parallelism in Algorithms and Architectures (SPAA 2007)*, (pp. 250–259). San Diego, CA: ACM Press.

Berkeley Lab. (2007). *Researchers are developing energy-efficient digital network technology*. Retrieved from http://www.lbl.gov/Science-Articles/Archive/EETD-efficient-networks.html.

Blumenthal, J., Reichenbach, F., & Timmermann, D. (2006). Minimal transmission power vs. signal strength as distance estimation for localization in wireless sensor networks. In *Proceedings of the 3rd IEEE International Workshop on Wireless Ad Hoc and Sensor Networks*, (pp. 761-766). Reston, VA: IEEE Press.

Boleng, J., & Camp, T. (2004). Adaptive location-aided mobile ad hoc network routing. In *Proceedings of the 23rd IEEE International Performance, Computing, and Communications Conference (IPCCC)*, (pp. 423-432). Phoenix, AZ: IEEE Press.

CARMEN. (2008). *Carrier grade mesh networks*. Retrieved from http://cordis.europa.eu/fetch?CALLER=FP7_PROJ_EN&ACTION=D&DOC=3&CAT=PROJ&QUERY=011b322267 17:c226:584c2e02&RCN=85283

Chiganmi, A., Baysan, M., Sarac, K., & Prakash, R. (2008). Variable power broadcast using local information in ad hoc networks. *Journal of Ad Hoc Networks*, 6(5), 675–695. doi:10.1016/j.adhoc.2007.06.002

Dai, F., Dai, Q., & Wu, J. (2005). Power efficient routing trees for ad hoc wireless networks using directional antenna. *Journal of Ad Hoc Networks*, 3(5), 621–628. doi:10.1016/j.adhoc.2004.08.008

Dutch Research Database. (2007). *Minimization of energy consumption in wireless communication networks with high demand for reliability*. Retrieved from http://www.onderzoekinformatie.nl/nl/oi/biza/d16000o/ OND1320539.

EU-MESH. (2008). *Enhanced, ubiquitous, and dependable broadband access using mesh networks*. Retrieved from http://cordis.europa.eu/fetch?CALLER=FP7_PROJ_EN&ACTION=D&DOC=1&CAT=PROJ&QUERY=011b322501 75:ea6a:60251d2d&RCN=85298.

Gelenbe, E., & Lent, R. (2004). Power-aware ad hoc cognitive packet networks. *Journal of Ad Hoc Network*, 2(3), 205–216. doi:10.1016/j.adhoc.2004.03.009

Halasa, A. (2010). *Development and performance evaluation of a location-based power conservation scheme for MANETs*. PhD Thesis. Amman, Jordan: The Arab Academy for Banking & Financial Sciences.

Huang, S., Jan, R., & Yang, W. (2008). SCPS: A self-configuring power-saving protocol for wireless ad hoc networks. *Journal of Computer Networks*, 52(6), 1328–1342. doi:10.1016/j.comnet.2008.01.007

Ingelrest, F., Simplot-Ryl, D., & Stojmenovic, I. (2006). Optimal transmission radius for energy efficient broadcasting protocols in ad hoc and sensor networks. *IEEE Transactions on Parallel and Distributed Systems*, 17(6), 536–547. doi:10.1109/TPDS.2006.74

Kaabneh, K., Halasa, A., & Al-Bahadili, H. (2009). An effective location-based power conservation scheme for mobile ad hoc networks. *American Journal of Applied Sciences*, 6(9), 1708–1713. doi:10.3844/ajassp.2009.1708.1713

Karayiannis, N., & Nadella, S. (2006). Power-conserving routing of ad hoc mobile wireless networks based on entropy-constrained algorithms. *Journal of Ad Hoc Networks*, 4(1), 24–35. doi:10.1016/j.adhoc.2004.04.006

Ko, Y., & Vaidya, N. (2000). Location-aided routing (LAR) in mobile ad hoc networks. *Journal of Wireless Networks*, 6(4), 307–321. doi:10.1023/A:1019106118419

Kohvakka, M., Suhonen, J., Kuorilehto, M., Kaseva, V., Hännikäinen, M., & Hämäläinen, T. (2006). Energy-efficient neighbor discovery protocol for mobile wireless sensor networks. *Journal of Ad Hoc Networks*, 7(1), 24–41. doi:10.1016/j.adhoc.2007.11.016

Mobile Group. (2008). *Green base station: The benefits of going green*. Retrieved from http://www.mobileeurope.co.uk/features/113824/greenbasestation_-_the_benefits_of_going_green.html.

Namboodiri, V., Gao, L., & Janaswamy, R. (2008). Power efficient topology control for static wireless networks with switched beam directional antennas. *Journal of Ad Hoc Networks*, 6(2), 287–306. doi:10.1016/j.adhoc.2007.01.003

Oikonomou, K., & Stavrakakis, I. (2006). Energy considerations for topology-unaware TDMA MAC protocols. *Journal of Ad Hoc Networks*, 4(3), 359–379. doi:10.1016/j.adhoc.2004.10.003

Pan, J., Hou, Y., Cai, L., Shi, Y., & Shen, S. (2003). Topology control for wireless sensor networks. In *Proceedings of 9th Annual International Conference on Mobile Computing and Networking (MOBICOM 2003)*, (pp. 286-299). San Diego, CA: IEEE Press.

Powell, O., Leonea, P., & Rolima, J. (2007). Energy optimal data propagation in wireless sensor networks. *Journal of Parallel and Distributed Computing*, 67(3), 302–317. doi:10.1016/j.jpdc.2006.10.007

Son, D., Krishnamachari, B., & Heidemann, J. (2004). Experimental study of the effects of transmission power control and blacklisting in wireless sensor networks. In *Proceedings of the 1st IEEE Conference on Sensor and Ad Hoc Communication and Networks*, (pp. 289-298). IEEE Press.

Sridhar, A., & Ephremides, A. (2008). Energy optimization in wireless broadcasting through power control. *Journal of Ad Hoc Networks*, 6(2), 155–167. doi:10.1016/j.adhoc.2006.11.001

University of South Florida. (2009). *The energy efficient internet project*. Retrieved from http://www.csee.usf.edu/~christen/energy/main.html.

Wang, L., & Kulkarni, S. (2008). Sacrificing a little coverage can substantially increase network lifetime. *Journal of Ad Hoc Networks*, 6(8), 1281–1300. doi:10.1016/j.adhoc.2007.11.013

Xu, Y., Lui, J., & Chiu, D. (2009). Improving energy efficiency via probabilistic rate combination in 802.11 multi-rate wireless networks. *Journal of Ad Hoc Networks*, 7(7), 1370–1385. doi:10.1016/j.adhoc.2009.01.005

Younis, M., Youssef, M., & Akkaya, K. (2003). Energy-aware management for cluster-based sensor networks. *Journal of Computer Networks*, 43(5), 649–668. doi:10.1016/S1389-1286(03)00305-0

Zarifzadeh, S., Nayyeri, A., & Yazdani, N. (2008). Efficient construction of network topology to conserve energy in wireless ad hoc networks. *Journal of Computer Communication*, 31, 160–173. doi:10.1016/j.comcom.2007.10.040

Zheng, R., & Kravets, R. (2005). On-demand power management for ad hoc networks. *Journal of Ad Hoc Networks*, 3(1), 51–68. doi:10.1016/j.adhoc.2003.09.008

## KEY TERMS AND DEFINITIONS

**Flooding Optimization Algorithms:** Algorithms which are developed to reduce the number of redundant retransmissions. As the number of retransmissions required for broadcasting is decreased, the bandwidth is saved and contention, collision, and node power consumption are reduced, and this will improve the overall network performance.

**LAR-1 Algorithm:** The location-aided outing (LAR) algorithm makes use of location information to reduce routing overhead. There are basically two LAR algorithms, namely, LAR-1 and LAR-2. They differ in the manner they use to determine the request zone. In this work, we mainly concern with the LAR-1 scheme. In LAR-1, it is assumed that the source node S knows the location of the destination node D at time $t_0$. It is also assumed that node S knows the speed ($u$) with which D can move. If at time $t_1$, node S initiates a route discovery for node D, it uses these information to define a region, which is called the expected zone, to be a circle of radius $R_e = u(t_1 - t_0)$ centered at the location of D. In addition, in LAR-1, another region is defined, which is called the request zone. It is defined as the smallest rectangle that includes current location of S and the expected zone.

**MANET:** A MANET (mobile ad hoc network) is defined as a collection of low-power wireless mobile nodes forming a temporary wireless network without the aid of any established infrastructure or centralized administration.

**Number of Retransmissions:** It is defined as the average number of retransmissions normalized to the total number of nodes on the network.

**Power Conservation Factor:** It is defined as the percentage save in the consumed energy.

**Probabilistic Algorithm:** It is a widely-used flooding optimization algorithm during route discovery in MANETs, which aims at reducing number of retransmissions probabilistically. In this algorithm, when receiving a RREQ packet, a node retransmits the packet with a certain retransmission probability, otherwise it discards the packet.

**Pure Flooding:** One of the earliest broadcast mechanisms proposed in the literature, which is also called simple or blind flooding. Although it is simple and reliable, pure flooding is costly where it costs $n$ transmissions in a network of $n$ reachable nodes. In addition, pure flooding in wireless networks results in serious redundancy, contention, and collisions in the network; such a scenario has often been referred to as the Broadcast Storm Problem (BSP).

**Reachability:** It is defined as the average number of reachable nodes by any node normalized to the total number of nodes on the network. It also can be interrupted as the probability of successfully delivering a RREQ message from source to destination nodes anywhere on the network.

**Route Discovery:** The first phase of the dynamic routing process, in which a route between source and destination nodes is established for the first time.

**Routing Protocol:** A routing protocol is a set of rules used by routers to determine the most appropriate paths into which they should forward packets towards their intended destinations.

# Chapter 10
# Comparing Various Route Discovery Algorithms in Ad Hoc Wireless Networks

**Hussein Al-Bahadili**
*Petra University, Jordan*

**Abdel Rahman Alzoubaidi**
*NYIT Amman Campus, Jordan*

**Ali Al-Khalidi**
*Yanbu University College, Saudi Arabia*

## ABSTRACT

*Dynamic (reactive or on-demand) routing protocols used in wireless ad hoc networks suffer from transmitting a huge number of control packets during the route discovery phase of the protocols, which increases the overhead significantly. Therefore, a number of optimization protocols have been developed throughout the years. This chapter compares the performance of various route discovery algorithms in ad hoc wireless networks, namely, pure flooding, probabilistic, Location-Aided Routing scheme 1 (LAR-1), LAR-1-Probabilsitic (LAR-1P), and Optimal Multipoint Relying (OMPR). The results obtained through the different simulations are analyzed and compared. This chapter will help practitioners of various kinds (academics, professionals, researchers, and students) grasp a solid understanding of the behavior of ad hoc wireless network route discovery algorithms and develop an appreciation for flooding optimization mechanisms. It also substantiates the case of experimenting via simulation with such models and shows how the different simulation parameters interplay.*

## INTRODUCTION

An ad hoc wireless network is a mobile, wireless network that does not necessitate a pre-existing infrastructure or centralized administration (Lang, 2008). A data packet in ad hoc networks is forwarded to other mobile nodes on the network through a reliable and an efficient route established by routing protocols. A routing protocol is part of the network layer software that is responsible for deciding which output path a packet should be transmitted on. Many routing protocols have been proposed for ad hoc networks (Graziani & Johnson, 2007). These algorithms differ in the approach they use for searching a new route

DOI: 10.4018/978-1-4666-0191-8.ch010

and/or modifying a known route, when nodes move. Each of the available routing algorithms has its own unique characteristic strengths and weaknesses. Routing protocols are classified into different categories according to their properties and applications (Ayub & Garrido, 2008). The most widely used mechanism for categorizing routing protocols is the one that is based on routing information update, which according to it, routing protocols are classified into proactive (static) or reactive (dynamic) or a combination of them (Royer & Toh, 1999).

A Dynamic Routing Protocol (DRP) consists of two main phases: route discovery and route maintenance. Route discovery is the process that allows any node on the network to dynamically discover a route to other nodes on the network (Rahman, et al., 2004). Reactive protocols such as Dynamic Source Routing (DSR) (Johnson & Maltz, 1996), Ad Hoc On-Demand Distance Vector (AODV) (Perkins & Royer, 1999), Zone Routing Protocol (ZRP) (Haas, et al., 2002), and Location Aided Routing (LAR) (Ko & Vaidya, 2000), or variations of them are widely used in MANETs.

It is usually assumed that the cost (in terms of bandwidth and power consumptions and delay) of information exchange during route discovery is higher than the cost of point-to-point data forwarding. Therefore, the process of route discovery should be done with minimum complexity, overhead, and bandwidth and power consumption (Rahman, et al., 2004).

Route discovery is used when a source node desires to send a packet to some destination node and does not already have a valid route to that destination; in which the source node initiates a route discovery process to locate the destination. It broadcasts a Route Request (RREQ) packet to its neighbours, which then forward the request to their neighbours, and so on until the expiration of the RREQ packet. During the forwarding process, the intermediate nodes record in their route tables the address of the node from which the first copy of the broadcast packet is received. Once the RREQ

reaches the destination, the destination responds with a Route Reply (RREP) packet back to the source node through the route from which it first received the RREQ (Royer & Toh, 1999).

Pure flooding is one of the earliest, simplest, and reliable mechanisms proposed in the literature for route discovery in MANETs. In pure flooding, each node rebroadcasts the message to its neighbours upon receiving it for the first time, starting at the source node. Although it is simple and reliable, pure flooding is costly where it costs $n$ transmissions in a network of $n$ reachable nodes. In addition, pure flooding in wireless networks, using the IEEE 802.11 protocol, results in serious redundancy, contention, and collisions in the network; such a scenario has often been referred to as the Broadcast Storm Problem (BSP) (Tseng, et al., 2002).

To eliminate the effects of BSP during route discovery in MANETs, a variety of flooding optimization algorithms have been developed, such as probabilistic broadcast (Haas, et al., 2006; Al-Bahadili, 2010a; Al-Bahadili & Kaabneh, 2010), locations-based (Ko & Vaidya 2000; Boleng & Camp 2004), Multipoint Relaying (MPR) (Qayyum, et al., 2002; Al-Bahadili & Jaradat, 2010), counter-based (Tseng, et al., 2002), distance-based (Tseng, et al., 2002), and cluster-based (Bettstetter, 2004) algorithms. They all try to limit the number of collisions by limiting the number of retransmissions. As the number of retransmissions required for broadcasting is decreased, the bandwidth is saved and contention and node power consumption are reduced, and this will improve the overall network performance.

The wireless network environment can be categorized, according to the presence of noise or packet-loss, into two types; these are (Al-Bahadili & Kaabneh, 2010):

1.  A noiseless (error-free) environment, which represents an ideal network environment, in which it is assumed that all data transmitted by a source node is successfully and

correctly received by a destination node. It is characterized by the following axioms or assumptions: the world is flat, all radios have equal range, and their transmission range is circular, communication link symmetry, perfect link, signal strength is a simple function of distance.

2. A noisy (error-prone) environment, which represents a realistic network environment, in which the received signal will differ from the transmitted signal, due to various transmission impairments, such as: wireless signal attenuation, free space loss, thermal noise, atmospheric absorption, multipath effect, refraction.

All of these impairments are represented by a generic name, noise, and the environment is called noisy environment. For modeling and simulation purposes, the noisy environment can be described by introducing a probability function, which referred to as the probability of reception ($p_c$). It is defined as the probability that a wireless transmitted data is survived being lost and successfully delivered to a destination node despite the presence of all or any of the above impairments.

This chapter compares the performance of a number of route discovery algorithms in noisy wireless ad hoc network through simulation using the Mobile Ad Hoc Network (MANET) Simulation (MANSim) (Al-Bahadili, 2010b). The compared algorithms include: pure flooding (Bani-Yassein, et al., 2006), probabilistic broadcast (Al-Bahadili, 2010a; Al-Bahadili & Kaabneh, 2010), Location-Aided Routing scheme 1 (LAR-1) (Ko & Vaidya, 2000), and LAR-1-Probabilistic (LAR-1P) (Al-Bahadili, et al., 2007), and Optimal MPR (OMPR) algorithms (Al-Bahadili & Jaradat, 2010). The simulations were aimed to estimate the variation of the number of Retransmissions (RET) and network Reachability (RCH) against $p_c$. This chapter can be a good reference as little efforts have been carried-out to investigate the performance of such algorithms in wireless ad hoc networks suffering from high packet-loss.

## DESCRIPTION OF THE ROUTE DISCOVERY ALGORITHMS

This chapter compares the performance of five route discovery algorithms, namely, pure flooding, probabilistic broadcast, LAR-1, LAR-1P, and OMPR algorithms. The pure flooding algorithm was described above, while the description of the other algorithms is presented next.

## Probabilistic Broadcast Algorithm

Probabilistic algorithm is widely-used for flooding optimization during route discovery in wireless ad hoc networks. It aims at reducing number of retransmissions, in an attempt to alleviate the effects of the BSP in MANETs (Al-Bahadili, 2010a; Al-Bahadili & Kaabneh, 2010; Bani-Yassin, et al., 2007). In this scheme, when receiving a RREQ packet, a node retransmits the packet with a certain retransmission probability ($p_t$) and with probability ($1-p_t$) it discards the packet. A node is allowed to retransmit a given RREQ packet only once, i.e., if a node receives a packet, it checks to see if it has retransmitted it before, if so then it just discards it, otherwise it performs its probabilistic retransmission check. Nodes usually can identify the RREQ packet through its sequence number. The source node $p_t$ is always set to 1, to enable the source node to initialize the RREQ. While, $p_t$ for intermediate nodes (all nodes except the source) is determined using a static or dynamic approach. In static approach, a pre-determined $p_t$ ($P_t$) ($0 \leq P_t \leq 1$) is set for each node on the networks. While, in dynamic approach, each node on the network locally calculates its $p_t$ using certain probability distribution function of one or more independent variables. Figure 1 outlines the probabilistic broadcast algorithm.

*Figure 1. The probabilistic broadcast algorithm*

---

**If** (IRange=1) **Then** {The receiving node is within the transmission range of the sender, in a noiseless
                    environment this guarantees request reception by the receiver. IRange=0 means the receiver
                    is not within the transmission range of the sender}
  **If** (IRet(i)=0) **Then** {The node has not retransmitted the request before (IRet(i)=0)}
    $\xi_1$=rnd() {$\xi_1$ some random number between 0 and 1}
    $p_t$=function_$p_t$()
    **If** ($\xi_1 <= p_t$) **Then**
      Retransmit RREQ
      IRet(i)=1 {Update the node retransmission index IRet(i) by equating it to 1}
    **End if**
  **End if**
 **End if**
**Function_$p_t$()** {Determining $p_t$}
 **If** (IProb="Static") **Then** {IProb is an integer indicates the approach to be used for determining $p_t$ whether it is
                    static or dynamic}
    $p_t$=constant value
**Else** (IProb="Dynamic")
    $p_t$=$f(k)$
**End If**

---

## Determination of Dynamic $p_t$

In a dynamic probabilistic algorithm, $p_t$ is usually calculated as a function of the number of first-hop neighbors ($k$), and it is referred to as $p_t(k)$. Many functions have been developed for calculating $p_t(k)$ (Al-Bahadili, 2010a; Bani-Yassin, et al., 2006; Hass, et al., 2002; Kim, et al., 2004; Sasson, et al., 2003; Scott & Yasinsac, 2004; Zhang & Agrawal, 2005).

In this work, $p_t(k)$ function presented in Al-Bahadili (2010a) is considered. This is because it demonstrated an excellent performance in comparison with other distribution functions in various network conditions, which is calculated as:

$$p_t = \begin{cases} p_{max} & for \quad k \leq N_1 \\ p_1 - \dfrac{k - N_1}{N_2 - N_1}(p_1 - p_2) & for \quad N_1 < k < N_2 \\ p_{min} & for \quad k \geq N_2 \end{cases}$$

(1)

Where $p_t(k)$ is the node retransmission probability; $k$ is the number of first-hop neighbor for the transmitting node; $p_{min}$ is the minimum $p_t$ that

could be assigned for a node; $p_{max}$ is the maximum $p_t$ that could be assigned for a node; $N_1$ is the number of nodes at or below which $p_t$ is equal to $p_{max}$; $N_2$ is the number of nodes at or above which $p_t$ is equal to $p_{min}$, $p_1$ and $p_2$ are the $p_t$s assigned to intermediate nodes surrounded by $k=N_1+1$ and $k=N_2-1$ nodes, respectively, $p_1$ and $p_2$ should lie between $p_{max}$ and $p_{min}$ (i.e., $p_{max} \geq p_{1/2} \geq p_{min}$), and also $p_1 \geq p_2$. Figure 2 shows the variation of $p_t$ with $k$. In general, selection of satisfactory distribution in the interval [$N_1+1, N_2-1$] and the values of $p_{max}$, $p_{min}, p_1, p_2, N_1$, and $N_2$ depend on a number of factors and need to be carefully considered for every network condition.

The reasons for selecting three ranges can be explained as follows:

1. Low node density neighborhood ($k \leq N_1$). In this case, $p_t$ of the intermediate node is set to $p_{max}$ to increase the probability of forwarding the RREQ packet across this low density neighborhood to ensure high reachability. Due to the small number of neighboring nodes this may incur an insignificant increase in the number of retransmissions.

*Figure 2. Retransmission probability as a function of k*

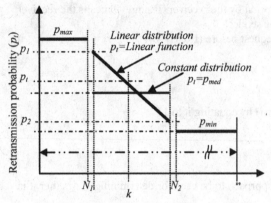

Number of first-hop neighbors (*k*)

2.  Medium node density neighborhood ($N_1 < k < N_2$). In this case, $p_t$ of the intermediate node is either a constant value or calculated using a linear function of *k*. In a linear relation, for example, $p_t$ can be assumed to decrease linearly from $p_1$ to $p_2$ with increasing *k*. This looks very acceptable, because as *k* increases, some of the intermediate nodes may fail retransmitting the RREQ packets, but still some will succeed, so that the chance of forwarding the RREQ packets remains high incorporating insignificant reduction in network reachability.

3.  High node density neighborhood ($k \geq N_2$). In this case, $p_t$ of the intermediate node is set to $p_{min}$ to reduce the probability of forwarding the RREQ packet. But, due to the high node density some nodes will success in forwarding the RREQ packet. Thus, the number of retransmissions is reduced incurring lower broadcast collision without sacrificing high reachability.

## Effect of Noise

It has been proved in the literature that the performance of probabilistic flooding, in particular, the network reachability is significantly affected in presence of noise, which is so common and unavoidable in MANET environment (Al-Bahadili, 2010a). This section shows how a noise negatively affects the performance of probabilistic algorithms. This can be explained with the help of Figure 3 as follows: Assume that nodes A and G are the source and destination nodes, and nodes B and C are intermediate nodes. Node G can be reached through nodes B and C. Figure 3a shows the RREQ packet dissemination from node A to G using pure flooding in noiseless environment, in which node G receives the RREQ packet twice through nodes B and C. However, it will send only one RREP through node B or C depending on which one forward the RREQ first.

On the other hand for the same network topology, if probabilistic flooding is used, there are three possibilities, these are: (1) both B and C, (2) either B or C, and (3) neither B nor C will retransmit the RREQ packet. Assume that only node B succeeds to retransmit the RREQ packet. For the same topology in noisy environment, assume that node A be unsuccessful in delivering the RREQ packet to node B (due to presence of noise) and be successful in delivering the RREQ packet to node C. Thus, the RREQ packet will not be delivered to node G, and node G appears as unreachable. This is because node B has no packet to retransmit and node C prohibits from retransmission by the probabilistic algorithm.

## Location-Aided Routing (LAR) Protocols

Location information can be used to reduce propagation of RREQ packets, to perform controlled flooding, to maintain valid routes in mobility conditions and to make simplified packet forwarding decisions. The basic advantage of using location information for wireless routing is to improve network scalability by reducing overall routing overhead. The routing protocols that are based on location information are called Location-Aided Routing (LAR) protocols (Blazevic, et al., 2005; Ko & Vaidya, 2002).

*Figure 3. Pure and probabilistic algorithms in various network conditions: (a) Pure flooding algorithm, (b) Probabilistic algorithm in noiseless environment, and (c) Probabilistic algorithm in noisy environment*

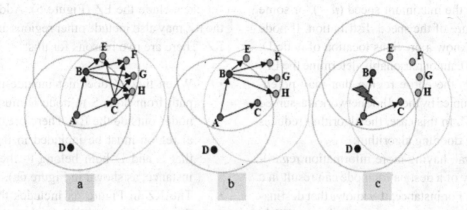

Location information used in the LAR protocol may be provided by the Global Positioning System (GPS). With the availability of GPS, it is possible for a mobile node to know its physical location. Even more, current GPS provides accurate three-dimensional location (latitude, longitude, and altitude), velocity and precise time traceable to coordinate Universal Time (UTC). In reality, position information provided by GPS includes some amount of error, which is the difference between GPS-calculated coordinates and the real coordinates. For instance, NAVSTAR GPS has positional accuracy of about 50–100 m and differential GPS offers accuracies of a few meters.

It is assumed that each node knows its current location precisely (i.e., no error). However, the ideas suggested here can also be applied when the location is known only approximately, and the mobile nodes are allowed to move in a two-dimensional plane.

Basically, there are two types of LAR protocols, namely LAR scheme 1 (LAR-1) and LAR scheme 2 (LAR-2). In this work, we concern with the first scheme, which is described below. However, before proceeding with the description of the LAR-1 protocol, we present definitions of some common terms that are used in LAR protocols, these are Expected Zone (EZ) and Request Zone (RZ).

## Expected Zone (EZ)

Consider a node S that needs to find a route to node D. Assume that node S knows that node D was at location L at time $t_0$, and the current time is $t_1$. Then, the EZ of node D, from the viewpoint of node S at time $t_1$, is the region that node S expects to contain node D at time $t_1$. Node S can determine the EZ based on the knowledge that node D was at location L at time $t_0$. For instance, if node S knows that node D travels with speed $u$, then S may assume that the EZ is the circular region of radius $u(t_1 - t_0)$, Figure 4a.

If the actual speed happens to be larger than the average, then the destination may actually be outside the EZ at time $t_1$ and vice versa. Thus, EZ is only an estimate made by node S to determine

*Figure 4. Examples of expected zones (Ko & Vaidya, 2000)*

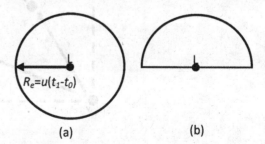

(a)  (b)

a region that potentially contains D at time $t_1$. In general, it is possible to define $u$ to be the average speed ($u_{av}$), the maximum speed ($u_{max}$), or some other measure of the speed distribution. If node S does not know a previous location of node D, then node S cannot reasonably determine the EZ, in this case, the entire region that may potentially be occupied by the ad hoc network is assumed to be the EZ. In this case, the algorithm reduces to the basic flooding algorithm.

In general, having more information regarding mobility of a destination node can result in a smaller EZ. For instance, if S knows that destination D is moving north, then the circular EZ in Figure 4a can be reduced to a semi-circle, as in Figure 4b (Ko & Vaidya, 2000).

## Request Zone (RZ)

Again, consider node S that needs to determine a route to node D. The LAR algorithms use pure flooding with one modification. Node S defines (implicitly or explicitly) a RZ for the RREQ. A node forwards a RREQ only if it belongs to the RZ (unlike pure flooding). To increase the probability that the RREQ will reach node D, the RZ should include the EZ (Figure 5). Additionally, the RZ may also include other regions around the RZ. There are two reasons for this:

- When the EZ does not include node S, a path from node S to node D must include nodes outside the EZ. Therefore, additional region must be included in the RZ, so that S and D both belong to the RZ (for instance, as shown in Figure 6a).

- The RZ in Figure 6a includes the EZ. Is this an adequate RZ? In the example in Figure 6b, all paths from S to D include nodes that are outside the RZ. Thus, there is no guarantee that a path can be found consisting only of the nodes in a chosen RZ. Therefore, if a route is not discovered within a suitable timeout period, the protocol allows S to initiate a new route discovery with an expanded RZ – in most simulations, the expanded zone includes the entire network space. In this event, howev-

*Figure 5. Illustration of the request and expected zones*

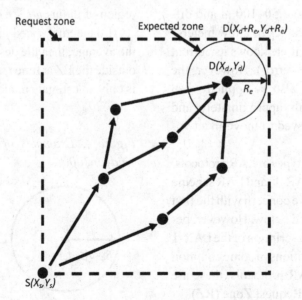

er, the latency in determining the route to D will be longer (as more than one round of RREQ propagation will be needed).

Note that the probabilities of finding a path (in the first attempt) can be increased by increasing the size of the initial RZ (Figure 6c). However, route discovery overhead also increases with the size of the RZ. Thus, there exists a trade-off between latency of route determination and the message overhead.

## Determining Membership of Request Zone (RZ)

As noted above, the LAR algorithms are essentially identical to pure flooding, with the modification that a node that is not in the RZ does not forward a RREQ to its neighbours. Recall that, in the pure flooding algorithm, a node forwards a RREQ if it has not received the request before and it is not the intended destination. Thus, implementing LAR algorithm requires that a node be able to determine if it is in the RZ for a particular RREQ – the two LAR algorithms presented here differ in the manner in which this determination is made.

## The LAR-1 Scheme

The LAR-1 scheme uses a RZ that is rectangular in shape, Figure 7. It is assumed that node S knows that node D was at location $(X_d, Y_d)$ at time $t_0$. At time $t_1$, node S initiates a new route discovery for destination D. It is also assumed that node S knows the speed $u$ with which D can move. Using this, node S defines the EZ at time $t_1$ to be the circle of radius $R_e=u(t_1 - t_0)$ centred at location $(X_d, Y_d)$. (As stated before, instead of the average speed, $u$ may be chosen to be the maximum speed or some other function of the speed distribution).

In LAR-1 algorithm, the RZ is defined to be the smallest rectangle that includes current location of S and the EZ (the circular region defined above), such that the sides of the rectangle are parallel to the X and Y axes. In Figure 7a, the RZ is the rectangle whose corners are S, A, B and C, whereas in Figure 7b, the rectangle has corners at point A, B, C and G. In Figure 7, current location of node S is denoted as $(X_s, Y_s)$.

The source node S can, thus, determine the four corners of the RZ. S includes their coordinates with the RREQ packet transmitted when initiating route discovery. When a node receives a RREQ,

*Figure 6. Examples of request zones (Ko & Vaidya, 2000)*

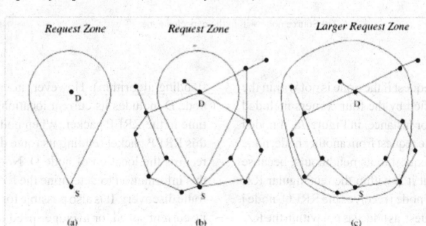

*Figure 7. The LAR-1 scheme (Ko & Vaidya, 2000)*

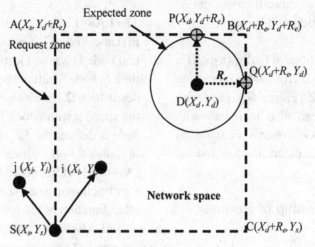

(a) Source node outside the expected zone

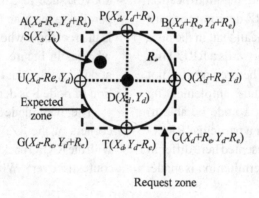

(b) Source node within the expected zone.

it discards the request if the node is not within the rectangle specified by the four corners included in the RREQ. For instance, in Figure 7a, if node i receives the route request from another node, node i forwards the request to its neighbours, because i determines that it is within the rectangular RZ. However, when node j receives the RREQ, node j discards the request, as node j is not within the RZ.

When node D receives the RREQ packet, it replies by sending a RREP packet (as in the pure flooding algorithm). However, in case of LAR, node D includes its current location and current time in the RREP packet. When node S receives this RREP packet (ending its route discovery), it records the location of node D. Node S can use this information to determine the RZ for a future route discovery. It is also possible for D to include its current speed, or average speed over a recent time interval, with the RREP packet. This information could be used in a future route discovery.

## Size of the Request Zone (RZ)

Note that the size of the rectangular RZ above is proportional to (1) average speed of movement $u$, and (2) elapsed time since the last known location of the destination was recorded. It is clear that the sender comes to know location of the destination only at the end of a route discovery (as noted in the previous paragraph). At low speeds, route discoveries occur after long intervals, because routes break less often (thus, $t_1$-$t_0$ is large). So, although factor (1) above is small, factor (2) becomes large at low speeds, potentially resulting in a larger RZ. At high speeds as well, for similar reasons, a large RZ may be observed. So, in general, a smaller RZ may occur at speeds that are neither too small, nor too large. For low speeds, it is possible to reduce the size of the RZ by piggybacking the location information on other packets, in addition to RREPs.

## LAR-1P Algorithm

The LAR-1P algorithm (Al-Bahadili, et al., 2007) is a combination of the two route discovery algorithms discussed above; these are: The LAR-1 and probabilistic algorithms. Therefore, it is referred to as the LAR-1P algorithm. The description of LAR-1P algorithm is straightforward. It is simply, when receiving a broadcast message, a node within the RZ rebroadcasts the message with a pre-defined $p_t$, the $p_t$ value decides that its LAR-1 or LAR-1P, and each node is allowed to rebroadcast the received message only once. This, of course, reduces the number of retransmissions and node average duplicate reception, thereafter the number of collisions and contentions.

This is at the cost of reducing the network reachability, because if the number of intermediate nodes within the RZ is small and some of them will not rebroadcast the request message, which may result in a failure of delivery of the request message to the destination, so that the source has to reinitiate a new request message. However, a significant advantage may be achieved if the number of intermediate nodes within the RZ is large. Figure 8 outlines the LAR-1P algorithm.

## The MPR Algorithms

The idea behind MPR algorithms is to define, for each node in the network, a set of nodes called MPRs or simply relay nodes, these relay nodes are a subset of the one-hop neighbors of the node, which can establish communication paths with all two-hop neighbors. They are responsible for

*Figure 8. The LAR-1P algorithm*

```
{
    Determine the requested zone for a specific source (S) and destination (D) nodes
    Determine the number of nodes within the request zone (z) and their IDs (node number 1 is the source
    node and node number z is the destination node)
    Loop over the number of nodes within the request zone (i=2 to z-1)
Perform probabilistic algorithm computation to find out the parameter iRet(i) as follows:
    On receiving a broadcast request at node i, do the following:
        If iRet(i) = 0 Then (The node has not retransmit the request before)
            ξ = rnd() (ξ some random number between 0 and 1)
            If ξ <=pt Then
                Retransmit request
                iRet(i)=1 {Update node retransmission index iRet(i) by equating it to 1}
            End if
        End if
}
```

forwarding the broadcast message (e.g., RREQ packet) upon receiving it for the first time, while non relay nodes will not forward the message. The set of MPRs or relay nodes of a particular node ($x$) is referred to as $MPR(x)$ (Qayyum, et al., 2002). The number of relay nodes in $MPR(x)$ is variable and it depends on the network topology, obviously it is less than or equal the number of one-hop neighbors. When the relay nodes are the same as the one-hop neighbors then this is pure flooding.

MPR algorithms require that each node knows the full list of its one-hop neighbor nodes ($N_1(x)$) and its two-hop neighbor nodes ($N_2(x)$). This information is collected via the periodic *HELLO* messages transmitted by mobile nodes. The *HELLO* messages contain the list of the one-hop nodes heard by the originator of the *HELLOs*. So that each node by collecting these *HELLO* messages can identify its one- and two-hop neighbor nodes, i.e., $N_1(x)$ and ($N_2(x)$).

Figure 9 illustrates how does an MPR algorithm works in a regular-geometry and noiseless environment. It shows that to diffuse a packet to the three-hops neighbors, a source node uniformly surrounded by 8, 16, and 24 one-, two-, three- hops neighbors, respectively, pure MPR algorithm needs 11 retransmissions as compared to 24 for pure flooding (Qayyum, et al., 2002).

It can be clearly seen from Figure 9 that an MPR algorithm may reduce the number of redundant retransmissions at no cost of the network

reachability. However, with high transmission errors, some of the forwarding nodes may not receive the packet due to a transmission error; this may result in a failure of delivery of the broadcast packet to all nodes in the network.

Figure 10a shows the use of MPR algorithms for flooding of a broadcast packet in a network that is characterized by a non-uniform node distribution and noiseless environment ($p_c$=1), while Figure 10b shows the flooding of a broadcast packet using MPR in a noisy environment. If using pure flooding, nodes F, G and H will have a chance to receive the packet from either node A, B, or C. While, using MPR nodes F, G, and H will have a chance to receive the packet from node B only. Thus, in a noisy environment, if the link between the source S and B is broken, then nodes F, G, and H will be isolated and no data can be delivered to them.

## Costs of MPR Algorithms

In order to calculate the forwarding nodes, a certain number of procedures and information are required. These requirements form the cost of the MPR selection algorithm. Four costs of MPR algorithms described as follows (Liang, et al., 2006):

- **Time complexity:** is the time required to complete the forwarding nodes calculations. A heuristic that requires much time

*Figure 9. Diffusion of broadcast packet using: (a) pure flooding. (b) MPR flooding*

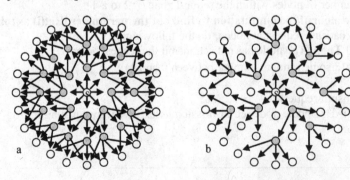

*Figure 10. Flooding using MPR algorithm in noiseless and noisy environments*

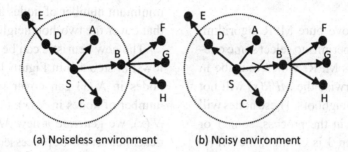

(a) Noiseless environment      (b) Noisy environment

to run the calculation may be too complex to be deployed. Furthermore, when the network topology changes rapidly, the frequency of a forwarding node calculation also increases, and thus the time consumption of the calculation is huge for a complex heuristic. Hence, an efficient heuristic that consumes less time is essential for the MPR set generation.

- **Message complexity:** is the number of *HELLO* messages required for the calculation of the MPR set. For any MPR scheme, a number of *HELLO* messages need to be exchanged between nodes in advance. These *HELLO* messages contain the necessary information for a heuristic to implement the forwarding node set calculation. Algorithms in different groups or even in the same group may require a different number of *HELLO* messages. However, frequent information exchange will consume the limited bandwidth of the link and also accelerate the energy consumption of mobile nodes. Therefore, the number of *HELLO* messages exchanged, which is regarded as the message complexity, can significantly affect the performance of an MPR algorithm.

- **Information range:** is the hop level of neighboring nodes information (i.e. two-hops, three-hops, etc.) needed for the calculation of MPRs. Generally, the larger information range an algorithm requires,

the more time and message exchange it will need depending on the algorithm. For example, an information range up to four hops may not be efficient for an MPR algorithm because messages need a long time to be transmitted to the source node and the information they carry may be outdated by then.

- **Source dependant:** in which a forwarding node needs to know from which node the packet was received in order to determine whether or not to retransmit this packet. If an algorithm is not source dependant, a forwarding node will broadcast all messages that are received for the first time. This requirement increases the complexity of both the message sending and receiving process in an algorithm.

## Pure MPR Algorithm

Pure MPR algorithm is designed to reduce the number of forwarding nodes and maintain the same network reachability, regardless of any other operation or optimization issues (e.g., QoS, reliability, power conservation, etc.). Therefore, the forwarding nodes selection heuristic is relatively simple. In addition, in pure MPR algorithm, using the neighbor-knowledge information obtained via periodic *HELLO* messages, each node can locally and independently calculate its own set of $N_1(x)$, $N_2(x)$ and *MPR(x)* nodes. Figure 11 outlines a simple pure MPR algorithm (Qayyum, et al., 2002).

To analyze the above pure MPR algorithm, first notice that step 3 permits to select some one-hop neighbor nodes as MPRs which must be in the $MPR(x)$ set. Otherwise the $MPR(x)$ will not cover all the two-hop neighbors. These nodes will be selected as MPRs in the process, sooner or later. Therefore, if step 3 is omitted, the MPRs set can still be calculated with success, i.e., it will cover all the two-hop neighbors. The presence of step 3 is for optimizing the MPR set. Those nodes which are necessary to cover the two-hop set $N_2(x)$ are all selected in the beginning, which helps to reduce the number of uncovered nodes of $N_2(x)$ at the start of the normal recursive procedure of step 4.

One drawback of pure MPR algorithm is that the selected forwarding set (i.e., $MPR(x)$) may not represent the optimum selection. This is because in step 4-a, there may be more than one nodes in $N_1(x)$ cover the same maximum number of nodes in $N_2(x)$. In step 4-b, one of nodes that covers this maximum number is selected, for example, by considering the node's ID, which not enough to ensure the optimum selection.

## Optimal Selection Heuristic

In this section, we describe a new heuristic for selecting the optimal $MPR(x)$ set, which is the set that has the minimum number of forwarding nodes. An optimal $MPR(x)$ set for a node is defined as a subset of the one-hop neighbors, which covers

the two-hop neighbors of that node, and it has the minimum number of nodes among all other sets that cover the two-hop neighbors of the node.

The new heuristic can be summarized as follows: in step 4-b in Figure 11, if more than one nodes in $N_1(x)$ can cover the same maximum number of nodes in $N_2(x)$, then for each node in $N_1(x)$, we generate a new $MPR(x)$ set and each generated set will be processed independently until all nodes in $N_2(x)$ are covered by the generated $MPR(x)$ set. Thus we will end up with a number of valid $MPR(x)$ sets. The $MPR(x)$ set selected is the one with minimum number of nodes. Figure 12 outlines the heuristic used for selecting the optimal $MPR(x)$ set.

## The OMPR Algorithm

The Optimal MPR (OMPR) algorithm uses the heuristic described above to select the optimal $MPR(x)$ set. It maximizes the performance of the network as it reduces the number of retransmission, which consequently reduces bandwidth and power consumption, contention, and collisions at the receiver.

Figure 13 outlines the implementation of the OMPR algorithm to calculate two main performance measures, namely: (1) number of retransmission (RET), which is defined as the average number of nodes that retransmit the RREQ normalized to the total number of nodes within the network ($n$); and (2) reachability (RCH), which represents the average number of reachable nodes by any node within the network normalized to $n$,

*Figure 11. The heuristic used for selecting the MPRs in pure MPR algorithm (Qayyum, et al., 2002)*

For each node, after receiving *HELLO* messages from its neighbors, do:
- (1) Construct its own set of $N_1(x)$ and $N_2(x)$ nodes
- (2) Start with an empty MPR set $MPR(x)$
- (3) First select those one-hop neighbor nodes in $N_1(x)$ as MPRs which are the only neighbor of some node in $N_2(x)$, and add these one-hop neighbor nodes to $MPR(x)$
- (4) While there still exist some nodes in $N_2(x)$ which are not covered by $MPR(x)$:
   - a.  For each node in $N_1(x)$ which is not in $MPR(x)$, compute the number of nodes that it covers among the uncovered nodes in the set $N_2(x)$.
   - b.  Add the node of $N_1(x)$ to $MPR(x)$ for which this number is maximum.

*Figure 12. The heuristic used for selecting the optimal MPRs*

For each node, after receiving *HELLO* messages from its neighbors, do:
(1)  Construct its own set of $N_1(x)$ and $N_2(x)$ nodes
(2)  Start with an empty MPR set $MPR(x)$
(3)  First select those one-hop neighbor nodes in $N_1(x)$ as MPRs which are the only neighbor of some node in $N_2(x)$, and add these one-hop neighbor nodes to the MPR set $MPR(x)$
(4)  Set $M=1$, where $M$ is the number of $MPR(x)$ sets
(5)  Set $m=1$, where $m$ is a counter for the number of $MPR(x)$ sets
(6)  While ($m \leq M$)
    a.  While there still exist some nodes in $N_2(x)$ which are not covered by $MPR(x)_m$:
        i.   For each node in $N_1(x)$ which is not in $MPR(x)_m$, compute the covered nodes
        ii.  Compute the maximum number of nodes among the uncovered nodes in the set $N_2(x)$ that is covered one or more nodes in the set $N_1(x)$
        iii. Compute the number of nodes ($K$) which cover this maximum
        iv. If ($K=1$)
                Add the node of $N_1(x)$ to $MPR(x)_m$
        Else ($K>1$)
                Compute the number of new generated set ($A$) as: $A=K-1$
                Select a node in $N_1(x)$ that covers this maximum
                Add the node of $N_1(x)$ to $MPR(x)_m$
                For ($i=1$ to A) (Each other node that covers this maximum)
                        Generates new set as follows:
                        Select a node in $N_1(x)$ that covers this maximum
                        Add the node of $N_1(x)$ to $MPR(x)_{M+i}$
                Compute the total number of sets ($M$) as: $M=M+K-1$
        End If
    b.  $m=m+1$
(7)  For all sets $MPR(x)_1$ to $MPR(x)_M$ select the MPR set with the least number of nodes as $MPR(x)$.

or it also can be defined as the probability that a RREQ packet initiated by any node (source node) will be successfully delivered to any other node (destination node) within the network.

Since each node needs to know its one-hop neighbor, in Figure 14 we present an algorithm for calculating the one-hop neighbor for each node in noisy ad hoc networks. This is done by presenting the noise level in terms of $p_c$. So that, for each node to discover its one-hop neighbor, it must be sure that the node is within its transmission range and the $p_c$ is equal to less than a certain random number $\xi$. However, the same algorithm can be used for noiseless environment by setting $p_c$ to unity.

## Features of the OMPR Algorithm

The main features of the OMPR algorithm can be summarized as follows:

- It is a neighbor-knowledge algorithm, in which each node needs to know the full list of its one-hop neighbors, and should pass this information back to all of them.
- Each node calculates its MPR set locally. Therefore, it is a source-dependent process.
- It generates an optimal MPR set for each node which has the minimum number of nodes among all other sets that cover the two-hop neighbors for that node.
- The number of relay nodes for each node depends on the network topology and it is highly affected by the node mobility.

*Figure 13. An algorithm for calculating RET and RCH using the OMPR algorithm*

---

(1) Generate nodes

(2) Calculate pause time ($\tau$=0.75*$R/u$) // $R$ is the transmission radius and $u$ is the average node speed

(3) Calculate number of mobility loops ($M=T_{sim}/\tau$) // Where $T_{sim}$ is the simulation time

(4) For ($m$=1 to $M$) Do

    a. For each node $x$ ($x$=1, 2, ..., $n$) // Where $n$ is the number nodes within the network

        Calculate node one-hop neighbors $N_1(x)$ using the algorithm in Figure 6

    b. For each node $x$ ($x$=1, 2, ..., $n$)

        Use the heuristic described in Section 5.1 to select the optimal MPR($x$) set

    c. For each node $x$ ($x$=1, 2, ..., $n$)

        Initiate RREQ

        Identify all nodes which are reachable by node $x$

        Construct the spanning tree starting with node $x$

        Use the MPR($x$) set

            Calculate the total number of nodes which receive the RREQ packet ($Rx$)

            Calculate the total number of nodes which retransmit the RREQ packet ($Tx$)

        Accumulate $Rx/(n$-1) into $accRx$ // The source node is excluded

        Accumulate $Tx/(n$-1) into $accTx$ // The source node is excluded

    d. Calculate average value $accRx/n$ and accumulate the result into $avgRx$

    e. Calculate average value $accTx/n$ and accumulate the result into $avgTx$

    f. Update nodes location

(5) Calculate average value $avgRx/m$ // Represents reachability (RCH)

(6) Calculate average value $avgTx/m$ // Represents number of retransmission normalized to $n$ (RET)

---

*Figure 14. Calculation of one-hop neighbor in a noisy MANET*

---

For a source node ($i$) Do:

    For each node within the network (except the source node $i$) Do:

        Calculate the distance ($d$) between two nodes ($i$ and $j$) using $d = \sqrt{(x_i - x_j)^2 + (y_i - y_j)^2}$

        If ($d{\leq}R$) Then             // Where $R$ is the source node transmission radius

        Generate a random number ($\xi$) ($0{\leq}\xi{<}1$)

        If ($\xi{\leq}p_c$) Then           // Where $p_c$ is the probability of reception

            Node is successfully delivered to node $j$

        Else ($\xi{>}p_c$)

            Node is failed to delivered to node $j$

        End If

    End If

---

- The performance of the OMPR may be extremely affected by the presence of noise. This is due to the fact that if the link between a source node and a relay node (a node in $N_1(x)$) is broken, then all nodes in $N_2(x)$ that are attained through this relay node are disconnected.

## SIMULATIONS AND RESULTS

The network simulator used in this work is MANSim (Al-Bahadili, 2010b). It is a MANET simulator especially developed to simulate and evaluate the performance of a number of flooding optimization algorithms for MANETs. It is written in C++ language, and it consists of four major modules, these are: network, mobility, computational, and algorithm modules.

In order to evaluate and compare the performance of the various route discovery algorithms (namely, pure flooding, probabilistic flooding with fixed $p_t$=0.8, probabilistic flooding with dynamic $p_t$, LAR-1, LAR-1P with $p_t$=0.8, and OMPR) in noisy wireless ad hoc networks, they all implemented on MANSim and a number of simulations were performed using MANSim. These simulations investigate the variation of RET and RCH with $p_c$. The input parameters for these simulations are listed in Table 1. The simulations results are plotted in Figures 15 and 16.

The main points that are concluded from these simulations can be summarized as follows:

- The probabilistic approach always achieves the highest possible RCH, but at the same time it introduces a low reduction in RET when it is compared with the other techniques.
- The LAR-1 and LAR-1P algorithms presents the highest reduction in RET but at the same time they provide the lowest RCH.
- The OMPR algorithm presents a moderate reduction in RET, when it is compared with probabilistic (fixed and dynamic $p_t$), LAR-1, and LAR-1P. It performs better than probabilistic and less than LAR-1 and LAR-1P for various values of $p_c$. The RCH it achieves is higher than that of LAR-1 and LAR-1P algorithms.

*Table 1. Input parameters*

| Parameters | Values |
|---|---|
| Geometrical model | Random node distribution |
| Network area | 1000x1000 m |
| Number of nodes ($n$) | 100 nodes. |
| Transmission radius ($R$) | 200 m |
| Average node speed ($u$) | 5 m/sec |
| Probability of reception ($p_c$) | From 0.5 to 1.0 in step of 0.1 |
| Simulation time ($T_{sim}$) | 300 sec |
| Pause time ($\tau$) | $\tau$=0.75*($R/u$)=30 sec |

*Figure 15. Variation of RET with $p_c$ for various algorithms*

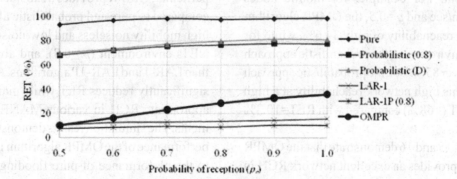

*Figure 16. Variation of RCH with $p_c$ for various algorithms*

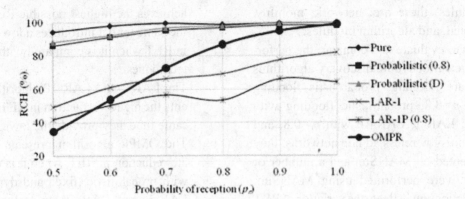

• The RCH of the OMPR algorithm is highly affected and ruined due presence of noise as shown in Figure 16.

Since the main objective of using flooding optimization during route discovery is to achieve a cost-effective RCH, which means a highest possible reachability at a reasonable number of retransmission. The obtained results demonstrated that the OMPR algorithm provides an excellent performance as it can achieve an excellent cost-effective reachability, for various network noise levels, as compared to other route discovery algorithms.

Figure 16 shows that the probabilistic and OMPR algorithms provide almost a comparative performance in noiseless and low-noise environments ($p_c$>0.8). But, in terms of network reachability, the probabilistic approach overwhelmed the performance of the OMPR algorithm in noisy environment. For example, for mobile nodes with $u$=5 m/sec and $p_c$=0.5, the OMPR algorithm achieves a reachability of only 34.6%, while for the same environment, the probabilistic approach achieves over 85%. But, the probabilistic approach achieves this high network reachability at a high cost of RET ($\approx$68%) compared with RET=10.3% for OMPR.

Figures 15 and 16 demonstrate that the OMPR algorithm provides an excellent network RCH in noisy environment, when compared with LAR-1 and LAR-1P. For example, when $p_c$=0.8, OMPR achieves a RCH of 86.6% compared with 69.2% and 53.4% for LAR-1 and LAR-1P, respectively. However, this is achieved at a cost of 28.8% RET compared with 13.8% and 8.9%, for LAR-1 and LAR-1P, respectively. The results also demonstrate that the OMPR algorithm is very sensitive to the variation in noise-level. Pure flooding is the least affected algorithm, then probabilistic algorithm, followed by the LAR-1 and LAR-1P algorithms.

## CONCLUSION

The main conclusion of this work is that the OMPR algorithm demonstrated an excellent cost-effective performance as compared to other route discovery algorithms, such as: pure flooding, probabilistic flooding, LAR-1 and LAR-1P algorithms In particular, OMPR provides a satisfactory RCH as compared to pure and probabilistic algorithms in high mobility noiseless and low-noise level MANETs environment ($p_c$≥0.8), and always higher than LAR-1 and LAR-1P algorithms. Also, OMPR significantly reduces RET while maintaining an appropriate RCH in various MANETs environments. The simulation results demonstrate that the performance of the OMPR algorithm is equivalent to the performance of pure flooding with minimum cost, when $p_c > 0.8$. The main drawback of the OMPR is its high sensitivity to noise-level as it yields the highest average rate of change in reachability in comparison with other algorithms.

# REFERENCES

Al-Bahadili, H. (2010a). Enhancing the performance of adjusted probabilistic broadcast in MANETs. *The Mediterranean Journal of Computers and Networks*, 6(4), 138–144.

Al-Bahadili, H. (2010b). On the use of discrete-event simulation in computer networks analysis and design. In Abu-Taieh, E. M. O., & El-Sheikh, A. A. (Eds.), *Handbook of Research on Discrete-Event Simulation Environments: Technologies and Applications* (pp. 414–442). Hershey, PA: IGI Global. doi:10.4018/978-1-60566-774-4.ch019

Al-Bahadili, H., Al-Basheer, O., & Al-Thaher, A. (2007). A location-aided routing-probabilistic algorithm for flooding optimization in MANETs. In *Proceedings of Mosharaka International Conference on Communications, Networking, and Information Technology (MIC-CNIT 2007)*. Amman, Jordan: IEEE Press.

Al-Bahadili, H., & Jaradat, R. (2010). Performance evaluation of an OMPR algorithm for route discovery in noisy MANETs. *The International Journal of Computer Networks and Communications*, 2(1), 85–96.

Al-Bahadili, H., & Kaabneh, K. (2010). Analyzing the performance of probabilistic algorithm in noisy MANETs. *International Journal of Wireless & Mobile Networks*, 2(3), 83–95. doi:10.5121/ijwmn.2010.2306

Ayub, J., & Garrido, G. (2008). *Routing in wireless mobile ad hoc networks*. Berlin, Germany: VDM Verlag.

Bani-Yassein, M., & Ould-Khaoua, M. (2007). Applications of probabilistic flooding in MANETs. *International Journal of Ubiquitous Computing and Communication*, 1(1), 1–5.

Bani-Yassein, M., Ould-Khaoua, M., Mackenzie, L., & Papanastasiou, S. (2006). Performance analysis of adjusted probabilistic broadcasting in mobile ad hoc networks. *International Journal of Wireless Information Networks*, 13(2), 127–140. doi:10.1007/s10776-006-0027-0

Bettstetter, C. (2004). The cluster density of a distributed clustering algorithm in ad hoc networks. In *Proceedings of 2004 IEEE International Conference on Communications (ICC 2004)*, (vol 7), (pp. 4336-4340). Paris, France: IEEE Press.

Blazevic, L., Boudec, J., & Giordano, S. (2005). A location-based routing method for mobile ad hoc networks. *IEEE Transactions on Mobile Computing*, 4(2), 97–110. doi:10.1109/TMC.2005.16

Boleng, J., & Camp, T. (2004). Adaptive location-aided mobile ad hoc network routing. In *Proceedings of the 23rd IEEE International Performance, Computing, and Communications Conference (IPCCC)*, (pp. 423-432). Phoenix, AZ: IEEE Press.

Graziani, R., & Johnson, A. (2007). *Routing protocols and concepts: CCNA companion guide*. New York: Cisco Press.

Haas, Z. J., Halpern, J. Y., & Li, L. (2006). Gossip-based ad hoc routing. *IEEE/ACM Transactions on Networking*, 14(3), 479–491. doi:10.1109/TNET.2006.876186

Haas, Z. J., Pearlman, M. R., & Samar, P. (2002). The zone routing protocol (ZRP) for ad hoc networks. *Mobile Ad Hoc Network Working Group, IETF Internet Draft*. Retrieved on 10 October 2009 from http://tools.ietf.org/id/draft-ietf-manet-zone-zrp-04.txt.

Johnson, D. B., & Maltz, D. A. (1996). Dynamic source routing in ad hoc wireless networks. In Imielinski, T., & Korth, H. (Eds.), *Mobile Computing* (pp. 153–181). Berlin, Germany: Kluwer Academic Publishers. doi:10.1007/978-0-585-29603-6_5

Kim, J. S., Zhang, Q., & Agrawal, D. P. (2004). Probabilistic broadcasting based on coverage area and neighbor confirmation in mobile ad hoc networks. In *Proceedings of the IEEE Global Telecommunications Conference Workshops (GlobeCom 2004)*, (pp. 96–101). Dallas, TX: IEEE Press.

Ko, Y., & Vaidya, N. (2000). Location-aided routing (LAR) in mobile ad hoc networks. *Journal of Wireless Networks*, 6(4), 307–321. doi:10.1023/A:1019106118419

Land, D. (2008). *Routing protocols for mobile ad hoc networks: Classification, evaluation, and challenges*. Berlin, Germany: VDM Verlag.

Liang, O., Sekercioglu, Y., & Mani, N. (2006). A survey of multipoint relay based broadcast schemes in wireless ad hoc networks. *IEEE Communications Surveys & Tutorials*, 8(4), 30–46. doi:10.1109/COMST.2006.283820

Perkins, C., & Royer, E. (1999). Ad-hoc on demand distance vector routing. In *Proceedings of the 2nd IEEE Workshop on Mobile Computing Systems and Applications (WMCSA)*, (pp. 90-100). New Orleans, LA: IEEE Press.

Qayyum, A., Viennot, L., & Laouiti, A. (2002). Multipoint relaying for flooding broadcast messages in mobile wireless networks. In *Proceedings of the 35th Hawaii International Conference on System Sciences (HICSS 2002)*, (pp. 3866- 3875). Hawaii, HI: IEEE Press.

Rahman, A., Olesinski, W., & Gburzynski, P. (2004). Controlled flooding in wireless ad hoc networks. In *Proceedings of IEEE International Workshop on Wireless Ad Hoc Networks (IWWAN 2004)*. Oulu, Finland: IEEE Press.

Royer, E., & Toh, C. (1999). A review of current routing protocols for ad hoc mobile wireless networks. *IEEE Personal Communication Magazine*, 6(2), 46-55.

Sasson, Y., Cavin, D., & Schiper, A. (2003). Probabilistic broadcast for flooding in wireless mobile ad hoc networks. In *Proceedings of IEEE Wireless Communications and Networking (WCNC 2003)*, (vol 2), (pp. 1124-1130). New Orleans, LA: IEEE Press.

Scott, D., & Yasinsac, A. (2004). Dynamic probabilistic retransmission in ad hoc networks. In H. R. Arabnia, L. T. Yang, & C. H. Yeh (Eds.), *Proceeding of the International Conference on Wireless Networks (ICWN 2004)*, (vol 1), (pp. 158-164). Las Vegas, NV: CSREA Press.

Tseng, T., Ni, S., Chen, Y., & Sheu, J. (2002). The broadcast storm problem in a mobile ad hoc network. *Journal of Wireless Networks*, 8(2-3), 153–167. doi:10.1023/A:1013763825347

Zhang, Q., & Agrawal, D. P. (2005). Dynamic probabilistic broadcasting in MANETs. *Journal of Parallel and Distributed Computing*, 65(2), 220–233. doi:10.1016/j.jpdc.2004.09.006

## KEY TERMS AND DEFINITIONS

**Flooding Optimization Algorithm:** Is defined as the algorithm that is developed to reduce the number of redundant retransmissions during the routing process.

**LAR-1P Algorithm:** Is a flooding optimization algorithm that is developed to alleviate the effect of the broadcast storm problem during route discovery by dynamic routing protocols. It utilizes two flooding optimization algorithms, namely, LAR-1 and probabilistic algorithms. It can also be used for data packets routing.

**Location-Aided Routing Scheme 1(LAR-1) Algorithm:** Is flooding optimization algorithm based on using the location information to reduce the number of retransmission during the route discovery process. It can also be used for data packets routing.

**MANET Simulator (MANSim):** It is an academic, research-level computer network simulator, which can be used to evaluate, analyze, and compare the performance of a number of flooding optimization algorithms in ideal and realistic ad hoc environments. It is written in C++ programming language, and consists of four main modules: network, mobility, computational, and algorithm modules.

**Multipoint Relaying (MPR) Algorithm:** Is a flooding optimization algorithm that is developed to alleviate the effect of the broadcast storm problem during route discovery by dynamic routing protocols. It defines, for each node in the network, a set of nodes called multipoint relays

(MPRs) or simply relay nodes, these relay nodes are a subset of the one-hop neighbors of the node, which can establish communication paths with all two-hop neighbors. They are responsible for forwarding the broadcast packet upon receiving it for the first time, while non relay nodes will not forward the message. It can also be used for data packets routing.

**Probabilistic Algorithm:** Is a flooding optimization algorithm aims at reducing the number of retransmissions probabilistically. In this algorithm, when receiving a route request packet, a node retransmits the packet with a certain retransmission probability, otherwise it discards the packet. It can be used for control or data packets routing. It can also be used for data packets routing.

**Route Discovery:** Is the process of finding the optimum, most appropriate, and available route between the source and destination nodes.

**Routing Protocol:** Is a set of rules used by routers to determine the most appropriate paths into which they should forward packets towards their intended destinations.

**Wireless Ad Hoc Network:** Is defined as a collection of low-power wireless mobile nodes forming a temporary network without the aid of any established infrastructure or centralized administration.

# Chapter 11
# Simulation in Amateur Packet Radio Networks

**Miroslav Škorić**
*University of Novi Sad, Serbia*

## ABSTRACT

*Computer programs that radio amateurs use in their packet radio networks give various opportunities in simulating real data communication systems. Such systems include radio-relay networks of digital repeaters that operate in cities or in rural and remote locations, email servers that handle amateur radio messaging and file exchange, and a variety of end-user stations at home or work. This chapter summarizes the results of recent experiments in network simulations by using amateur radio software in a local area network. We tested the main features of those amateur radio programs and their repercussions to the functionality of simulated networks and to the comfort and satisfaction in average network participants. Described tests help practitioners, students, and teachers in computer science and communication technologies, in implementing amateur radio within the existing computer networks and in planning and using telecommunication systems without making any investment in hardware infrastructure.*

## INTRODUCTION

Most of our schools, workplaces and homes are equipped with personal computers. Sometimes it is not only an isolated, single machine but also a Local Area Network (LAN) consisting of at least two or three machines, or even much more computers. In the simplest case there are two computers in a LAN, which is a suitable situation for simulating radio traffic between two different amateur radio facilities, such as digital amateur radio-relay systems - commonly called *digipeaters*

(a short of 'digital repeaters'), or *BBS* ('Bulletin Board Systems'; i.e., email servers). In addition, we can test the radio traffic between any of those facilities and the end-users who are sitting in front of their personal computers wired to the amateur radio transmitters. By simulating the amateur radio traffic, we become more familiar with technologies and protocols used in real amateur Radio Frequency (RF) networks – consisting of thousands radio-relay stations, radio email servers, and various home or work communicating solutions. The experiments with those technologies enlarge capacities in learners and educators alike to understand the implemented concepts, and

DOI: 10.4018/978-1-4666-0191-8.ch011

provide them with valuable tools for constructing new and building more effective and efficient systems for every day's communications. For you, researchers who already have experience in implementing real High Frequency (HF), VHF or UHF communications, these simulations will provide information on available amateur radio solutions that can give you some ideas on possible improvements in technical systems that are under your responsibility.

Furthermore, the software simulations that we are going to discuss in this chapter, would help you in finding most suitable solutions for your particular communication situation in the area of the amateur radio, and will help you in learning more about proper configuration of the subsystems in your amateur radio infrastructure. Finally, our experiments with the amateur radio in a LAN will help to all those who are already involved in this useful hobby, to 'relax' their working computer(s) from communicating devices such as radio-modems and transmitters, as well as accompanied programs and procedures that would, in turn, be moved to their 'playing' machine(s). By following principles in this book chapter, such a transition would be on behalf of all users of your computer(s) at home or work.

## BACKGROUND

"The healthiest way to increase the profits is by decreasing the costs" – told a professor of economics to his young audience some 20 years ago. As a remembrance of his words, the position I want to demonstrate in this chapter is that we should keep our educational experiments at low cost whenever possible. That means we do not always need to spend finances – that are often restricted nowadays, for obtaining brand new hardware and software resources for educative demonstrations and simulations in our computer rooms. In that manner, we support those solutions that offer enough opportunities for presenting behavior of

the real things we want to simulate, but without requiring additional funding for technical devices, or program upgrade subscriptions, or licensing fees, and so forth. One of the applicable solutions are 'ham radio' (= amateur radio) programs, which are globally available for occasional testing and later permanent use (if the experimenter decides to join the hobby). Although some of those programs do not belong to the categories of 'free' or 'shareware' software, they are freely available for installing and experimenting on the non-commercial basis. Despite the fact that most of amateur radio programmers do not allow using their software for making businesses or for establishing professional communications, scholarly experiments and demonstrations in front of young learners are the right ways of using the software.

Moreover, the authors of such programs acquired their programming skills during their own education and are happy to see their products finding place in the educational environments. The amateur radio code-writers are always seeking for feedback related to their products and possible ideas leading to software improvements. In that manner, if the pool of experimenters is larger – there are more chances in checking for inevitable errors and omissions in the program codes. Besides that, the amateur radio enthusiasts prefer to test all possible options and available features in their communication systems – in order to measure their functionalities and usefulness. If it is done in a familiar and safe environment, such as a computer room at home or work, without spending additional time and fuel for driving to remote locations, the better the chances for acquiring experience in maintaining existing communicating solutions and rethinking eventual improvements.

Despite the fact that the members of the amateur radio community have been doing the experiments 'in the wild' by using locally supplied hardware and software resources, they often miss to provide enough description of their experiments in the literature. Therefore, it is obvious that the lack of information may prevent conducting new, fresh experiments that, in turn, can lead us to the innovations. One of the purposes of this chapter is to close the gap between obvious shortage in describing our experiments, and the audience who might overlook a significant pool of opportunities in doing amateur radio simulations.

As Lucas, Jones, and Moore (1992) noted long ago, the amateur packet radio brought benefits to many groups and individuals who had strong links to the educational environment. We can add that the amateur radio is going to have its own benefits by attracting newcomers to join the hobby – by stimulating students and teachers to learn how to use the amateur radio software. One of the best ways of combining amateur non-professional investigations and scholarly research is by adding radio data communications to the daily events in our computer rooms. For example, an amateur radio BBS in a school might provide a *gateway* – the corridor to a school's LAN for those parents who belong to the amateur radio community (or vice versa). In addition, the school's amateur radio gateway would attract technical enthusiasts from the broader academic community because the 'ham radio' has already found its place at universities worldwide.

In that manner, Skoric (2009a) described some experiments in a LAN that you can reproduce in your school's computer room or at home. For the sake of simplicity, Skoric suggested using *telnet* command that was available in both *JNOS 1.11f* and *Xrouter 176c*, the two popular programs for MS DOS-based computers. The experiments with using *telnet* offered various opportunities in establishing TCP/IP connections:

- A link from a computer running JNOS or Xrouter, to a computer equipped with MS Windows operating system and appropriate mailbox program,
- A link from a computer equipped with Linux or MS Windows operating system, to a computer running JNOS or Xrouter, and

- A simulated link between two (or more) networking programs running on the same computer.

The author based his suggestion for using telnet command on the assumption that the majority of computer-educated teachers and students have already been familiar with TCP/IP networking operations and protocols. Although that hypothesis is yet to prove, a disadvantage of that approach is that telnet command is just a partial replacement for the *connect* command, which is the one that the radio amateurs use when they establish links between the entities in their packet radio networks. In other words, by using *connect* instead of *telnet*, the experimenters become more familiar with the amateur radio terminology and prepare themselves better for incoming experience on the real radio waves. Nevertheless, that does not mean that prospective experimenters should avoid using *telnet* in their scholarly experiments because that command is widely implemented in all popular operating systems nowadays. (It means that for the end-users of your simulated radio network, you do not need to install anything else but the operating system.)

In the other work, Skoric (2009b) examined the behavior of a packet radio network regarding two different procedures in accessing distant network entities: (a) by using manual, 'step-by-step' moving in a network; and (b) by using a 'semi-automatic' way of executing shortcuts that *netrom* protocol provides in the amateur data networks. The author explained how to use *connect* command for accessing an email server, which was physically connected to a remote networking node, where a starting point was another virtual node. Skoric constructed a two-node virtual network by implementing *bpqether* procedure that required two instances of virtual BPQ nodes linked together in a LAN. The first node ran *BPQ 4.08a* for MS DOS operating system and the other node ran *BPQ 4.10f* for MS Windows. Although the first tests were successful, the later experiments led to a discouraging conclusion that the bpqether–based networking did not prove as reliable in a long run. In fact, the link between two instances of BPQ software in the LAN tended to 'freeze' after some time and required the system administrator to re-boot the nodes as well as the computers used. As we will see later in this chapter, the author could have restored the full functionality of the bpqether–based networking by temporary disabling or uninstalling firewall programs used on the MS Windows computer. However, the problems with BPQ have challenged the author to investigate other options – one of them is *AXIP*.

Therefore, in this chapter we will present some of the experiments conducted by using AXIP links between simulated network entities. An AXIP link simulates the standardized amateur radio traffic of so-called *AX.25 Level 2* type by using the communication path between two computers in a LAN running standardized TCP/IP protocol. The AXIP works as a communicating 'tunnel' between two or more regular TCP/IP points where we encapsulate the AX.25 packets within the TCP/IP data packets. (The acronym AXIP stands for 'AX.25 over TCP/IP'.) The experiments with AXIP links will support using *connect* command instead of *telnet* (except in cases where we find *telnet* as unavoidable or significantly more suitable). Therefore, the implementation of AXIP links will not only make our network simulations more similar to real radio networks, but also these links will be necessary for running other software solutions in the LAN.

An alternative to AXIP is *AXUDP*. Although we did not implement AXUDP connections in our experiments, we suggest prospective experimenters to consult an online manual (McCosker, 2010) because it contains useful procedures that the document's author, Rod McCosker, VK4DOT, used when he installed some of the Xrouter nodes

in Australia. That document would help you in obtaining experience with the software and in configuring ADSL modems to access Xrouter-based nodes by using the Internet. Moreover, the author of Xrouter, Paula Dowie, G8PZT, made a presentation of her work on the software (Dowie, 2002), and her document will give you an inside look into the details of the program capabilities.

Some resources related to JNOS node/mailbox software are also available. Ian Wade, G3NRW, wrote one of the most suggested readings related to that software. Although his book was out of print long ago, some instructions from it appeared on the Internet in a copyrighted form (Wade, 1992). In my opinion, there should be even more parts of the Wade's book available in the electronic form – if not all. On the other side, the actual program maintainer of JNOS in version 2.xx, Maiko Langelaar, VE4KLM, provided some textual instructions related to the software installation, on his website (Langelaar, 2008). Although those instructions mentioned the possibility of using the network interface (i.e. the computer network card) within a JNOS station, they did not handle simulation-related opportunities of JNOS software in a network.

In Figure 1, we can see an imaginary amateur radio network, consisting of three radio relay stations (R1, R2, and R3), where two of them (R1 and R3) have accompanied mailboxes (BBS) being on the same physical locations of the relays – for example, at a university building and within a remote 'village' school area. In this chapter, we will focus our attention to the subsystems R1 and R3, where we are going to simulate three types of interactions in the network: 1) relay-relay communications, including relay-user communications, 2) mailbox-user communications, and 3) mailbox-mailbox communications.

*Figure 1. Simulated radio traffic between two radio-relays (R1, R3) and email servers (BBS) (Adapted from Skoric, 2009a)*

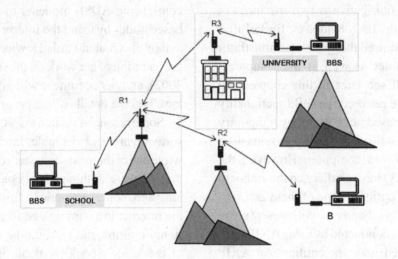

## SIMULATIONS OF INTERACTIONS IN A RADIO NETWORK

### Experiment 1: "Relay – Relay" Interaction

As mentioned in the literature review, the usage of BPQ software had some shortcomings. One of them was that the established links between two different generations of computers equipped with BPQ tended to become unreliable from unknown reasons, after just two or three minutes of intensive simulated 'radio traffic.' (Though, it worked well in an unloaded link between such BPQ nodes.) Secondly, the most popular versions of BPQ for MS/PC DOS operating system, *BPQ 4.08a* and *BPQ 4.09d*, did not support TCP/IP command *telnet*, as an alternative to the command *connect*. For that reason, we wanted to investigate other possibilities for DOS-based computers so we chosen *Xrouter*. An inventive amateur radio enthusiast, Paula Dowie, G8PZT, wrote that software as an alternative to BPQ. It was possible to configure Xrouter in different ways. For example, we were able to activate not only the main, radio-relay part of it, but also its *pms* section (means 'personal mailbox

system') as well as its *chat* section (a 'round-table' conferencing system). After we enabled all three mentioned subroutines in Xrouter, each of them appeared as a new node in our simulated radio network. That meant we got the response to the command **n**(odes), sent to the other node in our virtual network, as shown in Figure 2.

The upper part of Figure 2 shows the simulated radio traffic that ran throughout the simulated radio network. That traffic contained not only the information packets (E.g., *"Please register using …"*) but also the protocol-related packets (E.g., "DISC REQ"). In our simulations, the virtual nodes handle the traffic in a *simplex* regime. That means all stations must wait until a transmitting station finishes with its emission, in order to avoid inevitable collisions of multiplied transmissions on the same frequency. The simplex mode is the most common principle in real radio networks. (If we wanted our node to receive and send signals simultaneously, we should consider building a full duplex node, which would serve more than one radio station on different frequencies. When repeaters work in full duplex mode, amateur packet radio traffic can travel more efficiently.) The lower part of Figure 2 shows the

*Figure 2. Simulation of available "radio" nodes in a computer LAN*

node-list of our virtual node R3. The list consisted of three nodes: R1 (callsign *YT7M-1*), PMS (callsign *YT7M-2*), and CHAT (callsign *YT7M-3*). Now it is possible to connect each of them independently. Therefore, we were able do the following experiments at the command console of R3:

- To contact the chat section and investigate its opportunities (Figure 3);
- To contact the pms section and investigate its opportunities (Figure 4); and
- To contact the node R1 itself and investigate its opportunities (Figure 5).

The first command we sent, **c chat** (see Figure 3), established the link between our 'radio' station and remote conferencing system – 'chat server.' The chat server informed us that only one user was there and instructed us how to obtain help. The second command we sent, **/?**, returned a list of available commands within the conferencing system. (Note that all commands started with a slash – '/'.) Most of those commands sounded

familiar because they were similar to the commands for other round-table programs. Finally, we sent the command **/q** that disconnected our station from the conferencing system.

The next step in this experiment was to explore connections to the personal mailbox 'node' – PMS, as depicted in Figure 4.

The first command, **c pms** (see Figure 4), established the link between our station and remote personal mailbox (PMS). The second command we sent, **?**, returned a list of available commands within that type of a PMS. Be aware that in case of Xrouter's PMS, it is only possible to send (write) messages to the PMS owner – the system operator ('sysop') but not to the other visitors of the PMS.

The final step in this experiment was to explore the possibilities of the virtual network node itself, as shown in Figure 5.

The first command, **c r1** (see Figure 5), established the link between a network user at R3 (i.e., us, as experimenters) and the node R1. The second command, **?**, returned a short list of available commands of R1. As shown in Figure 5, in case

*Figure 3. Simulation of connecting to a "chat" node*

```
n
R3:YT7HPB-3) Nodes:
CHAT:YT7H-3        PHS:YT7H-2          R1:YT7H-1
c chat
R3:YT7HPB-3) Connected to CHAT:YT7H-3

Welcome to the chat server at R1.  There are 1 users
Type /HELP if you need help
Please register using "/N yourname"
/?
Full command list:


/?         /bye      /channel /exit     /help      /join      /leave
/links     /msg      /name    /personal /quit      /topic     /user
/version   /who
Use "/? <cmd>" for syntax of <cmd>
/q
```

*Figure 4. Simulation of connecting to a "PMS" node*

```
n
R3:YT7HPB-3) Nodes:
CHAT:YT7H-3        PHS:YT7H-2          R1:YT7H-1
c pms
R3:YT7HPB-3) Connected to PMS:YT7H-2
Welcome to YT7H's PMS

CMD(B/H/K/L/R/S/?)>
?

Help:
B)ye       Disconnect from PMS
K)ill n    Kill message n
L)ist      List messages
R)ead n    Read message n
S)end      Send msg to sysop

CMD(B/H/K/L/R/S/?)>
```

*Figure 5. Simulation of connecting to a "radio" node, getting information from it, and disconnecting*

```
n
R3:YT7HPB-3) Nodes:
CHAT:YT7H-3        PHS:YT7H-2          R1:YT7H-1
c r1
R3:YT7HPB-3) Connected to R1:YT7H-1
?

YT7H-1:R1) Basic commands:

<C)onnect <B>ye <I>nfo <H)heard <N>odes <P>orts <R>outes <U>sers <V>ersion

Use "? *" for full list
Use "? <cmd>" for specific help on <cmd>
b

YT7H-1:R1) Goodbye
```

of using Xrouter, it was possible to request a more detailed list of available commands, specific help text for each of them, and so forth. The last command **b** disconnected our station from the remote node.

After disconnecting from R1, we returned to R3 and checked the information about its own status (see Figure 6).

As shown in Figure 6, after the command **n**(odes), we sent **u**(sers) to see 'who was there', then **p**(orts) to see the available paths that link R3 to the outside world, and **v**(ersion) to get information about the software used in this simulation.

In Experiment 1, we used the version *176c* of Xrouter. As mentioned, it proved as a fast and memory efficient solution for those practitioners equipped with DOS-based computers in categories of CPU 80286 or similar. Comparing results we got by Xrouter running over an *axip*-based link in the LAN, it was clear that the AXIP connection did not suffer from the 'frozen' links we experienced with BPQ running over the *bpqether*–based link in the same LAN (including the same type of firewall). Although Xrouter 176c was a relatively old version of that software, it did not produce significant controversies or problems. As always, using any software is a compromise between different user's points of view and the author's points of view. For

example, we did not find an opportunity to run a mailbox program "on top" of an Xrouter node, which is a disadvantage when compared Xrouter to BPQ. On the other side, Xrouter gives more opportunities to networking practitioners, including the option of connecting it over the Internet or by telephone modems. As reported in the literature, it was possible to perform experiments with the same hardware and software we used in this experiment, by establishing 'telnet' connections to an Xrouter node from either Windows-based or Linux-based computers in a LAN.

It is important to say that an operator of the real hardware radio network would use the same set of commands as in Experiment 1 and would get the same type of responses from a remote network entity. During the steps mentioned in this experiment of connecting to the Xrouter 'node' in the LAN, we observed the main program window at the computer where Xrouter software was running. On the right top end of the screen, there was a free memory indicator that, in our case, varied around 195 kilobytes – regardless of particular commands mentioned in this experiment and different interactions we performed with the Xrouter subsystems. It is obvious that such memory management is very efficient because it does not require the Xrouter computer to read/write to its hard disk frequently.

*Figure 6. Simulation of getting information from a local "radio" node*

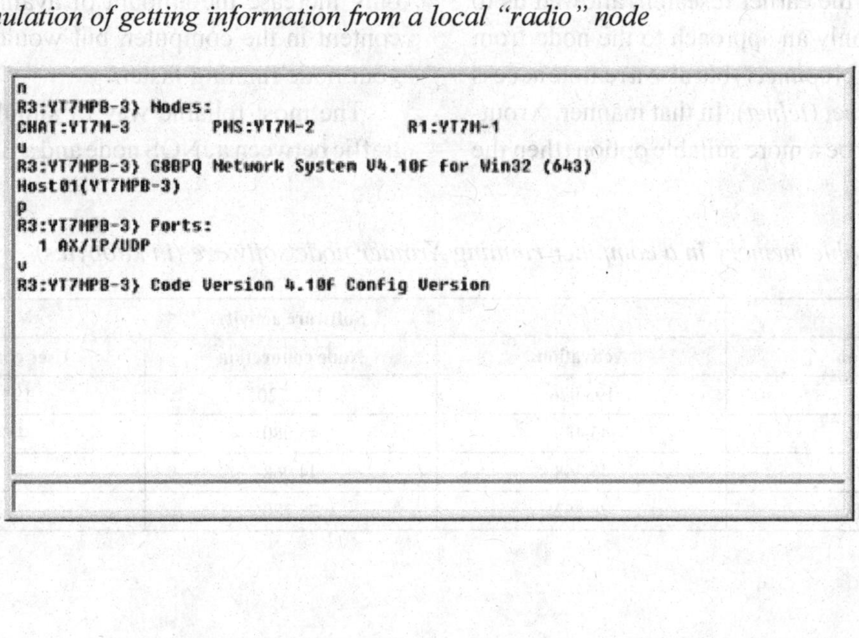

```
n
R3:YT7MPB-3} Nodes:
CHAT:YT7M-3          PMS:YT7M-2          R1:YT7M-1
u
R3:YT7MPB-3} G8BPQ Network System V4.10F for Win32 (643)
Host01(YT7MPB-3)
p
R3:YT7MPB-3} Ports:
   1 AX/IP/UDP
v
R3:YT7MPB-3} Code Version 4.10f Config Version
```

(This is important because in our next experiment with a node program *JNOS*, we will see an opposite situation where.) However, we performed similar memory tests with newer versions of Xrouter and the average values are in Table 1.

As we can see in Table 1, there was not much memory fluctuation within the same program version – regardless the level of the node's activity. However, there were significant differences in available memory after activation of the node – regarding the software versions (E.g., almost five times more free memory after the program initialization in version 176c, compared to version 187d, etc.). Probably some additional features, integrated in the newer program codes, produced the increased memory consumption, but we did not find significant and functional differences between the versions tested – that would approve that. (E.g., some of the versions with higher memory usage have introduced a sound signal – the 'beep' from computer speakers – when a connection to or a disconnection from the node occurred.)

Figure 7 illustrates the system administrator's connection to an Xrouter node. The 'users' list in the middle of the figure shows just one user (**YT7MPB**), who approached the node by using the local keyboard – the 'console' (**CON**).

Presented experiments with Xrouter, as well as those from the earlier research, allowed us to simulate not only an approach to the node from a radio network (*connect*) but also a remote access from the Internet (*telnet*). In that manner, Xrouter appeared to be a more suitable option (then the BPQ-based nodes) for 'sysops' who travel regularly and who want to check their nodes by using the Internet – as the only viable option in the absence of radio equipment abroad.

## Experiment 2: "Relay – Relay" Interaction

*JNOS* belongs to a diversified family of so-called 'NOS' programs ('NOS' stands for a '*N*etwork *O*perating *S*ystem'). A user can configure JNOS in different ways – one of which is a radio-relay node. In this experiment, we used an old version of that program, *JNOS 1.11f*, compiled for CPU 80286. (However, it is possible to compile JNOS executable file for different PC platforms, including Intel CPUs 8088, 80286, 80386, etc.) When our node started, its status line reported approximately 138 kilobytes of free system memory. Generally, the amount of free memory depends on the networking options chosen before compiling the program and the best practice is to include only the options that particular JNOS-node administrator plans for his or her node to provide to the network users. That means if you do not want your node to offer additional features, for example, working as an email server for the amateur radio messages, you should disable related options before compiling the program's executable file. That would not only increase the amount of available memory content in the computer, but would also enable your node running faster.

The most reliable way of simulating 'radio' traffic between a JNOS node and a BPQ32 node is

*Table 1. Available memory in a computer running Xrouter node software (in kilobytes)*

| Version | Software activity | | |
|---|---|---|---|
| | Activation | Node connection | User connection |
| 176c | 195.976 | 195.720 | 194.696 |
| 187d | 45.480 | 45.080 | 45.480 |
| 187f3 | 45.368 | 44.968 | 45.368 |
| 187f5 | 78.552 | 78.280 | 78.552 |

*Figure 7. Simulation of getting information from a local "radio" node*

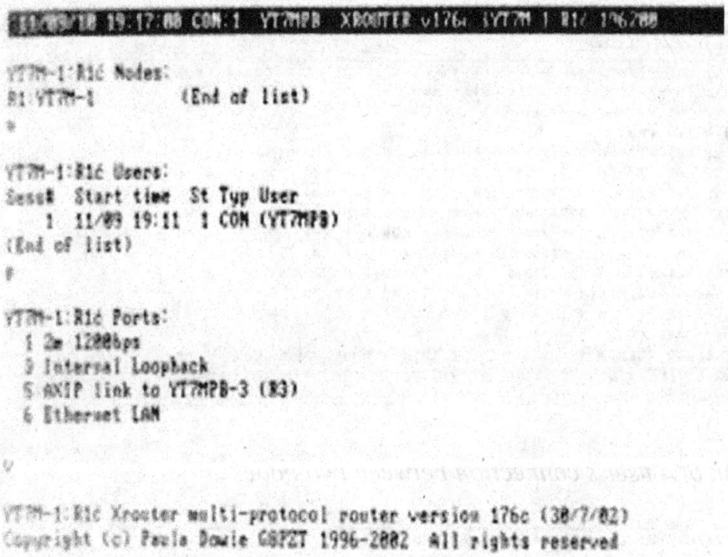

to establish an AXIP link between the two nodes. Both JNOS and BPQ32 support configuring AXIP interfaces, so it is not a problem to set up such a link in a LAN. The upper, monitoring part of Figure 8 describes two nodes, R1 (callsign YT7MPB-1) and R3 (callsign YT7MPB-3), broadcasting their 'nodes' lists and 'id' (software and alias) identifiers. In the screenshot of that seven-minute period, we can see that each node transmitted its 'nodes' and 'id' data only once – in order to avoid network congestion. (The usual interval between transmitting such data varies from 10 to 15 minutes.) However, every two minutes the nodes automatically re-checked their link.

As shown in Figure 8, the two virtual radio relays communicated each other fully automatically – regardless the different versions of software and computer platforms used. Establishing a simulated user's connection from R3 to R1 is shown in the lower part of Figure 9.

As shown in Figure 9, after successful connection to R1 ("… *Connected to R1:YT7MPB-1* …"), the user sent command **n** to check the 'nodes' list of R1 – where only one node, *R3:YT7MPB-3* was on the list; then the user sent command **nr** to

examine the 'routes' (i.e., physical paths) to the available node(s) – where only one direct or 'neighboring' route, *R3:YT7MPB-3* was on the list; and finally the user sent command **m** to see who were the users of that node – where only one user, *YT7MPB-3* who, by making a 'circuit' path starting from node *R3:YT7MPB-3*, was 'idling' on R1 at the time of sending the command.

This simple experiment has simulated the traffic over the radio frequencies. That means, any radio amateur who owns a radio transmitter would use the same commands to communicate between two (physically separated) radio-relay systems. For the sake of simplicity, we monitored the 'traffic' between just two virtual nodes. If you add more nodes to your LAN, you will expand this experiment - specifically in spotting visible delays that are inevitable in amateur radio systems due to time-sharing principle that serves more than two participants on the same 'frequency.'

During the experimentations with JNOS nodes, we managed to test only the basic, radio-relay functionality of that software. That means, when compared the tested features of Xrouter- and JNOS-based nodes, we did not activate eventual

*Figure 8. Simulation of "radio" traffic between two nodes*

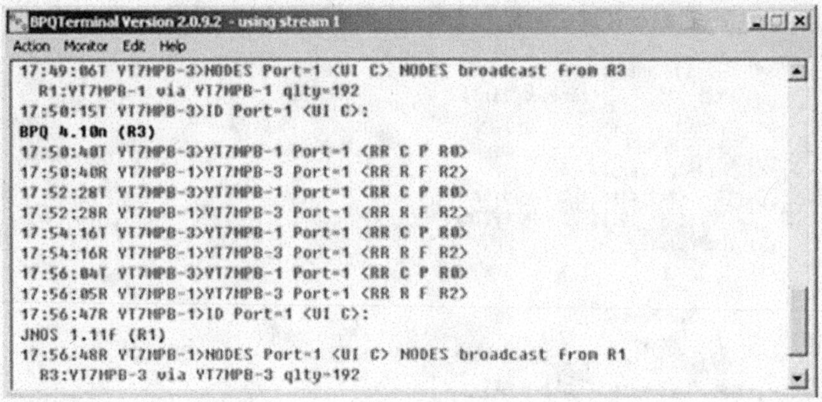

```
BPQTerminal Version 2.0.9.2 - using stream 1                    _|□|X|
Action  Monitor  Edit  Help
17:49:06T YT7MPB-3>NODES Port=1 <UI C> NODES broadcast from R3  ▲
  R1:YT7MPB-1 via YT7MPB-1 qlty=192
17:50:15T YT7MPB-3>ID Port=1 <UI C>:
BPQ 4.10n (R3)
17:50:40T YT7MPB-3>YT7MPB-1 Port=1 <RR C P R0>
17:50:40R YT7MPB-1>YT7MPB-3 Port=1 <RR R F R2>
17:52:28T YT7MPB-3>YT7MPB-1 Port=1 <RR C P R0>
17:52:28R YT7MPB-1>YT7MPB-3 Port=1 <RR R F R2>
17:54:16T YT7MPB-3>YT7MPB-1 Port=1 <RR C P R0>
17:54:16R YT7MPB-1>YT7MPB-3 Port=1 <RR R F R2>
17:56:04T YT7MPB-3>YT7MPB-1 Port=1 <RR C P R0>
17:56:05R YT7MPB-1>YT7MPB-3 Port=1 <RR R F R2>
17:56:47R YT7MPB-1>ID Port=1 <UI C>:
JNOS 1.11f (R1)
17:56:48R YT7MPB-1>NODES Port=1 <UI C> NODES broadcast from R1
  R3:YT7MPB-3 via YT7MPB-3 qlty=192                             ▼
```

*Figure 9. Simulation of a user's connection between two nodes*

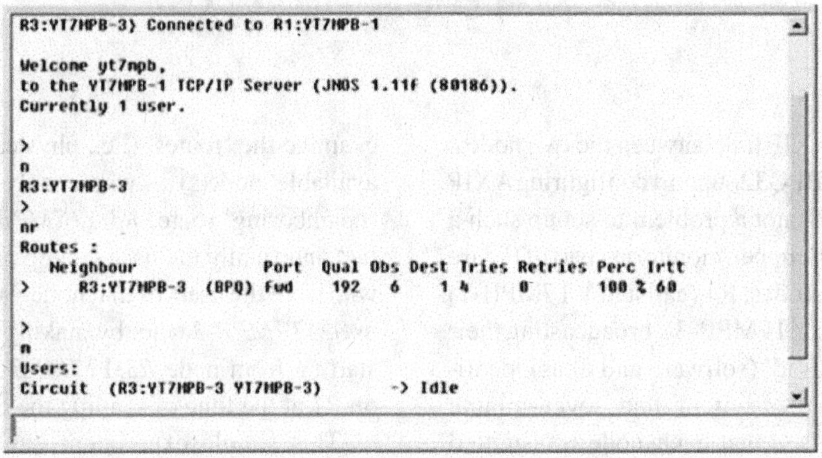

```
R3:YT7MPB-3) Connected to R1:YT7MPB-1                          ▲

Welcome yt7mpb,
to the YT7MPB-1 TCP/IP Server (JNOS 1.11f (80186)).
Currently 1 user.

>
n
R3:YT7MPB-3
>
nr
Routes :
  Neighbour           Port Qual Obs Dest Tries Retries Perc Irtt
> R3:YT7MPB-3 (BPQ) fwd  192   6   1 4    0          100 % 60

>
n
Users:
Circuit  (R3:YT7MPB-3 YT7MPB-3)      -> Idle                   ▼
```

option(s) in JNOS, such as PMS or CHAT. To be precise, we managed to activate both node and (regular) mailbox capabilities of JNOS – if we consider JNOS full 'mailbox' as a replacement to Xrouter's 'personal mailbox service.' The problem was that such combined activity of JNOS system was too memory consumptive and therefore unreliable in a long run on the old computer we used for testing JNOS.

## Experiment 3: "Mailbox – User" Interaction

As mentioned in Experiment 2, JNOS can be compiled as an amateur radio mailbox (with or without accompanied node). For this experiment, we compiled a newer version of JNOS software, *JNOS 2.0f*, (compiled for CPU i8088) as a stand-alone mailbox facility. The purpose of the experiment was to simulate an end-user access to the mailbox. Although we could simulate the user's access to

JNOS by using *HyperTerminal*, a program that is normally installed with Windows-based computers and which 'real' telnet connection, it does not provide a complete feeling of connecting to a JNOS station by using AX.25 protocol. For that purpose, we used the same AXIP link from the previous experiment to show that it was possible to 'connect' JNOS mailbox from a 'remote' node (which was, in our case, the BPQ32's console, as in Figure 10).

As shown in the console window (the lower part of Figure 10), we used the command **c yt7m** to establish the link with a 'distant' mailbox YT7M. The command of type 'c <callsign>' is completely the same command that users on radio frequencies send (in this case, from our radio relay 'R3'). As mentioned earlier, the AX.25 contacts do not require user authentication. The

only disadvantage in simulations of radio contacts between a user and a mailbox by using BPQ32's console is that it is not yet possible to change the user's *callsign*. In fact, the console user of BPQ32 node has the same *callsign* of the particular node. In this case, the user's callsign is 'YT7MPB-3' – the same as the node's callsign (see the upper part of Figure 10).

After connecting to a JNOS email server, the user can read stored bulletins, send new messages, and so forth. The lower part of Figure 11 describes a single 'page' of a long bulletin list the user received from the mailbox, while the upper part of the same figure describes the (simulated) radio-traffic between the mailbox (callsign YT7M) and the user (callsign YT7MPB-3) – delivering the same 'page' of data.

*Figure 10. Simulation of connecting to a JNOS "radio" mailbox*

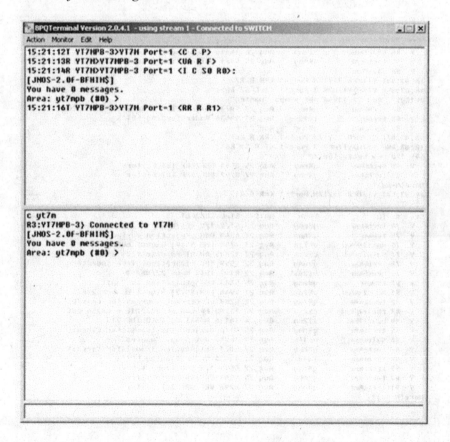

As we can see in Figure 11, the radio traffic was split into several parts, colloquially called 'packets,' and that is the reason why that type of the amateur radio transmissions has been called 'packet radio.'

As shown in Figures 11 and 12, there were no new messages for the user at the time of connections. That did not prevent the user to list available bulletins in the mailbox or to attempt establishing some outgoing AX.25 connections to the outside world, by using available radio ports of the mailbox. In our experiment, we tried to contact a fictive station 'YU7A' (Figure 12) and soon after we received a negative response from the mailbox, explaining that it did not success to contact that station (Figure 13).

Although the commands of a JNOS node may slightly differ from those of a JNOS mailbox, some commands result in same or similar outputs. For example, we saw in Figure 9 that the node command **m** had returned a list of actual users of the node. In case of a mailbox, the command **mbox** returned almost the same answer, see Figure 14.

In this case, the answer to the **mbox** command – *Uplink (YT7MPB-3 on port fwd)* informed that the user YT7MPB-3 had approached the mailbox by 'uplinking' the mailbox (i.e., connecting to it) by using its simulated radio channel 'fwd,' and the information that the particular user was doing nothing (*Idle*) at the time of answering the command.

Summarizing results from Experiment 2 and Experiment 3, we can say that the simulation of an outgoing attempt to connect a fictive nearby station (from the mailbox prompt), served us

*Figure 11. Simulation of getting the list of available messages in JNOS "radio" mailbox*

*Figure 12. Attempting an outgoing connection request from the real radio port of a JNOS mailbox*

```
c yt7m
R3:YT7MPB-3) Connected to YT7M
[JNOS-2.0f-BFHIH$]
You have 0 messages.
Area: yt7mpb (#0) >
p
Available AX.25 Ports:
fwd
vhf    : 2m, 1200 Bps.

Area: yt7mpb (#0) >
c vhf yu7a
Trying... The escape character is: CTRL-T
```

*Figure 13. Failure of the simulated outgoing connection from the radio port of a JNOS mailbox*

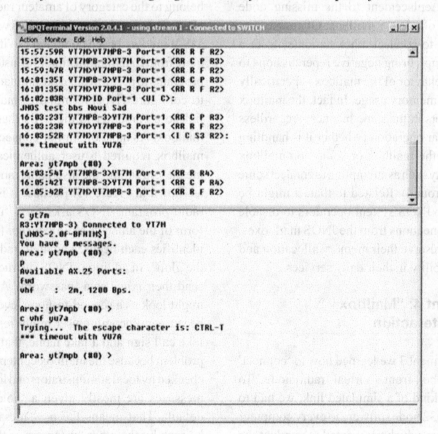

229

*Figure 14. Performing basic commands after connecting to a JNOS "radio" mailbox*

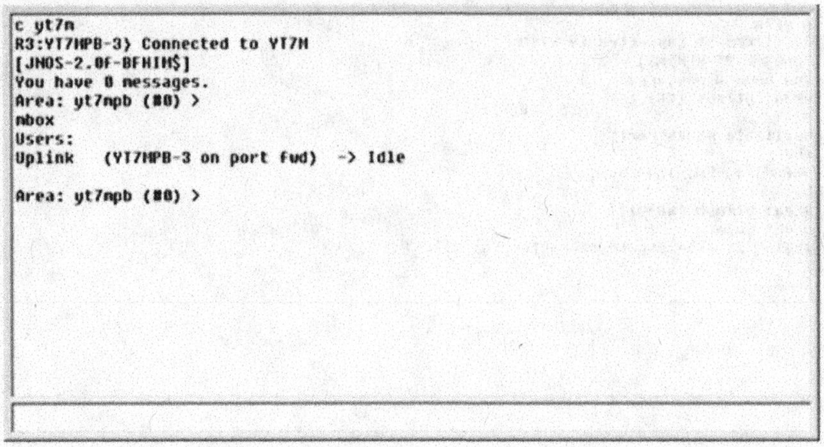

```
c yt7m
R3:YT7MPB-3) Connected to YT7M
[JNOS-2.0F-BFHIM$]
You have 0 messages.
Area: yt7mpb (#0) >
mbox
Users:
Uplink   (YT7MPB-3 on port fwd)  -> Idle

Area: yt7mpb (#0) >
```

as a partial replacement to the missing node functionality of a JNOS mailbox. Of course, any such attempt to connect other station(s) from a mailbox prompt, bring negative repercussions to the overall behavior of the mailbox –specifically regarding its memory usage. In fact, the mailbox serves its users in the same manner – regardless their particular operation (whether it is handling messages in the mailbox or some non-mailbox related activity such as attempting to connect some third party around). Related to that, it might be advisable for JNOS system operators to disable outgoing connections from the JNOS mailboxes, in order to preserve their memory allocation and to keep reliability in their daily services.

## Experiment 4: "Mailbox – User" Interaction

In the Experiment 3 we learned how to 'connect' a JNOS mailbox from a virtual 'radio node.' To achieve that kind of a simulated link, we had to install a BPQ32 node software to every computer in a LAN from which we wanted to conduct the Experiment 3. In opposite to that, we can simulate the same connection by using telnet protocol. As mentioned, one of the programs that support telnet is HyperTerminal. Whereas JNOS and BPQ32

belong to the category of amateur radio software, HyperTerminal is already installed within most of MS Windows-based computers so it does not require from LAN administrators to install additional programs to perform our next simulation. It is easy to configure HyperTerminal to make a 'telnet' link to a computer in the LAN that runs JNOS mailbox. As most of similar connections, JNOS mailbox required a user authentication, which meant providing the username and password, as shown in Figure 15. Because it is an amateur radio program, JNOS asks for a 'username' in form of the amateur radio *callsign* that uniquely identifies each licensed amateur radio station on the globe. In addition, JNOS instruct its users to send their *name* as a 'password.' Although that might look as a second-to-none level of security because an incoming user might respond with a fake call sign and a fake name, that is not a real problem because the mailbox content is regularly checked by local administrators and locally-stored messages are mostly given a 'hold' status per default. That means the new messages cannot be seen by the other customers of the mailbox - without a content check of the local administrator. Those messages cannot be even exchanged with other mailboxes without being reviewed by the local 'sysops.' The only difference between our simulations performed within a LAN and the real connection over radio frequencies is that a connection over 'the air' sends the call sign automatically and the password is not required per default. (However, JNOS can be compiled with mandatory passwords for stations that connect by using the real radio channels.)

In order to show the difference between users who reached the mailbox by simulated 'radio' paths (described in Figure 14) and those who accessed it by using 'telnet,' we sent the command **mbox** and received a different response, as shown in Figure 16.

As shown in Figure 16, the answer to the **mbox** command – *Telnet (yt7mpb @ 192.168.1.1)* informed that the user YT7MPB approached the mailbox by using 'telnet' connection, whereas 192.168.1.1 was the user's IP address.

After a successful connection by using *telnet*, the usage of mailbox commands is completely the same as in real amateur radio links. (You can compare the images in Figure 11 and in Figure 17.) That means a user has complete set of opportunities for listing and reading personal messages and bulletins that have been already deposited in the email server, as well as for composing new

messages and so on. Figure 17 describes a list of bulletins any user of HyperTerminal will get. The only difference between simulated access over the LAN and work with a real radio mailbox is a slightly but inevitable delay in the remote station's response, because of atmospheric conditions and time-sharing rules on the RF channels.

Having in mind that we used 'telnet' command to access those messages, it is obvious that we could use the same program, HyperTerminal, for accessing the mailbox content over the Internet. In that manner, this experiment of interacting JNOS and HyperTerminal in a LAN has also simulated the possibility of accessing the JNOS mailbox by using the Internet. That means if we want to add the option for handling the amateur radio email over the Internet, it is needed to obtain the ISP connection to the LAN. In that is the case, it would be also possible to compile JNOS mailbox to accept not only the amateur radio emails of the AX.25 type but also the TCP/IP mail that regularly travels via the Internet. A remote access to a JNOS facility from the Internet enables the sysop to check his or her system from a large distance (E.g. when on a vacation or business trip abroad, etc.).

*Figure 15. Simulation of connecting to a JNOS "radio" mailbox*

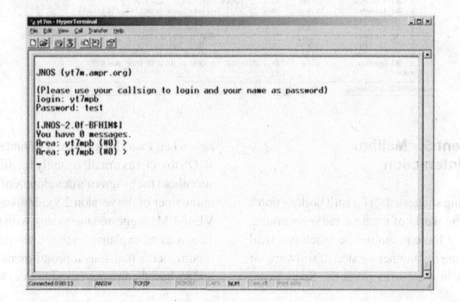

*Figure 16. Performing basic commands after connecting to a JNOS "radio" mailbox*

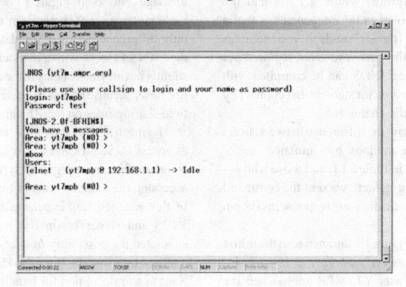

*Figure 17. Simulation of getting the list of available messages in JNOS "radio" mailbox*

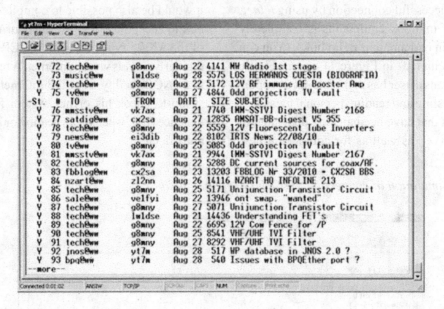

## Experiment 5: "Mailbox – User" Interaction

An old saying suggested: "If it isn't broke – don't fix it." In the world of amateur radio programs, it means that there might not be much practical use of looking for another version of software –if the version in use works properly. Some years ago, when I was looking for a suitable version of JNOS to run it as a mailbox-only facility, I was not sure about the program's development status. The maintainer of the version 2.xx, Maiko Langelaar, VE4KLM, suggested me to stay with the version 1.xx with an explanation that it would satisfy all requirements that I, as a proud owner of an old 80286-based computer, might have. Moreover, I did so. Soon after, I got an information from JNOS community that the version 1.xx had some minor, but annoying errors in the code that were never fixed since 2000 when the previous program maintainer, late James Dugal, N5KNX, released his last version, 1.11f (which solved then frightening Y2K problem). Therefore, I decided to upgrade my mailbox to the generation 2.xx (2.0f). However, as we saw in Experiment 2, a relay-relay interaction was simulated by using 1.11f. The reason was that I wanted to experiment with a version that was compiled and tested in a real network. Another amateur radio practitioner, Kerry Smith, N3NXO, provided his executable file accompanied with basic instructions about administering a network node. According to Smith (personal communication, August 2, 2010), he managed to run more than one JNOS 1.11f node on surrounding hilltops in his area. Having that experience in mind and the results of Experiment 2, I found it suitable to conduct another experiment with a mailbox-only version of JNOS 1.11f – in order to investigate differences between two software generations, 1.xx and 2.xx, and their eventual consequences in running on lower-end computer platforms. As mentioned earlier, one of the most important issues in experimenting with older computers and their programs is the memory management, which

means the level of efficiency in use of available random access memory (RAM). The experiment with the version 1.11f showed that JNOS started with approximately 131 kb of free memory if installed on an 80286-based computer equipped with 1024 kb RAM (Figure 18).

Furthermore, that content was likely to decrease by incoming connections. In that manner, after the first connection to the mailbox was made, the free memory amount went down to 126 kb, while the subsequent connections reduced the available memory to 118 kb and incoming new messages led to 111 kb (Figure 19). During the reversal process of disconnecting users, the tiny increment of the memory amount ended in relatively stable 120 kb. (In cases of low activity in the mailbox, which means without user activities or email exchange sessions with partnering systems, JNOS 1.11f remained on its initial 131 kb for longer periods of time.)

## Experiment 6: "Mailbox – User" Interaction

We performed our next experiment – a simulation of another 'mailbox-user' interaction by running two programs on one computer. The experiment was possible because both the mailbox program

*Figure 18. Available memory (130720 bytes) after initializing JNOS email server*

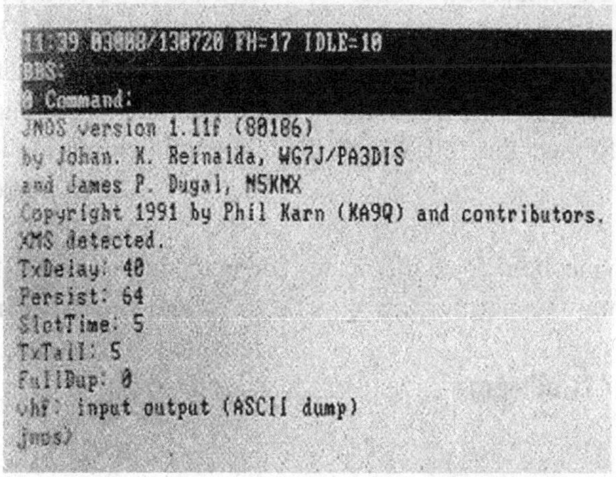

*Figure 19. Available memory (111392 bytes) during forwarding with JNOS email server*

```
17:43 13664/111392 FH=17 BBS=1 FWD=1 IDLE=10
BBS: ?yt7mpb
@ Command:
New mail for eu from <ok0nag%ok0nag.#boh.cze.
New mail for fwd from <cx2sa%cx2sa.lav.ury.sa
New mail for fwd from <cx2sa%cx2sa.lav.ury.sa
New mail for eu from <ok0nag%ok0nag.#boh.cze.
New mail for eu from <g4fvg%gb7cow.#44.gbr.eu
New mail for eu from <ok0nag%ok0nag.#boh.cze.
New mail for ww from <n9pmo%n9pmo.#sewi.wi.us
New mail for eu from <ok0nag%ok0nag.#boh.cze.
New mail for ww from <n9pmo%n9pmo.#sewi.wi.us
```

*WinFBB 7.00i*, and the user program *WinPack 6.80*, were capable to run in 'telnet' mode – in the same manner as they ran by using normal RF operations. Late Roger Barker, G4IDE, invented WinPack – the program that gained a lot of popularity among the radio amateurs worldwide. One of its most respected features is the capability of executing user-customized scripts. That means the users of WinPack can easily adapt accompanied program scripts to their particular situations (for example, to add specific connecting procedures for different types of mailboxes, or insert their user credentials to be sent to the email server, etc.) By adapting program scripts or writing their own scripts, the users of WinPack are able to perform many tasks fully automatically, by simple pressing function buttons on the keyboards.

For the purpose of this experiment, we customized the script called *F2 Connect to the local FBB*, to establish an automatic connection between WinPack and WinFBB, as shown in Figure 20.

Our customized script (activated by pressing F2 on the keyboard) performed the following actions:

1. "Initiate a telnet 'connection' to mailbox YT7MPB" (by using the script line **c 192.168.1.1:6300**)
2. "Wait for the prompt" (**Callsign:**)

3. "Send the callsign to telnet to my local BBS" (**yt7mpb**)
4. "Send the password to telnet to my local BBS" (**test**)

After running the script, we received the mailbox prompt *(1) YT7MPB BBS >* that was the starting point for entering manual commands.

Although most of the mailbox commands in WinFBB are simple one-character key strokes (E.g., **l** for list, **r** for read, etc.), it is not so easy to obtain the status of a system administrator. For security reasons, the administrative privileges require user authentication. If a mailbox visitor wants to activate the administrator's role, he or she has to do the following: (a) send **sys** command, (b) wait for the mailbox to send an MD2-based password *challenge*, (c) compute related MD2-based password *response*, and (d) send the response back to the mailbox. That procedure may take few minutes if done manually. By using scripts, WinPack is capable to perform the system administrator authorization in few seconds. Therefore, we customized the script called *F3 Send FBB sysop password*, which gave us the result depicted in Figure 21 (lower part of the picture).

As shown in Figure 21, our second script (activated by pressing F3 on the keyboard) did the following:

*Figure 20. Simulation of connecting to a WinFBB mailbox*

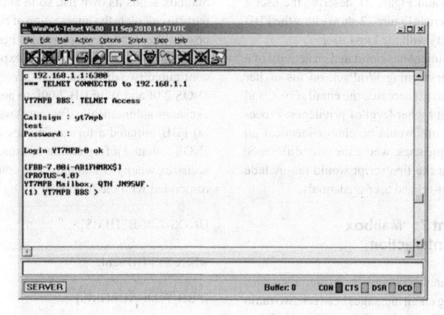

*Figure 21. Simulation of obtaining administrative rights in a FBB "radio" mailbox*

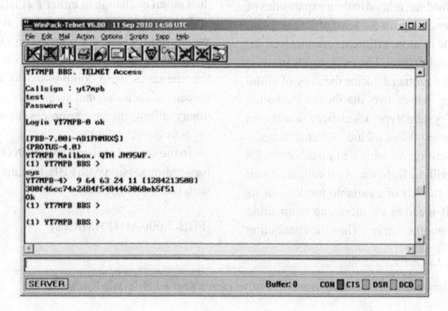

1. It sent the command asking for system administrator's privileges (**sys**)
2. It ran WinPack's subroutine *MD2PASS* (using **9 64 63 24 11 [1284213508]** as the 'key')
3. It sent the calculated response back to the BBS (**380f46cc7430d84f5484463068eb5f51**)

After successful running the script, we received the confirmation of the system administrator status (**Ok**), followed by the mailbox prompt *(1) YT7MPB BBS >* that was the starting point for typing administrator's commands.

Figure 20 and Figure 21 describe the user's interface, whereas Figure 22 shows how the FBB server interacts with the same user.

Our experiment has simulated an activity of a radio amateur running WinPack on his or her computer, who (a) accessed the email server, and (b) obtained a higher level of privileges. Procedures and results would be almost identical on the radio frequencies, where the only difference would be that the first script would not include sending telnet-related user credentials.

## Experiment 7: "Mailbox – Mailbox" Interaction

The radio amateurs colloquially call the procedures of exchanging email messages between two radio mailboxes as *forwarding*. It is particularly interesting to realize how different mailbox programs perform forwarding, related to their capabilities of doing email exchange in the least efficient 'plain text' mode, or in more efficient 'compressed binary' mode, and so forth. The exchanging mode is automatically negotiated during the stage of initial 'handshaking' where two mailboxes exchange their SIDs (*s*ystem type *id*entifiers, contained in square brackets) that include several 'flags' – letters representing the names of possible modes and other mailbox features. As usual, an email server sends the list of available modes (on its side) when it receives an incoming connection request from another server. Then the connecting

mailbox sends its own list, so to allow the other party to calculate the intersection of both systems' possibilities and implement the best one possible. For the purpose of our next experiment, we configured two different email server programs, JNOS 2.0f and WinFBB 7.00i, to perform email exchange automatically. Two cases were possible: (a) FBB initiated a forwarding session, and (b) JNOS initiated a forwarding session. In the first scenario, when FBB attempted to connect, JNOS responded with the following SID:

[JNOS-2.0f-BFHIM$]

where as FBB sent:

[FBB-7.00i-ABFHM$]

In this case, both parties were capable to conduct email exchange in either **F** (FBB text mode) or **B** (FBB compressed mode). In that situation the more efficient, compressed mode was used as it was less time-consuming. Prior to sending, the messages were compressed to some 30-45 percent of their original size. After arrival to the other mailbox, the reverse process of uncompressing was done.

In the second scenario, when JNOS initiated a forwarding session with FBB, the latter responded with the following SID:

[FBB-7.00i-AB1FHMRX$]

*Figure 22. Simulation of obtaining administrative rights in a FBB "radio" mailbox*

where as JNOS responses with the same SID as in the first scenario:

[JNOS-2.0f-BFHIM$]

It is obvious that FBB software has more capabilities than JNOS, including **1** (an extended version of 'B'-mode with 'resume' of suspended and partly-performed email transfer) and **X** (X-forwarding, a specially designed mode for FBB-to-FBB transfers). However, the lack of the last two capabilities in JNOS resulted in the compressed **B** mode, as in the first scenario.

In the left part of Figure 23, we can see a four-minute-long exchanging session between those two mailboxes, performing the first scenario. After the connection had been established, the first system (JNOS in this case) sent several blocks of so-called 'proposals' – even though the partnering system (FBB in this case) already had those messages (hence the refusing answers of type **FS -----**), but remained open for more proposals (**FF**). When the first station emptied its pool of proposals, it automatically cancelled the link (**FQ**). The next forwarding session was even shorter – less than a minute, because neither party had new email for exchange (the right part of Figure 23).

## Experiment 8: "Mailbox – Mailbox" Interaction

This experiment was an 'upgrade' to an experiment described in the literature review (a connection between two virtual nodes based on BPQ version 4.08a and BPQ32 version 4.10f). Because BPQ programs allow running email servers "on top" of the nodes, we installed the email server program *DosFBB 5.15c* alongside with BPQ 4.08a on the DOS-based computer, and performed a test of exchanging emails between that server and the server based on WinFBB v.7.00i that we used in our previous simulations. Our intention was to exercise message forwarding between two

FBB-based mailboxes *and* test some safety measures that had been written specifically for FBB software. Those safety measures are capable to protect email servers against unauthorized access performed by misusing callsigns of the other stations, including legitimate forwarding partners (a kind of a 'stealing identity').

In the amateur radio computer-related communication systems, it is not so easy to ensure that your correspondent on the other side of the link is really the person you are familiar with and not a strange person pretending to be your friend or close relative. The problem in the world of email servers is a fact that, from your forwarding partner's point of view, the station you are administering is nothing else but another user who attempts to make a connection to his or her server. We saw in Experiment 7 that FBB software is capable to handle incoming users' requests, which come in form of asking for administrative privileges, by implementing password procedures based on MD2 algorithm. Having in mind that the amateur radio mailboxes are mostly non-attended stations and the fact that forwarding cycles mostly happen in a regime of 24/7, which means non-stop, it is not possible to stay on guard all the time. Therefore, it is possible that an eventual amateur radio hacker can try to impersonate somebody else's identity by configuring his or her packet radio station to run under your mailboxes' callsigns. By misusing the callsign of an email server, a malicious person automatically plays the role of a legitimate forwarding partner and get an opportunity to dispatch an illegal content – say, some offensive bulletins filled by rude words or something like that. To prevent such scenario, it is possible to protect forwarding partners by additional programs that offer fully automatic password exchange without any human intervention. One of those protective programs is *Protus* that comes in versions for DOS, Windows and Linux variants of the FBB software (Skoric, 2010). It is important that the files of Protus that serve as secret keys never go visible "in the air," which means that system administrators should

*Figure 23. Simulation of two consecutive automated mail exchanges between "radio" mailboxes*

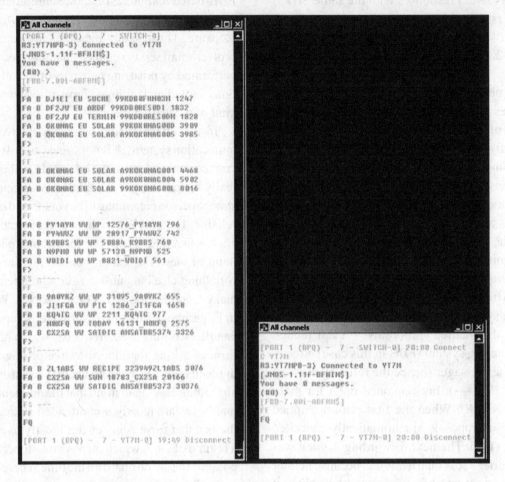

exchange them by using some other ways (E.g., by exchanging the keys on floppy diskettes, or by modem-to-modem communication over the phone line, or something like that).

Similarly to the WinPack's method of calculating MD2-based *responses*, the FBB mailboxes can now interchange the *challenge* and *response* fully automatically, as shown in Figure 24.

Figure 24 describes a short connection (which took only 5 seconds) between two mailboxes equipped with Protus. After the first station (WinFBB in this case) established the connection with the other station (DosFBB in this case), Protus on the DOS-based side sent its challenge **![1209754960]** back to the Windows-based system. Then, on the first side of the link, Protus

calculated the response in form of **0201ce8dfb4a-5ec8d98eef23e485ec4c** and sent it to the other end that did the same computation on its own and compared the results. Because both results were the same, the access was approved (**OK**). In Figure 25, you can see a similar example of password-related operations, which we recorded on the screen of the computer running DosFBB.

Despite encouraging results we got in this simulation, as well as an excellent ten-year-long experience with maintaining email servers based on DosFBB 5.15c from 1990 to 2000, we cannot use that version in real systems because it is not Y2K-compliant. Although there appeared newer versions of DosFBB that did not suffer from the 'millennium problem,' we have not experimented

*Figure 24. Simulation of an automated password exchange between two "radio" mailboxes*

```
All channels                                    _ □ ×
[PORT 2 (BPQ) - 27 - SWITCH-0] 20:03 Connect
C YT7M
WINNOD:YT7MPB-5) Connected to DOSBBS:YT7M
[FBB-5.15-AB1FHMR$]
{PROTUS-1.2}

![1209754960]
Running c_filter.dll ...
0201ce8dfb4a5ec8d98eef23e485ec4c
OK
1:YT7M)
[FBB-7.00i-AFHMR$]
FF
FQ

[PORT 2 (BPQ) - 27 - YT7M-0] 20:08 Disconnect
```

with them yet because they required CPUs faster than Intel 80286. In that manner, I strongly advise prospective experimenters to try newer versions of DosFBB by installing them on DOS-based computers of class Pentium™ 1.

## Experiment 9: "Mailbox – Mailbox" Interaction

We learned in Experiment 4 and Experiment 6 that it was not a problem to establish a connection between a mailbox and a user, or between two mailboxes by using *telnet*. Although the next section might look as another telnet-type simulation, it has already found its implementa-

tion in real amateur networks. In fact, since the mid-ninctics, the radio amateurs began using the Internet to bridge distances between amateur radio systems – in cases of unavailable RF connectivity. For example, if two mailbox administrators wanted to enable a long-haul intercontinental link between their systems, they had to provide an Internet access. Then, it was easy to configure the mailboxes to connect each other by using an automated version of *telnet* command and, after establishing the session, to exchange the email.

In that manner, we consider any telnet connection between two amateur radio mailboxes over the Internet as another simulation of the real RF links between similar systems. This author performs

*Figure 25. Simulation of an automated password exchange between two "radio" mailboxes*

```
$PORT 1 (BPQ) - 1 - YT7MPB-8Ć 19:02 Connect
$FBB-5.15-AB1FHMR$Ć
$PROTUS-1.2ć

!$1289751372Ć
18215d7bda82a2e4d4bef74984788b88
OK
1:YT7M)
$FBB-7.00i-AFHMR$Ć
FF
FQ
$PORT 1 (BPQ) - 1 - YT7MPB-8Ć 19:02 Disconnect
```

such connections between his FBB server and similar mailboxes on a regular basis. At present, the author's mailbox has contacts in many parts of the world, including Great Britain (Figure 26), Russia and Germany (Figure 29), Canada (Figure 30), Belgium, Japan, USA, and other countries. As shown in Figure 26, two partnering servers negotiated the mode of email transfer by mutual presenting their system type identifiers (as explained in Experiment 7) and accordingly 'agreed' on using the X-forwarding mode, which is the most efficient mail-exchanging regime for FBB-based email servers. (More samples of similar forwarding sessions are provided in Appendix 1. We have taken all screenshots during the real communications performed over the Internet and because of that the actual usernames and passwords are removed from the pictures.)

Bear in mind that you do not need to keep a permanent connection to the global network and perform forwarding 24 hours a day. In fact, it is enough to spend some 10-15 minutes of occasional links every so often, to exchange a plenty of the amateur radio email. However, it is advisable to keep such links on a regular basis – say, once a day or once in two days, or something similar.

Although some radio amateurs do not agree with the idea of using the Internet instead of or in addition to the real RF routes, we are sure that using modern technologies like the Internet will continue to support the existing amateur radio messaging systems worldwide. Nevertheless, we expect from the system administrators to keep running and maintaining their radio facilities for the VHF, UHF and HF coverage.

## Experiment 10: "Mailbox – Mailbox: Interaction

This experiment provides simulated radio traffic between the amateur radio mailboxes in two variants: (a) with 'live' radio nodes in the background of a mailbox, and (b) without such nodes.

To perform such experiments, we equipped our DOS-based computer with another type of mailbox software, *PZT 405* – running it "on top" of the BPQ node 4.09d. On the other side of the link, there was WinFBB 7.00i running on top of BPQ32 node, version 4.10n. To interconnect two BPQ nodes, we configured the *ethernet* connection, as described in Experiment 1. During the configuration stage, various changes in the computer setup led us to a conclusion that the firewall program, used at the Windows machine, caused the malfunctions in the link between two BPQ nodes. A temporary solution to avoid the occurrence of 'frozen' links was to disable the firewall. In our case, such an action did not bring any security risk because we experimented in an isolated, closed LAN. However, it still remains to investigate possible influence of firewall programs to the functionality of simulated radio network in a LAN.

In the first phase of Experiment 10, we planned to observe the functionality of the network and recognize eventual changes after adding additional load to the simulated 'radio' traffic. That meant we activated (a) an automated email exchange session ('forwarding') between the two mailboxes and, in parallel to that, we established (b) a manual connection from one node to the other as well as an outgoing connection request from the other node to an imaginary station 'in the field' around the second node, see Figure 27. Having in mind relatively low capacities of the DOS-based computer, we carefully observed its available memory content – before, during, and after inserting additional simulated traffic. In that manner, the unloaded system of the BPQ node + PZT mailbox responded with approximately 95.880 kilobytes of free memory. An incoming connection from the partnering WinFBB mailbox resulted in a temporary 3-step decrement in free memory. At first, it went down to 85.624 kilobytes (the connection itself). Then, it lowered to 85.144 kilobytes (during the process of receiving new messages from the other mailbox). In addition, it went further down to 84.616 kb (only during

*Figure 26. Using the Internet as a simulation of a radio link between two "radio" mailboxes*

```
[PORT 2 (TELNET) - 16 - GB7CIP-8] 07:56 Connect
*** Connected to GB7CIP


n
###############################################################
# Only Licensed Radio Amateurs are allowed to log into this system  #
# Please use your Amateur Radio Callsign issued by your local   #
# Telecommunications Agency. All access are logged.        #
#                              #
# If you have not previously registered, you can contact the system #
# administrator by providing your Radio Amateur Details contacting  #
# via internet paul@skywaves.demon.co.uk             #
# or  ampnet  g3apl@gb7cip.ampr.org  AX25 G3APL@GB7CIP.#32.GBR.EU  #
###############################################################

Callsign : Password :
Logon OK. Type MP to change password.

[FBB-7.04j-AB1FHMRX$]
GB7CIP Mailbox, QTH IO91WN.
(1) GB7CIP BBS >
[FBB-7.00i-AHMX$]
>
SX 16
298CW7LT
298BW7LT
1B4RE7DIH
52526_K9BBS
10783-W8IDI
32809_9AOVRZ
21499_H7YHE
21376_H7YHE
A281H7VSS
10769-W8IDI
21665_H7YHE
1B4RE7DIH
6FA3HBML
52682_K9BBS
4B35_KD4TG
11848-W8IDI
SY 16
298CW7LT
298BW7LT
1B4RE7DIH
52526_K9BBS
```

intensive database operations – such as comparing incoming bulletins against the existing state in bulletin databases, etc.). After the connection between two mailboxes was over, the system memory returned to the initial value of 95.880 kb.

The second step in Experiment 10 was to add some interactions between the nodes underlying bellow the servers exchanging email. It appeared that available commands of the BPQ 4.09d node (**connect**, **bye**, **info**, **nodes**, **ports**, **routes**, **users**, and **mheard**) did not make any change in the memory content the PZT mailbox was reporting – regardless it was the initial 95.880 kb or some

of the decreased amounts of memory mentioned in the first step. That was a positive consequence of the way of installing the BPQ node that was placed in the high memory area of DOS, so that the *node* activity seemed to be practically isolated from the *mailbox* activity. In order to check that hypothesis, we established another manual connection to the DOS-based computer – that time approaching the mailbox instead of the node. The connection to the mailbox immediately resulted with a decrease of available memory to 85.624 kb – identically as in the first step of Experiment 10. Furthermore, when we closed our

*Figure 27. Simulation of an automated mail exchange between two "radio" mailboxes (upper part), and the parallel user's interaction between two "radio" nodes (lower part)*

*Figure 28. Simulation of automated mail exchange between two "radio" mailboxes*

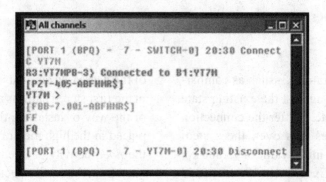

simulated connection to the mailbox, the memory content promptly returned to 95.880 kb, which was the same behavior as in the first phase of the experiment.

In the third phase of Experiment 10, we disabled node-related functionalities at the DOS-based computer. Actually, the BPQ program remained active there, but only as a support to the mailbox running "on top" of it. After activating that system configuration, PZT reported 95.880 kb of RAM. Similarly to the situation described in the first step of this experiment, an incoming connection – performed by the partnering WinFBB mailbox, resulted in a 2-step decrement in available memory: 85.624 kilobytes (the connection itself) and 85.144 kilobytes (the PZT's response to the partnering system). After the connection between the two systems was over, the memory content returned to 95.880 kb. Similar to the situation described in the second step of this experiment, a manual connection to the mailbox resulted in decreasing RAM to 85.624 kb, whereas a disconnection led to original 95.880 kb. Please note that from a functional point of view, the only difference was that a DOS-based node had not been available anymore. That means the 'nodes' list at a neighboring node (that was the Windows-based system in our case) listed only the mailbox entry on the opposite side of the link, but not the (now disabled) node entry. The consequence in functionality of the simulated network was that a visiting user could only access the mailbox on the DOS-based computer, but not its node.

In the fourth part of Experiment 10, we disabled the node features at the second simulated 'radio' system in our computer network, the Windows-based node. That meant the only activity was the interaction between two email servers (Figure 28). The result we got in that phase of our last experiment was that the memory fluctuation was identical as in the third phase: 95.880 kb without users connected, and 85.624 kb with one user connected to the mailbox.

To help prospective experimenters with setting up their stations, in Appendix 2 we provide the content of PORTS.SYS – the main configuration file in PZT mailbox.

## Solutions and Recommendations

During the tests of server programs in our simulations, we noticed that PZT mailbox was faster in handling new messages than the both versions of JNOS software. Therefore, we measured the difference in consuming simulated 'radio' resources during the email exchange (Table 2).

As shown in Table 2, PZT software transferred messages more efficiently than JNOS programs. In addition, and as Martin (2006b) noted, "it [i.e. JNOS] is not a simple system to install and can test the knowledge and patience of even third echelon IT professionals." About that, it might be a better solution to experiment with PZT if you have older computers. However, the situation with releasing newer versions of PZT software remains unclear because we were not able to locate any software updates on the web. Furthermore, the Internet mailing list for the users of PZT seemed to be too quiet. In contrary to that, the JNOS users' community has been very active on their mailing lists(s) and the current software maintainer regularly releases updated versions of that program.

Comparing node functionalities of Xrouter and JNOS software, we can say that Xrouter gives more to the network users. Besides the basic radio-relay features that are built-in, Xrouter offers an opportunity for connected radio amateurs to send

*Table 2. Efficiency in handling incoming messages by different mailbox programs*

| Version | Number of messages | Size (kilobytes) | Duration (minutes) | Speed[a] |
|---|---|---|---|---|
| PZT 405 | 101 | 350 | ~30 | 17.8 |
| JNOS 2.0f | 104 | 511 | ~75 | 43.2 |
| JNOS 1.11f | 130 | 560 | ~80 | 36.9 |

[a] Approximated time of transfer per message (in seconds).

a message to the node administrator, as well as to enter the 'round-table' conferencing system. In contrary to that, we did not find an easy way to do the same in JNOS nodes. From that perspective, we found Xrouter as a better solution than JNOS.

Related to the node-only programs for (particularly older types of) DOS-based computers, it is obvious that Xrouter is more modern and recently updated solution than BPQ. The experiments with Xrouter went smoothly and without any significant issue. As shown in Figure 7, our node included both an AXIP port (approachable by *connect* command) and an Ethernet LAN port (approachable by *telnet* command), and both ports were performing well by using the same, single network card in the computer running Xrouter. (To help you with making similar setup, we provide the content of XROUTER.CFG that is the main configuration file of Xrouter, in Appendix C.)

In opposite to the positive experience with the Xrouter node, we did not manage to find a similar way of activating two different protocols in parallel by using one network card with PZT mailbox software (made by the author of Xrouter). In addition, Xrouter is not a choice for practitioners who want to simulate both a node and a mailbox in the same computer. For those users, the combination of BPQ + PZT proved as a reliable solution.

When it comes to the MS Windows world, BPQ products in their 32-bit versions (BPQ32) give plenty of opportunities for the majority of node-related experiments. BPQ32 supports WinFBB family of mailbox programs very well. In addition, the BPQ author recently started with production of his own email server software, so the prospective experimenters will have more choices in networking simulations.

Considering all tested simulations, we can say that all programs performed more or less well in our local area network. Probably our biggest restriction in eventual achieving more competitive results was our low-end Intel 80286-based computer. Nevertheless, the results we got in the

presented experiments can approve that the average, more modern equipment, will ensure even better performances in the future network-related simulations.

## FUTURE RESEARCH DIRECTIONS

I hope that the simulations of radio traffic in the local area networks - which we presented in this chapter, are intriguing enough to challenge educators and students alike to replicate some of our virtual constructions in their local environments. One of the goals of this chapter is to encourage prospective experimenters and newcomers to the amateur radio hobby. For that purpose, we primarily focused on the simulations in DOS- and Windows-based computers in the local area networks, having in mind that Linux might not be the best 'entry-stage' solution for beginners in the amateur radio simulations. Therefore, we did not cover simulations using Linux in this study. Nevertheless, we strongly recommend Linux-related opportunities to more experienced users in computer- and radio-related technologies. Concerning that, we support research opportunities with widely available versions of FBB for Linux mailbox software, often referred as *LinFBB* (Skoric, 2010), as well as various node opportunities for the same operating system. LinFBB has several advantages compared to WinFBB: Its program code is regularly updated in the last decade, it shows less memory consumption during regular mailbox operations, it has the possibility of running as an invisible system service in the computer's background, it does not require any additional software for translating domain names into IP addresses – when used on the Internet, etc.

Future research opportunities with simulations of radio nodes and email servers are also feasible in DOS and Windows communities. Among the other opportunities, there might be a test of recently announced versions of JNOS and Xrouter software for Windows. To be specific, a 'beta' version of JNOS for Windows has already been released, although the complete software package is not yet available. When it comes to a development of node programs for both DOS and Windows market – other than BPQ program, you could try *FlexNet*. During the last two decades, FlexNet nodes have achieved significant popularity in the Western Europe. The authors of that program released a 'beta' version of their software for Windows platforms. Therefore, it would be a challenge to test both DOS and Windows variants of FlexNet in network simulations, and compare the results with those from our BPQ-related simulations. For the other experimenters who have spare DOS-based computers of Pentium™ 1 class in the LAN, we can suggest testing the installation of a BPQ 4.08a or 4.09d node, and a mailbox running DosFBB v. 7.00 – on the same machine, that should be another reliable solution for not-so-new generations of computer hardware.

In scholarly environments, we predict a perspective of giving a choice to the students in a computer room, to play with different amateur radio node, mailbox and the end-user solutions – some of which we presented in this chapter. It might be a challenge to summarize results of such experiments and to investigate eventual differences in preferred programs by different categories of software users (E.g. the students of different age, or different professional-career perception, etc.). The simulation experiments in a schoolroom could lead you to establishing real radio communications with the amateur radio community, including replicating well-known tests of radio communications between the schools and spacecraft crews.

## CONCLUSION

The experiments in this chapter, as well as the experience with the amateur radio programs described elsewhere, gave me a strong feeling that such software simulations deserve attention – particularly in educational environments. Although the amateur radio is a non-profit and hobbyist activity, it has already proved as a significant motivating factor to bring unnumbered technology enthusiasts into the worlds of computing and communications. As a member of societies such as IEEE and ACM, I am always pleasantly surprised when learn about distinguished peers in the engineering community who have been practicing amateur radio communications throughout their professional careers. As others also realized:

*Richard Campbell, an associate professor of computer and electrical engineering at Portland State University in Oregon, says ham radio helps him turn theoretical concepts into reality. Campbell, licensed as KK7B, is currently working on projects that are designed to add digital communications capabilities to the national power grid and to create remote sensors for use with ocean wave power generators.*

*Over the years, many hams have parlayed their radio experimentation into lucrative and even distinguished professional careers. Joe Taylor, licensed as K1JT, says the years he spent tinkering with radios led him into his current post as a Princeton University physics professor. "My practical knowledge of RF techniques, built up over years of enthusiastic pursuit of many amateur radio goals, turned out to be very useful when choosing and designing specialized equipment for unique studies of pulsars and other astrophysical objects," he says. In 1993, Taylor was awarded the Nobel Prize in Physics for the co-discovery of a new type of pulsar. (Edwards, 2009)*

For those who are not yet sure about making investments in the amateur radio hardware, needed for building real radio-relay and email server infrastructure, our software simulations are the best opportunity to expand existing computer-networking skills and test the level of interest in real communications as well as networking devices and procedures – both in their families, neighborhood, school and work.

## ACKNOWLEDGMENT

Teachers are not the only ones who are responsible for discovering new talents in the schoolrooms. The process of learning starts within the family so the parents should be able to recognize young potentials at homes too. This book chapter is dedicated to the late persons, Mr. Sava Skoric and Mrs. Radmila Skoric, who managed to recognize the exploring nature of their son during his early age. As brave parents, they did not punish him too much for his breaking and destroying various home devices – while inspecting the secrets of hidden mechanisms *living* inside. Instead, they supported their kid in his searching for new horizons in engineering and technology. Credits also go to all mentioned, known and unknown amateur radio enthusiasts who donated their time and willingness for a) making various ham radio programs, and b) participating in the correspondence needed to make this chapter.

## REFERENCES

Dowie, P. (2002). *Presentation: XROUTER network infrastructure software - Paula G8PZT*. Retrieved September 28, 2010, from http://www.g8pzt.pwp.blueyonder.co.uk/fourpak/2002_03.htm.

Edwards, J. (2009). Want to bone up on wireless tech? Try ham radio. *Computerworld*. Retrieved October 17, 2010, from http://www.computerworld.com/s/article/9139771/Want_to_bone_up_on_wireless_tech_Try_ham_radio.

Langelaar, M. (2009). *JNOS 2.0 - DOS install (the easy way)*. Retrieved September 13, 2010, from http://www.langelaar.net/projects/jnos2/documents/install/dos/.

Lucas, L. W., Jones, J. G., & Moore, D. L. (1992). *Packet radio: An educator's alternative to costly telecommunications*. Denton, TX: Texas Center for Educational Technology.

Martin, J. (2006). *JNOS operators guide*. Retrieved September 13, 2010, from http://www.nyc-arecs.org/JNOS_OpGuide.pdf.

Martin, J. (2006). *Whetting your feet with JNOS*. Retrieved October 17, 2010, from http://legitimate.org/iook/packet/jnos/whetting/whetting.htm.

McCosker, R. (2010). *Creating a XRouter remote node*. Retrieved September 28, 2010, from http://vk2dot.dyndns.org/XRouter/XRouter.htm.

Skoric, M. (2009). Amateur radio in education . In Song, H., & Kidd, T. (Eds.), *Handbook of Research on Human Performance and Instructional Technology* (pp. 223–245). Hershey, PA: IGI Global. doi:10.4018/978-1-60566-782-9.ch014

Skoric, M. (2009). The new amateur radio university network – AMUNET (Part 4). In *Proceedings of the 13th WSEAS International Conference on Computers,* (pp. 323-328). Athens, Greece: WSEAS Press.

Skoric, M. (2000-2010). FBB packet radio BBS mini-HOWTO. *The Linux Documentation Project*. Retrieved September 28, 2010, from http://tldp.org/HOWTO/FBB.html.

Wade, I. (1992). *NOSintro – TCP/IP over packet radio*. Retrieved September 28, 2010, from http://homepage.ntlworld.com/wadei/nosintro/.

## ADDITIONAL READING

Blystone, K., & Watson, M. (1995). *Alternative information highways: Networking school BBSs*. Denton, TX: Texas Center for Educational Technology.

Corley, A. (2010). Hams in Haiti. *IEEE Spectrum*. Retrieved October 17, 2010, from http://spectrum. ieee.org/telecom/wireless/hams-in-haiti/.

Davidoff, M. (1994). *The satellite experimenter's handbook*. Newington, CT: American Radio Relay League.

Diggens, M. (1990). Enhancing distance education through radio-computer communication. In R. Atkinson & C. McBeath (Eds.), *Open Learning and New Technology: Conference Proceedings*, (pp. 113-116). Perth, Australia: Australian Society for Educational Technology.

Erhardt, W. (2010). *Bill's amateur radio page*. Retrieved January 16, 2011, from http://www. k7mt.com/AmateurRadio.htm.

Ford, S. (1995). *Your packet companion*. Newington, CT: American Radio Relay League.

Ford, S. (1995). *Your HF digital companion*. Newington, CT: American Radio Relay League.

Hill, J. (2002). Amateur radio—A powerful voice in education. *QST, 86*(12), 52–54.

Hudspeth, D., & Plumlee, R. C. (1994). *BBS uses in education*. Denton, TX: Texas Center for Educational Technology.

Jones, G. (1996). *Packet radio: What? why? how?* Tucson, AZ: Tucson Amateur Packet Radio.

Kasal, M. (2010). *Experimental satellites laboratory*. Retrieved January 16, 2011, from http:// www.urel.feec.vutbr.cz/esl/.

Lucas, L. (1997). *Wide area networking guide for Texas school districts*. Denton, TX: Texas Center for Educational Technology.

Martin, J. (2006). *Linux - JNOS setup and configuration HOW-TO*. Retrieved October 17, 2010, from http://www.kf8kk.com/packet/jnos-linux/ linux-jnos-setup-9.htm.

McDonough, J. (2007). *The Michigan digital network*. Retrieved September 7, 2010, 2010, from http://packet.mi-nts.org/257/MIdigital.pdf.

McLarnon, B. (2008). *Packet radio technology: An overview*. Retrieved October 17, 2010, from http://www.friends-partners.org/glosas/ Tampere_Conference/Reference_Materials/ Packet_Radio_Technology.html.

Moxon, L. (1993). *HF antennas for all locations*. Potters Bar, UK: Radio Society of Great Britain.

Przybylski, J. (1997). *Home web SP1LOP*. Retrieved January 16, 2011, from http://www.sp1lop. ampr.org/.

Przybylski, J. (2009). *All Poland packet info server*. Retrieved January 16, 2011, from http:// www.packet.poland.ampr.org/.

Skoric, M. (2004). The amateur radio as a learning technology in developing countries. In *Proceedings of the 4th IEEE International Conference on Advanced Learning Technologies,* (pp. 1029-1033). Los Alamitos, CA: IEEE Press.

Skoric, M. (2005). The perspectives of the amateur university networks – AMUNETs. *WSEAS Transactions on Communications, 4*, 834–845.

Skoric, M. (2006). The new amateur radio university network – AMUNET (Part 2). In *Proceedings of the 10th WSEAS International Conference on Computers,* (pp. 45-50). Athens, Greece: World Scientific and Engineering Academy and Society.

Skoric, M. (2007). Summer schools on the amateur radio computing. In *Proceedings of the 12th annual SIGCSE conference on Innovation and Technology in Computer Science Education,* (p. 346). New York, NY: Association for Computing Machinery.

Skoric, M. (2008). The new amateur radio university network – AMUNET (Part 3). In *Proceedings of the 12th WSEAS International Conference on Computers: New Aspects of Computers,* (pp. 432-439). Athens, Greece: World Scientific and Engineering Academy and Society.

Sumner, D. (Ed.). (2003). *Proceedings of the 22nd ARRL and TAPR Digital Communications Conference*. Newington, CT: American Radio Relay League.

Sumner, D. (Ed.). (2007). *Proceedings of the 26th ARRL and TAPR Digital Communications Conference*. Newington, CT: American Radio Relay League.

Weiss, R. T. (2005). Ham radio operator heads south to aid post-Katrina communications. *Computerworld*. Retrieved October 17, 2010, from http://www.computerworld.com/newsletter/0,4902,104446,00.html?nlid=MW2.

Weiss, R. T. (2005). Ham radio volunteers help re-establish communications after Katrina. *Computerworld*. Retrieved October 17, 2010, from http://www.computerworld.com/securitytopics/security/recovery/story/0,10801,104418,00.html.

Wiseman, J. (2010). *BPQAXIP configuration*. Retrieved October 17, 2010, from http://www.cantab.net/users/john.wiseman/Documents/BPQAXIP%20Configuration.htm.

Wiseman, J. (2010). *BPQETHER ethernet driver for BPQ32 switch*. Retrieved October 17, 2010, from http://www.cantab.net/users/john.wiseman/Documents/BPQ%20Ethernet.htm.

## KEY TERMS AND DEFINITIONS

**AMUNET:** This acronym stands for the AMateur radio University computer NETwork, which is the proposed name for a wireless network of an amateur radio BBS at a local university, including one or more amateur radio 'digipeaters,' and one or more end-user computers in surrounding schools' computer labs, offices or homes.

**BBS:** An electronic Bulletin Board System, a software that usually operates on a personal computer equipped with one or more telephone lines, amateur radio stations and Internet connections, to provide communication between remote users such as electronic mail, conferences, news, chat, files and databases.

**Duplex:** Capability of some radio stations, including repeaters, to transfer data in two directions simultaneously. That is referred to as full duplex. When repeaters work in the full duplex mode, amateur packet radio traffic travels more efficiently.

**Forwarding:** In the amateur radio jargon, forwarding is the automated process of mutual exchange of e-mail and other files between BBS computers. Any two neighboring sysops have to negotiate working parameters of their systems due to a variety of BBS programs in use. The sysops must also coordinate working times of their systems, especially in cases when the servers are not 'on the air' all the time (24/7).

**Gateway:** A gateway is a computer that connects two different networks together. The gateway will perform the protocol conversions necessary to go from one network to the other. For example, a gateway could connect a local area network (LAN) of computers in a school to the Internet. In addition, an amateur radio BBS might provide a gateway for the school's LAN to the 'air,' or vice versa.

**Packet Radio:** A communication mode between the amateur radio stations where computers control how the radio stations handle the traffic. The computers and attached modems organize information into smaller chunks of it – often referred as 'packets' of data, and route those packets to intended destinations.

**Remote Access:** The ability to access a technical device (E.g. a computer running as the BBS, etc.) from outside a building in which it is installed. Remote access requires communications hardware, software, and actual physical links. Different users can have different access rights (user permissions) associated with their account on a BBS or a radio-relay system.

**Repeater:** In radio communications, a repeater is a device that amplifies or regenerates the signal in order to extend the distance of the transmission.

Repeaters are available for both analog (voice) and digital (data) signals. 'Digipeater' is the common short name for a 'digital repeater.'

**Sysop:** It is a short name for Systems Operator. That person maintains and runs an amateur radio BBS or a repeater. Some sources refer to the sysop as "system administrator."

## APPENDIX A

The following figures show a couple of *telnet* sessions that simulate radio communications between the amateur radio email servers. In Figure 29 we can see two consecutive sessions: The first one was established with UA6ADV server in Russia, and the second one with DB0ZAV in Germany. As shown in the figure, the second session started immediately after the first one was finished (at *07:56*). That practice enables the system operators to keep connecting times short and perform several sessions in a row, one after the other.

*Figure 29. Two consecutive telnet-type connections with a Russian (UA6ADV) and a German (DB0ZAV) email server*

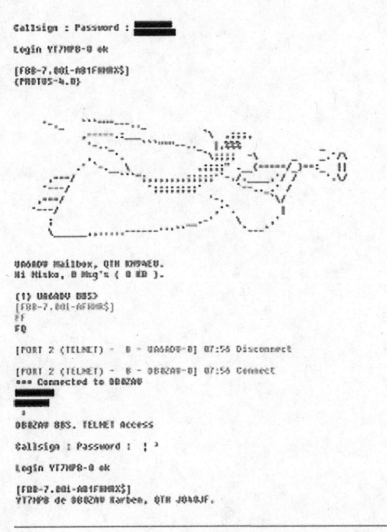

*Figure 30. A telnet-type connection to a Canadian (VE2PKT) email server*

```
[PORT 2 (TELNET) - 16 - VE2PKT-0] 07:56 Connect
*** Connected to VE2PKT


    n


    .........................................................
    .    ....... ......................... ........       .
    .    ........ LinFBB TELNET At VE2PKT .......          .
    .    ........ === Version 7.04r-pre8.0 === ........    .
    .                                                      .
    .              Bienvenue/Welcome                       .
    .                                                      .
    .            Full BBS TelNet Access                    .
    .          ve2pkt.dyndns.org Port 6300                 .
    .        or telnet 44.135.49.3 port 6300               .
    .........................................................
    . Premiere connection? Envoyer un message au           .
    .       Sysop avec mot de passe desirer.               .
    .........................................................
    . First time connections? Send a E-Mail to the         .
    .       Sysop with desire password.                    .
    :::::::::::::::::::::::::::::::::::::::::::::::::::::::::::
    .  Packet:   ve2pkt@ve2pkt.#qbc.qc.can.noam            .
    .  AMPR Net: ve2pkt@nos.ve2pkt.ampr.org                .
    .  Internet: ve2pkt@amsat.ca                           .
    .........................................................

Connected Stations to BBS:

Ch. 9   (TELNET) : F1BBI-0  - Mar 12/10/18 05:55
Ch. 18  (LINKODE) : 2L2BAB-8 - Mar 12/10/18 05:50
    via : VE2PKT-3
Ch. 19  (LINKODE) : VE2BVA-1 - Mar 12/10/18 05:50
    via : VE2PKT-4
Ch. 20  (LINKODE) : VE2PKT-4 - Mar 12/10/18 05:50
    via : VE2PKT-4

Callsign : Password :
Logon OK. Type HP to change password.

[FBB-7.04r-AB1FHMRX$]
OK Misko
4:VE2PKT>
[FBB-7.00i-AHMRX$]
>
```

To make incoming connections to their servers more likable and informative for visitors, local system administrators often insert additional visual and textual components at the beginning of the sessions, such as a 'simulated' picture in Figure 29, or a more detailed description of the system (Figure 30).

# APPENDIX B

The following content is the functional part of PORTS.SYS – the configuration file of the PZT mailbox software, as such we used in Experiment 10. Note that we removed unused portions and most of the comment lines in the file (the lines starting with semicolon).

```
; PORTS.SYS for G8PZT BBS versions 405 and above (Mandatory file)
;
; BPQ INTERFACES:
; =================
;
; Mode may be "raw" or "host"
;
; iface BPQ <stream> <mode>    <label>
; ---------------------------------
    iface bpq    64    raw     bpqraw
    iface bpq    1     host    host1
    iface bpq    2     host    host2
    iface bpq    3     host    host3
    iface bpq    4     host    host4
    iface bpq    5     host    host5
    iface bpq    6     host    host6
    iface bpq    7     host    host7
    iface bpq    8     host    host8
    iface bpq    9     host    host9
    iface bpq    10    host    host10
    iface bpq    11    host    host11
    iface bpq    12    host    host12
    iface bpq    13    host    host13
    iface bpq    14    host    host14
    iface bpq    15    host    host15
    iface bpq    16    host    host16
;
; COMMUNICATION CHANNELS:
; ========================
;
; Some interfaces may support several "streams" or "ports",
; e.g. up to 16 KISS TNCs may share one serial cable, or up to 16 radio
; ports may be connected to BPQ.
;
; You should define here one CHANNEL for every stream on every interface.
;
; The "stream" number used below is the one appropriate for the interface
; for example, BPQ radio ports are number 1 to 16, whereas KISS tncs use
; 0 - 15 (sometimes referred to by letters A - P).
; For interfaces which use only one stream, set the stream number to 0
;
;
```

```
; channel <name> <iface> <stream> <mtu>  <freq> [ip_address]
; -----------------------------------------------------------
;
  channel   bpq1    host1     0     240    BPQ_NODE
  channel   bpq2    host2     0     240    BPQ_NODE
  channel   bpq3    host3     0     240    BPQ_NODE
  channel   bpq4    host4     0     240    BPQ_NODE
  channel   bpq5    host5     0     240    BPQ_NODE
  channel   bpq6    host6     0     240    BPQ_NODE
  channel   bpq7    host7     0     240    BPQ_NODE
  channel   bpq8    host8     0     240    BPQ_NODE
  channel   bpq9    host9     0     240    BPQ_NODE
  channel   bpq10   host10    0     240    BPQ_NODE
  channel   bpq11   host11    0     240    BPQ_NODE
  channel   bpq12   host12    0     240    BPQ_NODE
  channel   bpq13   host13    0     240    BPQ_NODE
  channel   bpq14   host14    0     240    BPQ_NODE
  channel   bpq15   host15    0     240    BPQ_NODE
  channel   bpq16   host16    0     240    BPQ_NODE
;
; BBS PORT DEFINITIONS:
; =====================
;
; Mappings between channels and BBS ports
;
; Each bbs PORT should be attached to a seperate CHANNEL, except for TCP
; ports, which may share a channel, providing it uses KISS or BPQ RAW
; interface.
;
; Port#:     BBS port number (1-16)
; Type:      One of: tcp, bpq, modem, tnc2, tty
; Timeout:   Inactivity timeout in seconds
; Initstring: Initialisation string (e.g. for modem)
;
; PORT <port#> <type> <t/o> <channel> <initstring>
; ------------------------------------------------
  port      1       bpq     300   bpq1
  port      2       bpq     300   bpq2
  port      3       bpq     300   bpq3
  port      4       bpq     300   bpq4
  port      5       bpq     300   bpq5
  port      6       bpq     300   bpq6
  port      7       bpq     300   bpq7
```

```
     port    8     bpq    300    bpq8
     port    9     bpq    300    bpq9
     port    10    bpq    300    bpq10
     port    11    bpq    300    bpq11
     port    12    bpq    300    bpq12
     port    13    bpq    300    bpq13
     port    14    bpq    300    bpq14
     port    15    bpq    300    bpq15
     port    16    bpq    300    bpq16
;
; Set the default tracing for trace window
;
trace bpqraw 0
;
```

## APPENDIX C

The following content is the functional part of XROUTER.CFG – the configuration file of the Xrouter node software, as such we used in Experiment 1. Note that we removed unused portions and most of the comment lines in the file (the lines starting with semicolon).

```
; XROUTER.CFG  Configuration file for Xrouter version 1.76
; =========================================================
;
; =======================================================================
; Interface definitions - These MUST come before any port definitions
; =======================================================================
;
;
INTERFACE=1
     TYPE=ASYNC
     COM=1
     IOADDR=3F8
     INTNUM=4
     SPEED=9600
     PROTOCOL=KISS
     KISSOPTIONS=CHECKSUM
     MTU=256
ENDINTERFACE
;
```

```
;
INTERFACE=3
      TYPE=LOOPBACK
      PROTOCOL=KISS
      MTU=576
ENDINTERFACE
;
;
INTERFACE=7
      TYPE=AXIP
    MTU=256
ENDINTERFACE
;
;
INTERFACE=8
      TYPE=EXTERNAL
      PROTOCOL=ETHER
      MTU=256
      INTNUM=125
ENDINTERFACE
;
;
; ========================================================================
; Port definitions. Each one begins with PORT=n and ends with ENDPORT
; ========================================================================
;
;
PORT=1
      ID=2m 1200bps
      INTERFACENUM=1
      MHEARD=10          ; Mheard enabled, 10 calls
ENDPORT
;
;
PORT=3
      ID=Internal Loopback
      INTERFACENUM=3
      QUALITY=255
ENDPORT
;
;
PORT=5
      ID=AXIP link to YT7MPB-3 (R3)
      INTERFACENUM=7
```

```
    CHANNEL=A
    IPLINK=192.168.1.1
    MHEARD=10        ; Mheard enabled, 10 calls
ENDPORT
;
;
PORT=6
    ID=Ethernet LAN
    INTERFACENUM=8
    CHANNEL=A        ; Ignored
    FRACK=2000
    RESPTIME=100
    MAXFRAME=4
    PACLEN=256
    MHEARD=10        ; Mheard enabled, 10 calls
ENDPORT
;
;
```

# Chapter 12
# Modeling of TCP Reno with Packet–Loss and Long Delay Cycles

**Hussein Al-Bahadili**
*Petra University, Jordan*

**Haitham Y. Adarbah**
*Gulf College, Oman*

## ABSTRACT

*The Transport Control Protocol (TCP) is the dominant transport layer protocol in the Internet Protocol (IP) suite, as it carries a significant amount of the Internet traffic, such as Web browsing, file transfer, e-mail, and remote access. Therefore, huge efforts have been devoted by researchers to develop suitable models that can help with evaluating its performance in various network environments. Some of these models are based on analytical or simulation approaches. This chapter presents a description, derivation, implementation, and comparison of two well-known analytical models, namely, the PFTK and PLLDC models. The first one is a relatively simple model for predicting the performance of the TCP protocol, while the second model is a comprehensive and realistic analytical model. The two models are based on the TCP Reno flavor, as it is one of the most popular implementations on the Internet. These two models were implemented in a user-friendly TCP Performance Evaluation Package (TCP-PEP). The TCP-PEP was used to investigate the effect of packet-loss and long delay cycles on the TCP performance, measured in terms of sending rate, throughput, and utilization factor. The results obtained from the PFTK and PLLDC models were compared with those obtained from equivalent simulations carried-out on the widely used NS-2 network simulator. The PLLDC model provides more accurate results (closer to the NS-2 results) than the PFTK model.*

DOI: 10.4018/978-1-4666-0191-8.ch012

# INTRODUCTION

The TCP is a reliable connection-oriented protocol that allows a byte stream originating on one machine to be delivered without error to any other machine on the Internet (Forouzan, 2007). An Internet work differs from a single network because different parts may have different topologies, delays, bandwidths, packet sizes, and other parameters. The TCP was designed to be dynamically adaptable to outfit Internet work, robust in the face of many kinds of failures, handle flow control to make sure a fast sender cannot swamp a slow receiver with more messages than it can handle, and support full duplex and point-to-point connections (Tekala & Szabo, 2008).

The TCP only supports point-to-point connection in which the sending and receiving TCP entities exchange data in the form of TCP segments, and it does not support multicasting or broadcasting. The size of the segments are decided by the TCP software, which decides how big the segments should be, and can accumulate data from several writes into one segment or can split data from one write over multiple segments. Two parameters restrict the segment size, these are: the IP payload (each segment must fit in the 65515 Byte IP payload), and the network Maximum Transfer Unit (MTU) (each segment must fit in one MTU).

In practice, the MTU is generally 1500 bytes (the Ethernet payload size) and thus defines the upper bound on segment size. Segments can arrive out of order, so that some segment arrives but cannot be acknowledged because earlier segment has not turned up yet. Segments can also be delayed so long in transit that the sender times-out and retransmits them. The retransmissions may include different segment size than the original transmission. TCP must be prepared to deal with these problems and solve them in an efficient way. The definition of the components of the TCP segment header and more details on TCP protocol can be found in many computer networks textbooks and literatures (Tanenbaum, 2003).

The TCP was initially designed for wired networks for which a number of notable mechanisms have been proposed in the literature to improve the performance of TCP in such networks. For most of these mechanisms, analytical models have developed to predict and investigate their performance in wired networks in terms of the sending rate ($S$), throughput ($T$), and utilization factor ($U$). Unfortunately, these mechanisms demonstrated a poor performance in wireless networks due to presence of Packet-Loss (PL) and Long Delay Cycles (LDC) in such environment (Adarbah, 2008).

Presence of LDC leads to Spurious Retransmissions (STs) or Spurious Fast Retransmissions (SFRs), which produce serious end-to-end TCP performance degradation. However, since the emergent of wireless networks, new mechanisms have developed to enhance the performance of TCP in presence of STs and SFRs (Abouzeid & Roy, 2003; Chen, et. al., 2008). Consequently, new and adequate analytical models need to be developed to accommodate these new TCP mechanisms. This is because none of the existed models for wired networks considers the effect of STs and SFRs on the steady- state performance of TCP. This due to the fact that STs and SFRs do not occur frequently in wired networks, and also STs and SFRs are considered to be a transient state in a wired network, and thus cannot produce much impact on the steady-state performance of TCP (Yang, 2003). Practically, in wireless networks, STs and SFRs are more frequent and must be explicitly modeled to accurately estimate $S$, $T$, and $U$ of the TCP.

There are a number of mathematical models that have been developed throughout the years for evaluating the performance of a TCP connection in wireless networks (Abouzeid & Roy, 2003; Dunaytsev, 2006; Fu & Atiquzzaman, 2003). In this chapter, we present a description, derivation, implementation, and comparison of two well-known analytical models, these are:

1. **The PFTK analytical model.** This model is a relatively simple model developed for predicting the performance of the TCP protocol. It is call the PFTK model after the initials of the last names of its authors, namely, Padhye, Firoiu, Towsley, and Kurose (Padhye et. al. 2000). It considers parameters such as: PL, acknowledgment behavior, receiver's maximum congestion window size, and average Round Trip Time (RTT).

2. **The PLLDC analytical model.** This model is a comprehensive and realistic analytical model for evaluating the performance of the TCP protocol in wireless networks as it handles both PL and LDC; therefore, it was referred to as the PLLDC model (Adarbah, 2008). It considers parameters, such as: duration of LCD, interval between long delays, timeout, and slow-start threshold.

The two models are based on the TCP Reno flavor as it is one of the most popular implementation on the Internet. These two models are implemented in a user-friendly TCP Performance Evaluation Package (TCP-PEP). The TCP-PEP was used to investigate the effect of PL and LDC on the TCP performance measured in terms of $S$, $T$, and $U$. The results obtained from the PFTK and PLLDC models were validated against results obtained from equivalent simulations carried on the NS-2 simulator (Fall & Varadhan, 2008). The PLLDC model provides results closer to those obtained from the NS-2 simulator than the PFTK model.

# BACKGROUND

## Congestion of TCP

TCP is the dominant transport protocol On the Internet, and the current stability of the Internet depends on its end-to-end congestion control. Therefore, applications sharing a best-effort network need to positively respond to congestion to ensure network stability and high performance. Traditionally, congestion control algorithms have been implemented at the transport layer; therefore, it is referred to as congestion of TCP. One of the key elements for any TCP congestion control algorithm is the congestion signal that informs senders that congestion has or is about to occur. There is no explicit way that can be adopted by a TCP sender for congestion signal detection (Kung, et. al., 2007). However, there are two implicit approaches that have been identified for congestion signal detection, these are: PL-based and delay-based approaches (Widmer, 2001).

It is often not possible to draw sound conclusions on congestion from network delay measurements. Because it is difficult to find characteristic measures, such as the path's minimum $RTT$, due to persistent congestion at the bottleneck link or because of route changes. Consequently, PL is the only signal that senders can confidently use as an indication of congestion. A perceived PL is implemented either as a direct or an indirect trigger to throttle $S$; such flows are referred to as PL-responsive. In this sense, a TCP-based flow is a reliable PL-responsive flow.

One disadvantage of PL is that it is not unmistakable. Packets can get lost because of packet drops due to a buffer overflow at the bottleneck link or because of packet corruption due to a transmission error. The former indicates congestion, the latter does not. A sender is not able to discriminate among these events, because packet corruption usually leads to a frame checksum error and subsequent discard of the packet at the link layer.

Hence, transmission errors inevitably lead to an underestimation of available bandwidth for loss-responsive flows. As a consequence, applications can only fully utilize their share of bandwidth along the path if transmission errors are rare events. Due to the high error rate in wireless links, wireless links are often problematic, and the PL process and its consequences cannot be safely neglected as in wire line links.

There are two types of windows can be identified in a TCP connection, the congestion and advertised windows. The congestion window determines the number of bytes that can be outstanding at any time, or the maximum number of bytes can be transmitted without ACK that being received. This is a means of stopping the link between two places from getting overloaded with too much traffic. The size of this window is calculated by estimating how much congestion there is between the two places. Basically the size of the window, to a large degree, controls the speed of transmission as transmission pauses until there is ACK. The advertised window determines the number of bytes than can be sent over the TCP connection, which is imposed by the receiver. It is related to the amount of available buffer space at the receiver for this connection.

TCP congestion control consists of four mechanisms; these are (Voicu, et. al., 2007):

1. **Additive Increase/Multiplicative Decrease (AIMD):** This algorithm is a feedback control algorithm used in TCP congestion avoidance. Basically, AIMD represents a linear growth of the congestion window, combined to an exponential reduction when congestion takes place. The approach taken is to increase the transmission rate (window size), probing for usable bandwidth, until loss occurs. The policy of additive increase basically says to increase the congestion window by 1 maximum segment size (MSS) every *RTT* until a loss is detected. When loss is detected, the policy is changed to be one of multiplicative decrease which is to cut the congestion window in half after loss. The result is a saw tooth behavior that represents the probe for bandwidth (Altman et. al. 2005).

2. **Slow-Start (SS):** SS is part of the congestion control strategy used by TCP in many Internet applications, such as hyper text transfer protocol (HTTP), it is also known as the exponential growth phase. SS is used in conjunction with other algorithms to avoid sending more data than the network is capable of transmitting, that is, network congestion. The basic SS algorithm begins in the exponential growth phase initially with a congestion window size (*cwnd*) of 1 or 2 segments and increases it by 1 segment size (*SSize*) for each ACK received. This behavior effectively doubles the window size each *RTT* of the network.

   This behavior continues until the *cwnd* reaches the size of the receivers advertised window or until a loss occurs. When a loss occurs half of the current *cwnd* is saved as a SS threshold (*SST*) and SS begins again from its initial *cwnd*. Once the *cwnd* reaches the *SST* TCP goes into congestion avoidance mode where each ACK increases the *cwnd* by $SSize^2/cwnd$. This results in a linear increase of the *cwnd*.

3. **Fast Retransmit (FR):** Modifications to the congestion avoidance algorithm were proposed in 1990. Before describing the change, realize that TCP may generate an immediate ACK or a DUPACK, when an out of order segment is received. This DUPACK should not be delayed. The purpose of this DUPACK is to let the other end knows that a segment was received out of order, and to tell it what sequence number is expected.

   Since TCP does not know whether a DUPACK is caused by a lost segment or just a reordering of segments, it waits for a small number of DUPACKs to be received. It is assumed that if there is just a reordering of the segments, there will be only one or two DUPACKs before the reordered segment is processed, which will then generate a new ACK.

If three or more DUPACKs are received in a row, it is a strong indication that a segment has been lost. TCP then performs a retransmission of what appears to be the missing segment, without waiting for a retransmission timer to expire.

4. **Fast Recovery:** An improvement that allows a high throughput under moderate congestion, especially for large windows, is implemented as follows: After FR sends what appear to be the missing segment, then congestion avoidance but not SS is performed. This is called the fast recovery algorithm. The reason for not performing SS in this case is that the receipt of the DUPACKs tells TCP more than just a packet has been lost. Since the receiver can only generate the DUPACK when another segment is received, that segment has left the network and is in the receiver's buffer. In other words, there is still data flowing between the two ends, and TCP does not want to reduce the flow abruptly by going into SS.

The FR and fast recovery algorithms are usually implemented together as follows:

1. When the third DUPACK in a row is received, set *SST* to one-half the current *cwnd* but not less than two segments. Retransmit the missing segment. Set *cwnd* to *SST* plus 3 times the *SSize*. This inflates the congestion window by the number of segments that have left the network and which the other end has cached.
2. Each time another DUPACK arrives, increment *cwnd* by the *SSize*. This inflates the congestion window for the additional segment that has left the network. Transmit a packet, if allowed by the new value of *cwnd*.
3. When the next ACK arrives that acknowledges new data, set *cwnd* to *SST* (the value set in step 1). This ACK should be the ACK of the retransmission from step 1, one *RTT*

after the retransmission. Additionally, this ACK should acknowledge all the intermediate segments sent between the lost packet and the receipt of the first DUPACK. This step is congestion avoidance, since TCP is down to one-half the rate it was at when the packet was lost.

The FR algorithm first appeared in the Tahoe release, and it was followed by SS. The fast recovery algorithm appeared in the Reno release. Since, in this work we concern with TCP Reno, a description of this TCP flavor is given in the next section.

## TCP Reno

The TCP Reno implementation retained the enhancements incorporated into Tahoe, but modified the FR operation to include fast recovery. The new algorithm prevents the communication path from going empty after FR, thereby avoiding the need to SS to refill it after a single PL (Lulling, 2004; Lai & Yao, 2002; Vendicits, et al., 2003).

Fast recovery operates by assuming each DUPACK received represents a single packet having left the communication path. Thus, during fast recovery the TCP sender is able to make intelligent estimates of the amount of outstanding data. Fast recovery is entered by a TCP sender after receiving an initial threshold of DUPACKs. Once the threshold of DUPACKs is received, the sender retransmits one packet and reduces its congestion window by one half. Instead of SS, as is performed by a Tahoe TCP sender, the Reno sender uses additional incoming DUPACKs to clock subsequent outgoing packets.

During fast recovery the sender "inflates" its window by the number DUPACKs it has received, according to the observation that each DUPACK indicates some ACK has been removed from the network and is now cached at the receiver. After entering fast recovery and retransmitting a single packet, the sender effectively waits until half a window of DUPACKs have been received, and then sends a new packet for each additional DUPACK that is received.

Upon receipt of an ACK for new data (called a "recovery ACK"), the sender exits fast recovery. Reno's fast recovery algorithm is optimized for the case when a single packet is dropped from a window of data. The Reno sender retransmits at most one dropped packet per *RTT*. Reno significantly improves upon the behavior of Tahoe TCP when a single packet is dropped from a window of data, but can suffer from performance problems when multiple packets are dropped from a window of data (Xin & Jamalipour 2006, Lai & Yao 2002)

## Performance of TCP

A wireless network may suffer from extensive data loss due to: transmission errors in noisy environment, non-reliable wireless communication links, variable capacity links, frequent disconnections, limited communication bandwidth, broadcast nature of the communications, etc. Therefore, a wireless data communication session may involve a lot of data retransmission that degrades the performance of the networks. Data retransmissions reduce bandwidth utilization, and on the other hand increase delay and power consumption. These retransmissions are unavoidable and they are referred to them as factual retransmissions, because the data is lost and it will not reach the destination and they have to be retransmitted (Fu & Atiquzzaman, 2003).

There is another form of data retransmission that is initiated by the TCP sender, which is referred to it as SFR, which is occurred when segments get re-ordered beyond the DUPACK-threshold in the network before reaching the receiver, i.e. the reordering length is greater than the DUPACK threshold (three for TCP). There are two main reasons for SFR; these are (Ho, 2008; Weigle, et al., 2005):

1.   Timeout-based retransmission

2.   DUPACK-based retransmission

DUPACK-based retransmission is triggered when three successive (triple) DUPACKs (TD) for the same sequence number have been received, i.e., without waiting for the retransmission timer to expire.

Timeout-based retransmission can be explained as follows. Since, TCP was initially designed for wired networks, and hence performs poorly in the presence of delay spikes which are especially more frequent in wireless networks than in traditional wired network (Gurtov & Reiner, 2002).

These delay spikes may exhibit a sudden increase in the instantaneous *RTT* beyond the sender's Retransmission Timeout (RTO) (or simply abbreviated as TO) value causes retransmission ambiguity, resulting in Spurious Timeout (ST), which is defined as a TO which would not have happened if the sender waited long enough, and it results in retransmission due to a segment being delayed (but NOT lost) beyond TO. This produces serious end-to-end TCP performance degradation (Ludwig & Katz, 2000; Kesselman & Mansour, 2005).

One of the main reasons for the delay spikes to occur in a wireless environment is congestion and the lack of mechanisms through which the sender can detect or be informed about these congestions, and consequently prohibits SRs. However, there are other reasons for the delay spikes to occur in a wireless environment (Fu & Atiquzzaman, 2003).

## MODELING OF TCP

There are three basic techniques for performance evaluation of TCP connection in wireless networks; these are (Lulling & Vaughan, 2004; Fall & Floyd, 1996):

1.   Experimental measurement
2.   Computer simulation
3.   Mathematical modeling

Experimental measurement is rarely used to evaluate the performance of TCP connection, due to its difficulty, cost, limited flexibility, etc. On the other hand, due to the enormous development in computing resources and tools, computer simulation and mathematical modeling are extensively used to evaluate the performance of TCP connection algorithms. They have an equivalent importance as they are usually validated each other. In this work, we concern with analytical model of TCP connection, in particular TCP Reno.

## Essential of TCP Modeling

A number of notable models for TCP have been developed, which are either shed light on a particular aspect of the protocol or add a new level of generality to the process of modeling transport control within the Internet. It is very useful, however, to consider the similarities of all these models before focusing attention on any particular model, as this allows keeping the key features of the model in mind and not getting lost in the details of a specific model.

Earlier versions of the protocol do exist, which may not necessarily contain the features that are classed here as essential for proceeding with TCP modeling. Future TCP flavors may also depart from these essentials. In addition, there are some important dynamics of TCP, such as its SS procedure, and other phenomena, such as loss of ACK packets in queues, which are not generally included in mathematical models.

All TCP connections commence in SS and many spend their entire lives in SS, because only a few kilobytes of data are being transferred. Thus, it is important to understand that models do have their limitations in reflecting reality. There are two key processes that a model of TCP needs to include (Hassan & Jain, 2003):

1.    The dynamics of the window that defines the number of packets a TCP source can convey into the network.

2.    The PL process that indicates current traffic loads or congestion within the network.

One thing to notice about these processes is that they are both observed from the reference point of the TCP sender. This is obvious for window size, which is controlled by an algorithm within the source itself. The PL is also observed by the source. The loss process does not arise from any one particular node in the network but can be triggered by any node along the path of the TCP connection, with the source node observing the loss process as aggregation of information being generated along the connection path.

**Window dynamics:** The essential dynamics of this window size are its AIMD (Kesselman & Mansour 2005). During the interval in which TCP receives information (i.e., packets are not being lost in the network), TCP increases its window linearly. When the source deduces that a packet has been lost, it reduces its window by a factor of the current $W$ (i.e., multiplicatively). Implementation of TCP normally increases $W$ by one packet each round trip (in the linear increase phase) and reduce $W$ size by half in the event of a PL. Although, $W$ can be generalized in mathematical models of TCP, some models have been developed using $S$, as $S$ can ease the analysis that follows the development of the model. The standard assumption in this case is that $W$ is related to $S$ by $RTT$:

$$S = \frac{W}{RTT} \tag{1}$$

Where $S$ is the sending rate in packets/sec, $W$ is the window size, and $RTT$ is the RTT. This does assume that increasing $S$ has negligible effect on queuing delays at nodes within the network, so that $RTT$ is effectively constant. Regardless of whether a model uses $W$ or $S$, all models incorporate the AIMD dynamics of TCP.

2.  **Packet-Loss (PL) process:** The other main component of a TCP model is the PL process, which triggers the TCP source to reduce its *W*. As previously mentioned, this process aggregates information regarding network conditions at all nodes along the path of the TCP connection. The particular TCP connection being considered is competing for network resources, along its path, with other TCP connections that have routes intersecting with this path. It is also competing for network bandwidth with other network traffic in general. These variations in traffic load introduce uncertainty into the arrival of PL information at the TCP source.

This typically can be modeled as a stochastic process, either with regard to the probability *p* of losing a particular packet in the network or the intervals between instances when lost packets are detected (Abouzeid & Roy, 2003). The key point is that models usually incorporate the arrival of PL information, with the TCP source responding by decreasing its window. In fact, they do not necessarily need to consider the information being returned from the network as confirmation that packets have not been lost. Network information can take the form of explicit notification regarding congestion within the network, although individual congestion messages are most likely to still be coded as binary information. Regardless of whether the information is PL or explicit congestion information, TCP models must respond to the stream of network load information that is aggregated along the connection path.

## THE PFTK MODEL

This section presents a description and derivation of the TCP congestion control and avoidance model that was developed by Padhye, Firoiu, Towsley, and Kurose; therefore, it was referred

to it as the PFTK model after the initials of the last names of the authors (Padhye, et. al., 2000).

## Calculation of the TCP Sending Rate (*S*)

Many TCP receiver implementations send one cumulative ACK for consecutive packets (delayed ACK). Let *b* be the number of packets that are delayed and acknowledged by a single ACK. So that *b*=2 if one ACK is sent for two consecutive received packets. If *W* packets are sent in the first round and are all received and acknowledged correctly, then *W/b* ACKs will be received. Since each ACK increases *W* by 1/*W*, *W* at the beginning of the next round is then $W_r = W_{r-1} + 1/b$, where $W_r$ is *W* at round *r*. That is, during congestion avoidance and in the absence of loss, *W* increases linearly in time, with a slope of 1/*b* packets each *RTT*.

A PL can be detected at the TCP sender in one of two ways (Hassan & Jain, 2003):

1.  Reception of triple-DUPACK (TD), which is denoted as a TD loss indication.
2.  Timeout (TO), which is denoted as a TO loss indication.

The PFTK model is developed in three steps in accordance with its operating regimes, these are:

1.  Loss indications are exclusively TD
2.  Loss indications are both TD and TO
3.  The congestion *W* is limited by the receiver's advertised window

For each of the above operating regimes, an expression was derived for estimating *S*. A brief description and summary of the expressions are given below, while a detail description and derivation of equations can be found in (Padhye et. al. 2000).

***Loss indications are exclusively TD.*** At this stage, the loss indications are assumed to be exclusively of type TD, and that *W* is not limited by the receiver's advertised flow control window. A sample path of the evolution of congestion $W$ is given in Figure 1. Between two TD loss indications, the sender is in congestion avoidance, and $W$ increases by $1/b$ packets per round, and immediately after the loss indication occurs, $W$ is reduced by a factor of two.

The period between two TD loss indications is referred to it as a TD Period (TDP) and denoted by $(D_{TDP})$ as shown in Figure 1. A TDP starts immediately after a TD loss indication as shown in Figure 2. For the $i^{th}$ TDP, define $S_{TDP}$ to be the number of packets sent in the period $D_{TDP}$, which is the duration of the period, $W_i$ the window size at the end of the period, and $p$ the probability that a packet is lost, given that either it is the first packet in its round or the preceding packet in its round is not lost. Due to the stochastic nature of the loss process, the long-term steady-state value of $S$ of TCP source when loss indications are

*Figure 1. Evolution of $W$ over time when loss indications are TD*

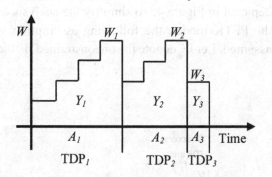

exclusively TD can be expressed as a function of $p$ and RTT as follows (Al-Bahadili & Adarbah, 2011; Padhye, et al., 2000):

$$E[S] = \frac{\dfrac{1-p}{p} + \dfrac{2+b}{3b} + \sqrt{\dfrac{8(1-p)}{3bp} + \left(\dfrac{2+b}{3b}\right)^2}}{RTT\left(\dfrac{2+b}{6} + \sqrt{\dfrac{2b(1-p)}{3p} + \left(\dfrac{2+b}{6}\right)^2} + 1\right)}$$

(2)

For small PL rate, the above equation can be simplified to:

$$E[S] = \frac{1}{RTT}\sqrt{\frac{3}{2bp}} + o\left(1/\sqrt{p}\right)$$

(3)

Furthermore, for $b=1$, Equation (3) can be reduced to the equation of the inverse square-root $p$ law or periodic model (Hassan & Jain, 2003) (see Figure 2).

***Loss indications are TD and TO***. In practice, it has been realized that in many cases the majority of window decreases are due to TO, rather than FR. Therefore, a good mathematical model should capture TO loss indications. This occurs when packets (or ACKs) are lost, and less than TD are received. In normal operation, the sender waits for a TO period denoted as $T_o$, and then retransmits non acknowledged packets. Following a TO, the congestion window is reduced to one, and one packet is thus resent in the first round after a TO. In the case that another TO occurs before successfully retransmitting the packets lost during the first TO, the period of TO doubles to $2T_o$; this doubling is repeated for each unsuccessful retransmission until a TO period of $64T_o$ is reached, after which the TO period remains constant at $64T_o$. Figure 3 illustrates an example on the evolution of congestion $W$.

*Exhibit 1.*

$$E[S] = \frac{\dfrac{1-p}{p} + \dfrac{2+b}{3b} + \sqrt{\dfrac{8(1-p)}{3bp} + \left(\dfrac{2+b}{3b}\right)^2} + Q \cdot \dfrac{1}{1-p}}{RTT\left(\dfrac{2+b}{6} + \sqrt{\dfrac{2b(1-p)}{3p} + \left(\dfrac{2+b}{6}\right)^2} + 1\right) + Q \cdot T_o \dfrac{f(p)}{1-p}} \tag{4}$$

In this case, due to the stochastic nature of the PL process, $S$ can be calculated as see in Exhibit 1.

Where $Q$, $E[W]$, and $f(p)$ are given by:

$$Q \approx \hat{Q}(E[W]) = \min\left(1, \frac{3}{E[W]}\right) \tag{5}$$

$$E[W] = \frac{2+b}{3b} + \sqrt{\frac{8(1-p)}{3bp} + \left(\frac{2+b}{3b}\right)^2} \tag{6}$$

$$f(p) = 1 + p + 2p^2 + 4p^3 + 8p^4$$
$$+ 16p^5 + 32p^6 = 1 + \sum_{i=1}^{6} 2^{i-1} p^i \tag{7}$$

***Impact of window limitation.*** So far, no limitation is considered on $W$. At the beginning of TCP flow establishment, the receiver advertises a maximum buffer size which determines a maximum congestion window size, $W_m$. As a consequence, during a period without loss indications, $W$ can grow up to $W_m$, but will not grow further beyond this value. An example of the evolution of $W$ is depicted in Figure 4. To simplify the analysis of the PFTK model, the following assumption is assumed. Let $W_u$ denote the unconstrained $W$, the

*Figure 2. Packets sent during a TDP*

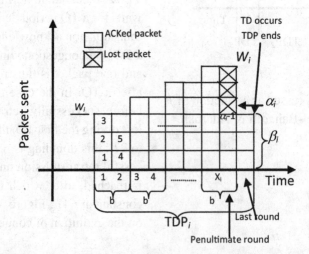

mean of which is derived by (Padhye, et. al., 2000) and it is given by Equation (6) with $W_u$ replaces $W$.

It is assumed that if $E[W_u]<W_m$, then the approximation $E[W]\approx E[W_u]$ is satisfactory. In other words, if $E[W_u]<W_m$, the receiver window limitation has negligible effect on $S$, and thus $S$ is given by Equation (4).

On the other hand, if $W_m \leq E[W_u]$, the approximation $E[W]\approx W_m$ can be considered as a satisfactory approximation. In this case, consider an interval $D_{TD}$ between two TO sequences consisting of a series of TDPs as in Figure 5. During the first TDP, the window grows linearly up to $W_m$ for $H$ rounds, afterwards remains constant for $L$ rounds,

and then a TD indication occurs. The window then drops to $W_m/2$, and the process repeats. According to the above discussion the following expression for $S$ can be derived:

$$E[S] = \frac{\dfrac{1-p}{p} + W_m + Q_m \cdot \dfrac{1}{1-p}}{RTT\left(\dfrac{b}{8}W_m + \dfrac{1-p}{pW_m} + 2\right) + Q_m \cdot T_O \dfrac{f(p)}{1-p}}$$

(8)

*Figure 3. Evolution of window size when loss indications are TD and TO*

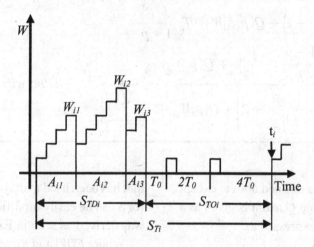

*Figure 4. Evolution of W limited by $W_m$*

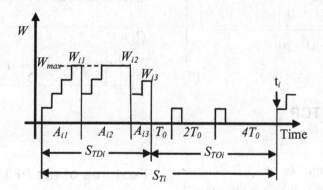

*Figure 5. Fast retransmit with window limitation*

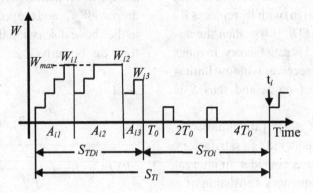

*Exhibit 2.*

$$E[T] = \begin{cases} \dfrac{\dfrac{1-p}{p} + \dfrac{E[W]}{2} + Q(p, E[W])}{RTT\left(E[W]+1\right) + Q(p, E[W]) \cdot T_o \dfrac{f(p)}{1-p}} & \text{for } E[W_u] < W_m \\[4ex] \dfrac{\dfrac{1-p}{p} + \dfrac{W_m}{2} + Q(p, W_m)}{RTT\left(\dfrac{W_m}{4} + \dfrac{1-p}{pW_m} + 2\right) + Q(p, W_m) \cdot T_o \dfrac{f(p)}{1-p}} & \text{Otherwise} \end{cases} \tag{10}$$

where all variables are as defined above, except $Q_m$, which is different from $Q$ and it is given as a function of $W_m$ and it is expressed as:

$$Q_m \approx \hat{Q}(w) = \\ \min\left(1, \frac{\left(1-(1-p)^3\left[1+(1-p)^3\left[1-(1-p)^{w-3}\right]\right]\right)}{1-(1-p)^w}\right) \tag{9}$$

## Calculation of the TCP Throughput (*T*)

The steady-state performance of TCP Reno is also be characterized by *T*, which is the amount of data received per unit time. The same analysis

that has been used to derive Equations (4) and (8) for *S* can be easily modified to calculate *T*, which was derived as seen in Exhibit 2.

Where $E[W]$ and $f(p)$ are defined in Equations (6) and (7), respectively, and $Q(p,w)$ was derived in (Padhye et. al. 2000) as:

$$Q(p, w) = \\ \min\left(1, \frac{\left(1-(1-p)^3\left[1+(1-p)^3\left[1-(1-p)^{w-3}\right]\right]\right)}{1-(1-p)^3}\right) \tag{11}$$

## Features of the PFTK Model

The main features of the PFTK model include:

1.  It is a relatively simple analytical model for predicting $S$ of a saturated TCP sender, i.e., a steady-state flow with an unlimited amount of data to send.

2.  It illustrates the congestion avoidance behavior of TCP and its impact on $S$, taking into account the dependence of congestion avoidance on:

    a.  ACK behavior.

    b.  The manner in which PL is inferred, whether by DUPACK detection and FR or by TO.

    c.  Limited $W$.

    d.  Average $RTT$.

3.  The model is based on the TCP Reno flavor as it is one of the more popular implementations in the Internet today.

4.  In this model, $W$ is increased by $1/W$ each time an ACK is received. Conversely, the window is decreased whenever a lost packet is detected, with the amount of the decrease depending on whether PL is detected by DUPACK or by TO.

5.  The model represents the congestion avoidance behavior of TCP in terms of rounds. A round starts with transmission of $W$ packets. Once all packets falling within the congestion window have been sent, no other packets are sent until the first ACK is received for one of these $W$ packets. This ACK reception marks the end of the current round and the beginning of the next round.

6.  The duration of a round is equal to $RTT$ and is assumed to be independent of $W$.

7.  The time needed to send all the packets in a window is smaller than the $RTT$.

8.  A PL in a round is entirely independent of PL in other rounds.

9.  PLs are correlated among the back-to-back transmissions within a round: if a packet is lost, all remaining packets transmitted until the end of that round are also lost.

## THE PLLDC MODEL

The detail mathematical derivation of the PLLDC model is presented in Adarbah (2008) and Al-Bahadili & Adarbah (2011). However, in this section, we present the final analytical form of model with limited details. Before we proceed with presenting the final form of the PLLDC model for estimating TCP Reno $S$ and $T$ in presence of PL and LDC, we introduce, first, the dynamics of sender window around a Long Delay (LD), and then the statistical modeling of the LD pattern.

***Dynamics of sender window around a LD.***
In order to analyze the dynamics of the sender window around a LD, it is important to be familiar with the evolution of sender's $W$ as represented by the number of packets that can be sent. This is shown in Figure 6. At each round $W$ is increased by $1/b$. After $X_i$ rounds, the LD begin, when some of the packets in the $X_i$-th round are delayed (packets marked "d") (Tekala & Szabo, 2008).

Since the LD is of a much larger timescale than a round, any extra packets that were sent in round $X_{i+1}$, corresponding to the ACKs of successfully delivered packets of round $X_i$, are also delayed. After $T_o$, which is the converged value of the TO when the $RTT$ is stable for a relatively long period of time, the sender will TO and reduce the window to one and retransmit the first delayed packet. If it is not acknowledged within $2T_o$, the sender will retransmit it again, and so on.

The number of retransmissions during the LD is denoted by $R_D$; all these retransmitted packets are also delayed. Eventually, when the ACK for the first delayed packets comes back after the LD has cleared, the sender will enter SS and spuriously retransmit all the delayed packets. The sender will exit SS when the window hits the $SST$.

The LD Period (LDP) is defined as consisting of two consecutive TDPs, one LD, and one SS as shown in Figure 6. Note that even though the first period, labeled with $TDP_i$ in the figure, does not end with a TD loss indication, the number of packets sent and the duration of $TDP_i$ is the same

*Figure 6. Packet sent during one LDP*

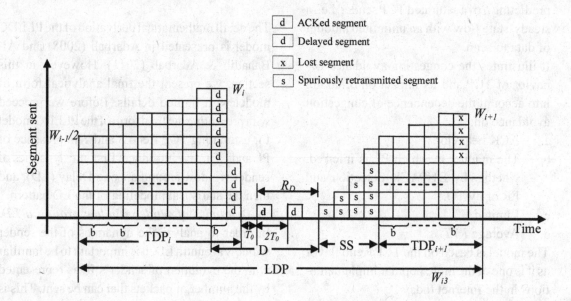

as other TDPs, so just TDP will be used for convenience. The sender's window was $W_{i-1}/2$ at the end of TDP$_{i-1}$; after the FR, it has been reduced to $W_{i-1}/2$, which is the sender's window at the start of TDP$_i$. TCP Reno starts FR after receiving TD.

***Statistical modeling of the LD pattern.*** It has been shown in Equation (1) that $S$ is obtained by dividing $W$ by the *RTT*, where *RTT* is the expected

value of RTT when there is no LD. However, in the presence of LD spikes, the actual time is much more than RTT, and the time measured by the sender is referred to as the LDs as illustrated in Figure 7a.

A two-state Markov chain is used to model the start and end of a LD as shown in Figure 7b (Altman et. al. 2005). The two states are: interval

*Figure 7. (a) variation of RTT showing four LDs, and (b) model of LDs*

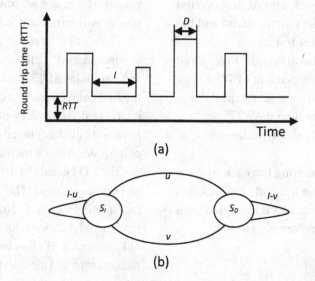

between LDs ($S_I$) and duration of LD ($S_D$). Here, it is assumed that the length of the $S_I$ and $S_D$ states are both exponentially distributed, with $u$ and $v$ being the transition probabilities from state $S_I$ to state $S_D$ and state $S_D$ to state $S_I$, respectively. By solving the Markov chain in Figure 7b, the relationship between $I$ and $D$ can be expressed as:

$$E[D] = \frac{u\,E[I]}{u + v} \tag{12}$$

Given a model for the lower layer events (such as link layer retransmission, mobile handoff, etc.) that cause LDs, the values of $D$, $I$, $u$, and $v$ can be obtained to be used in Equation (12).

## Calculation of the TCP Sending Rate ($S$)

A satisfactory mathematical model for estimating $S$ of wireless TCP source over an unreliable link with certain PL probability ($p$), and in the pres-ence of LD spikes, was derived in Al-Bahadili & Adarbah (2011) and it is expressed as:

$$E[S] = \frac{E[S_{LDC}]}{E[D_{LDC}]} = \frac{mE[S_{NP}] + E[S_{LDP}]}{mE[D_{NP}] + E[D_{LDP}]} \tag{13}$$

Where $S_{LDC}$ is the number of packets sent during one LDC, $D_{LDC}$ is the duration of the LDC. In the above equation, the numerator denotes the number of packets sent during one LDC and the denominator is the duration of an LDC.

The values of $E[S_{LDC}]$ and $E[D_{LDC}]$ are given as:

$$E[S_{LDC}] = m\,E[S_{NP}] + E[S_{LDP}] \tag{14}$$

$$E[D_{LDC}] = m\,E[D_{NP}] + E[D_{LDP}] \tag{15}$$

Where $m$ is the number of NPs in one LDC, $S_{NP}$ is the number of packets sent during one NP, $S_{LDP}$ is the number of packets sent during one LDP, $D_{NP}$ is the duration of one NP, and $D_{LDP}$ is the duration of one LDP. The variables in above two equations

*Exhibit 3.*

$$m = \frac{E[I] - 2E[D_{TDP}] - k \cdot RTT}{E[D_{NP}]} \tag{16}$$

$$E[S_{NP}] = \frac{1}{\min(1, \frac{3}{E[W]})} \left( \frac{1-p}{p} + \frac{2+b}{3b} + \sqrt{\frac{8(1-p)}{3bp} + \left(\frac{2+b}{3b}\right)^2} \right) + \frac{1}{1-p} \tag{17}$$

$$E[D_{NP}] = \frac{RTT}{\min(1, \frac{3}{E[W]})} \left( \frac{2+b}{6} + \sqrt{\frac{2b(1-p)}{3p} + \left(\frac{2+b}{6}\right)^2 + 1} \right) + T_o \frac{f(p)}{1-p} \tag{18}$$

$$E[S_{LDP}] = 2E[S_{TDP}] + E[R_D] + E[S_{SST}] \tag{19}$$

$$E[D_{LDP}] = 2E[D_{TDP}] + E[R_D] + (k-2)\,RTT \tag{20}$$

$m$, $E[S_{NP}]$, $E[D_{NP}]$, $E[S_{LDP}]$, and $E[D_{LDP}]$ are given as presented in Exhibit 3.

The values of $E[S_{TDP}]$, $E[D_{TDP}]$, $E[R_D]$, $E[D]$, $E[S_{SST}]$, and $k$ are given by:

$$E[S_{TDP}] = \frac{1-p}{p} + \frac{2+b}{3b}$$
$$+ \sqrt{\frac{8(1-p)}{3bp} + \left(\frac{2+b}{3b}\right)^2} \qquad (21)$$

$$E[D_{TDP}] =$$
$$RTT\left(\frac{2+b}{6} + \sqrt{\frac{2b(1-p)}{3p} + \left(\frac{2+b}{6}\right)^2} + 1\right) \qquad (22)$$

$$E[R_D] = \sum_{j=0}^{5}\left(e^{-\frac{2^j T_o}{E[D]}} - e^{-\frac{64 T_o}{E[D]}}\right) \qquad (23)$$

$$E[S_{SST}] = \sum_{j=1}^{k}\left(\frac{3}{2}\right)^j \approx 3\left(\frac{3}{2}\right)^k - 3 \qquad (24)$$

$$k = \left\lceil \frac{\ln\left(E[SST]\right)}{\ln\left(1.5\right)} \right\rceil \qquad (25)$$

## Derivation of the TCP Throughput ($T$)

$T$ can be determined by subtracting the spuriously retransmitted and lost packets from $S$. Referring to Figure 6, the delayed packets in the $X_i$ and $X_{i+1}$-th rounds of the first TDP are subsequently spuriously retransmitted, therefore, one window of packets $E[W]$ must be subtracted from $E[S_{TDP}]$.

Although, the spuriously retransmitted and lost packets are subtracted from the total number of packets received, the duration of an LDC remains unchanged. Therefore, $T$ can be determined as:

$$E[T] = \frac{E\left[S'_{LDC}\right]}{E[D_{LDc}]} \qquad (26)$$

Where $E[S'_{LDC}]$ represents the actual number of packets delivered to the receiver, and $E[D_{LDC}]$ is given in Equation (15) and it represents the duration of one LDC. $E[S'_{LDC}]$ is calculated as:

$$E[S'_{LDC}] = m\, E[S'_{NP}] + E[S'_{LDP}] \qquad (27)$$

Where $E[S'_{LDP}]$ and $E[S'_{NP}]$ are the net number of packets delivered to the receiver during one LDC and the net number of packets sent during $i^{th}$ NP ($i = 1, 2, ..., m$). They are given by:

$$E[S'_{LDP}] = E[S'_{TDP,1}] + E[R'_D]$$
$$+ E[S_{SST}] + E[S'_{TDP,2}] \qquad (28)$$

$$E[S'_{NP}] = \frac{1}{Q}\, E[S'_{TDP,2}] + E[R'_{NP}] \qquad (29)$$

The net number of packets send during the first TDP, $E[S'_{TDP,1}]$, can be expressed as:

$$E[S'_{TDP,1}] = E[S'_{TDP}] - E[W] \qquad (30)$$

Substituting $E[S_{TDP}]$ and $E[W]$ from Equations (21) and (6) into Equation (30) yields the following value for $E[S'_{TDP,1}]$:

$$E[S'_{TDP,1}] = \frac{1-p}{p} \qquad (31)$$

In the second TDP of the LDP period, the lost the delayed packets need to be subtracted from $S$, i.e., on the average, $E[W]/2$ must be subtracted. So that the net number of packets send during the second TDP, $E[S'_{TDP,2}]$, can be expressed as:

$$E[S'_{TDP,2}] = E[S_{TDP}] - \frac{E(W)}{2} \qquad (32)$$

Substituting $E[S_{TDP}]$ and $E[W]$ from Equations (21) and (6) into Equation (32) yields the following value for $E[S'_{TDP,2}]$:

$$E[S'_{TDP,2}] = \frac{1-p}{p}$$
$$+ \frac{1}{2}\left( \frac{2+b}{3b} + \sqrt{\frac{8(1-p)}{3bp} + \left(\frac{2+b}{3b}\right)^2} \right) \qquad (33)$$

## Derivation of the TCP Utilization Factor (*U*)

$U$ is determined as $T$ over $S$ and it is expressed mathematically as:

$$U = \frac{T}{S} \times 100 \qquad (34)$$

Substituting $T$ and $S$ from Equations (26) and (13) into Equation (34), yields the following equation for $U$:

$$E[U] = \frac{E[T]}{E[S]} \times 100$$
$$= \frac{m\,E[S'_{NP}] + E[S'_{LDP}]}{m\,E[S_{NP}] + E[S_{LDP}]} \times 100 \qquad (35)$$

Where $m$, $E[S'_{NP}]$, $E[S'_{LDP}]$, $E[S_{NP}]$, and $E[S_{LDP}]$ are given by Equations (16), (29), (28), (17), and (20), respectively.

## IMPLEMENTATION

The PFTK and PLLDC models described earlier are implemented in an interactive and user-friendly package using VB environment. The package can be used for TCP performance evaluation; therefore, we refer to this package as TCP-PEP. It can be used easily by professionals, researchers, and students to analyze the performance of the TCP Reno protocol in a realistic wireless environment and to investigate the effect of a number of parameters on the performance. The input parameters for TCP-PEP are listed in Table 1, while the code main computed parameters are given in Table 2. Each parameter is computed by the equation indicated in column #3 in Table 2. The computed parameters are ordered in the sequence by which they are computed. They are categorized into four main groups as shown in Table 2.

*Table 1. Definition of the code input parameters*

| Sym. | Description |
|---|---|
| $p$ | Packet-loss rate. |
| $D$ | Duration of the long delay. |
| $I$ | Interval between long delays. |
| $T_0$ | Timeout (TO) |
| $SST$ | Value of slow-start threshold at the end of a long delay $D$. |
| $b$ | Number of packets acknowledged by one ACK packet. |
| $RTT$ | Expected value of round trip time (RTT) when there is no long delay. |
| $W_m$ | The receiver's maximum advertised congestion window size. |

*Table 2. Definition of the code computed parameters*

| Sym. | Description | Equation |
|------|-------------|----------|
| Group 1: Length of each duration | | |
| $D_{TDP}$ | Duration of triple duplicate period (TDP), i.e. the time between two successive triple duplicate loss indications. | 22 |
| $f(p)$ | Polynomial function. | 7 |
| $W$ | TCP sender window size. | 6 |
| $Q$ | The probability that a loss indication in $W$ is TO. | 5 |
| $Q_m$ | The probability that a loss indication in $W_m$ is TO. | 9 |
| $k$ | The number of rounds needed to complete the SS stage after a long delay. | 25 |
| $m$ | Number of NPs in one long delay cycle (LDC). | 16 |
| $D_{LDP}$ | Duration of long delay period (LDP), which consists of one TDP, one long delay, one SS, and a second TDP. | 20 |
| Group 2: Number of packets sent during each duration | | |
| $S_{TDP}$ | Number of packets sent from the sender during one TDP. | 31 |
| $S_{NP}$ | Number of packets sent during $i^{th}$ NP, $i = 1, 2, ..., m$. | 17 |
| $R_D$ | Number of packets sent during long delay ($D$). | 23 |
| $S_{SST}$ | Number of packets sent during the SS stage in an LDP. | 24 |
| $S_{LDP}$ | Number of packets sent during one LDP. | 19 |
| $S_{LDC}$ | Number of packets sent during one LDC. | 14 |
| Group 3: Net number of packets sent during each duration | | |
| $S'_{TDP,1}$ | Net number of packets sent during the first TDP. | 31 |
| $S'_{TDP,2}$ | Net number of packets sent during the second TDP. | 32 |
| $S'_{LDP}$ | Net number of packets sent during one LDP. | 28 |
| $S'_{NP}$ | Net number of packets sent during $i^{th}$ NP, $i = 1, 2, ..., m$. | 29 |
| $S'_{LDC}$ | Net number of packets delivered to the receiver during one LDC. | 27 |
| Group 4: Main computed parameters | | |
| $S$ | Long-term steady-state sending rate of TCP connection. | 14 |
| $T$ | Long-term steady-state throughput of TCP connection. | 26 |
| $U$ | Long-term steady-state utilization factor. | 35 |

## RESULTS AND DISCUSSION

In order to assess the effectiveness of the TCP-PEP package in evaluating the performance of the TCP Reno protocol in a wireless networks suffering from PL and LDCs, it was used to investigate the variation of $S$, $T$, and $U$ against $p$ for various values of $D$. Also, to provide an insight into the behavior of TCP Reno in various wireless environments, the number of packets sent during different stages of the communication process was calculated, such

*Table 3. Input parameter*

| Parameter | Value |
|---|---|
| Packet-loss rate *(p)* | 0.001 to 0.5 |
| Duration of the long delay (*D*) | 6, 8, 10, 12 sec |
| Interval between long delays (*I*) | 30 sec |
| Round Trip Time *(RTT)* | 0.200 sec |
| Retransmission timeout or timeout ($T_o$) | 1.00 sec |
| Slow start threshold at the end of a long delay *D* (*SST*) | 2 |
| Number of packets acknowledged by one ACK packet (*b*). | 2 |
| Receiver's maximum congestion window size ($W_m$) | 800 packet |

*Figure 8. Variation of S with p for various values of D*

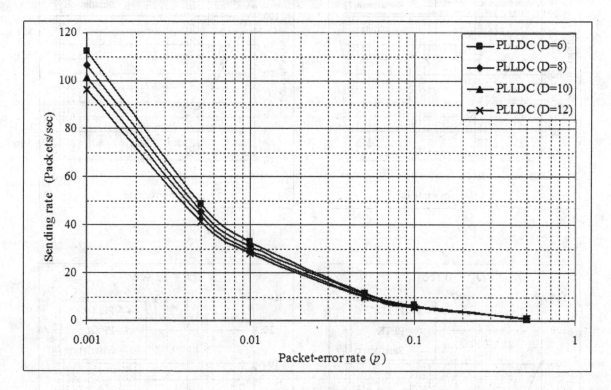

as: $S_{LDC}$, $S_{LDP}$, $S_{NP}$, $S_{TDP}$, $R_{NP}$, $R_D$, and $S_{SST}$. All input parameters are listed in Table 3.

**Calculation of S.** The TCP-PEP package was used to compute the variation of *S* with *p* for four various values of *D* (6, 8, 10, and 12 sec). The results obtained are plotted in Figure 8, which shows that *S* is inversely proportional to *p*, i.e., it is decreasing as *p* increases for all values of *D*. If all other network parameters are remained unchanged, *S* is slightly decreasing as *D* increases, in other word; *D* has only a slight effect on *S*.

The obtained results demonstrate that *D* has a recognizable effect on *S* at low *p* (*p*≤0.1) and has no effect at high *p* (*p*>0.1). In other words the dominant parameter at low *p* is *D* and vice-versa.

To numerically illustrate the variation of S as D changed, we define the following formula:

$$V = \frac{S_{D=x} - S_{D=6}}{S_{D=6}} \times 100 \qquad (36)$$

Where $V$ represents the variation with respect to a reference value ($S_{D=6}$). $S_{D=6}$ is the reference value ($D=6$ sec). $S_{D=x}$ is the sending rate at the same $p$ and $D$ takes any other valid value. For example, it can be deduced from Figure 8 that

*Figure 9. Comparison of S*

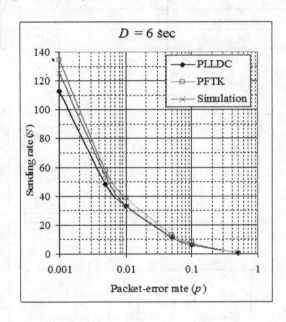

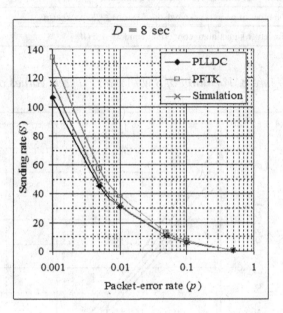

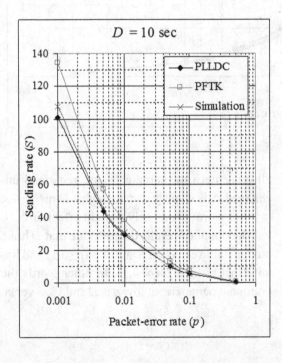

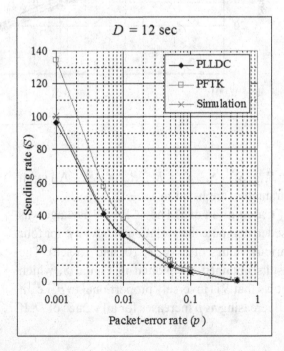

when *p*=0.01, and *D* is doubled (increased from 6 to 12 sec), *S* is reduced by 14.5% (from 32.80 to 28.09 packets/sec). A negative value indicates that *S* is decreasing as *D* increases.

In order to validate the accuracy of the models, their results are compared against results obtained

by the NS-2 network simulator as shown in Figure 9. It shows that the PLLDC model can predict *S* more accurately than the PFTK model. It also shows that when *D* increases, the gap between the PFTK model and the simulation results increases,

*Figure 10. Packets send during the different stages of LDC for various values of D*

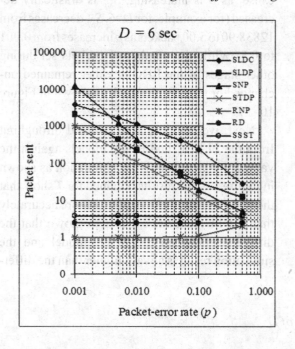
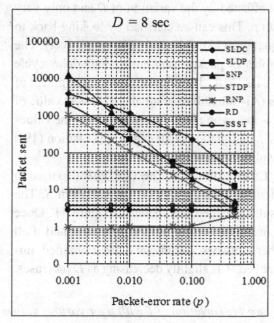
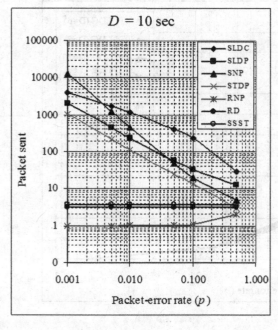
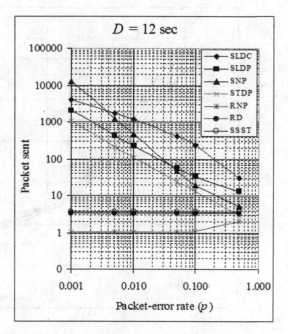

but the PLLDC model accommodates the increase of $D$ well.

In order to provide an insight into the behavior of TCP Reno in a PL environment and during LCD, the values of the number of packets sent during each time period within the LDC, namely, $S_{LDC}$, $S_{LDP}$, $S_{NP}$, $S_{TDP}$, $R_{NP}$, $R_D$, and $S_{SST}$ were computed and plotted in Figure 10. It can be seen from the results in Figure 10 that $S_{NP}$, $S_{TDP}$, and $S_{SST}$ are not affected by the variation of $D$ and only vary with $p$. This can be clarified by looking back to Equations (17), (21), and (24), respectively. The number of packets sent during long delay cycle ($D$), i.e., $E[R_{NP}]$ is calculated as the reciprocal of $1-p$ (Al-Bahadili & Adarbah 2011). The value of $R_D$ is increasing with $D$; consequently, the values of $S_{LDC}$ (Equation (14)) and $S_{LDP}$ (Equation (19)) are also increased.

**Calculation of $T$.** The TCP-PEP also used to calculate $T$ that is associated with each $S$. The results obtained are shown in Figure 11. Once again $T$ is inversely proportional to $p$, and if all other network parameters are remained unchanged, $T$ is slightly decreasing as $D$ increases.

Using Equation (35), our calculations show that $T$ is reduced by nearly 14% if $D$ is doubled, for all values of $p$. For example, when $p=0.01$ and $D$ is doubled (increased from 6 to 12 sec), $T$ is reduced by 14.44% (from 30.81 to 26.36 packets/sec). It can be deduced from Figure 8 and 11 that the difference between $S$ and $T$ is increasing as $p$ increases for all values of $D$. This is mainly because, as $p$ is increasing, $S_{NP}$ is drastically decreased (for example, for $D=6$, $S_{NP}$ decreases from 12838.90 to 5.00 packets as $p$ increases from 0.001 to 0.5. While the number of packets set during other stages of the LDC is either remained unchanged or slightly changed, as shown in Figure 10.

Next, we compare the predicted throughput from the PLLDC and PFTK models against the values obtained from NS-2 simulation as shown in Figure 12. The results obtained for $T$ show that the PLLDC model can predict $T$ more accurately than the PFTK model. It is also shown that the difference between the PFTK model and the simulation result is always higher than the differ-

*Figure 11. Variation of $T$ with $p$ for various values of $D$*

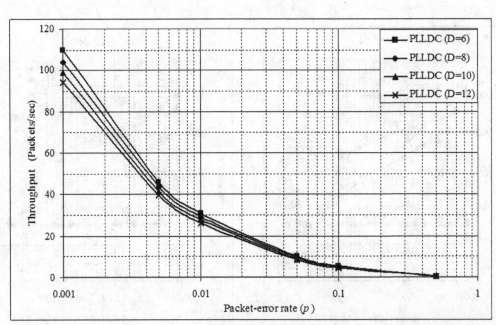

ence between the PLLDC model and the simulation results.

**Calculation of *U*.** The variation of *U* with *p* for various values of *D* is shown in Figure 13, which shows that *U* decreases as *p* increases due the fact that the difference between *S* and *T* is increasing as *p* increases, which has discussed above. For example, *U* decreases from around 97% to 60% as *p* increases from 0.001 to 0.5. In addition, presence of LCD almost equally effects *S* and *T* for all values of *D*, then the values of *U*, and consequently the performance of TCP Reno,

*Figure 12. Comparison of T*

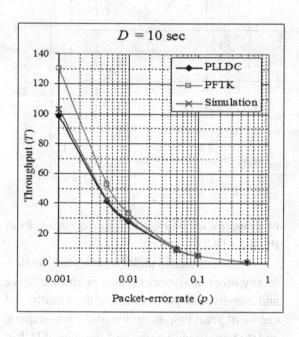
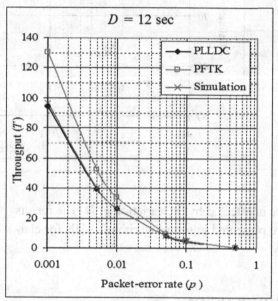
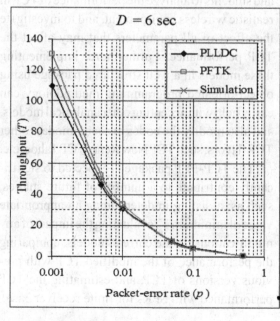
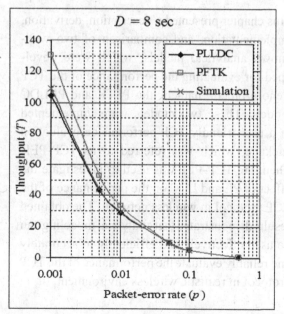

*Figure 13. Variation of U with p for various values of D*

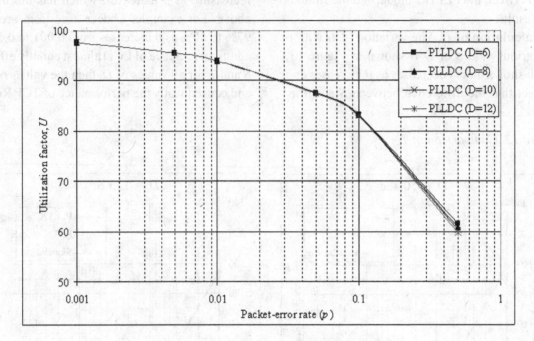

are unaffected by the variation in *D*. The results are presented in semi-logarithmic scale for clarity.

## CONCLUSION

This chapter presented a description, derivation, implementation, and comparison of two well-known analytical models, which were developed for evaluating the performance of the TCP Reno protocol, namely, the PFTK and PLLDC models. These two models were implemented in a user-friendly TCP performance evaluation package, which was referred to as TCP-PEP. Then, the TCP-PEP was used to investigate the effect of PL and LDC on the performance of the TCP protocol in wireless network. The obtained results demonstrated that analytical modeling can be used effectively and efficiently to accurately and reliably evaluate the performance of the TCP protocol in realistic wireless environment, or, in other words, a wireless environment suffers from PL and LDC.

Implementation of these two analytical models or any other analytical models in an interactive and user-friendly package can be done easily, and can be of great help to professional, researchers, and students to analyze the performance of TCP in realistic wireless environment, and to investigate the effect of all parameters that may affect the TCP performance. Furthermore, implementing these models in a well structured package using object-oriented programming methodology can easily help with accepting other analytical models, and also modify the codes to accommodate other TCP flavors, such TCP New Reno, TCP Tahoe, etc.

The TCP-PEP package is expected to significantly contribute to a number of future studies, such as: assisting in determining an appropriate value of minimum $T_o$, evaluating the impact of any modifications on the current models, comparing the performance of the modified TCP with previous versions of TCP, and estimating the TCP performance with SFRs for finite receiver case.

# REFERENCES

Abouzeid, A., & Roy, S. (2003). Stochastic modeling of TCP in networks with abrupt delay variations. *Journal of Wireless Networks, 9,* 509–524. doi:10.1023/A:1024644301397

Adarbah, H. (2008). *Modeling and analysis of TCP Reno with packet-loss and long delay cycles in wireless networks.* M.Sc Thesis. Amman, Jordan: Amman Arab University for Graduate Studies.

Al-Bahadili, H., & Adarbah, H. (2011). Effects of packet-loss and long delay cycles on the performance of the TCP protocol in wireless networks. In Abu-Taieh, E., El Sheikh, A., & Jafari, M. (Eds.), *Technology Engineering and Management in Aviation: Advancements and Discoveries.* Hershey, PA: IGI Global. doi:10.4018/978-1-60960-887-3.ch021

Altman, E., Barakat, C., & Ramos, V. (2005). Analysis of AIMD protocols over paths with variable delay. *Journal of Computer Networks, 48*(6), 960–971. doi:10.1016/j.comnet.2004.11.013

Chen, J., Gerla, M., & Zhong Lee, Y., & Sanadidi. (2008). TCP with delayed ACK for wireless networks. *Journal of Ad Hoc Networks, 6*(7), 1098–1116. doi:10.1016/j.adhoc.2007.10.004

Dunaytsev, R., Koucheryavy, Y., & Harju, J. (2006). The PFTK-model revised. *Journal of Computer Communications, 29*(13-14), 2671–2679. doi:10.1016/j.comcom.2006.01.035

Fall, K., & Floyd, S. (1996). Simulation-based comparison of Tahoe, Reno, and SACK TCP. *ACM Computer Communication Review, 26*(3), 5–21. doi:10.1145/235160.235162

Fall, K., & Varadhan, K. (2008). The NS manual. *The VINT Project.* Retrieved from http://www.isi.edu/nsnam/vint/.

Forouzan, B. A. (2007). *Data communications and networking* (4th ed.). New York: McGraw-Hill.

Fu, S., & Atiquzzaman, M. (2003). *Modeling TCP Reno with spurious timeout in wireless mobile environment.* Paper presented at the International Conference on Computer Communication and Networking. Dallas, TX.

Gurtov, A., & Reiner, L. (2002). *Making TCP robust against delay spikes.* Retrieved from draft-gurtov-tsvwg-tcp-delay-spikes-00.txt.

Hassan, M., & Jain, R. (2003). *High performance TCP/IP networking: Concepts, issues, and solutions.* Upper Saddle River, NJ: Prentice-Hall.

Ho, C. Y., Chen, Y. C., Chan, Y. C., & Ho, C. Y. (2008). Fast retransmit and fast recovery schemes of transport protocols: A survey and taxonomy. *Journal of Computer Networks, 52*(6), 1308–1327. doi:10.1016/j.comnet.2007.12.012

Kesselman, A., & Mansour, Y. (2005). Adaptive AIMD congestion control. *Special Issue on Network Design, 43*(1-2), 97–111.

Kesselman, A., & Mansour, Y. (2005). Optimizing TCP retransmission timeout. In *Proceedings of the 4th International Conference on Networking (ICN 2005),* (pp. 133-140). IEEE Press.

Kung, H. T., Tan, K. S., & Hsiao, P. H. (2003). TCP with sender-based delay control. *Journal of Computer Communications, 26*(14), 1614–1621. doi:10.1016/S0140-3664(03)00110-5

Lai, Y. C., & Yao, C. L. (2002). Performance comparison between TCP Reno and TCP Vegas. *Journal of Computer Communications, 25*(18), 1765–1773. doi:10.1016/S0140-3664(02)00092-0

Lestas, M., Pitsillinds, A., Ioannou, P., & Hadjipollas, G. (2007). Adaptive congestion protocol: A congestion control protocol with learning capability. *Journal of Computer Networks, 51*(13), 3773–3798. doi:10.1016/j.comnet.2007.04.002

Ludwig, R., & Katz, R. H. (2000). The Eifel algorithm: Making TCP robust against spurious retransmissions. *ACM Computer Communications Review, 1*(30).

Lulling, M., & Vaughan, J. (2004). A simulation-based performance evaluation of Tahoe, Reno and SACK TCP as appropriate transport protocols for sip. *Journal of Computer Communications, 27*(16), 1585–1593. doi:10.1016/j.comcom.2004.05.013

Padhye, J., Firoiu, V., Towsley, D., & Kurose, J. (2000). Modeling TCP Reno performance: A simple model and its empirical validation. *IEEE/ACM Transactions on Networking, 8*(2), 133–145. doi:10.1109/90.842137

Tanenbaum, A. (2003). *Computer networks* (4th ed.). Upper Saddle River, NJ: Prentice Hall.

Tekala, M., & Szabo, R. (2008). Dynamic adjustment of scalable TCP congestion control parameters. *Journal of Computer Communications, 31*(10), 1890–1900. doi:10.1016/j.comcom.2007.12.035

Vendicits, A., Baiocchi, A., & Bonacci, M. (2003). Analysis and enhancement of TCP Vegas congestion control in a mixed TCP Vegas and TCP Reno network scenario. *Journal of Performance Evaluation, 53*(3-4), 225–253. doi:10.1016/S0166-5316(03)00064-6

Voicu, L., Bassi, S., & Labrador, M. A. (2007). Analytical and experimental evaluation of TCP with an additive increase smooth decrease (AISD) strategy. *Journal of Computer Communications, 30*(2), 479–495. doi:10.1016/j.comcom.2006.09.010

Weigle, M. C., Jaffay, K., & Simith, D. (2005). Delay-based early congestion detection and adaptation in TCP: Impact on web performance. *Journal of Computer Communications, 28*(8), 837–850. doi:10.1016/j.comcom.2004.11.011

Widmer, J., Denda, R., & Mauve, M. (2001). A survey on TCP-friendly congestion control. *IEEE Network Magazine, 15*(3), 28–37. doi:10.1109/65.923938

Xin, F., & Jamalipour, A. (2006). TCP performance in wireless networks with delay spike and different initial congestion window sizes. *Journal of Computer Communications, 29*(8), 926–933. doi:10.1016/j.comcom.2005.06.012

Yang, Y. R., Kim, M. S., & Lam, S. S. (2003). Transient behaviors of TCP-friendly congestion control protocols. *Journal of Computer Networks, 41*(2), 193–210. doi:10.1016/S1389-1286(02)00374-2

## KEY TERMS AND DEFINITIONS

**Long Delay Cycles:** Delay is an expression of how much time it takes for a packet of data to get from one designated point to another. The contributors to network delay include: propagation delay, transmission delay, router and other processing delay, other computer and storage delays.

**Network Congestion:** It occurs when a link or node is carrying so much data that its quality of service (QoS) deteriorates. Typical effects include queuing delay, packet loss or the blocking of new connections. A consequence of these latter two is that incremental increases in offered load lead either only to small increase in network throughput, or to an actual reduction in network throughput.

**Packet-Loss:** It occurs when one or more packets of data traveling across a computer network fail to reach their destination. Packet loss is distinguished as one of the three main error types encountered in digital communications; the other two being bit-error and spurious packets caused due to noise.

**PFTK Analytical Model:** It is a relatively simple model developed for predicting the performance of the TCP protocol. It is call the PFTK model after the initials of the last names of its authors, namely, Padhye, Firoiu, Towsley, and Kurose. It considers parameters such as: packet-loss, acknowledgment behavior, receiver's maximum congestion window size, and average round trip time.

**PLLDC Analytical Model:** It is a comprehensive and realistic analytical model for evaluating the performance of the TCP protocol in wireless networks as it handles both packet-loss and long delay cycles; therefore, it is referred to as the PLLDC model. It considers parameters, such as: duration of long delay cycles, interval between long delays, timeout, and slow-start threshold.

**TCP Sending Rate:** It is the average rate of data transmitted over a communication channel. This data may be delivered over a physical or logical link, or pass through a certain network node. The sending rate is usually measured in bits or byte per second (bit/sec (bps) or byte/sec), and sometimes in data packets per second (packet/sec) or data packets per time slot.

**TCP Throughput:** It is the average rate of successful message delivery of data over a communication channel. This data may be delivered over a physical or logical link, or passed through a certain network node. The throughput is usually measured in bits or byte per second (bit/sec (bps)

or byte/sec), and sometimes in data packets per second (packet/sec) or data packets per time slot.

**Transport Control Protocol (TCP):** It is the dominant transport layer protocol in the Internet Protocol (IP) suite. It carries a significant amount of the Internet traffics, such as Web browsing, files transfer, e-mail, and remote access. It is a reliable connection-oriented protocol that allows a byte stream originating on one machine to be delivered without error to any other machine on the Internet.

**Wireless Networks:** It refers to any type of computer network that is wireless, and is commonly associated with a telecommunications network whose interconnections between nodes are implemented without the use of wires. Wireless telecommunications networks are generally implemented with some type of remote information transmission system that uses electromagnetic waves, such as radio waves, for the carrier and this implementation usually takes place at the physical level or layer of the network. There are different types of wireless networks, such as: wireless PAN (WPAN), wireless LAN (WLAN), wireless MAN (WMAN), wireless WAN (WWAN), and mobile ad hoc network (MANET).

# Chapter 13
# Wireless Identity Management:
## Multimodal Biometrics and Multilayered IDM

**Abdullah Rashed**
*University of Minho, Portugal*

**Henrique Santos**
*University of Minho, Portugal*

## ABSTRACT

*In the wireless era, digital users in the electronic world (e-world) are represented by sets of data called Digital Identities (ID), which they use, among other functions, for authentication purposes. Within the e-world it is risky to lose an identity and so security solutions are required to protect IDs. Information security should provide the necessary Identity Management (IDM) process to mitigate that threat. Moreover, efficient protection of digital identities would encourage users to enter the digital world without worries. The suggested solution depends on three dimensions: management, security solution, and security dimensions. The proposed model appears as a multi-layered security approach, since it tries to integrate different security technologies and multimodal biometrics tools and practices, such as wireless management, policies, procedures, guidelines, standards, and legislation. The advantages, limitations, and requirements of the proposed model are discussed.*

## INTRODUCTION

Wireless network and mobility have laid the foundation for a new era of computer users (Higby & Bailey, 2004), especially in Internet arena, and generated a lot of wireless clients everywhere (Yan, et al., 2009). This growth of the Internet has made it an integral part of many businesses' daily operations (Taylor, 2001). Today's user desires both flexibility and mobility (Keshariya & Hunt, 2008). The growth in the popularity of Internet services, increasing demands of mobile users together with a wide range of access technologies and mobile-networked devices, demands integration and inter-working of these heterogeneous access networks (Keshariya & Hunt, 2008). However,

DOI: 10.4018/978-1-4666-0191-8.ch013

this popularity has not been as eagerly received by network administrators. Because a great majority of these users lack the knowledge and/or experience to implement best practices, such as installing the latest security patches and antivirus software protection, or properly configuring firewalls, small networks are experiencing high levels of unwanted malicious activity (Yan, et al., 2009). Therefore, securing wireless networks in an untrustworthy open environment is always a challenging problem (Boudriga, et al., 2006). Network has facilitated some security vulnerabilities and malicious attacks. Even with good internal security practices, such as firewalls and virus protection, small networks are still vulnerable to malware, since wireless access on small networks allows the spread of computer viruses

and worms due to laptops moving between campus and less-protected networks (Yan, et al., 2009). Distributed security management would be used for preventing malicious behaviours (Boudriga, et al., 2006).

To enter the e-world users have to use some sort of credentials (ID) as shown in Figure 1. Authentication is a process of two different actions: provision and verification (Sklavos, et al., 2007) as shown in Figure 2.

Due to its fast and networked nature, e-world can provide that information for non expected purposes, such as business communications and marketing (Casassa & Thyne, 2006). Moreover, given the lack of face to face interaction, stolen or lost credentials can be easily abused to hide many types of e-crimes. Besides, users might be

*Figure 1. Authentication process*

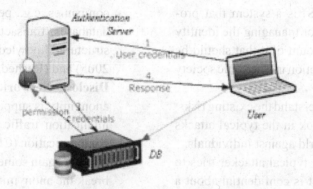

*Figure 2. A three-party authentication model (Sklavos, et al., 2007)*

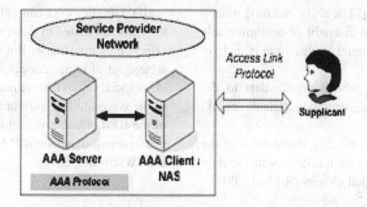

fooled into providing personal digital identity to rogue sites that redirect legitimate traffic (Madsen et al 2005). To illustrate that, we will use an example provided by (Claub, et al., 2005): when users visit a bookshop they do not need to show their unique numbers or any other personal information; in contrast, when they visit e-bookshop, they have to show, at least, their IP address but normally, sites are able to capture more information. To address these issues Identity Management (IDM) is a viable solution (Ahn & Lam, 2005) and it seems essential to protect the privacy of users in the electronic society (Claub, et al., 2005) and to make them feel safe.

Digital identity is defined as the digital representation of the known information about a specific individual or organization (Squicciarini, et al., 2008). By definition, IDM is a set of business processes and a supporting infrastructure for creation, maintenance and use of digital identity. An IDM system (IDMS) is a system that provides the control tools for managing the identity information and the amount of it that should be available for each interaction in electronic society (Claub, et al., 2005).

In order to better understand the existing risks, it is useful to have a look in the typical attacks perpetuated in the e-world against individuals.

Attacker Goals: The typical attacker tries to capture information that is confidential about a target, to gain some kind of advantage. Some examples are:

- **Blackmailing:** The act of extorting money by exciting to discredit or uncomfortable information would be disclosed (Claub, et al., 2005).
- **Revilement:** publish private data to destroy victims' reputation (Claub, et al., 2005).
- **Impersonate:** stealing the identity of the victims and communicate with society with their digital identity (Rashed, 2004).

- **Denying access:** when attackers obtain the identity of the victims they might change the credentials so the victims will not be able to access their information anymore (Rashed, 2004).
- **Identity attack by Phishing:** the act of luring the victims to provide their digital identity to rogue websites (Madsen, et al., 2005).
- **Attacking password:** it is well known that users have many accounts (about 40) and usually use the same password; so if a rogue site could get one of them, then the secret would be broken (Madsen, et al., 2005).
- **Privacy Attacking:** disclosing private information against user willing (Claub, et al., 2005).
- **Attacking Databases** that contain sensitive information about individuals or companies, e.g., person records, statistical databases, transaction databases, and unstructured knowledge bases (Claub, et al., 2005) and (Rashed, 2004).
- **Disclose Network Anonymity:** network anonymity is supposed to protect the communication traffic of a user, i.e. hide all communication (Claub, et al., 2005). When attackers gain some information they could break the anonymity. In addition, they will use this information to attack sensitive information or disclose the secrets.

IDM frameworks can help users to mitigate the risks associated to those attacks or the awful effects they may cause. But they also deal with a large set of issues concerning the privacy and other social values that are not equal for everyone in the e-world. To figure out the real extension of the IDM effect, it is useful to list the identity management dimensions (Madsen, et al., 2005) and (Wikipedia, 2011):

- **Technical issues:** concerning the infrastructure to support an IDMS.
- **Legal system:** especial legislation for data protection.
- **Information police:** for dealing with identity theft.
- **Social and humanity:** dealing with issues such as privacy.
- **Security components:** such as access control.
- Participating organizations.

We will discuss the IDM principals that can be applied to wireless networks and overview the work done by others. Moreover, we will present our model. This paper is organised as follows: In section 2 we overview the previous studies by a literature review. In section 3, we demonstrate our suggestion and discussion and finally, we conclude in section 4.

## LITERATURE REVIEW

There is a growing body of research focused on developing better ways to manage wireless network systems and multimodal security systems. Our literature review covers network security from controls to biometrics. Some of this research focused on various sections of the system and will be described next.

Boudriga et al (2006) presented an ad hoc architecture, communication and mobility schemes to offer an efficient monitoring system in an environment where targets have unpredicted motion. They concluded by presenting the simulation results in order to validate the effectiveness of the proposed schemes. They defined a network of wireless sensors for monitoring physical environments that have emerged as an important new application area for wireless technology. Major issues addressed in their paper include the continuity of environment monitoring, the mobility of sensors, the ad hoc communication scheme, and

a security scheme that protects against a large number of attacks including Denial-of-Service (DoS), replay and masquerading.

Xu (2009) reviewed the conceptualizations of information privacy through three different topics (information exchange, social contract and information control) as shown in Figure 3. They argued that consumers' privacy beliefs are influenced by the situational and environmental cues that signal the level of privacy protections in a particular environment. The framework developed for academic researchers, e-commerce vendors, legislators, industry self-regulators, and designers of privacy enhancing technologies.

Claub et al (2005) introduced some identity management techniques and their role to provide right anonymity and accountability. They overviewed the PRIME project, evaluated it and identified three fields (i.e. statistical database, network anonymity, and interactivity) from which, they believed attacks on IDM can be derived. Moreover they discussed the protection methods against these attacks.

The PRIME and PROTOTYPE projects were described in (Camenisch, et al., 2005), where authors showed the advantages of the proposed system. They assumed that individuals can limit the information collected about them by using pseudo-identities, certifications and cryptography, when performing online transactions. Their proposed solution include negotiation between individuals and the service providers for "privacy policies" that govern how disclosed personal data can be used and which precautions must be taken to safeguard it.

Madsen et al (2005) explored the online identity theft and IDM and the authors concluded that the federated IDM (FIDM) model may increase the risk of identity theft. Their argument was that if users' accounts at an identity provider were successfully phished, then attackers would have opportunity to access other linked service providers.

Rundle & Laurie (2005) studied the intersection of international law and technology in the area of

*Figure 3. Viewing information privacy through three theoretical lenses (Xu, 2009)*

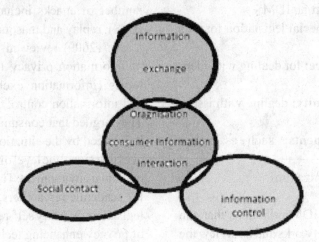

digital IDM. They discussed international treaties and guidelines concerning IDM. They discussed emerging IDM technologies and how they will enforce each other for enhancing accountability to the public.

Beres et al (2007) addressed the risk management for FIDM systems by presenting an identity assurance framework and its supporting technologies (as shown in Figure 4). They discussed the risk mitigation framework as a part of any identity assurance solution. They demonstrated how their model based on assurance technologies could be used to report success of an identity assurance program. In addition, they discussed how their approach could be used to gain trust within a FIDM solution, both by communicating the nature of the assurance framework and mitigating risks.

A delegation model for FIDM systems was introduced in (Gomi, et al., 2005). Their delegation framework is supposed to provide solutions for access control in the context of delegation. It had a function of transferring user's privileges across the entities encoded in delegation assertion extending Security Assertion Markup Language (SAML).

*Figure 4. IDM assurance systems (Beres, et al., 2007)*

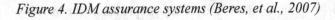

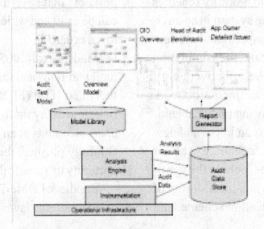

An identity-based signature scheme applicable in a mediated environment was proposed in (Candebat & Gray, 2006). In addition, they introduced a process whereby mobile users are only required to own one private key (for each) in order to protect their communications when accessing location-based services under different pseudonyms. They assumed that an identity-based PKI would simplify significantly key management by removing the need for digital certificates. In their scheme a mediated architecture would make key revocation easier and more efficient as it allows for instant revocation of security capabilities.

Goodrich et al (2006) proposed what they called notarized FIDM model. Their model was supposed to support efficient user authentication when providers are not known to each other. "Notary service," would be introduced by a trusted third-party. They presented a cryptographic solution to prevent the leaking of secret identity information.

Ahn & Lam (2005) demonstrated the importance of FIDM for internet identification. They investigated Microsoft Passport and Liberty Alliance approach concerning privacy issues in FIM, through possible business scenarios. They identified practical business scenarios and introduced their own systematic mechanisms to specify privacy preferences expression language in FIM.

In order to address explicit specification of policies, in (Memon, et al., 2007), it is proposed an architectural framework to adapt policy based access control. The authors analysed the wireless ad hoc communication environment with respect to security and proposed a layer where routine or dynamic analysis of adopted roles by devices can be formulated. They introduced analysis and showed that the framework, for these parameters, within a proposed layer, leads to better management during time critical operations of wireless ad hoc networks. They implemented a wireless monitoring system and demonstrated its effectiveness by characterizing typical computer science department WLAN traffic.

Policy-Based Management (PBM) layered framework is proposed in (Keshariya & Hunt, 2008). It would allow separate policy representations for both syntax and semantic analysis, while mapping translators between each layer maps policy from one representation to another. They explained and described the functionalities of each proposed layer followed and how they implemented a policy schema for manipulating high-level business policies using the NIST RBAC (role-based access control) scheme as well as extensions to the Role-Based Policy Information Model (RBPIM) as shown in Figure 5.

Squicciarini et al (2008) developed an approach to support privacy controlled sharing of identity attributes and harmonization of privacy policies in federated environments. They provided mechanisms for tracing the release of users' identity attributes within the federation. They found that the approach entailed a form of accountability since a non-compliant entity with the users original privacy preferences can be identified.

The Italian Electronic Identity card (IEID) (Arcieri, et al., 2000) was proposed to be fully equivalent to the paper based ID card, according to Italian Laws and can serve different purposes that need an authentication process.

Leitold et al (2002) tackled the security problems of the Austrian citizen card. They showed the infrastructure, the legal aspects and many of the security techniques used. They discussed the security requirements and architecture for e-government applications. They focused on the concept of the so-called "security layer" as the core part of the security architecture.

Yan et al (2009) presented a novel multimodal security enforcement framework built upon trust management and intrusion detection, merging the merits of both to guarantee correct services and guard against security attacks. They proposed a multimodal security enforcement framework in wireless ad hoc networks to address the node misbehaviours problem (Figure 6). They also introduce another layer of protection from intru-

*Figure 5. Proposed extended PBM model (Keshariya & Hunt, 2008)*

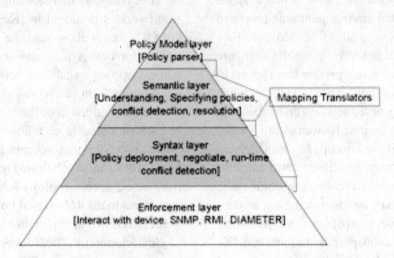

sion detection, once trust alone is insufficient to guarantee correct services of the network. In this way, selfish behaviours are mitigated and malicious behaviours in wireless ad hoc networks.

Lakshmi & Kannammal (2009) claimed that their multimodal biometrics proposal is an efficient authentication model. Their model depended on face and fingerprint. Their approach encrypted the face images and encoded them into fingerprint images. They found that the verification accuracy was high and considered it as a cheap solution for

spoofing and many other attacks. They found that their multimodal model could resist to various attacks (Lakshmi & Kannammal, 2009).

Figure 7 shows Ross's suggestion that consisted of a multimodal biometrics model to improve performance, increase population coverage, deter spoofing, and facilitate indexing. They addressed a limitation of biometrics multimodal systems which is the integration. However, they thought that the integration strategies can be adopted to consolidate information (Ross & Jain, 2004).

*Figure 6. Multimodal security enforcement framework (Yan, et al., 2009)*

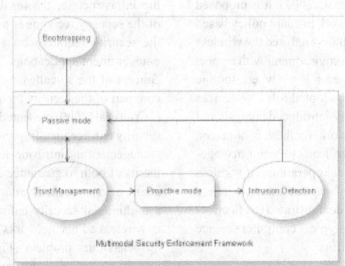

*Figure 7. Multimodal biometrics system scenarios (Ross & Jain, 2004)*

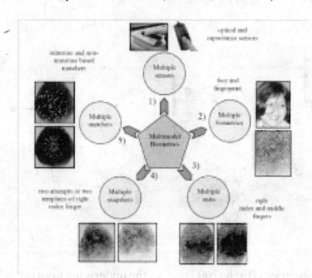

Zhou et al (2007) introduced spam multi-layered defence framework. They used a combination of anti-spamming methods. They stated that their layered structure improved the filtering accuracy and reduced the number of false positives.

Khan & Zhang (2006) presented multimodal biometrics model for authentication. Fingerprint templates were encrypted and encoded/embedded into the face images in such a way that the features, which are used in face matching, are not significantly changed during encoding and decoding. They found that the proposed scheme is an efficient and a cheap solution.

## IDM PROPOSED MODEL

In this section, we present a multimodal biometric technique within multilayered IDM model (Figure 9). Our assumptions of the proposed model are as follows:

### 1. Technological tools:

Technological tools (e.g., computer, cellphones, hardware, etc) would be supplied with biometric sensors that would enable the users to authenticate themselves using biometrics such as fingerprint, iris or odour. The digital ID is

*Figure 8. Consumer responses to the privacy protection measures framework (Xu, 2009)*

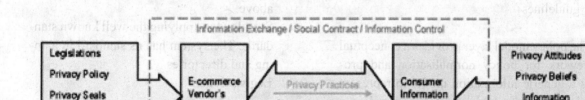

*Figure 9. Authentication process in the proposed model*

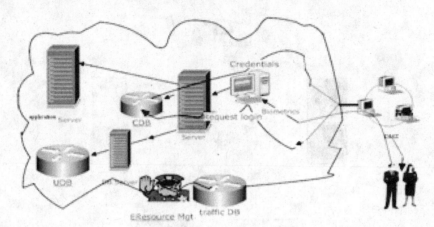

binding to multimodal biometrics (Birch, 2007). To overcome intrinsic biometric limitations, we suggest having multimodal biometrics:

- **Iris:** a camera would be attached to the screen (mobile, laptop or desktop) so the authentication process would be done without user cooperation.
- **Fingerprint:** The "enter button" would be the fingerprint scanner, to authenticate users in a stealth way, every time they press that button.
- **Odour:** when buying a computer the credentials should be issued so the computer could recognize the owner, using an odour sensor. This sensor can be hidden and it would work also in stealth mode.

2.  **Policy:** Policies/legislations, procedures, guidelines

The policy model layer provides a conceptual framework for policy normalisation and provides a generic information model to represent high-level policies which are then stored in a policy repository, and will be later analysed by the semantic layer. Policy which requires certain security functions for a wireless user regardless of

the underlying network infrastructure (Keshariya & Hunt, 2008).

- **Policies**
  - Users should be eligible and registered.
  - The SW will be automatically downloaded to authorized users to mitigate (SW piracy) and SW distribution.
  - Digital signature using a public key cryptosystem would mitigate the impersonation.
- **Guidelines:** guidelines would help users to understand the instructions of the system and how to use it in the correct manner: this would support the security system, and mitigate the intrusion operations.
- **Procedures:** Procedures are supposed to enhance the system security as mentioned above.
- **Standards:** Applying the well known standards. The system has its standard in naming and directories.
- **Legislations**.

The privacy laws of the European Union (EU) and the US represent the two major privacy regulatory models (Xu, 2009). Xu stated that privacy advocates and individual activists continue to demand stronger government legislation to restrain abuses of personal information by merchants (Xu, 2009), Figure 8 reflects that.

Therefore, in our model it is supposed to have laws that define who is eligible and organise the penalties such as fines for those who try to break the security in this system.

Users need to register at the organisation (e-resources management) and if they are eligible, they would be registered at Centralized Database (CDB) and get the credentials that enable them to join the organisation network as shown in Figure 10. Users may do a self registration at a web site and provide their personal information and other requested data. Some privacy preferences might also be asked and stored in a personal profile. Later on, users will be allowed to change their information and preferences by user account management.

When users need to access some resource or to use a specific application via organisation e-resources (via user account management), they need to ask to join the organization network and do the authentication process. After that, the access control system, using information stored in the CDB, would grant their permission if they are eligible to do that.

*Figure 10. Layers of the proposed model*

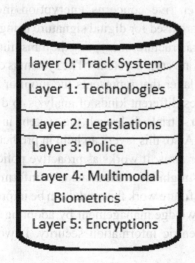

For more security: users will be as thin clients where the server will do everything. In this case, we achieve the security advantages:

- Users will not need to download the SW: they just authenticate themselves whenever they need to use the resources. Moreover, the SW piracy would be mitigated.
- It would be easy to control and analyze the traffic.

3. **IDM security tools:**

   ○ **Biometrics:** This would be used to authenticate users.

4. **Cryptography:** For more security public and private cryptosystems would be used as suggested by (Gayathre, et al., 2009) and by CISCO and Intel (Cisco, 2006).

5. **Access control:** The access will be controlled by user identity and applying access control standards.

6. **Governance:** CDB would be directed by the related department and the governance system should organize decision making in the system.

7. **Directories:** for identity and credentials

## MODEL IMPLEMENTATION

In this section we present a scenario of the proposed model implementation. The process starts at the end user side. When the new users buy the mobile device it should be capable to accept the new user's definitions which should be configured by the manufacturer. The new device would be programmed to authenticate the new owner as follows:

- Iris, odour, and finger prints would be captured by the sensors attached to the mobile; at the multimodal layer. The captured data would be used by user to authenticate himself in stealth way. This process should be supervised and controlled by the network department (according to the policies embedded in legislation layer) as they are in charge of monitoring and maintaining the traffic.

- Users are obliged to follow the policies as defined by the network department (or e-resource management) to guarantee the safety of the system. Each user should be eligible to register at the network (following the policies, procedures and guidelines) otherwise the policies procedures would prevent him and fines as penalties would be applied. Thus, eligible users will get (sent to his mobile for example) an exclusive link that would help them to register. This approach is followed by many website that required users to have cell-phone to send the links or passwords. When user is registered their credentials will be stored in CDB.
- The new devices would be issued both public and private keys to authenticate and encrypt communications.
- According to policies:
  - Users can change their information and preferences by user account management.
  - The SW will be automatically downloaded to authorized users only, which will mitigate SW piracy.
  - After the registration phase users can join the organization network to access specific resources they are authorized to. Thus they should authenticate themselves (using biometrics). The access control system, using information stored in the CDB, would grant their permission if they are eligible to do that.
- At server side, credentials will be verified depending on CDB. If they are authorized

then the request would be forwarded to DB server or application server depending on the resource type requested.

## CONCLUSION

IDM that applies management security solutions and dimensions was presented for a user authentication. Our proposed model was explained and assumptions are mentioned. The proposed model consists of interleaved multi-layers of security tools and techniques as shown in Figure 10. Layers play an important role in defending the system effectively against the opponents attack. One advantage of the layered security system is that it can discover (detect) attacks at earlier stages, when some layers are intruded. Moreover, benefits and advantages of multimodality are the ensuring of the accuracy in addition to decreasing the spoofing. Layer one concerns technologies such as firewall, router and proxy server which are placed at the demilitarized zone. Layer two concerns to legislation, governance, policies, procedures and guidelines that enhance the security and mitigate security threats. This layer is supported Layer three that represents the action that would be taken via police against those who do not respect the laws and try to misuse digital identity. Layer four implements multimodal biometrics.

Layer five concerns encryption methods, which are used for digital signature using public key infrastructure, encrypting the transmitted data via private cryptosystems. The system is covered with a layer that represents the monitor system and does different kinds of analysis to discover attackers' trials to breach the system in earlier stages. Also, this layer can help in predicting the attacker aims. It works as proactive policy: The system might block the attacker or inform police.

For future work the model can be improved to fit knowledge management by adopting knowledge centric information security. It would be applicable via adding knowledge management as another dimension.

# REFERENCES

Ahn, G., & Lam, J. (2005). Managing privacy preferences for federated identity management. In *Proceedings of the 2005 Workshop on Digital Identity Management*, (pp. 28–36). Fairfax, VA: IEEE Press.

Arcieri, F., & Ciclosi, M. Dimitr, Fioravanti, A., Nardelli, E., & Talamo, M. (2000). The Italian electronic identity card: Overall architecture and IT infrastructure. In *Proceedings of the 2nd International Workshop on Certification and Security in Inter-Organizational E-Services (CSES 2004)*, (pp. 5-18). Toulouse, France: IEEE Press.

Beres, Y., Baldwin, A., Casassa Mont, M., & Shiu, S. (2007). On identity assurance in the presence of federated identity management systems. In *Proceedings of the 2007 ACM Workshop on Digital Identity Management*, (pp. 27-35). ACM Press.

Birch, D. (Ed.). (2007). *Digital identity management: Technological, business and social implications*. Surrey, UK: Gower.

Boudriga, N., Baghdadi, M., & Obaidat, M. (2006). A new scheme for mobility, sensing, and security management in wireless ad hoc sensor networks. In *Proceedings of the 39th Annual Simulation Symposium (ANSS 2006)*, (pp. 61-67). Huntsville, AL: IEEE Press.

Camenisch, J., Abhi, S., Sommer, D., Fischer-Hübner, S., Hansen, M., Krasemann, H., et al. (2005). Privacy and identity management for everyone. In *Proceedings of the 2005 Workshop on Digital Identity Management*, (pp. 20-27). Fairfax, VA: IEEE Press.

Candebat, T., & Gray, D. (2006). Secure pseudonym management using mediated identity-based encryption. *Journal of Computer Security, 14*(3), 249–267.

Casassa Mont, M., & Thyne, R. (2006). Privacy policy enforcement in enterprises with identity management solutions. In *Proceedings of the 2006 International Conference on Privacy, Security and Trust: Bridge the Gap between PST Technologies and Business Services*, (vol 380). Markham, Canada: IEEE Press.

Cisco Systems. (2006). *Five myths of wireless networks*. Retrieved May 2011 from http://www.ciscosystems.lt/en/US/.../prod_white_paper0900aecd805287fc.pdf.

Claub, S., Kesdogan, D., & Kolsch, T. (2005). Privacy enhancing identity management: Protection against re-identification and profiling. In *Proceedings of the Workshop on Digital Identity Management*, (pp. 84-93). Fairfax, VA: IEEE Press.

Gayathri, T., Venkadajothi, S., Kalaivani, S., Divya, C., Dhas, S., & Sakunthala, R. (2009). Mobile multilayer IPsec protocol. *International Journal of Engineering and Technology, 1*(1), 23–29.

Gomi, H., Hatakeyama, M., Hosono, S., & Fujita, S. (2005). A delegation framework for federated identity management. In *Proceedings of the 2005 Workshop on Digital Identity Management*, (pp. 94-103). Fairfax, VA: IEEE Press.

Goodrich, M., Tamassia, R., & Yao, D. (2006). Notarized federated identity management for Web services. In *Proceedings of the 20th Annual IFIP WG 11.3 Working Conference on Data and Applications Security*, (pp. 133-139). Sophia Antipolis, France: IEEE Press.

Higby, C., & Bailey, M. (2004). Wireless security patch management system. In *Proceedings of the ACM Special Interest Group for Information Technology Education (SIGITE 2004)*, (pp. 165-168). Salt Lake City, UT: ACM Press.

Keshariya, M., & Hunt, R. (2008), A new architecture for performance-based policy management in heterogeneous wireless networks. In *Proceedings of the International Conference on Mobile Technology, Applications & Systems.* Ilan, Taiwan: IEEE Press.

Khan, M. K., & Zhang, J. (2006). Multimodal face and fingerprint biometrics authentication on space-limited tokens. *Journal of Neurocomputing, 71*(13-15), 3026–3031. doi:10.1016/j.neucom.2007.12.017

Lakshmi, B. P., & Kannammal, A. (2009). Secured authentication of space specified token with biometric traits–face and fingerprint. *International Journal of Computer Science and Network Security, 9*(7), 231–234.

Leitold, H., Hollosi, A., & Posch, R. (2002). Security architecture of the Austrian citizen card concept. In *Proceedings of the 18th Annual Computer Security Applications Conference,* (pp. 391-403). San Diego, CA: IEEE Press.

Madsen, P., Koga, Y., & Takahashi, K. (2005). Federated identity management for protecting users from ID theft. In *Proceedings of the Workshop on Digital Identity Management,* (pp. 77-83). Fairfax, VA: IEEE Press.

Memon, Q., Akhtar, S., & Aly, A. (2007). Role management in ad hoc networks. In *Proceedings of the Spring Simulation Multiconference, 2007,* 131–137.

Rashed, A. (2004). *Intelligent encryption decryption systems using genetic algorithms.* PhD Dissertation. Amman, Jordan: The Arab Academy for Banking & Financial Sciences.

Ross, A., & Jain, A. (2004). Multimodal biometrics: An overview. In *Proceedings of 12th European Signal Processing Conference (EUSIPCO),* (pp. 1221-1224). Vienna, Austria: IEEE Press.

Rundle, M., & Ben Laurie, B. (2005). *Identity management as a cybersecurity case study (research publication no. 2006-01).* Boston, MA: Harvard Law School.

Sklavos, N., Denazis, S., & Koufopavlou, O. (2007). AAA and mobile networks: Security aspects and architectural efficiency. In *Proceedings of the 3rd International Conference on Mobile Multimedia Communications (MobiMedia 2007).* Nafpaktos, Greece: IEEE Press.

Squicciarini, A., Czeskis, A., & Bhargav-Spantzel, A. (2008). Privacy policies compliance across digital identity management systems. In *Proceedings of the ACM GIS 2008 International Workshop on Security and Privacy in GIS and LBS (SPRINGL 2008),* (pp.72-81). Irvine, CA: ACM Press.

Taylor, D. S. (2001). *Multi-layered approach to small office networking.* Retrieved May 2011 from http://www.sans.org.

Wikipedia. (2011). *Identity management dimensions.* Retrieved May 2011 from http://www.en.wikipedia.org.

Xu, H. (2009). Consumer responses to the introduction of privacy protection measures: An exploratory research framework. *International Journal of E-Business Research, 5*(2), 21–47. doi:10.4018/jebr.2009040102

Yan, L., Abouzakhar, N., Xiao, H., & Qayyam, R. (2009). Multimodal security enforcement framework for wireless ad hoc networks. In *Proceedings of the IWCMC, 2009,* 921–925. doi:10.1145/1582379.1582580

Zhou, J., Chin, W., Roman, R., & Lopez, J. (2007). An effective multi-layered defense framework against spam. *Information Security Technical Report, 12*(3), 179–185. doi:10.1016/j.istr.2007.05.007

# Chapter 14
# Security Management and Simulation of Mobile Ad Hoc Networks (MANET)

**Ali H. Al-Bayatti**
*De Montfort University, UK*

**Hilal M. Al-Bayatti**
*Applied Science University, Bahrain*

## ABSTRACT

*This chapter provides a detailed description of a framework for designing, analyzing, deploying, and enforcing high level security management for Mobile Ad Hoc Networks (MANETs). The framework, which can be used by researchers, academics, security administrators, network designers, and post-graduate students, is designed and simulated using the object oriented Network Simulator-2 (NS-2). In this chapter, the authors also provide a full illustration of how to design and implement a secure MANET, while maintaining the security essentials using NS-2. Then, they describe the characteristics, applications, design, coding style, advantages/disadvantages, and implementation of the NS-2 simulator. Finally, this chapter provides a description of the future trend NS-3, which is the "eventual replacement" of NS-2.*

## INTODUCTION

Mobile Ad Hoc Networks (MANETs) have various defining characteristics that differentiate it from other wired and wireless networks, because MANET unique characteristics (i.e., infrastructureless, dynamic topology and constrained resources) nontrivial challenges will be raised, such as

security, routing, scalability, availability, deployment considerations, media access and Quality of Service (QoS) (Murthy & Manjo, 2004). As a result, providing security management as defined in ITU-TM.3400 (International Telecomunication Union, 2000) is essential in order to overcome the security threats (e.g., Denial of Service (DoS), host impersonation and information disclosure) MANET might encounter.

DOI: 10.4018/978-1-4666-0191-8.ch014

In order to evaluate the performance MANET and any other system; one of the available network simulators must be used. Many researchers have evaluated and simulated their work using various approaches and simulation tools. The most popular simulator is the Network Simulator version -2 (NS-2). As well known simulation tools in general and NS-2 in precise suffers from lack of credibility leading towards deceptive results from errors in simulation models or improper data analysis. As a result, to improve simulation credibility through open source simulation, Network Simulator version 3 (NS-3) was created targeting primarily researchers for academic purpose. NS-3 is intended to be the eventual replacement for NS-2; in this chapter we will highlight MANET characteristics, challenges and attacks, security requirements, security attacks, security management, NS-2 and NS-3 key elements and features showing the key difference with NS-2.

## MOBILE AD HOC NETWORKS (MANETS)

A MANET is a group of large autonomous wireless nodes interconnecting each other on a peer-to-peer basis in a heterogeneous environment with no pre-define infrastructure. The field of communications networks continues to evolve, a need for wireless connectivity and mobile communication is rapidly emerging. To meet the need for fast and reliable information exchange, communication networks have become an integral part of our society. The success of any corporation largely depends upon its ability to communicate. Ad hoc wireless networks will enhance communication capability significantly by providing connectivity from anywhere at any time, referring to the relatively newly emerging technology pervasive (or ubiquitous) networks. The principle behind ad hoc networking is multi-hop (a scenario of multi-hop will be shown later) relaying, which traces its roots back to 500 B.C. Darius I (533-486 B.C.),

the king of Persia, invented an innovative communication system that was used to send messages and news from his capital to the remote provinces of his empire by means of a line of shouting men positioned on tall structures or heights. This system was more than 23 times faster than normal messengers available at that time. The use of ad hoc voice communication was introduced in many ancient/ tribal societies with a string of repeaters of drums, trumpets or horns.

In 1970, DARPA (Defence Advanced Research Project Agency) (Dugan, 2010) had a project known as Packet Radio, where several wireless terminals could communicate with one another on a battlefield. Packet radio extended the concept of packet switching (evolved from point-to-point communication networks) to the domain of broadcast radio networks.

During the 1970s, a group of researchers led by Norman Abramson (and others including N. Gaarder and N. Weldon) invented ALOHAnet (Abramson, 1985), which linked the universities of the Hawaiian Islands together by broadcast property to send/receive data packets in a single radio hop system. Even though ALOHAnet was established for fixed single-hop wireless networks, the ALOHA project led to the development of a multi-hop multiple-access packet radio network (PRNET) under the sponsorship of the Advanced Research Project Agency (ARPA) (Dugan, 2010). Unlike ALOHA, PRNET permits multi-hop communications over a wide geographical area, helping to establish the notion of ad hoc wireless networking in the same year (Mohapatra & Krishnamurth, 2004).

## Characteristics of MANET

The study and development of infrastructure-less wireless networks have been very popular in recent years. MANET belongs to the class of networks which does not require the support of wired access points or base stations for intercommunication. A mobile ad hoc network is unlike a static network, as it has no infrastructure. It is a collection of mobile nodes where communication is established in the absence of any fixed foundation. The only possible direct communication is between neighbouring nodes. Therefore, communication between remote nodes is based on multiple-hop. These nodes are dynamically and arbitrarily located in such a manner that the interconnections between nodes are capable of changing on a continual basis. Each mobile node acts as a host and a router, relaying information from one neighbour to another (Royer, 1999). For example, in Figure 1, nodes *A* and *D* must enlist the aid of nodes *B* and *C* to relay packets between them in order to communicate.

MANETs have various defining characteristics that differentiate them from other wired and wireless networks, such as (Al-Jaroodi, 2002.) (Murthy & Manjo, 2004) (Toh, 2002):

- **Infrastructureless:** MANETs are formed based on the collaboration between independent, peer-to-peer nodes that wish to communicate with each other for a particular purpose. No prior organisation or base station is defined and all devices have the same role in the network. In addition, there are no pre-set roles such as routers or gateways for the nodes participating in the network unless specific arrangements are provided.

*Figure 1. A MANET of four nodes, node A communicates with node D*

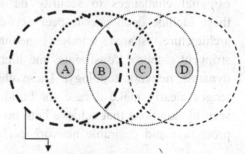

The range of node *A* radio transceiver

- **Dynamic Topology:** MANET nodes are free to move around; thus they could be in and out of the network, constantly changing its links and topology. In addition, the links between nodes could be bi-directional or unidirectional.
- **Low and Variable Bandwidth:** Wireless links that connect the MANET nodes have much smaller bandwidth than those with wires, while the effects of interference, noise and congestion are more visible, causing the available bandwidth to vary with the surrounding conditions and to be even more reduced.
- **Constrained Resources:** In general, most of the MANET devices are small handheld devices ranging from laptops, Smartphone and Personal Digital Assistants (PDA) down to cell phones. These devices have limited power (battery operated), processing capabilities and storage capacity.
- **Limited Device Security:** MANET devices are usually small and portable, and are therefore not restricted by location. As a result, these devices can be easily lost, damaged or stolen.
- **Limited Physical Security:** Wireless links make MANET more susceptible to physical layer attacks, such as eavesdropping, spoofing, jamming and Denial of Service (DoS). However, the decentralised nature of MANETs makes them better protected against single failure points.
- **Short Range Connectivity:** MANET depends on Radio Frequency (RF) or Infrared (IR) technology for connectivity, both of which are generally short range. Therefore, the nodes that wish to communicate directly need to be in close proximity to each other. To overcome this limitation, multi-hop routing techniques are used to connect distant nodes through intermediate nodes that act as routers.

Since ad hoc networks can be deployed rapidly without the support of a fixed infrastructure, they can be used in situations where temporary network connectivity is needed. Examples include conferences, meetings, crowd control, shared whiteboard applications (office workgroup), multi-user games, robotic pets, home wireless networks, office wireless networks, search and rescue, disaster recovery and automated battlefields. These environments do not naturally have a central administration or infrastructure available.

## MANET Challenges

The main challenges in the design and operation of MANET comes from the lack of a centralised entity (infrastructureless) - such as base stations, access points and servers, the possibility of rapid node movement and the fact that all communications are conducted over the wireless medium. Owing to the unique characteristics of wireless ad hoc networks, the major issues that affect the design, deployment and performance of an ad hoc wireless system and that are interesting research areas in MANETs are as follows:

- **Medium Access Scheme:** As ad hoc networks lack any centralised control, the distributed arbitration for the shared channel for transmission of packets is the primary responsibility of a Medium Access Control (MAC) protocol (Gouda & Jung, 2004; Yi & Kravets, 2002).
- **Routing:** The existence of mobility in ad hoc networks implies that links between nodes construct and break occasionally. Hence, new routing protocols are needed (Narasimha, et al., 2003; Luo, 2002).
- **Multicasting:** As ad hoc networks require point-to-multipoint and multipoint-to-multipoint voice and data communication, and as ad hoc networks are mobile, the nodes links need to reform periodically.

Moreover, most of the multicast protocols rely on the fact that routers are static, and that once the multicast tree is formed, tree nodes will not move. However, this is not so for MANET (Xu & Liviu, 2004).

- **Energy Management:** As MANET nodes act as host and routers, and are powered by small batteries with limited lifetime, consequently, necessary consideration must be taken (Lehane, et al., 2005).
- **TCP Performance:** Unfortunately, Transmission Control Protocol (TCP) is unable to distinguish the presence of mobility and network congestion. Hence, some enhancement or changes are needed to ensure that the transport protocol performs properly without affecting the end-to-end communication throughput (Zhu, et al., 2005; Hayes, 1994).
- **Service Location, Provision, and Access:** the question arises: should there be a continued assumption that the traditional client/Server RPC (Remote Procedure Call) paradigm is appropriate for MANET? Owing to the limitations in bandwidth and the heterogeneity of the devices in ad hoc networks, this may not be attractive. Also, how can a mobile device access a remote service in an ad hoc network or how it can advertise its desire to provide services to the rest of the devices in the network? All these issues demand research (Zhou & Haas, 1999).
- **Security:** The unique characteristics of MANET present a new set of serious and essential challenges to security design; these include open peer-to-peer network architecture, shared wireless medium, stringent resource constraints, and highly dynamic network topology. These challenges clearly make a case for building security solutions that achieve both broad protection and desirable network perfor-

mance (Zhou & Haas, 1999; Levijoki, 2000; Diffie & Hellman, 1976; Dewan & Dasgupta, 2003; Deng, et al., 2002).

Although MANETs are enjoying a growth in the number of applications and possess many attractive features, they nevertheless face several challenges, as is plainly shown above. Each of these challenges can be considered as a separate research area needing thorough examination.

## NETWORK SECURITY

When discussing network security in general, three important aspects need to be considered: security requirements, security attacks and security mechanisms.

Security requirements include the functionality necessary to provide a secure networking environment, while security attacks cover the methods that could be employed to break these requirements whereas, Security mechanisms are the fundamental structure blocks used to provide and enforce the security requirements.

## Security Requirements

Security requirements will be a vital solution to different attacks and threats (explained later in this chapter). If the key requirements are provided, then security will be much easier to achieve. In addition, those security requirements listed below should be implemented in any system in order to provide a high level of security; however, implementing all those requirements in one system is impossible. Researchers have tried implementing a set of key requirements to provide major security needs to any system.

The key requirements are being defined by several unions such as the International Telecommunications Union represented by their ITU-T Recommendation X.805 and X.800, and they are as follows (Al-Jaroodi, 2002; Murthy & Manjo,

2004; Stallings, 2003; Fokine, 2002): *Access control*; *Authentication*; *Non-repudiation*; *Data confidentiality*; *Data integrity*; *Availability* and *Privacy*.

**Authentication:** Authentication is essential to ensure that both end peers are who they claim to be (genuine) and not impersonators. Without proper authentication, no other requirement can be correctly implemented. For example, if two nodes are using symmetric-key encryption to exchange messages securely, and one of them becomes compromised as a result of the lack of proper authentication, then all encrypted material such as the shared key and the encryption algorithm will be readily available to that misbehaved node. Techniques to authenticate users securely are essential to the operation of MANET. Moreover, an adversary might masquerade nodes by gaining unauthorised access to resources and sensor information. Moreover, an adversary might interfere with the operation of other nodes in the network.

**Authorisation and Access Control:** This ensures that only authorised nodes have the permission and privilege to perform in the network. Nodes participating in the network need to have proper authorisation to access and share resources, services, applications and personal information on that network. There are various approaches to access control: Discretionary Access Control (DAC) offers a means for defining the access control to the users themselves. Mandatory Access Control (MAC) involves centralised mechanisms to control access to objects with a formal authorisation policy. Role Based Access Control (RBAC) enforces the notion of roles within the subjects and objects.

**Availability:** Essential services must be provided by a node at any time when they are needed, irrespective of attacks. In addition, availability of a network means that its services should be accessible, when needed, even in the event of break-ins.

**Data Confidentiality:** This concerns preventing unauthorised entities (intermediate nodes) from understanding the contents of the message.

Confidentiality is not restricted to survivability of users' information only, such as strategic or tactical military information, but also to the - survivability of the routing information. Confidentiality can be achieved using any of the available encryption techniques with proper key management systems.

**Data Integrity:** Guarantee data is not modified, deleted, removed, recorded, corrupted and re-transmitted by unauthorised entities either by radio failure or malicious attack. This is most essential in situations such as banking, military operations and equipment controls (e.g. trains or planes) where such changes could cause serious damage.

**Non-repudiation:** This ensures that the receiver and sender cannot deny receiving and sending packets to or from other nodes. This approach can detect and isolate the compromised node. If *A* received an erroneous message from *B* with the intention of breaking down *A*'s system, after that *A* can accuse *B* of providing proof of sending erroneous information, and expose *B* to other nodes to convince them that node *B* is a malicious node and not to route through *B* in the future. This is very important in cases of disputes or disagreement over some events. This can be achieved using techniques such as digital signatures that relate the data or action to the signer.

**Privacy:** Privacy ensures that the location and identity of nodes are protected against an adversary. Moreover, it provides protection of information flow so that an adversary cannot gain information by observing it.

Other requirements the system might need (Capkun, et al., 2002):

**Timeliness:** Routing updates should be delivered in a timely manner. Update messages that arrive late might reflect the wrong state of the network and might lead to a large loss in information.

**Isolation:** This requires that nodes should be able to identify misbehaving nodes and isolate them. Alternatively, routing protocols must be immune to malicious nodes.

**Lightweight computation:** Many devices connected to an ad hoc are assumed to be battery powered with limited computational ability. They might not be able to carry large cryptography algorithms.

**Self-stabilisation:** Nodes should be able to recover from attacks independently in real time without human intervention. If nodes are self-stabilising to malicious attacks, then the attacker will remain in the network, and continue sending erroneous messages in order to bring the system down, but it will be easier for nodes to locate the attacker.

**Survivability:** This is the capability of the system to fulfil its mission in a timely manner, in the presence of accidents, failures, intrusion or malicious attacks. Mission means restoring and maintaining essential services during and after the attack, even if a large portion of the system has been damaged or destroyed. Requirements of the survivability system are resistance to, recognition of, recover from, adoption and evaluation (Paul, et al., 2000).

**Anonymity:** Neither the node nor the system should by default expose information, such as MAC address and IP address, that might put the system at risk.

## Security Attacks

As mentioned, security in ad hoc wireless networks is very important, especially in military applications. The lack of any central administration makes MANET more vulnerable to attacks than wired networks. Consequently, attacks in ad hoc networks are generally divided into two broad categories, namely, *Passive* and *Active* attacks.

A passive attack refers to the attempts that are made by malicious nodes to perceive the nature of activities and to obtain information transacted in the network without disrupting the operation. For example, eavesdropping, active interference, leakage of secret information, data tempering, impersonation, message replay, message distortion and denial of service. Detection of passive attacks is complicated, since the operation of the network itself does not get affected. One way of overcoming such problems is to use effectual encryption mechanisms to encrypt the data being transmitted, thereby making it impossible for eavesdroppers to obtain any useful information from the data overheard.

An active attack refers to the attacks that attempt to alter, inject, delete or destroy the data being exchanged in the network. Those attacks can be executed by internal or external attackers, if the attacks are carried out by nodes that do not belong to the network (outside the network) that attack will be an *external attack*, which will be easier to defend, because users expect any act from an external node. Otherwise, if the attack comes from an insider node (part of the network), it will be an *internal attack*, which can cause considerable damage to the network because it is much harder to defend, as it is unfeasible to detect a malicious node and then prevent it from disrupting the network.

These attacks can be prevented by using regular security mechanisms such as encryption techniques and firewalls. Internal attacks come from compromised nodes that are actually part of the network; they are known as compromised nodes. Internal attacks are more serious and difficult to detect than external ones.

This section gives brief descriptions of some of the main active attacks known in most networks (Al-Jaroodi, 2002; Fei & Wenye, 2006; Fokine, 2002; Murthy & Manjo, 2004; Mishra, et al., 2004; Wen-Guey, 2002).

- **Denial of Service (DoS).** A DoS is an active attack that attempts to make resources unavailable to its intended users. The attacker tries to prevent legitimate users to access services offered by the network. DoS can be carried out in different ways, but in the end causing the same problems. It can be carried out in the classical way by flooding centralised recourses (e.g. base

stations) and permitting the system to crash or to interrupt its operation. Owing to the unique characteristics of ad hoc networks, DoS can be launched in different ways that do not exist in other wired or wireless networks and which can be launched at any layer of the protocol stack, for example, radio jamming and battery exhaustion on physical and MAC layers by disturbing the on-going transmissions at the wireless channels. On the network layer, an adversary could launch DoS on the routing protocols leading to a degrading in the QoS of the network by making routing protocols drop a certain number of packets. On higher layers, an adversary could bring down critical services, such as key management service.

- **Impersonation.** The attacker tries to copy the behaviour or the action of an authorised node to gain the same facilities of the original node, either to make use of the network resources that might be unavailable to it under normal circumstances, or in an attempt to disturb network functionality by injecting erroneous routing information (Holland & Vaidya, 1999). Man-in-the-middle attack is one form of impersonator. An adversary may read or falsify messages between legitimate users without letting either of them know that they have been attacked.

- **Disclosure.** A compromised node may try to disclose secret information to unauthorised nodes in the network; therefore communication must be protected against any eavesdropper trying to disclose confidential information that is being exchanged. Also, secret data must be protected from unauthorised access.

- **Repudiation.** In simple terms, this occurs when nodes tries to deny having any involvement in particular action or communication with other nodes.

## Routing Attacks

Those attacks occur on the network layer, when several types of attacks are mounted on the routing protocols which are aimed at disrupting the operation of the network. These are the major routing protocols attacks, which are described briefly:

- **Routing table overflow:** The main goal of this attack is to create an overflow of the routing table and to prevent new legitimate routes from being created, which can be achieved by an adversary node trying to create routes to non-existence nodes.
- **Location disclosure:** This type of attack can reveal some information about the location of the node or give a description of the network structure.
- **Blackhole attack:** In this attack, a malicious node tries to advertise itself as having the shortest path to the specific destination (falsify advertisement) whose packets it wants to intercept. After gaining access between the required communications, the malicious node can do anything, like performing a DoS attack or alternatively it can use its place on the route as the first step in a man-in-the-middle attack.
- **Packet Replication:** In this attack, an adversary node replicates stale packets. This devours additional bandwidth and battery power resources available to the elements, and also causes unnecessary confusion in routing process.
- **Sleep deprivation:** This attack occurs in Ad hoc networks only because of the power limitation that ad hoc networks have. Thus, an attacker will try to consume battery life by requesting unnecessary routes or forwarding Packets (garbage) to nodes, by using for example Blackhole attack.

## Military Attacks

Every network used by the military will need full protection, by providing maximum security. In a military environment, routing attacks can be divided into two types:

- **Strategic routing attacks:** Strategic routing attacks include intelligence gathering. This type of attacks might cover desolation of enemy networks in the preparation of battle. Additionally, because of the attack, the attacker could gain some information about where the enemy is about to strike next. Nevertheless, once a routing attack has finished, the network can usually be brought back into use in a short amount of time.
- **Tactical routing attacks:** Tactical attacks could be used most effectively during battles. This attack could use the information gathered about the topology of the network. The main goal could be to disable some important part of a network temporarily by using DoS attacks.

## Layers Attack

As seen in Figure 2, this section summarises the attacks that a MANET layer faces.

## Securely Managing MANET

Providing security management is critical for any system, and MANET is not exceptional; security management will be described upon the Recommendation ITU-T M.3400 perspective, showing three essential components (International Telecommunication Union, 2000):

- Security Administration
- Prevention and Detection
- Containment and Recovery

*Figure 2. The classification of security layer attacks (Murthy & Manjo, 2004)*

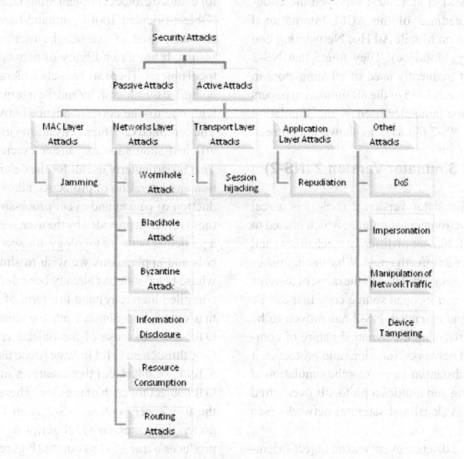

The *Security Administration* function sets are those needed for planning and administrating security policies and managing security related information. Owing to the lack of underlying infrastructure, depending on a central administration is impossible, raising one of the major issues ad hoc networks might face (Sun, et al., 2007).

*Prevention and Detection,* the prevention function sets, are those needed to prevent intrusion, whereas detection function sets are those needed to detect an intrusion.

The *Containment and Recovery* function sets are those needed to deny access to an intruder, repair damage done by an intruder, recover losses and to update the system whenever needed.

## MANET SIMULATION STUDIES

In order to evaluate the performance of any mechanism in terms of communication cost, it must be implemented using one of the available network simulators suitable for simulating such types of wireless network. Many researchers in MANET have evaluated and simulated their work using various approaches and simulation tools. The most popular network simulators are Network Simulator version 2 (NS-2) (Altman & Jimenez, 2003; The Network Simulator-NS-2, 2008), Global Mobile Information System Simulation Library (GloMoSim) (GloMoSim, 2007) and OPNET Modeller (OPNET Modeller, 2007). Some work has been simulated using self-developed code.

Kurkowski et al. (2005) surveyed the 2000-2005 proceedings of the ACM International Symposium on Mobile Ad Hoc Networking and Computing (MobiHoc). They found that NS-2 is the most frequently used of all simulators in MANET research: 35 of the 80 simulation papers that state the simulator used in the simulation study used NS-2 (43.8%), as shown in Figure 3.

## Network Simulator Version 2 (NS-2)

Network Simulator version 2 (NS-2) is a real network environment simulator, which is used to test the performance of different mechanisms and demonstrate its effectiveness. What distinguishes NS-2 from other simulators is the range of features it provides and its open source code that can be modified and extended. NS-2 has proven to be useful in analysing the dynamic nature of communication networks' functions and protocols, it provides substantial support for the simulation of TCP, routing and multicast protocols over wired and wireless (local and satellite) networks (see Figure 4).

NS-2 is a discrete event and an object-oriented simulator targeted at networking research; it was developed by the University of California at Berkeley and the VINT (Virtual InterNetwork Testbed) project (The Network Simulator, 2003). The NS-2 simulator has several versions and all of them are based on two languages: an object oriented simulator, written in C++ which is used

*Figure 3. Simulator usage from MobiHoc survey*

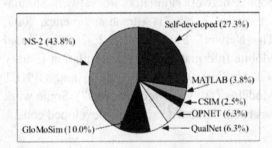

for detailed protocol implementation, and an OTcl (Object-oriented Tool Command Language) interpreter, used to execute the user's command scripts. It has a rich library of network and protocol objects. There are two-class hierarchies: the compiled C++ hierarchy and the interpreted OTcl, with one-to-one correspondence between them. The compiled C++ hierarchy allows us to achieve efficient simulation and faster execution times. This is particularly useful for the detailed definition and operation of protocols, allowing the reduction of packet and event processing time. In the OTcl script provided by the user, we can define a particular network topology, the specific protocols and applications we wish to simulate (and whose behaviour has already been defined in the compiled hierarchy) and the form of the output that we wish to obtain from the simulator. The OTcl can make use of the objects compiled in C++ through an OTcl linkage (done using tclCL: a Tcl/C++ interface) that creates a matching of OTcl object for each of the C++. Therefore, from the user's perspective, NS-2 is an OTcl interpreter that takes an OTcl script as input, and produces a trace file as output (Figure 5).

One of the compensations of this split-language programming is that it allows for the fast generation of large scenarios. This is because NS-2 can efficiently manipulate bytes and packet headers, and implement algorithms that run over large data sets. For these tasks, run-time speed is important. C++ is slow to modify, but its speed makes it appropriate for protocol implementation. On the other hand, a large element of network research involves slightly changing parameters and configurations, or exploring a number of scenarios. In these cases, iteration time (change the model and re-run) is more significant. Since configuration runs once (at the beginning of the simulations), run-time of this part is less important. OTcl runs slower but can be altered very quickly making it ideal for simulation configuration.

Nick McKeown, VINI public reviewer in the ACM Sigcomm 2006, quoted "For years, the community had to rely on simulators, which now seem a little dated, and it's not clear who was convinced to adopt anything new based on NS-2 simulations," in an overhead archive in sep. 2005

of the end2end-interest mailing list, researchers highlighted that around 50% of the NS-2 papers appeared to be bogus; therefore many researchers decided to move away from simulation focusing

*Figure 4. NS-2 animator (NAM)*

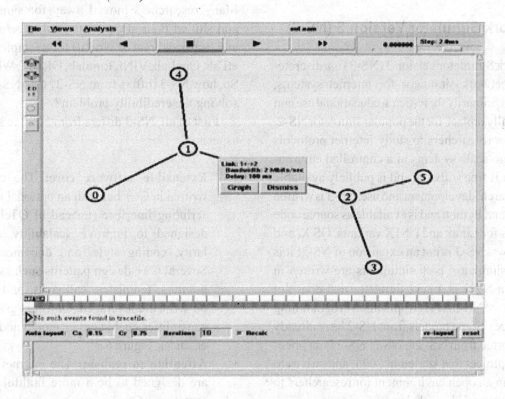

*Figure 5. Schematic structure for NS-2*

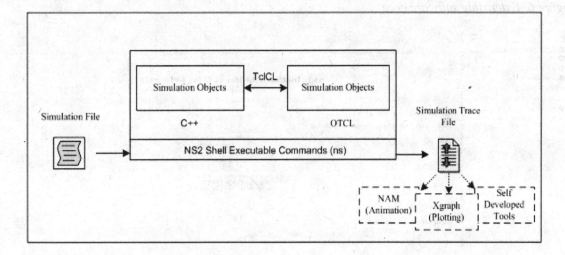

on experimental and test beds (real or virtual), yet providing such tools is hard to achieve. The question is can a replacement be found in different simulation tools or form? The answer is NS-3, but can NS-3 help with these problems i.e. align with how research is conducted now days and improve credibility.

## Network Simulator Version 3 (NS-3)

Network Simulator version 3 (NS-3) is a discrete-event network simulator for internet systems, targeted primarily for research educational use and eventually replace for the popular simulator NS-2. It allows researchers to study internet protocols and large-scale systems in a controlled environment; it is free software and is publicly available for research, development and use. NS-3 is written in C++ and Python and is available as source code releases for Linux and UNIX variants, OS X, and Windows. NS-3 is not an extension of NS-2; it is a new simulator; both simulators are written in C++ but NS-3 is a new simulator that does not support the NS-2 APIs (Application Programming Interface). Some models from NS-2 have already been ported from NS-2 to NS-3. NS-3 is an open-source project that started in 2006, and strives to maintain an open environment for researchers to contribute and share their software.

## Transition from NS-2 to NS-3

One of the major problems facing simulation tools including NS-2 is credibility (i.e. inaccurate and incorrect results), (Andel & Yasinsac, 2006) highlighted that the lack or rigor on simulation evaluating performances threatens credibility. Many researchers moved away for simulation and shifted their attention toward experimental and test-beds (real or virtual) for example, PlanetLab, OneLab, VINI, Emulab, ORBIT, WhyNet. So, how NS-3 differs from NS-2? Can NS-3 help solving the credibility problem?

First of all, NS-3 differs from NS-2 in several aspects:

- **Extensible software core:** The core is written in C++ but with an optional Python scripting interface (instead of OTcl), it is designed to improve scalability, modularity, coding style, and documentation. Several C++ design patterns such as smart pointers, templates, callbacks, and copy-on-write are leveraged. Object aggregation capabilities enable easier model and packet, check Figure 6.

- **Attention to realism:** The internet nodes are designed to be a more faithful representation of real computers, including the

*Figure 6. Extensible software core*

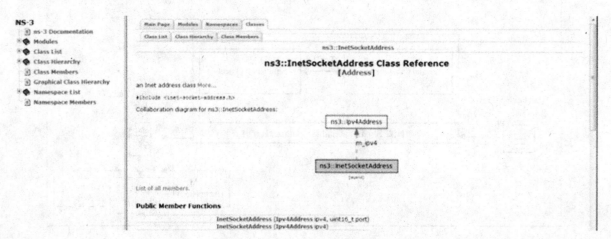

support for key interfaces such as socket and network devices, multiple interfaces per nodes, use of IP addresses, and other similarities.

- **Software integration:** An architecture to support the incorporation of more open-source networking software such as kernel protocol stacks, routing daemons, and packet trace analyser, reducing the need to port or rewrite models or tools for simulation, as seen in Figure 7.

- **Support for virtualisation:** Lightweight virtual machines are an attractive combination for current research; NS-3 planes to support a few modes of such operation including a native "process" environment where Posix-compliant applications can

be easily ported to run in simulation space with their own private stack, and including support for tying together virtual machines of various types.

- **Testbed integration:** NS-3 will enable the testbed based researcher to experiment with novel protocol stacks and emit/consume network packets over real device drivers or VLANs. The internal representation packets are network-byte order to facilitate serialisation, as seen in Figure 8.

- **Flexible tracing and statistics:** NS-3 is building a tracing and statistics gathering framework using callback-based design that decouples trace sources from trace sinks, enabling customisation of tracing or statistics output without building the sim-

*Figure 7. NS-3 trace viewed with Wireshark*

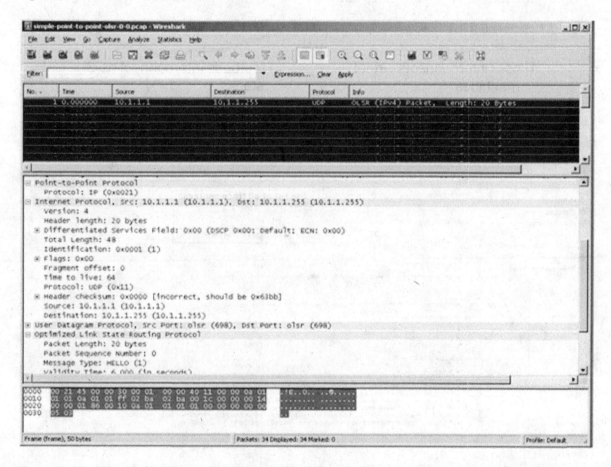

ulation core. Various trace sources (e.g., packet receptions, state machine transitions) are plumbed through the system, as seen in Figure 9.

Tracing system supports a statistical and data management architecture (currently under devel-

opment), which features: managing multiple runs of a scenario; assembling data into several output formats (e.g. databases with pre-run metadata); hooking into NS-3 trace sources; and interacting with the simulator at run-time (e.g. stopping simulation when counter reaches a value) (see Figure 10).

*Figure 8. NS-3 testbed framework*

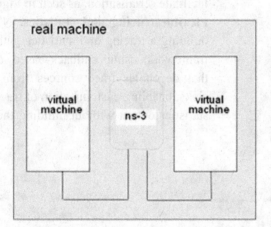
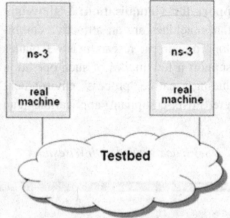

1) ns-3 interconnects virtual machines

2) testbeds interconnect ns-3 stacks

*Figure 9. NS-3 trace source example*

*Figure 10. Trace source architecture*

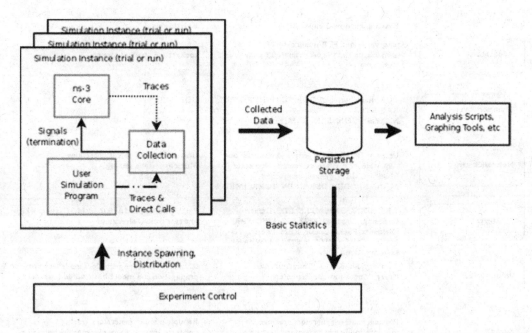

*Figure 11. NS-3 object attributes*

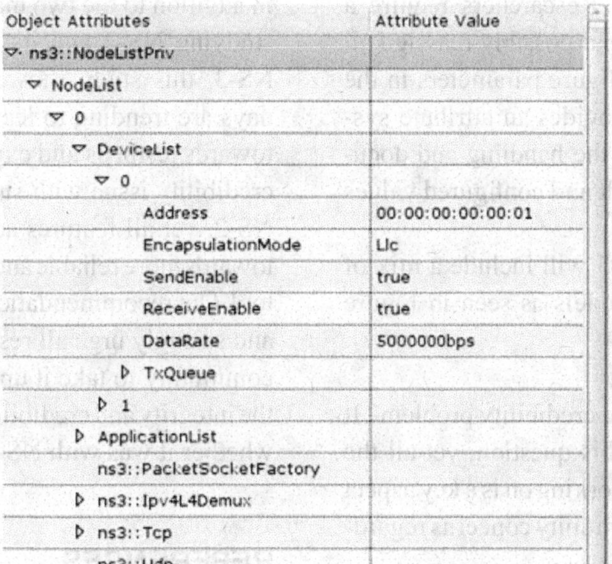

*Figure 12. NS-3 extended modules*

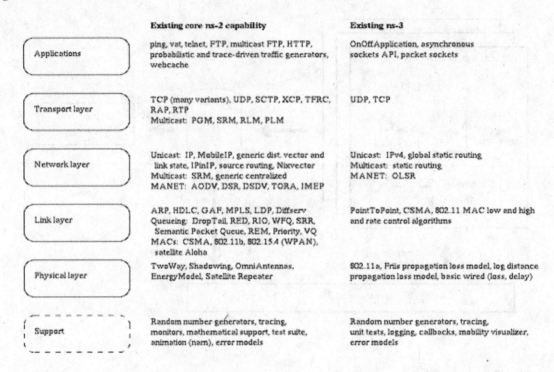

| | Existing core ns-2 capability | Existing ns-3 |
|---|---|---|
| Applications | ping, vat, telnet, FTP, multicast FTP, HTTP, probabilistic and trace-driven traffic generators, webcache | OnOffApplication, asynchronous sockets API, packet sockets |
| Transport layer | TCP (many variants), UDP, SCTP, XCP, TFRC, RAP, RTP Multicast: PGM, SRM, RLM, PLM | UDP, TCP |
| Network layer | Unicast: IP, MobileIP, generic dist. vector and link state, IPinIP, source routing, Nixvector Multicast: SRM, generic centralized MANET: AODV, DSR, DSDV, TORA, IMEP | Unicast: IPv4, global static routing Multicast: static routing MANET: OLSR |
| Link layer | ARP, HDLC, GAF, MPLS, LDP, Diffserv Queueing: DropTail, RED, RIO, WFQ, SRR, Semantic Packet Queue, REM, Priority, VQ MACs: CSMA, 802.11b, 802.15.4 (WPAN), satellite Aloha | PointToPoint, CSMA, 802.11 MAC low and high and rate control algorithms |
| Physical layer | TwoWay, Shadowing, OmniAntennas, EnergyModel, Satellite Repeater | 802.11a, Friis propagation loss model, log distance propagation loss model, basic wired (loss, delay) |
| Support | Random number generators, tracing, monitors, mathematical support, test suite, animation (nam), error models | Random number generators, tracing, unit tests, logging, callbacks, mobility visualizer, error models |

- **Attribute system:** Researchers require a means to identify and possibly reassign all values used to configure parameters in the simulator. NS-3 provides an attribute system that integrates the handling and documentation of default and configured values (see Figure 11).
- **NS-3 models:** NS-3 will include a mix of new and ported models as seen in Figure 12.

So, did NS-3 solve the credibility problem? It is still early to answer this question, yet all the aspects NS-3 project is working on is a key aspect towards solving the community concerns regarding the simulation results.

## CONCLUSION

This chapter presented a study of MANET showing its characteristics, applications and challenges in addition to the two main aspects of simulation studying NS-2 and its anticipated replacement NS-3, this study showed that researchers now days are trending to leave simulation and move towards testbeds and experiments because of the credibility issue with simulation tools including NS-2, yet all features added on NS-3 is leading towards more reliable and configurable simulation tool. Our recommendation is to shift towards NS-3 and strongly urge all researchers in the MANET community to take it upon themselves to ensure the integrity and credibility of published research, whether it was with NS-2 or NS-3.

## REFERENCES

Abramson, N. (1985). Development of ALOHANET. *IEEE Transactions on Information Theory*, *31*(2), 119–123. doi:10.1109/TIT.1985.1057021

Al-Jaroodi, J. (2002). *Security issues in wireless mobile ad hoc networks (MANET)*. Lincoln, Nebraska: University of Nebraska-Lincoln Press.

Altman, E., & Jimenez, T. (2003). *NS2 for beginners*. Paris, France: University of de Los Andes.

Andel, T., & Yasinsac, A. (2006). On the credibility of MANET simulation. *IEEE Computer Society, 39*(7), 48–51. doi:10.1109/MC.2006.242

Capkun, S., Buttyan, L., & Hubaux, J.-P. (2002). Small worlds in security systems: An analysis of the PGP certificate graph. In *Proceedings ACM New Security Paradigm Workshop (NSPW)*. ACM Press.

Deng, H., Li, W., & Agrawa, D. (2002). Routing security in wireless ad hoc networks. *IEEE Communications Magazine, 40*(10), 70–75. doi:10.1109/MCOM.2002.1039859

Dewan, P., & Dasgupta, P. (2003). Trusting routers and relays in ad hoc networks. In *Proceedings of the International Conference on Parallel Processing Workshops (ICPPW 2003)*. IEEE Press.

Diffie, W., & Hellman, M. (1976). New directions in cryptography. *IEEE Transactions on Information Theory, 22*(6), 29–40. doi:10.1109/TIT.1976.1055638

Dugan, R. (2010). *Defence advanced research project agency (DAPRA)*. Retrieved September 14, 2010, from http://www.darpa.mil.

Fei, X., & Wenye, W. (2006). Understanding dynamic denial of service attacks in mobile ad hoc networks. In *Proceedings of MILCOM*, (pp. 1-7). IEEE Press.

Fokine, K. (2002). *Key management in ad hoc networks*. Thesis. Linkping, Sweden: Linkping University.

GloMoSim. (2007). *Global mobile information system simulation*. Retrieved 2010 from http://pcl.cs.ucla.edu/projects/glomosim/#.

Gouda, M. G., & Jung, E. (2004). Certificate dispersal in ad-hoc networks. In *Proceedings of the 24th International Conference on Distributed Computing Systems (ICDCS 2004)*. IEEE Press.

Hayes, S. (1994). A standard for the OAM&P of PCS systems. *Personal Communications, 1*(4), 24–26. doi:10.1109/MPC.1994.337512

Holland, G., & Vaidya, N. (1999). Impact of routing and link layers on TCP performance in mobile ad hoc networks. In *Proceedings of the Wireless Communications and Networking Conference (WCNC)*, (pp. 1323-1327). IEEE Press.

International Telecomunication Union. (2000). *ITU-T recommendation M.3400—TMN Management Functions*. Retrieved from http://www.itut.org.

Kurkowski, S., Camp, T., & Colagrosso, M. (2005). *MANET simulation studies: The incredibles. ACM SIGMOBILE Mobile Computing and Communication Review* (pp. 50–61). ACM Press.

Lehane, B., Dolye, L., & Mahony, D. (2005). Ad hoc key management infrastructure. In *Proceedings of the International Conference on Information Technology: Coding and Computing (ITCC 2005)*. IEEE Press.

Levijoki, S. (2000). *Authentication, authorization and accounting in ad hoc networks*. Retrieved Septamber 11, 2010 from http://www.tml.hut.fi/Opinnot/Tik-110.551/2000/papers/authentication/aaa.htm.

Luo, H. (2002). Self-securing ad hoc wireless networks. In *Proceedings of the IEEE Symposium on Computers and Communications*. Taormina-Giardini Naxos, Italy: IEEE Press.

Mishra, A., Nadkarni, K., Patcha, A., & Tech, V. (2004). Intrusion detection in wireless ad hoc networks. *IEEE Wireless Communications, 11*(1), 48–60. doi:10.1109/MWC.2004.1269717

Mohapatra, P., & Krishnamurth, S. (2004). Ad hoc networks technology and protocols. *Ad Hoc Networks, 1*, 1–3.

Murthy, C., & Manjo, B. (2004). *Ad hoc wireless networks: Architectures and protocols*. Upper Saddle River, NJ: Prentice Hall.

Narasimha, M., Tsudik, G., & Yi, J. (2003). *On the utility of distributed cryptography in P2P and MANETs: The case of membership control*. Paper presented at the 11th IEEE International Conference on Network Protocols. Atlanta, GA.

NS-2. (2008). *The network simulator.* Retrieved October 1, 2010 from http://www.isi.edu/nsnam/ns/.

NS-2. (2010). *The network simulator.* Retrieved 3 October 2010 from http://www.isi.edu/nsnam/ns/.

OPNET. (2007). *Modeler.* Retrieved October 1, 2010 from http:// www.opnet.com/products / modeler/home.html.

Paul, K., Roy, R., & Bandyopadhyay, S. (2000). Survivability analysis of ad hoc network architecture. In *Proceedings of the European Commission International Workshop on Mobile and Wireless Communication*, (pp. 31-46). IEEE Press.

Royer, E. (1999). A review of current routing protocols for ad hoc mobile wireless networks. Retrieved from http://www.eecs.harvard.edu/~mdw/course/cs263/papers/royer-ieeepc99.pdf.

Stallings, W. (2003). *Cryptography and network security: Principles and practices*. Upper Saddle River, NJ: Prentice Hall.

Sun, B., Wu, K., Xiao, Y., & Wang, R. (2007). Integration of mobility and intrusion detection for wireless ad hoc networks. *International Journal of Communication Systems, 20*(6), 695–721. doi:10.1002/dac.853

Toh, C.-K. (2002). *Ad hoc mobile wireless networks: Protocols and systems*. Upper Saddle River, NJ: Prentice- Hall.

Wen-Guey, T. (2002). A secure fault-tolerant conference-key agreement protocol Computers. *IEEE Transactions on Computers, 51*(4), 373–379. doi:10.1109/12.995447

Xu, G., & Liviu, I. (2004). Locality driven key management architecture for mobile ad-hoc networks. In *Proceedings of the IEEE International Conference on Mobile Ad-hoc and Sensor Systems*, (pp. 436-446). IEEE Press.

Yi, S., & Kravets, R. (2002). Key management for heterogeneous ad hoc wireless networks. In *Proceedings of the 10th IEEE International Conference on Network Protocols (ICNP 2002)*. IEEE Press.

Zhou, L., & Haas, Z. (1999). Securing ad hoc networks. *IEEE Network, 13*(6), 24–30. doi:10.1109/65.806983

Zhu, B., Bao, F., Deng, R. H., Kankanhalli, M. S., & Wang, G. (2005). Efficient and robust key management for large mobile ad hoc networks. *IEEE Computer Networks, 48*(4), 657–682. doi:10.1016/j.comnet.2004.11.023

# Chapter 15
# Investigating the Performance of the TSS Scheme in Noisy MANETs

**Hussein Al-Bahadili**
*Petra University, Jordan*

**Shakir M. Hussain**
*Petra University, Jordan*

**Ghassan F. Issa**
*Petra University, Jordan*

**Khaled El-Zayyat**
*Al-Ahliyya Amman University, Jordan*

## ABSTRACT

*A Mobile Ad Hoc Network (MANET) suffers from high packet-loss due to various transmission impairments, such as: wireless signal attenuation, free space loss, thermal noise, atmospheric absorption, multipath effect, and refraction. All of these impairments are represented by a generic name, noise, and therefore such a network is referred to as a noisy network. For modeling and simulation purposes, the noisy environment is described by introducing a probability function, namely, the probability of reception ($p_c$), which is defined as the probability that transmitted data is successfully delivered to its destination despite the presence of noise. This chapter describes the implementation and investigates the performance of the Threshold Secret Sharing (TSS) node authentication scheme in noisy MANETs. A number of simulations are performed using the MANET Simulator (MANSim) to estimate the authentication success ratio for various threshold secret shares, number of nodes, node speeds, and noise-levels. Simulation results demonstrate that, for a certain threshold secret share, the presence of noise inflicts a significant reduction in the authentication success ratio, while node mobility inflicts no or an insignificant effect. The outcomes of these simulations are important to facilitate efficient network management.*

DOI: 10.4018/978-1-4666-0191-8.ch015

# INTRODUCTION

A mobile ad hoc network (MANET) is defined as a collection of low-power, wireless, mobile nodes forming a temporary network without the aid of any established infrastructure or centralized administration (Murthy & Manoj, 2004; Agrawal & Zeng, 2003; Toh, 2002). Despite the fact that MANETs offer a number of benefits over wired and other infrastructure wireless networks, still there are many challenges that need to be addressed for fully harvesting MANETs' benefits. These include: limited communication bandwidth, limited battery power and lifetime, size of the mobile devices, security, communication overhead, induced transmission errors, distributed control problem, nodes mobility and dynamic variation of network topology, scalability, meeting certain Quality-of-Service (QoS), etc (Stallings, 2003).

MANETs security is challenging for several reasons, such as (Huang & Medhi, 2008): security breach, node mobility, service ubiquity, network dynamics, network scale, etc. Furthermore, MANETs are very vulnerable to a number of security attacks, such as: passive eavesdropping over the wireless channel, Denial-of-Service (DoS) attacks by malicious nodes, and attacks from compromised entities or stolen devices (Kong, et al., 2001). As for any information exchange system, the main requirements that need to be carefully considered to ensure high-level of MANET security are: confidentiality, authentication, integrity, availability, and non-repudiation.

This paper is concerned with one of the main security requirements for MANETs, namely authentication. Authentication is the verification of the identity of a party who generated some messages, and of the integrity of the messages. In computer networks, two types of authentication can be identified, namely, message authentication and node authentication. Message authentication is a technique for verifying the integrity of a transmitted message. While node authentication enables a node to ensure the identity of the peer node it is communicating with. Without authentication, an adversary could masquerade a node, thus gaining unauthorized access to system resources and sensitive information and interfering with the operation of other nodes. There are two differences between message and node authentications, these are (Forouzan, 2008):

1.  Message authentication may not happen in real time; node authentication does. In message authentication, when a sender sends a message to a receiver, while the receiver authenticates the message; the sender may or may not be present in the communication process. On the other hand, when the sender requests node authentication, there is no real message communication involved until the sender is authenticated by the receiver. The sender needs to be online and takes part in the authentication process. Only after the sender is authenticated can message communicated between the two parties.

2.  Message authentication simply authenticates one message; the process needs to be repeated for each new message. Node authentication authenticates the sender for the entire duration of a session.

The most popular network authentication architectures are Kerberos (Kohl, et al., 1994), the X.509 standard (Aresenault & Turner, 2001), and Public-Key Infrastructure (PKI) trust model (Perlman, 1999), which are based on using a globally trusted Certificate Authority (CA) model (Balfanz, et al., 2002). Using a globally trusted CA model may work well in wired or infrastructure (access point) wireless networks, but not MANETs because: MANETs provide no infrastructure support (infrastructureless), each of the CA servers is exposed to a single point of compromises and failures, multihop communications over the error-prone wireless channel expose data transmissions to high packet-loss rate and large latency, and frequent route changes induced by node mobility, which makes locating and contacting CA servers in a timely fashion non-trivial (Yi & Kravets, 2003). Variations of the CA model, such as hierarchical CAs and CA delegations, can ameliorate but cannot addresses issues such as service availability and robustness (Perlman, 1999). Therefore, more efficient and reliable solutions are required to address the above issues. One alternative solution to address the problem of authentication in MANETs is to use the concept of secret share proposed by Adi Shamir in 1978 (Shamir, 1979).

The Shmir's concept of secret share was used in (Luo, et al., 2002) for developing an efficient scheme for self-securing wireless ad hoc networks, which we shall refer to as Threshold Secret Sharing (TSS) scheme. The work in (Luo, et al., 2002) and many other researches have been carried-out to investigate the performance of the TSS scheme in terms of authentication success ratio, average delay, overheads, etc (Huang & Medhi, 2008; Luo, et al., 2002; Kim & Bah, 2009; Mukherjee, et al., 2008; Yeun, et al., 2008; Chai, et al., 2007). All of these investigations have considered a noiseless (error-free) environment. In practice, MANETs suffer from high packet-loss due to the presence of noise and node mobility, which may significantly affect the performance of this scheme. In addition, we have realized that the literature is short of clear quantitative investigations on the variation of the performance of the TSS scheme with a number of network parameters, such as nodes densities, nodes speeds, and noise-levels.

The main objective of this chapter is to implement and investigate the performance of the TSS authentication scheme in noisy MANETs. The performance of the TSS scheme is evaluated through a number of simulations using the MANET Simulator (MANSim). In these simulations, the variation of the authentication success ratio is estimated for various threshold secret shares, number of nodes, nodes speeds, and network noise-levels. The chapter also introduces the concept of

Shamir secret share, authentication, authentication techniques, and authentication models. It also provides a comprehensive literature review.

## BACKGROUND

### Authentication

Authentication is the verification of the identity of a party who generated some messages, and of the integrity of the messages. In computer networks, two types of authentication can be identified, namely, message authentication and node authentication. Message authentication is a technique for verifying the integrity of a transmitted message. While node authentication is a technique to let one party prove the identity of another party. There are two differences between message authentication and node authentication; these are (Forouzan, 2008):

1.  Message authentication may not happen in real time; node authentication does. In message authentication, when a sender sends a message to a receiver, while the receiver authenticates the message; the sender may or may not be present in the communication process. On the other hand, when the sender requests node authentication, there is no real message communication involved until the sender is authenticated by the receiver. The sender needs to be online and takes part in the authentication process. Only after the sender is authenticated can message communicated between the two parties.
2.  Message authentication simply authenticates one message; the process needs to be repeated for each new message. Node authentication authenticates the sender for the entire duration of a session.

In this chapter, we concern with node authentication. In node authentication the sender must identify itself to the receiver. This can be done with one of the three kinds of witnesses; something known, something possessed, or something inherent (Brainard, et al., 2006).

1. Something known. This is a secret known only by the sender that can be checked by the receiver. Examples are password, a PIN number, a secret key, and private key.
2. Something possessed. This is something that can prove the sender identity. Examples are a passport, a driver's license, an identification card, a credit card, and a smart card.
3. Something inherent. This is an inherent characteristic of the sender. Examples are conventional signature, fingerprints, voice, facial characteristics, retinal pattern, and handwriting.

## Authentication Techniques

A number of node authentication techniques have been developed throughout the years, such as: password-based authentication, challenge-response authentication, Kerberos-based authentication, public-key cryptography, etc (Neuman, et al., 2005; Kohl, et al., 1994). In what follows a brief description is provided for each of them.

### Password-Based Authentication

The simplest and the oldest method of node authentication is the password, something that the sender possesses. A password is used when a user needs to access a system to use its resources (login). Each user has a user identification that is public and a password that is private. This authentication scheme is divided into two separate groups: the fixed password and the one-time password.

### Challenge-Response Authentication

In this type of authentication the sender proves that it knows a secret without actually sending it. In this scheme, the challenge is a time varying value sent by the receiver, and the response is the result of a function applied on the challenge. It can be divided into four categories: symmetric-key ciphers, keyed-hash functions, asymmetric-key ciphers, and digital signature.

### Kerberos-Based Authentication

Kerberos is a distributed authentication service that allows a sender (client) to prove its identity to a receiver (an application server, or just server) without sending data across the network that might allow an attacker or the receiver to subsequently impersonate the principal. Kerberos optionally provides integrity and confidentiality for data sent between the sender and receiver. Kerberos was developed in the mid-'80s as part of MIT's Project Athena (Champine, et al., 1990).

Kerberos is not effective against password guessing attacks; if a user chooses a poor password, then an attacker guessing that password can impersonate the user. Similarly, Kerberos requires a trusted path through which passwords are entered. If the user enters a password to a program that has already been modified by an attacker (a Trojan horse), or if the path between the user and the initial authentication program can be monitored, then an attacker may obtain sufficient information to impersonate the user.

To be useful, Kerberos must be integrated with other parts of the system. It does not protect all messages sent between two nodes; it only protects the messages from software that has been written or modified to use it. While it may be used to exchange encryption keys when establishing link encryption and network level security services, this would require changes to the network software of the hosts involved.

Kerberos does not itself provide authorization, but V5 Kerberos passes authorization information generated by other services. In this manner, Kerberos can be used as a base for building separate distributed authorization services (Neuman, et al., 2005).

The Kerberos authentication system uses a series of encrypted messages to prove to a receiver that a client is running on behalf of a particular sender. The Kerberos protocol is based in part on the Needham and Schroeder authentication protocol, but with changes to support the needs of the environment for which it was developed. Among these changes are the use of timestamps to reduce the number of messages needed for basic authentication, the addition of a "ticket-granting" service to support subsequent authentication without re-entry of a principal's password, and different approach to cross-realm authentication (authentication of a sender registered with a different authentication server than the receiver). Further information on Kerberos can be found in RFC 1510 for a more thorough description of the Kerberos protocol (Kohl, et al., 1994).

## Public-Key Cryptography

In public-key cryptography, encryption and decryption are performed using a pair of keys such that knowledge of one key does not provide knowledge of the other key in the pair (Forouzan, 2008; Forouzan, 2007; Stallings, 2003). One key is published and is called the public key, and the other key is kept private. Public-key cryptography has several advantages over conventional cryptography when used for authentication. These include more natural support for authentication to multiple recipients, support for non-repudiation (since the receiver does not know the private key, it cannot generate a message that purports to be from the authenticated sender), and the elimination of secret encryption keys from the central authentication server.

Public-key cryptography is well suited for use in authentication in store and forward applications such as electronic mail, and it is required by applications where a signature is verified by many readers. The most accepted algorithm for public-key cryptography is the RSA algorithm, which was proposed by R. Rivest, A. Shamir, and L. Adeleman (Rivest, et al., 1978). However, message encryption or decryption using the RSA algorithm is time consuming or expensive process.

Public-key encryption may also be used by authentication servers to exchange conventional cross-realm keys on-demand between authentication servers, with the cost amortized over many requests.

## Threshold Secret Sharing

Popular network authentication architectures, such as Kerberos (Neuman, et al., 2005), the X.509 standard (Aresenault & Turner, 2001), and PKI trust model (Perlman, 1999), are based on using a globally trusted Certification Authority (CA) model. However, using a globally trusted CA model may work well in wired or infrastructure (AP) wireless networks. But, it does not work well in MANETs environments for several reasons:

1. MANETs provide no infrastructure support. The cost of maintaining such CA may be prohibitively high.
2. Each of the CA servers is exposed to a single point of compromises and failures.
3. Multihop communications over the error-prone wireless channel expose data transmissions to high loss rate and large latency.
4. Frequent route changes induced by mobility also make locating and contacting CA servers in a timely fashion non-trivial.

Variations of the CA model, such as hierarchical CAs and CA delegations can ameliorate, but cannot addresses issues such as service availability and robustness (Kong, et al., 2001; Perlman, 1999). Therefore, more efficient and reliable solutions are required to address the above issues. One alternative solution is to use the concept of Threshold Secret Sharing (TSS) scheme proposed by Adi Shamir in 1978 (Rivest, et al., 1978).

Shamir's TSS scheme is working as follows: a secret ($S$) can be divided into a number of pieces (say $n$, where $n$ is the number of nodes within the network), in such a way that $S$ can be reconstructed from any number of pieces (say $k$), but even complete knowledge $k$-1 pieces is not enough to reconstruct $S$. This approach can be used to design self-securing networks, in which multiple nodes ($k$) collaboratively serve as a CA server. Therefore, the authority and functionality of the authentication server are distributed to each node's locality. Any local $k$ nodes are trusted as a whole and collaboratively provide authentication services.

Some pleasant features of this scheme are as follows. The system does not expose to any single point of compromise, single point of DoS attack, or single point of failure. Authentication can be performed in every network neighborhood; this feature is important to authenticate roaming users in a MANET. Furthermore, this solution scales to large network size.

## Authentication Models

A well-defined authentication (trust) model is fundamental in authentication protocols, therefore, a number of models have been developed, such as:

- The Trusted Third Party (TTP) model (Perlman, 1999).
- The Pretty Good Privacy (PGP) model (Garfinkel, 1995).
- The distributed trust model (Abdul-Rahman, 1997).
- The localized-trust model (Luo, et al., 2002).

In the TTP model, an entity is trusted (authenticated) only if it is verified by a CA. While implementations of the TTP model possess efficiency and manageability properties in centralized systems, they suffer from scalability and robustness problems. In the PGP model, each entity manages its own trust based on direct recommendation. It was developed by Philip R. Zimmermann (1991) and can be used to encrypt and decrypt e-mail over the Internet. It can also be used to send an encrypted digital signature that lets the receiver verify the sender's identity and know that the message was not changed en route. A number of distributed trust techniques were proposed to further quantify the notions of trust and recommendation. However, all of these three models were not enough to address the unique security issues in MANETs. Therefore, the localized-trust model was developed to address the unique security issues of MANETs.

In this section, we shall provide a detail discussion for the first and the forth models, namely, the TTP and the localized-trust models, while discussions of the PGP and the distributed trust models can be found in (Garfinkel, 1995) and (Abdul-Rahman, 1997), respectively.

## The TTP Model

In this model, an entity is authenticated only if it is verified by the system CA. The model is widely used in access point wireless networks, because of its simplicity, efficiency, and manageability. It only provides limited scalability and robustness. Furthermore, the availability of the system CA is one of critical issues, which needs to be carefully considered. There are four different cases for the availability of the system CA:

1. **CA always available**. The case that a CA is always accessible by all network nodes is generally not considered as an option in MANETs, because MANETs should be self-

organized after their initialization. If a CA is permanently available we could implement solutions that require certificates or implement Kerberos-like solutions where the TTP distributes session keys. However, in the future it might be reasonable to assume internet connection availability in MANETs. In this case we only need to cope with the resource constraints and mobility of the devices.

2. **CA available at network initialization phase and every time a node joins**. The second case comprises all scenarios where a CA is available to issue certificates, and generate and distribute key material and system parameters at the initial stage of the network. The CA is also available for all nodes that subsequently join the network in order to obtain the required system parameters and keys. The assumption that a CA is available every time a new node joins the network is not as restrictive as it might sound. The CA does not need to be accessible by all network nodes every time a new node joins a network. There could be implementations in which nodes contact a CA in order to receive the required data, such as a certificate of the public key or a symmetric key, before joining the network.

3. **CA available at network initialization phase**. This case is similar to the previous one, with the deference that subsequently added nodes cannot access the CA. After the initialization phase, the CA cannot be contacted anymore by any of the nodes, including the nodes in the networks and newly joining nodes. Usually this is called the self-organization property of the network. The present network nodes are responsible to take over the tasks of the CA, such as issuing, renewing, and revoking certificates.

4. **No CA available at any network phase**. If no CA is available at all and we still want to use public key encryption schemes, the nodes need to issue their own certificates or we need to implement a model that does not require any public key certificates. The first case can be realized by protocols in the self-organization model and the latter case by protocols in the certificateless public key model.

## The Localized-Trust Model

In this model, an entity is trusted if any $k$ trusted entities claim so within a certain time period $T$. These $k$ entities are typically among the entity's of the first-hop neighbors. Once a node is trusted by its local community, it is globally accepted as a trusted node. Otherwise, a locally distrusted entity is regarded as untrustworthy in the entire network. $k$ and $T$ are two important parameters with $T$ characterizing the time-varying feature of a trust relationship.

Two options for setting $k$ are as follows:

- The first is to set $k$ as a globally fixed parameter that is honored by each entity in the system. In this case, $k$ acts as a system-wide trust threshold.
- The second option is to set $k$ as a location-dependent variable. For instance, $k$ may be the majority of each node's neighboring nodes.

It is clear that the second option provides more flexibility to work in concert with diverse local network topology. However, there is no clear system-wide trust criterion. Due to lack of effective mechanisms to authoritatively determine a node's neighborhood in a mobile environment, the adversaries may take the advantage of this feature.

Trust management and maintenance are distributed in both $k$ and $T$ domains in this localized-trust model. This property is particularly appropriate for a large dynamic MANET, where centralized trust management would be difficult or expensive. Besides, a node indeed cares most the trustworthiness of its immediate neighbors in practice. This is because a node will communicate with the rest of the world via its one-hop neighbors.

## Previous Work

In this section we review some of the most recent work related to node authentication in MANETs. In (Chai, et al., 2007), a secure group key management (GKM) scheme for hierarchical MANETs was presented, which aimed to improve both scalability and survivability of GKM for large-scale MANETs. An architectural design of Mesh CA (MeCA) for Wireless Mesh Networks (WMNs) was presented in (Kim & Bahk, 2009). In MeCA, the secret key and functions of CA are distributed over several mobile routers using Fast Verifiable Share Redistribution (FVSR) scheme. Simulation results showed that MeCA does not disclose its secret key even under severe attacks while incurring low overhead compared to other existing schemes in MANETs.

A lightweight authenticated key establishment scheme with privacy preservation, to secure the communications between mobile vehicles and roadside infrastructure, in a Vehicular Ad Hoc Network (VANET), was proposed in (Li, et al., 2008). An entirely decentralized key generation mechanism was introduced in (Mukherjee, et al., 2008), in which keys can be established between group members with absolutely no prior communication. The approach relies on threshold cryptography and introduces a novel concept of Node-Group-Key (NGK) mapping. In (Wang, et al., 2008), a secure scheme for vehicular communication on VANETs was proposed. The scheme not only protects the privacy but also maintains liability using session keys for secure communications.

A novel authenticated group key agreement protocol for end-to-end security in MANETs was proposed in (Yeun, et al., 2008). A threshold password authentication scheme was presented in (Chai, et al., 2007), which meets both availability

and strong security requirements in MANETs. An ID-based version of the PKI cluster-based scheme was described in (Lee & Chang, 2007) providing secure communications in wireless ad hoc networks.

A non-interactive key agreement and progression (NIKAP) scheme for MANETs was described in (Li & Garcia-Luna-Aceves, 2007), which does not require an online CA. A Secure and Efficient Key Management (SEKM) framework for MANETs was presented in (Wu, et al., 2007). A novel hierarchical scheme based on threshold cryptography was proposed in (Zhu, et al., 2005) to address both security and efficiency issues of key management and certification service in MANET.

A fully self-organized public-key management system was proposed in (Capkun, et al., 2003). It allows users to generate their public-private key pairs, to issue certificates, and to perform authentication regardless of the network partitions and without any centralized services. The applicability of threshold cryptography for membership control in peer-to-peer networks was investigated in (Narasimha, et al., 2003). A self-securing MANET approach was described in (Luo, et al., 2002), in which multiple nodes collaboratively provide authentication services for other nodes in the network. A design that supports ubiquitous security services for mobile hosts and it is robust against break-ins was described in (Kong, et al., 2001).

## WIRELESS NETWORK ENVIRONMENTS

The wireless network environment can be categorized, according to the presence of noise into two types of environments; these are (Al-Bahadili & Jaradat, 2010):

1. A noiseless (error-free) environment, which represents an ideal network environment, in which it is assumed that all data transmitted by a source node is successfully and cor-

rectly delivered to destination nodes. It is characterized by the following axioms or assumptions: the world is flat, all radios have equal range, and their transmission range is circular, communication link symmetry, perfect link, signal strength is a simple function of distance.

2. A noisy (error-prone) environment, which represents a realistic network environment, in which the received signal will differ from the transmitted signal, due to various transmission impairments, such as: wireless signal attenuation, free space loss, thermal noise, atmospheric absorption, multipath effect, refraction.

All of these impairments are represented by a generic name, noise, and the environment is called noisy environment. For modeling and simulation purposes, the noisy environment can be described by introducing a probability function, which referred to as the probability of reception ($p_c$). It is defined as the probability that a wireless transmitted data is survived being lost and successfully delivered to a destination node despite the presence of all or any of the above impairments. Figure 1 outlines the steps of establishing the first hop-neighbors in noisy environment.

## CONCEPT OF SHAMIR'S SECRET SHARING SCHEME

The concept of Shamir's secret sharing scheme is to divide a data $D$ into $n$ pieces (shares) in such a way that $D$ is easily reconstructable from any $k$ shares, but even complete knowledge of $k$-1 shares reveals absolutely no information about $D$ (Shamir, 1979). The scheme is referred to as ($k$, $n$) threshold scheme. This scheme can be used to construct robust key management techniques for cryptographic systems that can function securely and reliably even when security breaches expose to $k$-1 shares. So that instead of having a central or distributed CA to control key distribution, the key can be divided into shares that are distributed between nodes, then each node can locally construct the key after collecting the shares of $k$ nodes.

According to Shamir, a data $D$ can be divided into $n$ shares $D_x$ ($x$=1, 2, ..., $n$) using the following polynomial:

$$q(x) = (a_0 + a_1x + \cdots + a_{k-1}x^{k-1}) = a_0 + \sum_{i=1}^{k-1} a_i x^i \tag{1}$$

In which $D_x$=$q(x)$ and $D$=$a_0$, so that it can expressed as:

*Figure 1. Calculating the first-hop neighbors in a noisy MANET environment*

```
For a node i  (i=1 to n)
    For node j  (j=1 to n)      // n is the total number of nodes within the network
        If (i≠j) Then
            // Test to see if the node j is a first-hop neighbor for node i
            Calculate the distance (r) between the two nodes as follows:

                    r = √((xᵢ − xⱼ)² + (yᵢ − yⱼ)²)  // x and y are the node location

            If (r<R) Then      // R is the radio transmission range of the source node
                // Test to see if data delivered successfully between nodes i and j
                ξ=rnd()  {ξ is a random number between 0 and 1}
                If (ξ ≤ pc) Then      // pc is the probability of reception
                    iRange = 1      // The two nodes are neighbors and succeed to exchange data
                Else
                    iRange = 0      // The two nodes are neighbors but fail to exchange data
                End If
            End If
        End If
```

Or $D_x = D + \sum_{i=1}^{k-1} a_i x^i$       (2)

Then, given any subset of $k$ of these $D_x$ values (together with their identifying indices), the coefficients ($a_0$ to $a_{k-1}$) of $q(x)$ can be evaluated by interpolation, and then evaluate $D=q(0)$ or $D=a_0$.

To make the above claim more precise, modular arithmetic is used instead of real arithmetic. Where, in order to make the interpolation possible all integer coefficients are taken as modulo of a prime number $p$, which is bigger than both $n$ and $D$. In other words, the integer coefficients $a_1$ to $a_{k-1}$ are either chosen between 0 and less than $p$ ($0 \leq a_i < p$) or calculated as $a_i = a_i \bmod p$, where $i=1$, 2, ..., $k$. Furthermore, the values of $D_x$ ($x=1, 2, ..., n$) are also computed modulo $p$. Thus, Equation 1 are expressed as:

$$D_x = D + \sum_{i=1}^{k-1} a_i x^i \bmod p \quad\quad (3)$$

Some of the useful properties of this $(k, n)$ threshold scheme (when compared to the mechanical locks and keys solutions) are:

1. The size of each share does not exceed the size of the original data.
2. When $k$ is kept fixed, $D_x$ shares can be dynamically added or deleted (e.g., when executives join or leave the network) without affecting the other $D_x$ shares. A piece is deleted only when a leaving executive makes it completely inaccessible, even to himself.
3. It is easy to change the $D_x$ shares without changing the original data $D$ - all we need is a new polynomial $q(x)$ with the same free term. A frequent change of this type can greatly enhance security since the pieces exposed by security breaches cannot be accumulated unless all of them are values of the same edition of the $q(x)$ polynomial.
4. By using tuples of polynomial values as $D_x$ shares, we can get a hierarchical scheme in which the number of shares needed to determine $D$ depends on their importance. For example, if we give each high importance node three values of $q(x)$, each moderate importance node two values of $q(x)$, and each low importance nodes one value of $q(x)$.

## THE TSS SCHEME

In a public-key based design, the system CA key pair is denoted as $\{SKR, SKU\}$, where $SKR$ is the system private key and $SKU$ is the system public key. $SKR$ is used to sign certificates for all nodes in the network. A certificate signed by $SKR$ can be decrypted only by the well-known public key $SKU$.

In a TSS scheme, $SKR$ is shared among network nodes. Each node $i$ holds a secret share $SKR_i$, and any $k$ of such secret share holders can collectively function as the role of CA. However, for better system security, the secrecy of $SKR$ is preserved all the time and it is not visible, known or recoverable by any network node. Besides the system key pair, each node $i$ also holds a personal RSA key pair $\{kr_i, ku_i\}$. To certify its personal keys, each node $i$ holds the certificate $C_i$ in the format of $<i, ku_i, T>$, which reads as: "It is certified that the personal public key of $i$ is $ku_i$ during the time interval $[t, t+T]$. A certificate is valid only if it is signed by system secret key $SKR$.

The TSS scheme makes an extensive use of the polynomial secret sharing scheme due to Shamir (Shamir, 1979). A secret, specifically the certificate-signing key $SKR$, is shared among all $n$ nodes in the network according to the following equation:

$$SKR_i = (SKR + \sum_{j=1}^{k-1} a_j\, i^j) \bmod p \quad\quad (4)$$

Where $SKR_i$ is the node secret share, $i$ is the node's ID, $SKR$ is the system private key, $k$ is the minimum number of shares required to recover $SKR$, $n$ is the total number of nodes within the network, and $p$ is a prime number bigger than $n$ and $SKR$. In other words, the integer coefficients $a_1$ to $a_{k-1}$ are either chosen between 0 and less than $p$ ($0 \leq a_j < p$) or calculated as $a_j = a_j$ mode $p$, where $j=1, 2, ..., k$. The same is for $SKR$ either it less than $p$ or it is calculated as $SKR = SKR$ mod $p$. A coalition of $k$ nodes with $k$ polynomial shares can potentially recover $SKR$. In fact there are two cases, these are:

1. A newly arrived node or a node that knows its partial share of $SKR$ ($SKR_x$), where $x$ is the node ID. In this case, it needs the IDs and shares of $k$-1 nodes to construct $k$ linear equations to solve for $SKR$.
2. A node $x$ does not know its partial share $SKR_x$. In this case, the node, first, needs the IDs and shares of $k$-1 nodes to calculate its share using Lagrange interpolation as follows:

$$SKR_x = \left( \sum_{j=1}^{k-1} SKR_j \, \ell_j(x) \right) \bmod p \qquad (5)$$

where $\ell_j(x) = \prod_{\substack{i=1 \\ i \neq j}}^{k-1} \frac{x-i}{j-i}$ \qquad (6)

Then, after having $k$ IDs and shares, a node $x$ can construct a set of $k$ linear equations to calculate $SKR$. In both cases, no coalition up to $k$-1 nodes can yield any information about $SKR$.

## The Localized Certification Procedure of the TSS Scheme

This section describes localized certification procedure of the TSS scheme for certificate issuing/renewal. In this scheme, a node $x$ firstly locates a coalition $B$ of $K$ neighbors ($K \geq k$) and broadcasts certification requests to them. A node $j \in B$ checks its monitoring data on $x$ to decide if certification service is granted, then it calculates its partial certificate and sends it back to node $x$. Upon receiving $k$ partial certificates from coalition $B$, node $x$ processes them together to recover its full certificate. Figure 2 outlines the main steps of the certification procedure for the TSS scheme.

There are two drawbacks in the above approach, these are:

1. If any node in coalition $B$ fails to respond due to node failures or moving out of range, all the other partial certificates become useless. The computation of other nodes is all wasted and node $i$ has to restart the whole process from the very beginning.
2. When node $j$ receives a certification request from $i$, its records may not provide enough

*Figure 2. The TSS scheme localized certification procedure*

```
For any node i which needs to get a new certificate or to renew its expired certificate:
        Locates a coalition B of K neighbors (K≥k);
        Broadcasts certification requests to them;
            For each node j∈B // After receiving certification request
                Check node I profile to decide if it is trustable or not.;
                If (Yes) Then
                        Calculates its partial certificate;
                        Sends it back to node i;
                Else (No)
                        Discard request;
                End If
        Upon receiving k partial certificates from coalition B at node i:
            Multiplies them together to recover its new full certificate;
```

information on $i$. It may be because the interaction between $i$ and $j$ does not last long enough. Moreover, $i$ may not exist in $j$'s records at all if they just met. Node $j$ has two options in this scenario. One is to serve $i$'s request, since no bad records are located. The risk is that a roaming adversary who cannot get a new certificate from his previous location may take the advantage. The other option is to drop the request, since no records can demonstrate $i$ well-behaving. The drawback of the second approach of dropping the request is that a legitimate mobile node may not be able to get a new certificate.

## SYSTEM, ADVERSARY, AND INTRUSION MODELS

### System Model

In this chapter, we consider a MANET in which mobile nodes communicate with one another via a bandwidth-constrained, error-prone (noisy), and insecure wireless channel. It is assumed that $n$ mobile nodes are randomly distributed within the networks area, and $n$ may be dynamically changing as mobile nodes join, leave, or fail over time. The network provides neither physical nor logical infrastructure support, and the reliability of multi-hop packet forwarding based on underlying transport layer and ad hoc routing is not assured. This is implemented in the simulation model by introducing a probability factor, namely, a probability of reception ($p_c$), which is defined as the probability of an authentication request packet being sent by a sender (source node) will be successfully delivered to the receiver (destination node). The following assumptions are also made:

1.  Each node has a unique nonzero ID and a mechanism to discover its one-hop neighbors.

2.  Communication between one-hop neighboring nodes is more reliable compared with multi-hop communication over the error-prone wireless channel.

3.  Each node has at least $k$ one-hop legitimate neighboring nodes. If a node could not find $k$ neighbors; it may wait for new nodes coming in or roam to a new location for more neighbors.

4.  Mobility is characterized by an average node moving speed ($u_{av}$).

5.  Each node is equipped with some local detection mechanism to identify misbehaving nodes among its one-hop neighborhood.

This last assumption is based on the observation that although intrusion detection in MANETs is generally more difficult than in wired networks (Zhang & Lee, 2000), detecting misbehaviors among one-hop neighbors is easier and practical due to the broadcast nature of the wireless transmission (Marti, et al., 2000).

### Adversary Model

There are two types of attacks that we are concerned with in this work, these are:

1.  Daniel-of-Service (DoS) attack
2.  Node break-ins attack

Adversaries may issue DoS attacks from various layers of the network stack ranging from network layer *Smurf* and *Teardrop*, transport layer *TCP flooding* and *SYN flooding*, and various attacks in application layer. For adversaries that seek to compromise networking nodes, we assume that the underlying cryptographic primitives such as RSA are computationally secure.

Occasional break-ins may occur through factors such as insecure OS, software bugs and backdoors, etc. Also, several adversaries may conspire to form a group. For ease of presentation, such an adversary group is denoted by a single adversary. Adversaries are characterized in one of the following two models, as proposed in (Asaeda, et al., 2005).

1.  **Model I:** During the entire lifetime of the network, the adversary cannot break into or control $k$ or more nodes.
2.  **Model II:** Consider the entire lifetime of the network is divided into intervals of length $T$. During any time interval $T$, the adversary cannot break into or control $k$ or more nodes.

Although, the adversary cannot break into or control $k$ or more nodes at a particular time, the adversary of model II can choose its victims at each time interval. As time goes on each node in the network can be broken during some time interval.

## Intrusion Model

At first we briefly discuss what kind of intrusions is allowed in this work. In the worst case, all information, whether public or private, is known to the intruder when a network entity is compromised. The intruder can forge, modify, and delete any information. The intruder can also do bookkeeping to facilitate future break-ins. However, the power of an intruder is set to be limited to make the problem tractable. Giving infinite power to the intruder simply makes any security design meaningless. Therefore, a more realistic intrusion model needs to be considered in the system.

Authentication is the basic building block for all security services. Fundamentally, it is assumed that each network entity has some information that is unknown to or unforgeable by the intruder. Otherwise, once an entity is broken, there is no way others can differentiate the intruder and the genuine entity. Two specific cases are considered:

1.  The entity private key will not be exposed for a certain period of time. Thus an entity is able to maintain its security identity by periodically renewing its private key via certificate renewal services.
2.  The entity ID is not forgeable by the intruder, or the intruder can be detected by intrusion detection mechanisms when it pretends to be the broken entity.

## PRACTICAL IMPLEMENTATION OF THE TSS SCHEME

In this section we discuss the main issues and challenges that are facing the practical implementation of the proposed TSS scheme in real MANETs. These are:

1.  Obtaining initial certificates. Any new node needs an initial certificate before it can join the network. Moreover, an admitted node has to maintain a valid certificate when it requests its certificate to be renewed. The localized certification never creates or issues a brand-new certificate. This policy is to prevent malicious node to have multiple certificates based by forged or stolen IDs. How to issue initial certificates poses the root of trust problem. A node may be issued an initial certificate by an offline authority through external means (e.g., in-person ID). Alternatively, we may use any coalition of $k$ networking nodes to issue an initial certificate via collaborative admission control for this new node. The admission control policy has to be consistent with the robustness of the overall trust model, system model and the adversary models.
2.  Bootstrapping of the first $k$ nodes. To initialize the very first $k$ nodes, we assume an offline authority who knows the full certificate signing key *SKR* and the associated polynomial in Equation 2 of degree $k$-1.
3.  Parameter $k$ revisited. The design so far assumes each node to have at least $k$ legitimate neighbors. This assumption is critical for

certification services to be robust against adversaries. The parameter $k$ also determines the availability of the services (successful authentication).

4.  Intrusion detection in ad hoc networks. As presented in the system model (Section 3.4), it is assumed that each node is equipped with some local detection mechanism to identify misbehaving nodes among its one-hop neighborhood. It is believed that as time goes, better local intrusion detection mechanism will be available to serve this purpose.

## THE MANET SIMULATOR (MANSIM)

MANSim is a computer network simulator written in C++ programming language. It consists of four major modules: network, mobility, computational, and algorithm modules (Al-Bahadili & Jaradat, 2007; Al-Bahadili, 2010). The network and mobility modules were explained in (Wu, et al., 2007). The TSS scheme described in Section 3 was implemented as part of MANSim algorithm module. The computational module of MANSim was modified to calculate a parameter called the success ratio ($S_R$), which is defined as the ratio between the number of nodes that are successfully authenticated or certified access to the network resources ($c$) and the total number of nodes on the network ($n$). Thus, $S_R$ can be calculated as: $S_R = c/n$. $S_R$ also reflects the probability with which a new arriving node can be successfully authenticated and certified access to the network resources. Using MANSim, the effect of a number of network parameters on $S_R$ can be investigated, such as: number of nodes ($n$), node speed ($u$), threshold ($k$), and reception probability ($p_c$).

The computational module can be explained as follows: a loop is performed over all nodes within the network to find out whether the node will be successfully authenticated. Then the number of authenticated nodes is divided by the total number of nodes within the network. This represents

the success ratio. Due to the stochastic nature of the process, each node is assumed to initiate $S$ authentication requests and the average value is calculated.

In order to consider node mobility, a simulation time is set. It is divided into a number of intervals ($nIntv$) that yields a time interval or pause time $\tau = T_{sim}/nIntv.$, where $T_{sim}$ is the total simulation time. The calculation is repeated for $nIntv$, and the results obtained for the computed parameters are averaged over $nIntv$. In general, it has been found that to obtain an adequate network performance, the pause time must be carefully chosen so that the distance traveled by the node, during location update interval, is less than the radio transmission range ($R$) of the nodes. Figure 3 outlines the computational modules for TSS scheme.

## RESULTS AND DISCUSSIONS

In order to evaluate and analyze the performance of the TSS scheme in a noisy environment, three scenarios were simulated using MANSim. These scenarios can be summarized as follows:

### Scenario #1: Investigate the Effect of Number of Nodes ($n$)

Scenario #1 investigates the variation of $S_R$ with $k$ for various $n$. In the following discussions, we shall interchangeably use the term node density, which is defined as the number of nodes divided by the network area ($A$). Since in all simulations $A$ remains unchanged, then the nodes density is directly proportional to $n$. The investigations were carried-out in both noiseless ($p_c=1.0$) and noisy ($p_c=0.8$) MANET environments. The input parameters for this scenario are given in Table 1.

Table 1 shows that the simulation time is 1800 sec and the pause time is 22.5 sec, which means the nodes locations are updated 80 times. Each time, $S_R$ is calculated by dividing the number of nodes that are successfully authenticated by $n$. A

*Figure 3. Computational module of the TSS scheme*

Loop over the number of intervals ($m=1, nIntv$)
    Loop over the number of nodes as source nodes ($i=1, n$)
        Loop over the number of transmitted request message ($j=1, S$)
            **If** (node $i$ successfully authenticated) **Then**
                $c = c + 1;$
            **End If**
        Compute $S_R(i)$ for node $i$ as follows: $S_R(i)=c/S$.

Compute the average value of $S_R(m)$ as follows: $S_R(m) = \sum_{i=1}^{n} S_R(i)/n$

Compute the average value of $S_R$ as follows: $S_R = \sum_{m=1}^{nIntv} S_R(m)/m$

node is considered as successfully authenticated if it establishes a link with $k$ or more nodes from its first-hop neighbors. The values of $S_R$ for all 80 trials are averaged to endow with the simulation $S_R$. Furthermore, due to the randomness of the process and to enhance the statistics of the results, each simulation is repeated for 20 runs, each run $S_R$ is calculated, and then the average of the $S_R$ values are calculated. The results for $S_R$ are shown in Figure 4.

The main outcomes of this scenario can be summarized as follows:

1. As $k$ increases, $S_R$ nonlinearly decreases regardless of the node density for both noiseless and noisy MANETs. This is because when $k$ increases, more first-hop neighbors

are required to ensure node authentication, a case which can not be satisfied by all nodes all the time due to the randomness of nodes distribution.

2. For the same value of $k$, $S_R$ is directly proportional to $n$, i.e., as $n$ increases a higher value of $S_R$ can be achieved. Since the node density increases the probability of having neighboring nodes $\geq k$ nodes is most likely to happen to help with or ensure node authentication.

3. For the same node density, when the noise-level increases (i.e., $p_c$ decreases), $S_R$ decreases. This may be explained as follows: When the node whose identity needs to be approved sends an authentication request packet asking for the secret shares of its first-hop neighbors, then due to presence of

*Table 1. Input parameters*

| Parameters | Scenario #1 | Scenario #2 | Scenario #3 |
|---|---|---|---|
| Geometrical model | Random distribution | Random distribution | Random node distribution |
| Network area ($A$) | 1000x1000 m | 1000x1000 m | 1000x1000 m |
| Number of node ($n$) | 100, 150, 200 nodes. | 150 nodes | 150 nodes |
| Transmission radius ($R$) | 150 m | 150 m | 150 m |
| Average node speed ($u$) | 5 m/sec | 2, 5, 10 m/sec | 5 m/sec |
| Simulation time ($T_{sim}$) | 1800 sec | 1800 sec | 1800 sec |
| Threshold secret shares ($k$) | 1, 3, 5, 7, 9, 11 | 1, 3, 5, 7, 9, 11 | 1, 3, 5, 7, 9, 11 |
| Probability of reception ($p_c$) | 0.8 and 1.0 | 0.8 and 1.0 | 0.5 to 1.0 in step of 0.1 |
| Pause time ($\tau$) | 22.5 sec | 56.5, 22.5, 11.25 sec | 22.5 sec |
| Number of runs | 20 runs | 20 runs | 20 runs |

*Figure 4. Variation of $S_R$ with k for various values of n and $p_c$*

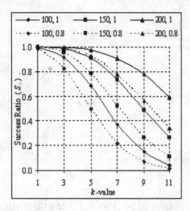

noise some of these packets may be lost or the requesting node fails to successfully receive its neighbors' replies. For example, if a node physically (distance-wise) has $f_1$ first-hop neighbors ($f_1 \geq k$), and due to the presence of noise some of the requests or reply packets are lost, and the node practically receives shares from $f_2$ nodes only ($f_2 < k$), so it can not be authenticated, and the node needs to re-initiate a new authentication request.

## Scenario #2: Investigate the Effect of Nodes Speed (*u*)

Scenario #2 investigates the variation of $S_R$ with $k$ for various $u$. The investigations are carried-out in both noiseless ($p_c = 1.0$) and noisy ($p_c = 0.8$) MANETs. The input parameters for this scenario are given in Table 1. The simulations were carried-out using MANSim. In this scenario three node speeds are examined, these are 2, 5, and 10 m/sec, which produce different pause times of 56.25, 22.50, and 11.25 sec, respectively. The results for the variation of $S_R$ with $k$ for various values of $u$ are shown in Figure 5.

The results show that $u$ has insignificant effects on $S_R$. The reason for that can be explained as follows: suppose at time ($t$), a node distribution in Figure 6-a shows three nodes (A, B, and C)

can be authenticated out of four nodes within the network, because they have first-hop neighbors equal to or greater than 5 ($k=5$). At time $t+\tau$ (Figure 6-b, the node distribution is changed as all nodes have randomly changed their locations. In this case, still one of the nodes (C) fails to gain access to the network resources because the number of its first-hop neighbors is less than $k$ nodes, so that it can not be authenticated. Therefore, $S_R$ is not (or slightly) affected as a result of node mobility.

It can also be seen in Figure 5 that the same conclusion above is applied to both noiseless and noisy MANETs. But due to the presence of noise some of the first-hop neighbors fail to exchange their secret share with the requesting node so that the requesting node fails to gather $k$ secret shares and it can not be authenticated. Consequently, $S_R$ is less for noisy MANETs as compared to equivalent noiseless MANETs.

## Scenario #3: Investigate the Effect of Probability of Reception (p_c)

In previous scenarios, all investigations were carried-out for noiseless and noisy MANET environments. For a noisy environment, only a single value of noise-level ($p_c = 0.8$) was considered. This may not provide a clear conclusion on the effect

*Figure 5. Variation of $S_R$ with k for various values of u and $p_c$*

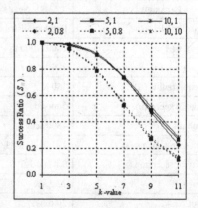

*Figure 6. Node distribution at time t and t+τ*

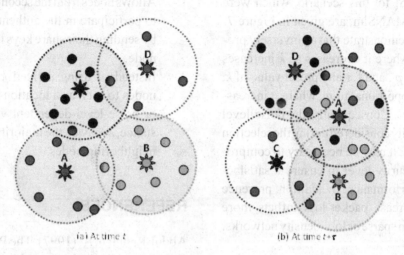

(a) At time *t*

(b) At time *t+τ*

*Figure 7. Variation of $S_R$ with k for various values of $p_c$*

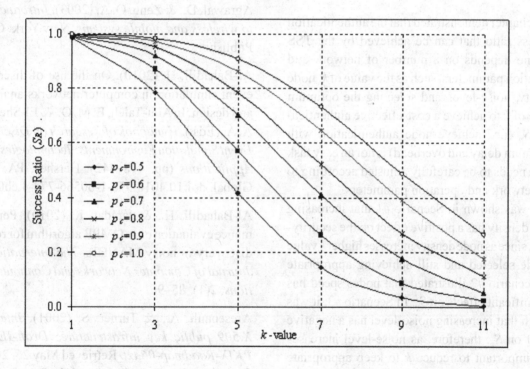

of $p_c$ on the performance of the TSS scheme and consequently the performance of the network. Therefore, scenario #3 investigates the variation of $S_R$ with $k$ for a range of $p_c$ values. In fact, the range of $p_c$ values, which were considered, is from 0.5 to 1.0 in step of 0.1. Where $p_c=1.0$ represents a noiseless MANET environment, while the value of $p_c=0.5$ is considered as a high noise-level MANET, where on average half of authentication request and/or reply packets exchanged between the requesting node and its neighbors are lost. The input parameters for this scenario are given in Table 1.

The results for $S_R$ for this scenario, which were obtained using MANSim, are given in Figure 7.

The results demonstrate that $S_R$ inversely proportional to $k$, where it decreases as $k$ increases for any value of $p_c$, and for any preset value of $k$, $S_R$ is directly proportional to $p_c$, where it increases as $p_c$ increases. Consequently, the noise-level should be carefully considered during the selection of $k$. Sometimes, it may be necessary to compromise on the security-level to ensure a satisfactory network performance. In addition, presence of noise or increase packet-loss inflicts more reduction on $S_R$ in sparse or low-density networks.

## CONCLUSION

This chapter demonstrated that the authentication success ratio that can be achieved by the TSS scheme depends on a number of network and operation parameters, such as the value of $k$, node density, noise-level, and selecting the optimum value of $k$ to achieve a cost-effective authentication $S_R$ (i.e., achieve node authentication with minimum delay and overhead) is not an easy task and $k$ needs to be carefully adjusted according to the network and operation parameters.

It was shown in Scenario #1 that increasing node density has a positive effect on the security-level, since as node density increases higher $k$ value can de selected and still achieving appropriate $S_R$. Scenario #2 illustrated that nodes speed has insignificant effects on $S_R$. In Scenario #3, it was shown that increasing noise-level has a negative effect on $S_R$, therefore, as noise-level increases it is important to reduce $k$ to keep appropriate value for $S_R$.

It is highly recommended to evaluate and investigate the variation of the performance of the TSS scheme in terms of other performance metrics, such as: load, thorough, bandwidth utilization, delay, power consumption. In addition, it is recommended to evaluate and investigate the variation of the success ratio considering the following:

1. Allows nodes from the second-hop neighbors to participate in the authentication process by sending their share keys to the requesting node.
2. Instead of using a fixed $k$ values, allows nodes to set $k$ as a location-dependent and/or noise-level-dependent variable. For instance, $k$ may be the majority of each node's neighboring nodes.

## REFERENCES

Abdul-Rahman, A. (1997). The PGP trust model. *The Journal of Electronic Commerce, 10*(3), 27–31.

Agrawal, D., & Zeng, Q. A. (2003). *Introduction to wireless and mobile systems*. New York: Cole Publishing.

Al-Bahadili, H. (2010). On the use of discrete-event simulation in computer networks analysis and design. In Abu-Taieh, E. M. O., & El-Sheikh, A. A. (Eds.), *Handbook of Research on Discrete-Event Simulation Environments: Technologies and Applications* (pp. 418–442). Hershey, PA: IGI Global. doi:10.4018/978-1-60566-774-4.ch019

Al-Bahadili, H., & Jaradat, R. (2010). Performance evaluation of an OMPR algorithm for route discovery in noisy MANETs. *The International Journal of Computer Networks and Communications, 2*(1), 85–96.

Aresenault, A., & Turner, S. (2001). *Internet X.509 public key infrastructure: Draft-IETF-PKIX-Roadmap-06.txt*. Retrieved May 26, 2011, from http://tools.ietf.org/html/draft-ietf-pkix-roadmap-06.

Asaeda, H., Rahman, M., & Toyama, Y. (2006). *Structuring proactive secret sharing in mobile ad-hoc networks*. Retrieved January 15, 2011, from http://www.sfc.wide.ad.jp/~asaeda/paper/ISWPC06_J1-2.pdf.

Balfanz, D., Smetters, D. K., Stewart, P., & Wong, H. C. (2002). Talking to strangers: Authentication in ad-hoc wireless networks. In *Proceedings of Network and Distributed System Security Symposium 2002 (NDSS 2002)*. San Diego, CA: ISOC Publications.

Brainard, J., Juels, A., Rivest, R., Szydlo, M., & Yung, M. (2006). Fourth factor authentication: Somebody you know. In *Proceedings of the ACM Computer and Communication Security (CCS 2006) Conference,* (pp. 168-178). Alexandria, VA: ACM Press.

Capkun, S., Buttyan, L., & Hubaux, J. (2003). Self-organized public-key management for mobile ad hoc networks. *IEEE Transactions on Mobile Computing, 2*(1), 52–64. doi:10.1109/TMC.2003.1195151

Chai, Z., Cao, Z., & Lu, R. (2007). Threshold password authentication against guessing attacks in ad hoc networks. *Journal of Ad Hoc Networks, 5*(7), 1046–1054. doi:10.1016/j.adhoc.2006.05.003

Champine, G. A., Geer, D. Jr, & Ruh, W. N. (1990). Project Athena as a distributed computer system. *Journal of IEEE Computer, 23*(9), 40–51. doi:10.1109/2.58217

Epperson, J. F. (2002). *An introduction to numerical methods and analysis*. New York: John Wiley and Sons.

Forouzan, B. A. (2007). *Data communications and networking* (4th ed.). New York: McGraw Hill.

Forouzan, B. A. (2008). *Introduction to cryptography and network security*. New York: McGraw Hill.

Garfinkel, S. (1995). *PGP: Pretty good privacy*. New York: O'Reilly & Associates Inc.

Huang, D., & Medhi, D. (2008). A secure group key management scheme for hierarchical mobile ad hoc networks. *Journal of Ad Hoc Networks, 6*(4), 560–577. doi:10.1016/j.adhoc.2007.04.006

Kim, J., & Bahk, S. (2009). Design of certification authority using secret redistribution and multicast routing in wireless mesh networks. *The International Journal of Computer and Telecommunications Networking, 53*(1), 98–109.

Kohl, J., Neuman, B. C., & Tso, T. Y. (1994). The evolution of the Kerberos authentication system. In *Distributed Open Systems* (pp. 78–94). New York: IEEE Computer Society Press.

Kong, J., Zerfos, P., Luo, H., Lu, S., & Zhang, L. (2001). Providing robust and ubiquitous security support for mobile ad-hoc networks. In *Proceedings of the 9th International Conference on Network Protocols (ICNP 2001)*. Riverside, CA: IEEE Press.

Lee, J. S., & Chang, C. C. (2007). Secure communications for cluster-based ad hoc networks using node identities. *Journal of Network and Computer Applications, 30*(4), 1377–1396. doi:10.1016/j.jnca.2006.10.003

Li, C., Hwang, M., & Chu, Y. (2008). A secure and efficient communication scheme with authenticated key establishment and privacy preserving for vehicular ad hoc networks. *Journal of Computer Communications, 31*(12), 2803–2814. doi:10.1016/j.comcom.2007.12.005

Li, Z., & Garcia-Luna-Aceves, J. J. (2007). Non-interactive key establishment in mobile ad hoc networks. *Journal of Ad Hoc Networks, 5*(7), 1194–1203. doi:10.1016/j.adhoc.2006.07.002

Luo, H., Zerfos, P., Kong, J., Lu, S., & Zhang, L. (2002). Self-securing ad hoc wireless networks. In *Proceedings of the 7th IEEE Symposium on Computers and Communications (ISCC 2002)*. IEEE Press.

Marti, S., Giuli, T., Lai, K., & Baker, M. (2000). Mitigating routing misbehavior in mobile ad hoc networks. In *Proceedings of the 6th ACM Annual International Conference on Mobile Computing and Networking (MOBICOM 2000),* (pp. 255 - 265). Boston, MA: ACM Press.

Mukherjee, A., Gupta, A., & Agrawal, D. P. (2008). Distributed key management for dynamic groups in MANETs. *Journal of Pervasive and Mobile Computing, 4*(4), 562–578. doi:10.1016/j.pmcj.2008.03.002

Murthy, C., & Manoj, B. (2004). *Ad hoc wireless networks: Architecture and protocols*. Upper Saddle River, NJ: Prentice Hall.

Narasimha, M., Tsudik, G., & Yi, J. H. (2003). On the utility of distributed cryptography in P2P and MANETs: The case of membership control. In *Proceedings from the IEEE International Conference on Networks and Protocols*, (pp. 336–345). IEEE Press.

Neuman, C., Yu, T., Hartman, S., & Raeburn, K. (2005). The Kerberos network authentication system (*RFC 4120*). Retrieved from http://www.ietf.org.

Perlman, R. (1999). An overview of PKI trust models. *IEEE Network, 13*, 38–43. doi:10.1109/65.806987

Rivest, L., Shamir, A., & Adleman, L. (1978). A method of obtaining digital signature and public key cryptosystem. *Communications of the ACM, 21*(2), 120–126. doi:10.1145/359340.359342

Shamir, A. (1979). How to share a secret. *Communications of the ACM, 22*(11), 612–613. doi:10.1145/359168.359176

Stallings, W. (2003). *Cryptography and network security* (4th ed.). Upper Saddle River, NJ: Prentice-Hall.

Toh, C. (2002). *Ad hoc mobile wireless networks: Protocols and systems*. Upper Saddle River, NJ: Prentice-Hall.

Wang, N., Huang, Y., & Chen, W. (2008). A novel secure communication scheme in vehicular ad hoc networks. *Journal of Computer Communications, 31*(12), 2827–2837. doi:10.1016/j.comcom.2007.12.003

Wu, B., Wu, J., Fernandez, E. B., Ilyas, M., & Magliveras, S. (2007). Secure and efficient key management in mobile ad hoc networks. *Journal of Network and Computer Applications, 30*(3), 937–954. doi:10.1016/j.jnca.2005.07.008

Yeun, C. Y., Han, K., Vo, D. L., & Kim, K. (2008). Secure authenticated group key agreement protocol in the MANET environment. *Journal of Information Security Technical Report, 13*(3), 158–164. doi:10.1016/j.istr.2008.10.002

Yi, S., & Kravets, R. (2003). MOCA: Mobile certificate authority for wireless ad hoc networks. *University of Illinois at Urbana-Champaign*. Retrieved May 26, 2011, from http://middleware.internet2.edu/pki03/presentations/06.pdf.

Zhang, Y., & Lee, W. (2000). Intrusion detection in wireless ad hoc networks. In Proceedings of the *6th ACM Annual International Conference on Mobile Computing and Networking (MOBICOM 2000)*. ACM Press.

Zhu, B., Bao, F., Deng, R. H., Kankanhalli, M. S., & Wang, G. (2005). Efficient and robust key management for large mobile ad hoc networks. *Journal of Computer Networks, 48*(4), 657–682. doi:10.1016/j.comnet.2004.11.023

## KET TERMS AND DEFINITIONS

**Authentication:** The verification of the identity of a party who generated some messages, and of the integrity of the messages. In computer networks, two types of authentication can be identified, namely, message authentication and node authentication.

**Certification Authority or a Certificate Authority (CA):** An entity that issues digital certificates.

**Digital Certificate:** Certifies the ownership of a public key by the named subject of the certificate.

**MANET:** A mobile ad hoc network (MANET) is defined as a collection of low-power wireless nodes forming a temporary network without the aid of any established infrastructure or centralized administration.

**MANSim:** An academic, research-level computer network simulator, which can be used to evaluate, analyze, and compare the performance of a number of flooding algorithms in ideal and realistic MANET environments. It is written in C++ programming language, and consists of four main modules: network, mobility, computational, and algorithm modules.

**Message Authentication:** A technique for verifying the integrity of a transmitted message.

**Node Authentication:** Enables a node to ensure the identity of the peer node it is communicating with.

**A Probability of Reception ($p_c$):** The probability of an authentication request packet being sent by a sender (source node) will be successfully delivered to the receiver (destination node).

**Secret Sharing:** Refers to method for distributing a secret amongst a group of participants, each of whom is allocated a share of the secret. The secret can be reconstructed only when a sufficient number of shares are combined together; individual shares are of no use on their own.

**Shamir's Secret Sharing:** An algorithm in cryptography. It is a form of secret sharing, where a secret is divided into parts, giving each participant its own unique part, where some of the parts or all of them are needed in order to reconstruct the secret.

**Success Ratio ($S_R$):** The ratio between the number of nodes that are successfully authenticated or certified access to the network resources ($c$) and the total number of nodes on the network ($n$). Thus, $S_R$ can be calculated as: $S_R = c/n$. $S_R$ also reflects the probability with which a new arriving node can be successfully authenticated and certified access to the network resources.

# Chapter 16
# A Hybrid Port–Knocking Technique for Host Authentication

**Ali H. Hadi**
*Philadelphia University, Jordan*

**Hussein Al-Bahadili**
*Petra University, Jordan*

## ABSTRACT

*This chapter presents the detail description of a Port-Knocking (PK) technique, which should avert all types of port attacks and meets all other network security requirements. The new technique utilizes four well-known concepts, these are: PK, cryptography, steganography, and mutual authentication; therefore, it is referred to as the Hybrid Port-Knocking (HPK) technique. It is implemented as two separate modules. One is installed and run on the server computer, either behind the network firewall or on the firewall itself, and the other one is installed and run on the client computer. The first module is referred to as the HPK server, while the second is the HPK client. In terms of data processing, the technique consists of five main processes; these are: request packetization and transmission, traffic monitoring and capturing, mutual authentication, request extraction and execution, and port closing. The HPK technique demonstrates immunity against two vital attacks, namely, the TCP replay and Denial-of-Service (DoS) attacks.*

## INTRODUCTION

The network security has become a primary concern on the Internet in order to provide protected communication between hosts/nodes in a hostile environment. In order to protect network resources, each service provider pose a number

DOI: 10.4018/978-1-4666-0191-8.ch016

of nontrivial challenges to security design and set its own policies for accessing resources on the network. These challenges make a case for building security solutions that achieve both broad protection and desirable network performance in terms of minimum data overhead and delay. It is so crucial to have computationally cheap and simple defense mechanisms that allow early protection against all types of attacks. In particular, it becomes very common and useful to have multiple progressively stronger layers of security, rather than attempting to have a single perfect security layer.

The Internet can be seen as a huge network of different nodes (computers or any microprocessor-based devices) connected together providing different services for a wide range of users. A node on the Internet can act as a host and/or client. It is classified as a host when it provides services to other nodes on the Internet, while it is classified as a client when it is a user to a service provided by a host on the Internet. The services on the Internet can be classified in different ways depending on the classification criterion. Based on who can access these services, services on the Internet are classified into public and private services. Public services are those services that can be accessed by all users on the Internet, while private services are those who can be accessed by authorized users only.

Any host connected to the Internet to provide private services needs to be secured against unauthorized intrusion and a number of network attacks. Example of these attacks may include: illegally access private resources, flood the network with redundant messages to deny other users from using the available network resources, impersonate some legal users, modify or re-direct exchanged messages, etc.

A first defense solution is implemented on the Internet represented by using the firewall (Rudis 2003). Firewalls are usually running on the network layer, so that it can only see IP addresses and its characteristics but not a user name and password, which can only be seen by the application layer. In addition, there are common attacks against which a firewall cannot protect. For example, firewalls do not protect against attempts to exploit bugs in application-level software. Such vulnerabilities occur because the Internet architecture assumes that services bound to a port should be accessible by any machine using the Internet protocols.

As a result a mechanism is required to open ports on a firewall to authorized users, and blocking all other traffic users (Krzywinski, 2003a). The best way to perform such a mechanism is to run port authentication service on firewalls, which validates the identity of remote users and modifies firewall rules according to per-user access policies. Such a mechanism was used in a number of applications, such as: block SSH guessers (Google Groups, 2006), Symantec security response, fast port scan detection (Jung et al 2004), exploration of modern network threats (Krivis, 2004), remote operating system detection (Fyodor, 1998), etc.

There are a number of techniques that have been developed by many researchers to create port authentication, such as: Port-Knocking (PK) technique, which will be referred to as Traditional PK (TPK) technique (Krzywinski, 2003b); PK with Single Packet Authentication (SPA) (Rash, 2006a; Rash, 2006b); a lightweight concealment protocol (Barham, et al., 2002; Murdoch & Lewis, 2005), etc.

The concept behind the PK-based techniques can be explained as follows: When a client requires accessing a certain service or performs a specific task on a server through the Internet (which we refer to as a request). For example, a network administrator requires to access a certain task on his network remotely or a client wish for accessing a music server, and that particular service or task is hidden behind an unknown or closed port, which is also hidden behind a firewall. At the same time an attacker is presented on the network.

In PK-based techniques, in order to gain access to the network resources and pass the firewall and access a server behind the firewall, the client sends a sequence of TCP SYN packets, which are called "knocks," to closed-ports, each of them has a different destination port number. In other work, the client sends a specified and agreed on ports sequence through a number of A TCP SYN packets to the server to gain access to the network resources. The number of SYN packets sent by the client is equal to the number of ports in the ports sequence. For example, for a port sequence of four ports: 1111, 2222, 3333, 4444, the client sends four SYN packets each one is sent with one of the ports as a destination port.

Investigations on the performance of current port authentication techniques in avoiding all possible types of port attacks have demonstrated that most of these techniques suffer from either one or more of the following issues: zero-day (0-day) attacks, sequence replay attacks, minimal data transmission rate, knock sequences and port scans, knock sequence busting with spoofed packets, failure if a client is behind a NATed network, failure if packets are received/delivered in out of order, a lack of association between authentication and connections being opened, flaws in how cryptography is applied to provide authentication, and data extraction from eavesdropped packets. Therefore, with increasing expansion of the Internet and the continuously increasing services that can be accessed through the Internet, and to maintain high network security, it is so vital to develop a PK technique for host authentication that should avert all types of port attacks and meet all other network security requirements.

In this chapter, we present the detail description of a new PK technique for host (user) authentication that can avert all types of port attacks and meets all other network security requirements. The new technique utilizes four well-known concepts, these are: PK, cryptography, steganography, and mutual authentication, therefore, it is referred to as the Hybrid Port-Knocking (HPK) technique. It also discusses the implementation of the HPK technique using Python and Scapy programming language on an Ubuntu GNU/Linux operating system. A number of simulations were performed to evaluate and compare the performance of the HPK technique against the performance of two current port authentication techniques, namely, the TPK and SPA techniques. Finally, based on the result obtained, a number of conclusions are drawn and recommendations for future work are pointed-out.

## PREVIOUS WORK

In this section, the most valuable researches related to PK are described in details and also identified the problems associated with each of them.

P. Barham et al (2002) proposed an approach to use multiple progressively stronger layers of security for hosts connecting to the Internet. This multi-layered approach allows early discard of packets associated with attacks. This reduces server vulnerability to computational Denial-of-Service (DoS) attacks via heavyweight cryptography calculations. They presented three techniques that allow TCP/IP services to be concealed from non-authorized users of said services, while still allowing access to the services for authorized users.

D. J. Bernstein (2002) proposed an approached based on using TCP SYN cookies. TCP SYN cookies are a well-known and effective technique for mitigating the effects of SYN-flood attacks on servers. The creation of the TCP control block is delayed until the 3-way handshake is complete; instead, the server returns an acknowledgment (ACK) with an initial sequence number which is a cryptographic hash of the incoming information in the SYN packet, plus a secret and a counter that changes every minute. SYN cookies were devised for the case of public servers where a shared secret between clients and server is neither feasible nor desirable, and concealment of the service's existence is explicitly not a goal. SYN cookies also provide no protection against more sophisticated attacks where the attacking machines set up TCP connections rather than simply ending SYNs. The approach is intended for cases where clients of the service are authorized in advance. The techniques not only defend against arbitrarily sophisticated DoS attacks by low-cost filtering most unauthorized traffic before it reaches the service itself, but also help conceal the existence of the service to port scanners and the like.

In Keromytis et al (2002), a Secure Overlay Services (SOS) were proposed by A. D. Keromytis as a method of securing IP communication against

DoS attacks. The assumptions of SOS are: a pre-determined (and pre-authorized) set of clients who should be allowed to access a service, and attackers with considerable resources but without prior knowledge of the location of the service. The SOS technique works by having the service only accept connections from a small number of authorized nodes, which participate in a much larger (several thousand node) overlay network. A client makes a connection to some overlay node, which then routes the connection to one of the authorized nodes over log(N) unpredictable hops in the overlay, where N is the total number of nodes. Much of the SOS work is concerned with how the system performs in the presence of some fraction of compromised overlay nodes.

Later on, work by P. Barham et al (2002) proposed three types of solutions with three different protocols, namely, Spread-Spectrum TCP (SSTCP), Option Keyed TCP (OKTCP), and Tail-Gate TCP (TGTCP). They observed that SSTCP, OKTCP and TGTCP all solve the same problem without the need to deploy a thousand-node overlay network, and without incurring the overhead of multi-hop overlay routing. However, they realized that one conceivable advantage of SOS over their techniques is that since SOS is filter-based, the filters can be pushed out from the server to an unmodified router at the other end of the access link, making it less practical to attack the system by simply saturating the link with traffic.

M. Doyle (2004) showed that the software tool *knockd* needs to be modified to support a number of different firewalls. *knockd* is only capable of modifying firewalls implemented with the *ipfilter* software package. It does this via the function *modify_ipfilter_firewall()*. It would not be difficult to implement functions that could modify firewalls based on other software packages, and allow the user to specify which function *knockd* should use.

The software tools *knockc* and *knockd* do not distinguish between the client IP address extracted

from the log entries and the IP address decrypted from the port knock sequence. *knockc* is designed in such a way that it allows the user to specify which IP address *knockd* will be granting access to. Thus, an authenticated user can grant access to whomever they choose. There are a number of reasons for and against this capability, and so *knockd* will eventually allow the administrator to specify whether or not this behavior will be allowed.

M. Doyle also proposed three areas of research for better network security, these are: Expansion of what the server can do when evaluating a knock sequence; solving the problem of log file pollution; and developing better authentication techniques.

D. Worth (2004) induced appropriate one-time-knocks to be generated by using a Web browser, if the Domain Name Spacing (DNS) server for a given domain is the target for knocks. For example, if the DNS server for www.foo.org, on which a restricted service is wanted to run, then COKd may run to point the browser to [OTP].foo.org. Using such approach, the DNS server will fail to resolve [OTP].foo.org, but COKd will act appropriately by processing the DNS query. Out-of-Bound (OOB) knocks using OOB protocol, such as Short-Message-Session (SMS), to transport knocks is perfectly reasonable and raises the ante for a man-in-the middle. To execute a man-in-the-middle attack against SMS one must recognize that knocking is occurring via the SMS network, and compromise it. This is not necessarily more difficult that compromising a router in the TCP/UDP context, it just requires more information.

R. deGraaf et al (2005) presented a novel PK architecture that provides strong authentication while addressing the weaknesses of existing PK systems. The conclusions of this research were that existing PK systems have three main flaws: they do not always work reliably in the presence of Network Address Translation (NAT) boxes; they fail if packets are delivered out of order, and they do not associate authentication exchanges with connections opened afterwards.

D. Isabel (2005) suggested implementing PK with authentication to resistant to replay attack and he also concluded that even with robust authentication, PK still needs some work before it is ready for the enterprise market.

M. Rash (2006a) proposed a Single Packet Authorization (SPA) technique, which combines a default-drop packet filter with a passively monitoring packet sniffer in a manner similar to port-knocking implementations. However, instead of transferring authentication data within packet header fields, SPA leverages payload data to prove possession of authentication credentials. Despite the security benefits that SPA offers for reducing the exposure of a service to potential attackers, it also has three main limitations; these are: Access piggybacking via NAT addresses; SPA server exposure; and Bogus replayed packets.

E. Y. Vasserman et al (2007) introduced a formal security model for PK that addresses issues, such as: how PK prevent attackers from discovering and exploiting potentially vulnerable services on a network host, while allowing authenticated users to access these services. They also described the design and analysis of SILENTKNOCK, an implementation of their protocol for the Linux 2.6 operating system that is provably secure, under the assumption that AES and a modified version of MD4 are pseudorandom functions, and integrates seamlessly with any existing application, with no need to recompile. Experiments indicated that the overhead due to running SILENTKNOCK on a server is minimal – on the order of 150 μsec per TCP connection initiation.

M. Marlinspike (2009) implemented a code that suppose to offer a possible solution to minimizing exposure, namely, *knockknock*. *knockknock* implementation code is very simple, and is written in Python language. While *knockknock*-daemon needs root privileges to adjust *iptables* rules, it employs privilege separation to isolate the code that actually runs as root to ~15 lines. So even though the entire code base is very small and very simple, the only part of the code actually running

with root privileges is even smaller and even simpler. When you run *knockknock*-daemon, it will fork out the privileged code and drop privileges everywhere else before processing knockknock requests. The communication protocol is a simple request encrypted using the Advanced Encryption Standard (AES) in Counter (CTR) mode, with an HMAC-SHA1 using the authenticate-then-encrypt paradigm. It protects against eavesdropping, replay attacks, and all known forms of cryptanalysis against IND-CCA secure schemes.

## THE HYBRID PORT-KNOCKING (HPK) TECHNIQUE

This section presents a detail description of the proposed HPK technique to be used as another front security layer next to the network firewall or may be on the network firewall. The proposed technique utilizes four well-known concepts, these are: PK, cryptography, steganography, and mutual authentication, therefore, it is referred to as the Hybrid Port-Knocking (HPK) technique. The HPK technique can be used for host authentication to make local services invisible from port scanning, provide an extra layer of security that attackers must penetrate before accessing or breaking anything important, act as a stop-gap security measure for services with known unpatched vulnerabilities, and provide a wrapper for a legacy or proprietary services with insufficient integrated security. Figure 1 shows the HPK network architecture.

### The Architectural Design of the HPK Technique

The HPK technique consists of two modules (Figure 2), each module consists of a number of software components (processes). These two main modules are:

1. The HPK server module. It is installed and run on a server computer or may be on the

*Figure 1. The network architecture*

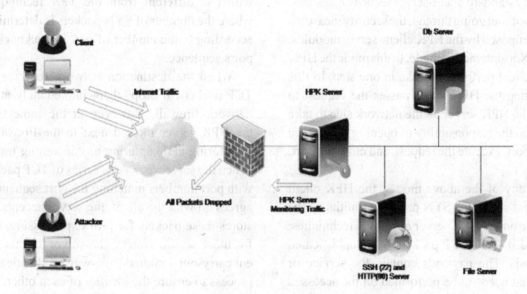

*Figure 2. A block diagram showing the architectural design of the HPK technique*

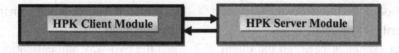

network firewall; therefore, it is referred to as the HPK server module or simply HPK server. The HPK server performs the following processes: traffic monitoring, traffic capturing, manage mutual authentication between the server itself and the client, TCP packets processing (i.e., TCP packets extraction, request re-assembling and decryption), execute request, and port opening/closing.

2. The HPK client module. It is installed and run on the client computer; therefore, it is referred to the HPK client. The HPK client is any node on the Internet requires accessing some resources on a network connected to the Internet and protected by a firewall and any service to be accessed needs special authorization. It performs the following processes: request initialization, request encryption, request hiding, packets craft-

ing, sending packets, and respond to mutual authentication instructions.

## Operation of the HPK Technique

The HPK technique is designed to work in two different modes without pre-adjustment or setting, we refer to these two modes as:

1. Interactive mode. In this mode the client performs its tasks in three steps, which are: communicate with HPK server to open port and gain access, execute the request interactively, and finally close the port. The first and the third steps performed by the HPK client module, while the second step performs by the requesting process at the client side on the target server on the network, and in this case the communication process comforted

by standard client-server security measures, without going through the security measures imposed by the HPK client-server modules.

2. Non-interactive mode. In this mode the HPK client performs it tasks in one step. In this step the HPK client passes the request to the HPK server on the network side to take on the responsibility of opening the service port, execute the request, and close the port.

In any of the above modes, the HPK client does not send TCP SYN packets to initialize the service on the HPK server as in TPK techniques; instead it sends TCP packets with sophisticated payloads. The payloads contain the service or task that needs to be performed on the accessed network or any of its servers. In the interactive mode, the payloads include a request for open port, specific request, or close port; while in the non-interactive mode; the payloads include the specific request only.

To secure data exchange between the client and server, the client performs the following tasks in order:

1. Initialize the request, which opens or closes port for the interactive mode and the actual request for the non-interactive mode.
2. Encrypt the request using the public key of the server.
3. Hide the encrypted request in an image file (e.g., PNG image file) using steganography.
4. Send the resulting image file in a number of TCP packets.

Thus, the TCP packets carry with them an encrypted and hidden request to the HPK server. The number of TCP packets ($P$), which are required to exchange the image file between the client and the server is determined by dividing the size of the image file ($S_{img}$) by the size of TCP packet ($S_{pac}$), i.e., ($P=S_{img}/S_{pac}$). Consequently, the number of ports in the knocking ports sequence is set equal to the number of required TCP SYN packets,

which is different from the TPK techniques, where the number of SYN packets is determined according to the number of port in the knocking ports sequence.

When the destination network receives the TCP packets, it drops them immediately at the network firewall. However, at the same time, the HPK server located next to the firewall is monitoring and capturing any incoming traffic. When the server receives a series of TCP packets with port numbers matching the port sequence it agrees on with the client, the server accepts and stores these packets for further processing. But, for more secure system, the server and the client carry-out a mutual (two-way) authentication process to ensure the identity of each other. The mutual authentication mechanism used in the HPK technique is considered as one other improvement over other PK techniques. Details of the two-way authentication process between the server and the client is given later.

If the two-way authentication process is successful and the server confirms the identity of the client, the server performs the following tasks in order:

1. Extract the payload of each TCP packets and re-assembles the image file.
2. Extract the hidden request from the image.
3. Decrypt the encrypted request using its private key.
4. Execute the request. In an interactive mode, it asks the firewall to open the requested port for the client IP, and wait for port closing. Otherwise, it closes port automatically after a pre-specified silent period. In a non-interactive mode, it takes on the responsibility to open the service port, execute the request, and close the port without any intervention from the client side.

For the sake of higher system security, if the client's request includes port opening to access some resources on the network local servers, the port should be closed safely. In fact, to ensure safe port closing, the HPK server closes the port due any of the following actions:

1.  Receive a port closing request from the HPK client. In this case, the client sends a request for port closing in the same way it sends a request for port opening, i.e., the client initializes, encrypts the request using the server public key, hides, splits the resultant image into *P* packets, sends the *P* packets each with one of pre-agreed on port sequence between the server and client. Then, when the server realizes the ports sequence matches the one it agrees on with the client for port closing, it carries on with the mutual authentication process. If the authentication passes is successful, the server performs locally the same steps for port-opening (extract payloads, extract request from the received image, decrypt the request using its own private key, and then execute the request, i.e., close the port).
2.  Automatically close the port after a specified silent period.

All TCP packets sent and received whether from the server or the client are crafted in certain ways to suite the techniques needs. Figure 3 outlines the main phases of the HPK technique for port opening or port closing.

## The Main Features of the HPK Technique

The HPK technique is developed to be used as an extra security layer in front of network services that need to be accessed securely from different locations on the Internet. It uses a new methodology that can communicate in an unseen or hidden manner, making TCP replay attacks hard to be issued against the new technique, and data extraction from eavesdropped packets useless. The implementation is also designed to listen to

no ports, or bind itself to no socket for packets exchange, so that it won't be exposed itself to a remote exploit, Denial of Service (DoS) attack, and completely hidden from port scanning regardless of the port-scanning technique used.

The proposed technique can be used to open TCP or UDP ports on a network firewall to authorized users, and block all other traffic. It can also be used to execute a task remotely, without the need to login to the remote server to do it. The technique for sure can also close the open ports that have been opened by a previous client request. This means that HPK can not only open and close ports, but even execute remote administration tasks, while all other PK techniques can just open/close ports.

The server is running as a host authentication service on the network firewall, which validates the identity of remote users and modifies firewall rules (plus other tasks) according to a mutual authentication process done between the HPK server and client.

## Processes of the HPK Technique

Based on the above discussion, we structured the HPK technique into five main processes; these are:

1.  Request packetization and transmission
2.  Traffic monitoring, sniffing, and capturing
3.  Mutual authentication
4.  Request extraction and execution
5.  Port closing

In this section a detail description for each of the above processes and where it is installed and run are presented. Figure 4 shows the HPK two modules and the main components or processes running on each of them.

*Request packetization and transmission.* This process is completely running on the HPK client. In this process, the client initializes, encrypts, hides, segments, packetizes, and transmits the request over the Internet to a particular network

*Figure 3. The HPK technique*

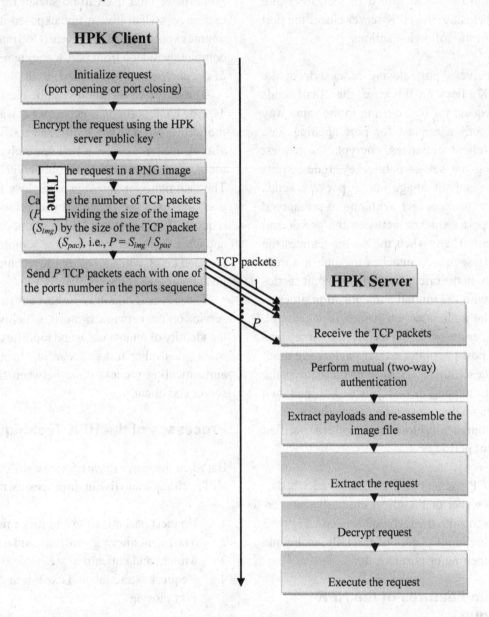

on which an HPK server is installed and running. The encryption of the request is carried out using asymmetric encryption algorithm, namely, the public key of the server. Then, the encrypted request is hidden in a PNG image file. Next, in this process, the client calculates $P$. Each packet is sent with one of the ports on the pre-agreed on port sequence between the server and client as its destination port to perform the knocking process.

Furthermore, for each TCP packets the SYN flag is set on so that these TCP packets will not be dropped by intermediate routers between the client and server. Finally, the TCP packets are sent on to the server on pre-defined ports sequence (ports agreed on between the server and the client) to perform the knocking phase.

*Traffic monitoring, sniffing, and capturing.* This process is installed and run on the HPK

*Figure 4. Main processes of the HPK technique*

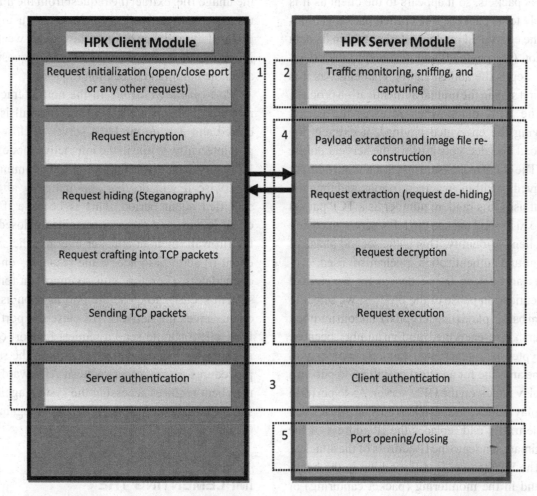

server. In which the server monitors all TCP packets arriving at the network firewall. Although all unauthorized TCP SYN packets or TCP packets with SYN flag set on/off are immediately dropped by the firewall, at the same time the server is designed to monitor the arriving packets and sniff those with pre-specified ports numbers and capture them. Traffic capturing means that the server captures the traffic that is destined to the pre-specified ports sequence, and the packets should have the SYN flag set.

This is the first packet checking process performed by the HPK server on the newly arrived packets. After the server checks and approves the ports sequence on the received $P$ packets, and the

SYN flag is set on all these $P$ packets, further processing will be done on the packet's payload as we shall explain next. In this case, only traffic that arrives from the HPK client is captured for further processing, while the traffic that arrives from an attacker is neglected.

*Mutual authentication.* After the HPK server makes sure that the payload is carrying an intended request, which have some specific format, it needs to make sure that it is communicating with a legitimate client. In order to do so we use the following procedure: The server selects a random number, encrypts it using the client public key and crafts a TCP packet using the information (source IP, TCP sequence number) received within the clients packets, so it appears to the client as it is a reply to its packets. The crafted packet is holding the encrypted random number within its data section (the payload) and destined to the client. This step is the authentication challenge, as it is the first step in the mutual authentication process.

The HPK client when receives the packet carrying the encrypted payload, it extracts the payload and decrypts it using the servers public key. The client makes sure that the random number received is within an agreed format, and then the client uses this random number as a TCP packet payload to send back to the HPK server to ensure its (client's) identity. This is the second phase of the mutual authentication mechanism used.

It can be seen in our design for the mutual authentication phase of the process; we select to return back a plain (unencrypted) random number, rather than re-encrypted random number, because encrypted or unencrypted random number will not be an issue for an attacker willing to perform a replay attack on the HPK server. As to perform a replay attack, the attacker only needs a copy of the traffic and replaces the IP address of the legitimate sender to the IP address of the attacker.

The HPK server is still working in the background in the monitoring (packet capturing) or sniffing state and receives a reply from the client. A check on the reply is done here, to make sure the packet payload holds the same random number that the server previously sent to the client as the challenge. The server extracts the payload and checks if the received message/payload holds the same number that was sent to the client. If the message is identified then this makes sure that the mutual authentication phases have passed successfully and the server moves to the execution phase. Otherwise, if the result of the request extraction reveals non-valid authentication parameters, the server blocks the IP address of the client that sent the knocks and the payload (image).

*Request extraction and execution.* The HPK server now goes back to TCP packets received from the HPK client, extract the payloads, re-construct the image file, extract the request from the image using steganography, decrypt the request using its private key, and then execute the request weather it's an open/close port on the firewall request, or a remote command execution request.

*Port opening/closing.* In the non-interactive mode no port open/close on the firewall is required and it is up the HPK server to close the port internally. While in the interactive mode, the HPK server will wait for port closing command, otherwise it will do that automatically after a specified silent period. This is because if the client leaves, and the port remains unclosed on the firewall, then an attacker may use the same client IP address to access the resources on the opened port. Therefore, it is so important for the system security to close the port as soon as the client leaves the network. To close the port the HPK client should send a request for port closing and this request will go exactly in the same procedures as any other request. Afterwards, if the client requires accessing the system again, it should initiate the whole HPK process again for the new request.

## IMPLEMENTING THE HPK TECHNIQUE

### The HPKTool

The HPK technique is implemented in a software tool called HPKTool using Python programming language (Python Programming Language, 2010) and Scapy (Scapy, 2010) on a Fedora GNU/Linux operating system (2010). The HPK technique requires a mechanism for crafting packets to meet the security and performance requirement. This mechanism is implemented using Scapy, which is a very useful tool for packet inspection, mangling, encapsulation, and complex packet crafting. Scapy gives the new technique the programming ability for complex packet crafting and inspection.

The HPK Tool is implemented as the technique architecturally designed in two modules, namely, the HPKServerModule and the HPKClientModule as shown in Figure 5. Figures 6 and 7 outline each of these two modules.

The HPKServerModule is installed and run on the server side of the network or may be on the network firewall. The HPKServerModule performs the following processes: traffic monitoring, traffic capturing, manage mutual authentication between the server itself and the client, TCP packets processing (i.e., TCP packets extraction, request re-assembling and decryption), execute request, and port opening/closing.

The HPKClientModule is installed and run on the client computer. The HPK client is any node on the Internet requires accessing some resources on a network connected to the Internet and protected by a firewall and any service to be accessed needs special authorization. It performs the following processes: request initialization, request encryption, request hiding, packets crafting, sending packets, and respond to mutual authentication instructions.

The implementation of the three concepts of cryptography, steganography, and mutual authentication is described below.

*Cryptography (GnuPG).* The main reason for using an asymmetric cipher in the HPK technique is not due to their high security only, but due to their strong key exchange capabilities. Key tampering is a major security weakness with public-key cryptography so the keys must be exchanged carefully using different media or using central

digital signature to make sure of the integrity of the keys (Jakobsson et al 2004).

The HPK server's GnuPG public key is used and exchanged with each legitimate client and each client in return exchanges its GnuPG public key with the HPK server too. The keys are used to encrypt the clients request, the mutual authentication security challenge sent by the HPK server to the client, and to decrypt the server's challenge by the client. GnuPG itself is a command-line tool without any graphical interface stuff. It is the real crypto engine which can be used directly from a command prompt, from shell scripts or by other programs, that why we use GnuPG in the HPK technique implementation, as it can be called directly from Python application.

*Steganography.* An embedded open source Python implementation of steganography called steganogra-py (2010) has been used in the HPK technique. The client uses steganogra-py to add its encrypted administration request to the PNG image file sent as the knocking TCP/IP packet payload. Each pixel in the image was based on a 24-bit color scheme. The implementation of steganogra-py in the HPK technique considered 3 bits from each pixel to be adjusted, 1 bit from red, 1 bit from green, and 1 bit from blue. This adjustment holds the clients request which is totally unlike to be noticed.

The Portable Network Graphics (PNG) is a bitmapped image format that employs lossless data compression (Miano, 1999). PNG was created to improve upon and replace Graphics Interchange Format (GIF) as an image-file format not requir-

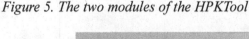
*Figure 5. The two modules of the HPKTool*

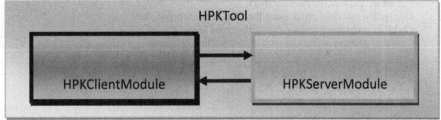

*Figure 6. The algorithm for the HPKServerModule of HPKTool*

```
{
    // Monitoring and capturing
        Do
                Sniff all arrived packets
                Capture TCP packets that are destined for a port number on the list of the predefined
                        ports sequence.
        Loop Until the ports sequence of received TCP packets matches the ports sequence agreed on
                        between the client and the server.
    // Mutual Authentication
            Generate a random number
            Encrypt the random number using the client GnuPG public key
            Craft a TCP packet and send it to the client using the information on the received TCP packet
                    (source IP address and packet sequence number)
            Wait for a reply from the client, the reply should include the same random number as a
                    payload.
            If (received random number ≠ transmitted random number) Then
                Terminate
            End If
    // Extract and execute the request
            Extract the payload from the P received packets and reconstruct the image file
            Extract the request from the image file
            Decrypt the request using the server GnuPG private key.
            If ("request" = "open port") Then
                Open port
                        Ask the firewall to open the required port for that particular IP address
            End If
            If ("request" = "close port") Then
                Close port
            End If
            If ("request" = "access a certain service") Then
                Open the port assigned for that particular service
                Execute the service
                Close port
            End If
}
```

*Figure 7. The algorithm for the HPKClientModule of HPKTool*

```
{
    // Request packetization and transmission
            Initialize request
            Encrypt request using the GnuPG public key of the HPK server
            Hide the encrypted request into a PNG image file
            Calculate the number of transmitted TCP packets (P) by dividing the size of the image file
                    (S_img) by the size of the load on each TCP packet (S_pac).
            Assign one of the ports on ports sequence for each TCP packet as a destination port
            Send the P TCP packets in order
    // Mutual Authentication
            Receive the authentication TCP packet
            Extract the payload (random number)
            Decrypt the random number using the GnuPG client private key
            Check its consistency and validity with agreed format
            Craft the random number and send it back to the HPK server
}
```

ing a patent license. PNG supports palette-based (palettes of 24-bit RGB or 32-bit RGBA colors), greyscale, greyscale with alpha, RGB, or RGBA images. PNG was designed for transferring images on the Internet, not for print graphics. PNG files nearly always use file extension "PNG" or "png," it was approved for this use by the Internet Engineering Steering Group (IESG).

*Mutual authentication or two-way authentication.* The HPK technique uses mutual authentication, so a connection can occur only when the server-client trusts each other. The HPKServer-Module generates a random number using the Linux/dev/random device, encrypts it using the client GnuPG public key and crafts a TCP packet using the information (source IP, TCP sequence number) received within the client TCP packets, so it appears to the HPKClientModule as it is a reply to its TCP packets. The crafted packet will hold the encrypted random number within its data section (payload) and destined to the HPK client. This is the first step in the authentication process.

When the HPK client receives the packet carrying the encrypted payload, it extracts the payload and decrypts it using its GnuPG private key. The HPK client makes sure that the random number received is within an agreed format, and then the client uses this random number as a TCP packet payload to send back to the HPK server to ensure its (client's) identity. This is the second phase of the mutual authentication mechanism used.

## Characteristics of the HPKTool

The main characteristics of HPKTool are:

- The modules codes are very simple and they are written completely using Python and Scapy.
- The modules codes are concise enough to be easily audited.
- The system does not listen on any TCP/UDP port, which means no sockets is used,

leaving port scanners or any other scanner useless in the attempt to detect the PK system running behind the scene.

- The system uses Scapy's capabilities to sniff the incoming traffic and the uses packet crafting techniques to reply back to a legitimate client only.
- The communication protocol is a simple secure encryption scheme that uses GnuPG keys with steganography constructions. An observer watching packets is not given any indication that the TCP packets transmitted by the system is a PK request, but even if they knew, there would be no way for them to determine which port was requested to open, or what task is requested to be done as all of that is first encrypted using GnuPG keys, and then hidden into an image (e.g., PNG image file) using steganography.
- An observer replaying the knock request later does them no good, and in fact does not provide any information that might be useful in determining the contents of future request. The mechanism works using a single packet for the mutual authentication or two-way authentication.

On the other hand, the HPK technique has some drawbacks. The main drawbacks are:

- The technique needs root privileges to adjust *iptables* rules, and perform remote tasks.
- Scapy cannot be used or run within an application without root privileges in order to construct, inspect, and evaluate the packets at a low level.
- The technique is currently implemented to run on a GNU/Linux operating system with netfilter (*iptables*) firewall capabilities only.

## PERFORMANCE MEASURES

In order to evaluate the performance of the PK techniques, it is so important to define efficient, reliable, unbiased, and practical measures that can be used in the evaluation process. One important measure that is critical for PK techniques is their resistance to different types of possible attacks that are usually carries by hackers. Examples of such attacks include: TCP replay attack, port scanning, knock sequences order check, data transmission rate and system load, busted spoofed knock packets, data extraction from eavesdropped packets, and exploiting the PK server.

The performance of the HPK technique is investigated and compared in two aspects, these are: the immunity of the techniques against certain types of attacks (replay attacks and DoS attacks) and complexity. The complexity of the HPK technique is evaluated by measuring the average authentication time $(T_a)$, which is defined as the time required for performing a successful port authentication in normal network operation condition.

The amount of data exchanged in each HPK session is equal to the size of the PNG image file plus the size of two TCP packets with payload equal to the size of the random number. However, because PK is not a continuous process, and clients only try to gain one access per session, the overall data overhead and delay will not be significant compared to the positive effect the implemented technique may have on the network security level.

## TESTING PLATFORM AND TOOLS

### Testing Platform

In order to simulate and evaluate the performance of the HPK technique and compare its performance against other PK techniques, it is so vital to develop an adequate and professional test platform. In this work, we develop a test platform that consists of three boxes; these are: ClientBox, ServerBox,

and AttackBox. They are all written with Ubuntu 10.04 (Lucid) operating system running in a Virtual Environment implemented using a GNU/Linux CentOS 5.4 64bit operating system and VMware Server v2.0.2 Build 203138. All boxes are using the bridged networking mode, so they all appear on the Internet as real devices, because each box has a unique IP address assigned to it so that it can be accessed across the network.

The description and role of each box in the simulation environment can be described as follows:

*ServerBox.* The role of this box is to simulate the server module of the PK technique. In this box, three PK servers, namely, TPK, SPK, and HPK servers, which will be tested in this work, are implemented. In order to access this box across the network, an IP address of 10.0.0.201 is assigned to it, and it is assumed to have a firewall with a default drop filtering policy installed on it. The HPKServerModule is implemented as a choice in the ServerBox with server modules of other techniques.

*ClientBox.* The role of this box is to simulate the client module of the PK technique. In this box, the client initializes its requests. For example, the client can initialize a request to access an SSH server on ServerBox. In order to access this box across the network, an IP address of 10.0.0.202 is assigned to it, and it is assumed to have a firewall with a default drop filtering policy installed on it. The HPKClientModule is implemented as a choice in the ClientBox with client modules of other techniques.

*AttackBox.* The role of this box is to simulate an observer (attacker) who will perform the attack. In this box, two types of attacks are implemented, these are: (1) the TCP replay attack, and (2) the DoS attack. In order to access this box across the network, an IP address of 10.0.0.203 is assigned to it, and it is assumed to have a firewall with a default drop filtering policy installed on it. A schematic shown how these boxes are interrelated is given in Figure 8.

*Figure 8. Schematic of the testing platform*

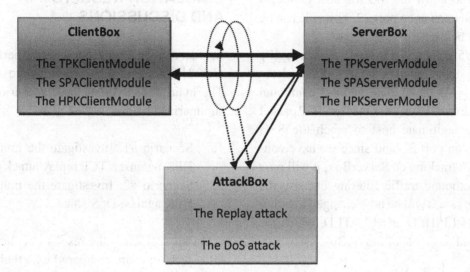

## Configuring the ServerBox

In order to start running the tests or simulations, the firewall rules set on ServerBox have to be configured to meet the requirements of the testing environments. The rules can be summarized as following:

1.  Rule #1: *iptables* -P INPUT DROP. The *iptables* command is used to enable the default policy (-P) for all inbound (INPUT) packets to be dropped (DROP), without giving any notification back to the host trying to interact with ServerBox. Furthermore, this means that any traffic trying to interact with ServerBox from any destination shall be dropped, except the packets that are allowed to pass through by predefined rules in the firewall's INPUT table.
2.  Rule #2: *iptables* -P FORWARD DROP. The *iptables* command is used to enable the default policy (-P) for all forwarding (FORWARD) packets to be dropped (DROP). This means that no routing is allowed to be done on ServerBox, except the packets that are allowed to pass through by

predefined rules in the firewall's FORWARD table.

3.  Rule #3: *iptables* -P OUTPUT DROP. This *iptables* command is used to enable the default policy (-P) for all outbound (OUTPUT) packets to be dropped (DROP). This means that any traffic going out of ServerBox to any destination shall be dropped, except the packets that are allowed to pass through by predefined rules in the firewall's OUTPUT table.
4.  Rule #4: *iptables* -A OUTPUT -m state --state ESTABLISHED, RELATED -j ACCEPT. The *iptables* command is used to enable connection tracking on the firewall for outbound traffic. All PK techniques that can be performed will be adjusting the GNU/Linux netfilter (*iptables*) firewall to open port 22. So we need netfilter (*iptables*) to make use of its checking capabilities to check the connection's information (states) of the packets trying to go out of ServerBox (outbound traffic). If the packet has an ESTABLISHED or RELATED state it shall be allowed to go out of ServerBox, else it will be dropped. When a successful knocking attempt is done on ServerBox, the PK server will execute

a rule to allow the specific host to access the SSH server on port 22. This rule can be found below.

5. Rule #5: *iptables* -A INPUT -s {Source_IP} -p tcp -m state --state NEW --dport {dest_port} -j ACCEPT. The *iptables* command when executed enables the first TCP packet of the legitimate host to reach the SSH server on port 22, and since we have connection tracking on ServerBox, it will pass the outbound traffic filtering because the packets state will be now changed to either ESTABLISHED or RELATED, which are allowed to go out of ServerBox.

## Testing Tools

In this work, a number of standard tools are used to perform network traffic monitoring, traffic capturing, and attacks. These standard tools include:

1. *Wireshark* tool. This tool is used for network protocol analysis (Wireshark, 2010).
2. *tcpwrite* tool. This tool is used for .pcap files editing and rewrite the TCP/IP and layer two packet headers [Web 8]. It is also used to change the IP addresses of the source and destination hosts.
3. *tcpreplay* tool. This tool is used for replaying captured network traffic (Tcpreplay, 2010), i.e., it is used to replay the edited .pcap files on the network.
4. *nmap* tool. This tool is used for network exploration and port scanning (Nmap, 2010), i.e., it is used to perform a port scan on the PK server.
5. *tcptrack* tool. This tool is used for sniffing and displaying information about TCP connections seen on a network interface (Tcpreplay, 2010), i.e., it is used to display information about source and destination addresses and ports, connection state, idle time, and bandwidth usage of TCP/IP connections.

## SIMULATION RESULTS AND DISCUSSIONS

In order to evaluate and compare the performance of the HPK technique, two scenarios are simulated. The main objectives of these scenarios can be summarized below:

1. Scenario #1: Investigate the immunity of HPK against a TCP replay attack
2. Scenario #2: Investigate the immunity of HPK against DoS attack.

In all scenarios, the results obtained for the HPK technique are compared with their equivalent results obtained for other two PK techniques, namely, the TPK and the SPA techniques. More scenarios and details of how to perform these scenarios can be found in (Al-Shemery, 2010).

## Scenario #1: TCP Replay Attack

In this scenario, we shall attempt to monitor or sniff the packets passing through the network in order to capture the packets that are performing the knocks that ClientBox is sending to ServerBox to access the SSH Server on port 22 on the ServerBox itself. The attacker on AttackBox run *Wireshark* to capture all network traffic on the line, and shall filter the output to only get packets that are from the source host (ClientBox) destined to the destination host (ServerBox) which is running the PK technique being tested.

Running *Wireshark* on a heavy traffic network captured a huge amount of traffic that makes it is very difficult to store and handle later on, so it is so important to filter out all unwanted traffic. To do so a *Wireshark* filter is used to filter out all unwanted traffic and save only the packets required to perform a TCP replay attack. In real world scenario the attacker has to capture packets and analyze them in order to figure out the knocking sequences and the exact packets used for each specific technique to perform the knock. The time that it will take to analyze these captured packets shall vary from network to another, and depends on the amount of noise being captured too.

All of the above activities are performed for the three PK techniques we are investigating. After investigating each case, the firewall rules on ServerBox needs to be reset to continue with the investigation of the case after. This means delete all rules and reinstall all the rules explained above. The results obtained for performing TCP replay attacks against the TPK, SPA, and HPK techniques are summarized in Table 1.

The TPK technique is found to be vulnerable to TCP replay attacks because the technique only uses TCP SYN packets destined to specific ports in order to request the ServerBox to open the port 22 for the ClientBox. The attacker on AttackBox only needs to capture the traffic, filter it, and then analyze it. After that it shall be clear to it that these certain knocks are performing some action on the destined firewall. All it needs is replay the whole process in order for the attacker to get the firewall open the port for its box.

The SPA technique is also found to be resisted to TCP replay attacks because the technique uses a single UDP packet with encrypted payloads by using GnuPG keys. Even if the attacker on AttackBox is able to distinguish the packet used to perform the knock, it will not be able to reply the packet because of its encrypted payload. The attacker needs to be able to get or crack the public/private key of both the ServerBox and the ClientBox, which is a very hard and time costly task to do.

The HPK technique is also resisting to TCP replay attacks because the technique uses two strategies for communication or performing the knocks. First it uses the GnuPG public/private keys encryption process. Second it uses mutual or two-way authentication. The attacker needs to be able to import the GnuPG public/private keys used by both the ServerBox and ClientBox. Then it needs to be able to crack the challenge packet sent from the ServerBox to the ClientBox for the mutual authentication process. Both tasks take huge time to be accomplished.

## Scenario #2: DoS Attack

In this scenario, three .pcap files are used on the AttackBox one for each PK technique to perform DoS attack. In particular, a type of DoS attack known as a SYN flood, which involves sending large numbers of SYN packets and ignoring the return, thereby forcing the server to keep track of a large number of half-open connections. Therefore, we only need to work on the AttackBox to perform the attacks, and on ServerBox monitoring the response of each attack against each technique. After investigating each technique, the firewall rules on ServerBox needs to be reset to continue with the investigation of another technique. This means delete all rules and reinstall all the rules explained above. Table 2 compares the results for performing DoS attacks against the three PK techniques investigated in this thesis.

When investigating the TPK technique, it can be found that it is vulnerable to DoS attack, be-

*Table 1. Comparing the immunity of the TPK, SPA, and HPK techniques against a TCP replay attack*

| Techniques | TCP replay attack | Explanation |
|---|---|---|
| TPK | Vulnerable | Uses TCP SYN packets for knocks. |
| SPA | Immune | Uses a single UDP packet with an encrypted payload for the knock. |
| HPK | Immune | Client sends TCP SYN packets and the Server responds with a challenge. The challenge is an encrypted (using GnuPG) random generated number as a payload. The Client responds back to the server using the decrypted (using GnuPG) random number in order to succeed. |

*Table 2. Comparing the immunity of the TPK, SPA, and HPK techniques against DoS attack*

| Technique | DoS attack | Explanation |
|---|---|---|
| TPK | Vulnerable | Doesn't have a detection capability, and it's vulnerable by default to a replay attack. |
| SPA | Vulnerable | Can only detect the flood of a spoofed knock packets (DoS) attack, but no countermeasure is done regarding the host causing the attack. |
| HPK | Immune | Has a built-in detection capability that can be adjusted to countermeasure after a specific number of failure attempts. And it's immune by default to a replay attack. |

cause the technique doesn't have any detection capability and is by default vulnerable to a TCP replay attack. The SPA technique is also found to be vulnerable to DoS attack, because the technique can only detect DoS attack, but cannot countermeasure against the host causing the attack. Finally, the HPK technique can be found to be immune to flooded spoofed knock packets or DoS attack, because the technique has a built-in detection capability that can be adjusted to countermeasure after a specific number of failure attempts.

The HPK technique is capable of using multi-processes or threads to handle a huge amount of traffic, and it is highly configurable for number of failure attempts. The technique can be configured to choose the minimum number of failed knocks before placing the IP address of that host in the temporary time period zone. If the period is finished the HPK technique will remove the firewall rule blocking that IP Address from the firewall table. If the same IP Address is seen again performing failed knocks, and reaches the maximum allowed of failure number of knocks which is also a configurable variable, it IP address will be blocked and placed in the permanent time period zone.

## CONCLUSION

The main conclusions of this work is that the proposed HPK technique can be easily implemented on any GNU/Linux firewall box, immune to TCP replay and DoS attacks, performing much better than TPK and SPA techniques, can be used with hosts behind the Network Address Translation (NAT) box of the network, can execute and perform remote tasks not just open/close firewall ports, the communication protocol used is a simple secure encryption scheme that uses GnuPG keys with steganography constructions, implemented using threads technology in case more HPK processes are needed (i.e., more clients requests are received), highly configurable to suite network needs, and completely open source and uses GNU General Public License version 3.

One main drawback of this technique is that the amount of data exchanged in each HPK session is equal to the size of the PNG image file plus the size of two TCP packets with payload equal to the size of a random number. Consequently, it takes relatively higher PK or authentication time. However, since PK is not a continuous process, and clients usually try to gain access only once per session, the overall data overhead and delay will not be significant compared to the positive effect the implemented technique may have on the network security level.

It is highly recommended to carry own research to use image compression to decrease the size of image file used for hiding the client's request; implement different encryption techniques (e.g., the Data Encryption Standard (DES); Advanced Encryption Standard (AES), etc) and not only limit the technique to use the GnuPG encryption tool; implement the HTTP protocol to carry the mutual authentication challenge; implement a Windows operating system client, in case client uses a Windows platform with putty running on it; implement a Web-based client to be used from a PDA, a Smart cards, an iPhone, or any mobile device. It also recommended to investigate the effect of the size of the image file, number of packets into which the image file is transmitted, size of the network (i.e., the number of hops between the client and the server), and speed of the links between the client and the server on the PK time.

# REFERENCES

Barham, P., Hand, S., Isaacs, R., Jardetzky, P., Mortier, R., & Roscoe, T. (2002). Techniques for lightweight concealment and authentication in IP networks. *Intel Research Berkeley, Technical Report IRB-TR-02-009*. Berkley, CA: Berkley University Press.

Bernstein, D. J. (2002). *SYN cookies*. Retrieved June 13, 2010, from http://cr.yp.to/syncookies.html.

DeGraaf, R., Aycock, J., & Jacobson, M. (2005). Port knocking with strong authentication. In *Proceedings of the 21st Annual Computer Security Applications Conference (ACSAC)*, (pp. 409-418). Tucson, AZ: IEEE Press.

Doyle, M. (2004). *Implementing a port knocking system*. MSc Thesis. Little Rock, AR: University of Arkansas.

Fedora GNU/Linux Operating System. (2010). *Fedoraproject*. Retrieved June 13, 2010, from https://fedoraproject.org/wiki/Fedora_Project_Wiki.

Fyodor, G. (1998). *Remote OS detection via TCP/IP stack finger printing*. Retrieved June 13, 2010, from http://nmap.org/nmap-fingerprinting-article.txt.

Google Groups. (2006). *Block SSH guessers*. Retrieved June 13, 2010, from http://groups.google.com/group/comp.os.linux.security/browse_thread/thread/30c8a88ddeed53dc/b75ee069451189fe?#b75ee069451189fe.

Hadi, A. H. (2010). *A hybrid port-knocking technique for host authentication*. PhD Thesis. AQmman, Jordan: The University of Financial Sciences.

Isabel, D. (2005). *Port knocking: Beyond the basics*. SANS Institute.

Jakobsson, M., Yung, M., & Zhou, J. (2004). Applied cryptography and network security. In *Proceedings of the 2nd Applied Cryptography and Network Security (ACNS) International Conference*. Yellow Mountain, China: ACNS Press.

Jung, J., Paxson, V., Berger, A., & Balakrishnan, H. (2004). Fast port scan detection using sequential hypothesis testing. In *Proceedings of IEEE Symposium on Security and Privacy*, (pp. 285-293). Oakland, CA: IEEE Press.

Keromytis, A., Misra, V., & Rubenstein, D. (2002). SOS: Secure overlay services. In *Proceedings of ACM SIGCOMM*, (pp. 61-72). Pittsburgh, PA: ACM Press.

Krivis, S. (2004). *Port knocking: Helpful or harmful? An exploration of modern network threats*. SANS Institute.

Krzywinski, M. (2003a). *How to: Port knocking*. New York: Linux Journal.

Krzywinski, M. (2003b). Port knocking: Network authentication across closed ports. *SysAdmin Magazine*, 12-17.

Marlinspike, M. (2009). *Knockknock: Using knockknock for single packet authorization*. Retrieved June 13, 2010, from http://www.thoughtcrime.org/software/knockknock/.

Murdoch, S., & Lewis, S. (2005). Embedding covert channels into TCP/IP. *Proceedings of 7th Information Hiding (IH)*, 37(27), 247–261.

Nmap. (2010). *Network exploration tool and security/Port scanner*. Retrieved June 13, 2010, from http://nmap.org.

Python Programming Language. (2010). *Python*. Retrieved June 13, 2010, from http://www.python.org/.

Rash, M. (2006a). *SPA: Single packet authorization. MadHat Unspecific and Simple Nomad*. New York: BlackHat Briefings.

Rash, M. (2006b). *Advances in single packet authorization. Paper presented at SchmooCon*. USA.

Rudis, B. (2003). *The enemy within: Firewalls and backdoors*. Retrieved June 13, 2010, from http://www.symantec.com/connect/articles/enemy-within-firewalls-and-backdoors.

Scapy. (2010). *Interactive packet manipulation program*. Retrieved June 13, 2010, from http://www.secdev.org/projects/scapy/.

Steganogra-py. (2010). *Steganography in Python*. Retrieved June 13, 2010, from http://code.google.com/p/steganogra-py.

Tcpreplay. (2010). *Replay captured network traffic*. Retrieved June 13, 2010, from http://tcpreplay.synfin.net/trac/.

Vasserman, E., Hopper, N., Laxson, J., & Tyra, J. (2007). SilentKnock: Practical, provably undetectable authentication. In *Proceeding of ESORICS*, (pp. 122-138). Palo Alto, CA: IEEE Press.

Wireshark. (2010). *Network protocol analyzer*. Retrieved June 13, 2010, from http://wireshark.org.

Worth, D. (2004). *COK - Cryptographic one-time knocking*. In *Proceedings of the Black Hat Conference*. USA.

Wuest, C. (2005). Phishing in the middle of the stream - Today's threats to online banking. In *Proceedings of the AVAR 2005 Conference*. Dublin, Ireland: AVAR Press.

## KEY TERMS AND DEFINITIONS

**Authentication:** Is the verification of the identity of a party who generated some messages, and of the integrity of the messages. In computer networks, two types of authentication can be identified, namely, message authentication and node authentication.

**Cryptography:** Is the field of studying encryption principles and methods.

**Denial-of-Service Attack: (DoS attack)** or **Distributed Denial-of-Service Attack (DDoS attack)**: Is an attempt to make a computer resource unavailable to its intended users. Although the means to carry out, motives for, and targets of a DoS attack may vary, it generally consists of the concerted efforts of person or persons to prevent an Internet site or service from functioning efficiently or at all, temporarily or indefinitely. Perpetrators of DoS attacks typically target sites or services hosted on high-profile web servers such as banks, credit card payment gateways, and even root nameservers. One common method of attack involves saturating the target machine with external communications requests, such that it cannot respond to legitimate traffic, or responds so slowly as to be rendered effectively unavailable.

**Firewall:** Is a dedicated appliance, or software running on a device installed between the Internal/private network of a system and public networks (Internet). It is designed to forward some packets and filter out others. Firewalls are usually classified into packet-filter firewall and proxy firewall.

**Mutual Authentication:** or **Two-Way Authentication:** (sometimes written as 2WAY authentication) refers to two parties authenticating each other suitably. In technology terms, it refers to a client or user authenticating themselves to a server and that server authenticating itself to the user in such a way that both parties are assured of the others' identity. When describing online authentication processes, mutual authentication is often referred to as website-to-user authentication, or site-to-user authentication. Typically, this is done for a client process and a server process without user interaction.

**Port-Knocking:** Is a port authentication service runs on the firewall, which can externally open ports on the firewall by generating a connection attempt on a set of prespecified closed ports. Once a correct sequence of connection attempts is received, the firewall rules are dynamically modified to allow the host which sent the connection attempts to connect over specific port(s).

**Replay Attack:** Is a form of network attack in which a valid data transmission is maliciously or fraudulently repeated or delayed. This is carried out either by the originator or by an adversary who intercepts the data and retransmits it, possibly as part of a masquerade attack by IP packet substitution (such as stream cipher attack).

**Steganography:** Is the art and science of writing hidden messages in such a way that no one, apart from the sender and intended recipient, suspects the existence of the message, a form of security through obscurity. The word steganography is of Greek origin and means "concealed writing" from the Greek words *steganos* meaning "covered or protected," and *graphei* meaning "writing." The advantage of steganography, over cryptography alone, is that messages do not attract attention to themselves. Plainly visible encrypted messages—no matter how unbreakable—will arouse suspicion, and may in themselves be incriminating in countries where encryption is illegal. Therefore, whereas cryptography protects the contents of a message, steganography can be said to protect both messages and communicating parties.

# Chapter 17
# The State of the Art and Future Prospective of the Network Security

**Alaa Hussein Al-Hamami**
*Amman Arab University, Jordan*

## ABSTRACT

*The continuous deployment of network services over the wide range of public and private networks has led to transactions and services that include personal, and sometimes quite sensitive, data. Examples of services include: pay-per-view, cable telephony, bill payments by phone, credit card charging, and Internet banking. Such services require significant effort not only to protect the sensitive data involved in the transactions and services but to ensure integrity and availability of network services as well. The requirement for employing heterogeneous networks and systems becomes increasingly important, and as the view of traditional distributed systems has changed to a network centric view in all types of application networks, therefore, the complexity of these systems has led to significant security flaws and problems. Existing conventional approaches for security service development over such complex and most often heterogeneous networks and systems are not satisfying and cannot meet users and applications needs; therefore, several approaches have been developed to provide security at various levels and degrees, such as: secure protocols, secure protocol mechanisms, secure services, firewalls, Intrusion Detection Systems (IDS), and later Intrusion Prevention System (IPS), etc. This chapter considers and addresses several aspects of network security in an effort to provide a publication that summarizes the current status and the promising and interesting future directions and challenges. The authors try to present the state-of-the-art in this chapter for the following topics: Internet security, secure services, security in mobile systems and trust, anonymity, and privacy.*

DOI: 10.4018/978-1-4666-0191-8.ch017

## INTRODUCTION

The continuous deployment of network services over this wide range of public and private networks has led to transactions and services that include personal, and sometimes quite sensitive, data. One only needs to consider simple, everyday services from pay-per-view and cable telephony to bill payments by phone, credit card charging and Internet banking. Such services require significant effort not only to protect the sensitive data involved in the transactions and services, but to ensure integrity and availability of network services as well.

It is easier to protect private networks than public one, so the typical approach is to provide services and increase security and dependability on private networks than public one. Internet has changed our lives including electronic business models, by providing ease of use, flexibility, and enabling service deployment with substantially lower cost. Even private networks are connected to the Internet in order to exploit its multiple advantages, and thus the role of network security is significantly more important in emerging network environments.

As the requirement for employing heterogeneous networks and systems becomes increasingly important, and as the view of traditional distributed systems has changed to a network centric view in all types of application networks, the complexity of these systems has led to significant security flaws and problems. The lack of systematic methods to design and implement secure end systems together with the traditional approach to network service development, using several layers and protocols, leads to vulnerabilities and difficulties in implementing and managing security. Attackers continuously find vulnerabilities at various levels, from the network itself to operating systems, and exploit them to crack systems and services.

Due to the conventional approaches for service development over such complex and most often heterogeneous networks and systems, several approaches are exist to provide security at various

levels and degrees: secure protocols, secure protocol mechanisms, secure services (e.g., phone), firewalls, IDS and later IPS, etc.

This chapter considers and addresses several aspects of network security, in an effort to provide a publication that summarizes the main current status and the promising and interesting future directions and challenges. We try to present the state-of-the-art in this chapter for the following topics: Internet security, secure services, security in mobile systems and trust, anonymity and privacy.

The ISO Open Systems Interconnection (OSI) reference model defines seven network layers as well as their interfaces. Each layer depends on the services provided by its intermediate lower layer all the way down to the physical network interface card and the wiring. It provides its services to its immediate upper layer, all the way up to the running application. The seven layers of the OSI reference model are described at the following, from the highest to the lowest one (Tanenbaum & Wetherall, 2010):

- **Layer 7: Application Layer.** It deals with the communication issues of an application. The availability of the communicating principals can be identified and established by this layer. It is also responsible to interface with the user. Examples of protocols include HyperText Transfer Protocol (HTTP), Session Initiation Protocol (SIP), File Transfer Protocol (FTP), Simple Mail Transfer Protocol (SMTP), and Telent.
- **Layer 6: Presentation Layer.** It is responsible for presenting the data to the upper application layer. It translates the data and performs tasks like data compression and decompression and data encryption and decryption. Some of standards and protocols of this layer include ASCII, ZIP, JPEG, TIFF, RTP, and MIDI format.
- **Layer 5: Session Layer.** It is responsible for initiating the contact between two

computers and setting up the communication lines. It maintains the end-to-end connection. Examples of the protocols are the Remote Procedure Call (RPC) and the Secure Sockets Layer (SSL) protocols.

*   **Layer 4: Transport Layer.** It defines how to address the physical locations of the network, establish connections between hosts, and handle network messaging. Also it maintains the integrity of the session and provides mechanisms to support session establishment for the upper layers. Examples of protocols are Transport Control Protocol (TCP) and User Datagram Protocol (UDP).
*   **Layer 3: Network Layer.** Its function is to send fragments of data called packets from a source to a destination host. It is responsible for routing and relaying the data between network hosts. IP belongs to this layer.
*   **Layer 2: Data Link Layer.** It establishes the link between the hosts over a physical channel. It ensures message delivery to the proper device and translates the transmitted bits for the lowest physical layer. Examples of protocols are Ethernet and Token Ring.
*   **Layer 1: Physical Layer.** It defines the physical connection between a host and a network. It converts the bits into physical signaling suitable for transmission, such as voltages or light impulse. Network cards, wireless cards, etc operate at this layer.

We have the following definitions for different parts of security:

*   **Computer Security:** generic name for the collection of tools designed to protect data and to thwart hackers.
*   **Network Security:** measures to protect data during their transmission.

*   **Internet Security:** measures to protect data during their transmission over a collection of interconnected networks.

## NETWORK SECURITY PROBLEMS

Due to the network nature, there are many security problems because of:

*   **Sharing:** Works and resources are shared by many people and for that; it is possible for any of them to have the ability to access the existing network systems.
*   **Complexity of System:** The operating system consists of complex programs and always the reliability of security is very difficult if it is not impossible to get it within working large systems.
*   **Unknown Perimeter**: The extension of connection with network leads to uncertainty and confidence about the network boundaries. May be one of the hosts is a node on two different networks, for that it is possible for resource on one network can be reached by second network users.
*   **Many Points of Attack:** When a file is stored in a network host far away from the user, the file could be passed through many hosts before it reached the user.
*   **Anonymity:** The attacker has the ability to execute the attack from a distance could be thousands of miles, and for that the attacker is not touching the attacked system or a relation with its administrative or users. It is possible for the attack to pass through many hosts for the purpose of hiding the originality of the attack. Security threats and attacks may involve any layer (ISO/OSI reference model), from the physical to the application. It is obvious that a successful attack in one layer may render useless the security measures taken in the other layers (Base & Mell, 2000).

Some basic network security attacks are described below:

- **Intercept transmitted data:** This attack consists of the unauthorized interception of network communication and the disclosure of the exchanged information. This can be performed in several different layers – e.g., in the network layer by sniffing into the exchanged packets or in the physical layer by physically wire tapping the access medium.

- **Logon Abuse Attacks:** Allow a user to obtain access with more privileges than authorized and would bypass the authentication and access control mechanisms due to a successful logon abuse attack.

- **Intrusion Attack:** They mean that unauthorized users gaining access to a system through the network. Such an attack would target specific vulnerabilities in assets. For example, when a Web service receives more data than it has been programmed to handle and thus reacts in unexpected and unpredicted ways. This attack is called buffer overflow attack.

- **Spoofing Attacks:** It is password forged or any definition to a program or user to disguise the identity by another user or program. It is the act of a subject asserting an identity that the subject has no right to use. A simple instance of this type of attacks is IP spoofing, through which a system is convinced that it is communicating with a known principal and thus provides access to the attacker.

- **Denial of Service (DoS) Attacks:** are the disruptions of an entire network, either by disabling the network or by overloading it with messages so as to degrade performance. A more advance type is the Distributed Denial of Service (DDoS) attacks, where the attacker uses resources from a distributed environment against a target host. The followings are some of the DoS attacks (Bergadano et al 2002):

  ○ **SYN Attack.** Here, the attacker exploits the inability of a server process to handle unfinished connection requests. The attacker floods a server process with connection requests, but it does not respond when the server answers those requests. Waiting for the proper acknowledgments of the initial requests will cause the attacked system to crash.

  ○ **Ping of Death.** The attacker sends a ping request that is larger than 65,536 bytes, which is the maximum allowed size for the IP, causing the system to crash or restart. Most of operating systems today have implemented measures against it.

- **Hijacking Attacks.** These are attempts to gain unauthorized access to a system by using a legitimate entity's existing connection. An example of session hijacking is the TCP sequence number attack. This attack exploits the communication session which was established between the target host and a legitimate host that initiated the session.

- **Application Level Attacks.** These attacks are concerned with the exploitation of weakness in the application layer and really focus on intrusion attacks, security weakness in the Web server, in the specific technology used in the website, or in faulty controls in the filtering of an input on the server side. Examples of these attacks include malicious software attacks (Viruses, Trojans, etc.), Web server attacks.

A useful categorization of these attacks is in terms of passive attacks and active attacks.

## Passive Attacks

They are eavesdropping on, or monitoring of, transmissions to obtain message contents, or monitor traffic flows. The goal of the opponent is to obtain information that is being transmitted. Two types of passive attacks are occurs (Stallings 4/e, 2011):

1. The release of message contents is easily understood. A telephone conversation, an E-mail message, and a transferred file may contain sensitive or confidential information. We would like to prevent the opponent from learning the contents of these transmissions.

2. The traffic Analysis is more subtle. Suppose that we had a way of masking the contents of messages or other information traffic so that opponents, even if they captured the message, could not extract the information from the message. The common technique for masking contents is encryption. If we had encryption protection in place, an opponent might still be able to observe the pattern of these messages. The opponent could determine the location and identity of communicating hosts and could observe the frequency and length of messages being exchanged. This information might be useful in guessing the nature of the communication that was taking place.

Passive attacks are very difficult to detect because they do not involve any alteration of the data. However, it is feasible to prevent the success of these attacks. Thus the emphasis in dealing with passive attacks is on prevention rather than detection.

## Active Attacks

It is a modification of data stream to masquerade of one entity as some other, replay previous messages, modify messages in transit, or denial of service.

These attacks involve some modification of the data stream or the creation of a false stream and can be subdivided into four categories (Stallings 5/e, 2011):

1. **Masquerade** takes place when one entity pretends to be a different entity. Its attack usually includes one of the other forms of active attacks. For example, authentication sequences can be captured and replayed after a valid authentication sequence has taken place, thus enabling an authorized entity with few privileges to obtain extra privileges by impersonating an entity that has those privileges.

2. **Replay** is retransmission of the passive capture subsequent of a data to produce an unauthorized effect.

3. **Modification of Messages** simply means to produce an unauthorized effect due to that some portion of a legitimate message is altered, delayed, or reordered. For example, a message meaning "Allow Alaa Hussein to read confidential file accounts."

4. **Denial of Service** prevents or inhibits the normal use or management of communications facilities. This attack may have a specific target, for example, an entity may suppress all message directed to a particular destination (e.g., the security audit service). Another form of service denial is the disruption of an entire network, either by disabling the network or by overloading it with messages so as to degrade performance.

Active attacks present the opposite characteristics of passive attacks. Whereas passive attacks are difficult to detect, measures are available to prevent their success. On the other hand, it is quite difficult to prevent active attacks absolutely, because to do so would require complete protection of all communications facilities and paths at all times. Instead, the goal is to detect them and to recover from any disruption or delays caused by them. Because the detection has a deterrent effect, it may also contribute to prevention.

## SECURITY SERVICES

It is something that enhances the security of the data processing systems and the information transfers of an organization. It is intended to counter security attacks by make use of one or more security mechanisms to provide the service. It is replicate functions normally associated with physical documents, e.g., have signatures, dates; need protection from disclosure, tampering, or destruction; be notarized or witnessed; be recorded or licensed.

It is possible to classify the security services as the following:

1. **Confidentiality.** It is protection of data from unauthorized disclosure. It is also the protection of transmitted data from passive attacks. With respect to the release of message contents, several levels of protection can be identified. The broadest service protects all user data transmitted between two users over a period of time. Variants of this service include *connection confidentiality* (when it involves all the layers of the communication), *connectionless confidentiality* (when it provides confidentiality in a connectionless service data unit), *selective field confidentiality* (when it protects selective fields of the data), and *traffic flow confidentiality* (when it protects information that could be potentially derived from observation of traffic flows).

2. **Authentication.** It is assurance that the communicating entity is the one claimed. The authentication service is concerned with assuring that a communication is authentic. In the case of a single message, such as a warning or alarm signal, the function of the authentication service is to assure the recipient that the message is from the source that it claims to be from (peer entity authentication). In the case of an ongoing interaction, such as the connection of a terminal to a host, two aspects are involved. First, at the time of connection initiation, the service assures that the two entities are authentic (that is, that each is the entity that it is not interfered with in such a way that a third party can masquerade as one of the two legitimate parties for the purposes of unauthorized transmission or reception.

3. **Integrity.** It is the assurance that data received is as sent by an authorized entity. This service ensures that during their transmission the data are not altered by unauthorized principals. As with confidentiality, integrity can apply to a stream of messages, a single message, or selected fields within a message. Again, the most useful and straightforward approach is total stream protection. A connection-oriented integrity with recovery service provides integrity of the data and also detects modification, insertion, deletion, and replay of data. In contrast, connection integrity with recovery does not attempt recovery. Selective field connection integrity provides integrity for selective data fields within a connection. Connectionless of the above services also exist for connectionless data units.

4. **Nonrepudiation.** It is a protection against denial by one of the parties in a communication. Nonrepudiation prevents either sender or receiver from denying a transmitted message. Thus, when a message is sent, the receiver can prove that the message was in fact sent by the alleged sender. Similarly, when a message is received, the sender can prove that the message was in fact received by the alleged receiver. This service may take one or both of two forms, proof of origin and proof of delivery.

5. **Access control.** This service can be used to protect the information assets and resources

363

available via OSI from unauthorized access. In the context of network security, access control is the ability to limit and control the access to host systems and applications via communications links. To achieve this control, each entity trying to gain access must first be identified, or authenticated, so that access rights can be tailored to the individual. This service may be applied to various types of access, such as read, write, or execute or combinations of the above. Access to resources may be controlled through various types of access policies, such as rule-based security policies.

6.  **Availability.** A variety of attacks can result in the loss of or reduction in availability. Some of these attacks are amenable to automated countermeasures, such as authentication and encryption, whereas others require some sort of physical action to prevent or recover from loss of availability of elements of a distributed system.

## NETWORK PROTECTION METHODS

It is possible to protect networks by using one or more of the following methods:

## Reliability (Encryption)

Encryption is an efficient tool to assure confidentiality, authentication, integrity, access control for data, and nonrepudation. It works by hiding the meaning of the message through hiding its existence. The original form of the message called plain text and the encrypted text called cipher text. To explain the process in more details, we may refer to the plain text message M as sequence of single codes M=(M1, M2,...Mn). Same thing for the cipher text where it is possible to write it as C=(C1, C2, .....Cn). To explain the transformation process between plain text and cipher text, we can write the following: C = E (M), for the encryption

process and M=D(C) for the Decryption process, where C is the cipher text, E is the encryption algorithm, M is the plain text, and D is decipher process. Of course we like to have cryptosystem as the following: M=D(E(M)).

## Integrity (Hashing Functions)

All the hashing functions work by using the following general principles: Input (message, file, ..., etc), and consider as sequence of blocks with size of n bits. The input will process every block separately in repeating way, to produce hash function with size n bits. One of the simplest hashing functions is using bit by bit Exclusive OR for every block. It is possible to express as the following:

$$C_i = b_{i1} + b_{i2} + \ldots\ldots + b_{in}$$

Where:

$C_i$: bit number I from the hash code $1 \leq i \leq n$.
M: Number of blocks with size n bit that exist in the input.
$b_i$: bit number i in block j.
+: Exclusive OR.

## Non-Repudiation (Digital Signature)

Digital signature is a protocol that has the same effect of the analog signature. It is a mark can be made by the sender only, but other users can recognize it easily that it belongs for the sender. Digital signature as the analog signature used for authentic message originality. When the message encrypted by the private key and nobody can use this private key and for that nobody can construct an encrypted message that can be decrypted by the public key, and for that the encrypted message will appear as a digital signature. In addition to that, it is not possible to change the message without having the private key. For that, this message is authentic for the source originality and integrity. It is important to emphasis that, the descript encryption process is not providing privacy. Thus, the message that has been send is secure from the change but is not from the exposure of its contents.

Digital signature must satisfy two basic conditions, these are:

1. **Unforgable:** If a user (p) likes to sign the message (M) by the signature S(P,M), it will be impossible for anybody else to get the pair [M, S(P,M)].
2. **Authentic:** If the user (R) received the pair [M, S(P,M)] from the user (P), user R can assure that signature truly belongs to user (P). Because (P) is the only user can use this signature, and this signature was truly been added to the message (M).

## SECURITY APPROACHES

### Intrusion Detection System (IDS)

Always there are set of tries to violate the computer resources or its security network that we consider it as intrusion. In addition to the available security services (e.g., confidentiality, integrity, authentication,… etc), Intrusion Detection Techniques (IDT) used to support the security systems and increase its resistance to the inside and outside attacks. These techniques can be applied by using IDS. The aim of the intruder is to access the system or to increase the access privilege range to the system. In general, this require from the intruder to access information that must be protected. In most cases, this information must be in a form of passwords to user. Knowing some of the passwords which belong to users, intruder can enter the system and violate it according to the user privilege that used his/her password. Intrusion is somebody tries to access or misuse computer system. Intrusion may be harm such as stealing secure data or misuse your E-mails. IDS is a system that used to detect such intrusion. There are two types of IDS (Caswell, et al., 2003):

1. **Network IDS (NIDS):** monitoring packets on the network communications attempting detection of intruder through comparing intruder pattern with database stored known attack samples. As an example, looking at a large number of communication request (SYN) TCP to different ports in the destination computer. Thus, it has been discovered if there is somebody attempt to examine TCP port. NIDS is stealing the network passage through monitoring all the network passage. Generally every NIDS consists of the following parts:

   a. **Packet Association Model.** This is most frequently referred to as the "sensor." In some distributed implementations this components may incorporate significant processing capability, and consequently a more abstract classification is appropriate. This processing capability can range from simple filtering and metadata extraction to complex statistical analysis.

   b. **Event Correlation and Detection (Core).** This component at the most basic level acts as a repository for aggregated packet association data. More commonly it also conducts the bulk of processing and correlating.

   c. **Graphical User Interface (GUI).** The presentation of output by the GUI is often accessible by multiple administrators throughout the network.

Communications between the components are facilitated by a variety of protocols. Communication between the packet association model and the core most often is some version of the Simple Network Management Protocol (SNMP). Likewise communication between the core and the GUI is often Web based, although just as often a vendor proprietary application protocol encapsulated inside a TCP socket is employed. Finally, communication between the IDS and other network devices can be by a wide variety of protocols depending on the vendor (Kuri, et al., 2003).

2.  **Host IDS:** HIDS doesn't monitor the network passage, but monitor what is happen in the real destination computer. It does that through monitoring security event record or validates the system changes, for example changes on the important system files or in the system recording. This system can be divide into the following:

    a.  **System Integrity Checkers:** It monitors system files and systems records for the change made by the intruder. There is some number of system/file integrity checkers like Tripwire or Languard.

    b.  **Log File Monitors:** Recording files monitoring can be generated by the computer system. Windows NT/2000 & XP systems generate security events around the important security topics which happened on the computer. (e.g., user requests admin/root level privilege). From retrieving and analysis these security events, one could discover the intruder.

    c.  IDSs depend on the analysis set of discrete events and time sequence for the misuse patterns. Location of source validation recognizes between IDSs based on the inserted information that we analysis. There are two types of IDSs and these are: Host based IDS and NIDS.

## DETECTION TYPES

There are two types of detections and these are anomaly and misuse intrusion detections.

## Anomaly Intrusion Detection

It refers to statistical anomaly detection and deals with certain anomaly detection in user behavior. Every computer's user has the ability to perform some objectives. In other words, for every user has certain ability within the system. Usually this activity is notable and can not change more in short time. System admin can access system components domains and perform statistics and audit and monitor application. This means it is possible to define set of activities performed usually by the user. This group called by the user appearance which describe the ordinary user behavior. After the definition of like this appearance, it is possible to follow the current user behavior and search of some confusion which is called anomaly and refers to the most interfere status. Anomaly detection performed by change detection in optimal usage pattern or system behavior. This performed through the construction of statistical model which contain derived metrics from system process and appear as input to the metric notable which has a statistical deviation clear from the model.

## Misuse Intrusion Detection

It refers to model corresponding detection. It refers to the intrusion resulted from good detection to the attack pattern which detect the weak message in system program and application. Nearly, it is possible to describe any intrusion in terms of its signs and pointers. Initially, models (sometimes called signatures) of the all known attacks must describe it in summary form and introduce to the IDS. These models been used later on by the IDS to define any intrusion. This can be done by study system validation information to find patterns correspondence with identified models to system intrusion. As an example to explore the way, is possible to be flooding SYN attack of denial of service. Their objective is to prevent destination host from accepting new connections on port IP. Misuse intrusion detection system has knowledge on the weak behavior or unaccepted which search about in direct way. It is very difficult for this system to learn, and here this type of systems is unable in attacks recognition which is not coded in sophisticated way in system. It is difficult to automate misuse detection because it needs to apply many rules or search for many models. It is nearly impossible to perform suitable test for these systems because of not enough information about the real intrusion states.

A third classification of IDS has recently been discussed called *specification–based detection*. Specification-based IDS are similar to anomaly detection systems in that they both detect deviations from a norm. The difference between the two is that anomaly detection systems base their norm on some machine-learned parameters. Specification based systems define their norm on manually developed specifications that describe legitimate system behaviors. The advantage of specification-based systems is they avoid false alarms that to anomaly detection systems might be legitimate but previously unlearned behaviors. The disadvantage of specification-based systems is that manual development of specifications can be very time consuming. Additionally, many commercial IDS implementations actually combine aspects of all classes of IDSs. These generally fall into a class which some refer to as hybrid HDSs.

## FIREWALLS

A firewall is a collection of components interposed between two networks that filter traffic between them according to some security policy. Typically, firewalls rely on restrictions in the network topology to perform this filtering (Rattle, 2004). One key assumption under this model is that everyone on the protected network(s) is trusted, since internal traffic is not seen by the firewall and thus cannot be filtered; if that is not the case, then additional, internal firewalls have to be deployed in the internal network. Most of the complexity

in using firewalls today lies in managing a large number of firewalls and ensuring they enforce a consistent policy across an organization's network (Cheswick & Belloving, 1994).

The aim of the Firewall is reduce the destruction which happened to the network and this is through the reduction of the outside access rights to the network. Firewall any device use to prevent the outsiders from gaining access to the network. This device is a mixture of software and hardware. Usually, firewall executes comprehensive methods or rules to isolate the desired addresses from the unwanted ones. Firewall as software system or hardware, it is designed for unwanted message filtration and allows for the legal communications only, see Figure 1.

For a firewall to be effective, it must be strategically placed so that all traffic between the internal network and the outside world passes thro0ugh it. This implies that firewalls traditionally are located at the points where the internal network is connected to the outside network (e.g., the Internet Service Provider). These are called the chock points. By placing the firewall at the chock point we control all traffic that enters or leaves the internal network.

The typical firewall usually comprises two packet filtering routers creating a restricted access network called the DMZ (Demilitarized Zone). The DMZ acts as a buffer between the internal (trusted) and external (untrusted) networks. The configuration attempts to satisfy a number of goals:

- Protect hosts on the internal (inside) network from attacks from the outside.
- Allow machines located in the DMZ to be accessed from the outside and thus be able to provide services to the outside world or serve as stepping stones linking hosts from the internal network to the hosts in the outside world.
- Enforce an organization wide security policy, which may include restrictions un-

*Figure 1. Simple firewall*

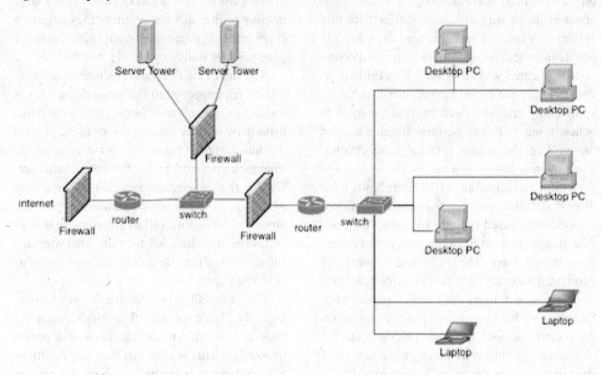

related to security, for example, access to certain websites during office hours.

There are another software companied the host firewall to support these central functions. Examples include Virus detection; records report tools, strong authentication and validation of file system integrity. Firewalls execute by using Screening Routers, Bastion, or the two together. It is possible to organize Screen Router to control the routing of the network packets that depends on the packet details, as an example Source address, Destination address, Port number, and direction, as in Figure 2.

Access to the Internet provides many advantages to the organization but it gives the ability to the outside world to access and interact with components of the Local network. This will create a threat to the organization while it is possible to supply every work station and server within the network by strong security system with excellent features such as intrusion protection but this

solution is impractical. The solution which is more acceptable is using firewall. Firewall interferes within network components and Internet network to gain a control link and to show an outside wall for the security. There are three basic techniques used for firewalls and these are:

1.  **Packet filtering:** It is a control mechanism on the network flow. Instead of processing or passage all arrived packets to the network node, packet filter judged to control rules for access before processing every packet. Packet filter router use set of rules for every coming IP packet and then sends or stopped the packet. The router will be organized basically to filter the directed packets in both sides. Filter rules depend on the existing fields in IP and address transfer (e.g.,. UDP or TCP), including IP address for the source and destination, field of IP protocol (which is known as transform protocol) and port number to TCP or UDP. Figure 3

*Figure 2. Address comparison*

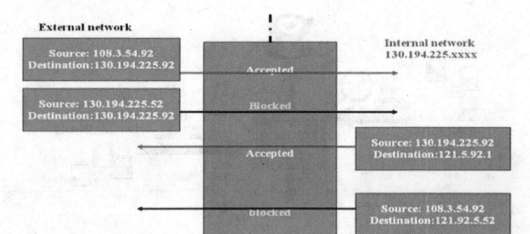

explains packet filter router. Packet filter will be put as a list of dependent rules for the correspondence to the fields in TCP or IP address. If there is one satisfy to one of the rules, this rule will be invoked to determine send or stop the packet.

2. **Application level gateway:** It is also called Proxy Gateway, it works as relay gateway for the flow of application level as explained in Figure 4. User contacts flow gateway by using TCP/IP application, as TELNET or FTP, the gateway will ask user about the remot host name that access required. When the user responds and introduce correct identification for user ID and authentication information, then the gateway contact the application exist on the remot host and also gateway of TCP divisions that contain on application data that exist between the two ends. If the gateway doesn't use proxy code for a certain application, then the service could not be introduced and it is not possible to pass the request through firewall.

3. **Circuit level gateway:** This gateway consider to be network flow between two connected hosts through virtual circuit for the network. Figure 5 explains Circuit level Gateway that doesn't allow to connect end-

to-end for TCP. One between itself and its user in inside host, and the other between itself and its user in outside host. The main advantage that we gain according to the application level gateway is, it doesn't need for proxy application limited for every new application which needs its flow outside the internal network.

4. **Bastion host:** It is a system that determined by the firewall manager as a strong main point in network security. Bastion serves as a platform to the application level gateway or Circuit Level Gateway as in Figure 6.

Firewalls also provide a number of additional services which, while not strictly part of the firewall "job description," have been used so widely that they are now considered an integral part of a firewall.

1. **Network Address Translation (NAT).** If hosts with private IP addresses require access to the Internet, they must use an intermediary host that has a global address. Such a host may act as a proxy, relaying the request to the final destination.

2. **Split-Horizon DNS.** DNS provides information related to the mapping between IP

*Figure 3. Packet filter router*

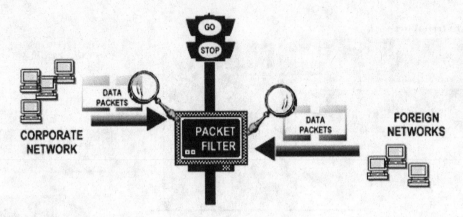

*Figure 4. Application level*

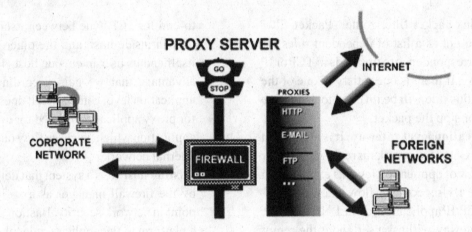

*Figure 5. Circuit level gateway*

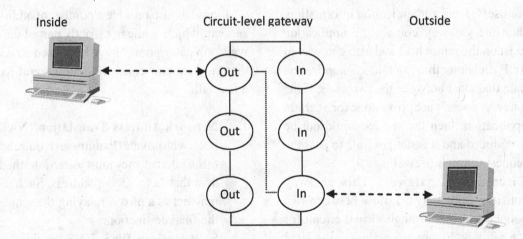

*Figure 6. Firewalls using bastion host*

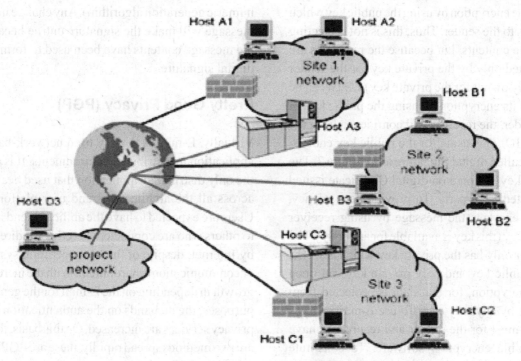

addresses and host names. This information may be used by an attacker to identify targets (e.g., a machine called mail-host is likely to be the mail server of the organization and hence have mail related services activated.

3. **Mitigating Host Fingerprinting.** Computer systems are to a large extent deterministic, and this can be used as a means of identification (fingerprinting) or, worse, as a means of subverting a system by anticipating its response to various events.

4. **IDSs.** It is imperative to have a strategy for detecting and responding to the security breach. IDSs are naturally placed within the DMZ and may be traffic monitors or booby-trapped hosts. Traffic monitoring systems tap into all traffic that crosses the DMZ and attempt to identify patterns that may indicate an attack.

## E-MAIL SECURITY

Security of E-mail can be preserved by using several methods, such as:

## Encryption

Encryption of E-mail techniques used in general asymmetric encryption which depends on pair of keys mathematically related. One of them used for encryption and the other one for opening data binary code. The pair of keys consists of public key which distributed publically to the others and private key which is available only for the user. It is possible to use the same pair of keys to provide the authentication for the sender ID and also the privacy of the message contents or the two together. To provide the authentication, sender encrypts the message by using the private key which belongs to the sender. Because the public key is available to anybody and for that it is available for anybody to break the encryption by using the public key which belongs to the sender. Thus, this is not protecting message contents, but because the messages are encrypted only by the private key for the sender (the only owner for the private key) which can be opened its encryption by using the public key of the sender, the receiver will confidence from the sender ID. This using for the public key encryption is called digital Signature as in Figure 7. The digital key is stored on digital Certificate issued by trusted third party. To provide data privacy, sender encrypts the message by using receiver public key (this key is available for anybody). The receiver only has the private key which is works with public key and only private key can open data encryption, for that data is protected from reading by anybody else. To use E-mail encryption, it must for the sender and receiver to have compatible encryption software. To constitute digital signature, software use private key and message contents (in its binary form) to gener-

ate number hashed (through its execution within numeric generation algorithm). Any change in the message will make the signature untrue because the message contents have been used to form the digital signature.

## Pretty Good Privacy (PGP)

Virtually, E-mail is heavily used network-based application in distributed environments. It is also the only distributed application that used heavily across all the architectures and user platforms. Users are expected to have the ability to send mail to others who are connected directly or indirectly by Internet, despite of the host operating system or communication environment. With the increase growth in depending on the E-mail for the general purposes, the demands on the authentication and privacy services are increased. On this basis, there are two methods spread rapidly, these are PGP and S/MIME. PGP consider as a remarkable method, and it is a great effort for one man called Phil

*Figure 7. Digital signature*

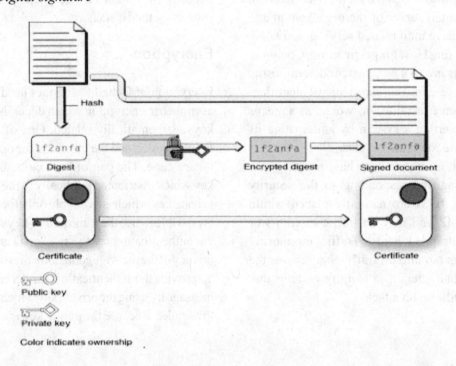

Zimmerman. PGP provides authentication and confidentiality services which can be used for the E-mail and file storage applications as in Figure 8.

In fact, Zimmerman has done the following:

1.  Selected the best available cryptographic algorithms as building blocks.
2.  Integrated these algorithms in general purpose application that is independent of operating system and processor and dependent on small groups of easy use instructions.
3.  Made the package and its documentation including the source code, available on the Internet, bulletin boards, and commercial networks such as CompuServe.
4.  Entered into agreement with a company (Vianypt) to provide a compatible, low cost commercial version of PGP.

## WEB SECURITY

Web Services can be defined as software objects that can be assembled over the Internet using standard protocols to perform functions or execute business processes. Web services connect com-

puters and devices with each other using widely accepted standards such as HTTP and eXtensible Markup Language (XML) aimed at addressing interoperability issues between different domains within independent environments.

The term Web services is also often used to denote a set of base protocols such as SOAP, WSDL, and UDDI, which form the initial specification for Web services:

*   **Simple Object Access Protocol (SOAP).** Defines the run time message that contains the service request and response. SOAP is independent of any particular transport and implementation technology.
*   **Web Services Description Language (WSDL).** Describes a Web service and the SOAP messages it understands. WSDL provides a structured way to describe what a service does, paving the way for automation.
*   **Universal Discovery, Description, Integration (UDDI).** UDDI is a cross industry initiative to create a standard for service discovery together with a registry

*Figure 8. PGP algorithm*

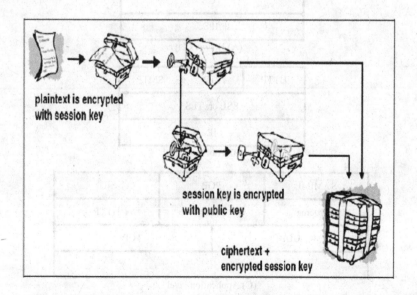

plaintext is encrypted
with session key

session key is encrypted
with public key

ciphertext +
encrypted session key

facility that facilitates the publishing and discovery processes.

There are several possible methods to assure the Website security. The different methods which are taken in consideration are similar in the services provided and sometimes are similar in the used tools but they are different according to their fields of implementations and locations within stack protocol TCP/IP. Figure 9 explains this difference. There is only one method to provide Web security is by using IP security. Figure 9-A, the advantage of using IP security is in its transparency according to the end users and applications and provide solution to the general purpose, more than that, IP security includes filtration ability to be a selective flow only which required effort for IP security processing.

Another solution relatively to the general purpose is to execute security only above TCP (Figure 9-B). A clear example to this procedure is SSL which belongs to the known Internet standard Transport Layer Security (TLS). In this level, there are two choices for execution. For the integral work it is possible to provide SSL or TLS as a part of defined protocol, for that it will be transparent to the applications. Another choice, it is possible to include SSL in limited packets, such as Netscape and Microsoft Explorer Browsers, which come and contain SSL and most of the Web servers have used the protocol. Security service of certain application is included within certain application. Figure 9-C examples cross this architecture. The advantage of this method is customizing the service to the required needs for used application. In the context of Web security, an important example for this method is Secure Electronic Transaction (SET).

## FUTURE RESEARCH AND DEVELOPMENT

We have discussed several topics concerning the security of networks. There are many develop-

*Figure 9. Implementation of network security on the TCP/IP protocol stack*

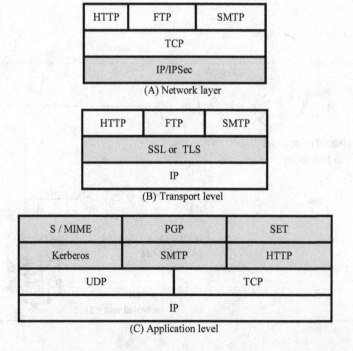

(A) Network layer

(B) Transport level

(C) Application level

ments can be done to the security components, such as the following:

- Although considerable research and development have been devoted in extending the capabilities of firewalls, further developments and refinements of the basic concept as well as increased deployment and use will be needed.

- Current trends in firewall design include the use of multiple firewalls at various locations at the perimeter and inside a network, extensive use of Virtual Private Network (VPN) capabilities to form Intranets and Extranets, integration of intrusion detection and prevention functionality, and use of quarantining mechanisms for containing DoS attacks and virus infestations.

- As security continues to be a critical issue in Internet communications, VPN technology will continue to see an accelerated growth in commercial, research, and military environments.

- Improving, mining, and reducing intrusion detection data are critical to dealing with the multisensor architectures of the future. Fast and flexible detection techniques are necessary to identify the vast variety of clever and unusual attacks we will undoubtedly encounter. Finally, cooperation with not only other IDS but also other network security components is mandatory to achieving a holistic network security posture for organizations of the future.

- DoS attacks are a serious problem on the Internet and their rate of growth and wide acceptance challenge the general public, a skeptical government, and business. It is clear that the wave of DoS attacks will continue to pose a significant threat; as new countermeasures are developed, new DoS attack modes will emerge. Since DoS attacks are complex and difficult to combat, there is no single-point solution; everyone is vulnerable and everyone's security is intertwined. A network infrastructure must be both robust enough to survive direct DoS attacks and extensible enough to adapt and embrace new defenses against emerging and unanticipated attack modes.

- While Web services make application interoperability possible, they add a new dimension in the security landscape. Web services move transactions beyond firewalls and enable outside entities to access sensitive data. Specific security issues must be addressed in order to establish a secure communication channel for messages traversing multiple application intermediates. Standard security technologies are utilized in this direction each addressing a specific or several security issues.

## REFERENCES

Base, R., & Mell, P. (2003). Intrusion detection systems. *NIST Special Publication SP 800-31*. Retrieved from http://www.csrc.nist.gov.

Bergadano, F., Gunetti, D., & Picardi, C. (2002). User authentication through keystroke dynamics. *ACM Transactions on Information and System Security*, 5(4), 367–397. doi:10.1145/581271.581272

Caswell, B., Beale, J., Foster, J., & Posluns, J. (2003). *Snort 2.0 intrusion detection*. Rockland, MA: Syngress Publishing.

Cheswick, W. R., & Belloving, S. M. (1994). *Firewalls and Internet security: Repelling the wily hacker*. Reading, MA: Addison Wesley.

Kuri, J., Novarro, G., & Me, L. (2003). Fast multi-pattern search algorithms for intrusion detection. *Fundamenta Informaticae*, 56, 23–49.

Rattle. (2004). *Using process infection to by-pass Windows software firewalls*. Retrieved from http://www.tech-forums.net/pc/f27/using-process-infection-bypass-windows-software-firewalls-86504/.

Stallings, W. (2011a). *Network security essentials: Applications and standards* (4th ed.). Upper Saddle River, NJ: Prentice-Hall.

Stallings, W. (2011b). *Cryptography and network security: Principle and practices* (5th ed.). Upper Saddle River, NJ: Prentice-Hall.

Tanenbaum, A. S., & Wetherall, D. J. (2010). *Computer networks* (5th ed.). Upper Saddle River, NJ: Prentice-Hall.

# Chapter 18
# Toward Distributed QoS Driven Wireless Messaging Infrastructure

**Souheil Khaddaj**
*Kingston University, UK*

**Bippin Makoond**
*Cognizant Technology Solutions, UK*

## ABSTRACT

*The Telecoms market is demanding more services which involve an increased mobile accessibility to the Internet, real time video transmission, real time games, Voice over IP (VOIP), and business critical transactions such as billing transactions and banking services. Meeting these challenges requires the mobile operators to change the way they design their telephony and messaging systems. As the mobile market moves to become more service centric, rather than technology centric, Quality of Service (QoS) has grown to become imperative, since in the Telecoms innovative services are very often short lived, where the quality aspects of a system and the provided services contribute as key differentiators. Thus, the main focus of this chapter is based around the QoS issues which have led to the consideration of a distributed messaging model to address the challenges faced in the Telecoms industry.*

## INTRODUCTION

Recent investigations of the undercurrent changes of the Telecoms market suggest that the key market differentiators of the mobile industry are found in the service provided and the technological

DOI: 10.4018/978-1-4666-0191-8.ch018

innovations, designed to facilitate the IP convergence (Gao & Damsgaard, 2007). Based on these facts we observe that the Telecoms business is being pressured by two major forces. One of these forces, initiated by the market, is urging the Telecoms operators to change their working model since there has been a shift in the way business is carried out over the last few years and this is referred to as the *pressure from outside*. The other force is attributable to the fact that the technology currently being used by the carriers also require some kind of transformation to adapt to the new Telecoms Economy and we refer to this as *pressure from the inside*.

In order to win in a very competitive market, organisations must differentiate their products from those of their competitors which is mainly caused by the outside pressure. Amongst the major Telecoms operators, there is almost no major differentiation in the technology they are using. They converge towards using the same technologies (GSM, GPRS, and 3G) and the same application which are heavily oriented towards messaging (SMS, MMS, and Video Messaging). To increase their differentiation, operators are campaigning to innovate and improve their service models which are leading to significant evolution in the characterization of the services provided.

The work carried out on service innovation in the Telecoms (Miyazakia & Wiggersb, 2005), present a sample of the major improvements introduced by the Telecommunication carriers to their organisations. Yet these studies only cover the traits of functionalities, tools and commercial innovations and fail to discuss the quality challenges inherent to these innovations. However, the fundamental differentiator that complements and reinforces new service introduction of the Telecoms is the Quality of Service (QoS), i.e. to what level of quality a particular service is being supplied. Moreover, the fact that there are external regulations from the increasing political influence to the Telecoms transactional model, operators are looking for more efficient and effective means to provide their services.

As far as the Pressure from inside is concerned, IP convergence is being regarded as the next technological shift of the new Telecoms economy. A report from the Learning Initiatives on Reform of Network Economies (Melody, et al., 2005) states that the introduction of Voice over IP services (VoIP) has raised a number of

issues of adjustment to the new environment by 1) Telecoms operators and service providers, 2) by policymakers and regulators, and 3) by the users. The report confirms that major technological improvements, which dramatically reduces unit costs and expands service capabilities, offer the potential of enormous benefits in terms of network and market expansion, cost and price reductions, and new service development. Yet it also brings the threat of significant losses to those benefiting from traditional ways of doing business, hence the obligation for the inherited structure of policies and regulations to be reassessed and modified to meet the new challenges and opportunities unfolding.

## MOBILE TELECOM: FROM TECHNOLOGY TO SERVICES

In his study of economic history, Joseph Schumpeter (Schumpeter, 1975) described the process of major technological change as *"creative destruction."* The convergence with IP is changing the strategic business model of Telecoms operators since they are not dealing with Telecoms specific and proprietary technological infrastructure any more. The new messaging model extends beyond the traditional SMS and MMS protocols to include the complexity of IP messaging systems. As a result, Telecoms operators are faced with the same problems as those of the IT departments, which are typically challenges of commoditisation, scaling resources, Information Technology management (IT and Cyber Parks) and efficient operational management. Telecoms operators are required to change their ways and culture of operating their business to include the aspects of economics, cost and earned value management of the IP technological models into their organisations.

Having considered the two major pressures, the Telecoms market tends to be more service centric, demanding a high level of Quality of Service (QoS) at low prices due to the consequence of fierce competition. However services are often short lived, for example, price packages and bundles are easy to copy and very soon new functionalities supplied by the operators are available to everyone and is not a differentiator any more.

Nevertheless, there are differentiators that tend to be longed-lived which are either based on having a genuine edge in customer-service standards, or by having a genuinely lower operational cost base, allowing pricing advantages to be sustained without financial damage. Over the years, Telecoms companies have tried hard to create value added differentiators. Call management services, fax, voicemail, cellular SMS, web hosting and email hosting all of which were launched as differentiators for connectivity service providers but lasted as products not as differentiators. Technology and innovative services can provide genuine, long-lasting differentiation in the Telecoms market, nonetheless pricing and QoS matter the most. In fact, QoS has a direct impact on the customer service standards and indeed an iterative process of QoS monitoring through consumer surveys and feedbacks will help to further improve the customer service standards. However to achieve lower operation cost base, the operator has to improve the management and the process of their systems which include their own internal "supply chain." These systems are the automated part of message logistics, such as messaging gateways and messaging service systems, which in essence is to manage the transportation of messaging across the networks.

In summary as the mobile market moves to become more service centric, rather than technology centric, Quality of Service (QoS) has grown to become imperative. Thus, decision makers of Telecoms are urging software architects, developers and engineers to build new communication infrastructure to reach for quality attributes such as horizontal scalability, high availability, economical resource management, performance and reliability. These are quality attributes that are now critical and characterise the survivability of an organisation. In many quality engineering fields, these attributes are referred to Key Quality Factors (KQFs) (Horgan, et al., 1999; Khaddaj & Horgan, 2004). The change in the Telecoms modus operandi is happening as the market waves more and more opportunities due to the expansion of the mobile community and in an attempt to grab those opportunities, software engineers realised that traditional architectures, with their centralised chassis, cannot evolve, thus they cannot support the load and exercise in the new Telecoms economy.

Hence the significance of distributed systems has changed the problem domain of building messaging systems and by virtue of illustrating the change, we introduce the concept of *Class of Problems* which is fundamentally a categorisation process, where a class can be regarded as an information system encapsulating the problem attributes that share common properties. The reason why the classification process is based on shared features is because common problem attributes may require the same knowledge and techniques for problem resolutions. Typically a class will not only state the problem attributes, their characteristics and relationships to each other but also specify the knowledge required, and techniques available to tackle these problems. The Class of Problems is, subsequently, a multi-disciplinary process in the way it defines a spectrum of tools and techniques required to resolve a set of problem attributes.

This led to the understanding that using purely classical software engineering tools were not sufficient to apprehend the problem of distributed messaging system in its entirety. Through the investigations, it has been observed that the aspect of communication and the interconnectivity of distributed nodes are too dynamic and too context dependent to be modelled entirely using structural design methods. However, structural design tools do add value to the design of the systems. Structural and formal methods can be used to construct distributed programs from hierarchical set of structured specifications of component instances and their interconnections. Composite component types are constructed from primitive computational components and these in turn can be configured into more complex composite types. From an infrastructural point of view, the formal approach provides a robust and specific formalism to build composite components that facilitates the process of managing systems structures. But, according to Garlan and Shaw, in their analysis on advances of software engineering (Shaw, 2001), there is a lack of scientific rigour within software engineering, wherein structural design alone cannot exhaustively define a software problem.

## QUALITY CHALLENGES OF MESSAGING SYSTEMS

With the worldwide installed base station of mobile phone owners is reaching many billions people and with most new mobile phones doubling as portable PCs and internet terminals, the Telecoms are urgently looking for alternative solutions to accommodate the expected surge in mobile services and mobile users. In this very dynamic market, quality presents a major challenge to the Telecoms. We identified two aspects of quality, namely 1) QoS for traffic engineering, and 2) Quality features of the system infrastructure.

### QoS and Traffic Engineering

QoS and traffic engineering is a type of quality assurance activity which is commonly practiced in software networking fields and very often referred to as "*test for quality.*" QoS is strongly linked to traffic engineering, where the investigations are focussed on the methods of obtaining and measuring metrics such as 1) traffic rate, 2) congestion rate 3) transition time or latency, 4) packet loss and 5) throughput. These metrics are usually diagnosed during the testing phase to validate and optimise the system performance against the specifications. There are several QoS measurement frameworks to compare the relative

benefits of using different types of traffic engineering mechanisms. The work carried out on adaptive QoS of network traffic (Medhi, 2002) considers QoS routing within the constraints of dynamic load conditions. Furthermore the assessment carried out on QoS based routing (Sun, 2002) evaluates several QoS routing algorithms and reports on their benefits and drawbacks. Another investigation on adaptive QoS in heterogeneous network environment (Gao, et al., 2003) suggests that a considerable amount of QoS research has been historically undertaken but the main portion still occurred in the context of individual architecture components where much less progress has been made in addressing the issue of an overall QoS architecture for the mobile Internet. The definition of QoS has changed within the Telecoms, which is mainly due to the IP Convergence, where not only, the aspect of QoS for Telecoms infrastructures is addressed, but operators are also required to understand the aspects of QoS for IP infrastructures. For recent years, many substantial research efforts for QoS support in IP infrastructures have been made. These are the new network challenges of the Telecoms in their endeavour to enforce quality methods in their automated operations.

### Quality Features of the System Infrastructure

Quality features for the system infrastructure falls into a different category, which we refer to as "*design for quality.*" The concept goes beyond the complexity of testing the system against specified QoS parameters. "*Design for quality*" inherently means that quality is modelled and built within the design of the system. This kind of approach is still not fully incorporated within the commercial software community and requires knowledge of more advanced quality methods which are in essence the ability to embed a quality model within the "genes" of the system. The main intention is to design quality into the system and to focus on some generic quality features that we currently believe have the biggest impact towards contributing as differentiator on the Telecoms market:

**Hot Deployment:** is the ability to deploy new components, packed with features onto a software platform at run time. As the Telecoms business develops into a more service centric model, the system has to support a flexible architecture to accommodate new services, which enable the construction of multi featured products. This is achieved by plugging new software components onto a base architecture by devising the necessary protocol links for inter-systems communication.

**Horizontal Scalability:** as the Telecoms business grows, the systems that support their functions (messaging or message logistics) also need to grow to handle more consumers, and process more data, without degrading the QoS. Williams and Smith demonstrate that, as businesses expand, it is important to maintain their performance (responsiveness or throughput) (Williams & Smith, 2004). Horizontal scaling offers a solution by tying multiple independent computers together to provide more processing power which is a resilient and viable solution as far as the evolution of the system is concerned. With growing demand in the Telecoms market to cover more economies and services, horizontal scalability, which allows the expansion of computing power, is a quality attribute becoming more stringent than ever.

**High Availability:** High availability refers to the availability of resources in a computer system, in the wake of components or nodes failure. This is achieved in a variety of ways, ranging from solutions that utilize custom and redundant hardware to ensure availability, to software that provides solutions using off-the-shelf hardware components. The former class of solutions provide a higher degree of availability, but are significantly more expensive. This has led to the popularity of off-the-shelf solutions, with almost all vendors of computer systems offering various high availability (cluster management) products. High availability is a critical quality attribute in many fields of automation, computerised transac-

tional systems and particularly in the Telecoms. Classically, in the Telecoms arena, messaging gateways are based on monolithic architectures and designers adopt the redundant hardware approach to build the system over an active vs. passive model. Active and Passive modes mean that two deployment nodes of the solution share a common database and at any given time one and only one node is active. Should the active node fail, the passive node reads the last defined states of the failed node from the database and becomes active.

**Evolution of system:** in an ever dynamic mobile market, the messaging systems have to adapt to its environment and manage its workload and interactivity. It has to be flexible to intelligently allocate new resources and distribute the resources using responsive work load distribution mechanism with regards to the economics (demand and supply) of the messaging systems. To elaborate, metrics are strategically positioned to measure and characterise the demand and supply of a messaging system in terms of message throughput, message processing / service (leading to resource consumption) and delivery rate, leading to designing the system for capacity. The economics involved in this approach of design uses to the concept of cost management, utility and earned value management.

**Content Agnostic:** in order to handle a large spectrum of messages packaged in different protocols, a messaging system is required to be content agnostic. At the very least this is a statement that many stakeholders believe to be critical for evolution. To build content agnostic servers is not trivial as it requires design methods that are dynamic enough to adapt and change their "nature" depending on the type of incoming and outgoing message. This adds new intensity to the work load of the logistics. In classical message service systems, designers use the concept of pluggable components designed specifically to react to certain protocols. However, as the infrastructure scales to accommodate more complex service and components, this approach shows drastic drop in the performance of the system. Thus, a new problem emerges that requires a consistent and adaptive communication model.

The reader would observe that most of the quality features required for the system infrastructure, "*design for quality*," naturally tallies with the mechanics of distributed systems rather than those of monolithic systems. When we envisaged how these quality features can be implemented within the architecture of messaging systems, we found out that that there are several reasons why distributed and autonomous systems are good candidates.

## DISTRIBUTED AND AUTONOMOUS SYSTEMS

As Gruber states in his work (Gruber, 2005), "*The mobile telecommunications industry is one of the most rapidly growing sectors around the world*," which is creating a market place governed by fierce competition, and as stressed in section 3, quality of service and service innovations are imperative for survivability and sustainability. Amongst the many quality factors, the Telecoms require systems that have to fundamentally meet three of the most important quality attributes, which are horizontal scalability, high availability and system evolution (Williams & Smith, 2004).

Horizontal scalability is a quality attribute that has been thoroughly assessed on both centralised systems and distributed systems. The flexibility of distributed architectures to scale over large heterogeneous network computing is very important factor whereas a centralised system imposes a burden on resource utility in the sense that it is sometimes intricate and uneconomical to expand or upgrade the system. In these circumstances, when utilities are to be added, it very often requires a physical upgrade of the existing machine's capability such as memory capacity or processors' speed. Furthermore, when it comes to High avail-

ability, historically, we have seen several works portraying the benefit of distributed systems to sustain high availability (Rossi & Turrini, 2005; Vilas, et al., 2005). Most of these works discuss the solution of clustering to ensure high availability within a distributed architecture. Vilas et al (2005) presented a technique of deploying web services with high availability features using clustering mechanism. This is based on the virtualization of the distributed web services by creating new virtual web services as requested by the clients. These clustering and high availability strategies are less costly and more effective than those of the hardware redundancies approaches, currently used for monolithic solutions of the Telecoms. The centralised solution is also reluctant to change, whereas distributed system would allow the replication of several operations and functions of messaging logistics on several dispersed nodes. These functions can be managed through distributed cluster management software which implements service discovery mechanism and can be deployed at run time when a typical failure occurs.

As far as system evolution is concerned, carriers have to design computerised system that will adapt to new dynamics and new requirements in order to keep the competitive edge. Several works have been dedicated to the evolution of computerised system in the domain of Telecoms. The work carried out on agent interoperability (Zhang, 2001) assessed the shortcomings of classical software design paradigm of interoperability and proposed a multi agent design on knowledge based understanding, which enabled a sophisticated system of co operation that can adapt to its environment unlike traditional semantic bases interoperability. In addition, the study on the management of software evolution (Mikkonen, et al., 2000) proposed a model of system abstraction to manage the evolution of Telecoms software through the concept of services. The services enable an abstract description of conceptual properties of the system disregarding their final relation to underlying software components of the implementation. As a result focus can be shifted from individual implementation components to their collaboration at varying levels of abstraction, thus providing autonomy. Another investigation carried out on the evolution of software systems within the Telecoms (Koutsoukos, et al., 2001) stressed on the problems of Telecoms systems to adapt to new requirements (flexibility) and proposes reconfigurable modelling primitive called coordination contract. It also presented a protocol design primitive that can support the evolution of requirements of a transactional processing system. The common feature amongst these studies is that they all inherently embrace the models of distributed systems whilst addressing the problem of system evolution. In a way distributed systems and autonomy seemed like a pre-requisite to designing a system that can adapt to its environment and evolve.

In the discussion on evolution of systems, Hugues Bersini (Bersini, 2005) states that of the many types of systems organisations models, those that are in the form of networks and which are based on distributed architectures are the ones that survive and are economically most viable. The study on dynamic evolution (Hay-Fung, et al., 2004) explains how one can easily achieve evolution in a component-based distributed system. In this paper, Hay Fung explains the abstraction of components and their connectors facilitates system structures to accommodate changes. Currently the software industry is in favour of the iterative and incremental development approach over the traditional waterfall model, in order to achieve flexible processes that handle requirements and reduce the risk by deploying smaller changes. In such an environment, dynamic evolution provides the flexibility in implementing changes to unforeseen and fluctuating business requirements which is very true for the development of messaging systems in the Telecoms.

Evolution is a key factor to software systems, because these systems are never isolated, but implicitly constrained by their users, the commu-

nication with external systems (machines or man) and the infrastructures (software or hardware) with which they communicate (Oudrhiri, 1980). Each adjustment or modification from any connecting peers may change or affect the internal system. The system may be provided with some resiliency and intelligence through predefined logic, to either protect itself from these changes or adapt itself to these changes, depending on the *hostility* of the environment. In other words some decision dominance may be given to the system, defining an aspect of autonomy, and since the working environment is non deterministic, the system will need to adapt and re-adapt itself, changing its course many times during its life time (Oudrhiri, 1980). Unfortunately, investments in software systems are mostly focus on designing systems based on strict protocols and precise specifications and constraints, thus restricting the systems from its external communication. If we agree that software systems are never isolated, these types of design approach (strict protocols and precise specifications) go against the natural progress of software systems. The need for evolution in the design of messaging system can be mapped to Lehman's 8 laws of software evolution (Lehman, 1980). We considered Lehman's 8 laws of evolution to guide the design and establish a framework of study to incorporate some aspects of evolution within the messaging system, however we are only focussing on following four laws:

Law (2) **Increasing Complexity** - "*As a program evolves, it becomes more complex, and extra resources are needed to preserve and simplify its structure.*" As the number of communication agents (content providers and network elements) increases, the communication model tend to become more complex and non deterministic. Within the Telecoms, the law also applies to the message, as the content of the message becomes more complex from SMS to MMS, and video messages, extra resources are needed to preserve or simplify the structure of the systems in terms of manageability and serviceability.

Law (6) **Continuing Growth** - "*The functional capability of systems must be continually increased to maintain user satisfaction over the system lifetime.*" Scalability of the functionalities is key in the design of messaging software solutions. Although Telecoms software solutions may be well structured internally using hierarchically structured class libraries, the programs have grown large and monolithic, with a high degree of interdependence of the internal modules. The size of the programs and their relatively high level, user oriented interface makes them inflexible and discomfited to use for the construction of new functions and applications. As a result, new applications usually have to be constructed at a relatively low level, as compiled programs, which are expensive and inflexible. The high degree of integration at the class library level makes it difficult to construct heterogeneous applications that use modules from different systems, since there is a lack of abstraction. This problem can be addressed by distributed systems which allow software modules to be represented as either stand alone or pluggable components in a distributed application through defined interface or resource adapters, hence scaling the capabilities of the systems.

Law (7) **Decline Quality** – "*Unless rigorously adapted to take into account for changes in the operational environment, the quality of a system will appear to be declining.*" In order to manage the quality of the system, a quality process has to be put in place to improve both the operational environment and the system itself. In many studies directed to the evolution of computerised system, (Zhang, 2001; Mikkonen, et al., 2000; Koutsoukos, et al., 2001), the aspect of quality management is very rarely considered. Yet, Lehman stresses that a decline in quality influences the viability of an evolutive system and for diverse reasons this is often the case for system that evolves.

Law (8) **Feedback System** – "*Evolution processes are multi-level, multi-loop, multi-agent feedback systems.*" Feedback is a strong manage-ment tool to revise and improve a system. Since, software systems are never isolated, a robust feedback mechanism is required to validate the compliance of system functions over which the system developers have little or no control. Due to the lack of control over the external components, the most economic development approach is to implement, obtain feedback on how the components and the interface behaves, and then evolve in the light of that feedback.

However, in order to design systems that evolve, one is also required to consider the aspect of autonomy within the distributed participants of the system. The study on the drive behind evolution of software architecture shows that systems are evolving under the pressure of a number of factors, which are: 1) distribution requires components to be more autonomous and to communicate through explicit means (not linked); 2) maintainability does not requires changing of the source code of components; 3) evolutivity and mobility require keeping components independent and autonomous and 4) Cost requires buying instead of building.

Autonomy is fundamentally about empowerment, giving responsibility to several parts of the system and hence these parts are governed by their own law (Bersini, 2005). In the study on the science of the artificial life (Simon, 1969), the author compares the natural and artificial worlds and concludes that "quasi-autonomy" from the outer environment is an essential characteristic of complex systems which are aggregations of "stable intermediate forms." Whilst the quasi-autonomous systems or subsystems maintain homeostatic relationships with their environment, they always operate within a set of environmental constraints that restrict the entity's autonomy (Oudrhiri, 1980). Communication between the autonomous entities relate to the exchanges of information that are performed through mutual presentations. This mutual presentation of information is a very important distinction between autonomous and non autonomous communications. Typically in autonomous systems, the presentation of information is based on a conversational communication model which is characterised by the information content, the syntactic structure, the morphologic code (the way data is coded, generally depending on the medium), the support (substratum or communication medium) and the rhythm of data exchange (the sends or receives). Yet, the nature of autonomy is constrained by organisational mechanisms and structures that are usually regarded as beneficial restrictions of an entity's autonomy in order to maintain viability and to achieve higher/social level goals. In the science of the artificial (Simon, 1969), the author defines five 'levels' of autonomy based on the constraints to which an entity is subjected to which are:

1. **No autonomy**, where an entity is told what actions to execute and it always attempts to execute them.
2. **Process autonomy**, where an entity is given a task to perform in the form of a goal state but it has some autonomy in what steps are executed in order to achieve that task.
3. **Goal-state autonomy**, where an entity is given an external goal, which may be satisfied by a number of states, e.g. an operating system that maintains processing capacity by deciding the run-time priority of processes.
4. **Intentional autonomy**, where an entity has the freedom to decide whether or not to satisfy external goals based on its own intentions, which can be either cooperative or competitive. A cooperative entity will fulfil the request if it can and collaborate to satisfy system goal. Competitive entity only collaborates if it receives sufficient reward based on a market system with the clear objectives of maximising its own utility.
5. **Constraint autonomy**, where an entity is prepared to violate norms or even rules to achieve its goals.

The fact that our problem domain is now addressing features of autonomy, evolution, qual-

ity modelling, and distributed systems, we are required to ensure an exhaustive comprehension of the problem attributes, and organize them into distinct classes, which we refer to as Class of Problems.

## THE CLASS OF PROBLEMS FOR DISTRIBUTED MESSAGING SYSTEMS

As the Telecoms shift their design towards distributed architectures, they observe a change in their problem domain. Distributed systems are complex and have brought new problem attributes to the process of building messaging systems. During our investigations, we looked at these emerging attributes and created a Class of Problems in an attempt to manage the complexity of the problem domain. The Class of Problems is similar to an information system, which means that it is a system of data records, (the problem attributes), activities that process the data (the methods related to the resolution of the problem attributes) and information arranged in a given category (specific problem domain of distributed messaging systems). The class is an entity that encapsulates attributes that share common features and the reason behind the classification process is typically because common problem attributes may require the same knowledge, methods and tools to be resolved. However, a class will not only state the problem attributes and their characteristics but also specify the required knowledge, methods and techniques to tackle these problems

The Class of Problems has been established based on the challenges from both the internal and external pressures to the Telecoms. Whilst the market and the business side revealed a service centric and quality oriented model, the technological side demands for the evolution of the system. A generic Class of Problems of distributed messaging systems (see Figure 1) presenting six classes of problems, (communication, substratum, dynamics, economics and quality), which together define the problem domain of enabling, managing and operating message logistics.

## Communication

Communication is the foundation of many systems and its understanding is fundamental to build the interaction of software entities such as objects, modules, components, agents etc. As we move from monolithic to distributed systems, the complexity of communication increases, where applications become increasingly dispersed with more connection interfaces, communication takes an ever more central role in modern software systems. Many different techniques and concepts have been proposed, in both academia and industry, for providing structure to the problems of communication in software systems. Recent developed communication structures such as Remote Message Send (RMS), also known as Remote Method Invocation (RMI) or Location-Independent Invocation (LII) are used for the management of distributed object based systems (Szyperski, 2006).

*Figure 1. Class of problems*

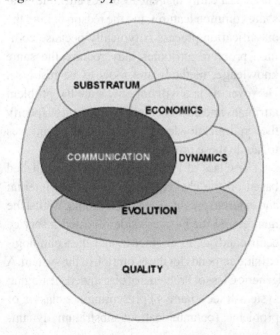

Another innovative communication structure, used for message oriented systems, is based on the message-oriented middleware that provides abstractions between the diverse communication layers (Lynch & Shvartsman, 2003). However, it has also become clear that while such abstractions are by themselves sufficient to expose the hard problems of distributed computing, they do not implicitly solve the complexity of the communication models. The need for advanced abstraction of communication system can be compared to the evolution of database management system in which the database model and the graphical user interfaces are examples of software elements that were once complicated to program but have, through the right abstractions and implementations, been greatly simplified.

The question central to our problem domain is whether similar abstractions can be devised for simplifying the communication within distributed applications. Just as successful database components required not only mechanisms for storing and retrieving data, but also abstractions like query languages and transactions, successful communication abstractions requires more than the mere ability to communicate, i.e. moving beyond the models data exchange (send and receive).

Thus, the development of a communication model that can adapt and evolve to the dynamics of the Telecoms is extremely important. Though several works have been achieved on the abstraction of communication model for distributed systems (Dedecker & De Meuter, 2003), our proposed approach's strength comes from the approach of adopting some aspects human conversation (the conversational dynamics) as metaphor to design and build a generic communication model for the domain of distributed messaging system (Khaddaj & Makoond, 2010). In doing so, we had to look at the elements of 1) dynamism in human conversation and 2) non deterministic behaviour or emergent behaviour during the conversation.

The aspect of non determinism is fundamental to the model of communication, because in employing the classical structural modelling tools such as ERD, Class Diagram and Flow Charts, to build a communication model, many factors mostly related to dynamic interaction and emergent behaviours cannot be represented. As a result we had to include dynamic modelling techniques such as simulations and prototyping in this research to depict the complexity involved when systems communicate.

The concept of dynamic interaction has been defined by G Bateson in his work on communication and language, (Batteson, et al., 1971), to demonstrate that the behaviour of a participant can induce a specific behaviour from his peer whilst conversing. This induction process of forcing (strongly influencing) a specific behaviour from peers is present in all the communication model of all systems or organisations; yet the effect can be implicit, explicit or both. The induction of behaviour by communicating peers defines the type of communication and it presents us with another aspect of communication which is the concept of *communication styles*. We used the concept of communication styles to enrich the management of communication for the proposed distributed messaging system.

## Substratum

According to Merriam Webster, a substratum is an underlying support or a foundation (Webster, 2005). In our case, the class substratum is fundamentally the structure (container) utilised to carry the information being exchanged in a given communication which relates to the communication medium. The class substratum has different interpretation depending on the scale or level at which it is being observed. In computerised networking, at the lowest level, the wiring over an open network, are communication mediums, yet as we move up to the Network Interface Card (NIC) and Kernel, the medium tend to be interpreted in a more virtual manner, for instance the memory allocated by the Kernel for network

copies. At the application level, or more precisely, to understand the communication amongst applications, we interpret the substratum as the type of memory in use, of which two types can be identified. On one hand we have the *"long term memory"* which relates to Storage (Databases and Database Management System). This category of medium perceives information to be stored for a long period of time often towards persistence. On the other hand we have the *"Short term memory"* which relates to the storage of information for a very short while often during a conversation; e.g. queues, stacks, array etc. Our approach focuses on the latter category and we understand that the communication styles influence the choice of communication medium and to illustrate, we provide the following analogy:

*The little boy was asked a simple mathematical calculation – "2 X 2." Promptly the little boy answered "4." The teacher then asked for a complex integration function – The little boy answered "I need pen and paper first!"*

For simple problem solving (communication style), the human mind usually allocate a small bit of memory (communication medium) to perform the calculations. But for complex problem, a different type of communication medium is required, that takes the form of long term memory (*pen and paper*). The economics behind the process of allocating resources (communication medium) for the different styles of communication play a major role in systems that need to evolve.

The concept of communication medium is of utmost importance for the design of communication models, since its abstraction is becoming more and more virtual, its management is being done at the application level. As a system becomes aware of the distinct communication styles, it may decide on the type of substratum to use as method of storage, either long term or short term, hence an intelligent way of managing resources. This however requires a communication model which is dynamic and can also evolve.

## Dynamics

Emergent behaviour is distinguishable when the behaviour of an entire system appears more coherent and engaged than the behaviour of individual parts of the system. Very often researchers use the analogy of an ant colony in the study of complex systems. Yet the analysis of the behaviour of individual parts (one ant) reveals very little about the systemic behaviour. This is a problem which is also relevant to the design of computer networks. The source and effects of emergent behaviour in computer networks, focuses on several QoS parameters particularly, traffic congestion, in the attempt to understand and control the dynamic behaviour of existing networks.

In a typical messaging system, there are many queues that communicate to each other. The control parameter of the queues, such as buffer size, no. of servers and throughput rate are usually factors that influence the dynamics of the system. In order to model and analyse these factors, one is required to adopt simulation and prototyping techniques, since classical structural model will not represent these characteristics.

## Economics

As software architectures move towards distributed models, there is the origination of a society, wherein software entities communicate to each other and in doing so they collaborate and compete for resources. Assuming that software entities are services, consumers or resources, an economic model can be applied to the society. The economies of the society can be defined by a consumer accessing a resource or a group of resources that are made available through a service. Since resources are scarce, the problem of resource management and resource allocation (distribution) within the

society is not only a problem of informatics anymore, but also a problem of economics.

In recent years, we observe several studies in the field of applying economic model to distributed systems in deployments such as grid computation. However, most studies on economic models for resource management and scheduling explore the usage of an economics-based paradigm for managing resource allocation in Grid computing environments, wherein an economic approach provided a fair basis in successfully managing distributed components and heterogeneity that is present in human economies (Buyya, et al., 2002). Competitive economic models provide algorithms/policies and tools for resource sharing within the Grid systems. There are two economic models which are based on bartering or prices models. In the bartering-based model, all participants need to own resources and trade resources by exchanges (e.g., storage space for CPU time). In the price-based model, the resources have a price, based on the demand, supply, value and the wealth in the economic system.

Classically, most of the related work in resource management for distributed systems and scheduling problems adopt the price based models (Chapin, et al., 1999). In these models the scheduling components manage resources by deciding which jobs are to be executed on certain cost functions and such cost functions are often driven by system-centric parameters that enhance system *throughput* and *utilisation* rather than improving the utility of application *processing*.

## Quality

The current push in the Telecoms industry is focused on ensuring that software applications consistently perform as desired. Software quality is the degree to which software possesses a desired combination of quality attributes, e.g. performance, safety, robustness, reliability, security, interoperability and correctness (Horgan, et al., 1999), also known as KQFs. In typical software development life cycle, most of these quality factors are assessed (test for quality) at the implementation and testing phase. However, recently, it has been observed that much of an application's quality aspects are determined by early design decisions, in which the design choices are carried out at the requirements, analysis and modelling phases. Consequently, quality assurance have shifted into the design phase (design for quality), changing the perspective of architecting software systems. When creating a software architecture for a given application domain, system designers often justify their creation by claiming that it supports and conforms to KQFs, commonly referred to as Non-Functional Requirements (NFR). The achievement of NFRs is attributable to many factors of the development process, such as coding styles, documentation and testing. However for larger and more complex systems, the achievement of NFRs, predominantly, rests in the software architecture and design.

## CONCLUSION

IP convergence is affecting the ways technology is being implemented by Telecoms operators to provide messaging service. Fierce competition is driving the market, collapsing what was once a Telecoms value chain, into a value web wherein the commercials are shared amongst many stakeholders, leading to a large variety of mobile services. This has resulted in a rapid expansion of the number of mobile users and mobile data applications. Consequently, the Telecoms are required to shift the current technology to distributed dynamic and evolutive systems to cope with the expanding market. To achieve these changes, quality engineering, to both the service and the technological dimensions, is essential, which means that quality has to be modelled throughout the development life cycle, spanning from the requirement, analysis, design, to the implementation and not just at the testing phase.

To survive the expanding Telecoms market, building messaging systems with adaptive and evolutive abilities is becoming more and more crucial. An important characteristic of evolution is the problem of co habitation which, in our case relates to IP convergence, where the classical messaging systems (the old) need to co habit with new IP infrastructures. To model the aspect of evolution into messaging systems, we explored Lehman's 8 laws of software evolution which led to the conceptualisation of autonomous participants. These autonomous entities, working on a distributed environment, tend to naturally conform to the framework of building adaptive and evolutive systems. These systems enable the abstraction of components from their connectors, thus facilitating the structure to accommodate changes. The fact that we regard distributed system as a group of distinct autonomous entities working together, introduces new complexities.

In order to understand the complexity, we devised a model that we refer to as a Class of Problems. The Class of Problems is primarily multidisciplinary as we observe that some classes require different approaches of modelling. For instance, within the class Dynamics, one of the requirements is to model the collaboration between software entities (components or agents) and analyse how they join and leave communication sessions. Using purely collaboration or sequence diagrams from UML is not sufficient due to their static characteristic. As a result we need to use dynamic and simulation modelling techniques, in order to investigate the model of communication from a systemic and holistic perspective.

From a quality engineering perspective, test for quality is not adequate anymore to ascertain the consistency of quality in distributed messaging systems. Within the class Quality, we are required to look at modelling tools, statistical and probabilistic techniques to measure, analyse and model quality of the system. Moreover, the class Communication demands a larger spectrum of modelling tools, ranging from structural modelling to dynamic modelling and simulation of communication amongst the peers to analyse the relationship between communication styles over the communication medium and most importantly the significance of non determinism within the communication.

The classical modelling approach, UML, ERD, flow charts and DFDs are principally structural and static in nature, but they add value by providing the formalism required to explain the structure of a system, the design and the flow of process. However, distributed messaging systems are social networks, with non deterministic behaviours, which only can be modelled by complementing the structural modelling techniques with the dynamic modelling approaches. Therefore, a blended modelling approach which employs tools and methods aspired from both the structural and dynamic arenas need to be adopted.

# REFERENCES

Batteson, G., Houseman, M., & Severi, C. (1971). *La cérémonie du Naven*. Paris, France: Minuit.

Bersini, H. (2005). *Des réseaux et des sciences – Biologie, informatique, sociologie: L'omniprésence des réseaux*. Paris, France: Vuibert.

Buyya, R., Abramson, D., Giddy, J., & Stockinger, H. (2002). Economic models for resource management and scheduling in Grid computing. In *Concurrency and Computation*. New York: John Wiley & Sons. doi:10.1002/cpe.690

Chapin, S., Karpovich, J., & Grimshaw, A. (1999). The legion resource management system. In *Proceedings of the 5th Workshop on Job Scheduling Strategies for Parallel Processing*. San Juan, Puerto Rico: Springer.

Dedecker, J., & De Meuter, W. (2003). *Communication abstractions through new language concepts*. Retrieved from http://soft.vub.ac.be/Publications/2003/vub-prog-tr-03-28.pdf.

Gao, P., & Damsgaard, J. (2007). *A framework for understanding mobile telecommunications market innovation: A case of china*. Manchester, UK: IDPM.

Gao, X., Wu, G., & Miki, T. (2003). QoS framework for mobile heterogeneous networks. In *Proceedings of the IEEE International Conference on Communications*, (pp. 933 – 937). IEEE Press.

Gruber, H. (2005). *The economics of mobile telecommunications*. Cambridge, UK: Cambridge University Press. doi:10.1017/CBO9780511493256

Hay-Fung, K., Low, G., & Bay, P. K. (2004). Embracing dynamic evolution in distributed systems Software. *IEEE, 21*(2), 49 – 55.

Horgan, G., Khaddaj, S., & Forte, P. (1999). An essential views model for software quality. In Kusters, R., Cowderoy, A., Heemstra, F., & Van Veenendaa, E. (Eds.), *Project Control for Software Quality*. New York: Shaker Publishing.

Khaddaj, S., & Horgan, G. (2004). The evaluation of software quality factors in very large information systems. *Electronic Journal of Information Systems Evaluation*, 43-48.

Khaddaj, S., & Makoond, B. (2010). Design and simulation of human conversational model for distributed systems. In *Proceedigns of the 9th International Conference on Distributed Computing and Applications for Business, Engineering and Science*. Hong Kong, China: IEEE Press.

Koutsoukos, G., Gouveia, J., Andrade, L., & Fiadeiro, J. L. (2001). Managing evolution in telecommunication systems. In *Proceedings of the IFIP TC6 / WG6.1 3rd International Working Conference on New Developments in Distributed Applications and Interoperable Systems*. IEEE Press.

Lehman, M. M. (1980). On understanding laws, evolution and conservation in the large program life cycle. *Journal of Systems and Software, 1*(3).

Lynch, N., & Shvartsman, A. (2003). *Communication and data sharing for dynamic distributed systems*. Heidelberg, Berlin: Springer-Verlag.

Medhi, D. (2002). Quality of service (QoS) routing computation with path caching: A framework and network performance. *IEEE Communication Magazine*.

Melody, W., Sutherland, E., & Tadayoni, R. (2005). *Convergence, IP telephony and telecom regulation*. Paper presented at the Workshop on Convergence, VoIP and Regulation. New Delhi, India: Telecommunication Regulatory Authority of India (TRAI).

Mikkonen, T., Lahde, E., Niemi, J., & Siiskonen, M. (2000). Managing software evolution with the service concept. In *Proceedings of International Symposium on Principles of Software Evolution*, (pp 46 – 50). IEEE Press.

Miyazakia, K., & Wiggersb, E. (2005). *Innovation in telecom services framework and analysis based on the case of international pre-paid calling cards in Japan*. Tokyo, Japan: Tokyo Institute of Technology.

Oudrhiri, R. (1980). *Une approche de l'évolution des systèmes- Application aux systèmes d'information*. Paris, France: Vuibert.

Rossi, D., & Turrini, E. (2005). Analyzing the impact of components replication in high available J2EE clusters. In *Proceedings of the Joint International Conference on Autonomic and Autonomous Systems and International Conference on Networking and Services*, (p. 56). IEEE Press.

Schumpeter, J. A. (1975). *Capitalism, socialism and democracy*. New York: Harper.

Shaw, M. (2001). The coming-of-age of software architecture research. In *Proceedings of ICSE*, (pp. 656–664). Pittsburgh, PA: Carnegie Mellon University.

Simon, H. A. (1969). *The sciences of the artificial*. Cambridge, MA: MIT Press.

Sun, W. (2002). *QoS, policy, constraint based routing*. Columbus, OH: Ohio State University.

Szyperski, C. (2006). Component-based software engineering. In *Proceedings of the 9th International Symposium, CBSE 2006*. Västeras, Sweden: IEEE Press.

Vilas, J. F., Arias, J. P., & Vilas, A. F. (2005). High availability with clusters of web service. In *Advanced Web Technologies and Applications* (*Vol. 3007*). Berlin, Germany: Springer. doi:10.1007/978-3-540-24655-8_70

Webster, M. (2005). *The Merriam-Webster dictionary*. New York: Merriam-Webster.

Williams, L. G., & Smith, C. U. (2004). *Web application scalability: A model-based approach*. New York: Software Engineering Research and Performance Engineering Services.

Zhang, T. (2001). *Agent-based interperability in telecommunications applications*. PhD Thesis. Berlin, Germany: University of Berlin.

# Chapter 19
# A Simulation Model for Large Scale Distributed Systems

**Ciprian Dobre**
*University POLITEHNICA of Bucharest, Romania*

## ABSTRACT

*The use of discrete-event simulators in the design and development of Large Scale Distributed Systems (LSDSs) is appealing due to their efficiency and scalability. Their core abstractions of process and event map neatly to the components and interactions of modern-day distributed systems and allow designing realistic simulation scenarios. MONARC 2, a multithreaded, process oriented simulation framework designed for modeling LSDSs, allows the realistic simulation of a wide-range of distributed system technologies, with respect to their specific components and characteristics. This chapter presents the design characteristics of the simulation model proposed in MONARC 2. It starts by first analyzing existing work, outlining the key decision points taken in the design of the MONARC's simulation model. The model includes the necessary components to describe various actual distributed system technologies and provides the mechanisms to describe concurrent network traffic, evaluate different strategies in data replication, and analyze job scheduling procedures.*

## INTRODUCTION

Large-scale grids and other federations of distributed resources that aggregate and share resources over wide-area networks present major new challenges for scientists. In this chapter we focus on the challenge to enable scalable, high-level, online simulation of applications, middleware, resources and networks to support scientific and systematic study of Large Scale Distributed Systems (LS-

DSs). The field of modelling and simulation was long-time seen as a viable alternative to develop new algorithms and technologies. It enables the development of LSDS when analytical validations are prohibited by the nature of the encountered problems.

In this chapter we describe the approach used to design and implement a generic simulator for distributed systems. We present the design characteristics of a model for the simulation of such systems that integrates components and mechanisms that enable realistic simulation

DOI: 10.4018/978-1-4666-0191-8.ch019

experiments for LSDS. The model incorporates the necessary components and characteristics that allow the complete and accurate design of realistic simulation experiments of complex Grid architectures, consisting of many resources and various technologies, ranging from data transferring to scheduling and data replication, with resources working together to provide a common set of characteristics. The proposed simulation model includes the components to describe various actual distributed system technologies, and provides the mechanisms to describe concurrent network traffic, evaluate different strategies in data replication, and analyze job scheduling procedures.

The model is part of a multithreaded, process oriented simulator for LSDS called MONARC 2. The first version of such a generic simulator for LSDS was developed in the late '90s (Dobre & Stratan, 2003). It started with the LHC physics experiments that needed data processing and storage capacities beyond what was available at that time. The size of the LHC experiments and the unprecedented scale of data resulted in the need to look at resources outside of European Organization for Nuclear Research (CERN). This context led to the proposal of the hierarchical distribution model (the Tier architecture), according to which facilities from all around the world are putting together resources in order to provide the necessary computing power and data storage space needed for the experiments (Legrand, et al., 2003). In many ways this architecture was the predecessor of modern LSDS. Still, because the architecture represented a novel approach, and to eliminate further suspicions that the model might not in fact deliver the envisioned processing and storing capacities, a mix team of researchers from CERN and California Institute of Technology designed and developed the first version of a generic simulator, called MOdels of Networked Analysis at Regional Centers (MONARC). It was actually used for the first validation experiments of the model that was later used in the processing of the data actual generated in the LHC experiments (Dobre & Cristea, 2007).

Still, the original simulator included only limited functionality. It was able to evaluate limited simple models, including several components needed in the physics experiments. Later on the author of this chapter redesigned the simulation model, adding new components and capabilities to allow the simulation of a wider range of distributed systems architectures. The model was evaluated in the implementation of the second generation of a more generic and flexible simulator, capable of delivering higher performance results. It was named MONARC 2. The simulator allowed the development of experiments with thousands of nodes and the evaluation of models ranging from Computational Grids to Data Grids, scheduling and replication algorithms, networking protocols, data warehouses, almost anything Grid related. MONARC 2 also took advantages of the current progress that was made by newer Java Virtual Machine implementations since the original MONARC project. The original simulation engine was redesigned to allow much larger systems to be simulated, comprising more components and running jobs. In the same time it improved the running performances by integrating state-of-the-art algorithms and structures. The simulation components were redesigned to consider many more parameters and others new were added into the simulation models. For example, the possibility to simulate data replication, distributed scheduling, fault tolerance, security, represent capabilities were introduced in the new simulation framework. The output representations of the simulations were redesigned. Higher aggregate functionalities were introduced to allow for a higher level analysis of the produced simulation results.

By incorporating state-of-the-art algorithms and technology solutions, the simulator allows the realistic simulation of a wide-range of distributed system technologies, with respect to their specific components and characteristics. The modelling instrument provides the means to faster simulate distributed system of larger scale, involving a large number of resources and applications. Its characteristics, such as its robust architecture, modular and extensible implementation, rich set of of-the-box components, made MONARC 2 a popular modelling instrument among users from various scientific fields. The use of monitoring technologies in the validation and design of the simulation framework consolidated the success of the project. The monitoring results were used to design realistic conditions for various simulation experiments.

## SPECIFIC SIMULATION REQUIREMENTS FOR MODERN LSDS

In the broad area of distributed systems researchers often ask questions such as which scheduling algorithm is best suitable for deploying an application on a Grid system or which caching strategy serves better a community of users that are working in distributed data analysis. Answers to such questions are obtained in several ways. A solution is to develop purely analytical or mathematical models, but this often leads to NP-complete problems, such as routing, partitioning or scheduling, for which no analytical solution can be found. Another solution consists in conducting live experiments. Unfortunately there are no standard approaches to conduct live experiments on LSDS. Real-world experiments can be time-intensive, since the execution of applications could last for hours, days, month or even more. And to make things worse, live experiments are limited to testbeds (the particular capabilities of the testbed can affect the outcome) and the obtained results cannot be reproduced by others (which is in fact the basis for scientific advances). Because of such problems simulation can prove to be a more elegant solution to conduct experiments.

However, the design and optimisation of LSDS requires a realistic description and modelling of the data access patterns, the data flow across the local and wide area networks, and the scheduling and workload presented by hundreds of jobs running concurrently and exchanging very large amounts of data. The first step in designing the simulation model of MONARC 2 was the survey of existing work. We wanted to provide a model that comprises the necessary components to design realistic simulations and that can offer a flexible and dynamic environment to evaluate the performance of a wide-range of possible data processing architectures.

## Distributed Systems and Their Influence on Simulation Models

Simulation is based on the use of formalized models of real-world systems that not only characterize the relationships inherent in the system, either mathematically, logically, or symbolically, but also are recognizable and executable by computers. In order to be useful, a simulation model designed for evaluating LSDS should incorporate several components and characteristics that are specific to the real-world systems.

The original distributed system architecture consists of a collection of autonomous machines connected by communication networks and running software systems designed to produce an integrated and consistent computing environment. Distributed systems represent a solution to enable people to cooperate and coordinate their activities more effectively and efficiently. The key characteristics of a distributed system are: resource sharing, openness, concurrency, scalability, fault-tolerance and transparency (Coulouris, et al., 1994).

In a distributed system, the resources – hardware, software and data – can easily be shared among users. For example, a database server can be shared among a group of users. The resource sharing characteristic is ensured by the use of networking components connecting various resources. This characteristic is also important for a simulation model. An adequate model should incorporate a wide set of networking components and protocols to facilitate the modeling of data communication between distributed resources.

The simulated entities, included in the model, should also easily share various resources (e.g., a database server could be modeled as being accessible to various tasks running in different locations).

The openness characteristic of a distributed system is related to specifying key software interfaces to the system and making them available to software developers so that the system can be extended in many ways. A modeling design preserves this characteristic by following an object-oriented programming approach. The user should also be presented with APIs for interfacing with existing simulated components. He should easily extend the modeling framework with its own modeling components. In addition, the simulated tasks should be able to access various modeling actors such as the networking stack, modeled database servers or processing units by using standard interfaces.

The processing concurrency can be achieved by sending requests to multiple machines connected by networks at the same time. For the simulation model this property is equivalent to many simulated processes competing for the same computational resources, as well as concurrent data transfers competing for the same networking resources. A simulation model should therefore incorporate special mechanisms to allow the modeling of concurrent data transfers and processes competing for the same resources. As an example, in MONARC 2 (Dobre & Cristea, 2007) concurrency is achieved using a specialized interrupt mechanism.

The scalability characteristic is important because a distributed system composed of a small number of machines should be easily extended to a large number of machines to increase the processing power. In order to preserve this property an adequate simulation model should consider the case of multiple resources connected by simulated networking entities. A modeled distributed system should, therefore, consist of many simulated machines; each composed of both computing and storage elements. A model should furthermore consider the case of a large number of simulated machines, and even allow the dynamical addition of many others. This could be accomplished using an object-oriented design for the simulation model, which could translate in allowing the addition of many instances into a simulation experiment. The number of simulated resources should only be limited by the physical resources available in the system where the simulation is being executed. The number of threads necessary to handle the various simulated actors is one physical limitation. The solution consists in allowing one thread to simultaneously handle multiple such actors, grouping them all together based on some logic. For example, all jobs being concurrently executed on a single processing unit could be handled in the simulation model by one single physical thread. The same idea could be applied in case of the network model, were all packets or flows traversing one network link could be handled, if necessary, by only one thread. An alternative (more expensive) solution consists in researching and using some form of distributed simulation algorithm such that to use the resources of multiple workstations.

Conducting simulation experiments is time consuming for several reasons. First, the design of sufficiently detailed models requires in depth modeling skills and usually extensive model development efforts. The availability of sophisticated modeling tools today significantly reduces development time by standardized model libraries and user friendly interfaces. Second, once a simulation model is specified, the simulation run can take exceedingly long to execute. This is due either to the objective of the simulation, or the nature of the simulated model. For statistical reasons it might for example be necessary to perform a whole series of simulation runs to establish the required confidence in the performance meters obtained by the simulation, or in other words make confidence intervals sufficiently small (Weske 2001) (see Table 1).

*Table 1. The characteristics of distributed systems and their influence on a simulation model*

| Characteristic | Possible influence on a simulation model |
|---|---|
| Resource sharing | Use of networking components and data sharing entities |
| Openness | Inclusion of easily extendable object-oriented modeling infrastructure and standard interfaces that allow access to the fabric components inside a running simulation experiment |
| Concurrency | Inclusion of mechanisms to model concurrent processes and networking transfers (possible based on some interrupt mechanisms) |
| Scalability | The adoption of an object-oriented simulation model and the use of advanced internal structures to make better use of available physical resources of the underlying stations |
| Fault-tolerance | Mechanisms to model the occurrence of faults and the possibility to include mechanisms to detect and recover from occurring faults |
| Transparency | Use of advanced routing algorithms, data replication algorithms, and scheduling algorithms to consider failure-transparency |

Possibilities to resolve these shortcomings can be found in several methods, one of which is the use of statistical knowledge to prune the number of required simulation runs. Statistical methods like variance reduction can be used to avoid the generation of "unnecessary" system evolutions. Statistical significance can be preserved with a smaller number of evolutions given the variance of a single random estimate can be reduced. Importance sampling methods can be effective in reducing computational efforts as well. Naturally, however, faster simulations can be obtained by using more computational resources, particularly multiple processors operating in parallel. It seems obvious, at least for simulation models reflecting real life distributed systems, consisting of components operating in parallel, that this inherent parallelism could be exploited to make better use of all physical computing resources more effectively. One way of copping up with the increasingly power demand coming from the simulation scenarios nowadays is to make use of more processor units, running on different architectures and dispersed around a larger area, in other words one way of keeping up with the simulating scenarios is to distribute the simulation application. Unfortunately, despite over two decades of research, the technology of distributed simulations has not significantly impressed the general simulation community (Fujimoto 1993). Considerable

efforts and expertise are still required to develop efficient simulation programs. There are no "golden rules" that a programmer can follow to guarantee an efficient program.

The fault-tolerance characteristic refers to the capability of distributed systems to detect and recover from faults occurring in various layers of the systems. The faults can be of various types, occurring in hardware or software; their occurrences can be transient or permanent. In distributed systems the failure of one machine can be tolerated, for example, if its functionality can be easily replaced by another redundant stand-by machine. So, machines connected by networks can be seen as redundant resources. A software system can be installed on multiple machines so that in the face of hardware faults or software failures, the faults or failures can be detected and tolerated by other machines. In order to validate fault-tolerance solutions for distributed systems a simulation model should at least incorporate the capability to simulate faults in various levels (applications, processing units, network links), to make use of various fault detection schemes or fault recovery procedures. Considering for example the case of a scheduler allocating jobs to be executed on the underlying distributed resources of a modeled system, a possible fault recovery solution that might be evaluated with a well-designed simulation model consists in allowing the scheduling algorithm to take immediate actions to use the remaining running resources.

Distributed systems can provide many forms of transparency such as location transparency, which allows local and remote information to be accessed in a unified way, failure transparency, which enables the masking of failures automatically, and replication transparency, which allows duplicating software/data on multiple machines invisibly. In order to preserve such characteristics into the designed experiment, a simulation model could include several possible mechanisms. For example, in case of network failures, the model could include algorithms that would automatically reroute, if possible, the transiting networking transfers. In case of data handling services failing, replication mechanisms could be used to ensure data consistency. Automation mechanisms could also run in the simulation scenario to ensure data consistency among replicas, as well as to save the data for longer-term usage (write the data in simulated tape deposits for example). A simulated scheduling algorithm could ensure, using various mechanisms, the correct execution of simulated jobs in case of failures occurring in the underlying resources under failure-transparency environments.

A useful simulation model must incorporate many, if not all, of the components and characteristics of Grid and P2P systems. An important aspect of a distributed system is the architecture that defines the system components, specifying the purpose and function of these components, and indicating their interactions. The analysis of the Grid and P2P architectures is a crucial aspect for developing useful simulation models. The functional requirements of the architecture influence the decision process on what the simulation model should comprise in terms of simulation entities and what properties and characteristics must be preserved.

## Characteristics of LSDSs

LSDSs, such as Grids, are complex systems that present specific characteristics. We are mainly referring to the characteristics of Grids because the hype around Grid computing is not about replacing current technologies but harnessing them all together (cluster computing, web services, P2P, etc.) to work as one unified utility. Grid computing incorporates many of these technologies, together with their characteristics.

According to Bote-Lorenzo (2002), the characteristics of a Grid system can be summarized into 10 main features. First of all, a Grid must be able to deal with a number of resources ranging from just a few to millions. The large scale characteristic of a Grid brings up the very serious problem of avoiding potential performance degradation as the grid size increases. In order to consider this characteristic, a simulation framework for Grids should allow the modeling of scenarios consisting of a large number of nodes (ranging from few hundreds to thousands). The model should also allow the dynamical addition of other nodes into a running simulation experiment. This could be possible by following an object-oriented approach, allowing the addition of many instances of a simulated resource. In this sense, the simulation model should be scalable, the number of resources being limited only by the amount of the physical resources of the system where the simulation is being executed. Careful consideration on the modeling engine implementation, the implementation of advanced structures and algorithms at this level, should allow the experimenting with scenarios involving a large number of resources.

Another characteristic of a Grid system is the geographical distribution of its resources. The resources pertaining to a grid may be located at distant places. A simulation model should consider that the underlying simulated system is composed of many resources organized into sites, each one being located in geographical distributed locations. The simulated networking stacks should also include special WAN components that connect such distributed farms of resources.

The heterogeneity, the vast range of technologies comprising a Grid system, both software and hardware, is one other characteristic. A Grid hosts both software and hardware resources, ranging from data, files, software components or programs to sensors, scientific instruments, display devices, computers, super-computers and networks. The simulation model can include various hardware components, each having different characteristics. For example, the simulation model can include both mobile components and several other types of hard servers. The diversity in hardware architectures can also be achieved by composing many different components. For example, a dual-processor server can be modeled by using two single-processor modeling nodes, together with several communication constructs. The software heterogeneity could also be modeled using various probability distributions that should be included the simulated model. For example, in case of a data transfer application, the effective quality of the transfer is subject to many influences coming from the software itself or from the underlying networking resources. The actual random fluctuations appearing in the data transfers can be modeled by generating various interrupts in the transmission according to various probability distributions. The network heterogeneity should also be considered by the network model, by means of diverse characteristics as well as protocols being used.

Resource sharing is one other characteristic. Resources in a Grid belong to many different organizations that allow other organizations (i.e. users) to access them. Resources, other than the local ones, can be used by applications, promoting efficiency and reducing costs. Yet, this is also one of the main stops in large-scale acceptance of Grid computing, due to problems such as server-hug-

ging or enterprise politics. The simulation model should preserve this characteristic by adopting a mature networking model, with components that simulate the connectivity among the resources being modeled (see Table 2).

The resource sharing characteristic is related to the multiple administrations feature. Each organization may establish different security and administrative policies under which their owned resources can be accessed and used. As a result, the already challenging network security problem is complicated even more with the need of taking into account all different policies. This characteristic can translate in the simulation model in the adoption of a distributed scheduler component. Each regional center can contain a local scheduler, and each scheduler can use its own policy to handle the locally available resources.

One other characteristic is resource coordination. The resources of a Grid must be coordinated in order to provide aggregated computing capabilities. A Grid aggregates many resources and therefore provides an aggregation of the individual resources into a higher capacity virtual resource. The capability of individual resources is preserved. As a consequence, from a global standpoint the Grid enables running larger applications faster (aggregation capacity), while from a local standpoint the Grid enables running new applications. In a simulation model, if the resource coordination capability is considered, a data replication scenario, for example, can be better simulated by using many geographically disparate sites with multiple simulated database servers, thus making good use of the underlying Grid resources. Such resource coordination mechanisms should be part of an adequate simulation model.

One important aspect provided by any Grid system is the transparent access, meaning the user should see the Grid as a single virtual computer. The Grid provides single-sign-on access to any user accessing the system. The possibility to ensure transparency in the simulation model was

*Table 2. The influence of the Grid characteristics on a simulator*

| Grid characteristic | Influence on the simulation framework |
|---|---|
| Large scale | Careful design consideration for the simulation model: the use of advanced internal structure could allow the modeling of experiments with many incorporated resources. |
| Geographical distribution | The inclusion of sites, geographically distributed, in the simulation model. The sites should be connected by special WAN modeled links. |
| Heterogeneity | Use of various models for hardware components; software architectures captured using probability distributions. |
| Resource sharing | Represented in the network model. |
| Multiple administration | Inclusion of a distributed scheduler. |
| Resource coordination | Resource coordination mechanisms. |
| Dependable access | Implementation of DAG scheduling algorithms. |
| Consistent access | Use of standard methods to access the resources. |
| Pervasive access | The scheduling framework detecting faults and taking appropriate actions. |

described in the analysis of the distributed systems presented in the previous section.

A Grid must also assure dependable access or the guaranty to deliver services under established Quality of Service (QoS) requirements. The need for dependable service is fundamental since users require assurances that they will receive predictable, sustained and often high levels of performance. In order to preserve this characteristic, a simulation model should also allow the definition of QoS metrics. In order to impose such metrics various politics could be implemented in several components. For example, the scheduler algorithm should consider deadline restrictions, the restrictions that job definitions impose (Dobre, et al., 2009). They should also allow the modeling of DAG scheduling algorithms, where the submitted job could have dependencies specified. In order to preserve QoS requirements, a simulation model should also include a monitoring component that reports when problem appear. This monitoring capability could be implemented, for example, with the help of a resource catalogue (Pop, et al., 2008).

According to the next characteristic, consistent access, a Grid must be constructed with standard services, protocols and interfaces, thus hiding the heterogeneity of the resources while allowing its

scalability. Without such standards, application development and pervasive use would not be possible. Every resource being simulated should extend a specific object abstraction in order to preserve this characteristic. The simulation model should also provide standard methods to access the simulated resources.

Finally, pervasive access means that a Grid must grant access to available resources by adapting to a dynamic environment in which resources do fail. This does not imply that resources are everywhere or universally available but that the Grid must tailor its behavior as to extract the maximum performance from the available resources. In the presence of faults in a simulation experiment the scheduling algorithm could take appropriate actions to use the remaining resources. To this date, not many simulators for distributed systems allow the evaluation of fault-tolerance solutions.

The characteristics of the Grid systems must influence the development process of a simulation model specifically designed for Grid technologies. To summarize the specific elements of the simulation model that enables the correct modeling of a Grid environment we can refer to the study conducted in Bagchi (1994). As such, the author presents the features that must be implemented by a simulation model in order to allow the correct modeling of a Grid environment. The identified set of features consists of: multi-tasking IT resources, job decomposition, task parallelization, heterogeneous resources, resource scheduling, and resource provisioning.

The simulation model must incorporate processing units, database servers, network links, and data storage devices (multi-tasking IT resources). The modeled processing unit should consider the case of several tasks being concurrently processed by the resource. An interrupt mechanism could ensure, for example, the modeling of concurrency. In this case, the time needed to complete a task is proportional with the number of other competing tasks. A detailed simulation of the task management within each resource is far too time-consuming when considering Grid environments, with hundreds of resources simulated for the duration of weeks. Instead, when a new task is submitted to a resource, the simulation framework should perform a good approximation of the multi-tasking behavior by re-estimating the completion time of all tasks being processed by that resource.

A workload could be composed of several jobs (job decomposition), each one having multiple resource requirements. In this sense, a simulated application could be composed of several jobs, handling various actions with several resource requirements. A job can, for example, be programmed by the user to request data from a database server, to perform some computation using the obtained records and then send the results for further processing to another job. The tasks performed by a job can be correlated with the tasks performed by another one. The dependencies between the jobs can be specified in the form of DAG structures in the simulation model.

A job can be furthermore decomposed into several tasks, each one representing a single resource requirement within the job. Each task in a job may be parallelizable. In the simulation model this can be accomplished if considering a job as being composed of several parallel jobs, each one

modeling the action of some task. A simulated job can start new simulated jobs, each one performing specific tasks. This, correlated with the job decomposition characteristic implemented using the DAG structures, can be used to handle the case of task parallelization.

Grid resources are heterogeneous by their nature. Therefore, the processing time of a task on a resource is subject to performance benchmarks. In the simulation model, the processing entities, as well as other simulated entities, must also be defined in terms of benchmarking units. The computation, data and network models should consider resources with various characteristics and their parameters be generically defined in order to simulate the heterogeneity of resources in the simulation experiments.

Also, a Grid simulator must be able to model scheduling policies used by resource brokers to determine on which resource a task will be executed. The simulation scheduler could provide a more advanced scheduling implementation, such as a meta-scheduler, allowing the execution the simulated jobs in a distributed manner, using all sites available. The meta-scheduler could also incorporate a wide-range of user-defined scheduling algorithms. Local scheduling is essential for a Grid simulation experiments. In the same time, user-defined scheduling algorithms should be easily added in a simulation experiment.

A simulation model should also incorporate the ability to provision resources for processing particular types of tasks. The provisioning policies could be either calendar-based or based on a more dynamic policy. The simulation model should consider the existence of background jobs to handle the execution of specific resource provisioning tasks. Such jobs can be used in dependency with other simulated jobs. In addition, the database server can perform programmed actions, being modeled as a special task in the simulation model. It can simulate special operations such as data archiving on a calendar based designed policy. The automation of resource provision is particularly important to the simulation model because it can be used to experiment with various data replication algorithms and provide flexibility to the simulation scenarios.

These characteristics describe the functionalities that a system must provide in order to be called correctly a Grid system. They are based on the various definitions of a Grid system. For example, the definition given in (Foster, 1998), "*A computational grid is a hardware and software infrastructure that provides dependable, consistent, pervasive, and inexpensive access to high-end computational capabilities,*" denote the dependable, consistent, and pervasive characteristics of the accesses a Grid system should provide. On the other hand, the definition given in (Foster, et al., 2001), "*The real and specific problem that underlies the Grid concept is coordinated resource sharing and problem solving in dynamic, multi-institutional virtual organizations,*" imply the resource sharing, resource coordination and pervasive access characteristics of a Grid system.

As presented, the characteristics of the Grids are well mapped on the simulation model. The simulation model allows the realistic simulation of a wide-range of Grid system technologies, with respect to their specific components and characteristics. There is one layer of the Grid that is in particular important to the simulation model. This layer is particularly responsible for interfacing with nodes so that they all can be accessed and used equally. The layer of software used to create this common interface is known as middleware. This layer is of particular importance since it ensures the main characteristics of the Grids. Generally, a grid middleware system consists of a set of components that can be used as part of a grid environment. The components provided by the middleware are the building blocks on which it is possible to create the environment where applications can use the resources available over the Grid. The following analysis presents the influence of the Grid middleware layer on the simulation model. In particular it presents the components

required to successfully conducting realistic Grid systems experiments.

The components of a Grid middleware allow the building of grid environments comprised of heterogeneous resources that would not otherwise be accessible without a user account on each machine and have different interfaces. A middleware system is made up of a set of components that provide the following functionalities: *authentication, security, fault detection/persistence, information service, data transfer, process creation, process monitoring, remote data access/storage, database replication*. A Grid middleware system provides the following main types of services: resource management, data management, information systems, monitoring, and security.

*Resource management* in Grids implies a quite large number of functionalities, from resource discovery to scheduling, execution management, status monitoring and accounting. Wieder et al (2005) distinguishes between two cases of Grid systems with respect to their requirements on resource management capabilities. The first identified case consists of specialized Grids for dedicated purposes, which are centred on a single or limited application domain and require high efficiency in execution. The Resource Management System (RMS) is itself adapted to a specific application, its workflow and the available resource configuration. Thus, the interfaces to the resources and the middleware are built according to the given requirements caused by the application scenario. While the Grid RMS is highly specialized, from the user perspective the handling is often easier as the know-how of the application domain is built into the system. The second case comprises the generic Grid Middleware, which has to cope with the complete set of the requirements to support applicability. Here, the Grid RMS is open for many different application scenarios.

Compared to the specialized Grids, generic interfaces are required and can be adapted to many front- and back-ends. However, the generic nature of this approach comes at the price of additionally overhead for providing information about the application. For instance, more information about a particular job has to be provided to the middleware, such as a workflow description, scheduling objectives, policies and constraints. The application-specific knowledge cannot be built into the middleware, and therefore must be provided at the front-end level. In this case, the consideration of security requirements is an integral aspect, which is more difficult to solve. It is possible to hide the additional RMS complexity of generic Grid infrastructures from the users or their applications by specialized components, which might be built on top of a generic middleware. Nevertheless, it can be concluded that in general a generic Grid middleware carries additional overhead with less efficiency at the expense of broader applicability. Current research is mostly focusing on the first case in which solutions are built for a dedicated Grid scenario in mind. However, for creating future generation Grids, suitable solutions for the second case are required. The two described case scenarios have an influence on the characteristics of the elements comprising the RMS. Despite the functional differences of the presented cases, any RMS presents a common architecture. From the simulation point of view, to conduct successful experiments the model incorporates the components of the RMS architecture. In the same time, the simulation model provides support for future functionalities to be later included by the user, allowing him the possibility to extend the model in order to run new possible modelling scenarios. The extendibility property is important because it allows the model to cope with future technologies as they appear.

Figure 1 shows the architecture of a general RMS. The Resource Information collected from the sensors of the service-provider forms one input of RMS. The other input is the Resource Requests from the users. The resource information interacts with the *Discovery* module of RMS. The *State Estimation* system converts the information, through the *Naming* system to a *Resource Informa-*

*tion* database. The *Resource Monitoring* system maintains the *Historical Data* and the current *Resource Status* databases. The *Dissemination* system is used to convey the resource information to users on the Grid. The *Request Interpreter* may format the request, or it may generate estimates of execution time for each task of the job request. The *Resource Broker* negotiates for the resources. It can use the *Resource Reservation* module to save information related to the reserved resources in the *Reservations* database. The *Scheduling* system puts the job in the *Job Queues*. Then the *Execution Manager* sends the job for execution to the allocated resources. The *Job Monitor* continuously monitors the job, as it is being executed. It stores the state of the job at checkpoints in the *Job Status* database.

The simulation model considers that a regional center contains a catalogue of available resources that is used by the simulated scheduler components (locally and/or meta-scheduler). This is the equivalent of the Resource Information presented as one input in the RMS architecture. In a simulation the user submits jobs that are executed on the resources that are available in the simulated system. A simulated job object has two properties. It programmatically specifies the functionality of the job, the sequence of simulated operations. The job also contains information regarding the specific resource requirements. The job contains information that specifies the amount of memory and processing power required to be successfully executed. This information, the equivalent of the Resource Request input in the RMS architecture, is used also by the scheduler inside the simulated system. Each regional center can incorporate a local scheduler. The entire ensemble of local schedulers, distributed in different regional centers, can exchange the data regarding the status of the existing resources and running jobs. The simulation model also allow for a job to be generated in one regional center and executed in a totally different center. This is particularly useful in simulation experiments designed

*Figure 1. Resource management system abstract structure*

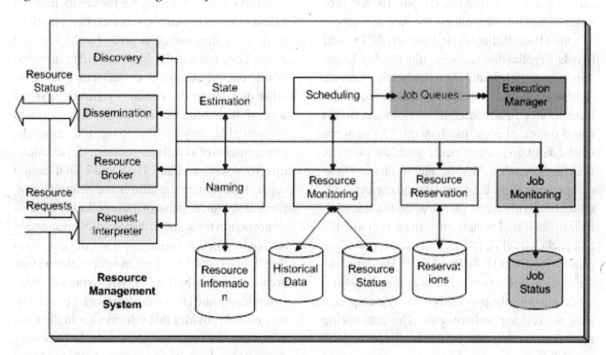

to analyze various job scheduling procedures. A series of successful scheduling simulation experiments that use this feature were presented in (Legrand, et al., 2003), and (Pop, et al., 2006).

The described functionality is further used to simulate various meta-scheduling algorithms or local-scheduling technologies. The three well-known *scheduler organization* categories (Hamscher, et al., 2002), centralized, hierarchical and decentralized, are well mapped on the scheduling architecture proposed by simulation model. In the *centralized scheduler* scenario all applications are added to a unique queue belonging to a centralized scheduler. This functionality is modelled by using distributed schedulers. In the simulation experiment the input jobs are sent to a designated central scheduler, responsible with the scheduling decision of sending the jobs for execution to the appropriate resources. The scheduling decision is based on the status of the entire system, on the dynamic information regarding the currently available resources. A *decentralized scheduler* has local queues at each site. It responds to requests for

service from local users and from other schedulers. This scheduler organization category is closest to the one used by the simulation model, where each regional center uses local queues. Finally, a *hierarchical structure* consists of local schedulers and higher-level schedulers, which work in concert. In the simulation model, the local schedulers of each regional center can work together using a distributed scheduling algorithm in order to provide the higher-level scheduling decisions. In conclusion, the simulation model allows the simulation of any scheduler organization, as well as the modelling of diverse scheduling algorithms. In fact, such scheduling simulation experiments were successfully conducted, and they are presented in the next chapters. Such experiments, proving the flexibility of the simulation framework to incorporate various scheduling technologies, generated modelling results that proved valuable for the testing and validation of modern decision-taking scheduling methods and techniques.

*Data management* solutions can be classified into data movement services and data replication services. For example the Globus Toolkit provides two main components for data movement – GridFTP and Reliable File Transfer (RFT) – and two data replication services – the Replica Location Service (RLS) and Data Replication Service (DRS). For data movement the simulation model incorporates an advanced network model that is based on an interrupt mechanism. The network model contains components such as network interfaces, LANs, WANs, and routers. These components allow the complete and correct modelling of a wide range of shared communication infrastructures. The data movement is simulated by a packet-level TCP/IP network stack, providing protocols such as IP, TCP and UDP. The networking stack is not closed to the user, the simulation model allowing the possibility to easily incorporate new networking technologies. The networking model allows the successful execution of several simulation experiments. For example, we managed to successfully simulate protocols such as FTP and NFS, data transfer technologies very useful in generating modern-day distributed system experiments. The simulation model also provides instruments for modelling replication services. The simulation model incorporates a global database index, which stores information about the entire data collections of the entire simulated system. This component is crucial in the implementation of the replication services, acting as the RLS of the simulated system. Also a database entity (database server, tape server) is simulated as a running task, containing an execution sequence. The database entity is connected to the simulated network model, this aspect preserving the resource sharing characteristics of the distributed systems. These aspects are specifically useful in the implementation of various data replication algorithms. Successful data replication experiments are presented in details in the next chapters.

*Resource information dissemination* is the way in which information about resources is propagated through the environment for it to be available to other entities. The information services provide discovery and monitoring for the components of a Grid system (resources, services, computations etc.). Their importance is given by the fact that a user does not usually have complete information about the resources or services offered by other users from the virtual organization. While several technologies for information services are available, they usually do not address all the requirements of a Grid environment (for example, directory services like LDAP and UDDI cannot support the dynamic addition and deletion of information sources, most of the monitoring systems do not permit the scalable discovery of information sources etc.). As a consequence, the developers of the Globus Toolkit designed an information service architecture suitable for Grid environments, MDS (Monitoring and Discovery Service). The simulation model provides this information in the form of resource catalogues that provide the necessary discovery and monitoring services to the modelled systems. The information regarding the existing computing and data resources are stored in the farm catalogue, being publicly available to the components of the simulated system. Their status is continuously being updated with the flow of the running simulation. The scheduler component, for example, bases its scheduling decisions on the status of the available resources. The database server uses the resource catalogue to find suitable storages for sending historical data, an automation mechanism for long time data storing also provided by the simulation model. The database server also uses the resource catalogue to handle the modelling of data replication algorithms. The simulated jobs are kept in two separate queues, one holding the jobs waiting to be scheduled for execution and the other one containing the jobs that are currently being executed. The second queue provides the job monitoring functionality, since the current status of the executed jobs is being continuously updated with the flow of a running simulation experiment. In conclusion, the simulation model provides the necessary discovery of monitoring services that are required to conduct realistic simulation experiments of a Grid middleware architecture.

*Grid monitoring* refers to the need of projects and organizations worldwide to track resource usage, network traffic, job distribution and many other quantities through the help of monitoring systems. The monitoring systems have the role of collecting information and presenting it in a way that allow making effective decisions. The systems also have to automatically troubleshoot and optimize very large Grid and network systems. While the initial target field of these applications were network and Grid systems supporting data processing and analysis for global high energy and nuclear physics collaborations, monitoring tools are broadly applicable to many fields of "data intensive" science, and to the monitoring and management of major research and education networks. An essential part of managing a global Data Grid is a monitoring system that is able to monitor and track the many site facilities, networks, and the many tasks in progress, in real time. The gathered monitoring information is also essential for developing the required higher level services and components of the Grid system that provide decision support and eventually some degree of automated decisions, to help maintain and optimize workflow through the Grid. The relevant efforts invested in this domain are reflected in the development of worldwide projects such as MonALISA, GridICE, R-GMA, and others. MonALISA, MONitoring Agents in a Large Integrated Services Architecture, is a global distributed monitoring system (Legrand, et al., 2004). MonALISA provides essential monitoring traces which were used to conduct realistic simulation experiments. The obtained results provided valuable feedback, used in implementing controlling functionality in the monitoring framework. For example, in one simulation experiment we showed that using a platform of agents capable to take intelligent decisions for the transferring of the data processed by the organizations involved in

the LHC experiments would increase significantly the performances of the global system.

For the simulation model the monitoring services are provided in the form of automated updates of the status of the various resources comprising a simulation scenario and of the executed jobs. The simulation engine automatically updates the catalogue that emulates the functionalities of the resource information dissemination services with the flow of a running simulation experiment. The catalogues are accessible to the user running the simulation research. This characteristic offers a global view of the status of the resources comprising the simulated scenario, such that the user can, for example, use the modelling framework for successfully testing a new scheduling algorithm that is based on the monitored status of the simulated system.

The *security* of a Grid system provides several specific characteristics: authentication, privacy, authorization, delegation and single sign-on. Authentication imply allowing entities to interact knowing each other identities (on top of authenticated identities, authorization, logging and pricing schemes can be implemented). Privacy means guaranteeing protection of data exchanged both against tampering and unwanted access. Authorization refers to the characteristic of establishing and enforcing policies under which clients and services can interact. Delegation enables entities/resources to act on behalf of other entities/resources/clients. Single Sign-on indicate the property of assuring that once an identity is authenticated/authorized, access can be obtained anywhere the entity is entitled to. Among the existing solution worth recalling we recall the Grid Security Infrastructure (GSI), proposed by Globus Toolkit, MyProxy Online Credential Repository, Community Authorization Service (CAS) or Virtual Organization Management Service (VOMS).

The proposed model considers the general case of security, as a mean to ensure that systems remain safe and reliable to the errors, threats or malicious changes. The model considers solutions for *data privacy, data integrity* and *system availability*. To ensure such objectives, we consider components designed to protect the services, data and offered information from threats such as *interruption, interception, change* or *forgery*. The most important security mechanisms considered are (Johnston 2004) *confidentiality* (the model includes mechanisms designed to ensure that an authenticated entity can access only the information that has been authorized to), *authentication* (the model includes mechanisms to identify entities involved in a communication or collaboration), *authorization* (the model guarantees that once the entity has been authenticated, its options will be restricted / limited to those operations that it is authorized to perform), and *audit* (the models includes the mechanisms to guarantee the non-repudiation of origin and content of a message).

For the particular case of Grid systems, an additional important concept, also considered by the security model, is the one of Virtual Organization (VO). In a VO different organizations (commercial companies, universities, governmental institutions or laboratories) collaborate to share resources and work together to solve common problems. Each company within a VO is managed independently and has its own security solutions such as Kerberos or PKI infrastructure (Public Key Infrastructure). The security model extends the regional center model. It includes extensions to all existing components of a distributed system (processing units, database server, jobs, job schedulers). We added a new secured job that carry authentication tokens or certificates, and is able to request data based on specific rights. The user can specify the use of X.509 certificate, together with a PKI infrastructure for example, or can easily add new means of authentication.

The model also includes the possibility to define VOs, based on specific security policies shared between regional centers. The model includes the mechanisms to evaluate various authentication solutions. Such authentication mechanisms are applied to the scheduler, processing unit, and even

when jobs request data from the database servers. For example, the job scheduler includes restrictions to where to execute specific jobs, based on the VO to which they belong. The processing units are capable to verify if a particular job is allowed to be executed. The access control verification can be implemented based on various schemas (RBAC, MAC, DAC, etc).

Also, we added delegation, a concept important especially in case of Grid experiments. Thus, a job is capable to delegate his rights (in the form of a certificate for example) to all the jobs that he further instantiates. The database server supports various security policies and includes mechanisms to verify authentication of incoming connections, and to support secured transport protocols. It also includes various mechanisms to certify the validity of data access requests. Similar to the processing unit, the database server maintains a list of VOs to which it belongs and the access policies for the data shared by the server with the other resources within the VO. For example, when a job accesses data on the server the model specifies a series of mechanisms to verify the identity of the requester (by default the model uses validation based on a PKI infrastructure and X.509 certificates) and if the job presents sufficient access rights. For compatibility with other experiments, a regional center can include both secured and non-secured database servers. The same applies for the processing units.

Within the networking simulation model, the model adds the possibility to include secured data transport protocols. For example, we included the SSL protocol to offer the possibility to encrypt the messages being exchanged between entities in a simulation experiment. We added the possibility to implement various handshake mechanisms (for protocols supporting authentication capabilities). The user can easily add and evaluate new protocols and mechanisms. The model includes mechanisms for data encryption, keys and certificate management, etc. In addition, it includes mechanisms for traffic filtering by specifying exclusion rules based on various metrics (ports, addresses, protocols, etc) and corresponding actions (reject for example).

The characteristics of the Grid systems positively influenced, as presented, the development process of the simulation model. To summarize the specific elements of the simulation model that enables the correct modelling of a Grid environment we can refer to the study conducted in (Bagchi, 2005). The author of the study presents the features that must be implemented by a simulation model in order to allow the correct modelling of a Grid environment. The identified set of features consists of: *multi-tasking IT resources, job decomposition, task parallelization, heterogeneous resources, resource scheduling,* and *resource provisioning.* Table 3 presents a comparison of the identified feature of a generic Grid environment simulator and their mapping on the simulation model.

As presented, all the features of the Grid environment are mapped on the simulation model. According to the table, the simulation model allows the realistic simulation of a wide-range of Grid system technologies, with respect to their specific components and characteristics.

## Simulation of Complex Computing Models

The simulation of complex realistic computing scenarios, incorporating the identified Grid and LHC requirements, present various research challenges. This section presents them and their influence on the model adopted by the presented simulation framework. The challenges were the result of the initial objective to allow the simulation of complex architectures such as Grids supporting the LHC computing model requirements, from the objective to allow the realistic simulation of distributed systems consisting of a great number of resources, where many jobs run concurrently, competing for tremendous amounts of processing power and data storage needs.

One of the objectives of the simulation framework is to save valuable time in determining the optimal parameters and configuration of a Grid system, answering important questions without resorting to trial and error with a real testbed. For example, the choice in the scheduling policy can have a dramatic effect on the job processing efficiency in various Grid systems. The choice of using a particular algorithm will affect not just the running of the submitted jobs, but also that of the system as a whole. The simulation model, with its presented characteristics, provides the means to test various resource selection policies, and measure the effect that they have on system performance.

The complexity of a simulation model results from many factors, including both non-technical and technical ones, but the most important one among them is unclear simulation objectives. In many cases, the same simulation objective can be achieved much more efficiently with a simplified model as opposed to a complex one. Hence, given a large, complex real system, it is important to develop the simulation model such that to contain the appropriate level of details to minimize the required computation, but in the same ensure its validity with respect to the simulation objective.

The need to incorporate adequate simplification techniques that preserve the properties of the system being modelled is better illustrated by the study presented in (Riley, et al., 2002. The authors studied the feasibility of simulating the Internet. They tried to answer the question of how much computation, memory, and disk space is required to simulate a large networking system, consisting of hundreds of millions of nodes. The study considered a conservative estimation of hosts, routers, links and traffic loads in Internet and also a discrete event simulator. It is estimated that simulating the an Internet-scale network for a single second generates $2.9 \cdot 10^{11}$ packet events, and needs 290000 seconds to finish if a 1 GHz CPU is used; it also requires $2.9 \cdot 10^{14}$ bytes of memory, and $1.4 \cdot 10^{13}$ bytes of disk space for logging the simulation results. In addition, in order to gain more confidence in the results from a simula-

*Table 3. Mapping of the grid environment features on the simulation model*

| Required feature of the simulation model (Bagchi 2005) | The implementation of the feature in the simulation model |
|---|---|
| **Multi-tasking IT resources:** Processors, database servers, network links, and data storage devices are all pre-emptive multi-tasking resources. Tasks submitted to such a resource goes immediately to the processing queue containing all the other tasks that are being processed by the resource. Each of these tasks get processed by the resource for a pre-defined time-slice and then put back to the processing queue (if not waiting for other resources). As a result of multi-tasking, the submission of a new task can change the completion time of existing tasks being processed by the resource. | The simulation model incorporates processing units, database servers, network links, and data storage devices. The processing unit has a queue of all the tasks being concurrently processed by the resource. An interrupt mechanism ensures modelling of tasks concurrency. The time needed to complete a task takes into account the number of other competing tasks. In this way the multi-tasking requirement is one of the characteristics implemented in the simulation model. A detailed simulation of the task management within each resource is far too time-consuming when considering grid environments with hundreds of resources simulated for the duration of weeks. Instead, when a new task is submitted to a resource, the simulation framework performs a good approximation of the multi-tasking behaviour by re-estimating the completion time of all tasks being processed by that resource. |
| **Job decomposition:** Each job from a workload may be composed of multiple resource requirements. The terminology of "task" is generally being used to define a single resource requirement within a job. Each resource requirement may be for a specific configuration of a server or a database. For example, a job may be composed of three tasks: get data from a customer database, perform data mining on a computational server, and add the results to a sales database. Job decomposition is important to model because grid designs typically focus on providing a certain type of resource (e.g., compute servers) on a grid and overlook the impact on other resources (e.g., databases, network bandwidth) needed by the job. | The simulated job is programmed to handle specific actions. A job can, for example, be programmed by the user to request data from a database server, to perform some computation using the obtained records and then send the results for further processing to another job. The tasks performed by a job can be correlated with the tasks performed by another one. The dependencies between the jobs can be specified in the form of DAG structures in the simulation model. |
| **Task parallelization:** Each task in a job (decomposed as described above) may be parallelizable. This is often the case with grid workloads. Parallelization could be of two types: "Embarrassingly parallel" tasks can simply be split up into as many chunks as available resources. The second category consists of parallel tasks that are more constrained and consist of a specific number of parallel paths, regardless of the number of available resources. | A simulated job can start new simulated jobs, each one performing specific tasks. This, correlated with the job decomposition characteristic implemented using the DAG structures, can be used to handle both described cases of task parallelization. |
| **Heterogeneous resources:** Grid resources can be of various vendor platforms, models, and operating systems. Therefore, the processing time of a task on a resource is subject to its performance benchmarks. A resource may be associated with multiple performance benchmarks that are relevant for different types of computing tasks. | The computing unit specified in computing power in the form of generic SI95 units, accommodating for a wide-range of performance benchmarks. The computation, data and network models all take into account resources with various amounts of resources to model the heterogeneity of resources in the simulation experiments. |
| **Resource scheduling:** The grid simulator must be able to model the scheduling policies used by resource brokers to determine which resource should process an arriving task. | The simulation model provides a meta-scheduling functionality, allowing the execution the simulated jobs in a distributed manner. The meta-scheduler can incorporate a wide-range of user-defined scheduling algorithms. Local scheduling algorithms can also be added in any user-defined experiments. |
| **Resource provisioning:** The ability to provision resources for processing particular types of tasks is another feature to be simulated. These provisioning policies could be either calendar based (e.g., a department needs a server to be an email server during 9AM to 5PM every workday and can release it to be a data-mining processor on the grid at other times) or based on a more dynamic policy that monitors workload arrivals and resource usage and reacts accordingly. Simulation of these provisioning policies in conjunction with the resource scheduling policies would allow grid designers to determine whether the respective policies are aligned and consistent with each other and providing the desired grid performance in terms of resource availability, workload throughput and processing times. | The simulation model allows the insertion of background jobs to handle the execution of specific resource provisioning tasks. Such jobs can be used in dependency with other simulated jobs. In addition, the database server can perform programmed actions, being modelled as a special task in the simulation model. It can simulate special operations such as data archiving on a calendar based designed policy. The automation of resource provision is particularly important to the simulation model because it can be used to experiment with various data replication algorithms and provide flexibility to the simulation scenarios. |

tion, a long simulation run or many independent simulation runs are necessary; this can further prolong the whole execution time. All these lead to a conclusion that packet-oriented simulation of an Internet-scale network is a computationally prohibitive task. The same conclusion can also be generalized to Grid systems. A high-granularity complete simulation of a world-wide Grid system is generally not feasible. In practice the simulation models are greatly simplified, using various techniques. The main idea is to try to reduce as much as possible the time needed to conduct the simulation experiment, possible by omitting various uninteresting details of the model being simulated or by making gross assumptions on the components being simulated.

The same principle is applied in the design of the simulation model used in MONARC 2. We used several simplification techniques in order to allow the simulation of large scale systems, while in the same time preserving the key characteristics of the underlying architecture and used technologies. The simplification techniques are exemplified in the following paragraphs.

The author in (Frantz, 1995) classified *model simplification techniques*, based on which components in the model are modified, into three categories: *boundary modification, behaviour modification,* and *form modification*.

The *boundary modification* approach aims to reduce the input variable space. It is done by either delimiting the range of a particular input parameter or by minimizing the number of input parameters. The latter case conforms to the parsimonious modelling principle, which prefers compact models among those that produce equally accurate results. Model sensitivity analysis can be used to identify input variables that hardly affect the simulation results, and these variables can be eliminated from the simulation model. The simulation model of MONARC 2 adopts this technique by minimizing the number of input parameters. The model considers only the parameters that affect the simulation results. For example, the input for the

processing power of the computation unit is not influenced by the background load of other possible existing processes. Instead the input is represented by the SI95 performance benchmark unit, an average measure that can be obtain from real systems using different monitoring techniques. Background influenced can be still modelled, if the experiment requires such behaviour, by using jobs specifically designed for this purpose. The variations in load can be modelled using the provided distributions in order to obtain realistic simulation experiments. The network does not consider by default background generated noise in the proposed model, but still such behaviour can be modelled if required by the experiment.

In case of *behaviour modification* the states of a simulation model are aggregated, in either space or time domain. At some time point in a simulation, the system state can be decomposed into a vector of state variables. Those variables that are closely correlated with each other in certain ways can be aggregated and then replaced by a single one in the simplified model. This is particularly useful when the dynamics of each state variable before aggregation is of little interest to the modeller and the property of the merged variable after aggregation can be easily defined. Aggregation in time domain, sometimes, can also reduce the complexity of simulation models. In case of discrete event simulation the simulation events may be aggregated together when their occurrence times are considerably close and they are thus deemed to happen simultaneously. The simulation model incorporates this technique in the simulation of the networking model. In case the dynamics of package flow is of no interest to the simulation experiment, the network model considers the arrival of a single package to be aggregated into the entire stream. The case of package lost is treated as if just inserting more simulation delay, as in the case of the TCP protocols.

The *Form modification* technique considers the simulation model as a "black-box." This means that the model generates results when inputs are fed into it. In contrast to the previous two approaches, this one replaces the original simulation model or submodel with a surrogate one that takes a different, but much simpler, form that does the same or approximate input-output transformation. A method to use this technique consists of generating a lookup table that maps from inputs to outputs directly. If the table size is small, this method provides an efficient substitute for the original model or submodel; however, as the latter grows in size and complexity, the lookup table can become extremely large. An alternative technique is called meta-modelling. It seeks a simpler mathematical approximation that statistically approaches the original model or submodel. Such a mathematical model can be inferred from the input/output data observed in real systems or deduced from the rules that govern the dynamics of real systems. Once such a mathematical model is established, it can be used in simulation to do input-output transformations and generate statistically equivalent results as with the original model. The simulation model of MONARC 2 incorporates various distributions that are used to implement this simplification technique. For example, the job that is being processed can encounter various interferences, therefore its completion time is considered to be generated according to some distribution. The model does not really consider executing background jobs in this case; instead it sees the processing of the job as a black-box, approximating its input-output transformation. The mathematical distributions, as presented in the architecture of the simulation framework, are quite frequently used in the simulation model as this simplification technique is quite useful in the large-scale distributed systems simulation.

Even if the model simplification techniques offer the possibility of accelerating simulation of large, complex systems, they come at a price. With details removed from a simulation model, its validity sometimes becomes doubtful. Therefore, it is always necessary to quantify loss of accuracy when a simplified model is adopted, especially in

the regions of the input space that are of modeller's interest. On the other hand, in order to minimize the computation costs, the real-system objects of the same type are often modelled at different abstraction levels. This is called multi-resolution modelling. Seamlessly integrating sub-models represented at multiple abstraction levels in the same simulation model is not always easy to accomplish. The simulation framework presents validation in the form of series of testbeds measurements, comparison of resource utilisation in real monitoring systems versus the observations drawn from the simulation experiments, or in the form of various queuing theory validity tests. All the validation efforts that are presented in further details in the next chapters proved the correctness of the simulation model in respect to the adopted simplifications techniques.

The presented simplifications techniques also lead to less errors being introduced in the design process of the simulation model or in the implementation of the modelling framework. Architects often assume without proof that although their simulator may make inaccurate absolute performance predictions, it will still accurately predict architectural trends. A classic example of simulation errors is presented in (Gibson et al 2000). The FLASH project at Standford was focusing on building large-scale shared-memory multiprocessors. They went from conception, to design, and in the end to actual hardware. Interesting to note is that during this process a total of six years were spent on simulation studies. When the project ended the authors went back and compared the simulation results with the real world results. Surprisingly, the simulations error was up to 30%. In the paper the author categorized the sources of errors into performance bugs, omission of large effects, and lack of sufficient detail. The conclusion of the authors is that a more complex simulator does not ensure better simulation. Surprisingly the simple simulators worked better than sophisticated ones, which were unstable and introduced more errors. What is vital in every simulator implementation in the end is the use of real world observations to tune or calibrate the simulator. The same conclusion is presented by the authors in (Vincent et al 2007). In respect with this observation we note that MONARC 2, besides using extensive validity tests, was also intensively analysed and fine-tuned based on real-world observations generated by the MonALISA monitoring framework (Dobre & Cristea 2007).

## A REALISTIC SIMULATION MODEL FOR EVALUATION OF LSDS

MONARC 2 is constructed using a process oriented approach for discrete event simulation, which is well suited to describe concurrent running programs, network traffic as well as all the stochastic arrival patterns, specific for such type of simulation. Threaded objects or "Active Objects" (having an execution thread, program counter, stack...) allow a natural way to map the specific

behavior of distributed data processing into the simulation program.

In order to provide a realistic simulation, all components of the system and their interactions were abstracted. The chosen model is equivalent to the simulated system in all the important aspects. A first set of components was created to describe the physical resources of the distributed system under simulation. The largest one is the regional center (Figure 2), which contains a farm of processing nodes (CPU units), database servers and mass storage units, as well as one or more local and wide area networks. Another set of components model the behavior of the applications and their interaction with users. Such components are the "Users" or "Activity" objects which are used to generate data processing jobs based on different scenarios. The job is another basic component, simulated with the aid of an active object, and scheduled for execution on a CPU unit by a "Job Scheduler" object.

*Figure 2. The regional center model*

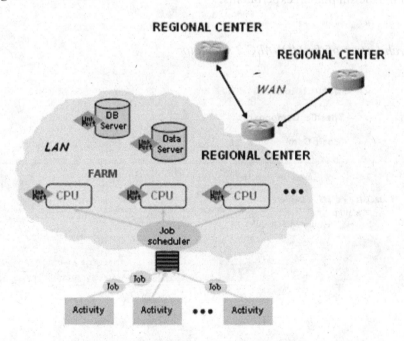

With this structure it is possible to build a wide range of models, from the very centralized to the distributed system models, with an almost arbitrary level of complexity (multiple regional centers, each with different hardware configuration and possibly different sets of replicated data). The analysis of the characteristics of various Grid architectures was essential in the design process of the simulation model. It influenced the decision on the type of components and interactions required to completely and correctly model various Grid related experiments.

One of the advantages of MONARC 2 is that it can be easily extended because of its *layered structure*. The layers and their interaction design (between themselves and with a monitoring instrument) are represented in Figure 3. The first layer contains the core of the simulator, called the "simulation engine." This layer provides discrete-event simulation capabilities. It incorporates components designed to handle simulation events, to schedule the execution of the simulation tasks, to manage the logical simulation clock. It basically provides all the elements that constitute the "engine" behind the simulation experiments.

The next layer comprises all the basic components of a distributed system (CPU/processing units, jobs, databases, networks, job schedulers etc.). On top of this layer are the components designed specifically for particular distributed systems models. This layer is needed for experiments involving specialized components, such as modelling the forthcoming HEP LHC experiments. All of the simulation components are open, meaning they can be extended by the user to handle the necessities of various simulation experiments or the particularities of some model used for distributed systems. The user can extend the architecture to incorporate different types of jobs, job schedulers with specific scheduling algorithms or database servers that support various data replication strategies.

Another layer is represented by the interaction with a monitoring instrument. The monitoring instrument is used to generate input traces for the simulation experiments or to validate the simulation model.

*Figure 3. The architecture of the MONARC 2 simulator*

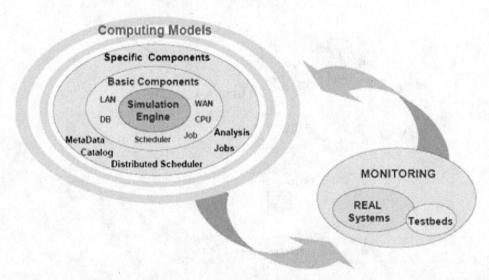

## Simulation Experiments

The generic simulation model allows the testing of various scheduling algorithms, data transport algorithms and infrastructures, data transfer protocols, replication algorithms, all with interesting results that were used in real-world. The model and simulator were successfully used in evaluating various data replications experiments, under the supervision of the author of this chapter. The results were presented in (Eremia, et al., 2010; Dobre, et al., 2008; Legrand, et al., 2003). The simulation experiments involved various replica strategies, mainly in the context of the LHC experiments at CERN. We were interested in the way the data availability influences the performances and increases the dependability property in LSDS. In several experimental scenarios we changed the amount of replicated data that is contained in the satellite regional centers and the bandwidth capabilities of the links connecting central data storage units. The obtained results showed how the performance improves when the data is located closer to the jobs, being greatly influenced also by the network characteristics. And because the proximity of the data represents the amount of locally replicated data in the experiment we can conclude that the replication of data have a great impact on the overall performances of the processing data applications.

A series of scheduling simulation scenarios were presented in (Dobre, et al., 2008; Pop, et al., 2006; Dobre, et al., 2003). These experiments evaluated the behavior of various distributed schedulers and scheduling policies and algorithms, under different conditions. Such simulations proved also useful for determining the optimal values for the network bandwidth or for the number of CPUs per regional centre to be consider in real-world scenarios.

Among the most extensive simulation scenarios is the one described in (Legrand, et al., 2005), later extended in (Dobre, et al., 2009). The experiment tested the behavior of the tier architecture envisioned by the two largest LHC experiments, CMS and ATLAS. The simulation study describes several major activities, concentrating on the data transfer on WAN between the T0 at CERN and a number of several T1 regional centers. The experiment simulated a number of activities specific for physics data production, the RAW data production, Production and DST distribution, the re-production and the new DST distribution and the detector analysis activity. We simulated the described activities alone and then combined.

The obtained results showed the role of using a data replication agent for the intelligent transferring of the produced data, as presented in Figure 4. The obtained results showed that the available capacity of 2.5 Gbps was not sufficient and in fact not far afterwards the link was upgraded to a current 30 Gbps based on our recommendations.

## CRITICAL ANALYSIS OF EXISTING WORK

In this section we present the categories of a taxonomy that best describes modeling instruments for Grid systems (Figure 5). The proposed taxonomy is focused on the simulation of Grid systems, hence it introduces categories such as motivation and Grid components that are particularly designed to better categorize the special family of Grid simulation instruments. The taxonomy considers both the design characteristics of the Grid systems being modeled and the implementation properties of simulators designed for such systems.

According to the adopted simulation model a simulator can be classified according to the *scope*, and *supported model*. The *scope* category refers to the extent and nature of the simulated systems, to the components supported by the simulation model.

A simulator designed for LSDS can include the components necessary to model Intranet or Internet systems, Web, Grid, Cloud, Farm, or Cluster

*Figure 4. The results obtained in the LHC simulation experiment, with and without the data transfer agent*

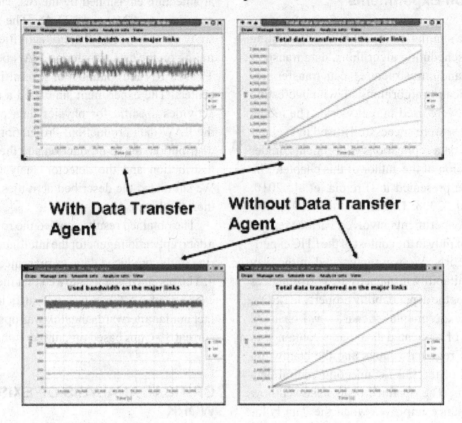

*Figure 5. A taxonomy of large scale distributed systems simulators*

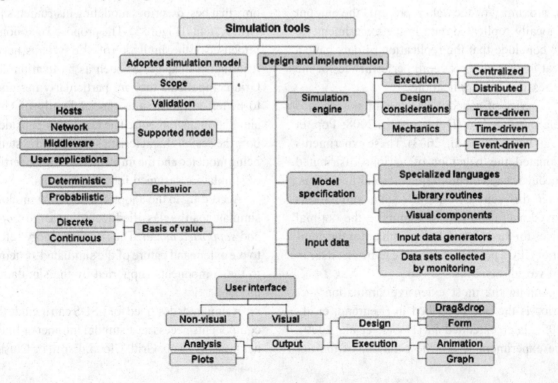

systems, P2P networks, distributed applications and other types of LSDS and applications. Many of existing simulators for LSDS were implemented to model only particular classes of problems. For example, some were implemented to simulate various scheduling algorithms; others were developed to simulate data transfer technologies. LSDS are complex by their nature. Because of this reason the simulation models also suffer from various limitations in the adopted scope.

According to this classification a simulator can be used to study data movement optimizations, to investigate scheduling algorithms, to evaluate replication solutions or to study a particular model of a Grid or P2P system. This category considers only the upper most scope. If, for example, we consider the case of a simulator designed specifically to study various scheduling algorithms, we can observe that in order to study such algorithms the simulator must also provide additional support, such as simulated underlying networks or processing nodes. If the underlying Grid components are also simulated then a scientist, with proper mediations, could also evaluate various other scenarios such as different file replication algorithms (assuming the simulator includes the possibility to also simulate data warehouses). But generally such modifications require some amount of work, and, except for the cases when the original developers of a simulator redesigned it at some point to comprehend some different classes of Grid related problems, such developments are virtually non-existent. The majority of the Grid simulators were developed in the context of the validation of the Large Hadron Collider (LHC) experiments in CERN and their proposed running conditions. For this reason we often see as possible motivation the categories identified by the authors of the taxonomy described in Venugopal (2006): Data Transport, Data Replication or Scheduling issues.

This classification is also important because it classifies simulators according to their capabilities to simulate the layers of the distributed architecture. For that we classify simulators based on the components of a distributed system that are supported by the simulation model. There are four types of components: hosts, network, middleware and user applications. It is very important to have a standardized, complete hierarchy of characteristics that are simulated for all four components of such systems. *Host characteristics* are used to describe the hosts within the distributed environments. Such hosts may contain computing, data storage, and other resources, grouped into single or distributed systems. In a simulation we are interested in the types of host resources capable of being modeled, their organization, as well as the characteristics that are considered for each type of resource. Examples of resource organization in simulation are the "central model" proposed by the Bricks project or the "tier model" proposed by the MONARC project (Dobre & Cristea, 2007). Of interest for this category are aspects such as how different simulators model the load of the computing nodes, the granularity of jobs being processed, or the types of data storage facilities.

The *Network characteristics* category describes the network elements interconnecting hosts within simulated distributed environments. Among network elements there are routers, switches and other devices. This category considers both the types of network devices and the communication protocols that are considered by the various simulation models. The infrastructure communication protocols refers to lower-level protocols such as TCP, UDP, etc. as well as higher-level application protocols such as FTP, NFS, etc.. This category also considers the granularity of the simulation. The simulation of the network can model in detail the flow of each packet through the network, a time consuming operation that leads to better output results, or it can model only the flows of packets going from one end to another in the network. The *middleware characteristics* are used to describe the middleware layer within the simulated environments. Amongst simulated middleware elements this category describes components such as schedulers and various security enforcement components. This category analyses how the middleware system schedules the jobs for execution inside a Grid system, for example. The *user applications* characteristics are used to describe the user applications within the large scale distributed environment.

In classifying different simulators based on their capability to model various distributed resources it is important to consider the ability to easily incorporate components dynamically defined during simulation runtime, for example by the user constructing the scenario experiment. This capability is crucial because it's almost impossible to provide the users with a complete set of predefined components to support all possible simulation scenarios. The vast majority of simulation tools provide this capability, but there are also exceptions (Bricks for example).

According to the *supported model* we can classify simulators based on their *behavior* and *time base*. The *behavior* category classifies simulators based on how the simulation proceeds. A *deterministic* simulation has no random events occurring, so repeating the same simulation will always return the same simulation results. In contrast, a *probabilistic* simulation has random events occurring. *Time base* specifies the values that the simulation time can contain. In a *discrete* simulation time has values within a finite range, but in a *continuous* simulation time has values within a finite range.

According to their implementation simulators for LSDS can be categorized based on several observations. Each simulator exploits a *simulation engine* to implement and execute the simulation model. According to their simulation engine simulators can be classified based on their *execution* implementation or based on their *mechanics*.

A simulator advances the simulation based on the *mechanics* defined in the simulation engine. The existing literature divides the types of possible mechanic designs into three categories: the *continuous*, *discrete-event* and *hybrid* categories. In a continuous simulation state changes occur continuously across time. In a Discrete-Event Simulation (DES) state changes only occur at specific time intervals. Finally, a hybrid simulation comprises both continuous and discrete-event simulations. In case of modeling distributed systems the continuous category identifies the particular case of emulators. While there are a number of particular good emulator projects for LSDS (MicroGrid, Grid eXplorer, etc.), we focus our analysis presented in the next section on simulators.

We also can classify furthermore discrete-event simulation based on how simulation proceeds. A discrete-event simulation adopts a queuing system where queues of events wait to be activated. A *trace-driven* DES proceeds by reading in a set of events that are collected independently from another environment and are suitable for modeling a system that has executed before in another environment. A *time-driven* DES advances by fixed time increments and is useful for modeling events that occur at regular time intervals. An *event-driven* DES advances by irregular time increments and is useful for modeling events that may occur at any time. An event-driven DES is more efficient than a time-driven DES since it does not step through regular time intervals when no event occurs.

Based on their execution, we can classify simulators for LSDS in *centralized* and *distributed*. Here execution refers to the capability of the simulators to make use of the underlying architectures. Sulistio et al (2004) present two modes of execution: serial and parallel. We argue that a better taxonomy should classify the simulators into centralized and distributed. Shared-memory parallel systems, comprising multiple processors, are becoming more and more accessible as home computing stations. In fact, a pure serial simulation execution, which would make use of only a single processor, cannot be a reality when addressing the problem of simulating LSDS, which are highly complex and in which multiple tasks/jobs are inherently being simultaneous processed. Modern simulators make use of at least the threading mechanisms provided by the underlying operating system; they use every processor existing on the underlying computing station.

According to this classification the simulators designed to use only a single computing unit, no matter if the underlying processing architecture provides multiple processing cores, are called centralized simulators. The second category comprises the simulators designed to make use of multiple processor units, running on different architectures and dispersed around a larger area. There are no pure distributed simulators for modeling LSDS. The reason for this is that, despite over two decades of research, the technology of distributed simulations has not significantly impressed the general simulation community (Fujimoto, 1993). Considerable efforts and expertise are still required to develop efficient simulation programs.

Of course, simulators also different between each others on aspects such as the queuing structures adopted in the design of the simulation engine for managing the event lists or the mapping of simulation jobs on physical threads or processes. These aspects, considered by the designers of the simulators, are important because they greatly influence the performance runtime and the capability to model systems consisting of many resources. A system using an $O(1)$ structure for the event list will behave better than another one using an $O(\log n)$ queuing structure. The time needed to run a complex simulation experiment can be quite huge when using the second queuing structure solutions, but the implementation of queuing solutions from the first category can take quite long and requires more time researching valuable results. Finding the best suitable queuing structure to be used for the simulation of large scale systems still represents a hot subject today. There is not a single unanimity accepted queuing structure that performs best when modeling distributed systems, they all tend to behave different depending on various parameters.

One other aspect to consider is the mapping of the simulation jobs on the underlying threads or processes. Reusing threads, using advanced mapping schemes in which multiple jobs can be simulated running in the same thread context, or any other aspect considered in this direction can yield higher simulation performances. This category considers the optimizations adopted in the design of the simulation engine to either improve the running performances or allow for advanced simulation models to be executed.

According to the *simulation model specification* simulators for LSDS can incorporate *specialized languages*, *general programming language and specialized library routines* or some other *visual* components (such as, for example, specific visual model components used in a drug-and-drop style for model construction).

A good design environment facilitates easy learning and fast usage. A language provides a set of defined constructs for the user to design simulation models. A library provides a set of routines to be used with a supporting programming language. A library-based simulation tool normally gives the user more flexibility in creating and controlling the simulation. An experienced user of the supporting programming language may fine-tune and optimize the simulation by exploiting certain libraries. A language-based simulation tool usually hides low-level implementation details from the user and thus provides less flexibility. Therefore, a language-based tool needs to provide a complete set of well-known constructs to ensure it supports the required level of flexibility. On the other hand, a language-based tool is often easier to learn and use since it is more high-level compared with a library-based tool.

Based on their *input data*, simulators can be further classified as including *input data generators* or as accepting *data sets collected by monitoring*. For example, MONARC 2 accepts both types of input (the monitoring data format is the one produced by MonALISA), while ChicagoSim accepts only input data generators.

The *user interface* determines how the user interacts with the simulator. Accordingly, we can classify simulators as having a *textual* or a *graphical output*. A visual user interface is preferred over a non-visual interface because graphical displays enable better interaction and they are easier to use and understand. A visual design interface allows the user to create a simulation model easier and faster compared with a non-visual interface, but the simulator that do provide this facility generally are restricting the types of simulation components that can be inserted in the modeling scene. Using a design interface the user can build the simulation model by dragging and dropping simulation objects and configuring the attributes and values (using forms for example). In contrast, a typical non-visual design interface requires the user to write programming code which requires more time and effort, but also extendibility support for the model. Examples of simulators providing visual design interfaces are GridSim and MONARC 2.

A visual execution interface provides a better representation of the simulation process. The user can more easily observe and analyze the simulation experiment. *Animations* provide a good visualization and display the flow of the simulation. Graphs give the graphical version of statistical data captured from the simulation. Without a visual execution interface the user encounters difficulties in analyzing and understanding the simulation results based on huge amounts of statistics and events captured. The visual interface can also include *interactivity* features, such as allowing the user to stop, suspend, resume, restart, change parameters or query the results database while the simulation is running.

The visual output analyzer is probably the most important graphical tool a simulator could have. Generally a simulation generates huge amounts of data. The data is difficult to be analyzed using a pure text format. Based on their visual analyzing support, there are two categories to classify simulators. The *plots* are the usual instruments used to represent the output data of the simulation in a graphical format that is more accessible to the end-user. Some tools provide high-level capabilities, being able to not only represent the data but also to analyze it and provide it in a modified and more meaningful way to the end-user. This category includes instruments such as 2D plots (bar graphs, scatter plots, contour maps) and 3D plots (such as surface rendering). The second category includes *analysis* of the original output results of the simulation, with possible comparison between different sets of results, often from different simulation runs. A simulation instrument that offers more visual capabilities to the end-user to better analyze the results of the simulation scenario is generally preferred by scientists.

Simulators can also be classified based on their capability to offer validation results. This classification refers to the process of assuring that the conceptual model accurately represents the behavior of a real system. According to this classification we can distinguish between simulators that provide appropriate validation tests or not. For those simulators providing validation proofs, we can further differentiate simulators as proving validation results based on mathematical comparison or based on comparison between simulation model and real-world testbed systems. Validation in this case represents a measure of the reliability offered to the end-user running different modeling scenarios. Validation is essentially a statistical problem because the number of performable experiments is limited and in general the magnitude of tolerable errors depends on the type of obtained results. To this date only a few simulators present validation studies (e.g. Bricks, MONARC and SimGrid).

## A Critical Analysis of Simulation Tools for Large Scale Systems

Using the categories of the proposed taxonomy, we present an analysis of the properties of six representative simulators for LSDS. This study presents an evaluation of most relevant work in the domain of distributed systems simulation, and tests the capabilities of the presented taxonomy to correctly investigate properties of the analyzed simulators.

Bricks was among the first simulation projects developed to investigate different resource scheduling issues using modeling techniques. The Bricks simulation framework allows the simulation of various behaviors: resource scheduling algorithms, programming modules for scheduling, network topology of clients and servers in global computing systems, and processing schemes for networks and servers. In its latest versions Bricks was extended, in order to evaluate the performance of various Data Grid application scenarios, with replica and disk management simulation capabilities. Bricks uses a model which the authors call the "central model." In this simulation model it is assumed that all the jobs are processed at a single site. In contrast with the model, MONARC also proposed another simulation model, called the "tier model," in which jobs are processed according to their hierarchical levels.

OptorSim is a Data Grid simulator project initially developed by a team of researchers working on the WorkPackage 2 of the European DataGrid project, which was responsible for replica management and optimization, and the emphasis is on this area. The objective of OptorSim is to investigate the stability and transient behavior of replication optimization methods. OptorSim adopts a Grid structure based on a simplification of the architecture proposed by the EU DataGrid project. According to this model the Grid consists of several sites, each of which may provide resources for submitted jobs. Given a Grid topology and resources, a set of jobs to be executed and an optimization strategy as input, OptorSim runs a number of Grid jobs on the simulated Grid. It provides a set of measurements which can be used to quantify the effectiveness of the optimization strategy under the considered conditions.

SimGrid is a simulation toolkit that provides core functionalities for the evaluation of sched-uling algorithms in distributed applications in a heterogeneous, computational distributed environment. SimGrid aims at providing the right model and level of abstraction for studying scheduling algorithms and generates correct and accurate simulation results. In its current form SimGrid can be used to simulate a single or multiple scheduling entities and timeshared systems operating in a Grid computing environment or to simulate distributed applications in the context of resource scheduling. SimGrid describes scheduling algorithms in terms of agent entities that make scheduling decisions. These agents interact by sending and receiving events via communication channels. SimGrid can be used to simulate compile time and running scheduling algorithms. In the first category, all scheduling decisions are taken before the execution. In the second category some decision are taken during the execution. In accordance with out proposed taxonomy, SimGrid does not provide any of the system support facilities as discussed in the taxonomy. A validation of SimGrid was presented in its very first paper (Casanova 2001). The validation consisted in comparing the results of the simulator with the ones obtained analytically on a mathematically tractable scheduling problem.

GridSim is a simulator developed by researchers from the Gridbus project to investigate effective resource allocation techniques based on computational economy. It allows simulation of entities in parallel and distributed computing systems-users, applications, resources, and resource brokers (schedulers) for design and evaluation of scheduling problems. It provides a comprehensive facility for creating different classes of heterogeneous resources that can be aggregated using resource brokers for solving compute and data intensive applications. GridSim supports modeling of heterogeneous computing resources (both time and space shared) from individual PCs to clusters, and various application domains from biomedical science to high energy physics. The focus is very much on scheduling and resource brokering. The GridSim toolkit can be used for modeling and simulation of application scheduling on various classes of parallel and distributed computing systems such as clusters, Grids, and P2P networks. GridSim focuses on Grid economy, where the scheduling involves the notions of producers (resource owners), consumers (end-users) and brokers discovering and allocating resources to users. Its design considers the existence of several brokers, which in SimGrid was introduced only since SimGrid2 (the Agents). GridSim is mainly used to study cost-time optimization algorithms for scheduling task farming applications on heterogeneous Grids, considering economy based distributed resource management, dealing with deadline and budget constraints. In some sense, GridSim is a higher-level simulator compared with SimGrid, which is basically designed to investigate interactions and interferences between scheduling decisions taken by distributed brokers.

The critical analysis of the simulators reveals the motivations, principles, implementations and applications of the instruments. The analysis (see Figure 6), based on the categories of the taxonomy presented in the previous section, describes the differences between the tools in terms of modeling, implementation and design. The evaluation of the analyzed simulators was mainly based on three criteria: (1) the ability to handle basic Grid functionalities; (2) the ability to schedule compute- and/or data-intensive jobs; and (3) the underlying network infrastructure.

The analysis highlights the specific characteristics of each analyzed simulator, from the simulation model to the internal properties to its implementation. There are advantages and disadvantages with each of the simulators. Interesting enough, even if many of them attack similar problems, being driven by comparable motivations, the simulators give a complementary approach to each others, allowing exploration of different areas of parameter space. Although the use of a particular simulator depends very much on the scope of the simulation being conducted and the skills of the user, they all cover important aspects of distributed systems, allowing exploration of different areas of parameter space.

## FUTURE TRENDS

LSDS are today regarded as the solution to developing increasingly large computing applications, designed to answer many of the problems of humanity. Commercially, LSDS are also becoming more and more appealing and this is reflected in the increasingly interest in the development of such systems coming from major industry players.

The development of solutions designed for LSDS, either applications running on top of them or technologies designed to help them, is facilitated by the use of adequate simulation instruments. However, today many of the simulators existing today are too focused on specific technologies, lacking the capability to model generic distributed systems. They do not include all the components and characteristics specific to such systems, leaving the user with the problem of implementing its own solutions on top simulation model. This translates into time and effort and is a reason why many prefer to implement a newly designed technology directly in real-world and evaluate its behavior at runtime.

In the future we believe this lack of generality in simulation model will be increasingly reduced, as designers start to invest more effort into providing more complete modeling solutions. Simulators such as MONARC 2 and ChicagoSim already started this trend. Users already see the potential of such simulators. As a consequence, MONARC 2 was already used to evaluate the specific behavior of the LHC experiments (Legrand, et al., 2005), providing valuable information without the need to implement the system in real-world. The experiment tested the behavior of the Tier architecture envisioned by the two largest LHC experiments, CMS and ATLAS. The obtained results indicated the role of using a data replication agent for the intelligent transferring of the produced data. The

*Figure 6. Design comparison of surveyed Grid simulation projects*

| No. | Simulation tool | Scope | Time base | Simulated components |
|-----|-----------------|-------|-----------|----------------------|
| 1 | Bricks | Resource scheduling in Grid systems | Discrete | Client-Server components organized in a central model;<br>Servers and networking elements modeled as queuing systems;<br>Scheduling Unit as the central simulation component. |
| 2 | OptorSim | Resource scheduling; Data replication strategies | Discrete | Grid sites composed of Computing Elements and Storage Elements;<br>Computing Elements run one job at a time;<br>Complex network model but lack routing, data transport, packetization;<br>GSs with modeled Resource Broker, Replica Manager and Replica Optimiser. |
| 3 | SimGrid | Resource scheduling | Discrete | Scheduling tasks;<br>Resource objects: modeled hosts and network links;<br>Grid model can be obtained from traces (ENV and NWS are supported). |
| 4 | GridSim | Resource scheduling; Simplistic data replication | Discrete | The modeling systems is composed of users, brokers and resources;<br>Both Computational and Data Grids are supported by the simulation model;<br>Networking model takes into consideration QoS, background traffic;<br>Well suited for algorithms designed for Nimrod-G? |
| 5 | EDGSIM | Resource Scheduling | Continuous | Jobs submitted using appropriate User Interface;<br>Resource Broker programmed with various Scheduling algorithms;<br>Replica Catalog mapping logical and physical file names;<br>Compute Element models the computation Resource of the Grid;<br>The network model is simple, without considering low-level functionality. |
| 6 | ChicagoSim | Resource scheduling; Data replication strategies | Discrete | Three modeled components: the site, the network and the driver;<br>Replica management is carried out at local level;<br>The modeled Grid includes any number of external schedulers, whilst the managing of the files is done locally by a dataset scheduler;<br>Support for modeling various scheduling algorithms and various replica methods. |
| 7 | MONARC 2 | Generic Grid simulator | Discrete | Processing units, Data Storage, farms, networking, HEP components;<br>Support for the modeling of scheduling algorithms, replica management, networking procedures, etc.<br>Strong support for modeling generic Grid architectures. |

| No. | Simulation tool | Execution | User interface | Validation |
|-----|-----------------|-----------|----------------|------------|
| 1 | Bricks | Centralized, event driven | Textual output, designed to be used with external tools | Performed by replacing the Predictor with NWS |
| 2 | OptorSim | Centralized, event and time driven | Graphical user interface, animations | Degenerate tests, fixed values, internal validity |
| 3 | SimGrid | Centralized, event driven | Graphical user interface, result analysis capabilities | Fixed values |
| 4 | GridSim | Centralized and distributed, event driven | Graphical user interface built on top of the simulator | N/A |
| 5 | EDGSIM | Centralized | Graphical user interface, drag-drop capability to construct scenarios | N/A |
| 6 | ChicagoSim | Centralized, event driven | Textual output, designed to be used with external tools | N/A |
| 7 | MONARC 2 | Centralized, event driven | Graphical user interface, animations | Model Validation<br>Monitored resource utilization vs simulated observations<br>Queuing theory tests |

obtained results also showed that the existing capacity of 2.5 Gbps was not sufficient and, in fact, not far afterwards the link was upgraded to a current 30 Gbps. Other simulators, such as GridSim, SimGrid, OptorSim and many others also are well underway to extend their simulation models to be more generically and address a wider set of possible simulation experiments.

Another problem with existing simulators for LSDS consists in the lack of evaluation results. A scientist wanting to use a simulator to evaluate a specific technology needs to have increased confidence in the obtained results. He needs evidence that the obtained results also are valid in real-world. Many of the existing simulators designed for LSDS do not present confidence because they lack proof of their validity. This is due to the nature of the LSDS, for which analytical models to be compared against the simulation models are hard to design. However, evaluation proof can be obtained in several ways. For example, a well-design simulator must present comparisons between experiments modeling small distributed systems against equivalent real-world testbeds. The comparison between the results obtained in simulation experiments and the monitored parameters of a real-world testbed should be made at least for the networking protocols, for the computing nodes and the storage facilities. If this simplified form of evaluation is conducted for each of the simulated component a general conclusion can be drawn, with higher confidence, for the entire simulation model. Another mechanism designed to facilitate the evaluation of the simulation models consists in the use of queuing theory. The formalism provided by the queuing models is important for the definition and validation of the simulation stochastic models. They provide an analytical model to the problem of testing the randomness introduced by various mathematical distributions. For example, in the simulation of network traffic pattern, queuing models are generally used to describe traffic generation, flows of the transmission and many intrusive problems related with the communication systems.

Another trend relates to the need to model very large distributed systems, consisting of a great number of resources. Many of today's simulators lack the capability to simulate large distributed systems because their simulation engines are limited to the physical resources of the workstations where the experiments are being executed. Today many researchers are interesting in finding solutions to facilitate the simulation of LSDS. The simulation engine can be optimized, in order to facilitate the evaluation of LSDS experiments, by using advanced priority queuing structures for the simulation events, by optimizing the way in which simulated entities are being scheduled in simulation for execution, by using various simplifications mechanisms or by using the underlying physical distributed resources of clusters of nodes.

With the advent of LSDS, today more than ever scientists are looking into simulation as the possible today to answer faster many of the faced problems. However, in order to be useful, a simulator must include solutions to be generic, to present evaluation capabilities and allow scalability.

## CONCLUSION

Large-scale grids and other federations of distributed resources that aggregate and share resources over wide-area networks present major new challenges for scientists. In this chapter we focus on the challenge to enable scalable, high-level simulation of applications, middleware, resources and networks to support scientific and systematic study of large scale distributed applications and environments. The contributions of the chapter are on the intelligent control of distributed systems where simulation is used in decision making as a way to predict future performance under some control law in question.

The field of modeling and simulation was long-time seen as a viable alternative to develop new algorithms and technologies and to enable the development of large-scale distributed systems, where analytical validations are prohibited by the nature of the encountered problems. The use of discrete-event simulators in the design and development of LSDS is appealing due to their efficiency and scalability. Their core abstractions of process and event map neatly to the components and interactions of modern-day distributed systems and allow the design of realistic scenarios. Compared with the alternative of implementing the new technology directly in real-world to demonstrate its viability, the simulation of distributed systems is a far better alternative because it achieves faster validation results, minimizing the costs involved by the deployment process.

In this chapter we described alternatives to designing and implementing simulation instruments to be used in the validation of distributed system technologies. We present the experienced accumulated by the author in developing a generic model for the simulation of distributed system technologies, integrating components and mechanisms to create realistic simulation experiments of large scale systems. The original model and framework (MONARC 2) incorporates all the necessary components and characteristics that allow the complete and accurate design of realistic simulation experiments of complex Grid architectures, consisting of many resources and various technologies, ranging from data transferring to scheduling and data replication, with resources working together to provide a common set of characteristics.

In this chapter we present the design characteristics of the simulation model proposed in MONARC. Designed as a generic simulation framework for distributed systems, MONARC encompasses many of the characteristics of distributed systems. We present the characteristics of such systems that influenced the design process

of MONARC 2. We demonstrate that this model includes the necessary components to describe various actual distributed system technologies, and provides the mechanisms to describe concurrent network traffic, evaluate different strategies in data replication, and analyze job scheduling procedures.

We also presented a critical comparison study of the most important simulation projects involved in the modeling of distributed systems. Previous work addressed either the general categories of computing systems simulation, without focusing on the specific issues related to simulating large-scale heterogeneous systems, or overviewed the current work being done in this field without comparing the various surveyed simulation instruments. We presented a comparison survey study of a number of seven most representative simulation instruments. The analysis highlights their specific characteristics, from the types of simulation models or internal simulation design to the implementations of the respective instruments. We demonstrated that, although the use of a particular simulation instrument depends very much on the scope of the simulation being conducted and the skills of the user, they all cover important aspects of distributed systems, allowing exploration of different areas of parameter space. Among these projects, we demonstrate that MONARC is the most generic one, being capable to handle a wider range of simulation scenarios. It also offers the highest number of capabilities, being able to consider many parameters, capabilities and components that any other existing simulation instrument for distributed systems.

## REFERENCES

Bagchi, S. (1994). Simulation of grid computing infrastructures: Challenges and solutions. In *Proceedings of the Winter Simulation Conference*, (pp. 1773-1780). ACM Press.

Bagchi, S. (2005). *Simulation of grid computing infrastructures: Challenges and solutions*. In Proceedings of the Winter Simulation Conference, (pp. 131-135). ACM Press.

Bote-Lorenzo, M., Dimitriadis, Y., & Gomez-Sanchez, E. (2002). *Grid characteristics and uses: A grid definition. Technical Report CICYT*. Valladolid, Spain: University of Valladolid.

Coulouris, G., Dollimore, J., & Kindberg, T. (1994). *Distributed systems – Concepts and design* (2nd ed.). Reading, MA: Addison-Wesley.

Dobre, C., Pop, F., & Cristea, V. (2008). A simulation framework for dependable distributed systems. In *Proceedings of the 37th International Conference on Parallel Processing (ICPP-08)*, (pp. 181-187). Portland, Oregon: IEEE Press.

Dobre, C., Pop, F., & Cristea, V. (2009). Simulation Framework for the Evaluation of Dependable Distributed Systems. *International Journal for Parallel and Distributed Computing, 10*(1), 13–23.

Dobre, C., & Stratan, C. (2003). MONARC 2 - Distributed systems simulation. In *Proceedings of the 14th International Conference on Control Systems and Computer Science*, (pp. 145-149). Bucharest, Romania: IEEE Press.

Dobre, C. M., & Cristea, V. (2007). A simulation model for large scale distributed systems. In *Proceedings of the 4ᵗʰ International Conference on Innovations in Information Technology*, (pp. 526-530). Dubai, UAE: IEEE Press.

Dobre, C. M., & Stratan, C. (2004). *MONARC simulation framework*. Paper presented at the RoEduNet International Conference. Timisoara, Romania.

Eremia, B., Dobre, C., Pop, F., Costan, A., & Cristea, V. (2010). Simulation model and instrument to evaluate replication techniques. In *Proceedings of the International Conference on, P2P, Paralel, Grid, Cloud and Internet Computing*, (pp. 541-547). Fukuoka, Japan: IEEE Press.

Foster, I., & Kesselman, C. (1998). *The GRID: Blueprint for a new computing infrastructure*. New York: Morgan Kaufmann.

Foster, I., Kesselman, C., & Tuecke, S. (2001). *The anatomy of the grid: Enabling scalable virtual organizations*. Retrieved from http://www.globus.org/alliance/publications/papers/anatomy.pdf.

Frantz, F. K. (1995). A taxonomy of model abstraction techniques. In *Proceedings of the 1995 Winter Simulation Conference*, (pp. 1413-1420). Arlington, VA: IEEE Press.

Fujimoto, R. M. (1993). Parallel discrete event simulation: Will the field survive? *ORSA Journal on Computing, 5*(3), 213–230.

Gibson, W. (2000). FLASH vs (simulated) FLASH: Closing the simulation loop. *ACM Transactions on Modeling and Computer Simulation, 35*(11).

Hamscher, V., Schwiegelshohn, U., Streit, A., & Yahyapour, R. (2000). Evaluation of job-scheduling strategies for grid computing. In *Proceedings of the First IEEE/ACM international Workshop on Grid Computing*, (pp. 191-202). London, UK: Springer-Verlag.

Johnston, S. (2004). *Modeling security concerns in service-oriented architectures*. Retrieved from http://www.ibm.com/developerworks/rational/library/4860.html.

Legrand, I. C., Dobre, C. M., Voicu, R., Stratan, C., Cirstoiu, C., & Musat, L. (2005). *A simulation study for T0/T1 data replication and production activities*. Paper presented at the 15th International Conference on Control Systems and Computer Science. Bucharest, Romania.

Legrand, I. C., Newman, H., Dobre, C. M., & Stratan, C. (2003). *MONARC simulation framework*. Paper presented at the International Workshop on Advanced Computing and Analysis Techniques in Physics Research. Tsukuba, Japan.

Legrand, I. C., Newman, H., van Lingen, F., Dobre, C., Stratan, C., & Paschen, K. (2003). A processes oriented, discrete event simulation framework for modelling and design of large scale distributed systems. In *Proceedings of the IX International Workshop on Advanced Computing and Analysis Techniques in Physics Research*. Tsukuba, Japan: IEEE Press.

Legrand, I. C., Newman, H. B., Voicu, R., & Cirstoiu, C. (2004). *MonALISA: An agent based, dynamic service system to monitor, control and optimize grid based applications*. Paper presented at the Computing in High Energy and Nuclear Physics (CHEP 2004). Interlaken, Switzerland.

Pop, F., Dobre, C. M., Godza, G., & Cristea, V. (2006). A simulation model for grid scheduling analysis and optimization. In *Proceedings of the International Symposium on Parallel Computing in Electrical Engineering (PARELEC 2006)*, (pp. 133 – 138). Bialystok, Poland: IEEE Press.

Pop, P., Dobre, C., & Cristea, V. (2008). Evaluation of multi-objective decentralized scheduling for applications in grid environment. In *Proceedings of the 2008 IEEE 4th International Conference on Intelligent Computer Communication and Processing*, (pp. 231-238). Cluj-Napoca, Romania: IEEE Press.

Riley, G. F., & Ammar, M. H. (2002). Simulating large networks – How big is big enough? In *Proceedings of the First International Conference on Grand Challenges for Modelling and Simulation*. IEEE Press.

Sulistio, A., Yeo, C. S., & Buyya, R. (2004). A taxonomy of computer-based simulations and its mapping to parallel and distributed systems simulation tools. *Software, Practice & Experience, 34*(7), 653–673. doi:10.1002/spe.585

Venugopal, S., Buyya, R., & Ramamohanaro, K. (2006). A taxonomy of data grids for distributed data sharing, management and processing. *ACM Computing Surveys, 38*(1). doi:10.1145/1132952.1132955

Vincent, J. M., & Legrand, A. (2007). *Discrete event simulation*. Paper presented at the Laboratory ID-IMAG. Paris, France.

Weske, M., & Wirtz, G. (2001). Integrated modeling of distributed software systems and workflow applications. In *Proceedings of the 34th Annual Hawaii international Conference on System Sciences (HICSS-34)*, (Vol. 9). Hawaii, HI: HICSS Press.

Wieder, P., Schwiegelsholn, U., & Yahyapour, R. (2005). *Resource management for future generation grids*. Berlin, Germany: CEI.

## KEY TERMS AND DEFINITIONS

**Complex Model:** Is a network of large number of heterogeneous components that interact nonlinearly, to give rise to emergent behavior for the system it represents.

**Distributed Computing:** Is a field of computer science that studies distributed systems. It also refers to the use of distributed systems to solve computational problems. In distributed computing, a problem is divided into many tasks, each of which is solved by one or more computers.

**Distributed Program:** Is a computer program that runs in a distributed system.

**Distributed Programming:** Is the process of writing such distributed programs.

**Distributed System:** Is a system that consists of multiple autonomous computers that communicate through a computer network. The computers interact with each other in order to achieve a common goal.

**Evaluation:** Is systematic determination of merit, worth, and significance of something or someone using criteria against a set of standards. It often is used to characterize and appraise subjects of interest in a wide range of systems.

**Large Scale Distributed System:** Is a distributed system that consists of large number of autonomous and heterogeneous computers or networks that communicate through various communication technologies.

**Modeling:** Is the process of generating abstract, conceptual, graphical and/or mathematical models. A model can provide a way to read elements easily which have been broken down to a simpler form. It is an essential and inseparable part of all scientific activity, and many scientific disciplines have their own ideas about specific types of modeling. There is an increasing attention for scientific modeling in many fields of science and engineering.

**Tier Architecture** (or **N-Tier Architecture**): Is a client–server architecture in which the presentation, the application processing, and the data management are logically separate processes. It provides a model for developers to create a flexible and reusable application. By breaking up an application into tiers, developers only have to modify or add a specific layer, rather than have to rewrite the entire application over. The concepts of layer and tier are often used interchangeably. However, one fairly common point of view is that there is indeed a difference, and that a layer is a logical structuring mechanism for the elements that make up the software solution, while a tier is a physical structuring mechanism for the system infrastructure.

# Chapter 20
# Future Approach of Next Generation Cellular Mobile Communications

**Muzhir Shaban Al-Ani**
*Amman Arab University, Jordan*

## ABSTRACT

*The tremendous use of telecommunication services and the existence of various types of mobile devices and networks impose a huge need for a new technology that can integrate these devices and networks to provide adequate services and applications to satisfy the user's needs. The new technology tries to eliminate all boundaries of telecommunications and leads to a universal approach that is able to demonstrate an easy and efficient technique to overcome all technical and managerial issues. This chapter, first, studies and analyzes the performance of existing mobile systems and their services and estimates the future aspects of next generation mobile communications. Second, a new approach is proposed and investigated. The new approach is based on using the abilities of satellite communications as part of the mobile communication systems. Such an approach introduces advanced communication solutions that could be set up anywhere/anytime subject to the existence of satellite coverage.*

## INTRODUCTION

Mobile communication and networking becoming one of the biggest dominate media in the word, it penetrates the customer networks and it becomes the bridge to the future. Mobile devices deals with mobile PCs, cellular mobiles, satellites, TV devices, radio devices, handset devices, game consoles and all wireless devices and networks. The customer required the network that has the ability to offer many performances such as high throughput, high degree of scalability, capabilities of quality of service, reasonable degree of security, reasonable degree of flexibility and reasonable degree of coverage. These performances lead to compromise between quality and cost, and offers comfortable services to the customer. The world is going toward mobility in every need of

DOI: 10.4018/978-1-4666-0191-8.ch020

life, so a big amount of investments go to mobile technology, mobile platforms, mobile services, mobile infrastructure, and the related advertising companies. In order to lead these investments in a right way it must be follow the customer needs of mobile applications and services.

Recently, mobile systems and networks are distributed all over the world. Some countries of the developed world have implemented the advanced four generation mobile system with high speed data transfer up to 50 Mbps, and some other countries have implemented third generation mobile system with moderate speed data transfer up to 10 Mbps, but many other countries of the developing world still using the second generation mobile system with low speed data transfer up to 2 Mbps.

## BACKGROUND ON ITU

### About ITU

International Telecommunication Union (ITU) is the leading United Nations agency for information and communication technology issues, and the global focal point for governments and the private sector in developing networks and services. For 145 years, ITU has coordinated the shared global use of the radio spectrum, promoted international cooperation in assigning satellite orbits, worked to improve telecommunication infrastructure in the developing world, established the worldwide standards that foster seamless interconnection of a vast range of communications systems and addressed the global challenges of our times, such as mitigating the impact of natural disasters and climate change and strengthening cyber-security.

ITU also organizes worldwide and regional exhibitions and forums, such as ITU TELECOM WORLD, bringing together the most influential representatives of government and the telecommunications and Information and Communication Technologies (ICT) industry to exchange ideas,

knowledge and technology for the benefit of the global community, and in particular the developing world.

From broadband Internet to latest-generation wireless technologies, from aeronautical and maritime navigation to radio astronomy and satellite-based meteorology, from convergence in fixed-mobile phone, Internet access, data, voice and TV broadcasting to next-generation networks, ITU is committed to connecting the world (ITU, 2010).

### ITU Definitions

Before we start with the statistics related to this chapter let us explain briefly some of the definitions related to the growth of ICT issued by ITU (PCBS, 2010):

- **Fixed telephone lines** refers to the active line connecting the subscriber's terminal equipment to the Public Switched Telephone Network (PSTN) and which has a dedicated port in the telephone exchange equipment.
- **Mobile cellular telephone subscriptions** refers to the subscriptions to a public mobile telephone service and provides access to Public Switched Telephone Network (PSTN) using cellular technology, including number of pre-paid SIM cards active during the past three months. This includes both analogue and digital cellular systems (IMT-2000 Third Generation [3G] and Fourth Generation [4G]) subscriptions.
- **Total fixed (wired) Internet subscriptions** refers to the number of total Internet subscriptions with fixed (wired) Internet access, which includes dial-up and total fixed (wired) broadband subscriptions. Only active subscriptions that have used the system within the past 3 months should be included.

- **Total fixed (wired) broadband Internet subscriptions** refers to subscriptions to high-speed access to the public Internet (a TCP/IP connection), at downstream speeds equal to, or greater than, 256 kbit/s. This can include for example cable modem, DSL, fibre-to-the-home/building and other fixed (wired) broadband subscriptions.
- **Total Wireless broadband subscriptions** refers to the sum of satellite, terrestrial fixed wireless and terrestrial mobile wireless subscriptions.

## ITU Sectors

ITU have four main sectors:

1. **ITU Radiocommunication Sector (ITU-R):** This sector manages the international radio-frequency spectrum and satellite orbit resources. ITU is mandated by its constitution to allocate spectrum and register frequency assignments, orbital positions and other parameters of satellites, "in order to avoid harmful interference between radio stations of different countries." The international spectrum management system is therefore based on regulatory procedures for frequency notification, coordination and registration (ITU-R, 2010).

2. **Telecommunication Standardization Sector (ITU-T):** ITU's standards-making efforts are its best-known — and oldest — activity. Working at the coalface of the world's fastest changing industry, today's ITU-T continues to evolve, adopting streamlined working methods and more flexible, collaborative approaches designed to meet the needs of increasingly complex markets. Specialists drawn from industry, the public sector and R&D entities worldwide meet regularly to thrash out the intricate technical specifications that ensure that each piece of communications systems can interoperate seamlessly with the myriad elements that make up today's complex ICT networks and services (ITU-T, 2010).

3. **Telecommunication Development Sector (ITU-D):** The ITU-D was established to help spread equitable, sustainable and affordable access to ICT as a means of stimulating broader social and economic development. Held every four years, the World Telecommunication Development Conference (WTDC) establishes concrete priorities to help achieve these goals. Through a series of regional initiatives together with comprehensive national programs, activities on the global level and multiple targeted projects, the Sector works with partners in government and industry to mobilize the technical, human and financial resources needed to develop ICT networks and services to connect the unconnected. To that end, we are pushing for the expansion of global broadband connectivity that is pervasive, simple and affordable for all and enables the migration towards Next-Generation Networks (NGN) (ITU-D, 2010).

4. **ITU TELECOM Sector:** It brings together the top names from across the ICT industry as well as ministers and regulators and many more for a major exhibition, a high-level forum and a host of other opportunities. Through all that they offer, the events provide a networking platform for the world's ICT community to come together, meet, network, showcase the latest technologies, explore the latest trends and get business done. ITU TELECOM began life in 1971 when the first event was held in Geneva, Switzerland. Since then, ITU TELECOM has built up a wealth of experience organizing events across the world. An ITU TELECOM event is held in a different world region each year, with the flagship ITU TELECOM WORLD taking place every 3 years (ITU-Telecom, 2010).

## ICT STATISTICS

To look for the importance of future aspects of the mobile communication, we start to illustrate the importance of ICT development in each country of the world, then we will take into account some of the statistics published by ITU related to this subject. There are many ICT trends that mentioned the ICT revolution over the world and these trends issued by ITU.

### Global ICT Trends

The global ICT trends as mentioned by ITU are shown in Figure 1. This figure measures the statistics during ten years (1998-2009). A small growth is mentioned for fixed broadband subscription and mobile broadband subscription also a small decrement mentioned in fixed telephone lines. Significant growths are mentioned in both Internet users and mobile cellular telephone subscription. Internet users penetration shows a normal increment from 2% to 26.8% but mobile cellular telephone subscription penetration shows a high increment from 5% to 68.2%. This indicates that mobile cellular telephone is an important issue

via ICT factors that attract most of the investment of the next few years (ITU-ICT-Trends, 2010).

### Internet Users

The Internet users' trends for developed and developing countries as mentioned by ITU are shown in Figure 2. It is clear from this figure that the growth of Internet penetration for the developed countries is much greater that for the developing countries. This difference because of many reasons such as economy, technology, human think, as well as cellular mobile started in many years ago in developed countries before started in developing countries (ITU-Internet-Trends, 2010).

The total number of Internet users as issued by ITU is shown in Figure 3. This figure shows about 1.8 Billions subscribers are registered in 2009 (6.8 Billions world population in 2009) where as about 800 million subscribers are registered in 2000. This indicates that during few years total number of Internet users will be duplicated (ITU-Internet-Users, 2010).

The Internet subscriptions for developed and developing countries as issued by ITU are shown in Figure 4. This figure shows that in 2003 there

*Figure 1. Global ICT trends (ITU-ICT-Trends, 2010)*

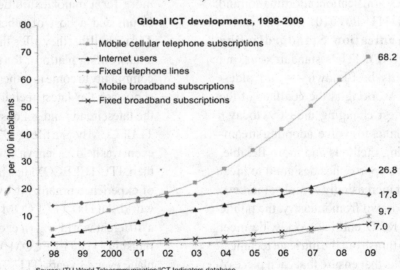

*Figure 2. Internet users trends for developed and developing countries (ITU-Internet-Trends, 2010)*

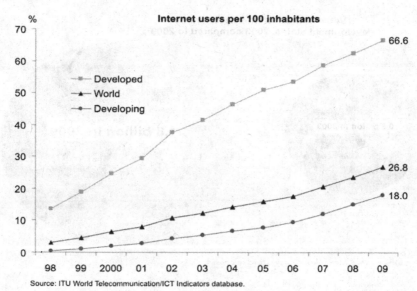

*Figure 3. Number of Internet users (ITU-Internet-Users, 2010)*

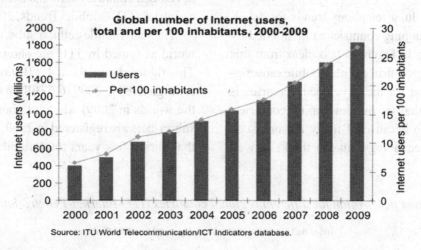

was a wide area of Internet subscriptions for developed countries (about 70% of the total). This measures was opposite in 2009 means there was a wide area of Internet subscriptions for developing countries (about 60% of the total). This indicates that the future of developing countries has a huge market for Internet technology (ITU-Internet-Subscriptions, 2010).

The Internet penetration for different regional countries as issued by ITU is shown in Figure 5. It is clear that Africa denotes a minimum penetration (about 8.8%), where Europe denotes maximum penetration (about 62.9%). This indicates that Africa and Asia have a wide future market for Internet technology (ITU-Internet-Penetration, 2010).

*Figure 4. Internet subscriptions for developed and developing countries (ITU-Internet-Subscriptions, 2010)*

**Global number of Internet users by development status, 2003 compared to 2009**

Developing

0.8 billion in 2003

Developed

Developing

**1.8 billion in 2009**

Developed

Source: ITU World Telecommunication/ICT Indicators database.

## Mobile Cellular Telephony Users

The mobile cellular telephony trends for developed and developing countries as mentioned by ITU are shown in Figure 6. It is clear from this figure that the growth of cellular mobile subscription penetration for the developed countries is much greater that for the developing countries. This difference because of many reasons such as economy, technology, human think, as well as cellular mobile started in many years ago in developed countries before started in developing countries (ITU-Mobile-Trends, 2010).

The total mobile cellular subscriptions for the world as issued by ITU are shown in Figure 7. This figure shows about 4.7 Billions subscribers are registered in 2009 (6.6 Billions inhabitants of the worlds in 2009) where as about 700 million subscribers are registered in 2000. This indicates that during few years total mobile cellular sub-

*Figure 5. Internet penetration for different regional countries (ITU-Internet-Penetration, 2010)*

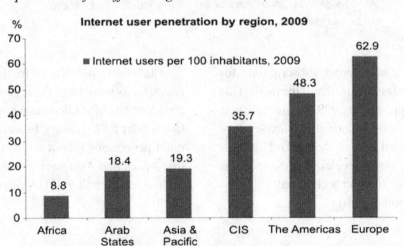

**Internet user penetration by region, 2009**

■ Internet users per 100 inhabitants, 2009

| Region | % |
| --- | --- |
| Africa | 8.8 |
| Arab States | 18.4 |
| Asia & Pacific | 19.3 |
| CIS | 35.7 |
| The Americas | 48.3 |
| Europe | 62.9 |

Source: ITU World Telecommunication/ICT Indicators database.

*Figure 6. Mobile cellular telephony trends (ITU-Mobile-Trends, 2010)*

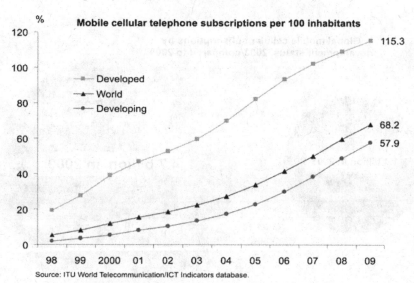

Source: ITU World Telecommunication/ICT Indicators database.

scriptions will reach inhabitants of the worlds (ITU-Mobile-Subscriptions, 2011).

The total mobile cellular subscriptions for developed and developing countries as issued by ITU are shown in Figure 8. This figure shows that in 2003 there was a wide area of mobile cellular subscriptions for developed countries (about 2/3 of the total). This measures was opposite in 2009 means there was a wide area of mobile cellular

subscriptions for developing countries (about 2/3 of the total). This indicates that the future of developing countries has a huge market for mobile cellular technology (ITU-Cellular-Subscriptions, 2010).

The mobile cellular penetration for different regional countries as issued by ITU is shown in Figure 9. It is clear that Africa denotes a minimum penetration (about 37.5%), where CIS denotes

*Figure 7. Total mobile cellular subscriptions (ITU-Mobile-Subscriptions, 2010)*

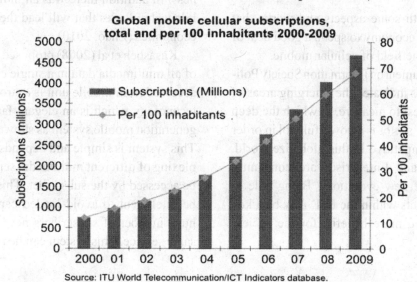

Source: ITU World Telecommunication/ICT Indicators database.

*Figure 8. Cellular subscriptions for developed and developing countries (ITU-Cellular-Subscriptions, 2010)*

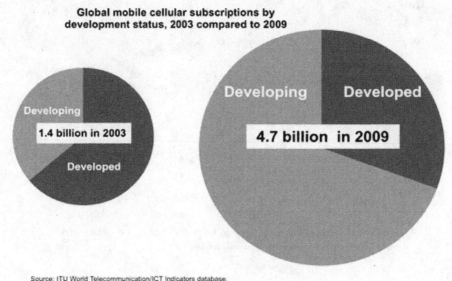

Source: ITU World Telecommunication/ICT Indicators database.

maximum penetration (about 127.8%). This indicates that Africa and Asia have a wide future market for mobile cellular technology (ITU-Mobile-Penetration, 2010).

## MAIN FOCUS OF THE CHAPTER

### ICT and Cellular Mobile Trends

Let us start with some aspects and works that push the global economy to spend a good deal of investment in the field of cellular mobile.

Madrid Document on Information Society Policies and Metrics indicated the emerging areas of particular interest to measure, in which the deep knowledge ICT sector is a powerful tool in order to be more competitive in this globalize world. Governments and Enterprises are constantly adapting to the new evolutions. Being able to emerging markets within the ICT, may be a key issue to achieve more benefits for the society (Madrid, 2011).

ITU deputy security – general, Houlin Zhao in his Speech at WESIS Forum indicate that high speed networks are also a focus of the new report (National e-Strategies for Development) said realised yesterday, which shows that, across the globe, governments are looking to ICT for a successful future. Also share computing power that called cloud computing is becoming more and more important for scientists and for business. In addition there was an indication to mobile technologies that will lead the way in many economies (Zhao, 2010).

Kasasbeh et al (2008) proposed the impaction of all multimedia data in a single channel can be accessed from mobile unit is a strong and power technology which is an elegant face of the next generation mobile system as shown in Figure 10. This system is simple and depends on the multiplexing of different multimedia services that can be accessed by the subscriber. This system must be intelligent to avoid loaded capacity when a huge number of subscribers need to access the same service. This system can be reach its maxi-

*Figure 9. Mobile cellular penetration for different regional countries (ITU-Mobile-Penetration, 2010)*

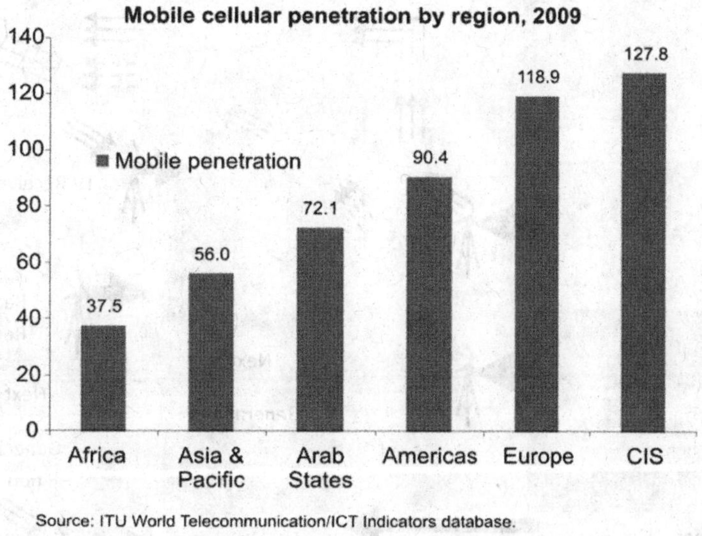

Source: ITU World Telecommunication/ICT Indicators database.

mum efficiency, when the next generation well be reachable and accessible with their adaptable high speed of transmission, high verity of services, high capacity of channels, high quality and performance of mobile units with high screen resolution (Kasasbeh, et al., 2008).

Al-Ani (2009) proposed the demonstration of the advance and future technologies that serve for E-commerce and M-commerce as shown in Figure 11. This approach deals with the demonstration of commerce technologies and concentration on the next generation technologies. The development of high advance technologies in telecommunications such as internet and mobile telephony leads to massive support for digital commerce. Many problems will appear through the integration of different multimedia technologies. The suggested system will use the feature of speed technology of transmission (100 Mbps). This system has the capability to operate on real-time multimedia technologies. The globalization of industry, business, marketing, information and technologies lead to this integrity of commerce. The new system supports specific features such as high speed, standard, intelligent, secure and simple (Al-Ani, 2009).

Al-Ani et al (2009) proposed a new communication system has been proposed to integrate the usage of GSM over the available satellites infrastructures as shown in Figure 12. The proposed system divides the world into areas that each area contains on a number of countries and can be covered by one geosynchronous satellite, so it is possible to assume that 24 satellites can be cover all the areas of the world (as in Geographic Information System). This system could be used to facilitate and get benefits of both systems to achieve competitive services over the world. This system is concentrated on a global communications system that served all over the world and gives some specialization and privacy for each country. This approach is attempted to show how to implement mobile communications over satellite systems in an efficient, flexible, and cost-effective manner (Al-Ani, et al., 2009).

## Future Aspects

The ICT statistics for Internet and mobile cellular growth indicate that there is a huge amount of raw market for future investment in these technologies.

435

*Figure 10. The proposed real TV over mobile (Kasasbeh, et al., 2008)*

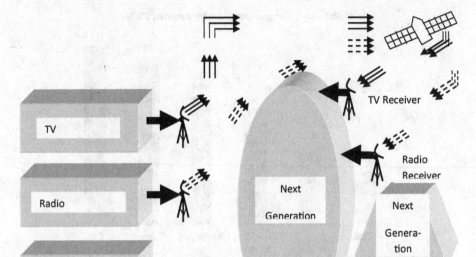

*Figure 11. The proposed integrated multisystem (Al-Ani, 2009)*

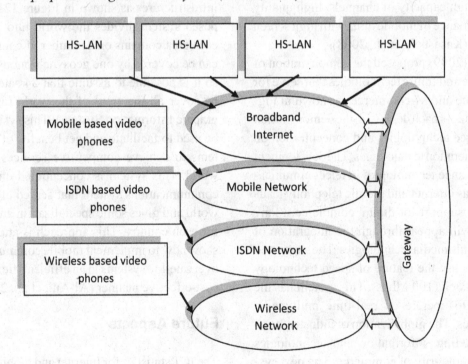

*Figure 12. The proposed GSM over satellites (Al-Ani, et al., 2009)*

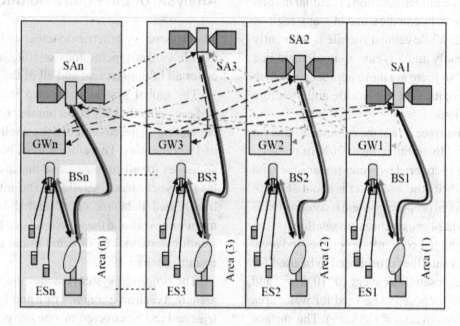

This leads to deep investigations of new technologies to overcome many new services.

The population growth rate is about 1.1%, means it is expected that the human population will reach about 7.3 billion by 2015. In addition, according to the Internet Usage and World Population Statistics at June 30, 2010, there were about 2 Billions of Internet users and Internet penetration about 28.7%, and about 40% of these users are found in Asia.

Furthermore there were about 5 Billions of mobile users and about 80% of mobile penetration. This indicates that there are huge business and huge investment in this field.

According to the normal growth of population and corresponding growth in Internet and mobile users we can estimate that during the five next years (2015) the Internet users will reach about 3.5 Billions (with the increment of 1.7 Billions) while mobile users will reach about 7 Billions (with the increment of 2.3 Billions). Also we can say that the real mobile users number may be more than this estimated number because of the future trend of new mobile technologies.

From this brief introduction of the future aspects and from the previous proposed related cellular mobile systems we can introduce a future architecture of a hybrid mobile – satellite system that can help to adapt new services (IWS, 2011).

## Future Next Generation Cellular Mobile

According to the ICT indicators and to the previous introduction of this chapter we can mentioned that telecommunications including cellular mobiles, satellites, wireless networks and wireless technologies are main aspects of future investments in the world. So the proposed approach is concentrated on the integration of cellular mobile communications over satellite systems. Flexibility, reliability, high quality, acceptable cost, as well as you can manage and do your job any where any time; these are the main factors that must be considered in any proposal for future mobile system architecture.

Due to the growth of the subscription of cellular mobile all over the world and this growth will reach approximately the population of the world in the year 2015. The implementation of cellular mobile over satellite is in common use in many regions of the world. While cellular mobile is inherently satellite friendly and it is easy to implement in a simple way, so there are more approaches which can lead to significant bandwidth, and therefore cost, reductions.

The total surface area of the continental is about $510*10^6$ km$^2$. In addition about 70% of the total surface area is covered by water (means the land is about $150*10^6$ km$^2$ and water is about $360*10^6$ km$^2$). The global proposed system is constructed to be covered via 24 geosynchronous satellites (s1, s2 … s24) in which it concentrates on the land area. Therefore 15 satellites is proposed to be used for land area (each satellite covers $10*10^6$ km$^2$) and 9 satellites is proposed to be used for water area (each satellite covers $40*10^6$ km$^2$). The surface areas are different from one country to another, so the coverage area of each satellite may cover one or more countries.

The proposed system is illustrated in Figure 13, in which floating cells (FC1, FC2 … FCn) are constructed (with no more than one kilometer in height) and these cells are normally distributed in each country, these cells have identical address for each country that related to a certain satellite via a bidirectional gate way (GW1, GW2 … GW192) means there are many gate ways corresponding to a certain satellite. The gate way is used to identify and verify all communication links from any mobile station uplink and downlink (MS1, MS2 … MSz). The integration of the cellular mobile cells is done by the encapsulation of the mobile frame via satellite frame.

Many important aspects must be considered through the design of this system such as; multimedia data transmission, frame format, data propagation, bit rate, protocols between floating cells, protocols between gate ways, protocols between mobile and satellite and protocols between countries.

## Analysis of the Future Solution

The proposed system tries to integrate the cellular mobile via geosynchronous satellite in a way to cover all of the services and all of the countries.

The global system is divided into 24 areas and each area divided into a number of countries depending on the coverage of the satellite, in total of 192 countries. Therefore it must be 192 fixed addresses for all countries, and that are indicated by geosynchronous satellites. The international transmitted data are encapsulated by internal mobile network and then encapsulated by external satellite network and directed to the destination country (one of 192).

The proposed system divides the world into areas that each area contains on a number of countries and can be covered by one geosynchronous satellite, so it is possible to assume that 24 satellites can be cover all the areas of the world (as in Geographic Information System). The proposed system as shown in Figure 13 can be divided into two parts; the first one is the Global Extra Communication System (GECS), that concern with the satellite communication between users outside of areas and countries. GECS depends on geostationary satellite through Earth Stations (ESs), where the communications of each area goes through a GateWay (GW) unit, that make security and privacy for each country as well as identify the authority and legality for each user. The second one is the Local Intra Communication System (LICS), that concern with the mobile communication between users inside of areas and countries. LICS depends on mobile communication systems networks through Base Stations (BSs), where the communications through of each area goes through a central center that dominant all the internal communications and operates as a pre-filter link to the gateway to achieve the external communications.

*Figure 13. The future proposed system*

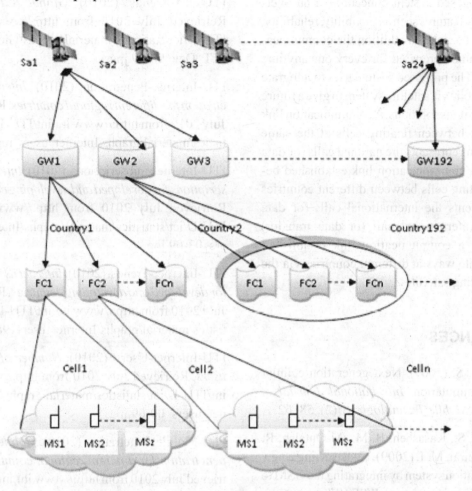

The local operation (internal access) starts when a signal is transmitted to a local subscriber, so this operation passes through a mobile network, then to the nearest base station, then to the indicated subscriber. The global operation (external access) starts when a signal is transmitted to a global subscriber, so this operation passes through a satellite network to the area gateway of the source subscriber, then via inter-satellite links passes to the area gateway of the destination subscriber, then to the indicated subscriber.

## CONCLUSION

Many subjects are explained in this chapter such as ITU and ICT trends, Internet users and Internet penetration, cellular mobile users and cellular mobile penetration, also ICT statistics and trends are discussed. Then the cellular mobile trends are explained to overcome a hybrid mobile – satellite system. Then future aspects of next generation cellular mobile system integrated via satellite system are proposed to introduce new and future services.

The proposed system concentrated on overcomes many features such as flexibility, reliability, quality, cost … etc. In addition the communication link can be prepared for every one anytime anywhere. The proposed system tries to integrate cellular mobile via satellite system to give a future communications solutions. A communication link established between floating cells at the same country that represents the national calls (or data transfer). A communication link established between floating cells between different countries that represents the international calls (or data transfer). International call (or data transfer) occurs via a communication link established between gate ways at different countries via the corresponding satellites.

# REFERENCES

Al-Ani, M. S. (2009). Next generation cellular mobile commutation. *International Journal of Interactive Mobile Technologies*, *3*(2), 58–62.

Al-Ani, M. S., Kasasbeh, B. M., Al-Qutaish, R. E., & Muhairat, M. I. (2009). Constructing a new communication system by integrating the GSM to the satellites infrastructure. *WSEAS Transactions on Communications*, *8*(2), 217–226.

ITU. (2010). *Information about ITU*. Retrieved June, 2010, from http://www.itu.int/net/about/.

ITU-Cellular-Subscriptions. (2010). *Cellular subscriptions for developed and developing countries*. Retrieved July 2010 from http://www.itu.int/ITU-D/ict/statistics/material/graphs/Mobile_cellular_03-09.jpg.

ITU-D. (2010). *Telecommunication development sector*. Retrieved June 2010 from http://www.itu.int/net/about/itu-d.aspx.

ITU-ICT-Trends. (2010). *Global ICT trends*. Retrieved July 2010 from http://www.itu.int/ITU-D/ict/statistics/material/graphs/Global_ICT_Dev_98-09.jpg.

ITU-Internet-Penetration. (2010). *Internet penetration for different regional countries*. Retrieved July 2010 from http://www.itu.int/ITU-D/ict/statistics/material/graphs/Internet_users_reg-09.jpg.

ITU-Internet-Subscriptions. (2010). *Internet subscriptions for developed and developing countries*. Retrieved July 2010 from http://www.itu.int/ITU-D/ict/statistics/material/graphs/Internet_users_03-09.jpg.

ITU-Internet-Trends. (2010). *Internet users trends for developed and developing countries*. Retrieved July 2010 from http://www.itu.int/ITU-D/ict/statistics/material/graphs/Internet_users_98-08.jpg.

ITU-Internet-Users. (2010). *Number of internet users*. Retrieved July 2010 from http://www.itu.int/ITU-D/ict/statistics/material/graphs/Internet_users_00-09.jpg.

ITU-Mobile-Penetration. (2010). *Mobile cellular penetration for different regional countries*. Retrieved July 2010 from http://www.itu.int/ITU-D/ict/statistics/material/graphs/mobile_reg-09.jpg.

ITU-Mobile-Subscriptions. (2010). *Total mobile cellular subscriptions*. Retrieved July 2010 from http://www.itu.int/ITU-D/ict/statistics/material/graphs/Global_mobile_cellular_00-09.jpg.

ITU-Mobile-Trends. (2010). *Mobile cellular telephony trends*. Retrieved July 2010 from http://www.itu.int/ITU-D/ict/statistics/material/graphs/Mobile_cellular_98-08.jpg.

ITU-R. (2010). *Radio communication sector*. Retrieved June 2010, from http://www.itu.int/net/about/itu-r.aspx.

ITU-T. (2010). *Telecommunication standardization sector*. Retrieved June 2010 from http://www. itu.int/net/about/itu-t.aspx.

ITU-Telecom. (2010). *ITU telecom*. Retrieved June 2010 from http://www.itu.int/net/about/telecom.aspx.

IWS. (2011). *Internet usage and world population statistics*. Retrieved May 2011 from http://www. internetworldstats.com/stats.htm.

Kasasbeh, B. M., Al-Qutaish, R. E., Al-Ani, M. S., & Al-Sarayreh, K. (2008). Real digital TV accessed by cellular mobile system. *European Journal of Scientific Research, 20*(4), 914–923.

Madrid. (2011). *Madrid document on information society policies and metrics*. Retrieved May 2011 from http://www.mityc.es/telecomunicaciones/Presidency/actos/Junio/Documents/2010-06-14_BackgroundMadridDocumentonISpoliciesandmetrics.pdf.

PCBS. (2010). *Definitions of world telecommunications/ICT indicators*. Retrieved June 2010, from www.pcbs.gov.ps/Portals/_PCBS/ICT/ICT_Escwa.pdf.

Zhao, H. (2010). *Broadband applications for tomorrow*. Paper presented at WESIS Forum. Arlington, VA.

# Chapter 21
# Evaluation of Simulation Models

**Sattar J Aboud**
*Iraqi Council of Representatives, Iraq*

## ABSTRACT

*Simulation is employed widely to evaluate complicated systems involving telecommunication networks. This chapter reviews and evaluates different types of discrete event simulation models that are widely used for modeling network models in a practical time-frame. Different methods are presented, but special attention is given to systems that use spatial decomposition. This involves data that may have to be transmitted by mediator tiles to its purpose depending on the decomposition post. For congruent simulation the challenge is to decompose the tool in order to make effective use of the original processor design. This chapter reviews a number of methodologies and architectural design that have been developed for efficient simulation model decomposition.*

## INTRODUCTION

Simulation is the implementation of a model, denoted by a program code that provides information regarding the scheme being inspected. Simulation models are employed to carry out tests that are costly, risky or time consuming to be performed using analytical or experimental approaches. There are a number of methodologies that can be used to classify the existing simulation models. In particular, simulation models can be classified

DOI: 10.4018/978-1-4666-0191-8.ch021

according to one of the following criteria, which are widely-used in classifying the different types of simulation models: time-variation of the state of the system variables, simulation termination procedure, and input-traffic pattern. Based on the time-variation of the state of the system variables, simulation models can be classified into continuous-valued or discrete-event (Al-Bahadili, 2010; Sinclair, 2004; Law & Kelton, 2000; Roth, 1987). Discrete simulation is the modeling of a scheme; it changes over time by which state variables alters in time at a countable number of points. At these stages an event is happen and is taken to be an immediate event this could alter the situation of a scheme. The standard simulation of packet-switched networks typically includes the use of discrete event simulators which is model every separate packet during the network, usually entitled packet-level simulation. Every packet departure from or arrival at a network position is denoted by an event. Too big number of packets should be simulated to get trust in the results. This needs long simulation period, usually totaling many hours to simulate a few packets.

## Discrete Event

Traditionally, discrete-event system simulations have been done in a sequential manner. A variable clock holds the time up to which the physical system has been simulated. A data structure, called the event list, maintains a set of messages, with their associated times of transmissions, that are scheduled for the future. Each of these messages is guaranteed to be sent at the associated time in the physical system, provided the sender receives no message before this message transmission time. At each step, the message with the smallest associated future time is removed from the event list, and the transmission of the corresponding message in the physical system is simulated. Sending this message may, in turn, cause other messages to be sent in the future, which then are added to the event list or cause previously scheduled messages to be canceled which are removed from the event list. The clock is advanced to the time of the message transmission that was just simulated (Moorsel, 1991).

This form of simulation is called event driven, because events, message in the physical system are simulated chronologically and the simulation clock is advanced after simulation of an event to the time of the next event. There is another important simulation scheme, time-driven simulation in which the clock advances by one tick in every step and all events scheduled at that time are simulated.

Discrete event simulation model is dynamic physically, thus there is a requirement for a method to move forward the simulation time from one event to another. This needs a simulation clock which provides the existing state of the elapsed simulated value. Also, certain means of saving the present predictable events queued to happen within the scheme is needed. This data structure usually takes the type of a specific time ordered cycle of event minutes title an event-list. The simulation clock can be later consistent with either of two main time-progression policies, entitled fixed-increment time progression. The fixed-increment time progression technique of time has been commonly employed in the simulation of schemes such that events are known to happen at fixed regular time.

The simulation clock increase by constant numbers, named ticks. After every tick, a test is generated to determine when any events must happen in the preceding time period. When one or more events are queued, they are considered to happen at the end of the period (Walrand, 1987). The scheme situation is then updated. The system can be unproductive when the tick degree is not carefully measured. Selecting a small value decreases the chance of events happening with a tick age and thus raises the possibility of simulator operation cycles that have no practical event work. Choosing a big tick time decreases the event time solution. With subsequent event time progression the times of happening of next events are created. Then, the simulation clock is moved to the time of the initial event, which is then handled. The scheme is updated to display the results of this event then the simulation clock is moved to the following most pending event and so on. This is the most general method used, since times of used in the scheme are neglected because the entire state modifies only happen at event times. This exclusion of used periods permits the simulation to carry on effectively, particularly if the time between following events is big.

## Generating Event Times

If it is essential to choose a proper time for the execution of certain future event, the simulator can employ one of the two main methods.

- A method that can use determined data from an actual scheme such data is inserted into the simulator as a sequence of events. However this method provides authenticity, it have a drawback that for certain duration of simulation, a large amount of storage is needed.
- A generally chosen technique is to employ a random number generator with sort of the sources, from which specific event times can be computed if needed.

Actually, random number series includes a completely random stream of numbers that are in result un-reproducible. This stream is usually found by viewing some obviously random physical operation for example the radioactive decay of a matter. In practice this can show to be a hard job in terms of fixing an untried biases and preserving a satisfactory creation rate. Storage of the resulting data stream may also introduce a challenge. For these causes, methods for making pseudo random numbers have been presented broadly (Parekh & Walrand, 1989). The standard of such pseudo random number generator process is that to a viewer it seems a random in character. Pseudo random number generator is used since the creation of each number is accurately defined as indicated by certain algorithm and thus reproducibility of a known statistical experiment is possible. This is very helpful in debugging software. Furthermore, the storage and execution requirements of the generator are very traditional and ease many coding algorithms regarding high-speed making rate. These algorithms are entirely non random and are periodic, but the finding stream of values is to show random to a viewer. But, offered the relationship between values is insignificant, and

the age of the random number generator is big, then the finding performance is typically measured as an independent of a generator.

## Verification and Validation

In order to adequately rearrange simulation system verification and validation are essential. Verification is an operation of comparing the program code with the system to guarantee that the code is an accurate execution of the system, while validation is the operation of comparing the system result with the performance of the occurrence. However, validation involves evaluating the system to actuality (Aboud, et al., 2010). Additional consideration is calibration. This is an operation of factor evaluation for a system. Calibration is an alteration of existing values and generally does not include the introduction of new ones, altering the system framework. In the situation of optimization, calibration is an optimization process included in model identification or in new plan.

Verification and validation is the multi-disciplinary process of demonstrating credibility in simulation results. Credibility is built by collecting evidence that:

- The numerical model is being solved correctly
- The simulation model adequately represents the appropriate physics

The former activity is called verification and requires intimate knowledge of the mathematical model representing the physics, the numerical approximation derived from that model, software quality engineering practices, and numerical error estimation methods. The latter, termed validation is accomplished by comparing simulation output with experimental data and quantifying the uncertainties in both. Broad knowledge of modeling and experimentation, augmented with a deep understanding of statistical methods, are necessary for validation.

Computer simulations are used for analysis of all aspects of weapon systems, as well as the analysis and interpretation of experiments. The credibility of simulation capability is central to the credibility of the certification of the nuclear stockpile and is established through rigorous and quantitative verification and validation analyses. Regardless of whether or not we return to nuclear testing, verification and validation establishes credibility by providing evidence to support questions such as, "Why should we trust the simulation's results?" Insufficient confidence or credibility in our simulations, will lead us to an incorrect decision pertaining to the reliability, performance and safety of the nuclear weapons.

## Simulation Challenges

When the network simulation starts by an empty state at the proposed time the simulator is employed, then an initial bias will all times be there in the outputs. Clearly, when this is correct the model being considered as an attractive characteristic. Suppose that the empty state is far deleted from the standard processing conditions of the network, its result might become too obvious. The problem can be decreased, and even removed, through the adoption by one of following:

- Execute the simulator for such a long time that this initial result becomes an insignificant influence on the steady-state measures.
- Observed data after a preparation period once an appropriate steady-state has been accomplished.
- If an appropriate steady-state has been accomplished, the status of the whole network is stored.

In all three above simulation executes, the network is restarted from this frozen state.

An extra challenge with simulation is fixing the steady state. The word steady state is useful to methods that have achieved a state of balance (Nicola, et al., 1990). But, with most stochastic methods, there is no determined steady state. One method to determining a balance condition can be impose a tolerance on the result information such that if the value of interest continued within some bounds of variability for a set number of handled events, then the result could be measured to be in balance. The concern with this technique is deciding on an acceptable open-mindedness. When it is very large the values may be incorrect and choosing too small a tolerance might effect in an ending value by no means being reached. Sometimes remark of the real system can assist to fix appropriate bounds.

The chief concern of this chapter is to explore the ways in which simulation studies and their findings could be described as valid. If we truly believe in the benefits of simulations, just like any other well established research method, effort must be committed to ensuring the approach is valid, or at least to establish its strengths and weaknesses. The rest of this chapter is organized as follows. In Section 2 the simulation methods including (races and hazards, concurrency, distributed simulation, decomposition, look ahead, and Optimistic Scheme) are described. In Section decomposing techniques including (federated simulations and Multi-Threaded Parallel Simulation) are explained. Section 4 depicts fast simulation methods including (impact sampling, hybrid simulation and emulation). Whereas section 5 gives the conclusion and future works

## SIMULATION METHODS

The types of simulation methods needs a considerable quantity of data to be collected for results is statistically feasible. To allow such simulation researches happen within a reasonable amount of real time, the designer can run the program on a rapid sequential computer or decompose the system into divide analytical and simulation components, a method entitled as hybrid simulation. An extra method is to employ concurrent processing manners by a number of processors in certain coherent technique to able some tasks to be executed in parallel. Both functional and spatial types of decomposition are probable.

## Races and Hazards

It is worth in many schemes encompassing multiple linked, but there is a possibility of races and hazards happening. The race is a competition between bodies where the winner is the one that achieves certain task, or arrives at certain point. This is a usual characteristic of many schemes, but the creator should ensure that this feature is dealt with accurately. The Hazard is an accidental race whose result can alter the performance of the system and so cause an incorrect scheme characterization. Though races are parallel occurrence, they can still be represented using traditional trail simulation. The creator should be careful regarding the processing of events listed to happen at the same time. There are various modes of failure of asynchronous sequential logic circuits due to timing problems. There is a mechanism common to all forms of hazards and to detestable states. A similar mechanism is complication to characterize critical races. Means for defeating various types of hazards and critical races are using one-sided delay constraints. A circuit technique is available also for extending a previously known technique for defeating detestability problems in self-timed systems. It is important to emphasis that the use of simulation for verifying the correctness of a circuit with given bounds on the branch delays cannot be relied upon to expose all timing problems. An example is that refutes a plausible conjecture that replacing pure delays with inertial delays can never introduce, but only eliminate glitches. It is often desired or required to code asynchronous sequential switching circuits such that noncritical races occur (Goyal, et al., 1992). The effect of these races on hazard-free circuit operation

should investigate. It is important to say that the removal of single-input-change static hazards it the networks realizing the next-state functions is not, in general, sufficient to prevent static hazards if a noncritical race is happen. A necessary and sufficient condition for hazard-free realization of a flow table containing noncritical races is given; a hazard-free realization is always possible.

## Concurrency

Traditional event-driven simulations use an international clock to show the present simulated time during the scheme. This clock is just advanced once all of the scheme's processes programmed to happen at the present time immediate have been achieved; this lets every of these processes to be handled in sequence, though they may continue in parallel in the network system. The restriction of this traditional sequential simulation is that just a single instruction series is supported that operations an individual data stream. This sequential simulation of instructions is known as the Von Neumann principle. To enhance operation, the CPU power should be improved (Saouma & Sivaselvan, 2008). This guides to a possible bottleneck as the use of a single memory interface during all information and control data should pass.

Events are reported to be parallel if they overlap to certain degree in time. This possible concurrency exists at different levels in an application. For instance, concurrency may be exploited from the simulator design, by letting irrelevant simulator behavior to proceed in concurrency. Possible concurrency can also exist within the network type itself. By parallel simulation, it is meant that certain way is available to support the dedicated processing of two or more programming jobs in overlapping time. Supposing an infinite quantity of processors to execute $i$ tasks, every needing $t$ units of processor time, preferably all the jobs must be finished in $t/i$ units of time. Associations between single tasks may need that some jobs be achieved before others can start, resultant in reduced performance. This relationship between behaviors is named as coupling. Certain jobs can proceed independently, but others are associated. This combination results in turn dependencies and stopping some tasks from being processed until others have been finished. Not just does this arranging lower the possible implementation, but also combination by its very nature involves that certain data is associated between processes to determine if successor tasks may be processed. These dependencies can be known as a directed graph allowing analysis to be employed to assess an asymptotic upper bound on the possible concurrency of a scheme. Order dependencies between individuals can also determine the processing series of actions listed to happen at the same time. To model schemes of this kind, extra knowledge is needed to implement this ordering.

In distributed simulation, certain technique is always needed to ensure consistency of the system. This involves that the processing of events within the system remains analogous to a performance of the real system, and that event causality relationship are in no way violated. The synchronous method for preserving consistency uses a determined time-synchronous hand-shaking scheme between the parallel event processing behaviors. The simulation time then go forwards from event to event at any provided time. However, the simulated time over the system is the same, and is equivalent to the international first event-time. The asynchronous approach reduces this limit fairly, but remaining reliable, so that processing areas stay within bounded restrictions of certain international first time range of simulated time which is supported by the simulation system, without infringing consistency, is fixed by the look-ahead value.

## Distributed Simulation

The distributed simulation of multi-processor system identifies that many simulation researches take the type of a repeated sequence of experiments, differing just in random number generator seed numbers, to allow batches of observed results of a parameter to be gathered. Entity runs are only appointed to individual processors and implemented congruently. The separate results are gathered and processed by one of the processors on end of the composite run. The application of this method is that it is easy to execute, with no communication needed between the processors until the completion of the trial, and values in around $i$-fold performance gains. An option means of employing a multi-processor resource to enhance functioning is decomposition.

Distributed simulation offers a radically different approach to simulation. Shared data objects of sequential simulation-the clock and event list-are discarded. In fact, there are no shared variables in its algorithm. We believe that an algorithm in which one machine may simulate a single physical process; messages in the physical system are simulated by message transmissions among the machines. The synchronous nature of the physical system is captured by encoding time as part of each message transmitted between machines. We stress that machines may operate concurrently as long as their physical counterparts operate autonomously; they must wait for message receptions to simulate interactions of the corresponding physical processes. Distributed simulation offers many other advantages in addition to the possible speedup of the entire simulation process. It requires little additional memory compared with sequential simulation. There is little global control exercised by any machine (Barel, 1985). Simulation of a system can be adapted to the structure of the available hardware; for instance, if only a few machines are available for simulation, several physical processes may be simulated sequentially on one machine. Several distributed simulation algorithms are available. They all employ the same basic mechanism of encoding physical time as part of each message. The basic scheme they use may cause deadlock. Various distributed simulation algorithms differ in the way they resolve the deadlock issue.

## Decomposition

Several types of decomposition exist for parallelizing use. These can be generally categorized as functional and spatial decomposition. By functional decomposition, simulation program contain several functions that work on data structures. Splitting these to a number of piece processes is named functional decomposition. This method is named Algorithmic Parallelism. On the other hand, by spatial decomposition the scheme is decomposed into insecurely coupled network pieces, which are assigned to individual processes. These processes can then be recorded in separate processors for parallel implementation. This method is named Geometric Parallelism.

Functional parallelism separates insecurely coupled functional pieces that are, at least to certain extent, independent of every other and so can work in parallel. It permits the decomposition method to be customized to the existing resources. For instance, mathematically difficult functions can be located on processors providing an integral Floating Point Unit. The use of Task Farming is acutely applicable and can give outstanding speedups. It is also a policy that is inherently load-balancing. Certain authors have selected to separate the event-list management functionality from that of the network system processing (Jones, 1986). The achievable performance is mainly related to the inherent parallelism in the method. By spatial parallelism every spatial unit preserves its own local clock of how far it has advanced in elapsed simulated time and provides certain data structure of listed future events, which will happen at this place. The processing of an event is usually coupled with certain alter of situation in the physical processes it forms; processing events can also generate alters of situation within other spatial domains needing data to be moved between them. Certain synchronized form of

time-progression is also needed. By Synchronous methods, similar to their time-driven counterparts, a global clock is executed either in a centralized or distributed method.

Asynchronous event-driven systems based on time-stamped messages to communicate timing data between the processes, every of which preserves a local clock record of elapsed time. In order to make the decomposition successful it is useful to arrange for the processing algorithm to be prearranged into rude granularity construction where every processor can accept an important quantity of practical jobs between intervals if it has to connect with other scheme elements. This is since communication is typically decelerate relative to the processing of information thus avoiding undue communication, by custody the processor busy performing local deeds, enhances the amount of time spent satisfying certain functional process. Also, to decrease the time spent by processors waiting to begin a communication, decoupling buffers can operate as mediators, which temporarily keep the information until the recipient is ready. Lastly, enhanced act is reached if the work assignment positions more tasks that are computationally more difficult, on processors with better performance (Reynolds, 1980). If the processors provide the same processing ability, greatest performance is gained if the workload is allocated likewise, and time spent unused is least.

## Look-Ahead

An important value that increases the capability of processors to act in parallel is look-ahead (Lin & Lazowska, 1990). Look-ahead describes the quantity of time into the prospect of a process that can predict its performance categorically. It can as a minimum be dimensioned to a minimum servicing time of every part in the network system. This is named a network look-ahead parameter. Events in spatially individual regions of a network system should be independent of every other offered the dissimilarity between their queued implementation times differs by less than this network wide look-ahead value. They can so be processed in parallel, even while these times are not the same, meaningful that the processing of following events cannot later invalidate resultant state alters in the network system. It is by this way that the inherent in parallel of the network system can be utilized. The expression look-ahead is employed if a look-ahead result is invariant and is identified before the beginning of the simulation.

Specific requirements for various sequential and parallel simulation protocols to execute models with simultaneous events are derived using either of the preceding tie-breaking mechanisms. These requirements are derived in terms of the look-ahead properties of the model. Look ahead is the ability of a simulation object to predict its future. It is known to be an important determinant of the performance of parallel simulation protocols, especially the conservative ones. Look ahead is also widely believed to be required in a simulation model in order for the model to be executed using parallel conservative protocols, whereas the global event list and parallel optimistic protocols are often perceived to be free from such a requirement. In this article we show that most existing protocols, including the commonly used sequential and optimistic ones, require some look ahead to be available in the model in order to ensure that simultaneous events are processed in a deterministic order specified by the program. The article shows that, in general, the look-ahead requirements needed to implement the user-consistent mechanism are stronger than those required to implement the arbitrary mechanism. Also, the look-ahead requirements to implement a given tie-breaking mechanism vary considerably among the different protocols.

## Optimistic Scheme

In traditional optimistic distributed simulation protocols, a logical process receiving a straggler rolls back and sends out anti-messages. Receiver of an anti-message may also roll back and send out more anti-messages. So a single straggler may result in a large number of anti-messages and multiple rollbacks of some logical processes. In our protocol, a logical process receiving a straggler broadcasts its rollback. On receiving this announcement, other logical processes may roll back but they do not announce their rollbacks. So each logical process rolls back at most once in response to each straggler (Jefferson, 1985). Anti messages are not used. This eliminates the need for output queues and results in simple memory management. It also eliminates the problem of cascading rollbacks and echoing, and results in faster simulation. All this is achieved by a scheme for maintaining transitive dependency information. The cost incurred includes the tagging of each message with exam dependency information and the increased processing time upon receiving a message. We also present the similarities between the two areas of distributed simulation and distributed recovery. We show how the solutions for one area can be applied to the other area.

Distributed simulation approaches should support certain type of synchronization method to ensure the system properly simulates the actions of the model being formed. This can be attained by either using positive synchronization strategies. Optimistic systems let a module to process messages; even if there is doubt. This provides increase to a hazard of unpredictable performance whereas the simulated elapsed time of the element might go beyond that of the time-stamps of messages so far to arrive. Optimistic systems let a processor to simulate as far ahead in time as it needs, without respect for the danger of having its simulation past involved, resultant in time warping over the system. When its past is altered it should then be capable to roll-back (Gafni, 1980) in time and accurate every mistaken action it has taken in its fake future.

## DECOMPOSITION TECHNIQUES

Some types of decomposition are now existed. The first one relied on (Jones, 1986), entitled centralized event-list and employs a grouping of functional and spatial parallelism with a separate event-list processor for events occurring from every spatial area. Inter-processor communication usually presents an important performance penalty, provoked if messages have to be transmitted by mediators. It is shown in Figure 1.

In this system functional parallelism lets the event-list running to proceed in parallel with the modernizing of a network system in the spatial areas. Also, a look-ahead windowing method is used by the event-list to allow multiple state-changes to occur congruently. The process of this Moving Time-Window method (Sokol, et al., 1988) is illustrated in Figure 2.

To commence with (A) as certain events fall within the present look-ahead window they are passed for processing. Depend on coming from the event-2-update the parallel event record is erased (B). Though, as the event at time 0 is yet outstanding, no more deed is taken (C). The ar-

rival of the event update at time 0 that links to the top outstanding event produces the removal of the parallel event record (D). Also, thus there are no more events outstanding at the moment, the window can be complex, thus not the entire of the presently outstanding event updates have returned (E).

An important drawback of this method is that there is generally a large performance expenses in shifting every one of events between the event-list processor and the spatial area processors. To offset this, another system, named the distributed event-list is to decompose the event-list into single ones connected with every spatial area (Nicol, et al., 1989). This decreases the communication load but it needs coordination between these spatial area processors to ensure the performance stays steady. Figure 3 illustrates the distributed event-list decomposition.

In addition to time-stamped packet communication, spatial area processors switch first event times in turn for the Global Virtual Time is recognized from that local look-ahead bounds is resulting. This system does much better than the centralized event-list method if the distribution

*Figure 1. Centralized event-list decomposition*

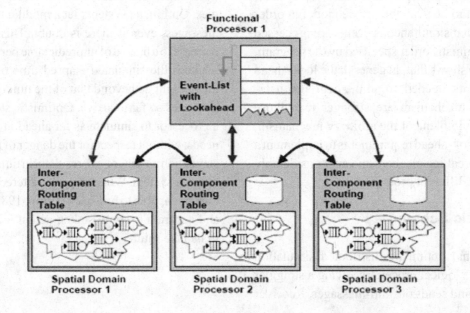

*Figure 2. Moving time window example*

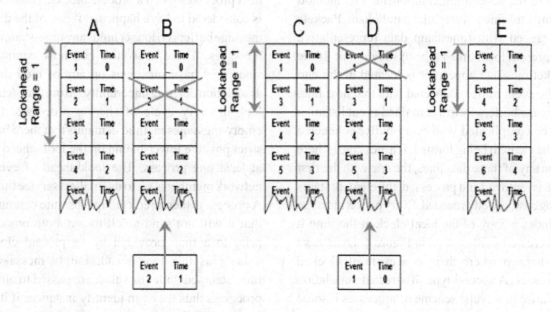

*Figure 3. Distributed event-list decomposition*

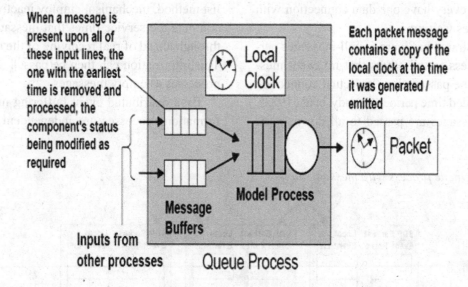

of the network system districts to the different area processes restrictions their communication. While a network-wide look-ahead value can be employed to decide which events is processed without breaching consistency limitations, more look-ahead is used between the spatial areas when the network system relations between them can be arranged thus they are connected with sched-

ules that have a substantial service time comparative to the schedules within every area.

A more entire type of decomposition is that of allocated event buffering relied on (Chandy & Misra, 1981). In this system the event-list is dispersed. Every scheduling element is considered separately with its own event treatment ability in the type of a message buffer connected with every data to the scheduling component. The method permits for fine grain spatial parallelism. Packets are tagged with timestamp data representative the present local time at the upstream unit. If the packet message appears it is located at the end of the event buffer connected with that next line. Message buffers form a contained event list must not be complicated with every buffer connected by the element being formed. If a message is there upon any of these data lines, the one with the first time is removed and processed, the element status being customized as needed. Every packet message includes a copy of the local clock at the time it was created as illustrated in Figure 4. Deadlocks can happen where there is a cycle of blocked processes. A second type of arrested simulation can arise in a cyclic scheme of processes if some pathways, which end in a merge point, are not employed. Neither of these schedules can proceed since they every have one data connection with no messages waiting.

As illustrated in Figure 5, null-messages permit a process to tell others that no event messages will be passed along an actual connection for a provided time period (Chandy, et al., 1983). Empty messages are passed to all downstream next processes when a process blocks. The block is considered to have happened if one of the data message buffers no longer holds any time-stamped messages. These schedules can now continue since they have messages on any of their data association deleting uncertainty. To prevent deadlock in every cycle of sharing processes, the empty-messages method demands that there be a strict positive lower-bound on the look-ahead of at least one process. The look-ahead of every network member is set to its smallest service time. A process is then predicted by absolute certainty that it will not send a cell to a remote process prior to a time provided by its present clock value plus this look-ahead. Empty messages, time-stamped with this value, are passed to other processes thus they can identify instances if it is legal to handle event messages waiting on their other data. By implied look-ahead, with a future list method, mechanism employ inactive time to compute the service times that message will go through ahead of real receiving of the messages. This information can then be passed as to other processes as empty messages.

By a distributed event buffering method information processes are independent naturally

*Figure 4. Queue process with message buffers*

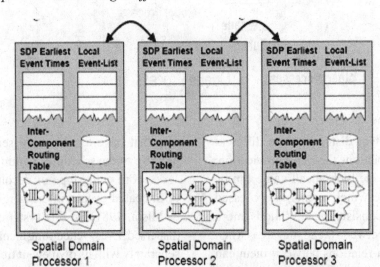

*Figure 5. Arrested simulation and the use of null messages*

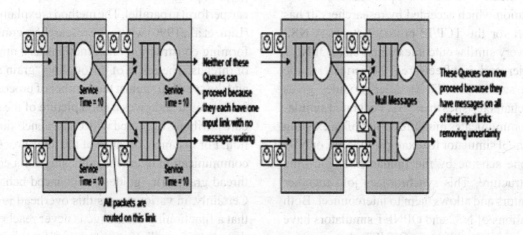

and thus can create messages constantly, until certain simulation preventing criterion without needing data from other processes. This can be very undesirable. Flow control is essential to stop message buffer saturation. To prevent an inordinate number of flow control messages, hysteresis is used as shown in Figure 6.

## Federated Simulations

OPNET Modeler® is the foremost business software for network simulation (OPNET, 2011). It contains a widespread well-document library of schemes and an influential state-machine typed representation of processes. Schemes are denoted

*Figure 6. Flow control to regulate autonomous source processes*

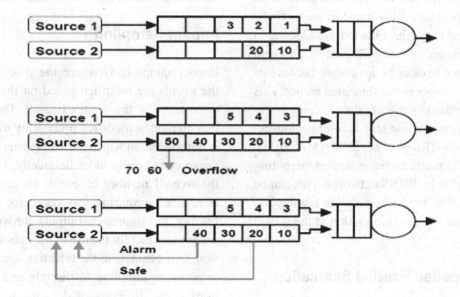

hierarchically. A NS2 is an open source network simulation which accepted by researchers. It has support for the TCP/IP protocol stack. A NS2 gives very similar outcome compared to OPNET Modeler and is "freeware." Nevertheless, the whole set of OPNET Modeler modules gives more characteristics thanNS2. Federated simulation communicates multiple copies of an existing sequential simulator for example OPNET or NS2 into one scheme by the fundamental run-time infrastructure. This synchronizes join together simulators and allows them to interconnect. Both federations of NS2 and OPNET simulators have been tried (Wu, 2001). In OPNET, the existence of zero look-ahead interactions, global data structures, and pointers guide to dependencies between parts of the simulation that are difficult to recognize, making parallelization hard and long low level communications.

The architecture of NS2 is a simulation of big networks which is very complicated, when not impossible, because of undue memory and CPU time needs. It employs a "federated simulation" method where individual instantiations of NS forming dissimilar sub-networks perform on different processors. Distributed *ns* uses a traditional method to synchronization. No federate in the congruent simulation will process an event that may later have to be invalidate because of receiving messages in the simulated earlier. This prevents the want to execute state keeping in the existing $ns_2$ code while still accomplishing excellent speedup (Riley, et al., 2004; IMA, 2011). PDNS also contains emulation support for routing real uses traffic by PDNS networks. This can be accomplished by the Veil emulation framework, which catches the use information at the socket API layer.

## Multi-Threaded Parallel Simulation

A thread is a fragment of a program that can implement independently. Operating systems that support multi-threading allows researchers to propose programs with threaded components that can perform in parallel. The method is explained in (Lim, et al., 1990) where the researchers consider forming construction line functions as a number of threads. The result of decoupling "grain size" and the speedup against the number of processors is illustrated and gives a good picture of the standard attributes observed with congruence simulation. For instance, because of the inter-processor communication overhead, choosing for a coarse thread granularity guides to enhanced behavior. Certainly, in various cases this overhead is such that a functioning advantage is never reached, as the stage of parallel cannot pay off for this price. Even if it does, the speedup tends to stage as the inherent parallelism of the fundamental form is attained.

## FAST SIMULATION METHODS

Additionally, there are different other ways of improving the behavior of simulations. Several of these methods are concisely discussed in this section, commencing with impact sampling.

### Impact Sampling

Impact sampling is where the probabilities of the events are modified based on their relative importance to the required result. Therefore in this method, a modified probability distribution is introduced, in which the rare events of interest are forced to occur more frequently. This means the overall number of events to be simulated is reduced, requiring less computer resources. Further, the simulation outputs are weighted in order to correct for the use of the biased distribution. One obstacle to the effective application of importance sampling to discrete event simulations is the difficulty of deciding how to alter the probability measure. Calculating the optimal change of probability measure is hard, since the calculation requires knowledge of the quantity to be estimated. Researchers have, therefore, focused on finding good heuristics for particular types of models, such as models of dependable systems and certain classes of queuing networks. For an alternative approach to the rare event problem, see Van Moorsel, et al. (Moosel, 1991). Two problems hindering importance sampling researchers are that there is no simple representation for importance sampling heuristics, and that there is no easy way to experiment with new heuristics. To date, most researchers have hand-coded simulation programs for each problem. The main benefit of this approach is the high degree of flexibility available to the simulation programmer. On the other hand, it is very time consuming to program, validate, debug, etc., for each new problem or importance sampling heuristic.

## Hybrid Simulation

Hybrid simulation deals with a rapidly evolving technology combining computer simulation typically of a finite element model and physical laboratory testing of two complementary substructures. It is a cost-effective alternative to physical testing of an entire system, and allows for the improved understanding of complex coupled systems. Traditionally, numerical simulation and physical tests have been uncoupled and performed separately. In the hybrid simulation paradigm, the coupled nature of the simulation allows for improved understanding, and more efficient design since the factor of safety does not have to be arbitrarily inflated to account for uncertainties due to uncoupling. It is a multidisciplinary technology which relies heavily on computational dynamics, control theory, and numerical methods and finds applications in aerospace, civil, and mechanical engineering.

This method focuses the simulation on a portion of the network of special interest and models the remainder of the network using analytic techniques (Schormans, et al., 2001). It can be used to model network functions or characteristics with varying degrees of precision. For example traffic can be decomposed into foreground flows modeled with simulation and background flows analytically that simply influence the foreground traffic. As an example of hybrid simulation it is possible to classify the network traffic into Fore Ground traffic and Back Ground traffic, and only the Fore Ground Traffic is simulated. The Back Ground Traffic is handled analytically; the service times of the Fore Ground Traffic are adjusted to compensate for the missing Back Ground traffic. The magnitude of speed up depends on the ratio of Fore Ground, BG traffic. This gives a substantial reduction in the overall number of events to be simulated; however, validation tests typically show that there are some differences between the original and accelerated models. The analytical models do not capture nuances of protocol behaviors such as the feedback mechanism of TCP whereby the state of the network affects the source behavior and, in turn, alters the network state. A further challenge remains how to interface data between the constituent tools such as network simulators and statistical analysis tools. There is no economical open-standard. A further form of hybrid simulation is the use of aggregated models of sources to replace N multiplexed sources by a single equivalent source, such as an ON-OFF model. This equivalent source generates traffic flows with the same characteristics as if they were derived from many individual sources. As the number of sources has a major impact on the run-time of a simulation, this aggregation can provide substantial performance benefits.

## Emulation

Emulation is the ability of a program to imitate another program. Traditionally emulator implies hardware, and simulator is considered emulation by software. However, it is possible to employ e-circuits to mimic the actions of routers and other telecommunications devices, though speedup is greatly affected by the complexity of the design

(Xu, 2001). A simple example would be to model simple queuing systems with hardware microcells within a Field-Programmable Gate Array (FPGA), originally expressed with VHDL (VHDL is an abbreviation for VHSIC hardware description language; and VHSIC is an abbreviation for very high speed integrated circuit) and then suitably synthesized. Re- configuration is possible by reprogramming the FPGA. Packet flows can be represented in a simplified form only containing fields such as the destination address and the length of the packet. The approach appears to be relatively inflexible, except for modeling particular specific systems.

## CONCLUSION

There is a great reason for developing a quicker simulation. The stability of the Internet could seem to need large-scale forms to hold the complex interactions between autonomous systems. Larger performance CPUs remain to be fabricated permitting legacy code to execute faster but the computer design can stay a bottleneck. Hybrid simulation is attractive but often guides to compromises in the correctness of the information that is created because of simplifications required to make the systems tractable. Congruence simulation seems attractive as there is no loss of features and scalable structural design is possible. However overheads, naturally in the type of communication holdup, can outweigh the gains. The trade-off decisions concerning decomposing a system into feasible areas thus the workload is balanced is not minor and typically needs suitable selection of quick simulation tool with particular calibration for every formed milieu. Recent engineering developments are likely to reinvigorate interest in congruent simulation. Intel Company, for instance, are considering multi-processor designs for high performance calculating that try to address space, power and thermal considerations connected

with great performance calculating (Intel, 2001). If inter-processor communication is essential a high-speed routing part on every tile gives four connections to neighboring tiles. This involves that data may have to be transmitted by mediator tiles to its purpose depending on the decomposition post. For congruent simulation the challenge is to decompose the tool in order to make effective use of the original processor design. Within preceding congruent processing schemes efficient post has usually based on handcrafted configuration. But, compilers that are sensitive to the hardware design are likely to receive large attention as they encounter analogous challenges addressed by the place and route algorithms for hardware fusion.

## REFERENCES

Aboud, S. J., Al-Fayoumi, M., & Al-Nuaimi, M. (2010). Verification and validation of simulation models. In Abu-Taieh, E. M. O., & El Sheikh, A. A. (Eds.), *Handbook of Research on Discrete Event Simulation Environments: Technologies and Applications* (pp. 58–74). Hershey, PA: IGI Global.

Al-Bahadili, H. (2010). On the use of discrete-event simulation in computer networks analysis and design. In Abu-Taieh, E. M. O., & El-Sheikh, A. A. (Eds.), *Handbook of Research on Discrete-Event Simulation Environments: Technologies and Applications* (pp. 418–442). Hershey, PA: IGI Global. doi:10.4018/978-1-60566-774-4.ch019

Barel, M. (1985). Performance evaluation of the discrete event simulation computer DESC. In *Proceeding of the 18th Annual Simulation Symposium*, (pp. 1-13). Tampa, FL: IEEE Press.

Chandy, K. M., & Misra, J. (1981). Asynchronous distributed simulation via a sequence of parallel computations. *ACM Communications, 24*(11), 198–206. doi:10.1145/358598.358613

Chandy, K. M., Misra, J., & Haas, L. (1983). Distributed deadlock detection. *ACM Transactions on Computer Systems, 1*(2), 144–156. doi:10.1145/357360.357365

Gafni, A. (1988). Rollback mechanisms for optimistic distributed simulation systems. In *Proceeding SCS Multi-Conference on Distribution Simulation*, (pp. 61-67). IEEE Press.

Goyal, A., Shahabuddin, P., Heidelberger, P., Nicola, V., & Glynn, P. (1992). A united framework for simulating Markovian models of highly dependable systems. *IEEE Transactions on Computers, 41*(1), 36–51. doi:10.1109/12.123381

IMA. (2003). *Website*. Retrieved from http://www.ima.umn.

Intel. (2011). *Teraflops research chip*. Retrieved 25 May 2011 from http://techresearch.intel.com/ProjectDetails.aspx?Id=151.

Jefferson, D. (1985). Virtual time. *ACM Transactions on Proceeding Languages and Systems, 7*(3), 404–425. doi:10.1145/3916.3988

Jones, D. (1986). Concurrent simulation: An alternative to distributed simulation. In *Proceeding of the Winter Simulation Conference (WSC 1986)*, (pp. 417-423). Washington, DC: IEEE Press.

Law, A., & Kelton, W. D. (2000). *Simulation modeling and analysis* (3rd ed.). New York: McGraw-Hill Higher Education.

Lim, C. C., Low, Y. H., Cai, W., Hsu, W. J., Huang, S. Y., & Turner, S. J. (1998). An empirical comparison of runtime systems for conservative parallel simulations. In *Proceedings of the 2nd Workshop on Runtime Systems for Parallel Programming*, (pp. 123-134). Miami: FL: IEEE Press.

Lin, Y., & Lazowska, E. (1990). Exploiting look-ahead in parallel simulation. *IEEE Transactions on Parallel and Distributed Systems, 1*(4), 457–469. doi:10.1109/71.80174

Moorsel, V., Haverkort, B., & Niemegeers, I. (1991). Fault injection simulation: A variance reduction technique for systems with rare events. In *Proceedings of the 2nd International Working Conference on Dependable Computing for Critical Applications*, (pp. 57-64). Tucson, AZ: IEEE Press.

Nicol, D., Michael, C., & Inouye, P. (1989). Efficient aggregation of multiple LPs in distributed memory parallel simulations. In *Proceeding of the Winter Simulation Conference (WSC 1989)*, (pp. 680-685). Washington, DC: IEEE Press.

Nicola, V., Nakayama, M., Heidelberger, P., & Goyal, A. (1990). Fast simulation of dependability models with general failure, repair and maintenance processes. In *Proceedings of the 12th Annual International Symposium on Fault-Tolerant Computing*, (pp. 491-498). Newcastle Upon Tyne, UK: IEEE Press.

OPNET. (2011). *Website*. Retrieved from http://www.opnet.com/products/modeler/home.

Parekh, S., & Walrand, J. (1989). A quick simulation method for excessive backlogs in networks of queues. *IEEE Transactions on Automatic Control, 34*(1). doi:10.1109/9.8649

Reynolds, P. (1988). A spectrum of options for parallel simulation. In *Proceeding of the Winter Simulation Conference (WSC 1988)*, (pp. 325-332). San Diego, CA: IEEE Press.

Riley, G. F., Ammar, M. H., Fujimoto, R. M., Park, F., Perumalla, K., & Xu, D. (2004). A federated approach to distributed network simulation. *ACM Transactions on Modeling and Computer Simulation, 14*(2), 116–148. doi:10.1145/985793.985795

Roth, P. F. (1987). Discrete, continuous and combined simulation. In *Proceeding of the Winter Simulation Conference (WSC 1987)*, (pp. 56-60). Atlanta, GA: IEEE Press.

Saouma, V., & Sivaselvan, M. V. (Eds.). (2008). *Hybrid simulation: Theory, implementation and applications*. New York: Taylor & Francis.

Schormans, J., Liu, E., Cuthbert, L., & Pitts, J. (2001). A hybrid technique for the accelerated simulation of ATM networks and network elements. *ACM Transactions on Modeling and Computer Simulation*, *11*(2), 182–205. doi:10.1145/384169.384172

Sinclair, J. B. (2004). *Simulation of computer systems and computer networks: A process-oriented approach*. Houston, TX: Rice University.

Sokol, L., Briskoe, D., & Wieland, A. (1988). MTW: A strategy for scheduling discrete simulation events for concurrent execution. In *Proceeding of SCS Western Multi-Conference on Advances in Parallel and Distributed Simulation*, (pp. 34-42). Orlando, FL: IEEE Press.

Walrand, J. (1987). Quick simulation of queuing networks: An introduction. In *Computer Performance and Reliability*, (pp. 275-286). North Holland: Verlag.

Wu, H., Fujimoto, R. M., & Riley, G. (2001). Experiences parallelizing a commercial network simulator. In *Proceedings of Winter Simulation Conference (WSC 2001)*, (pp. 1353-1360). Arlington, VA: IEEE Press.

Xu, D. (2001). *Hardware-based parallel simulation of flexible manu-factoring systems*. PhD Dissertation. Blacksburg, VA: Virginia Polytechnic Institute and State University.

## KEY TERMS AND DEFINITIONS

**Computer Simulation:** Is used for analysis of all aspects of weapon systems, as well as the analysis and interpretation of experiments.

**Concurrency:** Events are reported to be parallel if they overlap to certain degree in time. This possible concurrency exists at different levels in an application. For instance, concurrency may be exploited from the simulator design, by letting irrelevant simulator behavior to proceed in concurrency.

**Discrete Simulation:** Is the modeling of a scheme; it changes over time by which state variables alters in time at a countable number of points.

**Distributed Simulation:** Is the type of a repeated sequence of experiments, differing just in random number generator seed numbers, to allow batches of observed results of a parameter to be gathered.

**Functional Decomposition:** Simulation program contain several functions that work on data structures. Splitting these to a number of piece processes is named functional decomposition. This method is named Algorithmic Parallelism.

**Races and Hazards:** The race is a competition between bodies where the winner is the one that achieves certain task, or arrives at certain point. This is a usual characteristic of many schemes. The Hazard is an accidental race whose result can alter the performance of the system and so cause an incorrect scheme characterization.

**Simulation:** Is the implementation of a model, denoted by a program code that provides information regarding the scheme being inspected.

**Simulation Model:** Is employed to carry out tests that could be costly, risky or very time consuming with actual schemes. But, given such model is enough description of actuality.

**Spatial Decomposition:** The scheme is decomposed into insecurely coupled network pieces, which are assigned to individual processes. These processes can then be recorded in separate processors for parallel implementation. This method is named Geometric Parallelism.

**Verification and Validation:** To measure the accuracy and validity of every intermediate result separately.

# Chapter 22
# Analyzing and Evaluating Current Computer Networks Simulation Models

**Jafar Ababneh**
*World Islamic Sciences and Education University, Jordan*

**Hussein Abdel-Jaber**
*World Islamic Sciences and Education University, Jordan*

**Firas Albalas**
*University of Jadara, Jordan*

**Amjad Daoud**
*World Islamic Sciences and Education University, Jordan*

## ABSTRACT

*Computer simulation is widely-used in investigating the performance of existing and proposed systems in many areas of science, engineering, operations research, and management science, especially in applications characterized by complicated geometries and interaction probabilities, and for dealing with system design in the presence of uncertainty. This is particularly true in the case of computer systems and computer networks. Therefore, it is very important to have efficient, reliable, and accurate methodologies for simulating these systems to ensure effective, reliable, and accurate evaluation and analysis of performance and to create the optimum design parameters for communication and computer networks. Although practical experiments and simulations are the most widely used, several efforts have also been directed towards mathematical models. The main objectives of this chapter are to: present the methodologies and techniques used to evaluate and analyze the performance of communication and computer networks routers, such as mathematical analysis, computer simulations techniques, and empirical measurements; identify the workload required for accomplishing a simulation model or mathematical analysis; identify the main metrics used to evaluate, manage, and control the performance of the computer networks; present the advantage and disadvantage of these techniques; and identify the challenges facing these different methodologies.*

DOI: 10.4018/978-1-4666-0191-8.ch022

# 1. INTRODUCTION

In order to propose and design enhanced communication and computer networks, it is essential to be able to assess network performance. Methods that may be engaged in this assessment are applied mathematical analysis, computer simulation studies, empirical measurements, or combinations of these techniques. The use of one or a combination of the previous techniques should be applied before the actual use of developed methods and should not be ignored. Ignoring the use of any previous techniques before actual use will cause lose of time, effort, and a lot of opportunities. This is imprudent to come up to many difficulties such as:

- The problems related to performance issues are regularly not brought in premature time for the design stages.
- From beginning to the end of the tuning stages, not all design phases matters are always repaired.
- It is not achievable for fixing architectural problems
- Designing issues is ,not always possible for the best solving techniques and they are usually very expensive and not professional.

When you create a performance models, you categorize application scenarios and your performance objectives. To achieve these objectives, suitable performance metrics should be chosen, such as:

- Response time.
- Throughput (how much work in how much time)
- Resource utilization (CPU, memory, disk I/O, and network I/O).

The next step after getting the performance metrics results is to analyze these results to build your vision for the resources, difficulties, and limitations.

Although it has disadvantages, Performance modeling provides a lot of imperative gains, such as:

- The documentation of categorized state of affairs that you prepared can assist you to judge what is significant, important, and essentials that answers many questions:
  ◦ Where to instrument
  ◦ What to test for
  ◦ Does the design support performance goals?
  ◦ How to know that you are on the map for achieving your performance goals.
- Knowing that design decisions are influenced by performance and the constraints performance puts on future design decisions. Frequently, these decisions if not captured, can lead to huge maintenance efforts that work against your original goals.
- When your appliance is released you stay away from disclosures in terms of performance.
- At the end of the day performance turns out to be a component of your design.

Most performance modeling techniques has history since 1947, based on continuous-time perceptions, and discrete-time approach. Discrete-time approach is considered and used in computer communication networks, where the time span is divided into slots of certain length, and packets are allowed to arrive at the beginning of time slots and depart at the end of time slots. On the other hand the continuous-time perceptions, the basic time unit can be used to reflect such things as time slotting in the physical system, and which they consider thorny to submit an application to digitized computer communication networks.

The rest of this chapter is outlined as follows: Section 2 introduces a literature review about performance modeling and evaluation methodologies in communication and computer networks, explaining the methodologies and techniques based on continuous or discrete-time approach. Section 3 explains the performance which is used to evaluate and analyze performance of these system, what is the workload levels to be considered among simulation or modeling. Section 4 identifies the main metrics used to evaluate the performance of the computer networks. Section 5 explains the performance models of the computer networks and communication. Section 6 explains the Modeling formalisms related to mathematical procedure; Progression algebra, queuing computer networks and communication, and petri nets. Section 7 explains and mentions different simulation models for computer networks with advantages and disadvantages for each. Finally, in section 8 conclusions and suggestions for future work are given.

## 2. LITERATURE REVIEW

This section presents a short description for the most recent and related researches on performance modeling and evaluation methodologies of communication and computer networks. Also a detailed discussion for the most recent analytical performance evaluation models for the existing queuing systems related to continuous or discrete-time approach.

Ababneh et al (2010a) proposed a derivation of discrete-time queuing network analytical model to manage and control congestion in early stages before it occurs, which is referred to as the 3QN model. The proposed model consists of three interconnected queue processing nodes. Expressions were derived to calculate performance metrics, namely; throughput, and average queuing delay. In order to investigate and analyze the effectiveness and flexibility of the proposed model by perform-

ing two scenarios; these scenarios investigate the variation of packets arrival probability against throughput, and average queuing delay.

Al-Bahadili & Ababneh (2009) presented a derivation of an analytical model to evaluate the performance of a multi-queue nodes network router, which is referred to as the mQN model. They derived expressions to calculate two performance metrics, namely, the queue node and system utilization factors. For demonstrating the flexibility and effectiveness of the mQN model in analyzing the performance of a multi-queue nodes network router, two scenarios were performed; variation of queue node and system utilization factors against queue node dropping with probability for various numbers of queue nodes, and packets arrival routing probabilities. The performed scenarios demonstrated the flexibility and effectiveness of the mQN model.

Abdel-Jaber et al (2008a) proposed a discrete-time queuing network analytical model based on DRED algorithm (James et al 2002) consisting of two queue nodes to control congested networks. They compared between the proposed analytical model and three well-known AQM algorithms, DRED (James et al 2002), RED (Floyd et al 1993) and adaptive RED (Floyd et al 2001). They experimentally compared the queue nodes of the proposed analytical model and the three AQM methods in terms of different performance measures to determine the queue node that offers better performance.

Ho & Lin (2008) proposed an autonomous random early detection (AURED) technique that allows a complete autonomous adjustment process without having to assume the existence of a known combination of optimal parameter. By tuning the packet drop probability variable according to the performance variation between two consecutive sampling periods, this technique does not require a target setting value to adapt to, thus allowing more flexibility to accommodate for various situations.

Hoflack et al (2008) considered a discrete-time queuing model with infinite storage capacity and one single output line. Users can start and end sessions during which they are active and send packets to the queuing system. Each active user generates a random but strictly positive number of packets per time slot. This model applied to study the traffic of a file server, where one file download by a user corresponds to one session. The steady-state probability generating functions of the number of active sessions, buffer occupancy (number of packets stored in the buffer) and packet delay were derived. They also derived an approximation for the tail probabilities of the buffer occupancy. This allowed them to study the influence of the different system parameters.

Liu et al (2008) used an existing nonlinear dynamic model of TCP to design AQM controllers based on improved neuron adaptive PIDC for network congestion control. They introduced a new type of neural networks controller based on proportion, sum, and differential (PSD) arithmetic to improve the lack of fixed gain in single neuron adaptive PIDC. They compared the performances of single neuron adaptive and PSD using NS-2 simulation platform to support their design. They concluded that using back propagation arithmetic to adjust the coefficients of the PIDC provides better performance at dynamic network load.

Walraevens et al (2008) analyzed a discrete-time priority queue model with session-based arrivals. They considered a user population, where each user can start and end sessions. Sessions belong to one of two classes and generate a variable number of fixed-length packets which arrive to the queue at the rate of one packet per slot. The lengths of the sessions are generally distributed. Packets of the first class had transmission priority over the packets of the other class. The model was motivated by a web server handling delay-sensitive and delay-insensitive content. By using probability generating functions, some performance measures of the queue such as the moments of the packet delays of both classes were calculated. There was an impact of the priority scheduling discipline and of the session nature of the arrival process.

Wang et al (2008) developed an analytical performance model for priority-based AQM subject to heterogeneous bursty traffic modeled by Markov-modulated Poisson processes (MMPP) and non-bursty traffic modeled by Poisson processes. Individual thresholds for each traffic class and pre-emptive resume priority scheduling mechanism are adopted to control traffic injection rate and support differential QoS. The model derived the expression of the aggregate and marginal performance metrics of the priority-based AQM system. The credibility of the model was demonstrated by comparing the analytic results with those obtained through extensive simulation experiments. The proposed model was used to investigate the impact of the squared coefficient of variation of bursty traffic on the performance of AQM.

Zhang et al (2008) proposed a new AQM algorithm called auto-tuning reference queue (ARQ) for measuring performance, which can be incorporated in any existing AQM algorithms with fixed reference queue length, such as RED and PI. According to the average packet drop probability, AQM algorithms with ARQ adjust the reference queue length. It demonstrates low-delay by keeping low reference queue length when the network traffic is light. On the other hand, it attends low-packet loss ratio by increasing the reference queue length in the case of heavy traffic. The simulation results showed that AQM algorithms with ARQ can make a good tradeoff between delay, packet-loss ratio and throughput.

Abdel-Jaber et al (2007a) presented a discrete-time DRED-based queue analytical model consisting of one queue node to deal with network congestion incipiently. They compared their proposed analytical model with the original DRED algorithm with reference to packet-loss probability, average queue length, throughput, and average queuing delay. Their results clearly showed that when the traffic load increases, DRED router buffer drops packets on a higher rate than the proposed analytical model, which consequently degrades the throughput performance. The packet-loss rate for the proposed analytical model is often stable, and it is not affected with the increase of the traffic loads, and thus stabilized the throughput performance.

Abdelhafez et al (2007) studied the behavior of TCP based worms in mobile ad hoc networks (MANETs). They developed analytical models for the spread of TCP worms in the MANET environment that account for payload–size, bandwidth sharing, radio range, nodal density, packet discards and several other parameters specific to MANETs. They presented numerical solutions for the models and verify the results using high fidelity packet–level simulations. The results showed that the analytical model developed matches the results of the packet–level simulation in all cases except when topologies result in a high probability of disconnected clusters. Their simulation studies showed that under many cases, due to the resource constrained nature of the MANET and its underlying wireless layers, the TCP-based worms rapidly become self-throttling, which may benefit the design of effective mitigation technologies in such critical networking environments.

Argyriou & Madisetti (2006) presented a joint performance evaluation model of TCP and TCP-friendly rate control (TFRC) protocol, with the underlying IP-based mobility protocols. They developed stochastic models that can characterize the protocol performance during handoffs between heterogeneous wireless networks like WLAN, cellular, or WMAN. They presented performance evaluation results for validating the developed models under a set of different handoff scenarios. Their developed model can be utilized as a basis for further analytical evaluation of new mobility management protocols, allowing thus a fast and accurate comparison.

Budhiraja et al (2004) described a new analytic model for the dynamic behavior of CP windows as they respond to congestion indicated by data loss in the network developed a stochastic differential equation to describe the dynamic evolution of the congestion window size of a single TCP session over a network.

Aweya et al (2007) determined the stability bounds for the DRED AQM algorithm using a previously developed nonlinear dynamic model of TCP. They developed a second-order linear model with time delay by linearizing the nonlinear model. Using the Pade approximation of time-delayed system $e^{-R_0 s}$, where $R_0$ is the delay in the system, then they determined the range of stabilizing gains of DRED when controlling the second-order system with time delay $R_0$. They presented examples showing the stability bounds of the DRED controller gain for networks with different parameters such as link capacity, load level, and round-trip time (RTT). In addition, they described an efficient implementation of the DRED AQM algorithm.

Baccelli & McDonal (2007) introduced a simplified model of such a HTTP flow, which consists of a succession of idle and download periods. The file downloads are subject to a fixed packet-loss probability. The same TCP connection is possibly used for the download of a random number of files, for which the effect of the slow start is taken into account. For this stochastic model, they derive a closed form formula for the stationary throughput obtained by a flow. They also derived closed form expressions for the mean time to transfer a file and for the distribution of the throughput. Several laws of file sizes and idle times were considered including heavy tailed distributions. Furthermore, they briefly discussed how the formulas can be applied to predict bandwidth sharing among competing HTTP flows.

Byun & Baras (2007) developed a new AQM algorithm, namely, the adaptive virtual queue RED (AVQRED) algorithm, by feeding virtual queue size to the RED algorithm. The objective of the new algorithm was to improve overall performance by: keeping link utilization high, link utilization stable, queuing delay low, and consecutive packet drop rate low. They compared AVQRED with six other well-known AQM methods in a realistic emulation environment. To provide fair comparisons, the AQM parameters were fine-tuned by exploring many different parameter settings via emulations. The emulation results concluded that AVQRED improves overall performance by 8 to 25%. To provide intuitive properties and validate the emulation results, a mathematical model was derived and fed to MATLAB and the results from MATLAB and emulations were compared.

Guan et al (2007) proposed a two-dimensional discrete-time Markov chain to model the RED mechanism for two traffic classes, where each dimension corresponds to a traffic class with its own parameters. This mechanism took into account the reduction of incoming traffic arrival rate due to packets dropped probabilistically with the drop probability increasing linearly with system contents. The stochastic analysis of the queue considered could be of interest for the performance evaluation of the RED mechanism for a multi-class traffic with short range dependent traffic characteristics. The results clearly demonstrated how different threshold settings can provide different trade-offs between loss probability and delay to suit different service requirements. The effects on various performance measures of changes in the input parameters and of burstiness and correlations exhibited by the arrival process are presented. The model can also be applied to high-speed networks which use slotted protocols.

Ohsaki et al (2007) proposed an AQM mechanism called SPRED (Smith predictor for RED) for measuring performance wide-area networks. The notable feature of SPRED is realizing high steady-state and transient-state performance by using a delay compensator called Smith predictor for compensating a large feedback delay. They showed the effectiveness of SPRED by both analysis and simulation experiments.

Yamagaki et al (2007) proposed a new flow-based queue management scheme, called dual metrics fair queuing (DMFQ), to improve the fairness and QoS per flow. DMFQ discards arrival packets by considering not only the arrival rate per flow but also the flow succession time. They evaluated the performance of DMFQ with computer simulations using standard simulators. In addition, they implemented DMFQ to confirm its feasibility.

Wang et al (2007) proposed a novel AQM algorithm that achieves better performance with respect to fast response time and yet good robustness. The algorithm, called loss ratio-based RED (LRED), measures the latest packet-loss ratio, and uses it as a complement to queue length for adaptively adjusting the packet drop probability. They developed an analytical model for LRED, which demonstrated that LRED is responsive even if the number of TCP flows and their persisting times vary significantly. It also provides a general guideline for the parameter settings in LRED. The performance of LRED was further examined under various simulated network environments, and compared to existing AQM algorithms. Simulation results showed that, with comparable complexities, LRED achieves shorter response time and higher robustness. More importantly, it trades off the good put with queue length better than existing algorithms, enabling flexible system configurations.

Awan et al (2006) presented a framework for the performance analysis of queuing networks with blocking under AQM scheme. The analysis was based on a queue-by-queue decomposition technique. The use of queue thresholds is a well-known technique generalized exponential distribution which can capture the bursty property of network traffic. The analytical solution was obtained using the maximum entropy principle. The forms of the state and blocking probabilities were analytically established at equilibrium via appropriate mean value constraints. The initial numerical results demonstrated the credibility of the proposed analytical solution.

Wu et al (2006) designed an efficient AQM algorithm, namely, server fairness RED (SF-

RED) that aims to provide inter-server fairness service in a simple and scalable manner to enhance performance system. In the TCP/IP network, it happens that one may intentionally, but in a legal way, generates many "flows" for the same job in order to grab more bandwidth. This will lead to servers/bandwidth allocation unfair and will thus make ISP price based services policy enforcement difficult. They defined this as an inter-server fairness problem. They studied the inter-server fairness problem in traditional AQM, and proposed a novel server based AQM algorithm for providing fair services to different servers without affecting congestion control performance. They proved the effectiveness of their approach with extensive simulations using the widely-used network simulator, namely, the NS-2 simulator.

Wang et al (2006) developed an analytical performance model for a finite capacity queuing system with AQM mechanisms based on the instantaneous number of packets in the queue. They considered two different traffic classes modeled by Poisson arrival processes. Expressions for the aggregated and marginal performance measures including the mean queuing length, response time, system throughput, probability of packet-losses and mean waiting time were derived. The validity of the analytical results was demonstrated by comparing the analytical results and those obtained from simulation experiments.

Kim & Park (2006) presented a wavelet neural network (WNN) controller based on adaptive learning rates (ALRs) method, for AQM in end-to-end TCP network in order to improve performance. The AQM is important to regulate the queue length and short RTT in TCP network. The WNN controller using ALRs adaptively controls the dropping probability of the TCP network. Also the proposed controller is intelligently trained by GD algorithm. The parameters of WNN are tuned by ALRs method. They applied Lyapunov theorem to verify the stability of WNN controller using ALRs. The simulation results showed that the performance of WNN controller using ALRs is superior to that of WNN controller using fixed learning rates.

Kulkarni et al (2006) presented a proactive prediction based AQM called PAQMAN that captures variations in the underlying traffic accurately and regulates the queue size around the desirable operating point. PAQMAN harnesses the predictability in the underlying traffic by applying the recursive least squares algorithm to estimate the average queue length for the next prediction interval given the average queue length information of the past intervals. This predicted average queue length then drives the computation of the packet drop probability. The performance of PAQMAN had been evaluated and compared against the RED scheme through NS-2 simulations that encompass a wide variety of network conditions. In addition to its simplicity and a negligible computational overhead, PAQMAN maintains a relatively low queue size, high link utilization and low packet-loss (and hence better QoS) in comparison to RED as was shown by their simulation results. Moreover, it does not maintain any per flow state and hence scalability is not an issue.

Chen (2005) proposed a general functional optimization model for designing AQM schemes to boost system performance. Unlike the previous static function optimization models based on the artificial notion of utility function, the proposed dynamic functional optimization formulation allowed them to directly characterize the desirable system behavior of AQM and design AQM schemes to optimally control the dynamic behavior of the system. Such a formulation also allowed adaptive control, which enables the AQM scheme to continuously adapt to dynamic changes of networking conditions. He presented the portraying minimum principle, a necessary condition, for the functional optimization model of AQM with TCP adaptive increase multiple decrease (AIMD) congestion control. Chen also investigated queuing stability criteria and applied the necessary conditions to optimize the functional model.

Cho et al (2005) introduced an AQM technique based on a dynamic neural network (NN) using the back-propagation (BP) algorithm to regulate a queue size close to a reference level to provide highest TCP performance. The dynamic NN was designed to perform as a robust adaptive feedback controller for TCP dynamics after an adequate training period. They evaluated the performances of the NN AQM approach using simulation experiments. The approach yields superior performance with faster transient time, larger throughput, and higher link utilization compared to two existing schemes: RED and proportional-integral (PI)-based AQM. The neural AQM outperformed PI control and RED, especially in transient state and TCP dynamics variation.

Gao et al (2005) proposed a novel AQM algorithm, namely, PFED, which is based on network traffic prediction to increase performance of the networks. The main properties of PFED are:

- Stabilizing queue length at a desirable level with consideration of future traffic, and using a minimum mean square error (MMSE) predictor to predict future network traffic.
- Imposing effective punishment upon misbehaving flow with a full stateless method.
- Maintaining queue arrival rate bounded by queue service rate through more reasonable calculation of packet drop probability.

To verify the performance of PFED, PFED was implemented in NS-2 and was compared with RED and Choke with respect to different performance metrics. Simulation results showed that PFED outperforms RED and Choke in stabling instantaneous queue length and in fairness. They also showed that PFED enables the link capacity to be fully utilized by stabilizing the queue length at a desirable level, while not incurring excessive packet loss ratio.

Ku et al (2005) proposed a method aimed to provide users with better services in terms of end-to-end delay and packet-loss ratio with all performance issues. The method captures a significant traffic increase at an early stage and signals TCP sources to slow down. In this way, TCP can quickly adjust the transmission rate, and thereby prevent overloading the network. In addition to RED, another two prominent AQM schemes, namely, random early marking (REM) and ARED, are compared with the proposed method. Simulation results showed that under various network loads and a range of network propagation delays, their method achieved lower end-to-end delay and packet-loss ratio, compared with all aforementioned schemes.

Liu et al (2005) introduced and analyzed a decentralized network congestion control algorithm which has dynamic adaptations at both user ends and link ends, a so-called general primal-dual algorithm. They obtained sufficient conditions for local stability of this algorithm in a general topology network with heterogeneous round-trip delays. Then, as an implementation of this algorithm in the Internet, they introduced an AQM scheme called exponential-RED (E-RED), which outperforms RED and is inherently stable when combined with TCP-Reno or its variants for high-speed networks.

Aweya & Ouellette (2004) extended the DRED with multiple packet drop precedence to allow for priority treatment of traffic in a network. In this new scheme, packets marked with higher dropped probability are preferentially dropped in order to make buffer room for packet marked with lower dropped probability. The main advantage of using the DRED algorithm is the lower parameter configuration complexity it offers and the ease of configuration for a wide range of network conditions.

Joshi et al (2004) proposed multiple average-multiple threshold (MAMT) AQM as a solution for providing available and dependable service to traffic from emergency users after disasters. MAMT is a simple but effective approach that can be applied at strategic network locations, where heavy congestion is anticipated. It can provide low loss to emergency packets while dropping non-emergency packets only as much as necessary. Fluid flow analysis and simulation was conducted to provide guidelines for proper MAMT design, especially regarding the queue size and averaging parameters that are most important. It considered non-responsive traffic exclusively, since non-responsive traffic types are currently getting the most attention from emergency management organizations. Plus, very little work had been performed regarding AQM and non-responsive traffic. It demonstrated queue oscillation problems that previously may have been attributed to the interactions between TCP and AQM, but which are actually inherent to AQM and can be greatly reduced with proper parameter settings. MAMT showed to perform well over a range of loads and can effectively protect emergency traffic from surges in non-emergency traffic.

Zhang & Sun (2004) presented a comparative study among a number of AQM algorithms, such as: PI controller, DRED, SRED, BLUE, REM, and proportional derivative RED (PD-RED) algorithms using simulations. The performance metric used in the study was queue length. There results demonstrated that PD-RED is more effective at stabilizing the queue length, and the performance of PD-RED is obviously better than all of the above algorithms there were compared.

Aweya et al (2003) described an improved AQM scheme which dynamically changes its threshold settings as the number of connections and system load changes. This technique allows network devices to effectively control packet-losses and TCP timeouts while maintaining high link utilization, which all for getting better performance.

Joo et al (2003) proposed a new AQM algorithm that combines the more effective elements of recent algorithms with a RED core. Throughout analysis and simulations, they demonstrated improved performance in stability and response time with

straightforward selection of parameters for both steady load and changes in loads.

Puigjaner (2003) stated that managing and controlling any system; communication and computer network; wired, wireless and cellular, banking system, etc, can be performed by measuring its performance.

Yanfei et al (2003) proposed PID controller to speed up the responsiveness of AQM system and overcame the pure transient performance of the proportional-integral (PI) controller for AQM designed by C. Hollot. The controller parameters are tuned based on the determined gain and phase margins. The simulation results showed that the integrated performance of the PID controller is obviously superior to that of the PI controller.

Fen et al (2002) proposed, implemented, and evaluated a fundamentally different AQM algorithm, called BLUE. BLUE uses packet-loss and link idle events to manage congestion. Using both simulation and controlled experiments, BLUE showed to perform significantly better than RED, both in terms of packet-loss rates and buffer-size requirements in the network. As an extension to BLUE, a novel technique based on Bloom filters was described for enforcing fairness among a large number of flows. In particular, they proposed and evaluated stochastic fair BLUE (SFB), a queue management algorithm which can identify and rate-limit non responsive flows using a very small amount of state information.

Wydrowski et al (2002) introduced a new AQM algorithm called generalized random early evasion network (GREEN). GREEN provides high link utilization whilst maintaining low-delay and packet-loss. It enabled low latency interactive applications such as telephony and network games. Simulations showed that GREEN outperforms a number of AQM algorithms.

Aweya et al (2001) described a technique for enhancing the effectiveness of RED schemes by dynamically changing the threshold settings as the number of connections (and system load) changes. Using this mechanism, routers and switches can effectively control packet losses and TCP timeouts while maintaining high link utilization. This mechanism is attractive for the deployment of large IP networks supporting a wide range of connections and large aggregations of traffic.

AlWehaibi et al (2000) carried out a comprehensive study to investigate the performance behavior of four selected policing mechanisms for the Internet namely: Token Bucket (Ts). Jumping Window (JW), Triggered Jumping Window (TJW) and Exponentially Weighted Moving Average (EWMA). Three types of bursty sources modeled as On/off Poisson and Batched Poisson processes are utilized. Three criteria are used to evaluate the performance behavior of the selected policing mechanisms. These are the average packet delay, the average packet loss probability and the average number of lost credits. They used computer simulations to arrive at various conclusions regarding the dependence of performance on source traffic characteristics and policing mechanism parameters. Furthermore, a comparison of the performance behavior of the selected policing mechanisms was carried for different input traffic characteristics.

From the previous literature review, we can notice that all the publishers concentrate on one or no more than two things in order to increase, enhance, and improve the performance of the networks through creating a model; analytical or through simulation, to predict the behavior of the system during measuring and evaluating theses metrics.

## 3. PERFORMANCE MODELING

Performance modeling is defined in many ways, one of these is a structured and repeatable approach to modeling the performance of your software. It begins during the early phases of your application design and continues throughout the application life cycle. Another definition for performance system is how hardware is used by software when they are serving and helping the workload generated by the user's demands. From the definitions we can conclude that any performance model consists of three main aspects: system structure, the operational strategy, and statistical properties. The first two parts are considered as machine deterministic, but the last one is a user deterministic. (i.e. internal and external user one; operational and administrator user).

All agree that the performance measures are not taken into account until main problems countered the system. When it is time to measure the performance, the easiest way is to measure the performance of running an entire existing system, as opposed to a partially existing system. However what if this system that you want to measure is partially existing? Then what do you do? With this situation there aren't many options, it may be an inflexible and hard job to implement and control your structure but could be the only chance to use the performance models.

Performance modeling psychotherapy, research, examination investigation, psychoanalysis and testing have been maintained to be of grand practical and theoretical significance in research areas of the design development and optimization of computer and communication systems and applications; ranging from using experimental techniques, passing through using analytical models ending up with simulation up to using.

It is obvious that the main types of performance measures used for managing and controlling the computer networks are Practical experiments, simulations, and analytical models. Practical experiments and simulations are the most widely-used methodologies for analyzing the performance of multi-queue systems during congestion (Robertazzi, T. G., 2000; Welzl, M., 2005). However, several efforts have also been directed towards mathematical modeling of multi-queue systems in congested computer networks. This is because mathematical models are cheaper and easier to use than experimental or simulation applications, and they can improve understanding of the real problem to set-up appropriate and flexible solutions that suit the network and design requirements (Al-bahadili, H. 2009; Robertazzi, T. G., 2000).

Analytical models were developed (Ababneh et al, 2010a; Ababneh et al, 2010b; Abdeljaber et al, 2008a; Abdeljaber et al 2007) to evaluate the performance of a discrete-time active-queue management (AQM) based queuing systems of one, two, and three-queue nodes; where analytical expressions were derived to calculate a number of performance networks metrics, such as: average queue length, throughput, average queuing delay, and packet-loss rate. The mathematical models can be used to improve understanding of the real problem of a multi-queue nodes router to set-up appropriate and flexible parameters that suit the network and design requirements, and meet all sources' (users, services, and applications) needs with respect to computer networks.

Due to the enormous development and wide spread of computer networks and the Internet, managing and controlling the computer networks becomes a critical issue, which needs to be efficiently solved to achieve optimum performance (Ababneh et al, 2010a; Ababneh et al, 2010b; Abdeljaber et al, 2008a; Abdeljaber et al 2007). Congestion is considered a computer networks issue which touch the heart of the performance and the utilization of computer networks, which usually occurs at the network router buffer when the number of incoming packets exceeds the available network resources, such as buffer space and processing speed of the network router. Multi-queue systems are widely used as a practical solution to the computer network congestion problem. Therefore, it is very important to have efficient, reliable, and accurate models to evaluate and analyze the performance of the network and consequently to contrivance optimum designs for the congestion avoidance queuing system at the network router (Ababneh et al, 2010a; Ababneh et al, 2010b; Abdeljaber et al, 2008a; Abdeljaber et al 2007; Aweya, J. et al, 2001.; Rob, T.G., 2000). Due to Performance computer networks there is an important issue in the design and implementation of an efficient Internet congestion control policing mechanism that is related to performance behavior. The effectiveness of such a mechanism can be measured by packet loss probability, bandwidth allocation, packet delay, throughput or other quality of service measures.

# 4. PERFORMANCE METRICS

A number of network parameters are considered to evaluate, analyze, and compare the performance of the proposed computer networks and communications models. These criteria are commonly used to measure the performance of these models and they are recommended by the IETF also RFC 2309 (Bra, et al, 98). These performance metrics are used to determine the proposed model QoS with reference to traffic loads in the network. Some of these main performance metrics are as follow:

- **Average Queue Length:** it is the number of packets that the queue can hold. Keeping the Average Queue Length as low as possible to maintain the router queue in computer networks from building up its size, and thereby the router queue avoids the congestion incident. In addition, Average Queue Length metric helps in computing the average queuing delay.
- **Throughput:** it can be defined as the number of packets that successfully pass through the queue of the computer networks from all arrived packets at router queue. Moreover, throughput represents the fraction of time that the router queue of the computer networks is busy (Woodward, M.E., 2003).
- **Average Queuing Delay:** it can be considered as the average waiting time for packets at the router queue of the computer networks. It can be evaluated using the little law formula (Woodward, M.E., 2003).

- **Packet Loss Rate:** this metric denotes the number of packets lost the service from all the arrived packets at router queue for computer networks. (Woodward, M.E., 2003). Defined it as the fraction of messages that are lost due to no buffer space being available at the time of their arrival in the computer networks, this measure is important in assessing the transmission quality for certain types of data such as voice or video.

Beside what we mentioned we can add another performance metrics such as; resource utilization, response time and jitter. These are a part of (but not limited to) performance networks measurements. Also we can categorize them to two different types: internal performance measures and external performance measures, or we can discriminate them from end user point view and administrator system respect view.

## 5. PERFORMANCE MODELING TECHNIQUES

Evaluating performance of the computer networks depends on the system itself as we mentioned above, it is comparatively trouble-free, straightforward and uncomplicated if and only if your system is in reality operation. This is because you can get the system efficiency and performance of the computer networks with multi easy ways. But suppose you have a situation which is considered the hardest way; when your system is virtual and you can't touch or measure performance of the computer networks, or the second choice requires you to use some type of performance model or performance evaluation or management techniques, such as simulation. So one of the main performance modeling of the computer networks goal is to gain understanding of a computer system's performance on various applications, by means of measurement and analysis, and then

to encapsulate these characteristics in a compact formula for computer networks in general.

The resulting computer networks and communication models can be used to gain greater understanding of the performance phenomena involved and to project performance to other system/application combinations. We said that performance models of the computer networks and communication are experimental, analytical and simulations used to calculate performance measures approximately.

Generally, from the broad definition we can realize and understand that many requirements are needed. There are general requirements for computer networks and communication model that must be possible to verify the model and determine the model parameters from scrutinized data, these requirements are called functional and non-functional requirements. Both should be practicable, feasible and practical to submit an application to the computer networks and communications model.

The above definitions will shed a light on few questions. Some of these questions, what is the system performance? What are the components of the system that evaluate the performance? What are the metrics that decide the quality of services (QoS)? What are performance variables? What are the problems faced through evaluating performance? What are the challenges encountered? These questions and others will be answered due to computer network and communication environments.

Through developing performance model for computer network and communication many questions can be answered, such as which protocol gives best delay? Buffer size to manage overflow? Response time? throughput? utilization? packet dropping?, etc.

When modeling performance of the computer networks and communication, your aim is to model workload of a computer networks and communication system, where this kind of performance can be observed at different stages; the first one and considered largest one is connection stage, for this stage proposed models are used to take performance of the communications and computer networks in general (Erlang, A.K., 1909) and the performance measurements that used for are loss probability, and chunking or blocking probability. The second stage that can be observed for performance of computer networks and communication is burst stage. We can call these stages as macroscopic and microscopic level to be considered among simulation or modeling computer networks and communication. The second and third level are complex ones and we can call them microscopic level because they modeled jointly permitting to investigate cell or packet loss probability, delay, etc.

# 6. MATHEMATICAL FORMALISMS

Progression algebra, queuing computer networks and communication, and petri nets are formalisms related to mathematical procedure. They are all considered part of Markov chains and used to model computer networks and communication. Starting with theories which make available tools and equipment for defining machine deterministic structure (hardware), strategy (software) and user demands (stochastic) and explain the behavior of the computer networks and communication models. Process idioms and activities are considered fundamental structure for this approach, where Algebra of communicating processes (ACP) and Communication Sequential Processes (CSP) are an example for this process. Using this approach guide to build up stochastic process algebras (SPA), where delay of uncertain length integrated to its activities. As we mentioned before, process terms are basic fundamentals for this approach. These processes are made up of in order components running parallel and coordinate by shared activities with other processes. Compositional-

ity of the algebra method can be utilized in all levels of computer network and communication performance modeling; construction, production, building, generalization and solution of the model (Bau, et al 1996; Hillston 1996).

The second approach is queuing computer networks and communication, we can define a queuing system as a job waiting in a holding competence or service facility. Systems act as a job that achieves services from the node, and then goes to next node. We can call one queue a node, such as packet switching network, cell, telecommunication systems, etc. What takes this service may be a job, customer, source, person, message, packet or program. Network queue explains circumstances where the input from one queue is the output from one or more, and it has very significant and essential application of queuing theory. Where the queuing theory was published by Erlang in 1908 and dealt with queuing systems that has service time constant. As an example, the central server network; this consists of central processing units to perform the tasks. The second part is the storage unit (which also has its queue) consists of how the queues are ordered or all jobs in the queues treated equally. The jobs in the queue can be treated one by one serially, or a priority queuing is applied such as; First in First out(FIFO) this means jobs are performed in the order that they arrived, First Come First Served (FCFS), Last in First out (LIFO) which is opposite to FIFO, Smallest Job First (SJF) it executes the tasks in terms of the smallest one first, but some method need to imply the need for applying Emption and pre-Emption; when a job with high priority (mouse event) arrives in queue headed by low priority job (mouse event), in this case pre-emption is applied where queue stopped the current entry half way and the new job with high priority entered. In queuing networks there are two types: closed and open queuing networks. Where in closed queuing networks the number of customers is fixed but in open queuing networks the customer's numbers are varying. Besides that there are some terms related to queuing networks such as queue length, waiting time through, etc, where total sojourn time including delay and service time is the waiting time, total number of tasks in the node also including delayed and served tasks.

Generally, every queuing system network and communication systems can be described by several notations. The most widely used notations are proposed by Kendall; therefore, they were referred to as Kendall's notations (Kendall 1953):

1.  **The arrival process (A):** A stochastic process explaining how packets arrive to the queuing system.
2.  **The service process (B):** A stochastic process that illustrates the time-span spent by the server processing the packet.
3.  **The number of servers (C):** The number of server in the system.
4.  **The system capacity (K):** The maximum number of packets inside the buffer (waiting in queue) including packets currently in the service. In this thesis, it is referred to as K.
5.  **The customer population (P):** It represents the maximum number of packets who participate in the arrival process.
6.  **Queuing service discipline:** The rules and laws for deciding which packet in the queuing system should be served, i.e. first come first served (FCFS), last come first served (LCFS), round robin (RR), etc.

The fourth and fifth notation K and P components are optional, they can be removed where in this case they assumed by default infinite values. It should be noted that C, K and P notations are positive integers only, where the first and second notations are selected based on the set of descriptors such as:

*   **Deterministic (C):** Where the inter-arrival and service time distribution are constant.
*   **Markovian (M):** Where the distribution can be used depending on system time as follows:
    *   **Continuous-time system:** the inter-arrival and service time's distributions are exponentially distributed. For instance, the inter-arrival time is Poisson process and the service time is exponentially distributed.
    *   **Discrete-time system:** the inter-arrival and service times are geometrically distributed, but if the arrivals and departures are multiple, exponential distributions can be used.
*   **Generally distributed (G):** In this case no restraints can be used on the distributions types.

Network queuing has many applications such as; computer networks, network communication as circuit switching or packet switching, broadcasting radio or digital communication, markov chain and Jackson queuing network, etc.

As we mentioned above that mathematical techniques are based on queuing computer networks and communication, process algebras and finally Petri nets. In 1962 Carl Adam Petri invented Petri nets, where its explanation of the concurrency and synchronization inherent computer networks and communication systems, it consists of graph, two kinds of nodes; places and transitions and unidirectional arcs between them, where according to firing rules enforcing by transitions tokens moves between places. Petri nets are so helpful, practical and accommodating for studying qualitative or logical properties of computer networks systems concurrent and synchronous evaluation and for that time must be taken in Petri nets definition (Ajmone marsan, M., et al, 1995; Bause, f. et, al., 1996; Bolch, G. el al., 1998; Peterson, J. L., 1981; Silva, M. 1993).

# 7. SIMULATION

Simulation can be defined by so many definitions. One definition is depicting the timing activities of the system by software, while execution the program you mimicking the fruition of the system along the time, also we can summarized main most of these definitions:

- **Paul & Balmer defined simulation as:** Analyst builds a model of the system of interest, writes computer program which embody the model and uses a computer to initiate the system's behavior when subject to a Varity of operating policies. Thus the most desirable policy may be selected (Paul, R. J. & Balmer, D. W. 1998).

- **Nylor defined simulation as:** (computer) simulation is a numerical techniques for conducting experiments on a digital computer, which involves certain types of mathematical and logical models that describes the behavior of a business or economic system (or some component thereof) over extended periods of real time (Paul, R. J. & Balmer, D. W. 1998).

- **Mize and Cox defined it as:** The process of conducting experiments on a model of a system in lieu of either (i) direct experimentation with the system itself, or (ii) direct analytical solution of some problem associated with the system (Paul, R. J. & Balmer, D. W. 1998).

- **Shannon define simulation as:** the process of designing a model of a real system and conducting experiments with this model for the purpose of either understanding the behavior of the system or of evaluating various strategies for the operation of the system (Paul, R. J. & Balmer, D. W. 1998).

- **El Sheikh defines simulation a comprehensive definition:** Simulation is the use of a model to represent over time essential characteristics of a system under study (El Sheikh, A. 1987).

- Also simulation has many advantages over mathematical and experimental methods; it is widely used in investigating and the performance of existing and proposed computer networks designs, protocols, models to get better quality of services and effectiveness of the network design and modeling, but Banks sum up the advantages of computer networks (Paul, R. J. & Balmer, D. W. 1998).
  - Making correct choices
  - Compressing and expanding time
  - Understanding "Why"
  - Exploring possibilities
  - Diagnosing problem
  - Developing understanding
  - Building consensus
  - Preparing for change
  - Training the team
  - Specifying requirements

- Despite a lot of advantages, simulation still has minor disadvantages; the effort time and cost spent debugging and developing, also quality is proportional to the square root the number of events, simulation languages, elasticity and complexity, but most of them are mentioned by (Paul, R. J. & Balmer, D. W. 1998).
  - Model building requires special training
  - Simulation results may be difficult to interpret
  - Simulation modeling and analysis can be time-consuming and expensive
  - Simulation may be used inappropriately

Time-flow handling, behavior of the system, and change handling are features must be put forward during computer simulation proposed by (Pidd 1998).

Most performance modeling techniques in relation with time are based on continuous-time perceptions model, which has former history since 1947, and the packets are allowed to arrive or depart at any time during the time span, but applying to computer communication networks consider multifaceted and difficult, so using a discrete-time approach is the nature, where the time span is divided into slots of certain length, and packets are allowed to arrive at the beginning of time slots and depart at the end of time slots. There is at most one arrival or departure per one time slot.

The last mathematical formalism solution techniques that provides most general solution technique because most of the other procedures are ultimately Markov chains, which can (in principle) be constructed unambiguously; despite the well known and universal procedure, it suffer from the huge size where billion states and orders moderate system has, that will need parallel computation, (Ajmone Marsan et al, 1995; Bause,& Kritzinger 1996; Bolch et al 1998; Wang 1998)

In the beginning performance computer networks and communication models are generated in document structure by using the means of your choice, then the document turns into a communication point for other team members. Performance of computer networks and communication models contains a lot of explanation information, including application description, goals, hardware requirements, network consideration such as bandwidth, shared resources, budgets, scenarios, performance objectives, workloads goals, and baseline hardware, QoS and workload requirements and other keys, where it plays out possibilities and evaluates alternatives, before committing to a design or implementation decision. You need to measure to know the cost of your to model. Besides that performance of computer networks and communication modeling process has an input and output input, from these inputs that are required; scenarios and design documentation about cases, workload requirements, application design and target in-frastructure limitations, and QoS requirements, where the output from performance of computer networks and communication modeling are; test cases, goals, and a performance model document. In broad-spectrum the process of the performance computer networks and communication can recapitulate to eight steps as following; first step is categorize explanation scenarios, second step is identifying workload, and the third step is categorizing performance of the computer network and communication objectives, the fourth step is identifying budget, the fifth step is identifying processing steps, then the sixth step is allocating budget, the seventh step is assessing and evaluating, the eighth and final step is validating.

## 8. CONCLUSION AND FUTURE RESEARCH DIRECTIONS

It is obvious that performance modeling, evaluation, management and simulation of computer networks have its information, risk management, processes, parameters, objectives, workload goals in every phase in it is life cycle.

It is very important to have efficient, reliable, and accurate methodologies or techniques to evaluate and analyze the performance and to contrivance the optimum designs for communication and computer networks, where practical experiments and simulations are the most widely used beside that several efforts have also been directed towards mathematical models for many reasons. Beginning performance modeling early on helps you expose key issues and allow you to quickly see places to make tradeoffs in design or help you identify where to spend your efforts. A practical step in the right direction is simply capturing your key scenarios and breaking them down into logical operations or steps. Most importantly, you identify your performance goals such as response time, throughput, and resource utilization with each scenario.

Again the most important goals of this chapter is to: Present performance modeling and evaluation methodologies of communication and computer networks; explain the methodologies and techniques used to evaluate and analyze performance of these system, categorizing the important measurements used to evaluate, manage and control the performance of the computer networks from model designer point of view, so its person or group disction, so its partially correct not completely (100%) correct because evaluating performance of the computer networks depends on the system itself, also we present the advantage and disadvantage of these techniques especially simulation techniques over other techniques. The resulting networks model used to expand grater sympathetic and perceptive of the performance phenomena engrossed and to project them to other applications.

We planned in near future to write chapter or even book related to methods and techniques for evaluating performance of multi -queue nodes based on active queue management in discrete-time and compare them with simulation and analytical performance models using multi-performance measures.

# REFERENCES

Ababneh, D. (2009). *Development of a discrete-time DRED-based multi-queue nodes network analytical model*. PhD Thesis. Amman, Jordan: The Arab Academy for Banking & Financial Sciences.

Ababneh, J., Thabtah, F., Abdel-Jaber, H., Hadi, W., & Badarneh, E. (2010). Derivation of three queue nodes discrete-time analytical model based on DRED algorithm. In *Proceedings of the 7th IEEE International Conference on Information Technology: New Generations (ITNG 2010)*, (pp. 885-890). Las-Vegas, NV: IEEE Press.

Ababneh, J., Thabtah, F., Abdel-Jaber, H., Hadi, W., & Badarneh, E. (2010). Discrete-time analytical model for evaluating the performance of three queue nodes based on dynamic RED algorithm. In *Proceedings International Journal Aviation Information Technology, Engineering and Management (IJATEM) Inauguration Conference*, (pp. 152-164). New Orleans, LA: IJATEM Press.

Abdel-Jaber, H., Woodward, M. E., Thabtah, F., & Abu-Ali, A. (2008). Performance evaluation for DRED discrete-time queuing network analytical model. *Journal of Network and Computer Applications*, *31*(4), 750–770. doi:10.1016/j.jnca.2007.09.003

Abdel-Jaber, H., Woodward, M. E., Thabtah, F., & Etbega, M. (2007). A discrete-time queue analytical model based on dynamic random early drop. In *Proceedings of the 4th IEEE International Conference on Information Technology: New Generations (ITNG 2007)*, (pp. 71-76). Las Vegas, NV: IEEE Press.

Ajmone Marsan, M., Balbo, G., Conte, G., Donatelli, S., & Franceschinis, S. (1995). *Modeling with generalized stochastic petri nets* (2nd ed.). New York: John Wiley and Sons.

Al-Bahadili, H. (2010). On the use of discrete-event simulation in computer networks analysis and design. In Abu-Taieh, E. M. O., & El-Sheikh, A. A. (Eds.), *Handbook of Research on Discrete-Event Simulation Environments: Technologies and Applications* (pp. 418–442). Hershey, PA: IGI Global. doi:10.4018/978-1-60566-774-4.ch019

Athuraliya, S., Li, V. H., Low, S. H., & Yin, Q. (2001). REM: Active queue management. *IEEE Network*, *15*(3), 48–53. doi:10.1109/65.923940

Aweya, J., Ouellette, M., & Montuno, D. Y. (2001). A control theoretic approach to active queue management. *Journal of Computer Networks*, *36*(2–3), 203–235. doi:10.1016/S1389-1286(00)00206-1

Banks, J., Carson, J. S. II, & Nelson, B. L. (1996). *Discrete-event system simulation* (2nd ed.). Upper Saddle River, NJ: Prentice-Hall.

Bause, F., & Kritzinger, P. S. (1996). Stochastic petri nets: An introduction to the theory. In *Advances in Computer Science*. Wiesbaden, Germany: Verlag Vieweg.

Bolch, G., Greiner, S., de Meer, H., & Trivedi, K. S. (1998). *Queueing networks and Markov chains: Modeling and performance evaluation with computer science applications*. New York: John Wiley & Sons. doi:10.1002/0471200581

Braden, R., Clark, D., Crowcroft, J., Davie, B., Deering, S., Estrin, D., et al. (1998). *Recommendations on queue management and congestion avoidance in the Internet (RFC 2309)*. Retrieved from http://www.ietf.org.

Brakmo, L., & Peterson, L. (1995). TCP Vegas: End to end congestion avoidance on a global internet. *IEEE Journal on Selected Areas in Communications*, *13*(8), 1465–1480. doi:10.1109/49.464716

Brandauer, C., Iannaccone, G., Diot, C., Ziegler, T., Fdida, S., & May, M. (2001). Comparison of tail drop and active queue management performance for bulk-data and web-like Internet traffic. In *Proceeding of ISCC*, (pp. 122–129). IEEE Press.

Chengyu, Z., Oliver, W. W., Aweya, J., Ouellette, M., & Delfin, Y. (2002). A comparison of active queue management algorithms using the OPNET modeler. *IEEE Communications Magazine*, *40*(6), 158. doi:10.1109/MCOM.2002.1007422

El Sheikh, A. (1987). *Simulation modeling using a relational database package*. Unpublished PhD Thesis. London, UK: The London School of Economics.

Erlang, A. K. (1909). The theory of probabilities and telephone conversations. In *The Life and Works of A.K. Erlang, E. Brockmeyer, H.L. Halstr m og Arne Jensen* (pp. 131–137). Copenhagen, Denmark: Verlag.

Feng, W., Kandlur, D., Saha, D., & Shin, K. G. (1999). *Blue: A new class of active queue management algorithms. Technical report UM CSE-TR-387-99*. Ann Arbor, MI: University of Michigan.

Feng, W., Kandlur, D., Saha, D., & Shin, K. G. (2001). Stochastic fair blue: A queue management algorithm for enforcing fairness. In *Proceedings of IEEE INFOCOM* (*Vol. 3*, pp. 1520–1529). IEEE Press.

Floyd, S., & Jacobson, V. (1993). Random early detection gateways for congestion avoidance. *IEEE/ACM Joint Transactions on Networking*, *1*(4), 397–413.

Floyd, S., Ramakrishna, G., & Shenker, S. (2001). *Adaptive RED: An algorithm for increasing the robustness of RED's active queue management. Technical Report*. New York: ICSI.

Hillston, J. A. (1996). *Compositional approach to performance modeling*. Cambridge, UK: Cambridge University Press. doi:10.1017/CBO9780511569951

Kang, J., & Nath, B. (2004). Resource-controlled MAC-layer congestion control scheme in cellular packet network. In *Proceedings of the Vehicular Technology Conference*, (vol 4), (pp. 1988–1992). IEEE Press.

Kendall, D. (1953). Stochastic processes occurring in the theory of queues and analysis by means of the imbedded Markov chain. *Annals of Mathematical Statistics*, *24*, 338–354. doi:10.1214/aoms/1177728975

Lapsley, D., & Low, S. (1999). Random early marking for Internet congestion control. In *Proceeding of GlobeCom 1999* (pp. 1747–1752). IEEE Press. doi:10.1109/GLOCOM.1999.832461

Leeuwaarden, J., Denteneer, D., & Resing, J. (2006). A discrete-time queuing model with periodically scheduled arrival and departure slots. *Performance Evaluation, 63*(4), 278–294. doi:10.1016/j.peva.2005.03.001

Paul, J. R. (1993). Activity cycle diagrams and the three-phase method. In *Proceeding of the 25th Conference on Winter Simulation*, (pp. 123-131). Los Angeles, CA: IEEE Press.

Pentikousis, K., & Badr, H. (2002). *On the resource efficiency of explicit congestion notification.* Berlin, Germany: Springer.

Peterson, J. L. (1981). *Petri net theory and the modeling of systems.* Englewood Cliffs, NJ: Prentice-Hall.

Pidd, M. (1998). *Computer simulation in management science* (4th ed.). Chicester, UK: John Wiley.

Puigjaner, R. (2003). Performance modelling of computer networks. In *Proceedings of IFIP/ACM Latin America conference on Towards a Latin American Agenda for Network Research*, (pp. 106-123). ACM Press.

Richard., & Stevens, W. (2001). TCP slow start, congestion avoidance, fast retransmit, and fast recovery algorithms. *IETF RFC*. Retrieved from http://www.ietf.org.

Robertazzi, T. (2000). *Computer networks and systems: Queuing theory and performance evaluation* (3rd ed.). Berlin, Germany: Springer Verlag.

Silva, M. (1993). *Introducing petri nets: Practice of petri nets in manufacturing.* New York: Chapman & Hall.

Wang, J. (1998). *Stochastic petri net: Theory and application.* PhD Thesis. Nanjing, China: Nanjing University of Science and Technology.

Wang, J. (1998). *Timed petri nets: Theory and application. Norwell, Ma.* Kluwer Academic Publishers.

Wang, L., Min, G., & Awan, I. (2006). Modeling active queue management with different traffic classes. In *Proceedings of the 20th International Conference on Advanced Information Networking and Applications*, (pp. 442-446). IEEE Press.

Welzl, M. (2005). *Network congestion control: Managing internet traffic.* New York: John Wiley & Sons. doi:10.1002/047002531X

Woodward, M. E. (2003). *Communication and computer networks: Modeling with discrete-time queues.* London, UK: Pentech Press.

Wydrowski, B., & Zukerman, M. (2002). GREEN: An active queue management algorithm for a self managed internet. In *Proceedings of ICC 2002*, (vol 4), (pp. 2368-2372). IEEE Press.

## KEY TERMS AND DEFINITIONS

**Active Queue Management (AQM):** Is a technique that consists in dropping or marking packets before a router's queue is full, they operate by maintaining one or more drop/mark probabilities, and probabilistically dropping or marking packets even when the queue is short. There are a number of AQM algorithms that have been developed by many researchers; RED, DRED, GRED, GREEN, BLUE, SRED.

**Average Queuing Delay:** It can be considered as the average waiting time for packets at the router queue of the computer networks. It can be evaluated using the little law formula. Also he defined it as the time interval, in units of the average transmission time of the computer networks.

**Average Queue Length:** Keeping the Average Queue Length as low as possible to maintain the router queue in computer networks from building up its size, and thereby the router queue avoids the congestion incident. In addition, Average Queue Length metric helps in computing the average queuing delay.

**Discrete-time Analytical Model:** Non- continues time that can be utilized as a congestion control method in fixed and wireless networks, a basic time unit called slot is used, where in each slot, single or multiple events can occur.

**Markov Chain:** Mathematical formalism solution techniques that provides most general solution technique, which can (in principle) be constructed unambiguously; despite the well known and universal procedure, it suffer from the huge size where billion states and orders moderate system has, that will need parallel computation.

**Packet Loss Rate:** This metric denotes the packets ratio that has lost the service from all the arrived packets at router queue for computer networks. Defined it as the fraction of messages that are lost due to no buffer space being available at the time of their arrival in the computer networks, this measure can be important in assessing the transmission quality for certain types of data such as voice or video.

**Packets Loss Probability:** The proportion of packets that lost the service at the router buffer from all the packets that were arrived is evaluated

**Performance Modeling:** A structured and repeatable approach to modeling the performance of your software

**Petri Nets:** It is explanation of the concurrency and synchronization inherent computer networks and communication systems, it consists of graph, two kinds of nodes; places and transitions and unidirectional arcs between them, where according to firing rules enforcing by transitions tokens moves between places.

**Quality of Service:** Is the ability to provide different priority to different applications, users, or data flows, or to guarantee a certain level of performance to a data flow, packet dropping probability, average queue length.

**Simulation:** Is a numerical techniques for conducting experiments on a digital computer, which involves certain types of mathematical and logical models that describes the behavior of a business or economic system (or some component thereof) over extended periods of real time.

**Throughput:** It can be defined as the number of packets that successfully pass through the queue of the computer networks from all the arrived packets at router queue or the number of successfully transmitted messages per mean transmission time of message. Moreover, throughput represents the fraction of time that the router queue of the computer networks is busy.

# Chapter 23
# Network Simulation Tools for Supporting Teaching in Computer Networks

**Shao Ying Zhu**
*University of Derby, UK*

**Gerald Schaefer**
*Loughborough University, UK*

## ABSTRACT

*Computer networks have evolved dramatically in recent years and consequently qualified and experienced network administrators are highly sought after, which in turn has led to the development of specialised computer networking courses at many universities. In this chapter, the authors investigate the use of network simulation tools as an alternative to be employed in computer networking laboratories. Network simulation tools provide students with the opportunity to freely experiment with virtual computer networks and equipment without the expensive costs associated with real networking hardware. The results of their research show that students appreciate the use of network simulators and see them as an effective approach to learning computer networking concepts and gaining the relevant experience. This was also confirmed by the actual performance of students who experienced different levels of exposure to networks simulators during their studies. The authors furthermore investigate the use of interactive, electronically assessed lab sessions, where students get immediate and interactive feedback while they are going through lab exercises. Their research shows that this approach not only releases the lecturer from less demanding students to better support weaker students, but that this will also lead to improved student performance and better student retention.*

DOI: 10.4018/978-1-4666-0191-8.ch023

## INTRODUCTION

Computer networks have evolved dramatically in recent years. The growing demand in terms of security, mobile computing and voice-over-IP among others, has led to the development of new protocols and algorithms to meet these challenges. Qualified and experienced network administrators are therefore highly sought after, which in turn has led to the development of specialised computer networking courses at many universities. Training for CISCO's Certified Network Associate Certification (CCNA) is an integral part of the BSc Computer Networks course in the School of Computing at the University of Derby. During their study, students take four Cisco related modules: Network Fundamentals, Routing Protocols and Concepts, LAN Switching and Wireless, and Assessing the WAN. Network Fundamentals and Routing Protocols and Concepts are stage 1 modules, while LAN Switching and Wireless and Accessing the WAN are stage 2 modules.

Computer networking courses clearly need the support of a lab-based approach due to the practical nature of the subject (Sarkar, 2006; Goldstein, et al., 2005; Javidi & Sheybani, 2008; Dixon, et al., 1997). However, the initial costs of the equipment, as well as costs for maintenance and frequent upgrading as demanded by ever changing technologies is extremely high. Due to these costs, students are often provided only with limited network equipment during their studies. In addition, typically only a small number of students can use the equipment at any one time, which puts restrictions on class sizes and teaching resources. The size and location of physical laboratories further restrict the students' experience. Moreover, some of the functionality (e.g., some WAN technologies) cannot actually be experimented with by the students. Due to these reasons, we have decided to use network simulation programs for lab exercises. This is also backed up by a number of studies reported in the literature (Sarkar, 2006; Goldstein, et al., 2005;

Javidi & Sheybani, 2008) which have confirmed the usefulness of network simulation programs.

The remainder of this chapter is organised as follows. The following section compares physical and simulation based network laboratories, while the next section reports our investigation of using network simulation software for teaching computer network concepts. This is followed by a session which provides details on our study of employing e-assessment based laboratories for networking, before the last section concludes the chapter.

## PHYSICAL LABORATORIES VS. SIMULATION SOFTWARE

Physical networking laboratories have the following limitations:

1. They are expensive. The cost of network components is high and sometimes beyond the reach of higher education institutions.
2. They are difficult to maintain. Networking equipment and software need to be upgraded regularly.
3. They are hard to secure. The safety of the equipment cannot be guaranteed, and it is difficult to prevent accidental damages to the hardware by inexperienced student.
4. They lack flexibility. Students need to conduct lab session on campus within a certain time limit (2 hours). It is difficult to replicate the same lab without wasting time on initial setup. After the lab, the students have to leave the room to make way for another class. Therefore, if they have not finished their exercises, they will need to wait for the next available timeslot to continue with their lab session. Also, time is wasted in reconfiguring the network equipment to the former network topology.

On the other hand, simulation software is less expensive and easy to upgrade. They are flexible and there is no need to purchase new network equipment regularly. Students can conduct network labs both on campus and off campus (or even on the move with mobile computing). Some labs (such as the one shown in Figure 1) which are impossible to complete in reality due to the demand of a large setup of networking equipment become possible with network simulation programs.

## NETWORK SIMULATION TOOLS FOR TEACHING

In our research (Zhu & Schaefer, 2009) we investigate the use of a network simulation package, namely Packet Tracer™, developed and distributed by the Cisco Learning Institute, as an alternative to help students learn the relevant networking concepts in our Network Interfaces module and gain practical experience in learning Cisco CCNA integrated computer networking. The

module Network Interfaces focuses on advanced IP addressing techniques such as Variable Length Subnet Masking (VLSM), intermediate routing protocols such as RIPv2, single-area OSPF, and EIGRP, command-line interface configuration of switches, Ethernet switching, Virtual LANs (VLANs), Spanning Tree Protocol (STP), and VLAN Trunking Protocol (VTP). The module is delivered through a combination of lectures, tutorials and laboratories. Our aim is to find out whether network simulation programs can replace laboratories based on physical equipment. To this extent, we have designed a questionnaire for the students on the course, which was followed up by research through interview and observation.

## Questionnaire Design and Results

Questionnaires were designed to judge the effectiveness of network simulation tools as perceived by students and were given to the students on the module. 19 students (17 males and two females)

*Figure 1. Sample screen shot of a simulated lab*

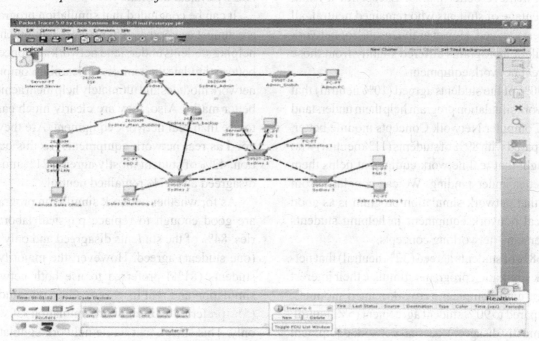

aged between 18 and 45 (mean age: 23) attended and completed the questionnaire.

58% of the students consider Network Interfaces as a technical module for which it is hard to understand the underlying concepts. Only 5 percent (one student who had previous experience in computer networks) disagreed. This is not surprising, as without previous exposure to networking concepts, many of the study areas are indeed very technical by design so as to prepare the students for more advanced material later on in the course. All students agree that hands-on experience is important in helping them to understand computer network related modules. This agrees with other literature (Sarkar, 2006; Goldstein, et al., 2005; Javidi & Sheybani, 2008) in the field. 74% of the students have not used network simulation program before they came to study at the University of Derby.

Another question aimed to demonstrate whether students perceive network simulation program and real network equipment as useful tools to stimulate their interest in learning computer networking related modules, help them understand computer network concepts and help them achieve better marks. Except for a small percentage of students who remained neutral, all students agreed. However the results for network simulation programs differed slightly from those for real network equipment.

90% of the students agreed (10% neutral) that network simulation program help them understand the Computer Network Concepts module better, compared with 89% of students (11% neutral) who thought that real network equipment helps them to better understanding. We can conclude from this that network simulation program is as good as real network equipment in helping students understand networking concepts.

68% of students agreed (32% neutral) that network simulation programs stimulate their interest in learning computer network related modules, compared to 90% student agreement (5% neutral, 5% mostly disagree) that real network equipment

stimulates their interest. We can conclude that real network equipment can stimulate more students' interest in learning networking related modules.

78% of students agreed (22% neutral) that network simulation programs help them achieve better marks. In contrast, 84% of students agreed (16% neutral) that real network equipment helps them achieve better mark. These results are hence very similar. It should be noted that it was reported in (Javidi & Sheybani, 2008) that students learning with the help of simulation programs achieved higher marks than those who learnt with the help of physical laboratories.

This confirms that network simulators are indeed very useful and also of sufficient functionality to simulate real hardware. How easy is it to learn to use network simulation program? 68% of the students consider Packet Tracer easy to learn, while 32% of the students consider it intermediate and none consider it is hard. 100% of students consider it is harder to do practicals using real network equipment. This might help explain the question posted in study (Javidi & Sheybani, 2008) why students using simulation program achieved higher scores than students using physical laboratory.

It can be concluded that simulation programs are almost as good as real network equipment in helping students understand networking concepts better, stimulate their interest in learning computer network modules and ultimately help them achieve better marks. Also, they are clearly much easier to use than real network equipment. Are they as good as real network equipment? To this question, 42% of student mostly agreed, 21% mostly disagreed and 37% remained neutral.

As for whether network simulation programs are good enough to replace physical laboratories, 84% of the students disagreed and only 5% (one student) agreed. However, the majority of students (81%) preferred to use both network simulation and real hardware. Only one student (5%) preferred to use network simulation software only. This shows that while network simulation programs are indeed very useful, they cannot replace training on real networking equipment. Almost all students state that simulators should not completely replace physical laboratories. This is the case although all students agree that network physical laboratories are much harder than those based on network simulation software.

## Interviews, Observation, and Further Results

As the results of the questionnaire have shown, network simulation software can play an effective role in helping students understand networking concepts. It also stimulates their interest in the subject, which is also observed during the actual laboratory sessions.

We have also conducted follow-up interviews with several of the students to gain some more insights into the results obtained through the questionnaire. In particular, we were interested in finding out how students perceive laboratories based on network simulators compared to those based on real networking equipment. Sample interview questions were:

- Why do you think it is harder to do practicals with physical laboratory than with network simulation program?
- Why don't you think that network simulation programs can replace physical laboratories?

As the questionnaire has shown, students prefer to have both types of experience and do not want to lose physical laboratories. During the interviews we learnt that students like the use of simulators while physical laboratories, though very important, are much harder to do. During the laboratory, students can experience all kinds of problems. 90% of these problems are physical, such as faulty cables, wrong type of cable, or due to the configuration of the clock rate on the wrong router. Time wasted on troubleshoot-

ing such problems varied from 10 minutes to 30 minutes and hence meant that often the students were unable to finish their assigned exercises. Such problems were much reduced when using network simulators and students were hence able to focus on the task at hand and make more efficient use of their laboratory time.

Following our observations we have decided, over the last three years, to reduce the use of physical laboratories while at the same time increasing the use of network simulators. While in 2006/07 only 10% of laboratory time was spend on network simulation tools and 90% on real equipment, this changed to 60%-40% in 2007/08, while in 2008/09 students spent 90% of their lab time using network simulation program and only 10% using real network equipment. Students who were prompted stated that they felt that the laboratory time now is spent much more effectively. At the same time, we are happy to confirm that the marks achieved by students during those three years show no significant deviation, i.e. that those students that use network simulation programs most of the time perform as well as those that were trained almost exclusively on real network equipment which further confirms the usefulness of network simulation programs in learning and teaching. In addition, after using network simulation programs, the number of questions that were related to network troubleshooting was reduced significantly.

## E-ASSESSMENTS FOR TEACHING

The majority of our lab sessions consist of step-by-step instructions for the students to follow. Inevitably, students make various mistakes such as missing commands, allocating wrong IP addresses, etc. without realising this until the end of the session. Several students may need assistance simultaneously and it is therefore difficult if not impossible for one lecturer to give timely individual feedback, especially when many students finish at approximately the same time. Due to the time constraints of lab sessions and the number of students, some students may not be able to get the help they need in time to continue and finish their lab session. This in turn adds to students' frustration and affects students' performance and satisfaction. In some further research (Zhu & Schaefer 2010), we therefore set out to improve this situation by using interactive, electronically assessed lab sessions for teaching our stage 2 LAN Switching and Wireless module. The module focuses on LAN design, basic switch concepts and configuration, Virtual LANs (VLANs), VLAN Trunking Protocol (VTP), Spanning Tree Protocol (STP), Inter-VLAN routing and basic wireless concepts and configuration. The module is delivered through a combination of lectures, tutorials and laboratories.

In this context, we investigated the use of Packet Tracer's e-assessment capabilities, namely Packet Tracer Activity, as an alternative to help students understand the material of the LAN Switching and Wireless module. Packet Tracer Activity consists of two parts as shown in Figures 2 to 4. The first part comprises the instructions,

which include the activity title, learning objectives, introduction and step-by-step instructions. At the bottom of the screen, the elapsed time and current percentage of exercise completion are displayed, so that students can check how long it takes them to finish an exercise, and to observe their progress through the exercise. If they want to know more details such as which parts of the exercise they haven't finish yet, they can click on the Check Results button, upon which the screen will change to the Activity Results screen as shown in Figure 3.

In the Activity Results screen, students can see the list of assessment items, status, points, components and feedback. On the top right corner of the screen shot, it lists the required items, completed items and total points. For the assessment items that the student has finished, a green tick is displayed next to it. Unfinished items are denoted by a red cross next to it. This simple feedback provides a clear indication of problem areas which the student should work on. A summary is also provided which lists the number of points achieved and the number of completed tasks. Students will thus get instant and interactive

*Figure 2. Packet tracer activity example exercise*

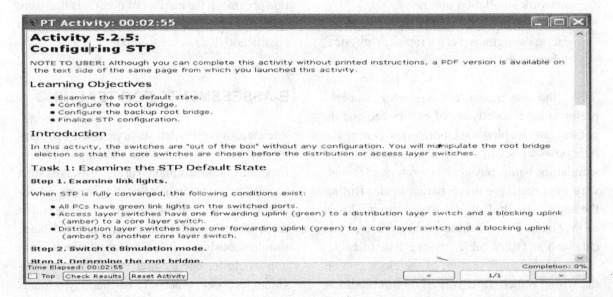

*Figure 3. Packet tracer activity results screen*

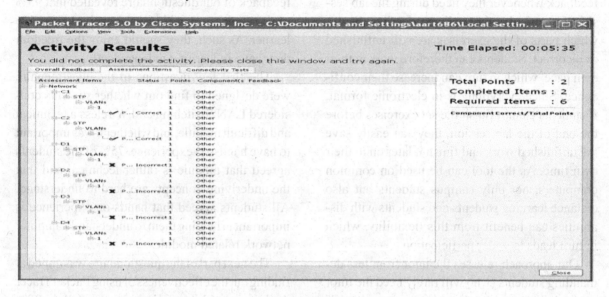

*Figure 4. Packet tracer activity sample network configuration*

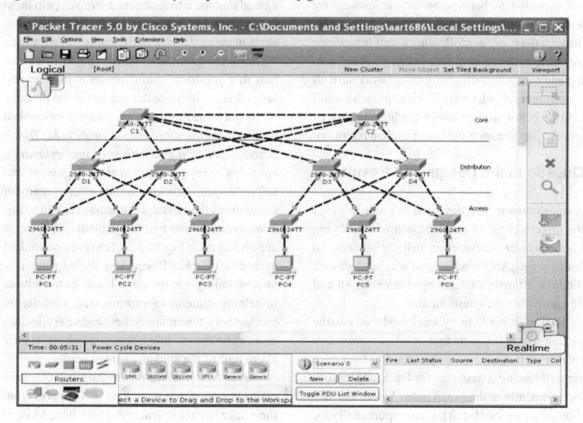

feedback whenever they need during the lab session. In particular, the feedback clearly indicates which parts of the exercises are still unfinished or incorrect. Students can therefore work at their own pace, which in turn can increase their confidence. Since everything is in electronic format, if students cannot finish the set exercises before the end of the lab session, they can easily save the unfinished work and finish it later on in their own time. As the tool can be used on common computers, not only campus students but also distance learning students and students with disabilities can benefit from this flexibility, which in turn leads to wider participation.

Our approach releases the tutor from less demanding students (who will rarely need the tutor to check their work), to be able to support weaker students better. Getting instant feedback, students are expected to become reflective learners by learning from their mistakes. They can proceed through the exercises following a simple process: implement the lab, check for errors, troubleshooting and continue configuring the network until all errors are resolved. Overall, this approach should lead to better student understanding, improved student performance and better student retention.

## Questionnaire Design and Results

A questionnaire was designed in order to judge the effectiveness of our approach of employing Packet Tracer Activities in helping students to learn for the LAN Switching and Wireless Network module. 20 male students aged between 18 and 35 completed the questionnaire.

Packet Tracer Activity was introduced into the module to encourage students to take a more active role in their study by troubleshooting their own errors through e-assessment feedback, and to work independently at their own pace. Active learners would be comfortable in taking responsibility for their own learning and setting their own pace, while passive learners would feel more uncomfortable by being forced into self-paced, active learning. The

feedback of our questionnaire revealed that 95% of the students considered themselves as active learner. As such, they should enjoy the freedom they have in learning independently.

The first few questions of the questionnaire were designed to find out whether students considered LAN Switching and Wireless a technical and difficult module, and whether it was important to have hands-on experience. 75% of the students agreed that module is rather technical and that the underlying concepts are hard to understand. All students agreed that hands-on experience is important in helping them to understand computer network related modules.

The next part of the questionnaire was aimed at finding out the effectiveness of using Packet Tracer Activity in teaching and learning the module. 90% of the students (the remaining 10% were neutral) agreed that the e-assessment exercises help them to better understand computer networking concepts in general and in particular to improve their understanding of the module. They also agreed that this approach stimulates their interest and helps them achieve better marks for the module.

To get some more insight, students were asked the following question: *Do you think Packet Tracer Activity will help you with your understanding, confidence, productivity, time management and self reflection?* Students could select as many of the items as they liked. 18 students replied to this question; the other two left it blank. The results are displayed in Figure 5. All except one student agreed that Packet Tracer Activity helps them in understanding. On the other hand, its usefulness in helping students to improve their confidence, productivity, time management and self reflection in learning the module is less convincing as only about half of the students agreed here.

90% of the students (the remaining 10% were neutral) agreed that they need less support from their tutor in Packet Tracer Activity labs. Most of them (61%) did not find it stressful to use the instant assessment feedback offered to help them to learn for the module. However, 11% of the

*Figure 5. Results of question designed to find out which aspects e-assessment exercises support and improve*

| Candidate | Understanding | Confidence | Productivity | Time management | Self reflection |
|---|---|---|---|---|---|
| 1 | √ | √ | √ | | √ |
| 2 | √ | | | | |
| 3 | | | | √ | |
| 4 | √ | | √ | √ | |
| 5 | √ | √ | √ | √ | |
| 6 | √ | √ | √ | | |
| 7 | √ | | | √ | |
| 8 | √ | √ | | | |
| 9 | √ | √ | √ | √ | √ |
| 10 | √ | | | | |
| 11 | √ | | | √ | |
| 12 | √ | | | √ | |
| 13 | √ | √ | | | √ |
| 14 | √ | | √ | | |
| 15 | √ | √ | √ | √ | √ |
| 16 | √ | | √ | √ | √ |
| 17 | √ | | | | √ |
| 18 | √ | √ | √ | | √ |
| Total agreed | 17 | 8 | 9 | 9 | 7 |

students found it stressful and the remaining 28% were neutral. According to students' feedback, one of the main causes of stress is that the automatically calculated percentage completion does not reflect the actual completion rate. For example, some steps may not be taken into account when calculating the completion rate, while trivial mistakes (such as typing in a switch name in lower case) may cause the loss of 5% total completion marks.

75% of the students agreed that it was easy to learn using Packet Tracer Activity. 85% (the remaining 15% were neutral) considered that it was harder to implement practicals using real network equipment as compared to using Packet Tracer Activity. However, 85% of the students (the remaining 15% were neutral) disagreed that Packet Tracer Activity could replace actual real network equipment-based labs, which confirms what we found in our earlier research (Zhu & Schaefer, 2009). The majority of students (80%) therefore preferred to use both Packet Tracer Activity and real network equipment, while the remaining 20% preferred to use real network equipment only. Some of the reasons students gave were:

- *"PT is just a virtual environment. You need to physically do it to understand the equipment. Select what cable you need rather than selecting cable virtually on packet tracer."*

- *"You need real experience with network equipment. Because it cannot be 100% accurate to real life situations. You need to see it happening in real time."*

- *"You need to do both to keep interested, you need both to achieve the highest grade."*

- *"Physical lab has a lot more real world application. You need to see/use physical equipment to see how it is implemented. Things often work slightly differently on the real equipment"*

Students found that Packet Tracer is a helpful tool in creating scenarios of real life examples, without the hassle of using real network equipment. It is flexible and can be used independently of location and time constrains. At the same time, it helps to test students' knowledge and provides them with an instant completion score. Therefore, it helps students to identify errors and missing tasks, and students thus learn from their own mistakes. However, it is not very suitable for passive learners. Also, one student noted that *"it is boring to use PT, it is just sitting down, clicking mouse and reading text instructions."*

## CONCLUSION

In our study we set out to investigate the usefulness of network simulation programs for teaching computer networking concepts and obtaining hands-on experience in network configuration. We have shown that students perceive network simulators indeed as a valuable learning tool, which helps them to focus on the tasks at hand and helps them to make more efficient use of their laboratory time. While a simulation can never replace experience with real networking equipment, it is of certain benefit to all parties involved, i.e. to students who gain more experience in their courses, to lecturers who can better focus on the actual aims of the laboratory sessions, and to the department which will appreciate the reduced costs involved.

Packet Tracer Activity is an interactive, electronically assessed lab session tool, which we employ for supporting computer networks modules. It provides students with immediate and interactive feedback whenever they need it, and helps them to keep track of their progress and mistakes. By doing so, it encourages students to learn independently, effectively and in a self-reflective manner. At the same time, it allows teaching staff to focus on weaker students who need more help during lab sessions. Due to the virtual environment employed, students can work anywhere, anytime and at their own pace. This benefits not only students on campus but also distance learning students and students with disabilities, and provides a more flexible, encouraging, interactive and interesting way for students to learn.

While our courses and hence the tools employed in our studies are based on Cisco material and software, there exist of course other network simulation tools with similar functionality like OPNET or ns-2. The conclusions drawn in this chapter should certainly not be considered as being Cisco specific and should be applicable to other, similar, network simulation software.

## REFERENCES

Dixon, M. W., Mcgill, T. J., & Karisooon, J. M. (1997). Using a network simulation package to teach the client-server model. In *Proceedings of the 2nd Conference on Integrating Technology into Computer Science Education,* (pp. 71-73). IEEE Press.

Goldstein, G. M., Leisten, S., Stark, K., & Tickle, A. (2005). Using a network simulation tool to engage students in active learning enhances their understanding of complex data communications concepts. In *Proceedings of the 7th Australasian Conference on Computing Education,* (pp. 223-228). IEEE Press.

Javidi, G., & Sheybani, E. (2008). Content-based computer simulation of a networking course: An assessment. *Journal of Computers, 3*(3), 64–72. doi:10.4304/jcp.3.3.64-72

Sarkar, N. I. (2006). Teaching TCP/IP networking using practical laboratory exercises. *International Journal of Information and Communication Technology Education, 2*(4), 39–50. doi:10.4018/jicte.2006100104

Zhu, S. Y., & Schaefer, G. (2009). Using network simulation tools to support teaching in computer networks. In *Proceedings of the International Conference on Education and New Learning Technologies*. IEEE Press.

Zhu, S. Y., & Schaefer, G. (2010). E-assessments to support teaching computer networks - A case study. In *Proceedings of the International Conference on e-Commerce, e-Administration, e-Society, e-Education, and e-Technology*. IEEE Press.

## KEY TERMS AND DEFINITIONS

**CCNA (Cisco Certified Network Associate):** Is a popular networking certification programme developed by Cisco Systems.

**Computer Network:** Is a collection of electronic devices connected together to share resources and information.

**E-Assessment:** Is assessment related activity performed in electronic form.

**E-Learning:** Is the use of a range of electronic technologies such as Internet, multimedia, simulation programs to support people to learn independently at their own pace at anytime and anywhere.

**LAN (Local Area Network):** Is a network in small area such as in a room, an office building or within a campus.

**Network Simulation Program:** Is a software program that simulates the behaviour of computer networks such as the interaction between different network entities (routers, switches, hubs, servers, etc.) under different network conditions. It can be used, among others, to monitor network behaviour, analyse network performance and facilitate visual analysis of trends.

**Network Topology:** Refers to either the physical or logical layout of a network environment.

**Packet Tracer:** Is a network simulation program developed and distributed by Cisco Learning Institute to help people that participate in the Cisco Academic Program to learn various Cisco academic courses.

**WAN (Wide Area Network):** Is a computer network that spans a large geographic area such as a county or country.

# Chapter 24

# Wire and Wireless Local Area Networks Simulation:
## OPNET Tutorial

**Ali Maqousi**
*Petra University, Jordan*

**Tatiana Balikhina**
*Petra University, Jordan*

## ABSTRACT

*There has been a tremendous increase in the use of wire/wireless Local Area Networks (LAN) with different network configurations. Therefore, it is vital to have an accurate and a reliable generic platform to enable network developers, managers, security mangers, researchers, and students evaluating and investigating the performance of LANs of different technologies and configurations. Many network simulators have been developed throughout the years, such as: the Optimized Network Engineering Tool (OPNET), the Network Simulator (NS), the Global Mobile Simulator (GloMoSim), etc. One of the most widely-used and powerful general-purpose network simulators is OPNET, which is an object-oriented simulation environment. This chapter provides two walk through tutorials on using OPNET IT Guru (Academic Edition of OPNET) for wire/wireless LANs simulations. These tutorials demonstrate in step-by-step fashion, the procedures of initiating new simulation, setting up the simulation parameters, running the simulation, and viewing the results. The first tutorial (Tutorial #1) simulates a wired LAN of 10 computers and one server connected to a single switch, and the second tutorial (Tutorial #2) simulates a wireless ad hoc network of 10 mobile nodes and one server. This chapter demonstrates that OPNET IT Guru is a powerful tool that can be used by a range of professional users to simulate, evaluate, and investigate the performance of wire and wireless LANs. Moreover, it encourages and helps students to easily perform network simulation for better understanding of the network performance under different network conditions.*

DOI: 10.4018/978-1-4666-0191-8.ch024

# INTRODUCTION

There has been an impressive advancement in computer networks' and Internet architecture, technologies, and protocols. Furthermore, it can be easily noticed that there has been an exponential growth in the use of Local Area Networks (LANs) that utilizes different communication technologies (wire and wireless), and also different network configurations. One enabling technology for such advancement and growth is the tremendous development in computer simulation methodologies and tools. Simulation tools enable and encourage network researchers and developers to easily and cost-effectively simulate, evaluate, and investigate the performance of LANs of different technologies and configurations to look for the most efficient, reliable, and cost-effective design.

Network developers use simulation and performance evaluation as an integral component of the development effort. The developers rely on the simulation model to provide guidance in choosing among alternative design choices, to detect bottlenecks in network performance, or to support cost-effective analyses. As part of this process, the developers may use the simulation output to modify the network abstraction, model, and implementation as opposed to the system itself, in order to include detail that may have not been considered in the previous abstraction, or to modify the network model or the implementation, for example to collect additional or alternative types of data (Sinclair, 2004; Law & Kelton, 2000).

The application of computer simulation can potentially improve the quality and effectiveness of the network model. In general, modeling and simulation can be considered as a decision support tool in deciding the optimum technology, design, and configuration of computer network. It provides us with a more economical and safer option in order to learn from potential mistakes - that is to say, it can reduce cost, risk, and improve the understanding of the real life networks that are being investigated. It also can be used to investigate and analyze the performance of the network model under extreme working environment.

Network simulation translates some aspects of the physical world into a mathematical model (description) followed by regenerating that model on a computer – which can be used instead of performing an actual physical task. For instance, simulations are widely used to evaluate the performance of routing protocols in wireless ad hoc networks characterized by presence of noise and high node mobility (Al-Bahadili & Kaabneh, 2010), measure packet delay in data networks (Fusk, et al., 2003), simulate TCP/IP applications (Ahmed & Shahriari, 2001). In addition, computer modeling and simulation can be used as a computer network learning tool (Asgarkhani, 2002).

It is generally unfeasible to implement computer networks algorithms before valid tests are being performed to evaluate their performance. It is clear that testing such implementations with real hardware is quite hard, in terms of the manpower, time, and resources required to validate the algorithm, and measure its characteristics in desired realistic environments. External conditions also can affect the measured performance characteristics. The preferred alternative is to model these algorithms in a detailed simulator and then perform various scenarios to measure their performance for various patterns of realistic computer networks environments (e.g., connection media, node densities, node mobility, radio transmission range, transmission environment, size of traffic, etc.).

Many network simulators have been developed throughout the years, such as: the Optimized Network Engineering Tool (OPNET) (OPNET Technologies, 2008), the Network Simulator (NS) (Fall & Varadhan, 2008), the global mobile simulator (GloMoSim) (GloMoSim, 2010; Nuevo, 2004), etc. One of the most widely–used and powerful general-purpose network simulators is OPNET, which is an object-oriented simulation environment. This chapter is concerned with OPNET, in particular, it concerns with the academic edition of OPNET modeler, namely, OPNET IT Guru.

This chapter provides two walk through tutorials on using OPNET IT Guru for wire and wireless LANs simulations. These tutorials demonstrate in step-by-step fashion, the procedures of initiating new simulation, setting up the simulation parameters, running the simulation, and viewing the results. The first tutorial (Tutorial #1) simulates a wired LAN of 10 computers and one server connected to a single switch, and the second tutorial (Tutorial #2) simulates a wireless ad hoc network of 10 mobile nodes and one server. The structure and contents of these tutorials are prepared in a simple and clear way. This is done in order to make it easy to be read and practiced by a range of users (developers, researchers, professionals, network managers, academics, students). The chapter also aims to introduce OPNET IT Guru network simulation software, provide understandable and easy to use OPNET document, provide users with hands on material to practice some theoretical networking concepts, encourage users to analyze statistics gathered from the simulation runs, and encourage users to write reports on the results gained from the simulation runs.

This chapter ends with a conclusion that OPNET IT Guru is a powerful tool that can be used by a range of professional users to simulate, evaluate, and investigate the performance of wire and wireless LANs. Moreover, it encourages and helps students to easily perform network simulation for better understanding to the network performance under different network conditions.

## BACKGROUND: NETWORK SIMULATORS

There are a number of computer network simulators that have been developed throughout the years to support computer networks analysis and design. Some of them are of general-purpose use and other dedicated to simulate particular types of computer networks. A typical network simulator can provide the programmer with the abstraction of multiple threads of control and inter-thread communication. Functions and protocols are described either by finite-state machine, native programming code, or a combination of the two. A simulator typically comes with a set of predefined modules and user-friendly GUI. Some network simulators even provide extensive support for visualization and animation (Chang, 1999). Examples of network simulators include (Al-Bahadili, 2010):

- *REAL* is a network simulator that has been developed for studying the dynamic behavior of flow and congestion control schemes in packet switch data networks. Network topology, protocols, data and control parameters are represented by scenarios, which are described using Net Language, a simple ASCII representation of the network. About 30 modules are provided which can exactly emulate the actions of several well-known flow control protocols.

- *INSANE* is a network simulator designed to test various IP-over-ATM algorithms with realistic traffic loads derived from empirical traffic measurements. Its ATM protocol stack provides real-time guarantees to ATM virtual circuits by using Rate Controlled Static Priority (RCSP) queuing. A protocol similar to the Real-Time Channel Administration Protocol (RCAP) is implemented for ATM signaling. A TK-based graphical simulation monitor can provide an easy way to check the progress of multiple running simulation processes.

- *NetSim* is intended to offer a very detailed simulation of Ethernet, including realistic modeling of signal propagation, the effect of the relative positions of stations on events on the network, the collision detection and handling process and the transmission deferral mechanism. But it cannot be extended to address modern networks.

- *Maisie* is a C-based language for hierarchical simulation, or more specifically, a language for parallel discrete-event simulation. A logical process is used to model one or more physical processes; the events in the physical system are modeled by message exchanges among the corresponding logical processes in the model.
- *Network Simulator (NS)* is a discrete event simulator targeted at networking research. It has a version NS-2 and new release called NS-4. It provides substantial support for simulation of TCP, routing, and multicast protocols over wired and wireless (local and satellite) networks. It runs under a variety of platforms, such as UNIX, LUNIX, and Microsoft Windows. The simulator is written in C++, it uses OTCL (Object-orientated of Tool Command Language) as a command and configuration interface.
- *CNET* is network simulator that enables experimentation with various data link layer, network layer, routing and transport layer protocols, and with various network configurations. It runs under a variety of UNIX and LUNIX platforms and it does not run on Windows. CNET requires network protocols to be written in C programming language. CNET uses TCL and it provides a graphical representation of the network.
- *Global Mobile Information System Simulator (GloMoSim)* is a scalable simulation environment for large wireless and wireline communication networks. It uses the Parsec compiler (Parsec is a C-based simulation language) to compile the simulation protocols. GloMoSim has a visualization tool that is platform independent because it is coded in Java. To initialize the visualization tool, we must execute from the *java gui* directory. This tool al-

lows to debug and verify models and scenarios; stop, resume and step execution; show packet transmissions, show mobility groups in different colors and show statistics.
- *OPNET IT Guru Academic Edition (OPNET)* is a powerful simulation tool with wide variety of possibilities to simulate computer and mobile networks using various protocols. It was created by OPNET Technologies, Inc for introductory level networking courses and designed to be used with popular classroom lab manuals. OPNET is quite expensive for commercial use and fortunately, OPNET IT Guru Academic Edition is a free license for educational purposes. University students may obtain a free license from OPNET website (www.opnet.com) to use the product. OPNET IT Guru allows to design and study communication networks, devices, protocols, and applications. It is a high level event based network level simulation tool. It has a huge library of OPNET specific functions written in C/C++ code. Users may add their own code in C/C++. OPNET application areas include: network planning and analysis of performance and problems prior to actual implementation, wireless and satellite schemes and protocols, protocol development and management, and routing algorithm evaluation for routers.

In this work, we concern with OPNET IT Guru Academic Edition, therefore, in the next section, we provide an introduction to the software, and how it can be obtained, installed, and how to obtain a license for using the software. Then using illustrations we describe the process of installing the software. Finally, we provide description to the main parts of the software.

## OPNET IT GURU ACADEMIC EDITION

OPNET IT Guru Academic Edition is a free license software tool; however, each user is required to have a renewable 6-month license to use this product. In this section, we present the process of obtaining the license and the software, we also present the steps to install the software, and finally, we describe the main parts of the software.

### Software License and Installation

A user should register and create an account on the company's website (http://www.opnet.com/university_program/itguru_academic_edition/) to be able to download the software. Then a user can login to OPNET IT Guru Academic Edition home page to download the software and to learn the system requirements. Having the software (ITG_Academic_Edition_vXXXX.exe, where XXXX is the year of the freely offered version), user may install it on his/her PC and at the end of the installation, the user will be asked to get a license for the software as shown in Figure 1.

In order to get a license for the software, click on License Management, then through a number of screens belongs to Perform License Transaction window do the following: first, you will get a License Request Code (12-digit), copy it to clip-

*Figure 1. OPNET IT Guru screen after completion of installation asking for license management*

board and then submit it to IT Guru License Activation Confirmation page, then you will receive an License Approval Code (24-digit), again copy it and paste it at the License Transaction window and click Next. Then you will get a message that indicates the completion of the activation of the code (your license has been activated) as shown in Figure 2. You, then, need to restart the application to use the license.

Now, after running OPNET IT Guru, the screen shown in Figure 3 will be displayed and the software is ready to use.

### The OPNET IT Guru Academic Edition

OPNET Modeler is the industry's leading network development software first introduced in 1986 by MIT graduate (OPNET Technologies, 2003; Hassan & Jain, 2003). OPNET allows to design and study communication networks, devices, protocols, and application. Modeler is used by the world's most prestigious technology organizations to accelerate the research and development (R&D) process. Some of the strategic users of OPNET include Pentagon, MIT, UIC, and many more.

OPNET's object-oriented modeling approach and Graphical User Interface (GUI) enable relatively easy means of developing models from the actual world network, hardware devices, and protocols. Modeler supports all major network types and technologies, allowing you to design and test various scenarios with reasonable certainty of the output results. The application areas of OPNET include:

- Network planning (both LAN and/or WAN) and analysis of performance and problems prior to actual implementation
- Wireless and Satellite communication schemes and protocols
- Microwave and Fiber-optic based Network Management
- Protocol Development and management

*Figure 2. OPNET IT Guru screen after license activation*

- Routing algorithm evaluation for routers, switches, and other connecting devices.

Some promiscuous features of features that make OPNET such a comprehensive tool are as follows:

- Hierarchical network models (The model can be nested within layers)
- Object oriented modeling (Model can be reference and used as logical extension of object concepts.)
- Multiple scenarios can be simulated concurrently and compared.
- The traffic patterns can be imported into the modeling software
- Ability to analyze using built-in graphing tools.

OPNET allows to model network topologies with nested sub-networking approach. This software allows nodes and protocols to be modeled as classes with all features of object oriented design It facilitates modeling the behavior of individual objects at the "Process Level" and interconnect them to form devices at the "Node Level" So that user can interconnect devices using links to form networks at the "Network Level." User also can organize multiple network scenarios into "Proj-

ects" to compare designs and aggregate traffic from LANs or "Cloud" nodes.

OPNET has highly efficient simulation engine and with user's ability to modify memory utilization during the simulation. Very granular simulation can be accomplished in relatively short amount of time. This, in part, is due to the complied nature of the model when it is executed. The OPNET model in its very core consists of C++ codes. These codes are complied and executed just like the C++ program. This enables very detailed control of the model by the user (if the user is proficient in C++).

## Model Construction

OPNET developed by OPNET Technologies Inc. (formerly called Mil3 Inc.). OPNET is a very popular tool used by many researchers and practitioners for TCP/IP simulation. OPNET built-in model libraries contain most popular TCP/IP protocols and applications, including

- Multiprotocol Label Switching (MPLS)
- IP Quality of Service (QoS)
- Resource Reservation Protocol (RSVP)

OPNET models a wide range of computer network equipment (e.g., routers, switches, links, etc.) manufactured by leading network equip-

*Figure 3. OPNET IT Guru starting screen*

ment vendors including (Cisco, Bay Networks (acquired by Nortel), and Fore Systems (acquired by Marconi). It can be run on either UNIX (e.g., Solaris, HP) or Windows NT/Windows 2000, also it supports concurrent users.

Modeling in OPNET is structured in three hierarchical levels, these are

- Network level modeling
- Node level modeling
- Process level modeling

The detailed operation of a given modeling level is hidden from its adjacent higher level, making it easier to use the tool at any level.

*Network level modeling* is the highest modeling level used to construct a network by interconnected network nodes. The interface for network-level modeling is activated by opening the Project Editor from OPNET's main menu. A network can be constructed by "dragging and dropping" objects from an object palette. For example, construction of an IP network by interconnecting two RSVP clients with their corresponding servers via two routers. Network models can also be created automatically by using the Rapid Configuration facility, which supports numerous network topologies, such as star, bus, mesh, and so on. In addition to the manual and automatic configuration of the network topology, the network model can also be constructed by importing network topology information collected from a real network.

*Node-level modeling* is used to model the internal architecture of a given network node by using node-level objects (transmitters, receivers, queues, etc.). Node modeling is used to model the internal structure of a network node (workstation, router, switch, etc.). A node model is composed of a number of modules, which are the fundamental "building blocks" of a node model. At node modeling level, each module models some aspect of the behavior of a network node (data transmission, data reception, routing, etc.). Node Editor is used

as a modeling tool, which are used to create and edit node models.

*Process-level modeling* is used to precisely describe the functional behavior of a given node-level object using Finite State Machines (FSM) and writing the necessary source codes to describe the states. There are five different types of modules, these are:

- Processor model which represents a generic process.
- Generator model which is used to model packet generation as specified by PDF and packet format.
- Queue models which is a queuing process and may consist of any number of sub queues.
- Transmitter which is used to model packet transmission.
- Receiver which is used to model packet reception.

Another type of node object is "streams" which are used to connect modules (e.g., generator, queue, transmitter/receiver modules, etc.). OPNET defines three different types of streams:

- Packet streams represent packet flow between two modules.
- Statistic streams (statistic wire) which do not carry data packets, they are used to convey statistics from module to module.
- Association streams which do not carry any information at all, they are used to logically associate a transmitter with a receiver to form a "transceiver." A transceiver is used to send packets to a link and receive packets from the link.

The Process Editor is used to create and edit process models at the process modeling level. OPNET graphically depicts a process in the form of Finite State Machine (FSM). An FSM consists of a number of states and transition between them.

A process is represented by a collection of states, transitions, and the conditions that control the transition between the states. States are mutually exclusive, which means that a process can be in only one state at any given time. Actions taken in s state are called executives in OPNET terminology. Executives of a state are split into two parts:

- Enter executives which are executed when a process enter a state. Executives can be composed in an editing pad.
- Exit executives which are executed when the process leave the state.

## Parameter Setting

In OPNET, the parameters of an object are configured using the parameter editors. All configurable parameters are grouped in four parameter models, each having its own parameter editor:

- Link model is used to model the parameters (attributes) of link objects using a Link Editor. It specifies a particular type of communication link (e.g., PPP, bus, etc.). Attributes of a link model can be set in advance, promoted to the higher level, or hidden from the high-level models if necessary.
- Packet format model defines the structure of data packets, and can be created and edited using the Packet Editor. It specifies the format of packets (e.g., TCP, IP, ATM, etc.) that are generated by a generator module. Packet Editor allows users to specify the name, length, and data type of each field in a packet. A packet field can be edited in attributes dialog box by right clicking on the field.
- ICI model specifies the format of a data structure that is used to support interrupt-based communications between processes.

The ICI may contain a pointer to a packet, when there is packet stream interrupt at destination, the destination can extract the packet pointer from the ICI and pick up the packet. ICIs are used to exchange control information between protocol layers. ICI models are composed by the ICI Editor, which allows various ICI fields to be defined.

- Probability Density Function (PDF) model defines statistical distribution; in particular it defines the parameters of the traffic generators. PDF is usually used to specify the traffic profile, for example, the distribution of inter packet generation time, the distribution of packet length, and so on. PDF models can be created and edited by the PDF.

## Data Collection

In OPNET, advanced data collection is supported by the Probe Editor, which is activated by selecting Choose Statistics (Advanced) operation from the simulation pull-down menu. The Probe Editor is used to create probe objects the specify where to collect statistics and what statistics to be collected. A probe object also has a set of attributes that can be configured to specify the name of the probe, statistic, the precise location of data collection, and so on.

There are seven action buttons on the main menu bar of the Probe Editor. Each action button can be used to create a specific type of probe object on subnets, nodes, links, and modules. Probe objects created in the Probe Editor are saved in a profile file, which can be used as an attribute of a simulation object. There are a number of probe objects which can be created in the Probe Editor, such as: node statistic, link statistic, global statistic, simulation attribute, automatic animation, custom animation, and statistic animation.

## Simulation Execution

In OPNET, users can define their own simulation sequences and control the execution of simulation. A simulation sequences may consist of any number of simulation objects, each containing a set of configurable attributes. A simulation object may define one or more simulation runs, depending on the values of some application-specific attributes. A simulation sequence can saved in a file for later use.

The simulation tool in OPNET provides the following capabilities:

- Definition of simulation sequences
- Collection of both vector and scalar statistics
- Control of simulation execution

The Simulation Tool is activated by selecting Configure Simulation (advanced) from the Simulation pull-down menu.

Simulation can be classified whether they are single or multiple into:

- Single simulation. A simulation sequence that consists of one simulation object.
- Multiple simulations. A simulation sequence may consist of more than one simulation object. Each simulation object may contain different simulation attributes. Multiple values for an application-specific attribute result in multiple simulation runs. It is possible to specify more than one simulation object in a simulation sequence. Each simulation object may even have different set of attributes (e.g., different network models, probe files, durations, etc.). The simulation sequence can be executed unattended.

A simulation sequence can be executed as a shell command, which realized by the OPNET utility program (op_runsim). When running simulation in a shell, the only required argument is the name of the network model. Simulation sequences can also be defined via shell scripts (or batch files for Windows NT), just like other shell commands.

In OPNET, simulation can be run in the debugger mode supported by OPNET Debugger (ODB). ODB enables users to interactively control the simulation execution and track down modeling problems quickly and efficiently. Numerous ODB commands have been developed to allow users to set breakpoints, access state variables, modify object attributes, and so on.

## Presentation of Results

OPNET has built-in facilities for visual presentation of simulation results, it is known as Analysis Tool. The Analysis Tool in OPNET provides the capability to manipulate and present the simulation results graphically. Simulation results are saved in the output vector file or output scalar file during the simulation execution. Analysis Tool extracts data from vector/scalar files and displays them in the analysis panels. The Analysis Tool is usually used to process statistics specified in the probe objects created in the Probe Editor.

The Analysis Tool is activated by selecting the View Results (Advanced) operation from the Results pull-down menu. Action buttons on the menu bar in the Analysis Tool support operation to create vector panels and scalar panels, which are used to display vector statistics and scalar statistics, respectively. Other services provided by the Analysis Tool include:

- Apply numerical processing to statistics
- Edit trace color, style, and thickness, etc
- Make graph template
- Export data to spreadsheet

## SIMULATION WITH OPNET IT GURU

This section provides a walk through tutorials on performance modeling of two types of networks using OPNET IT Guru. The first tutorial (Tutorial #1) simulates a wire LAN uses the IEEE 802.3 protocol, and the second tutorial (Tutorial #2) simulates a wireless ad hoc network uses the IEEE 802.11 protocol. These tutorials cover how to create a new scenario, setting up simulation parameters, running simulations and getting simulation results.

### Tutorial #1: Simulation of a Wire LAN

This section provides a walk through tutorial on building a small LAN of 10 nodes using OPNET IT Guru. OPNET IT Guru has a Startup Wizard that can be used to create the project and its scenario. The following steps can be used to build this scenario and any other project/scenario on OPNET IT Guru.

### Step 1: Create a Project and a Scenario

From the main menu, select File, New, then select Project from the pull-down window and then click OK. You will be asked to enter the project and scenario names, type the names (you may use the software-supplied names (project1 and scenario1) and change them later to new names when you save the project. The "Startup Wizard: Initial Topology" window opens as shown in Figure 4, from this window select "Create Empty Scenario" and click on Next.

The "Startup Wizard: Choose Network Scale" opens and through the dialog windows selects: Network Scale (Office), Specify Size (100x100 m), and Select Technology (Sm_Int_Model_List)

*Figure 4. The "startup wizard: initial topology" window*

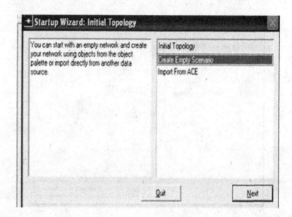

as shown in Figures 5, 6, and 7. Then "Startup Wizard: Review" window that shows a summary of selections is opened as shown in Figure 8. Click Next and a workplace with the object palette for the selected technologies will open.

The workplace is the area where the user can construct the project. The palette contains the technology model family of objects that has been selected by the user, in this scenario it is Sm_Int_Model_List as shown in Figure 9.

*Figure 5. The "startup wizard: choose network scale" window*

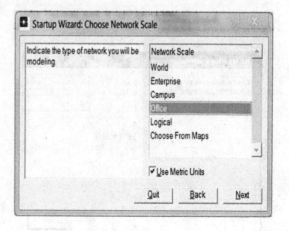

*Figure 6. The "startup wizard: specify size" window*

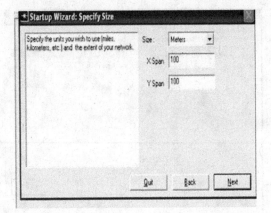

*Figure 7. The "startup wizard: select technologies" window*

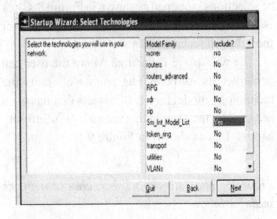

*Figure 8. The "startup wizard: review" window*

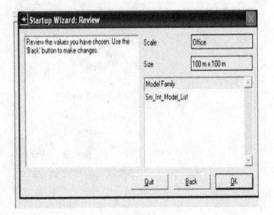

## Step 2: Build Network Topology Model

At the workplace user starts creating the network topology model, there are three ways to create the model:

- Import the topology
- Drag objects from the palette into the workplace
- Use rapid configuration

The first one is used when you have an existed network topology model and you want to use it again. The second way is preferable when you add single or few objects to the workplace. The third one is better to use when you create the model for the first time and in case you have a number of repeated objects configured in one of network listed topologies. This tutorial uses the third way (Rapid Configuration) to build the network model.

Rapid configuration allows user to create a network model by configuring the network topology (such as Bus, Ring, Star, Tree, etc...), the types of nodes and their numbers, types of connecting links, and finally model placement at the workplace. From the application's main menu select Topology and then click on Rapid Configuration. Figure 10 shows Rapid Configuration in use to create a star network that is consist of 10 workstations, switch as a central connecting node, 10BaseT links, and the placement of the network model. Figure 11 shows part of a network topology model in the workplace.

## Step 3: Adding Server

The object palette contains all technologies that have been added (selected) by the user at project's creating phase (Figure 12). A user can select, drag, and paste any of the objects located in the palette into the workplace. For example if we want to

*Figure 9. The workplace with object palette*

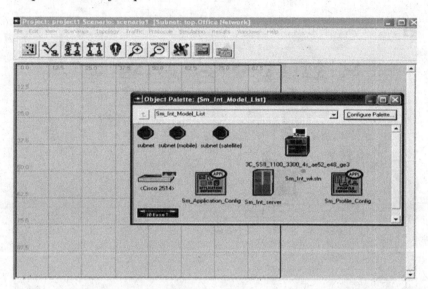

add a server to the network topology model, we select the server icon (Sm_Int_server), we drag it and paste it into the workplace, we do the same to add the link 10BaseT that connects the server to the central node the result is shown in Figure 13.

## Step 4: Adding Applications and User Profile to the Model

In order to use the created network model, a user needs to add two models: an application definition model and a traffic profile definition model. The application definition model is used to describe the application(s) on the network such as database, email, or web applications. The traffic profile definition describes which application(s) will be used by each client (workstation). For the purpose of this tutorial we need just to add them to the network model from the Object Palette (node 12 and node13) as we did previously with adding the server to the network model. The workplace now looks as in Figure 14. Now a network model of one server and 10 workstations connected via a 10BaseT cables is created. The Object Palette window can be closed.

## Step 5: Define Objects and Global Statistics

Statistics on individual object or node in the network (object statistics) or statistics for the entire network (global statistics) can be collected to build the baseline results. This baseline results can be used to compare statistics gathered from different scenarios of different configurations and parameters. To collect object statistics (e.g., the

*Figure 10. The "rapid configuration: star" window*

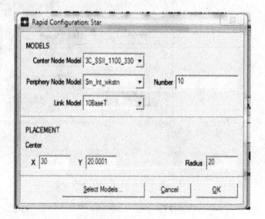

*Figure 11. The network topology model in the workplace*

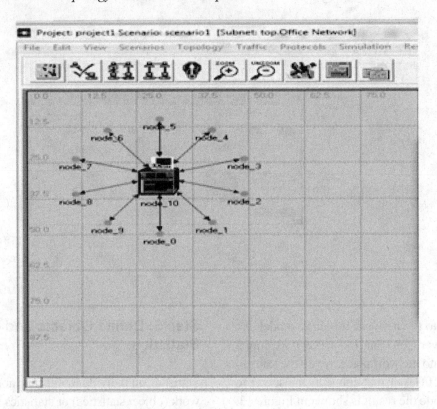

*Figure 12. The object palette: (Sm_Int_Model_List)*

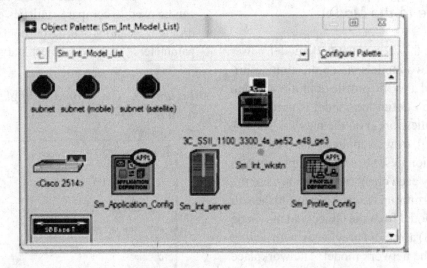

*Figure 13. The network topology model in the workplace after adding the Sm_Int_server*

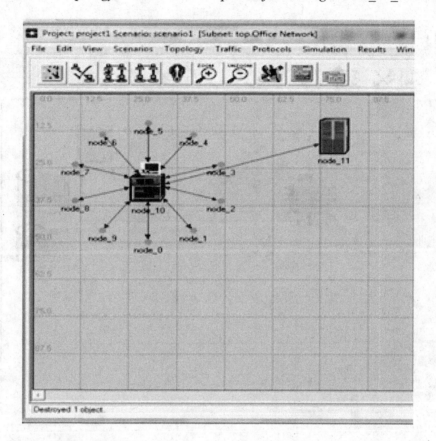

server load), user can right click on server node; a pull down menu will appear as shown in Figure 15. Select Choose Individual Statistics and click on it, a Choose Results window will appear (Figure 16). Expand the Ethernet option by clicking on plus box and select the Load (bits/sec). User may select more than one statistic.

To collect global statistics (e.g. Delay (sec)), user can right click anywhere in the workplace but not on any object, and then select Choose Individual Statistics, a Choose Results window will appear with three options: Global Statistics, Node Statistics, and Link Statistics. Expand Global Statistics and then expand Ethernet and select Delay (sec). Now it's time to save the scenario. To save the scenario, from the main menu select File then Save.

## Step 6: Running the Simulation

To run the simulation, from the main menu user can select Simulation then select Configure Discrete Event Simulation (or by clicking on Configure/ Run Icon from the Icons Bar). One of the main attributes of simulation run is the simulation's duration time which can be edited through the Configure Simulation window.

Figures 17 and 18 show the simulation in progress and after its completion respectively. Its worth noted that the simulation in progress takes time depending on the simulation duration time, and if the simulation completed successfully a Simulation Sequence window will provide a report about the starting time, ending time, and duration time, and number of events. The Simulation

*Figure 14. Snapshot of the complete network model*

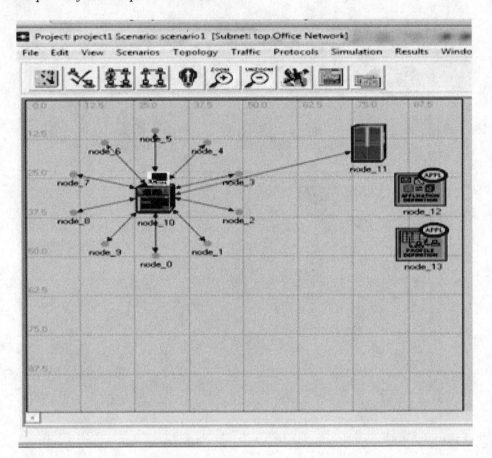

Sequence window will also report any errors in case of any failure.

## Step 7: Viewing Results

To view results of objects statistics user can select the object and right click, then select View Results, a View Results window will appear and user expands Ethernet and selects Load (bits/sec) (this is exactly the statistic(s) that has been previously selected by the user). Figure 19 shows the View Results window. A graph representation of the results is placed at the right side of the window (number of bits/sec over time). This graph representation can be changed into one of other

representations (Figure 20). Some of the most popular representations are Probability Density Function (PDF), cumulative distribution function (CDF), histogram (sample distribution) and average. As it seen in the Figure 19 the maximum load values for the server is below 1100 bits/sec.

To see the results of Global Statistics (Delay [sec]), user may right click on any place on the workplace and select View Results, then expand the Ethernet option and select Delay (this is again exactly the Global Statistics that has been selected previously by the user). Figure 21 shows the results and it is noted that the network delay is approximately 4 msec.

*Figure 15. Selecting the individual (object: server) statistics*

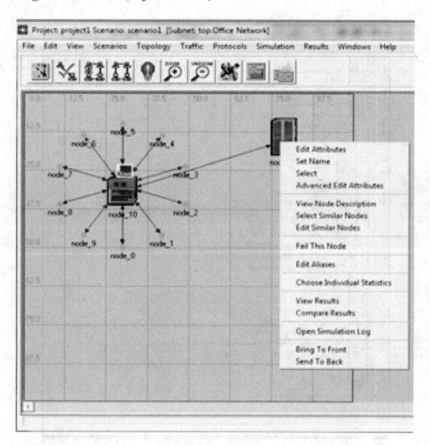

## Tutorial #2: Simulation of a Wireless Ad Hoc Network

This section provides a walk through tutorial on building a wireless ad hoc network of 10 wireless nodes using OPNET IT Guru. Nodes will be randomly distributed in a 100x100 m area.

### Step 1: Create a Project and a Scenario

This step is similar to Step 1 explained earlier, except from the "Startup Wizard: Select Technologies" window, select wireless_lan and wireless_lan_adv as shwown in Figure 22. The "Startup Wizard: Review" is shown in Figure 23. Click Next and a workplace with the object palette for the selected technologies will open.

### Step 2: Build Network Topology Model

At the workplace we can start creating the network topology model, in this tutorial as in Tutorial #1; we shall use the "Rapid Configuration" to construct the network topology model. From the "Rapid Configuration" window, select "Unconnected Nodes" as shown in Figure 24, and then press OK. The "Rapid Configuration: Unconnected" window will open. In this window specify the node model (wlan_wkstn_adv), type (mobile), and number (10) as shown in Figure 25, and then press OK to see the network topology model in the workplace in Figure 26. Because of WLAN modeling, there is no need to define a connection between the nodes.

*Figure 16. Choose results (load in bits/sec) window*

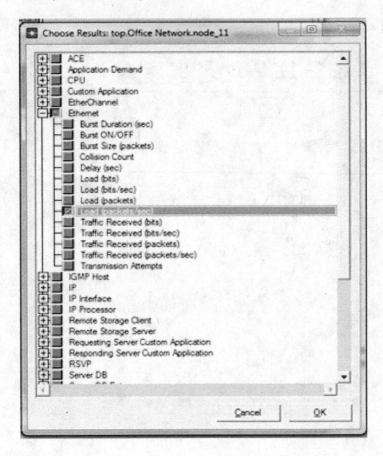

## Step 3: Adding Server

The object palette contains all technologies that have been added (selected) by the user at project's creating phase (Figure 27). A user can select, drag, and paste any of the objects located in the palette into the workplace. For example if we want to add a server to the network topology model, we select the server icon (e.g., wlan_server_adv (fix)), we drag it and drop it into the workplace as shown in Figure 28.

## Step 4: Adding Applications and User Profile to the Model

As described in Tutorial #1, in order to use the created network model, a user needs to add two models: an application definition model (Application Config) and a traffic profile definition model (Profile Config). The application definition model is used to describe the application(s) on the network such as database, email, or Web applications. The traffic profile definition describes which application(s) will be used by each client (node). These two models can be added as follows: Drag and drop them from the "Object Palette" window (Figure 27) to the workplace window (Figure 26). The workplace now looks as in Figure 28. Now a network model of one server and 10 mobile nodes connected via wireless links is created. The "Object Palette" window can be closed. One can easily assign custom name to each component on the workplace by right clicking on it and selecting the "Set Name" option from the context menu.

*Figure 17. The simulation in progress window*

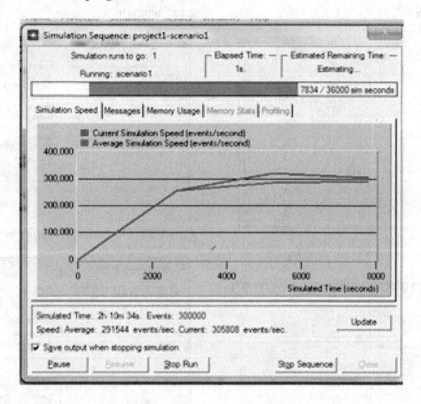

*Figure 18. The simulation after completion window*

*Figure 19. The results for the object statistics (load in bits/sec)*

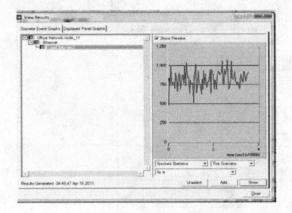

*Figure 20. Types of representations for the results*

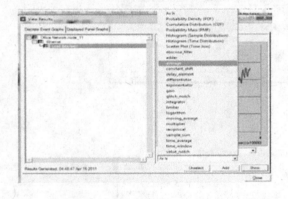

*Figure 21. The results for the global statistics (delay in sec)*

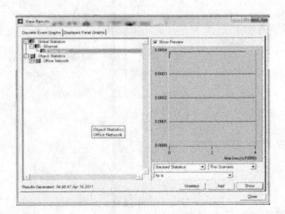

*Figure 22. The "startup wizard: select technologies" window*

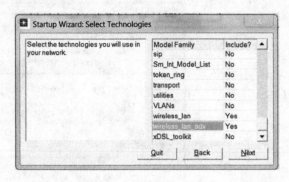

*Figure 23. The "startup wizard: review" window*

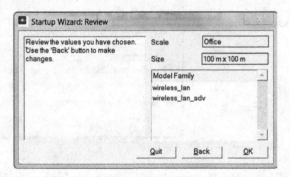

*Figure 24. The "rapid configuration" window*

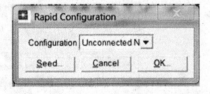

*Figure 25. The "rapid configuration: unconnected" window for tutorial #2*

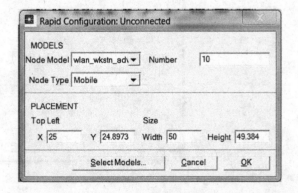

*Figure 26. The network topology model in the workplace for tutorial #2*

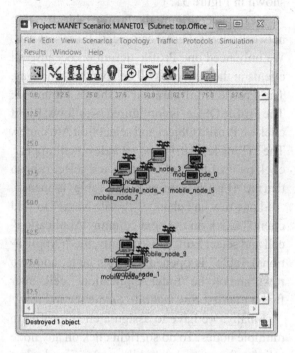

*Figure 27. The object palette*

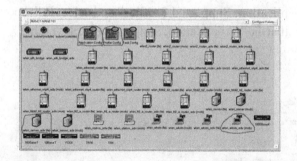

*Figure 28. The network topology model in the workplace after adding all components*

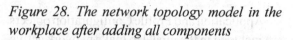
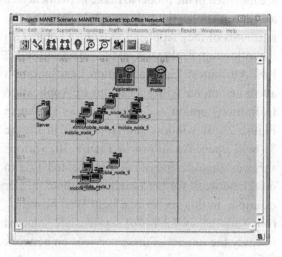

*Figure 29. Application attributes menu*

*Figure 30. Assigning a service behavior*

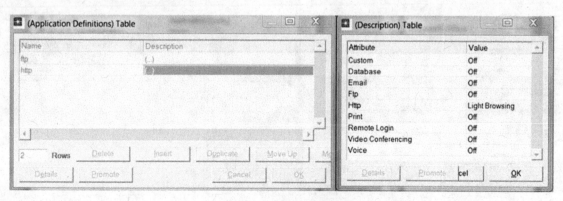

Application and Profile Configuration objects are included in the model to make network active and to run applications (Figure 28). To set up the attributes of the "Application Config" object do the following: Right click on the object and select Edit Attributes. The Application Configuration attributes menu will appear, go to Application Definitions option and select Edit as shown in Figure 29. A window similar to that in Figure 31 will open. As shown in Figure 30, various services (applications) can be selected to run on the network for performance evaluation. For example, in this scenario, a light Web browsing (http) and heavy load (ftp) services are selected to study the impact of these services on network performance. By creating two new rows in Application Definitions table and assigning them to ftp and http, we now have two network services available to the nodes.

We then need to set up Server attributes and assign services to the Server (Figure 31). This can be done as follows: Right click on the Server and select Edit Attributes. Click on "Application Supported Services" and select Edit. The Application: Support Services table will be opened. Create two

rows, one named ftp and the other one http as shown in Figure 31.

Next, we configure the Profile Object so that network users (clients) can access these services. We only need one Profile definition because all clients in the network will behave the same way. The Profile Configuration is shown Figure 32. The Profile Object is configured as follows: Right click on Profile Object and select Edit Attributes. The "(Profile) Attributes" window will appear, click on Profile Configuration and select Edit so that the "(Profile Configuration) Table" is opened. Add one row and change "Profile Name" to "std client." Click on the next column "Application" cell and select Edit, consequently, the "(Applications) Table" is opened. On this table, add two rows, and on the "Enter Applications" cell, enter ftp on the first row and http on the second row.

Finally, we have to assign a client profile to multiple nodes. To do so, right click on any node (client); for example "mobile_node_4" and select Edit Attributes. The "(mobile_node_4) Attributes" window is opened. Then click on the field "Application: Supported Profiles" and select Edit so that the "(Application: Supported Profiles) Table"

*Figure 31. Assigning services to the server*

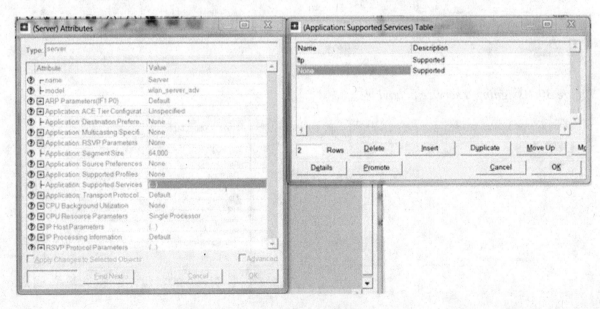

*Figure 32. Setting up client profile*

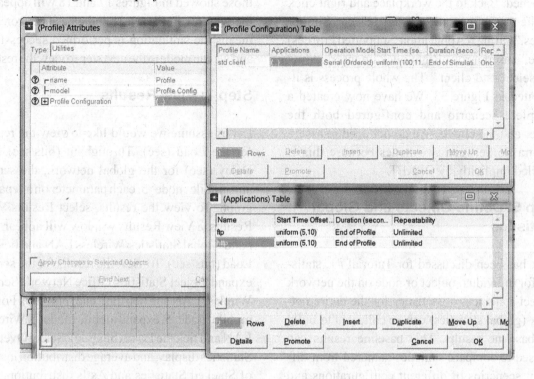

*Figure 33. Assigning a client profile to multiple nodes*

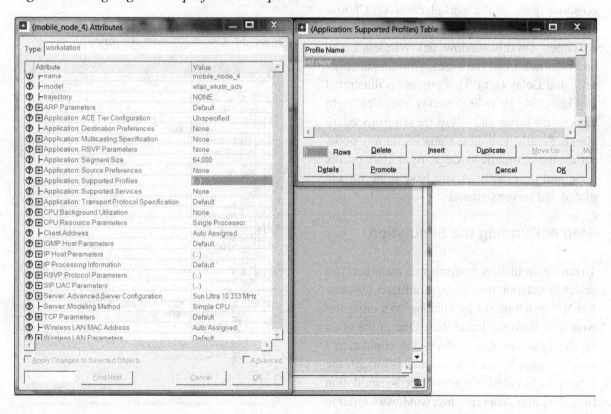

is opened. Back to the workplace and right click on the "mobile_node_4" and select "Similar Nodes." On the "(Application: Supported Profiles) Table," insert a row. Right click on inserted row and select "std client." The whole process is illustrated in Figure 33. We have now created a complete scenario and configured both the server and the clients. We do not need to assign any traffic between two nodes because this is handled implicitly by OPNET.

## Step 5: Define Objects and Global Statistics

As it has been discussed for Tutorial #1, statistics for individual object or node on the network (object statistics) or statistics for the entire network (global statistics) can be collected to build the baseline results. This baseline results can be used to compare statistics gathered from different scenarios of different configurations and parameters. To collect global statistics, right click on some space on the workplace, select Choose Individual Statistics, a Choose Results window will open. On this window, tick Wireless LAN, and then tick Load (bits/sec), Throughput (bits/sec), and Delay (sec). This process is illustrated in Figure 34. To collect Server statistics, right click on the server and follow the same procedure above. Finally, to collect statistics for any node, for example, mobile_node_5, right click on the node and do exactly as you have done for the global and server statistics.

## Step 6: Running the Simulation

To run the simulation, from the main menu user can select Simulation then select Configure Discrete Event Simulation (or by clicking on Configure/Run Icon from the Icons Bar). One of the main attributes of simulation run is the simulation's duration time which can be edited through the Configure Simulation window. Set the simulation time to 15 min. After running, windows similar to those showed in Figures 17 and 18 will appear, if the window in Figure 18 indicates no error, that means the simulation is performed successfully and we can mode to the next step to view the results.

## Step 7: View Results

Let us assume we would like to view the results for the Load (sec), Throughput (bits/sec), and Delay (sec) for the global network, the server, and mobile_node_5, each parameter on a separate graph. To view the results, select Results/View Results, a View Results window will appear. Expand Global Statistics/Wireless LAN and tick the Load (bits/sec). To view the results for the server, expand Object Statistics/Office Network/Server/Wireless LAN and tick the Load (bits/sec). For the mobile_node_5, expand mobile_node_5/Wireless LAN and tick the Load (bits/sec). Select Overlaid Statistics display, and average distribution instead of Stacked Statistics and As Is distribution. The load distribution against time will be displayed

*Figure 34. Choose results window*

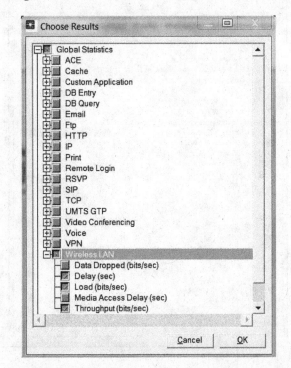

*Figure 35. The results of tutorial #2*

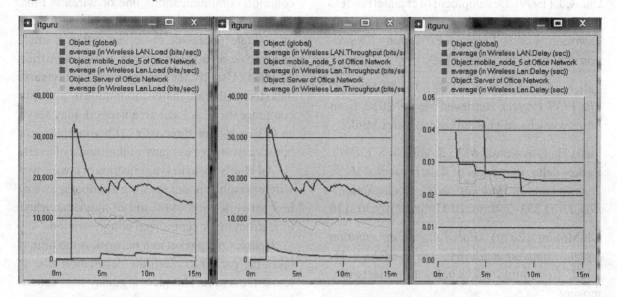

as in Figure 35a. Follow the same procedure to display the results for the Throughput (bits/sec) and Delay (sec). The results will be displayed as shown in Figure 35.

## CONCLUSION

This chapter provided two OPNET tutorials on modeling and simulation of wire and wireless LAN networks. The tutorials cover how to initiate a new network simulation model, create the scenarios, setting up simulation parameters, running the simulation, and viewing the results. The level of detailed simulation offered by OPNET IT Guru suggests that this particular simulator is suitable for performance modeling of both wire and wireless networks. The chapter stresses the importance of using a good simulator for performance modeling of wire and wireless networks. The simplicity in explaining theses two tutorials can be of great help for researchers, professionals, and students who are new to use OPNET. It can be considered a first step towards launching more complicated and realistic simulations.

## REFERENCES

Ahmed, Y., & Shahriari, S. (2001). *Simulation of TCP/IP applications on CDPD channel*. MSc Thesis. Stockholm, Sweden: Chalmers University of Technology.

Al-Bahadili, H. (2010). On the use of discrete-event simulation in computer networks analysis and design. In Abu-Taieh, E. M. O., & El-Sheikh, A. A. (Eds.), *Handbook of Research on Discrete-Event Simulation Environments: Technologies and Applications* (pp. 414–442). Hershey, PA: IGI Global. doi:10.4018/978-1-60566-774-4.ch019

Al-Bahadili, H., & Kaabneh, K. (2010). Analyzing the performance of probabilistic algorithm in noisy MANETs. *The International Journal of Wireless & Mobile Networks, 2*(3), 83–95.

Asgarkhani, M. (2002). *Computer modeling and simulation as a learning tool: A preliminary study of network simulation products*. Christchurch, New Zealand: Christchurch Polytechnic Institute of Technology (CPIT).

Chow, J. (1999). Development of channel models for simulation of wireless systems in OPNET. *Transaction of the Society for Computer Simulation International, 16*(3), 86–92.

Fall, K., & Varadhan, K. (2008). The NS manual. *The VINT Project*. Retrieved May 9, 2010, from http://www.isi.edu/nsnam/ns/doc/index.html.

Fusk, H., Lawniczak, A. T., & Volkov, S. (2001). Packet delay in models of data networks. *ACM Transactions on Modeling and Computer Simulation, 11*(3), 233–250. doi:10.1145/502109.502110

GloMoSim. (2010). *Global mobile information systems simulation library*. Retrieved June 15, 2010, from http://pcl.cs.ucla.edu/projects/glomosim/.

Hassan, M., & Jain, R. (2003). *High performance TCP/IP networking: Concepts, issues, and solutions*. Upper Saddle River, NJ: Prentice-Hall.

Law, A., & Kelton, W. D. (2000). *Simulation modeling and analysis* (3rd ed.). New York: McGraw-Hill Higher Education.

Nuevo, J. (2004). A comprehensible GloMoSim tutorial. *University of Quebec*. Retrieved June 15, 2010, from www.ccs.neu.edu/course/csg250/Glomosim/glomoman.pdf.

Sinclair, J. B. (2004). *Simulation of computer systems and computer networks: A process-oriented approach*. Houston, TX: Rice University.

Technologies, O. P. N. E. T. (2008). *OPNET*. Retrieved September 15, 2010, from www.opnet.com.

## KEY TERMS AND DEFINITIONS

**A Local Area Network (LAN):** Is a group of computers and associated devices that share a common communications line or wireless link. Typically, connected devices share the resources of a single processor or server within a small geographic area (for example, within an office building). Usually, the server has applications and data storage that are shared in common by multiple computer users. A local area network may serve as few as two or three users (for example, in a home network) or as many as thousands of users.

**Ad Hoc Network:** Is a collection of low-power wireless mobile nodes forming a temporary wireless network without the aid of any established infrastructure or centralized administration.

**Delay:** Of a packet in a network is the time it takes the packet to reach the destination after it leaves the source. The queueing delay at the source is not taken into account, since users interest is in the network delay. The average packet delay for a network with $n$ nodes, $D(n)$, is obtained by averaging over all packets, all source-destination pairs, and all random network configurations. In a fixed network, the delay equals the sum of the times spent at each relay. In a mobile network also, the delay is the sum of the times spent at each relay. However, in this case, delay depends on the velocity, $v(n)$, of each relay.

**Load or Network Load:** Is a term in data communication networks that is a common measure of data speed for transmission media or carrier in bits per second (abbreviated as bit/sec or bps). As the term implies, the speed in bps is equal to the number of bits transmitted or received each second.

**OPNET:** Is a discrete-event, object-oriented, general purpose network simulator (commercial simulation package).

**OPNET IT GURU:** Is an academic version of OPNET, which is available at no cost under OPNET academic program.

**Throughput:** or **Network Throughput:** Is a term in communication networks, such as Ethernet or packet radio, which represents the average rate of successful message delivery over a communication channel. This data may be delivered over a physical or logical link, or pass through a certain network node. The throughput is usually measured in bits per second (bit/sec or bps), and sometimes in data packets per second or data packets per time slot. The system throughput or aggregate throughput is the sum of the data rates that are delivered to all terminals in a network.

The throughput can be analyzed mathematically by means of queueing theory, where the load in packets per time unit is denoted arrival rate $\lambda$, and the throughput in packets per time unit is denoted departure rate $\mu$. Throughput is essentially synonymous to digital bandwidth consumption.

# Compilation of References

3GPP. (2008a). *3GPP technical specification services and system aspects: Evolved universal terrestrial radio access (E-UTRA) - Packet data convergence protocol (PDCP) specification: 3GPP TS 36.323 v8.2.1 (Release 8)*. Retrieved June 14, 2011, from ftp://ftp.3gpp.org/specs/2008-12/Rel-8/36_series/.

3GPP. (2008b). *3GPP technical specification services and system aspects: General packet radio services (GPRS) enhancements for evolved universal terrestrial radio access network (EUTRAN) specification: 3GPP TS 23.401 v8.2.0 (Release 8)*. Retrieved June 14, 2011 from ftp://ftp.3gpp.org/specs/2008-12/Rel-8/23_series/.

3GPP. (2010). *3GPP technical specification group radio access network: Evolved universal terrestrial radio access (E-UTRA) - Physical layer procedures: 3GPP TS 36.213 v9.3.0*. Retrieved June 14, 2011from ftp://ftp.3gpp.org/specs/2008-12/Rel-8/36_series/.

Ababneh, D. (2009). *Development of a discrete-time DRED-based multi-queue nodes network analytical model*. PhD Thesis. Amman, Jordan: The Arab Academy for Banking & Financial Sciences.

Ababneh, J., Thabtah, F., Abdel-Jaber, H., Hadi, W., & Badarneh, E. (2010). Derivation of three queue nodes discrete-time analytical model based on DRED algorithm. In *Proceedings of the 7th IEEE International Conference on Information Technology: New Generations (ITNG 2010)*, (pp. 885-890). Las-Vegas, NV: IEEE Press.

Ababneh, J., Thabtah, F., Abdel-Jaber, H., Hadi, W., & Badarneh, E. (2010). Discrete-time analytical model for evaluating the performance of three queue nodes based on dynamic RED algorithm. In *Proceedings International Journal Aviation Information Technology, Engineering and Management (IJATEM) Inauguration Conference*, (pp. 152-164). New Orleans, LA: IJATEM Press.

Abaii, M., Yajian, L., & Tafazolli, R. (2008). An efficient resource allocation strategy for future wireless cellular systems. *IEEE Transactions on Wireless Communications, 7*(8), 2940–2949. doi:10.1109/TWC.2008.060161

Abdelatif, M., Kalebaila, G., & Chan, H. (2007). A joint IEEE802.21 and cross layer model. *The International Journal of Computer and Telecommunications Networking, 51*(17), 4849–4866.

Abdel-Jaber, H., Woodward, M. E., Thabtah, F., & Etbega, M. (2007). A discrete-time queue analytical model based on dynamic random early drop. In *Proceedings of the 4th IEEE International Conference on Information Technology: New Generations (ITNG 2007)*, (pp. 71-76). Las Vegas, NV: IEEE Press.

Abdel-Jaber, H., Woodward, M. E., Thabtah, F., & Abu-Ali, A. (2008). Performance evaluation for DRED discrete-time queuing network analytical model. *Journal of Network and Computer Applications, 31*(4), 750–770. doi:10.1016/j.jnca.2007.09.003

Abdulai, J., Ould-Khaoua, M., & Mackenzie, L. (2007). Improving probabilistic route discovery in mobile ad hoc networks. In *Proceeding of the 32nd IEEE Conference on Local Computer Networks (LCN 2007)*, (pp. 739-746). Dublin, Ireland: IEEE Press.

Abdulai, J., Ould-Khaoua, M., Mackenzie, L., & Bani-Yassin, M. (2006). On the forwarding probability for on-demand probabilistic route discovery in MANETs. In *Proceeding of the 7th Annual Postgraduate Symposium on the Convergence of Telecommunications, Networking and Broadcasting (PGNET 2006)*, (pp. 120-125). Liverpool, UK: IEEE Press.

Abdul-Rahman, A. (1997). The PGP trust model. *The Journal of Electronic Commerce, 10*(3), 27–31.

Aboud, S. J., Al-Fayoumi, M., & Al-Nuaimi, M. (2010). Verification and validation of simulation models. In Abu-Taieh, E. M. O., & El Sheikh, A. A. (Eds.), *Handbook of Research on Discrete Event Simulation Environments: Technologies and Applications* (pp. 58–74). Hershey, PA: IGI Global.

Abouzeid, A., & Roy, S. (2003). Stochastic modeling of TCP in networks with abrupt delay variations. *Journal of Wireless Networks, 9,* 509–524. doi:10.1023/A:1024644301397

Abramson, N. (1985). Development of ALOHANET. *IEEE Transactions on Information Theory, 31*(2), 119–123. doi:10.1109/TIT.1985.1057021

Abuzanat, H., Trouillet, B., & Toguyeni, A. (2008). Routing fairness model for QoS optimization in wireless network. In *Proceedings of the 2nd International Conference on Sensor Technologies and Applications (SENSORCOMM 2008),* (pp. 776-781). Cap Esterel, France: IEEE Press.

Adarbah, H. (2008). *Modeling and analysis of TCP Reno with packet-loss and long delay cycles in wireless networks.* M.Sc Thesis. Amman, Jordan: Amman Arab University for Graduate Studies.

Agrawal, D., & Zeng, Q. A. (2003). *Introduction to wireless and mobile systems.* New York: Cole Publishing.

Ahmed, Y., & Shahriari, S. (2001). *Simulation of TCP/IP applications on CDPD channel.* MSc Thesis. Stockholm, Sweden: Chalmers University of Technology.

Ahn, G., & Lam, J. (2005). Managing privacy preferences for federated identity management. In *Proceedings of the 2005 Workshop on Digital Identity Management,* (pp. 28–36). Fairfax, VA: IEEE Press.

Ajmone Marsan, M., Balbo, G., Conte, G., Donatelli, S., & Franceschinis, S. (1995). *Modeling with generalized stochastic petri nets* (2nd ed.). New York: John Wiley and Sons.

Al-Ani, M. S. (2009). Next generation cellular mobile commutation. [IJIM]. *International Journal of Interactive Mobile Technologies, 3*(2), 58–62.

Al-Ani, M. S., Kasasbeh, B. M., Al-Qutaish, R. E., & Muhairat, M. I. (2009). Constructing a new communication system by integrating the GSM to the satellites infrastructure. *WSEAS Transactions on Communications, 8*(2), 217–226.

Alawieh, B., Assi, C., & Mouftah, H. (2009). Power-aware ad hoc networks with directional antennas. *Journal of Ad Hoc Networks, 7*(3), 486–499. doi:10.1016/j.adhoc.2008.05.004

Al-Bahadili, H., & Jaradat, Y. (2007). Development and performance analysis of a probabilistic flooding in noisy mobile ad hoc networks. In *Proceedings of the 1st International Conference on Digital Communications and Computer Applications (DCCA 2007),* (pp. 1306-1316). Irbid, Jordan: IEEE Press.

Al-Bahadili, H., Al-Basheer, O., & Al-Thaher, A. (2007). A location-aided routing-probabilistic algorithm for flooding optimization in MANETs. In *Proceedings of Mosharaka International Conference on Communications, Networking, and Information Technology (MIC-CNIT 2007).* Amman, Jordan: IEEE Press.

Al-Bahadili, H. (2010). On the use of discrete-event simulation in computer networks analysis and design. In Abu-Taieh, E. M. O., & El-Sheikh, A. A. (Eds.), *Handbook of Research on Discrete-Event Simulation Environments: Technologies and Applications* (pp. 414–442). Hershey, PA: IGI Global. doi:10.4018/978-1-60566-774-4.ch019

Al-Bahadili, H. (2010a). Enhancing the performance of adjusted probabilistic broadcast in MANETs. [MEDJCN]. *The Mediterranean Journal of Computers and Networks, 6*(4), 138–144.

Al-Bahadili, H. (2010b). On the use of discrete-event simulation in computer networks analysis and design. In Abu-Taieh, E. M. O., & El-Sheikh, A. A. (Eds.), *Handbook of Research on Discrete-Event Simulation Environments: Technologies and Applications* (pp. 414–442). Hershey, PA: IGI Global. doi:10.4018/978-1-60566-774-4.ch019

Al-Bahadili, H., & Adarbah, H. (2011). Effects of packet-loss and long delay cycles on the performance of the TCP protocol in wireless networks. In Abu-Taieh, E., El Sheikh, A., & Jafari, M. (Eds.), *Technology Engineering and Management in Aviation: Advancements and Discoveries.* Hershey, PA: IGI Global. doi:10.4018/978-1-60960-887-3.ch021

Al-Bahadili, H., Issa, G., & Sabri, A. (2011). Enhancing the performance of the DNDP algorithm. [IJWMN]. *The International Journal of Wireless and Mobile Networks*, *3*(2), 113–124. doi:10.5121/ijwmn.2011.3210

Al-Bahadili, H., & Jaradat, R. (2010). Performance evaluation of an OMPR algorithm for route discovery in noisy MANETs. [IJCNC]. *The International Journal of Computer Networks and Communications*, *2*(1), 85–96.

Al-Bahadili, H., & Kaabneh, K. (2010). Analyzing the performance of probabilistic algorithm in noisy MANETs. [IJWMN]. *International Journal of Wireless & Mobile Networks*, *2*(3), 83–95. doi:10.5121/ijwmn.2010.2306

Al-Bahadili, H., & Sabri, A. (2011). A novel dynamic noise-dependent probabilistic algorithm for route discovery in MANETs. [IJBDCN]. *International Journal of Business Data Communications and Networking*, *7*(1), 52–67. doi:10.4018/jbdcn.2011010103

Al-Jaroodi, J. (2002). *Security issues in wireless mobile ad hoc networks (MANET)*. Lincoln, Nebraska: University of Nebraska-Lincoln Press.

Altman, E., Barakat, C., & Ramos, V. (2005). Analysis of AIMD protocols over paths with variable delay. *Journal of Computer Networks*, *48*(6), 960–971. doi:10.1016/j.comnet.2004.11.013

Altman, E., & Jimenez, T. (2003). *NS2 for beginners*. Paris, France: University of de Los Andes.

Altman, E., Kherani, A. A., Michiardi, P., & Molva, R. (2004). *Non-cooperative forwarding in ad hoc networks (Report 5116)*. Sophia-Antipolis, France: INRIA.

Altwelib, H., Ashibani, M., & Shatwan, F. (2007). *Performance evaluation of an integrated vertical handover model for next generation mobile networks using virtual MAC addresses*. Paper presented at the Southern Africa Telecommunication Networks and Applications Conference (SATNAC). Johannesburg, South Africa.

Andel, T., & Yasinsac, A. (2006). On the credibility of MANET simulation. *IEEE Computer Society*, *39*(7), 48–51. doi:10.1109/MC.2006.242

Arcieri, F., & Ciclosi, M. Dimitr, Fioravanti, A., Nardelli, E., & Talamo, M. (2000). The Italian electronic identity card: Overall architecture and IT infrastructure. In *Proceedings of the 2nd International Workshop on Certification and Security in Inter-Organizational E-Services (CSES 2004)*, (pp. 5-18). Toulouse, France: IEEE Press.

Aresenault, A., & Turner, S. (2001). *Internet X.509 public key infrastructure: Draft-IETF-PKIX-Roadmap-06.txt*. Retrieved May 26, 2011, from http://tools.ietf.org/html/draft-ietf-pkix-roadmap-06.

Arora, A., & Krunz, M. (2007). Power-controlled medium access for ad hoc networks with directional antennas. *Journal of Ad Hoc Networks*, *5*(2), 145–161. doi:10.1016/j.adhoc.2005.10.001

Asaeda, H., Rahman, M., & Toyama, Y. (2006). *Structuring proactive secret sharing in mobile ad-hoc networks*. Retrieved January 15, 2011, from http://www.sfc.wide.ad.jp/~asaeda/paper/ISWPC06_J1-2.pdf.

Asgarkhani, M. (2002). *Computer modeling and simulation as a learning tool: A preliminary study of network simulation products*. Christchurch, New Zealand: Christchurch Polytechnic Institute of Technology (CPIT).

Athuraliya, S., Li, V. H., Low, S. H., & Yin, Q. (2001). REM: Active queue management. *IEEE Network*, *15*(3), 48–53. doi:10.1109/65.923940

Aweya, J., Ouellette, M., & Montuno, D. Y. (2001). A control theoretic approach to active queue management. *Journal of Computer Networks*, *36*(2–3), 203–235. doi:10.1016/S1389-1286(00)00206-1

Axelrod, R. (1984). *The evolution of cooperation*. New York, NY: Basic Books.

Ayub, J., & Garrido, G. (2008). *Routing in wireless mobile ad hoc networks*. Berlin, Germany: VDM Verlag.

Bagchi, S. (2005). *Simulation of grid computing infrastructures: Challenges and solutions*. In Proceedings of the Winter Simulation Conference, (pp. 131-135). ACM Press.

Balfanz, D., Smetters, D. K., Stewart, P., & Wong, H. C. (2002). Talking to strangers: Authentication in ad-hoc wireless networks. In *Proceedings of Network and Distributed System Security Symposium 2002 (NDSS 2002)*. San Diego, CA: ISOC Publications.

Bani-Yassein, M., & Ould-Khaoua, M. (2007). Applications of probabilistic flooding in MANETs. *International Journal of Ubiquitous Computing and Communication, 1*(1), 1–5.

Bani-Yassein, M., Ould-Khaoua, M., Mackenzie, L., & Papanastasiou, S. (2006). Performance analysis of adjusted probabilistic broadcasting in mobile ad hoc networks. *International Journal of Wireless Information Networks, 13*(2), 127–140. doi:10.1007/s10776-006-0027-0

Banks, J., Carson, J. II, Nelson, B., & Nicol, D. (2010). *Discrete-event system simulation* (5th ed.). New York, NY: Prentice Hall.

Barel, M. (1985). Performance evaluation of the discrete event simulation computer DESC. In *Proceeding of the 18th Annual Simulation Symposium*, (pp. 1-13). Tampa, FL: IEEE Press.

Barham, P., Hand, S., Isaacs, R., Jardetzky, P., Mortier, R., & Roscoe, T. (2002). Techniques for lightweight concealment and authentication in IP networks. *Intel Research Berkeley, Technical Report IRB-TR-02-009*. Berkley, CA: Berkley University Press.

Bari, F., & Leung, V. (2007). Application of ELECTRE to network selection in a heterogeneous wireless network environment. In *Proceedings of IEEE Wireless Communications and Networking Conference (WCNC 2007)*, (pp. 3810-3815). IEEE Press.

Bari, A., Wazed, S., Jaekel, A., & Bandyopadhyay, S. (2008). A genetic algorithm based approach for energy efficient routing in two-tiered sensor networks. *Journal of Ad Hoc Networks, 7*(4), 665–676. doi:10.1016/j.adhoc.2008.04.003

Barrett, C., Eidenbenz, S., Kroc, L., Marathe, M., & Smith, J. (2005). Parametric probabilistic routing in sensor networks. *Journal of Mobile Networks and Applications, 10*(4), 529–544. doi:10.1007/s11036-005-1565-x

Base, R., & Mell, P. (2003). Intrusion detection systems. *NIST Special Publication SP 800-31*. Retrieved from http://www.csrc.nist.gov.

Batteson, G., Houseman, M., & Severi, C. (1971). *La cérémonie du Naven*. Paris, France: Minuit.

Bause, F., & Kritzinger, P. S. (1996). Stochastic petri nets: An introduction to the theory. In *Advances in Computer Science*. Wiesbaden, Germany: Verlag Vieweg.

Berenbrink, P., Cooper, C., & Hu, Z. (2007). Energy efficient randomized communication in unknown ad hoc networks. In *Proceedings of 19th ACM Symposium on Parallelism in Algorithms and Architectures (SPAA 2007)*, (pp. 250–259). San Diego, CA: ACM Press.

Beres, Y., Baldwin, A., Casassa Mont, M., & Shiu, S. (2007). On identity assurance in the presence of federated identity management systems. In *Proceedings of the 2007 ACM Workshop on Digital Identity Management*, (pp. 27-35). ACM Press.

Bergadano, F., Gunetti, D., & Picardi, C. (2002). User authentication through keystroke dynamics. [TISSEC]. *ACM Transactions on Information and System Security, 5*(4), 367–397. doi:10.1145/581271.581272

Berkeley Lab. (2007). *Researchers are developing energy-efficient digital network technology*. Retrieved from http://www.lbl.gov/Science-Articles/Archive/EETD-efficient-networks.html.

Bernstein, D. J. (2002). *SYN cookies*. Retrieved June 13, 2010, from http://cr.yp.to/syncookies.html.

Bersini, H. (2005). *Des réseaux et des sciences – Biologie, informatique, sociologie: L'omniprésence des réseaux*. Paris, France: Vuibert.

Bettstetter, C. (2004). The cluster density of a distributed clustering algorithm in ad hoc networks. In *Proceedings of 2004 IEEE International Conference on Communications (ICC 2004)*, (vol 7), (pp. 4336-4340). Paris, France: IEEE Press.

Bianchi, G. (2000). Performance analysis of the IEEE 802.11 distributed coordination function. *IEEE Journal on Selected Areas in Communications, 18*(3), 535–547. doi:10.1109/49.840210

Birch, D. (Ed.). (2007). *Digital identity management: Technological, business and social implications*. Surrey, UK: Gower.

Blankenship, Y. W., Sartori, P. J., Classon, B. K., Desai, V., & Baum, K. L. (2004). Link error prediction methods for multicarrier systems. In *Proceedings of the IEEE 60th Vehicular Technology Conference (VTC 2004)*, (vol 6), (pp. 4175-4179). Los Angeles, CA: IEEE Press.

Blazevic, L., Boudec, J., & Giordano, S. (2005). A location-based routing method for mobile ad hoc networks. *IEEE Transactions on Mobile Computing, 4*(2), 97–110. doi:10.1109/TMC.2005.16

Blumenthal, J., Reichenbach, F., & Timmermann, D. (2006). Minimal transmission power vs. signal strength as distance estimation for localization in wireless sensor networks. In *Proceedings of the 3rd IEEE International Workshop on Wireless Ad Hoc and Sensor Networks*, (pp. 761-766). Reston, VA: IEEE Press.

Bolch, G., Greiner, S., de Meer, H., & Trivedi, K. S. (1998). *Queueing networks and Markov chains: Modeling and performance evaluation with computer science applications*. New York: John Wiley & Sons. doi:10.1002/0471200581

Boleng, J., & Camp, T. (2004). Adaptive location-aided mobile ad hoc network routing. *Proceedings of the 23rd IEEE International Performance, Computing, and Communications Conference (IPCCC)*, (pp. 423-432). Phoenix, AZ: IEEE Press.

Bote-Lorenzo, M., Dimitriadis, Y., & Gomez-Sanchez, E. (2002). *Grid characteristics and uses: A grid definition. Technical Report CICYT*. Valladolid, Spain: University of Valladolid.

Boudriga, N., Baghdadi, M., & Obaidat, M. (2006). A new scheme for mobility, sensing, and security management in wireless ad hoc sensor networks. In *Proceedings of the 39th Annual Simulation Symposium (ANSS 2006)*, (pp. 61-67). Huntsville, AL: IEEE Press.

Braden, R., Clark, D., Crowcroft, J., Davie, B., Deering, S., Estrin, D., et al. (1998). *Recommendations on queue management and congestion avoidance in the Internet (RFC 2309)*. Retrieved from http://www.ietf.org.

Brainard, J., Juels, A., Rivest, R., Szydlo, M., & Yung, M. (2006). Fourth factor authentication: Somebody you know. In *Proceedings of the ACM Computer and Communication Security (CCS 2006) Conference*, (pp. 168-178). Alexandria, VA: ACM Press.

Brakmo, L., & Peterson, L. (1995). TCP Vegas: End to end congestion avoidance on a global internet. *IEEE Journal on Selected Areas in Communications, 13*(8), 1465–1480. doi:10.1109/49.464716

Brandauer, C., Iannaccone, G., Diot, C., Ziegler, T., Fdida, S., & May, M. (2001). Comparison of tail drop and active queue management performance for bulk-data and web-like Internet traffic. In *Proceeding of ISCC*, (pp. 122–129). IEEE Press.

Breslau, L., Estrin, D., Fall, K., Floyd, S., Heimann, J., & Helmy, A. (2000). Advances in network simulation. *Computer, 33*(5), 59–67. doi:10.1109/2.841785

Broch, J., Maltz, D., Johnson, D., Hu, Y.-C., & Jetcheva, J. (1998). *A performance comparison of multi-hop wireless ad hoc network routing protocols*. Paper presented at the ACM International Conference on Mobile Computing and Networking (Mobi-Com 1998). Dallas, TX.

Buyya, R., Abramson, D., Giddy, J., & Stockinger, H. (2002). Economic models for resource management and scheduling in Grid computing. In *Concurrency and Computation*. New York: John Wiley & Sons. doi:10.1002/cpe.690

Camenisch, J., Abhi, S., Sommer, D., Fischer-Hübner, S., Hansen, M., Krasemann, H., et al. (2005). Privacy and identity management for everyone. In *Proceedings of the 2005 Workshop on Digital Identity Management*, (pp. 20-27). Fairfax, VA: IEEE Press.

Candebat, T., & Gray, D. (2006). Secure pseudonym management using mediated identity-based encryption. *Journal of Computer Security, 14*(3), 249–267.

Capkun, S., Buttyan, L., & Hubaux, J.-P. (2002). Small worlds in security systems: An analysis of the PGP certificate graph. In *Proceedings ACM New Security Paradigm Workshop (NSPW)*. ACM Press.

Capkun, S., Buttyan, L., & Hubaux, J. (2003). Self-organized public-key management for mobile ad hoc networks. *IEEE Transactions on Mobile Computing, 2*(1), 52–64. doi:10.1109/TMC.2003.1195151

CARMEN. (2008). *Carrier grade mesh networks*. Retrieved from http://cordis.europa.eu/fetch?CALLER=FP7_PROJ_EN&ACTION=D&DOC=3&CAT=PROJ&QUERY=011b32226717:c226:584c2e02&RCN=85283

Carson, J. S., II. (2004). Introduction to modeling and simulation. In *Proceedings of 2004 Winter Simulation Conference*, (pp. 1283-1289). IEEE Press.

Casassa Mont, M., & Thyne, R. (2006). Privacy policy enforcement in enterprises with identity management solutions. In *Proceedings of the 2006 International Conference on Privacy, Security and Trust: Bridge the Gap between PST Technologies and Business Services*, (vol 380). Markham, Canada: IEEE Press.

Cassady, R. (1967). *Auction and auctioneering.* Berkeley, CA: University of California Press.

Caswell, B., Beale, J., Foster, J., & Posluns, J. (2003). *Snort 2.0 intrusion detection.* Rockland, MA: Syngress Publishing.

Chai, Z., Cao, Z., & Lu, R. (2007). Threshold password authentication against guessing attacks in ad hoc networks. *Journal of Ad Hoc Networks*, 5(7), 1046–1054. doi:10.1016/j.adhoc.2006.05.003

Chakeres, I., & Perkins, C. (2010). Dynamic MANET on-demand (DYMO) routing. *IETF Internet Draft.* Retrieved from http://www.ietf.org.

Champine, G. A., Geer, D. Jr, & Ruh, W. N. (1990). Project Athena as a distributed computer system. *Journal of IEEE Computer*, 23(9), 40–51. doi:10.1109/2.58217

Chandy, K. M., & Misra, J. (1981). Asynchronous distributed simulation via a sequence of parallel computations. *ACM Communications*, 24(11), 198–206. doi:10.1145/358598.358613

Chandy, K. M., Misra, J., & Haas, L. (1983). Distributed deadlock detection. *ACM Transactions on Computer Systems*, 1(2), 144–156. doi:10.1145/357360.357365

Chapin, S., Karpovich, J., & Grimshaw, A. (1999). The legion resource management system. In *Proceedings of the 5th Workshop on Job Scheduling Strategies for Parallel Processing.* San Juan, Puerto Rico: Springer.

Chen, W.-T., Jian, B.-B., & Lo, S.-C. (2002). An adaptive retransmission scheme with QoS support for the IEEE802.11 MAC enhancement. In *Proceedings of the 55th IEEE Vehicular Technology Conference*, (pp. 70-74). IEEE Press.

Chengyu, Z., Oliver, W. W., Aweya, J., Ouellette, M., & Delfin, Y. (2002). A comparison of active queue management algorithms using the OPNET modeler. *IEEE Communications Magazine*, 40(6), 158. doi:10.1109/MCOM.2002.1007422

Chen, J., Gerla, M., & Zhong Lee, Y., & Sanadidi. (2008). TCP with delayed ACK for wireless networks. *Journal of Ad Hoc Networks*, 6(7), 1098–1116. doi:10.1016/j.adhoc.2007.10.004

Cheswick, W. R., & Belloving, S. M. (1994). *Firewalls and Internet security: Repelling the wily hacker.* Reading, MA: Addison Wesley.

Chiganmi, A., Baysan, M., Sarac, K., & Prakash, R. (2008). Variable power broadcast using local information in ad hoc networks. *Journal of Ad Hoc Networks*, 6(5), 675–695. doi:10.1016/j.adhoc.2007.06.002

Chowdhury, P. K., Atiquzzaman, M., & Ivancic, W. (2006). SINEMO: An IP-diversity based approach for netwrok mobility in space. In *Proceedings of the 2nd IEEE International Conference on Space Mission Challenges for Information Technology (SMC-IT 2006)*, (pp. 109–115). Pasadena, CA: IEEE Press.

Chow, J. (1999). Development of channel models for simulation of wireless systems in OPNET. *Transaction of the Society for Computer Simulation International*, 16(3), 86–92.

Cisco Systems. (2006). *Five myths of wireless networks.* Retrieved May 2011 from http://www.ciscosystems.lt/en/US/.../prod_white_paper0900aecd805287fc.pdf.

Cisco. (2001). *Introduction to mobile IP.* Retrieved March 14, 2010 from http://www.cisco.com/en/US/docs/ios/solutions_docs/mobile_ip/mobil_ip.html.

Claub, S., Kesdogan, D., & Kolsch, T. (2005). Privacy enhancing identity management: Protection against re-identification and profiling. In *Proceedings of the Workshop on Digital Identity Management*, (pp. 84-93). Fairfax, VA: IEEE Press.

Clausen, T., & Jacquet, T. (2003). Optimized link state routing protocol (OLSR). *IETF RFC 3626.* Retrieved from http://www.ietf.org.

Clincy, V. A., & Mudiraj, P. (2007). The future leading mobility protocol: Mobile IPv4 or Mobile IPv6? *Journal of Computing Sciences in Colleges, 22*(6), 197–203.

CMU Monarch Project. (2011). *Webpage*. Retrieved January 5, 2011 from http://www.monarch.cs.cmu.edu.

Cole, R. G., & Rosenbluth, J. (2001). Voice over IP performance monitoring. *Journal of ACM SIGCOMM Computer Communications Review, 31*(2), 9–24. doi:10.1145/505666.505669

Colson, G., & Bruyn, C. (1989). Models and methods in multiple objectives decision making. *Mathematical and Computer Modelling, 12,* 1201–1211. doi:10.1016/0895-7177(89)90362-2

Coucheney, P., Touati, C., & Gaujal, B. (2009). Selection of efficient pure strategies in allocation games. In *Proceedings of the International Conference on Game Theory for Networks (GameNets 2009),* (pp. 658-666). Istanbul, Turkey: IEEE Press.

Coulouris, G., Dollimore, J., & Kindberg, T. (1994). *Distributed systems – Concepts and design* (2nd ed.). Reading, MA: Addison-Wesley.

Dai, F., Dai, Q., & Wu, J. (2005). Power efficient routing trees for ad hoc wireless networks using directional antenna. *Journal of Ad Hoc Networks, 3*(5), 621–628. doi:10.1016/j.adhoc.2004.08.008

Das, A., Neishaboori, A., & Kesidis, G. (2009). Wireless mesh networking games. *In Proceedings of the International Conference on Game Theory for Networks (GameNets 2009),* (pp. 565-574). Istanbul, Turkey: IEEE Press.

DaSilva, A., & Srivastava, V. (2004). *Node participation in peer-to-peer and ad hoc networks: A game theoretic formulation.* Paper presented at the Workshop on Games and Emergent Behaviour in Distributed Computing. Birmingham, UK.

Das, S. R., Castaneda, R., & Yan, J. (2000). Simulation-based performance evaluation of routing protocols for mobile ad hoc networks. *Mobile Networks and Applications, 5*(1), 179–189. doi:10.1023/A:1019108612308

Dedecker, J., & De Meuter, W. (2003). *Communication abstractions through new language concepts.* Retrieved from http://soft.vub.ac.be/Publications/2003/vub-prog-tr-03-28.pdf.

DeGraaf, R., Aycock, J., & Jacobson, M. (2005). Port knocking with strong authentication. In *Proceedings of the 21st Annual Computer Security Applications Conference (ACSAC),* (pp. 409-418). Tucson, AZ: IEEE Press.

Deng, H., Li, W., & Agrawa, D. (2002). Routing security in wireless ad hoc networks. *IEEE Communications Magazine, 40*(10), 70–75. doi:10.1109/MCOM.2002.1039859

Dewan, P., & Dasgupta, P. (2003). Trusting routers and relays in ad hoc networks. In *Proceedings of the International Conference on Parallel Processing Workshops (ICPPW 2003).* IEEE Press.

Diffie, W., & Hellman, M. (1976). New directions in cryptography. *IEEE Transactions on Information Theory, 22*(6), 29–40. doi:10.1109/TIT.1976.1055638

Dixon, M. W., Mcgill, T. J., & Karisooon, J. M. (1997). Using a network simulation package to teach the client-server model. In *Proceedings of the 2nd Conference on Integrating Technology into Computer Science Education,* (pp. 71-73). IEEE Press.

Dobre, C. M., & Cristea, V. (2007). A simulation model for large scale distributed systems. In *Proceedings of the 4th International Conference on Innovations in Information Technology,* (pp. 526-530). Dubai, UAE: IEEE Press.

Dobre, C. M., & Stratan, C. (2004). *MONARC simulation framework.* Paper presented at the RoEduNet International Conference. Timisoara, Romania.

Dobre, C., & Stratan, C. (2003). MONARC 2 - Distributed systems simulation. In *Proceedings of the 14th International Conference on Control Systems and Computer Science,* (pp. 145-149). Bucharest, Romania: IEEE Press.

Dobre, C., Pop, F., & Cristea, V. (2008). A simulation framework for dependable distributed systems. In *Proceedings of the 37th International Conference on Parallel Processing (ICPP-08),* (pp. 181-187). Portland, Oregon: IEEE Press.

Dobre, C., Pop, F., & Cristea, V. (2009). Simulation Framework for the Evaluation of Dependable Distributed Systems. [SCPE]. *International Journal for Parallel and Distributed Computing, 10*(1), 13–23.

Dowie, P. (2002). *Presentation: XROUTER network infrastructure software - Paula G8PZT*. Retrieved September 28, 2010, from http://www.g8pzt.pwp.blueyonder.co.uk/fourpak/2002_03.htm.

Doyle, M. (2004). *Implementing a port knocking system*. MSc Thesis. Little Rock, AR: University of Arkansas.

Dricot, J.-M., & De Doncker, P. (2004). High-accuracy physical layer model for wireless network simulations in ns-2. In *Proceedings of 2004 International Workshop on Wireless Ad-Hoc Networks*, (pp. 249-253). IEEE Press.

Dugan, R. (2010). *Defence advanced research project agency (DAPRA)*. Retrieved September 14, 2010, from http://www.darpa.mil.

Dunaytsev, R., Koucheryavy, Y., & Harju, J. (2006). The PFTK-model revised. *Journal of Computer Communications, 29*(13-14), 2671–2679. doi:10.1016/j.comcom.2006.01.035

Dutch Research Database. (2007). *Minimization of energy consumption in wireless communication networks with high demand for reliability*. Retrieved from http://www.onderzoekinformatie.nl/nl/oi/biza/d16000o/OND1320539.

Dutta, P. K. (2001). *Strategies and games: Theory and practice*. Boston, MA: MIT Press.

E3 Project. (2009). *Website*. Retrieved from http://cordis.europa.eu/fetch?CALLER=FP7_PROJ_EN&ACTION=D&DOC=1& CAT=PROJ&QUERY=011b322313b1:7666:291412e1&RCN=85443.

Edwards, J. (2009). Want to bone up on wireless tech? Try ham radio. *Computerworld*. Retrieved October 17, 2010, from http://www.computerworld.com/s/article/9139771/Want_to_bone_up_on_wireless_tech_Try_ham_radio.

El Sheikh, A. (1987). *Simulation modeling using a relational database package*. Unpublished PhD Thesis. London, UK: The London School of Economics.

Epperson, J. F. (2002). *An introduction to numerical methods and analysis*. New York: John Wiley and Sons.

Eremia, B., Dobre, C., Pop, F., Costan, A., & Cristea, V. (2010). Simulation model and instrument to evaluate replication techniques. In *Proceedings of the International Conference on, P2P, Paralel, Grid, Cloud and Internet Computing*, (pp. 541-547). Fukuoka, Japan: IEEE Press.

Erlang, A. K. (1909). The theory of probabilities and telephone conversations. In *The Life and Works of A.K. Erlang, E. Brockmeyer, H.L. Halstr m og Arne Jensen* (pp. 131–137). Copenhagen, Denmark: Verlag.

Ernst, T. (2007). *Network mobility support goals and requirements (RFC 4886)*. Retrieved March 18, 2011, from http://www.rfc-archive.org/getrfc.php?rfc=4886.

Ernst, T., & Lach, H. Y. (2007). *Network mobility support terminology (RFC 4885)*. Retrieved 18 May 2011 from http://www.isi.edu/in-notes/rfc4885.txt.

Ernst, T. (2006). *The information technology era of the vehicular industry. ACM SIGCOMM Computer Communication Review* (2nd ed.). New York, NY: ACM Press.

ETS. (2005). *European telecommunications standards institute ETS 300 726 v6.0.1:2005: Digital cellular telecommunications system (Phase 2+) (GSM): Enhanced full rate (EFR) speech transcoding: GSM 06.60 version 5.2.1*. Retrieved June, 14, 2011 from http://zmailer.org/p/mea/ham/GSM/.

EU-MESH. (2008). *Enhanced, ubiquitous, and dependable broadband access using mesh networks*. Retrieved from http://cordis.europa.eu/fetch?CALLER=FP7_PROJ_EN&ACTION=D&DOC=1&CAT=PROJ&QUERY=011b32250175:ea6a:60251d2d&RCN=85298.

Fall, K., & Varadhan, K. (2008). The NS manual. *The VINT Project*. Retrieved from http://www.isi.edu/nsnam/vint/.

Fall, K., & Varadhan, K. (Eds.). (2010). *The network simulator ns-2: Documentation*. Retrieved from http://www.isi.edu/nsnam/ns/ns-documentation.html.

Fall, K., & Floyd, S. (1996). Simulation-based comparison of Tahoe, Reno, and SACK TCP. *ACM Computer Communication Review, 26*(3), 5–21. doi:10.1145/235160.235162

Fantacci, R., Pecorella, T., & Habib, I. (2004). Proposal and performance evaluation of an efficient multiple-access protocol for LEO satellite packet networks. *IEEE Journal on Selected Areas in Communications, 22*(3), 538–545. doi:10.1109/JSAC.2004.823437

Fedora GNU/Linux Operating System. (2010). *Fedora-project*. Retrieved June 13, 2010, from https://fedaproject.org/wiki/Fedora_Project_Wiki.

Fei, X., & Wenye, W. (2006). Understanding dynamic denial of service attacks in mobile ad hoc networks. In *Proceedings of MILCOM*, (pp. 1-7). IEEE Press.

Felegyhazi, M., Buttyan, L., & Hubaux, J. P. (2004). Equilibrium analysis of packet forwarding strategies in wireless ad hoc networks – The dynamic case. In *Proceeding of the 2nd Workshop on Modelling and Optimization in Mobile, Ad Hoc and Wireless Networks (WiOpt 2004)*. Cambridge, UK: IEEE Press.

Felegyhazi, M., Cagalj, M., Bidokhti, S., & Hubaux, J. (2007). Non-cooperative multi-radio channel allocation in wireless networks. In *Proceedings of the 26th IEEE International Conference on Computer Communications (INFOCOM 2007)*, (pp.1442-1450). Anchorage, AK: IEEE Press.

Felegyhazi, M., Buttyan, L., & Hubaux, J. P. (2006). Nash equilibria of packet forwarding strategies in wireless ad hoc networks. *IEEE Transactions on Mobile Computing*, 5(5), 463–476. doi:10.1109/TMC.2006.68

Feng, W., Kandlur, D., Saha, D., & Shin, K. G. (1999). *Blue: A new class of active queue management algorithms. Technical report UM CSE-TR-387-99.* Ann Arbor, MI: University of Michigan.

Feng, W., Kandlur, D., Saha, D., & Shin, K. G. (2001). Stochastic fair blue: A queue management algorithm for enforcing fairness. In *Proceedings of IEEE INFOCOM* (*Vol. 3*, pp. 1520–1529). IEEE Press.

Floyd, S., & Jacobson, V. (1993). Random early detection gateways for congestion avoidance. *IEEE/ACM Joint Transactions on Networking*, 1(4), 397–413.

Floyd, S., Ramakrishna, G., & Shenker, S. (2001). *Adaptive RED: An algorithm for increasing the robustness of RED's active queue management. Technical Report.* New York: ICSI.

Fokine, K. (2002). *Key management in ad hoc networks.* Thesis. Linkping, Sweden: Linkping University.

Forouzan, B. A. (2007). *Data communications and networking* (4th ed.). New York: McGraw-Hill.

Forouzan, B. A. (2008). *Introduction to cryptography and network security.* New York: McGraw Hill.

Foster, I., Kesselman, C., & Tuecke, S. (2001). *The anatomy of the grid: Enabling scalable virtual organizations.* Retrieved from http://www.globus.org/alliance/publications/papers/anatomy.pdf.

Foster, I., & Kesselman, C. (1998). *The GRID: Blueprint for a new computing infrastructure.* New York: Morgan Kaufmann.

Frantz, F. K. (1995). A taxonomy of model abstraction techniques. In *Proceedings of the 1995 Winter Simulation Conference*, (pp. 1413-1420). Arlington, VA: IEEE Press.

Fu, S., & Atiquzzaman, M. (2003). *Modeling TCP Reno with spurious timeout in wireless mobile environment.* Paper presented at the International Conference on Computer Communication and Networking. Dallas, TX.

Fujimoto, R. M. (1993). Parallel discrete event simulation: Will the field survive? *ORSA Journal on Computing*, 5(3), 213–230.

Fusk, H., Lawniczak, A. T., & Volkov, S. (2001). Packet delay in models of data networks. *ACM Transactions on Modeling and Computer Simulation*, 11(3), 233–250. doi:10.1145/502109.502110

Fyodor, G. (1998). *Remote OS detection via TCP/IP stack finger printing.* Retrieved June 13, 2010, from http://nmap.org/nmap-fingerprinting-article.txt.

Gafni, A. (1988). Rollback mechanisms for optimistic distributed simulation systems. In *Proceeding SCS Multi-Conference on Distribution Simulation*, (pp. 61-67). IEEE Press.

Gallardo-Medina, J., Pineda-Rico, U., & Stevens-Navarro, E. (2009). VIKOR method for vertical handoff decision in beyond 3G wireless networks. In *Proceedings of IEEE International Conference on Electrical Engineering, Computing Science and Automatic Control (CCE 2009)*. IEEE Press.

Gao, X., Wu, G., & Miki, T. (2003). QoS framework for mobile heterogeneous networks. In *Proceedings of the IEEE International Conference on Communications*, (pp. 933 – 937). IEEE Press.

Gao, P., & Damsgaard, J. (2007). *A framework for understanding mobile telecommunications market innovation: A case of china*. Manchester, UK: IDPM.

Garcia, A., & Jimenez, O. (2008). *Software prototype for network re-selection in heterogeneous wireless environments*. Paper presented at IEEE Communications Colombian Congress. Bogata, Colombia.

García, A., Escobar, L., Navarro, A., Arteaga, A., Guerrero, F., & Salazar, C. (2010). *Simulation of vertical handover algorithms with NCTUns*. Paper presented at 2010 Summer Simulation Multiconference. Ottawa, Canada.

Garfinkel, S. (1995). *PGP: Pretty good privacy*. New York: O'Reilly & Associates Inc.

Gayathri, T., Venkadajothi, S., Kalaivani, S., Divya, C., Dhas, S., & Sakunthala, R. (2009). Mobile multilayer IPsec protocol. *International Journal of Engineering and Technology, 1*(1), 23–29.

Gelenbe, E., & Lent, R. (2004). Power-aware ad hoc cognitive packet networks. *Journal of Ad Hoc Network, 2*(3), 205–216. doi:10.1016/j.adhoc.2004.03.009

Gentleman, R., & Ihaka, R. (2010). *R-project*. Retrieved from http://www.r-project.org.

Gibson, W. (2000). FLASH vs (simulated) FLASH: Closing the simulation loop. *ACM Transactions on Modeling and Computer Simulation, 35*(11).

GloMoSim. (2010). *Global mobile information systems simulation library*. Retrieved June 15, 2010, from http://pcl.cs.ucla.edu/projects/glomosim/.

Goldstein, G. M., Leisten, S., Stark, K., & Tickle, A. (2005). Using a network simulation tool to engage students in active learning enhances their understanding of complex data communications concepts. In *Proceedings of the 7th Australasian Conference on Computing Education,* (pp. 223-228). IEEE Press.

Gomi, H., Hatakeyama, M., Hosono, S., & Fujita, S. (2005). A delegation framework for federated identity management. In *Proceedings of the 2005 Workshop on Digital Identity Management*, (pp. 94-103). Fairfax, VA: IEEE Press.

Goodrich, M., Tamassia, R., & Yao, D. (2006). Notarized federated identity management for Web services. In *Proceedings of the 20th Annual IFIP WG 11.3 Working Conference on Data and Applications Security*, (pp. 133-139). Sophia Antipolis, France: IEEE Press.

Google Groups. (2006). *Block SSH guessers*. Retrieved June 13, 2010, from http://groups.google.com/group/comp.os.linux.security/browse_thread/thread/30c8a88ddeed53dc/b75ee069451189fe?#b75ee069451189fe.

Gouda, M. G., & Jung, E. (2004). Certificate dispersal in ad-hoc networks. In *Proceedings of the 24th International Conference on Distributed Computing Systems (ICDCS 2004)*. IEEE Press.

Goyal, A., Shahabuddin, P., Heidelberger, P., Nicola, V., & Glynn, P. (1992). A united framework for simulating Markovian models of highly dependable systems. *IEEE Transactions on Computers, 41*(1), 36–51. doi:10.1109/12.123381

Graziani, R., & Johnson, A. (2007). *Routing protocols and concepts: CCNA companion guide*. New York: Cisco Press.

Greis, M. (2011). *Ns-2 tutorial*. Retrieved January 5, 2011 from http://www.isi.edu/nsnam/ns/tutorial/index.html.

Gruber, H. (2005). *The economics of mobile telecommunications*. Cambridge, UK: Cambridge University Press. doi:10.1017/CBO9780511493256

Guardini, L., Demaria, E., & La Monaca, M. (2007). *Mobile IPv6 deployment opportunities in next generation 3GPP networks*. Paper presented at the 16th IST Mobile and Wireless Communications Summit. Budapest, Hungary. Retrieved June 2011 from http://www.ist-enable.eu/pdf/ist_mobile_summit_07/session3-paper2.pdf.

Gurtov, A., & Reiner, L. (2002). *Making TCP robust against delay spikes*. Retrieved from draft-gurtov-tsvwg-tcp-delay-spikes-00.txt.

Haas, Z. J., Pearlman, M. R., & Samar, P. (2002). The zone routing protocol (ZRP) for ad hoc networks. *Mobile Ad Hoc Network Working Group, IETF Internet Draft*. Retrieved on 10 October 2009 from http://tools.ietf.org/id/draft-ietf-manet-zone-zrp-04.txt.

Haas, Z. J., Halpern, J. Y., & Li, L. (2006). Gossip-based ad hoc routing. *IEEE/ACM Transactions on Networking*, *14*(3), 479–491. doi:10.1109/TNET.2006.876186

Hadi, A. H. (2010). *A hybrid port-knocking technique for host authentication*. PhD Thesis. AQmman, Jordan: The University of Financial Sciences.

Halasa, A. (2010). *Development and performance evaluation of a location-based power conservation scheme for MANETs*. PhD Thesis. Amman, Jordan: The Arab Academy for Banking & Financial Sciences.

Hamscher, V., Schwiegelshohn, U., Streit, A., & Yahyapour, R. (2000). Evaluation of job-scheduling strategies for grid computing. In *Proceedings of the First IEEE/ACM international Workshop on Grid Computing*, (pp. 191-202). London, UK: Springer-Verlag.

Hanash, A., Siddique, A., Awan, I., & Woodward, M. (2009). Performance evaluation of dynamic probabilistic broadcasting for flooding in mobile ad hoc networks. *Journal of Simulation Modeling Practice and Theory*, *17*(2), 364–375. doi:10.1016/j.simpat.2008.09.012

Hassan, M., & Jain, R. (2003). *High performance TCP/IP networking: Concepts, issues, and solutions*. Upper Saddle River, NJ: Prentice-Hall.

Hayes, S. (1994). A standard for the OAM&P of PCS systems. *Personal Communications*, *1*(4), 24–26. doi:10.1109/MPC.1994.337512

Hay-Fung, K., Low, G., & Bay, P. K. (2004). Embracing dynamic evolution in distributed systems Software. *IEEE*, *21*(2), 49 – 55.

Hechenleitner, B., & Entacher, K. (2002). On shortcomings of the ns-2 random number generator. In Znati, T., & McDonald, B. (Eds.), *Communication Networks and Distributed Systems Modeling and Simulation* (pp. 71–77). New York: The Society for Modeling and Simulation International.

Hegedus, A., Maggio, G. M., & Kocarev, L. (2005). A ns-2 simulator utilizing chaotic maps for network-on-chip traffic analysis. In *Proceedings of the IEEE International Conference on Circuits and Systems (ISCAS 2005)*, (pp. 3375-3378). IEEE Press.

Higby, C., & Bailey, M. (2004). Wireless security patch management system. In *Proceedings of the ACM Special Interest Group for Information Technology Education (SIGITE 2004)*, (pp. 165-168). Salt Lake City, UT: ACM Press.

Hillston, J. A. (1996). *Compositional approach to performance modeling*. Cambridge, UK: Cambridge University Press. doi:10.1017/CBO9780511569951

Ho, C. Y., Chen, Y. C., Chan, Y. C., & Ho, C. Y. (2008). Fast retransmit and fast recovery schemes of transport protocols: A survey and taxonomy. *Journal of Computer Networks*, *52*(6), 1308–1327. doi:10.1016/j.comnet.2007.12.012

Holland, G., & Vaidya, N. (1999). Impact of routing and link layers on TCP performance in mobile ad hoc networks. In *Proceedings of the Wireless Communications and Networking Conference (WCNC)*, (pp. 1323-1327). IEEE Press.

Holloway, D. (2003). *Wireless networking: A guide to wireless networking and deployment*. Retrieved September 25, 2003 from http://www.hill.com/archive/pub/papers/2003/01/paper.pdf.

Hong, C., Kang, T., & Kim, S. (2005). An effective vertical handoff scheme supporting multiple applications in ubiquitous computing environment. In *Proceedings of the Second International Conference on Embedded Software and Systems*, (pp. 407–440). IEEE Press.

Horgan, G., Khaddaj, S., & Forte, P. (1999). An essential views model for software quality. In Kusters, R., Cowderoy, A., Heemstra, F., & Van Veenendaa, E. (Eds.), *Project Control for Software Quality*. New York: Shaker Publishing.

Houser, D., & Wooders, J. (2001). *Reputation in auctions: Theory and evidence from eBay (working paper)*. Phoenix, AZ: University of Arizona.

Huang, D., & Medhi, D. (2008). A secure group key management scheme for hierarchical mobile ad hoc networks. *Journal of Ad Hoc Networks*, *6*(4), 560–577. doi:10.1016/j.adhoc.2007.04.006

Huang, S., Jan, R., & Yang, W. (2008). SCPS: A self-configuring power-saving protocol for wireless ad hoc networks. *Journal of Computer Networks*, *52*(6), 1328–1342. doi:10.1016/j.comnet.2008.01.007

Hui, S. K., & Yeung, K. H. (2003). Challenges in the migration to 4G mobile systems. *IEEE Communications Magazine*, *41*(12), 54–59. doi:10.1109/MCOM.2003.1252799

IEEE Draft Standard 802.11S. (2009). *Telecommunications and information exchange between systems-local and metropolitan area networks: Specific requirements-Part 11: Wireless LAN medium access control (MAC) and physical layer (PHY) specifications-Amendment 10: Mesh networking*. New York: IEEE Press.

IEEE Standard 1003.1-2008. (2008). *Portable operating system interface (POSIX)*. New York: IEEE Press.

IEEE Standard 802.11-2007. (2007). *Telecommunications and information exchange between systems-local and metropolitan area networks: Specific requirements - Part 11: Wireless LAN medium access control (MAC) and physical layer (PHY) specifications*. New York: IEEE Press.

IEEE Standard 802.15.4-2006. (2006). *Telecommunications and information exchange between systems- local and metropolitan area networks: Specific requirements part 15.4: Wireless medium access control (MAC) and physical layer (PHY) specifications for low-rate wireless Personal area networks (WPANs)*. New York: IEEE Press.

IMA. (2003). *Website*. Retrieved from http://www.ima.umn.

Ingelrest, F., Simplot-Ryl, D., & Stojmenovic, I. (2006). Optimal transmission radius for energy efficient broadcasting protocols in ad hoc and sensor networks. *IEEE Transactions on Parallel and Distributed Systems*, *17*(6), 536–547. doi:10.1109/TPDS.2006.74

Intel. (2011). *Teraflops research chip*. Retrieved 25 May 2011 from http://techresearch.intel.com/ProjectDetails.aspx?Id=151.

International Telecomunication Union. (2000). *ITU-T recommendation M.3400—TMN Management Functions*. Retrieved from http://www.itut.org.

Isabel, D. (2005). *Port knocking: Beyond the basics*. SANS Institute.

ISI. (2010). *Network animator*. Retrieved June 5, 2010 from http://www.isi.edu/nsnam/nam/.

ISI. (2011). *ns-2 contributed code*. Retrieved January 5, 2011 from www.isi.edu/nsnam/ns/ns-contributed.html.

ITU. (2010). *Information about ITU*. Retrieved June, 2010, from http://www.itu.int/net/about/.

ITU-Cellular-Subscriptions. (2010). *Cellular subscriptions for developed and developing countries*. Retrieved July 2010 from http://www.itu.int/ITU-D/ict/statistics/material/graphs/Mobile_cellular_03-09.jpg.

ITU-D. (2010). *Telecommunication development sector*. Retrieved June 2010 from http://www.itu.int/net/about/itu-d.aspx.

ITU-ICT-Trends. (2010). *Global ICT trends*. Retrieved July 2010 from http://www.itu.int/ITU-D/ict/statistics/material/graphs/Global_ICT_Dev_98-09.jpg.

ITU-Internet-Penetration. (2010). *Internet penetration for different regional countries*. Retrieved July 2010 from http://www.itu.int/ITU-D/ict/statistics/material/graphs/Internet_users_reg-09.jpg.

ITU-Internet-Subscriptions. (2010). *Internet subscriptions for developed and developing countries*. Retrieved July 2010 from http://www.itu.int/ITU-D/ict/statistics/material/graphs/Internet_users_03-09.jpg.

ITU-Internet-Trends. (2010), *Internet users trends for developed and developing countries*. Retrieved July 2010 from http://www.itu.int/ITU-D/ict/statistics/material/graphs/Internet_users_98-08.jpg.

ITU-Internet-Users. (2010). *Number of internet users*. Retrieved July 2010 from http://www.itu.int/ITU-D/ict/statistics/material/graphs/Internet_users_00-09.jpg.

ITU-Mobile-Penetration. (2010). *Mobile cellular penetration for different regional countries*. Retrieved July 2010 from http://www.itu.int/ITU-D/ict/statistics/material/graphs/mobile_reg-09.jpg.

ITU-Mobile-Subscriptions. (2010). *Total mobile cellular subscriptions*. Retrieved July 2010 from http://www.itu.int/ITU-D/ict/statistics/material/graphs/Global_mobile_cellular_00-09.jpg.

ITU-Mobile-Trends. (2010). *Mobile cellular telephony trends*. Retrieved July 2010 from http://www.itu.int/ITU-D/ict/statistics/material/graphs/Mobile_cellular_98-08.jpg.

ITU-R. (2010). *Radio communication sector*. Retrieved June 2010, from http://www.itu.int/net/about/itu-r.aspx.

ITU-T. (1988). *Recommendation ITU-T G.711: Pulse code modulation (PCM) of voice frequencies: Approved in November 1988*. Retrieved June 14, 2011 from http://www.itu.int/rec/T-REC-G.711-198811-I/en.

ITU-T. (1996). *Recommendation P.800: METHODS for subjective determination of transmission quality: APPROVED in August 1996*. Retrieved June 14, 2011 from http://www.itu.int/rec/T-REC-P.800-199608-I/en.

ITU-T. (2007). *Recommendation ITU-T G.729A: Coding of speech at 8 kbit/s using conjugate-structure algebraic-code-excited linear prediction (CS-ACELP): Approved in January 2007*. Retrieved June 14, 2011 from http://www.itu.int/rec/T-REC-G.729/en.

ITU-T. (2010). *Telecommunication standardization sector*. Retrieved June 2010 from http://www.itu.int/net/about/itu-t.aspx.

ITU-Telecom. (2010). *ITU telecom*. Retrieved June 2010 from http://www.itu.int/net/about/telecom.aspx.

IWS. (2011). *Internet usage and world population statistics*. Retrieved May 2011 from http://www.internetworldstats.com/stats.htm.

Jakobsson, M., Yung, M., & Zhou, J. (2004). Applied cryptography and network security. In *Proceedings of the 2nd Applied Cryptography and Network Security (ACNS) International Conference*. Yellow Mountain, China: ACNS Press.

Javidi, G., & Sheybani, E. (2008). Content-based computer simulation of a networking course: An assessment. *Journal of Computers*, 3(3), 64–72. doi:10.4304/jcp.3.3.64-72

Jefferson, D. (1985). Virtual time. *ACM Transactions on Proceeding Languages and Systems*, 7(3), 404–425. doi:10.1145/3916.3988

Jianwei, H., Zhu, H., Mung, C., & Poor, H. V. (2008). Auction-based resource allocation for cooperative communications. *IEEE Journal on Selected Areas in Communications*, 26(7), 1226–1237. doi:10.1109/JSAC.2008.080919

Joa-Ng, M., & Lu, I. (1999). A peer-to-peer zone-based two-level link state routing for mobile ad hoc networks. *IEEE Journal on Selected Areas in Communications*, 17(8), 1415–1425. doi:10.1109/49.779923

Johnson, D., Hu, Y., & Maltz, D. (2007). *The dynamic source routing protocol (DSR) for mobile ad hoc networks for IPv4 (RFC 4728)*. Retrieved from http://www.ietf.org.

Johnson, D., Perkins, C., & Arkko, J. (2004). *Mobility support in IPv6 (RFC 3775)*. Retrieved June 14, 2011 from http://www.ietf.org/rfc/rfc3775.txt.

Johnson, D. B., & Maltz, D. A. (1996). Dynamic source routing in ad hoc wireless networks. In Imielinski, T., & Korth, H. (Eds.), *Mobile Computing* (pp. 153–181). Berlin, Germany: Kluwer Academic Publishers. doi:10.1007/978-0-585-29603-6_5

Johnston, S. (2004). *Modeling security concerns in service-oriented architectures*. Retrieved from http://www.ibm.com/developerworks/rational/library/4860.html.

Jo, J., & Cho, J. (2008). A cross-layer optimized vertical handover schemes between mobile WiMAX and 3G networks. *KSII Transactions on Internet and Information Systems*, 2(4), 64–69. doi:10.3837/tiis.2008.04.001

Jones, D. (1986). Concurrent simulation: An alternative to distributed simulation. In *Proceeding of the Winter Simulation Conference (WSC 1986)*, (pp. 417-423). Washington, DC: IEEE Press.

Jung, J., Paxson, V., Berger, A., & Balakrishnan, H. (2004). Fast port scan detection using sequential hypothesis testing. In *Proceedings of IEEE Symposium on Security and Privacy*, (pp. 285-293). Oakland, CA: IEEE Press.

Kaabneh, K., Halasa, A., & Al-Bahadili, H. (2009). An effective location-based power conservation scheme for mobile ad hoc networks. *American Journal of Applied Sciences*, 6(9), 1708–1713. doi:10.3844/ajassp.2009.1708.1713

Kang, J., & Nath, B. (2004). Resource-controlled MAC-layer congestion control scheme in cellular packet network. In *Proceedings of the Vehicular Technology Conference*, (vol 4), (pp. 1988 – 1992). IEEE Press.

Kannan, R., Sarangi, S., & Iyengar, S. S. (2002). A simple model for reliable query reporting in sensor networks. In *Proceedings of the 5th International Conference on Information Fusion*, (pp. 754-759). Annapolis, MD: ACM Press.

Kannan, R., Sarangi, S., Iyengar, S. S., & Ray, L. (2003). Sensor centric quality of routing in sensor networks. In *Proceeding of the 22nd Annual Joint Conference of the IEEE Computer and Communications (INFOCOM 2003)*, (vol 2), (pp. 693-701). San Francisco, CA: IEEE Press.

Kannan, R., Sarangi, S., & Iyengar, S. S. (2004). Game-theoretic models for reliable path-length and energy-constrained routing with data aggregation in wireless sensor networks. *IEEE Journal on Selected Areas in Communications*, *22*(6), 1141–1150. doi:10.1109/JSAC.2004.830937

Kannan, R., Sarangi, S., & Iyengar, S. S. (2004). Sensor-centric energy constrained reliable query routing for wireless sensor networks. *Journal of Parallel and Distributed Computing*, *64*, 839–852. doi:10.1016/j.jpdc.2004.03.010

Karayiannis, N., & Nadella, S. (2006). Power-conserving routing of ad hoc mobile wireless networks based on entropy-constrained algorithms. *Journal of Ad Hoc Networks*, *4*(1), 24–35. doi:10.1016/j.adhoc.2004.04.006

Kasasbeh, B. M., Al-Qutaish, R. E., Al-Ani, M. S., & Al-Sarayreh, K. (2008). Real digital TV accessed by cellular mobile system. *European Journal of Scientific Research*, *20*(4), 914–923.

Kash, W., Ward, J., & Andrusenko, J. (2009). Wireless network modeling and simulation tools for designers and developers. *IEEE Communications Magazine*, *47*(3), 120–127. doi:10.1109/MCOM.2009.4804397

Kassar, M., Kervella, B., & Pujolle, G. (2008). An overview of vertical handover decision strategies in heterogeneous wireless networks. *Computer Communications*, *31*(10), 2607–2620. doi:10.1016/j.comcom.2008.01.044

Kendall, D. (1953). Stochastic processes occurring in the theory of queues and analysis by means of the imbedded Markov chain. *Annals of Mathematical Statistics*, *24*, 338–354. doi:10.1214/aoms/1177728975

Keromytis, A., Misra, V., & Rubenstein, D. (2002). SOS: Secure overlay services. In *Proceedings of ACM SIGCOMM*, (pp. 61-72). Pittsburgh, PA: ACM Press.

Keshariya, M., & Hunt, R. (2008). A new architecture for performance-based policy management in heterogeneous wireless networks. In *Proceedings of the International Conference on Mobile Technology, Applications & Systems*. Ilan, Taiwan: IEEE Press.

Kesselman, A., & Mansour, Y. (2005). Optimizing TCP retransmission timeout. In *Proceedings of the 4th International Conference on Networking (ICN 2005)*, (pp. 133-140). IEEE Press.

Kesselman, A., & Mansour, Y. (2005). Adaptive AIMD congestion control. *Special Issue on Network Design*, *43*(1-2), 97–111.

Khaddaj, S., & Horgan, G. (2004). The evaluation of software quality factors in very large information systems. *Electronic Journal of Information Systems Evaluation*, 43-48.

Khaddaj, S., & Makoond, B. (2010). Design and simulation of human conversational model for distributed systems. In *Proceedigns of the 9th International Conference on Distributed Computing and Applications for Business, Engineering and Science*. Hong Kong, China: IEEE Press.

Khan, I., Javaid, A., & Qian, H. (2008). Coverage-based dynamically adjusted probabilistic forwarding for wireless mobile ad hoc networks. In S. Giordano, W. Jia, P. M. Ruiz, S. Olariu, & G. Xing (Eds.), *Proceedings of the 1st ACM International Workshop on Heterogeneous Sensor and Actor Networks (HeterSanet 2008)*, (pp. 81-88). Hong Kong, China: ACM Press.

Khan, M. K., & Zhang, J. (2006). Multimodal face and fingerprint biometrics authentication on space-limited tokens. *Journal of Neurocomputing*, *71*(13-15), 3026–3031. doi:10.1016/j.neucom.2007.12.017

Kim, J. S., Zhang, Q., & Agrawal, D. P. (2004). Probabilistic broadcasting based on coverage area and neighbor confirmation in mobile ad hoc networks. In *Proceedings of the IEEE Global Telecommunications Conference Workshops (GlobeCom 2004)*, (pp. 96–101). Dallas, TX: IEEE Press.

Kim, J. S., Zhang, Q., & Agrawal, D. P. (2004). Probabilistic broadcasting based on coverage area and neighbor confirmation in mobile ad hoc networks. In *Proceedings of the IEEE Global Telecommunications Conference Workshops (GlobeCom 2004)*, (pp. 96–101). Dallas, TX: IEEE Press.

Kim, J., & Bahk, S. (2009). Design of certification authority using secret redistribution and multicast routing in wireless mesh networks. *The International Journal of Computer and Telecommunications Networking, 53*(1), 98–109.

Kleijnen, J. P. C. (1979). The role of statistical methodology in simulation. In Zeigler, B. P. (Ed.), *Methodology in Systems Modelling and Simulation. North Holland.* The Netherlands: Academic Press. doi:10.1145/1102786.1102793

Kohl, J., Neuman, B. C., & Tso, T. Y. (1994). The evolution of the Kerberos authentication system. In *Distributed Open Systems* (pp. 78–94). New York: IEEE Computer Society Press.

Kohvakka, M., Suhonen, J., Kuorilehto, M., Kaseva, V., Hännikäinen, M., & Hämäläinen, T. (2006). Energy-efficient neighbor discovery protocol for mobile wireless sensor networks. *Journal of Ad Hoc Networks, 7*(1), 24–41. doi:10.1016/j.adhoc.2007.11.016

Kong, J., Zerfos, P., Luo, H., Lu, S., & Zhang, L. (2001). Providing robust and ubiquitous security support for mobile ad-hoc networks. In *Proceedings of the 9th International Conference on Network Protocols (ICNP 2001)*. Riverside, CA: IEEE Press.

Koodli, R. (2005). *Fast handovers for mobile IPv6 (RFC 4068)*. Retrieved March 21, 2010 from http://www.ietf.org/rfc/rfc4068.txt.

Koutsoukos, G., Gouveia, J., Andrade, L., & Fiadeiro, J. L. (2001). Managing evolution in telecommunication systems. In *Proceedings of the IFIP TC6 / WG6.1 3rd International Working Conference on New Developments in Distributed Applications and Interoperable Systems.* IEEE Press.

Ko, Y., & Vaidya, N. (2000). Location-aided routing (LAR) in mobile ad hoc networks. *Journal of Wireless Networks, 6*(4), 307–321. doi:10.1023/A:1019106118419

Krishna, V. (2009). *Auction theory* (2nd ed.). London, UK: Elsevier.

Krivis, S. (2004). *Port knocking: Helpful or harmful? An exploration of modern network threats.* SANS Institute.

Krzywinski, M. (2003b). Port knocking: Network authentication across closed ports. *SysAdmin Magazine*, 12-17.

Krzywinski, M. (2003a). *How to: Port knocking.* New York: Linux Journal.

Kung, H. T., Tan, K. S., & Hsiao, P. H. (2003). TCP with sender-based delay control. *Journal of Computer Communications, 26*(14), 1614–1621. doi:10.1016/S0140-3664(03)00110-5

Kuri, J., Novarro, G., & Me, L. (2003). Fast multi-pattern search algorithms for intrusion detection. *Fundamenta Informaticae, 56*, 23–49.

Kurkowski, S. (2006). *Credible mobile ad hoc network simulation-based studies.* PhD Dissertation. Boulder, CO: Colorado School of Mines.

Kurkowski, S., Camp, T., Mushell, N., & Colagrosso, M. (2005). A visualization and analysis tool for ns-2 wireless simulations: iNSpect. In *Proceedings of the 13th IEEE International Symposium on Modeling, Analysis, and Simulation of Computer and Telecommunication Systems*, (pp. 503-506). IEEE Press.

Kurkowski, S., Camp, T., & Colagrosso, M. (2005). *MANET simulation studies: The incredibles. ACM SIGMOBILE Mobile Computing and Communication Review* (pp. 50–61). ACM Press.

Kuznetsov, N. A., & Fetisov, V. N. (2008). Enhanced-robustness Dijkstra algorithm for control of routing in the IP-networks. *Automation and Remote Control, 69*(2), 247–251. doi:10.1134/S0005117908020069

L'Ecuyer, P. (2001). Software for uniform random number generation: Distinguishing the good and the bad. In *Proceedings of the 2001 Winter Simulation Conference*, (pp. 95-105). Arlington, VA: IEEE Press.

L'Ecuyer, P., Richard, S., Chen, E. J., & Kelton, W. D. (2001). An object-oriented random number package with many long streams and substreams. *Operations Research*, *1*(1).

Laffont, J., & Maskin, E. (1980). Optimal reservation prices in the Vickrey auction. *Economics Letters*, *6*, 309–313. doi:10.1016/0165-1765(80)90002-6

Lai, Y. C., & Yao, C. L. (2002). Performance comparison between TCP Reno and TCP Vegas. *Journal of Computer Communications*, *25*(18), 1765–1773. doi:10.1016/S0140-3664(02)00092-0

Lakshmi, B. P., & Kannammal, A. (2009). Secured authentication of space specified token with biometric traits–face and fingerprint. [IJCSNS]. *International Journal of Computer Science and Network Security*, *9*(7), 231–234.

Land, D. (2008). *Routing protocols for mobile ad hoc networks: Classification, evaluation, and challenges.* Berlin, Germany: VDM Verlag.

Langelaar, M. (2009). *JNOS 2.0 - DOS install (the easy way)*. Retrieved September 13, 2010, from http://www.langelaar.net/projects/jnos2/documents/install/dos/.

Lapsley, D., & Low, S. (1999). Random early marking for Internet congestion control. In *Proceeding of GlobeCom 1999* (pp. 1747–1752). IEEE Press. doi:10.1109/GLOCOM.1999.832461

Lassoued, I., Bonnin, J., Hamouda, Z., & Belghith, A. (2008). A methodology for evaluation vertical handoff decision mechanisms. In *Proceedings of the International Conference on Networking*, (pp.377-384). IEEE Press.

Law, A., & Kelton, W. D. (2000). *Simulation modeling and analysis* (3rd ed.). New York: McGraw-Hill Higher Education.

Lee, J. F., Liao, W., & Chen, M. C. (2008). An incentive-based fairness mechanism for multi-hop wireless backhaul networks with selfish nodes. *IEEE Transactions on Wireless Communications*, *7*(2), 697–704. doi:10.1109/TWC.2008.060631

Lee, J. S., & Chang, C. C. (2007). Secure communications for cluster-based ad hoc networks using node identities. *Journal of Network and Computer Applications*, *30*(4), 1377–1396. doi:10.1016/j.jnca.2006.10.003

Lee, S., Sriram, K., Kim, K., Kim, Y., & Golmie, N. (2009). Vertical handoff decision algorithms for providing optimized performance in heterogeneous wireless networks. *IEEE Transactions on Vehicular Technology*, *58*(2), 5164–5169.

Leeuwaarden, J., Denteneer, D., & Resing, J. (2006). A discrete-time queuing model with periodically scheduled arrival and departure slots. *Performance Evaluation*, *63*(4), 278–294. doi:10.1016/j.peva.2005.03.001

Legrand, I. C., Dobre, C. M., Voicu, R., Stratan, C., Cirstoiu, C., & Musat, L. (2005). *A simulation study for T0/T1 data replication and production activities*. Paper presented at the 15th International Conference on Control Systems and Computer Science. Bucharest, Romania.

Legrand, I. C., Newman, H. B., Voicu, R., & Cirstoiu, C. (2004). *MonALISA: An agent based, dynamic service system to monitor, control and optimize grid based applications*. Paper presented at the Computing in High Energy and Nuclear Physics (CHEP 2004). Interlaken, Switzerland.

Legrand, I. C., Newman, H., Dobre, C. M., & Stratan, C. (2003). *MONARC simulation framework*. Paper presented at the International Workshop on Advanced Computing and Analysis Techniques in Physics Research. Tsukuba, Japan.

Legrand, I. C., Newman, H., van Lingen, F., Dobre, C., Stratan, C., & Paschen, K. (2003). A processes oriented, discrete event simulation framework for modelling and design of large scale distributed systems. In *Proceedings of the IX International Workshop on Advanced Computing and Analysis Techniques in Physics Research*. Tsukuba, Japan: IEEE Press.

Lehane, B., Dolye, L., & Mahony, D. (2005). Ad hoc key management infrastructure. In *Proceedings of the International Conference on Information Technology: Coding and Computing (ITCC 2005)*. IEEE Press.

Lehman, M. M. (1980). On understanding laws, evolution and conservation in the large program life cycle. *Journal of Systems and Software*, *1*(3).

Leitold, H., Hollosi, A., & Posch, R. (2002). Security architecture of the Austrian citizen card concept. In *Proceedings of the 18th Annual Computer Security Applications Conference*, (pp. 391-403). San Diego, CA: IEEE Press.

Leon-Garcia, A. (1994). *Probability and random processes for electrical engineering* (2nd ed.). Oxford, UK: Addison-Wesley.

Lestas, M., Pitsillinds, A., Ioannou, P., & Hadjipollas, G. (2007). Adaptive congestion protocol: A congestion control protocol with learning capability. *Journal of Computer Networks, 51*(13), 3773–3798. doi:10.1016/j.comnet.2007.04.002

Levijoki, S. (2000). *Authentication, authorization and accounting in ad hoc networks*. Retrieved September 11, 2010 from http://www.tml.hut.fi/Opinnot/Tik-110.551/2000/papers/authentication/aaa.htm.

Liang, O., Sekercioglu, Y., & Mani, N. (2006). A survey of multipoint relay based broadcast schemes in wireless ad hoc networks. *IEEE Communications Surveys & Tutorials, 8*(4), 30–46. doi:10.1109/COMST.2006.283820

Liao, H.-C., Ting, Y.-W., Yen, S.-H., & Yang, C.-C. (2004). Ant mobility model platform for network simulator. In *Proceedings of the International Conference on Information Technology: Coding and Computing (ITCC 2004)*, (pp. 380-384). IEEE Press.

Li, C., Hwang, M., & Chu, Y. (2008). A secure and efficient communication scheme with authenticated key establishment and privacy preserving for vehicular ad hoc networks. *Journal of Computer Communications, 31*(12), 2803–2814. doi:10.1016/j.comcom.2007.12.005

Lim, C. C., Low, Y. H., Cai, W., Hsu, W. J., Huang, S. Y., & Turner, S. J. (1998). An empirical comparison of runtime systems for conservative parallel simulations. In *Proceedings of the 2nd Workshop on Runtime Systems for Parallel Programming*, (pp. 123-134). Miami: FL: IEEE Press.

Lin, Y., & Lazowska, E. (1990). Exploiting look-ahead in parallel simulation. *IEEE Transactions on Parallel and Distributed Systems, 1*(4), 457–469. doi:10.1109/71.80174

Li, Z., & Garcia-Luna-Aceves, J. J. (2007). Non-interactive key establishment in mobile ad hoc networks. *Journal of Ad Hoc Networks, 5*(7), 1194–1203. doi:10.1016/j.adhoc.2006.07.002

Lucas, L. W., Jones, J. G., & Moore, D. L. (1992). *Packet radio: An educator's alternative to costly telecommunications*. Denton, TX: Texas Center for Educational Technology.

Ludwig, R., & Katz, R. H. (2000). The Eifel algorithm: Making TCP robust against spurious retransmissions. *ACM Computer Communications Review, 1*(30).

Lulling, M., & Vaughan, J. (2004). A simulation-based performance evaluation of Tahoe, Reno and SACK TCP as appropriate transport protocols for sip. *Journal of Computer Communications, 27*(16), 1585–1593. doi:10.1016/j.comcom.2004.05.013

Luo, H. (2002). Self-securing ad hoc wireless networks. In *Proceedings of the IEEE Symposium on Computers and Communications*. Taormina-Giardini Naxos, Italy: IEEE Press.

Luo, H., Zerfos, P., Kong, J., Lu, S., & Zhang, L. (2002). Self-securing ad hoc wireless networks. In *Proceedings of the 7th IEEE Symposium on Computers and Communications (ISCC 2002)*. IEEE Press.

Lynch, N., & Shvartsman, A. (2003). *Communication and data sharing for dynamic distributed systems*. Heidelberg, Berlin: Springer-Verlag.

MacKenzie, A. B., & deSilva, L. A. (2006). *Game theory for wireless engineering*. New York, NY: Morgan & Claypool.

Madrid. (2011). *Madrid document on information society policies and metrics*. Retrieved May 2011 from http://www.mityc.es/telecomunicaciones/Presidency/actos/Junio/Documents/2010-06-14_BackgroundMadridDocumentonISpoliciesandmetrics.pdf.

Madsen, P., Koga, Y., & Takahashi, K. (2005). Federated identity management for protecting users from ID theft. In *Proceedings of the Workshop on Digital Identity Management*, (pp. 77-83). Fairfax, VA: IEEE Press.

Mahrenholz, D., & Ivanov, S. (2004). Real-time network emulation with ns-2. In *Proceedings of the Eighth IEEE International Symposium on Distributed Simulation and Real-time Applications (DS-RT 2004)*, (pp. 29-36). IEEE Press.

Mäkelä, J. (2008). *Effects of handoff algorithms on the performance of multimedia wireless networks*. Academic dissertation. Oulu, Finland: University of Oulu.

Marlinspike, M. (2009). *Knockknock: Using knock-knock for single packet authorization*. Retrieved June 13, 2010, from http://www.thoughtcrime.org/software/knockknock/.

Marti, S., Giuli, T., Lai, K., & Baker, M. (2000). Mitigating routing misbehavior in mobile ad hoc networks. In *Proceedings of the 6th ACM Annual International Conference on Mobile Computing and Networking (MOBICOM 2000)*, (pp. 255 - 265). Boston, MA: ACM Press.

Martin, J. (2006). *JNOS operators guide*. Retrieved September 13, 2010, from http://www.nyc-arecs.org/JNOS_OpGuide.pdf.

Martin, J. (2006). *Whetting your feet with JNOS*. Retrieved October 17, 2010, from http://legitimate.org/iook/packet/jnos/whetting/whetting.htm.

Martinez-Morales, J. D., Pineda-Rico, U., & Stevens-Navarro, E. (2010). Performance comparison between MADM algorithms for vertical handoff in 4G networks. In *Proceedings of IEEE International Conference In Automatic Control, Computing Science and Electronic Engineering (CCE 2010)*, (pp. 309-314). IEEE Press.

Mathworks. (2010). *MATLAB and Simulink for technical computing*. Retrieved 28 June 2010 from http://www.mathworks.com.

Matsumoto, M., & Nishimura, T. (1999). Mersenne twister: A623-dimentionally equidistributed uniform pseudorandom number generator. *ACM Transactions on Modeling and Computer Simulation, 7*(1), 3–30.

McAfee, R., & McMillan, J. (1987a). Auctions and bidding. *Journal of Economic Literature, 25*, 699–738.

McAfee, R., & McMillan, J. (1987b). Auctions with a stochastic number of bidders. *Journal of Economic Theory, 43*, 1–19. doi:10.1016/0022-0531(87)90113-X

McAfee, R., & McMillan, J. (1992). Bidding rings. *The American Economic Review, 82*, 579–599.

McCosker, R. (2010). *Creating a XRouter remote node*. Retrieved September 28, 2010, from http://vk2dot.dyndns.org/XRouter/XRouter.htm.

McHaney, R. (2009). *Understanding computer simulation*. Frederiksberg, Denmark: Ventus Publishing APS. Retrieved December 20, 2010 from http://bookboon.com/us/textbooks/it/understanding.

McHaney, R. (1991). *Computer simulation: A practical perspective*. San Diego, CA: Academic Press.

Medhi, D. (2002). Quality of service (QoS) routing computation with path caching: A framework and network performance. *IEEE Communication Magazine*.

Melia, T., Vidal, A., De la Oliva, A., Soto, I., Corujo, D., & Aguiar, R. (2006). *Toward IP converged heterogeneous mobility: A network controlled approach*. Paper presented at the Seventh International Conference on Networking on Mobile Data Management. Nara, Japan.

Melody, W., Sutherland, E., & Tadayoni, R. (2005). *Convergence, IP telephony and telecom regulation*. Paper presented at the Workshop on Convergence, VoIP and Regulation. New Delhi, India: Telecommunication Regulatory Authority of India (TRAI).

Memon, Q., Akhtar, S., & Aly, A. (2007). Role management in ad hoc networks. In [Philadelphia, PA: IEEE Press.]. *Proceedings of the Spring Simulation Multiconference, 2007*, 131–137.

Menezes, F. M., & Monteiro, P. K. (2004). *An introduction to auction theory*. Oxford, UK: Oxford University Press.

Michiardi, P., & Molva, R. (2005). Analysis of coalition formation and cooperation strategies in mobile ad hoc networks. *Journal of Ad Hoc Networks, 3*(2), 193–219. doi:10.1016/j.adhoc.2004.07.006

Mikkonen, T., Lahde, E., Niemi, J., & Siiskonen, M. (2000). Managing software evolution with the service concept. In *Proceedings of International Symposium on Principles of Software Evolution*, (pp 46–50). IEEE Press.

Milgrom, P. R. (1985). A theory of auction and competitive bidding. *Journal of Econometrics, 50*(5), 1089–1122.

Mishra, A., Nadkarni, K., Patcha, A., & Tech, V. (2004). Intrusion detection in wireless ad hoc networks. *IEEE Wireless Communications, 11*(1), 48–60. doi:10.1109/MWC.2004.1269717

MiXiM Project. (2010). *Website*. Retrieved from http://mixim.sourceforge.net.

Miyazakia, K., & Wiggersb, E. (2005). *Innovation in telecom services framework and analysis based on the case of international pre-paid calling cards in Japan.* Tokyo, Japan: Tokyo Institute of Technology.

Mobile Group. (2008). *Green base station: The benefits of going green.* Retrieved from http://www.mobileeurope. co.uk/features/113824/greenbasestation_-_the_benefits_of_going_ green.html.

Mohapatra, P., & Krishnamurth, S. (2004). Ad hoc networks technology and protocols. *Ad Hoc Networks, 1,* 1–3.

Montgomery, D. C. (2006). *Applied statistics and probability for engineers* (4th ed.). New York: John Wiley.

Montgomery, D. C. (2009). *Design and analysis of experiments* (7th ed.). New York: John Wiley.

Moore, N. (2006). *Optimistic duplicate address detection (DAD) for IPv6 (RFC 4429).* Retrieved June 14, 2011 from http://tools.ietf.org/html/rfc4429.

Moorsel, V., Haverkort, B., & Niemegeers, I. (1991). Fault injection simulation: A variance reduction technique for systems with rare events. In *Proceedings of the 2nd International Working Conference on Dependable Computing for Critical Applications,* (pp. 57-64). Tucson, AZ: IEEE Press.

Motorola Labs & INRIA PLANETE Team. (2002). *Mobi-Wan: NS-2.1b6 extensions to study mobility in wide-area IPv6 networks.* Retrieved May 18, 2010 from http://www.inrialpes.fr/planete/mobiwan/.

Mukherjee, A., Gupta, A., & Agrawal, D. P. (2008). Distributed key management for dynamic groups in MANETs. *Journal of Pervasive and Mobile Computing, 4*(4), 562–578. doi:10.1016/j.pmcj.2008.03.002

Murdoch, S., & Lewis, S. (2005). Embedding covert channels into TCP/IP. *Proceedings of 7th Information Hiding (IH), 37*(27), 247–261.

Murthy, C., & Manjo, B. (2004). *Ad hoc wireless networks: Architectures and protocols.* Upper Saddle River, NJ: Prentice Hall.

Namboodiri, V., Gao, L., & Janaswamy, R. (2008). Power efficient topology control for static wireless networks with switched beam directional antennas. *Journal of Ad Hoc Networks, 6*(2), 287–306. doi:10.1016/j.ad-hoc.2007.01.003

Narasimha, M., Tsudik, G., & Yi, J. (2003). *On the utility of distributed cryptography in P2P and MANETs: The case of membership control.* Paper presented at the 11th IEEE International Conference on Network Protocols. Atlanta, GA.

Narasimha, M., Tsudik, G., & Yi, J. H. (2003). On the utility of distributed cryptography in P2P and MANETs: The case of membership control. In *Proceedings from the IEEE International Conference on Networks and Protocols,* (pp. 336 – 345). IEEE Press.

Nasser, N., Hasswa, A., & Hassanein, H. (2006). Handoffs in fourth generation heterogeneous networks. *IEEE Communications Magazine, 44*(10), 96–103. doi:10.1109/MCOM.2006.1710420

Nasser, N., Hasswa, A., & Hassanein, H. (2006). Handoffs in fourth generation heterogeneous networks. *IEEE Communications Magazine, 44*(10), 96–103. doi:10.1109/MCOM.2006.1710420

Neuman, C., Yu, T., Hartman, S., & Raeburn, K. (2005). The Kerberos network authentication system (*RFC 4120).* Retrieved from http://www.ietf.org.

Nicol, D., Michael, C., & Inouye, P. (1989). Efficient aggregation of multiple LPs in distributed memory parallel simulations. In *Proceeding of the Winter Simulation Conference (WSC 1989),* (pp. 680-685). Washington, DC: IEEE Press.

Nicola, V., Nakayama, M., Heidelberger, P., & Goyal, A. (1990). Fast simulation of dependability models with general failure, repair and maintenance processes. In *Proceedings of the 12th Annual International Symposium on Fault-Tolerant Computing,* (pp. 491-498). Newcastle Upon Tyne, UK: IEEE Press.

Nicopolitidis, P., Obaidat, M. S., Papadimitriou, G. I., & Pomportsis, A. S. (Eds.). (2003). *Wireless networks.* New York: John Wiley & Sons, Ltd.

Ni, S., Tseng, Y., Chen, Y., & Sheu, J. (1999). The broadcast storm problem in a mobile ad hoc network. *Journal of ACM/Springer. Wireless Networks, 8*(2), 153–167.

Nmap. (2010). *Network exploration tool and security/Port scanner.* Retrieved June 13, 2010, from http://nmap.org.

NSL. (2010). *NCTUns network simulator and emulator*. Retrieved 20 June 2010 from http://nsl.csie.nctu.edu.tw/nctuns.

Nuevo, J. (2004). A comprehensible GloMoSim tutorial. *University of Quebec*. Retrieved June 15, 2010, from www.ccs.neu.edu/course/csg250/Glomosim/glomoman.pdf.

Oikonomou, K., & Stavrakakis, I. (2006). Energy considerations for topology-unaware TDMA MAC protocols. *Journal of Ad Hoc Networks*, *4*(3), 359–379. doi:10.1016/j.adhoc.2004.10.003

OPNET. (2007). *Modeler*. Retrieved October 1, 2010 from http:// www.opnet.com/products /modeler/home.html.

OPNET. (2011). *Webpage*. Retrieved June 14, 2011 from http://www.opnet.com.

OPNET. (2011). *Website*. Retrieved from http://www.opnet.com/products/modeler/home.

Oudrhiri, R. (1980). *Une approche de l'évolution des systèmes- Application aux systèmes d'information*. Paris, France: Vuibert.

Padhye, J., Firoiu, V., Towsley, D., & Kurose, J. (2000). Modeling TCP Reno performance: A simple model and its empirical validation. *IEEE/ACM Transactions on Networking*, *8*(2), 133–145. doi:10.1109/90.842137

Pan, J., Hou, Y., Cai, L., Shi, Y., & Shen, S. (2003). Topology control for wireless sensor networks. In *Proceedings of 9th Annual International Conference on Mobile Computing and Networking (MOBICOM 2003)*, (pp. 286-299). San Diego, CA: IEEE Press.

Parekh, S., & Walrand, J. (1989). A quick simulation method for excessive backlogs in networks of queues. *IEEE Transactions on Automatic Control*, *34*(1). doi:10.1109/9.8649

Park, M. K., Lee, J. Y., Kim, B. C., & Kim, D. Y. (2008). Design of fast handover mechanism for multiple interfaces mobile IPv6. In *Proceedings of IEEE International Symposium on Wireless Prevasive Computing*, (pp. 697-701). IEEE Press.

Park, S. K., & Miller, R. W. (1988). Random number generators: Good ones are hard to find. *Communications of the ACM*, *31*(10), 1192–1201. doi:10.1145/63039.63042

Parrsch, H. J., & Robert, J. (2003). *Testing equilibrium behaivour at first-price, sealed-bid auctions with discrete bid increments (working paper)*. Montreal, CA: CIRANO. Retrieved from http://econpapers.repec.org/paper/circirwor/2003s-32.htm.

Patten, R. W. (1970). *Tatworth candle auction*. London, UK: Taylor & Francis.

Paul, J. R. (1993). Activity cycle diagrams and the three-phase method. In *Proceeding of the 25th Conference on Winter Simulation*, (pp. 123-131). Los Angeles, CA: IEEE Press.

Paul, K., Roy, R., & Bandyopadhyay, S. (2000). Survivability analysis of ad hoc network architecture. In *Proceedings of the European Commission International Workshop on Mobile and Wireless Communication*, (pp. 31-46). IEEE Press.

Pawlikowski, K. (1990). Steady-state simulation of queuing processes: A survey of problems and solutions. *ACM Computing Surveys*, *1*(2), 123–170. doi:10.1145/78919.78921

Pawlikowski, K., Jeong, H.-D. J., & Lee, J.-S. R. (2002). On credibility of simulation studies of telecommunication networks. *IEEE Communications Magazine*, *40*(1), 132–139. doi:10.1109/35.978060

PCBS. (2010). *Definitions of world telecommunications/ICT indicators*. Retrieved June 2010, from www.pcbs.gov.ps/Portals/_PCBS/ICT/ICT_Escwa.pdf.

Pentikousis, K., & Badr, H. (2002). *On the resource efficiency of explicit congestion notification*. Berlin, Germany: Springer.

Perkins, C., & Royer, E. (1999). Ad-hoc on demand distance vector routing. In *Proceedings of the 2nd IEEE Workshop on Mobile Computing Systems and Applications (WMCSA)*, (pp. 90-100). New Orleans, LA: IEEE Press.

Perkins, C., Belding-Royer, E., & Das, S. (2003). *Ad hoc on-demand distance vector (AODV) routing, (RFC 3561)*. Retrieved from http://www.ietf.org.

Perlman, R. (1999). An overview of PKI trust models. *IEEE Network*, *13*, 38–43. doi:10.1109/65.806987

Peterson, J. L. (1981). *Petri net theory and the modeling of systems*. Englewood Cliffs, NJ: Prentice-Hall.

Pidd, M. (1998). *Computer simulation in management science* (4th ed.). Chicester, UK: John Wiley.

Pop, F., Dobre, C. M., Godza, G., & Cristea, V. (2006). A simulation model for grid scheduling analysis and optimization. In *Proceedings of the International Symposium on Parallel Computing in Electrical Engineering (PARELEC 2006)*, (pp. 133 – 138). Bialystok, Poland: IEEE Press.

Pop, P., Dobre, C., & Cristea, V. (2008). Evaluation of multi-objective decentralized scheduling for applications in grid environment. In *Proceedings of the 2008 IEEE 4th International Conference on Intelligent Computer Communication and Processing*, (pp. 231-238). Cluj-Napoca, Romania: IEEE Press.

Powell, O., Leonea, P., & Rolima, J. (2007). Energy optimal data propagation in wireless sensor networks. *Journal of Parallel and Distributed Computing, 67*(3), 302–317. doi:10.1016/j.jpdc.2006.10.007

Proctor, W., & Drechsler, M. (2003). *Deliberative multi-criteria evaluation: A case study of recreation and tourism options in Victoria, Australia*. Paper presented at European Society for Ecological Economics, Frontiers 2 Conference. Tenerife, Canary Islands.

Puigjaner, R. (2003). Performance modelling of computer networks. In *Proceedings of IFIP/ACM Latin America conference on Towards a Latin American Agenda for Network Research*, (pp. 106-123). ACM Press.

Python Programming Language. (2010). *Python*. Retrieved June 13, 2010, from http://www.python.org/.

Qayyum, A., Viennot, L., & Laouiti, A. (2002). Multipoint relaying for flooding broadcast messages in mobile wireless networks. In *Proceedings of the 35th Hawaii International Conference on System Sciences (HICSS 2002)*, (pp. 3866- 3875). Hawaii, HI: IEEE Press.

Qiu, Q., Zhang, D., & J., M. (2004). GPRS network simulation in ns-2. In *Proceedings of the 10th Asia-Pacific Conference on Communications and 5th International Symposium on Multi-Dimentional Mobile Communications*, (pp. 700-704). APCC Press.

Rahman, A., Olesinski, W., & Gburzynski, P. (2004). Controlled flooding in wireless ad hoc networks. In *Proceedings of IEEE International Workshop on Wireless Ad Hoc Networks (IWWAN 2004)*. Oulu, Finland: IEEE Press.

Rahman, M., Pakštas, A., & Zhigang, F. (2009). Network modelling and simulation tools. *Simulation Modelling Practice and Theory, 17*(6), 1011–1031. doi:10.1016/j.simpat.2009.02.005

Rajaraman, R. (2002). Topology control and routing in ad hoc networks. *ACM Special Interest Group on Algorithms and Computation Theory (SIGACT). News, 33*(2), 60–73.

Rappaport, T. (2001). *Wireless communications: Principles and practice* (2nd ed.). Upper Saddle River, NJ: Prentice Hall.

Rash, M. (2006b). *Advances in single packet authorization. Paper presented at SchmooCon*. USA.

Rashed, A. (2004). *Intelligent encryption decryption systems using genetic algorithms*. PhD Dissertation. Amman, Jordan: The Arab Academy for Banking & Financial Sciences.

Rash, M. (2006a). *SPA: Single packet authorization. MadHat Unspecific and Simple Nomad*. New York: BlackHat Briefings.

Rasmusen, E. (2006). *Games and information: An introduction to game theory* (4th ed.). Oxford, UK: Blackwell Publishers.

Rattle. (2004). *Using process infection to bypass Windows software firewalls*. Retrieved from http://www.tech-forums.net/pc/f27/using-process-infection-bypass-windows-software-firewalls-86504/.

Reliarisk. (2010). *Reliability and risk management: Criticality analysis*. Retrieved 20 March 2010 from http://www.reliarisk.com.

Resnick, P., & Zeckhauser, R. (2002). Trust among strangers in Internet transactions: Empirical analysis of eBay's reputation system. In Baye, M. R. (Ed.), *The Economics of the Internet and E-Commerce: Advances in Applied Microeconomics (Vol. 11)*. Amsterdam, The Netherlands: Elsevier Science. doi:10.1016/S0278-0984(02)11030-3

Reynolds, P. (1988). A spectrum of options for parallel simulation. In *Proceeding of the Winter Simulation Conference (WSC 1988)*, (pp. 325-332). San Diego, CA: IEEE Press.

Rice, S. O. (1948). Mathematical analysis of a sine wave plus random noise. *The Bell System Technical Journal, 27*(1), 109–157.

Richard., & Stevens, W. (2001). TCP slow start, congestion avoidance, fast retransmit, and fast recovery algorithms. *IETF RFC*. Retrieved from http://www.ietf.org.

Riley, G. F., & Ammar, M. H. (2002). Simulating large networks – How big is big enough? In *Proceedings of the First International Conference on Grand Challenges for Modelling and Simulation*. IEEE Press.

Riley, G. F., Ammar, M. H., Fujimoto, R. M., Park, F., Perumalla, K., & Xu, D. (2004). A federated approach to distributed network simulation. *ACM Transactions on Modeling and Computer Simulation, 14*(2), 116–148. doi:10.1145/985793.985795

Rivest, L., Shamir, A., & Adleman, L. (1978). A method of obtaining digital signature and public key crypto-system. *Communications of the ACM, 21*(2), 120–126. doi:10.1145/359340.359342

Robertazzi, T. (2000). *Computer networks and systems: Queuing theory and performance evaluation* (3rd ed.). Berlin, Germany: Springer Verlag.

Ross, A., & Jain, A. (2004). Multimodal biometrics: An overview. In *Proceedings of 12th European Signal Processing Conference (EUSIPCO)*, (pp. 1221-1224). Vienna, Austria: IEEE Press.

Rossi, D., & Turrini, E. (2005). Analyzing the impact of components replication in high available J2EE clusters. In *Proceedings of the Joint International Conference on Autonomic and Autonomous Systems and International Conference on Networking and Services*, (p. 56). IEEE Press.

Roth, P. F. (1987). Discrete, continuous and combined simulation. In *Proceeding of the Winter Simulation Conference (WSC 1987)*, (pp. 56-60). Atlanta, GA: IEEE Press.

Royer, E. (1999). A review of current routing protocols for ad hoc mobile wireless networks. Retrieved from http://www.eecs.harvard.edu/~mdw/course/cs263/papers/royer-ieeepc99.pdf.

Royer, E., & Toh, C. (1999). A review of current routing protocols for ad hoc mobile wireless networks. *IEEE Personal Communication Magazine, 6*(2), 46-55.

Rudis, B. (2003). *The enemy within: Firewalls and backdoors*. Retrieved June 13, 2010, from http://www.symantec.com/connect/articles/enemy-within-firewalls-and-backdoors.

Rundle, M., & Ben Laurie, B. (2005). *Identity management as a cybersecurity case study (research publication no. 2006-01)*. Boston, MA: Harvard Law School.

Saaty, T. (1980). *The analytic hierarchy process*. New York, NY: McGraw-Hill.

Sakurai, Y., & Katto, J. (2004). AODV multipath extension using source route lists with optimized route establishment. In *Proceedings of the 2004 International Workshop on Wireless Ad-Hoc Networks*, (pp. 63-67). IEEE Press.

Saouma, V., & Sivaselvan, M. V. (Eds.). (2008). *Hybrid simulation: Theory, implementation and applications*. New York: Taylor & Francis.

Sargent, R. G. (2004). Validation and verification of simulation models. In *Proceedings of the 2004 Winter Simulation Conference*, (pp. 17-28). IEEE Press.

Sarkar, N. I. (2010). *Capacity estimation of wireless LANs*. Retrieved March 15, 2010 from http://elena.aut.ac.nz/homepages/staff/Nurul-Sarkar/capacity/.

Sarkar, N. I., & McHaney, R. (2006). Modeling and simulation of IEEE 802.11 WLANs: A case study of a network simulator. In *Proceedings of the 2006 Information Resources Management Association International Conference*, (pp. 715-718). Washington, DC: IEEE Press.

Sarkar, N. I., & Sowerby, K. W. (2005). Buffer unit multiple access (BUMA) protocol: an enhancement to IEEE 802.11b DCF. In *Proceedings of the IEEE Global Telecommunications Conference (GLOBECOM 2005)*, (pp. 2584-2588). St. Louis, MO: IEEE Press.

Sarkar, N. I., & Sowerby, K. W. (2006). Wi-Fi performance measurements in the crowded office environment: A case study. In *Proceedings of the 10th IEEE International Conference on Communication Technology (ICCT 2006)*, (pp. 37-40). Guilin, China: IEEE Press.

Sarkar, N. I. (2006). Teaching TCP/IP networking using practical laboratory exercises. *International Journal of Information and Communication Technology Education, 2*(4), 39–50. doi:10.4018/jicte.2006100104

Sarkar, N., & Pawlikowski, K. (2002). A delay-throughput performance improvement to the pi-persistent protocol. *Pakistan Journal of Applied Sciences, 2*(3), 390–399.

Sasson, Y., Cavin, D., & Schiper, A. (2003). Probabilistic broadcast for flooding in wireless mobile ad hoc networks. In *Proceedings of IEEE Wireless Communications and Networking (WCNC 2003)*, (vol 2), (pp. 1124-1130). New Orleans, LA: IEEE Press.

Saunders, S., & Aragón-Zavala, A. (2007). *Antennas and propagation for wireless communication systems* (2nd ed.). Chichester, UK: John Wiley.

Scapy. (2010). *Interactive packet manipulation program.* Retrieved June 13, 2010, from http://www.secdev.org/projects/scapy/.

Schmeiser, B. (2004). Simulation output analysis: A tutorial based on one research thread. In *Proceedings of the 2004 Winter Simulation Conference*, (pp. 162-170). IEEE Press.

Schormans, J., Liu, E., Cuthbert, L., & Pitts, J. (2001). A hybrid technique for the accelerated simulation of ATM networks and network elements. *ACM Transactions on Modeling and Computer Simulation, 11*(2), 182–205. doi:10.1145/384169.384172

Schumpeter, J. A. (1975). *Capitalism, socialism and democracy.* New York: Harper.

Scott, D., & Yasinsac, A. (2004). Dynamic probabilistic retransmission in ad hoc networks. In H. R. Arabnia, L. T. Yang, & C. H. Yeh (Eds.), *Proceeding of the International Conference on Wireless Networks (ICWN 2004)*, (vol 1), (pp. 158-164). Las Vegas, NV: CSREA Press.

Shamir, A. (1979). How to share a secret. *Communications of the ACM, 22*(11), 612–613. doi:10.1145/359168.359176

Shaw, M. (2001). The coming-of-age of software architecture research. In *Proceedings of ICSE*, (pp. 656–664). Pittsburgh, PA: Carnegie Mellon University.

Shubik, M. (2004). *The theory of money and financial institutions* (*Vol. 1*). Cambridge, MA: MIT Press.

Silva, M. (1993). *Introducing petri nets: Practice of petri nets in manufacturing.* New York: Chapman & Hall.

Simon, H. A. (1969). *The sciences of the artificial.* Cambridge, MA: MIT Press.

Sinclair, J. B. (2004). *Simulation of computer systems and computer networks: A process-oriented approach.* Houston, TX: Rice University.

Siringoringo, W., & Sarkar, N. I. (2009). Teaching and learning Wi-Fi networking fundamentals using limited resources. In Gutierrez, J. (Ed.), *Selected Readings on Telecommunications and Networking* (pp. 22–40). Hershey, PA: IGI Global. doi:10.4018/9781605660943.ch003

Sklavos, N., Denazis, S., & Koufopavlou, O. (2007). AAA and mobile networks: Security aspects and architectural efficiency. In *Proceedings of the 3rd International Conference on Mobile Multimedia Communications (MobiMedia 2007)*. Nafpaktos, Greece: IEEE Press.

Skoric, M. (2000-2010). FBB packet radio BBS mini-HOWTO. *The Linux Documentation Project.* Retrieved September 28, 2010, from http://tldp.org/HOWTO/FBB.html.

Skoric, M. (2009). The new amateur radio university network – AMUNET (Part 4). In *Proceedings of the 13th WSEAS International Conference on Computers,* (pp. 323-328). Athens, Greece: WSEAS Press.

Skoric, M. (2009). Amateur radio in education. In Song, H., & Kidd, T. (Eds.), *Handbook of Research on Human Performance and Instructional Technology* (pp. 223–245). Hershey, PA: IGI Global. doi:10.4018/978-1-60566-782-9.ch014

Sokol, L., Briskoe, D., & Wieland, A. (1988). MTW: A strategy for scheduling discrete simulation events for concurrent execution. In *Proceeding of SCS Western Multi-Conference on Advances in Parallel and Distributed Simulation,* (pp. 34-42). Orlando, FL: IEEE Press.

Son, D., Krishnamachari, B., & Heidemann, J. (2004). Experimental study of the effects of transmission power control and blacklisting in wireless sensor networks. In *Proceedings of the 1st IEEE Conference on Sensor and Ad Hoc Communication and Networks,* (pp. 289-298). IEEE Press.

Squicciarini, A., Czeskis, A., & Bhargav-Spantzel, A. (2008). Privacy policies compliance across digital identity management systems. In *Proceedings of the ACM GIS 2008 International Workshop on Security and Privacy in GIS and LBS (SPRINGL 2008)*, (pp. 72-81). Irvine, CA: ACM Press.

Sridhar, A., & Ephremides, A. (2008). Energy optimization in wireless broadcasting through power control. *Journal of Ad Hoc Networks*, *6*(2), 155–167. doi:10.1016/j.adhoc.2006.11.001

Srinivasan, V., Nuggehalli, P., Chiasserini, C. F., & Rao, R. R. (2003). Cooperation in wireless ad hoc networks. In *Proceeding of the 22nd Annual Joint Conference of the IEEE Computer and Communications (INFOCOM 2003)*, (vol 2), (pp. 808-817). San Francisco, CA: IEEE Press.

Stallings, W. (2011a). *Network security essentials: Applications and standards* (4th ed.). Upper Saddle River, NJ: Prentice-Hall.

Stallings, W. (2011b). *Cryptography and network security: Principle and practices* (5th ed.). Upper Saddle River, NJ: Prentice-Hall.

Steganogra-py. (2010). *Steganography in Python*. Retrieved June 13, 2010, from http://code.google.com/p/steganogra-py.

Stepanov, I., Hahner, J., Becker, C., Tian, J., & Rothermel, K. (2003). A meta-model and framework for user mobility in mobile networks. In *Proceedings of IEEE International Conference*, (pp. 231-238). IEEE Press.

Stevens-Navarro, E., & Wong, V. (2006). Comparison between vertical handoff decision algorithms for heterogeneous wireless networks. In *Proceedings of the IEEE Vehicular Technology Conference*, (pp. 947-951). IEEE Press.

Stockholm Auction House. (2011). *About the company*. Retrieved 5 March 2010 from http://www.auktionsverket.se/historike.htm.

Suciu, L., Guillouard, K., & Bonnin, J. (2006). A methodology for assessing the vertical handover algorithms in heterogeneous wireless network. In *Proceedings of the Workshop on Broadband Wireless Access for Ubiquitous Networking*, (p. 196). ACM Press.

Sulistio, A., Yeo, C. S., & Buyya, R. (2004). A taxonomy of computer-based simulations and its mapping to parallel and distributed systems simulation tools. *Software, Practice & Experience*, *34*(7), 653–673. doi:10.1002/spe.585

Sun, B., Wu, K., Xiao, Y., & Wang, R. (2007). Integration of mobility and intrusion detection for wireless ad hoc networks. *International Journal of Communication Systems*, *20*(6), 695–721. doi:10.1002/dac.853

Sun, W. (2002). *QoS, policy, constraint based routing*. Columbus, OH: Ohio State University.

Syuhada, M., Mahamod, I., & Firuz, W. (2008). *Performance evaluation of vertical handoff in fourth generation (4G) networks model*. Paper presented at the 6th National Conference on Telecommunication Technologies and IEEE 2008 2nd Malaysia Conference on Photonics. Putrajaya, Malaysia.

Szyperski, C. (2006). Component-based software engineering. In *Proceedings of the 9th International Symposium, CBSE 2006*. Västeras, Sweden: IEEE Press.

Tanenbaum, A. (2003). *Computer networks* (4th ed.). Upper Saddle River, NJ: Prentice Hall.

Tanenbaum, A. S., & Wetherall, D. J. (2010). *Computer networks* (5th ed.). Upper Saddle River, NJ: Prentice-Hall.

Taylor, D. S. (2001). *Multi-layered approach to small office networking*. Retrieved May 2011 from http://www.sans.org.

Tcpreplay. (2010). *Replay captured network traffic*. Retrieved June 13, 2010, from http://tcpreplay.synfin.net/trac/.

Technologies, O. P. N. E. T. (2008). *OPNET*. Retrieved September 15, 2010, from www.opnet.com.

Tekala, M., & Szabo, R. (2008). Dynamic adjustment of scalable TCP congestion control parameters. *Journal of Computer Communications*, *31*(10), 1890–1900. doi:10.1016/j.comcom.2007.12.035

The Network Simulator NS-2. (2011). *Website*. Retrieved May 18, 2011 from http://www.isi.edu/nsnam/ns.

Tickoo, O., & Sikdar, B. (2003). On the impact of IEEE 802.11 MAC on traffic characteristics. *IEEE Journal on Selected Areas in Communications*, *21*(2), 189–203. doi:10.1109/JSAC.2002.807346

Toh, C. (2002). *Ad hoc mobile wireless networks: Protocols and systems*. Upper Saddle River, NJ: Prentice-Hall.

Tseng, T., Ni, S., Chen, Y., & Sheu, J. (2002). The broadcast storm problem in a mobile ad hoc network. *Journal of Wireless Networks, 8*(2-3), 153–167. doi:10.1023/A:1013763825347

Tsirtsis, G., Giaretta, G., Soliman, H., & Montavont, N. (2011). *Traffic selectors for flow bindings (RFC 6088)*. Retrieved June 14, 2011 from http://www.faqs.org/rfcs/rfc6088.html.

Tsirtsis, G., Soliman, H., Montavont, N., Giaretta, G., Montavont, N., & Kuladinithi, K. (2010). *Flow bindings in mobile IPv6 and NEMO basic support (RFC 6089)*. Retrieved June 14, 2011 from http://tools.ietf.org/id/draft-ietf-mext-flow-binding-09.html.

University of Bonn. (2010). *BonnMotion: A mobility scenario generation and analysis tool*. Retrieved from http://net.cs.uni-bonn.de/wg/cs/applications/bonnmotion.

University of South Florida. (2009). *The energy efficient internet project*. Retrieved from http://www.csee.usf.edu/~christen/energy/main.html.

Urpi, A., Bonuccelli, M., & Giordano, S. (2003). Modeling cooperation in mobile ad hoc networks: A formal description of selfishness. In *Proceeding of the 1st Workshop on Modeling and Optimization in Mobile, Ad Hoc and Wireless Networks (WiOpt 2003)*. Sophia-Antipolis, France: IEEE Press.

Valentin, S. (2006). *ChSim: A wireless channel simulator for OMNeT++*. Paper presented at the TKN TU Berlin Simulation Workshop. Berlin, Germany. Retrieved June 14, 2011 from http://www.cs.uni-paderborn.de/en/research-group/research-group-computer-networks/publications/talks-without-proceeding.html.

Varga, A. (2010a). *OMNeT++ user manual*. Retrieved May 2011 from http://www.omnetpp.org/doc/omnetpp41/manual/usman.html.

Varga, A. (2010b). *INET-framework*. Retrieved from http://inet.omnetpp.org.

Varga, A. (2010c). *Omnetpp R package*. Retrieved from http://github.com/omnetpp/omnetpp-resultfiles/wiki/Tutorial-for-the-omnetpp-r-package.

Varoli, J. (2007). Swedish auction house to sell 8 million Euros of Russian art. *Bloomberg News*. Retrieved 3 March 2010 from http://www.bloomberg.com/apps/news?pid=20601088&sid=aGlwT7.MHwzw&refer=muse.

Vasserman, E., Hopper, N., Laxson, J., & Tyra, J. (2007). SilentKnock: Practical, provably undetectable authentication. In *Proceeding of ESORICS*, (pp. 122-138). Palo Alto, CA: IEEE Press.

Vendicits, A., Baiocchi, A., & Bonacci, M. (2003). Analysis and enhancement of TCP Vegas congestion control in a mixed TCP Vegas and TCP Reno network scenario. *Journal of Performance Evaluation, 53*(3-4), 225–253. doi:10.1016/S0166-5316(03)00064-6

Venugopal, S., Buyya, R., & Ramamohanaro, K. (2006). A taxonomy of data grids for distributed data sharing, management and processing. *ACM Computing Surveys, 38*(1). doi:10.1145/1132952.1132955

Vickrey, W. (1961). Counter speculation, auctions, and competitive sealed tenders. *The Journal of Finance, 16*, 8–37. doi:10.2307/2977633

Vilas, J. F., Arias, J. P., & Vilas, A. F. (2005). High availability with clusters of web service. In *Advanced Web Technologies and Applications* (*Vol. 3007*). Berlin, Germany: Springer. doi:10.1007/978-3-540-24655-8_70

Vincent, J.-M., & Legrand, A. (2007). *Discrete event simulation*. Paper presented at the Laboratory ID-IMAG. Paris, France.

Viswanath, K., & Obraczka, K. (2005). Modeling the performance of flooding in wireless multi-hop ad hoc networks. *Journal of Computer Communications, 29*(8), 949–956. doi:10.1016/j.comcom.2005.06.015

Voicu, L., Bassi, S., & Labrador, M. A. (2007). Analytical and experimental evaluation of TCP with an additive increase smooth decrease (AISD) strategy. *Journal of Computer Communications, 30*(2), 479–495. doi:10.1016/j.comcom.2006.09.010

Wade, I. (1992). *NOSintro – TCP/IP over packet radio*. Retrieved September 28, 2010, from http://homepage.ntlworld.com/wadei/nosintro/.

Wakikawa, R., Devarapalli, V., Tsirtsis, G., Ernst, T., & Nagami, K. (2009). *Multiple care-of addresses registration (RFC 5648)*. Retrieved June 14, 2011 from http://www.faqs.org/rfcs/rfc5648.html.

Wakikawa, R., Ernst, T., & Nagami, K. (2009). *Multiple care-of addresses registration (RFC 5648)*. Retrieved May, 5, 2010 from http://tools.ietf.org/html/rfc5648.

Walrand, J. (1987). Quick simulation of queuing networks: An introduction. In *Computer Performance and Reliability*, (pp. 275-286). North Holland: Verlag.

Wang, J. (1998). *Stochastic petri net: Theory and application*. PhD Thesis. Nanjing, China: Nanjing University of Science and Technology.

Wang, L., Min, G., & Awan, I. (2006). Modeling active queue management with different traffic classes. In *Proceedings of the 20th International Conference on Advanced Information Networking and Applications*, (pp. 442-446). IEEE Press.

Wang, S., Chou, C., Lin, C., & Huang, C. (2008). *The GUI user manual for the NCTUns 5.0 network simulator and emulator*. Retrieved from http://nsl10.csie.nctu.edu.tw/support/documentation/GUIManualNCTUns5.0.pdf.

Wang, S., Chou, C., Lin, C., & Huang, C. (2008). *The protocol developer manual for the NCTUns 5.0 network simulator and emulator*. Retrieved from http://nsl10.csie.nctu.edu.tw/support/documentation/DeveloperManual.pdf.

Wang, J. (1998). *Timed petri nets: Theory and application. Norwell, Ma*. Kluwer Academic Publishers.

Wang, L., & Kulkarni, S. (2008). Sacrificing a little coverage can substantially increase network lifetime. *Journal of Ad Hoc Networks*, *6*(8), 1281–1300. doi:10.1016/j.adhoc.2007.11.013

Wang, N., Huang, Y., & Chen, W. (2008). A novel secure communication scheme in vehicular ad hoc networks. *Journal of Computer Communications*, *31*(12), 2827–2837. doi:10.1016/j.comcom.2007.12.003

Wang, S., Chou, C., & Lin, C. (2007). The design and implementation of the NCTUns network simulation engine. *Simulation Modelling Practice and Theory*, *15*, 57–81. doi:10.1016/j.simpat.2006.09.013

Webster, M. (2005). *The Merriam-Webster dictionary*. New York: Merriam-Webster.

Weigle, M. C., Jaffay, K., & Simith, D. (2005). Delay-based early congestion detection and adaptation in TCP: Impact on web performance. *Journal of Computer Communications*, *28*(8), 837–850. doi:10.1016/j.comcom.2004.11.011

Wellens, M., Petrova, M., Riihijarvi, J., & Mahonen, P. (2005). Building a better wireless mousetrap: Need for more realism in simulations. In *Proceedings of the Second Annual Conference on Wireless On-Demand Network Systems and Services (WONS 2005)*, (pp. 150-157). IEEE Press.

Welzl, M. (2005). *Network congestion control: Managing internet traffic*. New York: John Wiley & Sons. doi:10.1002/047002531X

Wen-Guey, T. (2002). A secure fault-tolerant conference-key agreement protocol Computers. *IEEE Transactions on Computers*, *51*(4), 373–379. doi:10.1109/12.995447

Weske, M., & Wirtz, G. (2001). Integrated modeling of distributed software systems and workflow applications. In *Proceedings of the 34th Annual Hawaii international Conference on System Sciences (HICSS-34)*, (Vol. 9). Hawaii, HI: HICSS Press.

Widmer, J., Denda, R., & Mauve, M. (2001). A survey on TCP-friendly congestion control. *IEEE Network Magazine*, *15*(3), 28–37. doi:10.1109/65.923938

Wieder, P., Schwiegelsholn, U., & Yahyapour, R. (2005). *Resource management for future generation grids*. Berlin, Germany: CEI.

Wikipedia. (2011). *Identity management dimensions*. Retrieved May 2011 from http://www.en.wikipedia.org.

Williams, L. G., & Smith, C. U. (2004). *Web application scalability: A model-based approach*. New York: Software Engineering Research and Performance Engineering Services.

Wireshark. (2010). *Network protocol analyzer*. Retrieved June 13, 2010, from http://wireshark.org.

Woodward, M. E. (2003). *Communication and computer networks: Modeling with discrete-time queues*. London, UK: Pentech Press.

Worth, D. (2004). *COK - Cryptographic one-time knocking*. In *Proceedings of the Black Hat Conference*. USA.

Wu, H., Fujimoto, R. M., & Riley, G. (2001). Experiences parallelizing a commercial network simulator. In *Proceedings of Winter Simulation Conference (WSC 2001)*, (pp. 1353-1360). Arlington, VA: IEEE Press.

Wu, B., Wu, J., Fernandez, E. B., Ilyas, M., & Magliveras, S. (2007). Secure and efficient key management in mobile ad hoc networks. *Journal of Network and Computer Applications*, *30*(3), 937–954. doi:10.1016/j.jnca.2005.07.008

Wuest, C. (2005). Phishing in the middle of the stream - Today's threats to online banking. In *Proceedings of the AVAR 2005 Conference*. Dublin, Ireland: AVAR Press.

Wydrowski, B., & Zukerman, M. (2002). GREEN: An active queue management algorithm for a self managed internet. In *Proceedings of ICC 2002*, (vol 4), (pp. 2368-2372). IEEE Press.

Xin, F., & Jamalipour, A. (2006). TCP performance in wireless networks with delay spike and different initial congestion window sizes. *Journal of Computer Communications*, *29*(8), 926–933. doi:10.1016/j.comcom.2005.06.012

Xu, D. (2001). *Hardware-based parallel simulation of flexible manu-factoring systems*. PhD Dissertation. Blacksburg, VA: Virginia Polytechnic Institute and State University.

Xu, G., & Liviu, I. (2004). Locality driven key management architecture for mobile ad-hoc networks. In *Proceedings of the IEEE International Conference on Mobile Ad-hoc and Sensor Systems*, (pp. 436-446). IEEE Press.

Xu, H. (2009). Consumer responses to the introduction of privacy protection measures: An exploratory research framework. *International Journal of E-Business Research*, *5*(2), 21–47. doi:10.4018/jebr.2009040102

Xu, Y., Lui, J., & Chiu, D. (2009). Improving energy efficiency via probabilistic rate combination in 802.11 multi-rate wireless networks. *Journal of Ad Hoc Networks*, *7*(7), 1370–1385. doi:10.1016/j.adhoc.2009.01.005

Yang, O., Choi, S., Choi, J., Park, J., & Kim, H. (2006). A handover framework for seamless service support between wired and wireless networks. *International Conference on Advanced Communication Technology (ICACT 2006)*, (Vol. 3), (pp. 1791-1796). IEEE Press.

Yang, D., & Chen, M. (2008). Efficient resource allocation for wireless multicast. *IEEE Transactions on Mobile Computing*, *7*(4), 387–400. doi:10.1109/TMC.2007.70739

Yang, Y. R., Kim, M. S., & Lam, S. S. (2003). Transient behaviors of TCP-friendly congestion control protocols. *Journal of Computer Networks*, *41*(2), 193–210. doi:10.1016/S1389-1286(02)00374-2

Yan, L., Abouzakhar, N., Xiao, H., & Qayyam, R. (2009). Multimodal security enforcement framework for wireless ad hoc networks. In [Leipzig, Germany: IEEE Press.]. *Proceedings of the IWCMC*, *2009*, 921–925. doi:10.1145/1582379.1582580

Yan, X., Sekercioglu, Y., & Narayanan, S. (2010). A survey of vertical handover decision algorithms in fourth generation heterogeneous wireless networks. *Computer Networks: The International Journal of Computer and Telecommunications Networking*, *54*(11), 1848–1863.

Yeun, C. Y., Han, K., Vo, D. L., & Kim, K. (2008). Secure authenticated group key agreement protocol in the MANET environment. *Journal of Information Security Technical Report*, *13*(3), 158–164. doi:10.1016/j.istr.2008.10.002

Yi, S., & Kravets, R. (2002). Key management for heterogeneous ad hoc wireless networks. In *Proceedings of the 10th IEEE International Conference on Network Protocols (ICNP 2002)*. IEEE Press.

Yi, S., & Kravets, R. (2003). MOCA: Mobile certificate authority for wireless ad hoc networks. *University of Illinois at Urbana-Champaign*. Retrieved May 26, 2011, from http://middleware.internet2.edu/pki03/presentations/06.pdf.

Younis, M., Youssef, M., & Akkaya, K. (2003). Energy-aware management for cluster-based sensor networks. *Journal of Computer Networks*, *43*(5), 649–668. doi:10.1016/S1389-1286(03)00305-0

Yuan, J., & Yu, W. (2008). Joint source coding, routing and power allocation in wireless sensor networks. *IEEE Transactions on Communications*, 56(6), 886–896. doi:10.1109/TCOMM.2008.060237

Zahran, A., & Liang, B. (2005). Performance evaluation framework for vertical handoff algorithms in heterogeneous networks. In *Proceedings of the IEEE International Conference on Communications*, (pp. 173-178). IEEE Press.

Zahran, A., Liang, B., & Saleh, A. (2006). Signal threshold adaptation for vertical handoff in heterogeneous wireless network. *Mobile Networks and Applications*, 11(4), 625–640. doi:10.1007/s11036-006-7326-7

Zaikiuddin, I., Hawkins, T., & Moffat, N. (2005). Towards a game-theoretic understanding of ad hoc routing. [ENTCS]. *Electronic Notes in Theoretical Computer Science*, 119(1), 67–92. doi:10.1016/j.entcs.2004.07.009

Zarifzadeh, S., Nayyeri, A., & Yazdani, N. (2008). Efficient construction of network topology to conserve energy in wireless ad hoc networks. *Journal of Computer Communication*, 31, 160–173. doi:10.1016/j.comcom.2007.10.040

Zhang, T. (2001). *Agent-based interoperability in telecommunications applications*. PhD Thesis. Berlin, Germany: University of Berlin.

Zhang, W. (2004). Handover decision using fuzzy MADM in heterogeneous networks. In *Proceedings of IEEE Wireless Communications and Networking Conference (WCNC 2004)*, (pp. 653-658). IEEE Press.

Zhang, Y., & Lee, W. (2000). Intrusion detection in wireless ad hoc networks. In Proceedings of the *6th ACM Annual International Conference on Mobile Computing and Networking (MOBICOM 2000)*. ACM Press.

Zhang, Q. T. (2003). A generic correlated Nakagami fading model for wireless communications. *IEEE Transactions on Communications*, 51(11), 1745–1748. doi:10.1109/TCOMM.2003.819216

Zhang, Q., & Agrawal, D. P. (2005). Dynamic probabilistic broadcasting in MANETs. *Journal of Parallel and Distributed Computing*, 65(2), 220–233. doi:10.1016/j.jpdc.2004.09.006

Zhao, H. (2010). *Broadband applications for tomorrow*. Paper presented at WESIS Forum. Arlington, VA.

Zheng, R., & Kravets, R. (2005). On-demand power management for ad hoc networks. *Journal of Ad Hoc Networks*, 3(1), 51–68. doi:10.1016/j.adhoc.2003.09.008

Zhou, J., Chin, W., Roman, R., & Lopez, J. (2007). An effective multi-layered defense framework against spam. *Information Security Technical Report*, 12(3), 179–185. doi:10.1016/j.istr.2007.05.007

Zhou, L., & Haas, Z. (1999). Securing ad hoc networks. *IEEE Network*, 13(6), 24–30. doi:10.1109/65.806983

Zhu, S. Y., & Schaefer, G. (2009). Using network simulation tools to support teaching in computer networks. In *Proceedings of the International Conference on Education and New Learning Technologies*. IEEE Press.

Zhu, S. Y., & Schaefer, G. (2010). E-assessments to support teaching computer networks - A case study. In *Proceedings of the International Conference on e-Commerce, e-Administration, e-Society, e-Education, and e-Technology*. IEEE Press.

Zhu, B., Bao, F., Deng, R. H., Kankanhalli, M. S., & Wang, G. (2005). Efficient and robust key management for large mobile ad hoc networks. *Journal of Computer Networks*, 48(4), 657–682. doi:10.1016/j.comnet.2004.11.023

Zhu, F., & McNair, J. (2006). Multiservice vertical handoff decision algorithms. *URASIP Journal on Wireless Communications and Networking*, 2, 52–64.

Zhu, H., & Liu, K. J. R. (2005). Noncooperative power-control game and throughput game over wireless networks. *IEEE Transactions on Communications*, 53(10), 1625–1629. doi:10.1109/TCOMM.2005.857136

# About the Contributors

**Hussein Al-Bahadili** received his B.Sc degree in Engineering from College of Engineering (University of Baghdad, Iraq) in 1986. He received his M.Sc and PhD degrees in Engineering from Queen Mary College (University of London, UK) in 1988 and 1991, respectively. His field of study was parallel computers. He is currently working as an Associate Professor at Petra University, Jordan. He is a visiting researcher at the Wireless Networks and Communications Centre (WNCC) at the University of Brunel, UK. He is also a visiting researcher at the School of Engineering, University of Surrey, UK. He has published many papers and book chapters in different fields of science and engineering in numerous leading scholarly and practitioner journals, books, and presented at leading world-level scholarly conferences. His research interests include parallel and distributed computing, wireless communications, computer networks, cryptography and network security, data compression, image processing, and artificial intelligence and expert systems.

\* \* \*

**Jafar Ababneh** received his PhD degree from the Arab Academy for Banking and Financial Sciences in Jordan in 2009. He received his M.Sc degree in Computer Engineering from University of Yarmouk in Jordan in 2005. He earned his B.Sc in Telecommunication Engineering from University of Mu'ta in Jordan in 1991. In 2010, he joined The World Islamic Sciences and Education (WISE) University. He has published many research papers and book chapters in different fields of science in refereed journal and international conference proceedings. His research interest include: development and performance evaluation of multi-queue nodes queuing systems for congestion avoidance at network routers using discrete and continuous time, also his research interests include computer networks design and architecture, wire and wireless communication, artificial intelligence and expert system, knowledge base systems, security systems, data mining, and information.

**Hussein Abdel-Jaber** graduated and was awarded a BSc in Computer Sciences and Computer Information Systems from Philadelphia University, Jordan in 2003. He received his MSc in Mobile Computing from the University of Bradford, U.K. in 2004 and from the same university he received his PhD in the Research of Congestion Control of Networks and Network Performance Engineering. In 2009, he joined The World Islamic Sciences and Education (WISE) University as a head of the Departments of Computer Information Systems and Network Systems in the school of Information Technology. His research interests are in congestion control of networks (i.e. Internet), queuing networks analysis using discrete-time queues or continuous-time queues, networks performance engineering, fuzzy logic control, and data mining. He has several research papers in the previous research interests.

**Sattar J Aboud** is a Professor and Advisor for Science and Technology at Iraqi Council of Representatives. He received his education in United Kingdom. Aboud has served his profession in many universities and he was awarded the Quality Assurance Certificate of Philadelphia University, Faculty of Information Technology in 2002. Also, he was awarded the Medal of Iraqi Council of Representatives for his conducting the First International Conference of Iraqi Experts in 2008. His research interests include the areas of both symmetric and asymmetric cryptography, area of verification and validation, performance evaluation, and e-payment schemes.

**Haitham Y. Adarbah** is a Lecturer at the Department of Computer Science, Faculty of Computing Studies, Gulf College in Sultanate of Oman, which is affiliated with Staffordshire University, UK, since April, 2009. He Received the B.Sc. degree in Computer Science from AL-Zaytoonah University, Jordan, in 2004. He received his M.Sc degree in Computer Science from Amman Arab University for Graduate Studies, Jordan, in 2008. His research title is: "Modeling and Analysis of TCP in Wireless Networks." He has published many papers and book chapters. His research interests include: studying the performance of TCP protocol in wireless networks, developing efficient dynamic routing protocols for mobile ad hoc networks, wireless networks management and security, and ad hoc networks modeling and simulation.

**Muzhir Shaban Al-Ani** received his PhD in Computer and Communication Engineering Technology, ETSII, Valladolid University, Spain, 1994. He acted as Dean Assistant at Al-Anbar Technical Institute in Iraq (1985), Head of Electrical Department at Al-Anbar Technical Institute, Iraq (1985-1988), Head of Computer and Software Engineering Department at Al-Mustansyria University, Iraq (1997-2001), Dean of Computer Science and Information System Faculty at University of Technology in Iraq (2001-2003). In 2003, he worked as an Associate Professor at Applied Science University in Jordan. In 2005, he joined Amman Arab University in Jordan till now. His research interests include digital signal processing, parallel processing, digital filters, digital image processing, image compression, computer vision, information hiding, steganography, computer networks, wireless networks, next generation cellular mobile communications, management information systems, and management information technology.

**Ali H. Al-Bayatti** is currently a Research Fellow at Software Technology Research Laboratory – De Montfort University (UK). He received his PhD from the School of Technology at De Montfort University in 2009. He Obtained his BSc in Computer Engineering and Information Technology at Technology University (Iraq) in 2006. His research interests include mobile ad hoc networks, vehicular ad hoc networks, context-aware systems, ubiquitous and pervasive computing, and network and mobile Security. Ali has published a number of books, several papers, and articles in highly reputable journals and international conferences.

**Hilal Mohammed Al-Bayatti** received his Bachelor's degree in Mathematics from the College of Science, University of Baghdad (Iraq) in 1970. In 1977, he earned his M.Sc Degree in Computer Science from University of London (UK). He got his Ph.D. in Computer Science from Loughborough University of Technology (UK) in 1986. Prof. Al-Bayatti has more than 30 years experience in the computer sector as an IT consultant, and as a system project manager. In the field of education, he has more than 25 years experience in lecturing undergraduate and postgraduate courses in different universities. He has also supervised numerous postgraduate students projects leading towards M.Sc and Ph.D degrees. He received his professorship in January 2001. Prof. Al-Bayatti is a Vice President of Applied Science University at Kingdom of Bahrain since September 2007. His research interests include computer security, digital watermarking, cryptography, software engineering, and parallel computing.

**Alaa Al-Hamami** is presently Professor of Database Security and Dean of Computer Sciences and Informatics College, Amman Arab University, Jordan. He is a reviewer for several national and international journals and a keynote speaker for many conferences. He is supervising many PhD, MSc, and Higher Diploma thesis. His research is focused on distributed databases, data warehouse, data mining, cryptography, steganography, and network security.

**Ali Al-Khalidi** holds an M.Sc degree in Computer, Information, and Network Security from Depaul University of Illinois. He positioned himself in the IT industry when working as an R&D Network Systems Engineer at Texum Technologies, Inc. in Long Beach, CA, providing consultancies for SMEs in system consolidation and integration. Before that, he was a lead software engineer working for LEAD Technologies, Charlotte, NC, where he was involved in porting LEAD's award-wining toolkits (raster, vector, and medical imaging) to the Linux platform. His recent endeavors include: a consultancy job to employ NFC technology in tourism, as well as managing the IT infrastructure for the e-learning environment at King Khalid University, in Saudi Arabia, and prior to that he was leading a team of system administrators at Araby.com, the Arabic search engine of Maktoob.com, before it was acquired by Yahoo. Throughout his career, he served under different capacities, including software engineer, R&D engineer, senior systems and network administrator, and IT manager in both the private and public (government and education) sectors; maintaining a breadth wise coverage of technologies, yet an in-depth and hands-on experience in each. He holds industry certifications from Sun Microsystems, as well as GNU Linux, and he is a career-long advocate of the open source movement and its technologies. He is currently involved in building a virtual supercomputer for use in scientific computing while serving the capacity of a lecturer at Yanbu University College in Saudi Arabia.

**Hamed Al-Raweshidy** joined the Optoelectronics Group at Strathclyde University in 1987 after completing the postgraduate course in Optical Information Processing at Glasgow University. He subsequently obtained his PhD degree for work in the area of spread spectrum multiplexing for communication networks. Between 1990 and 1993 he worked as a research fellow at Oxford University where his main area of investigation was spread spectrum in satellite applications. During the summer of 1992, he worked with the Fiber Access Network Group at British Telecom Laboratories. In January 1993, he joined the Department of Electrical and Electronic Engineering at Manchester Metropolitan University as a Senior Lecturer. In November 1998, he joined the Department of Electronics at the University of Kent. He is currently a Professor and Group Leader of the Wireless Communications and Networks Research Group at Brunel University. He is a member of IEE and New York Academy of Sciences. He has been awarded a Nuffield research grant as a newly appointed university lecturer in science and engineering and UK-Dutch Scientific Research in collaboration with the International Research Centre for Telecommunications-Transmission and Radar, Delft University, Netherlands, for work involving the development of radio over fiber for 3G microcellular mobile communications. He has acted as guest editor for the *International Journal of Wireless Personal Communications Special Issue on Radio over Fibre Systems Technologies and Applications.* He is a member of several international conference advisory committees, such as VTC, PIMRC, and GLOBECOM, and has organized several workshops on wireless lightwave interaction and radio over fiber for 3G mobile communications in Europe and Japan. He is a member of journal editorial boards such as *Communications and Mobile Computing* and *Wireless Personal Communications*. His main areas of interest are radio over fiber, software radio networks, and IP mobility. He has published over 100 learned journal and conference papers in these areas. He is editor of a book entitled *Radio over Fiber Technologies for Mobile Communications Networks* (March 2002).

**Firas Albalas** completed his PhD degree in Computer Science on Feb 2009, in the area of Routing over Wireless Ad Hoc Networks from Glamorgan University, UK. After that he worked as an Assistant Professor at the University of Applied Science for one year then he moved to Jadara University as a Chairman for Computer Networks Department. His research interest includes computer networks, distributed systems, and simulation tool development.

**Abdel Rahman Alzoubaidi** is Associate Professor in the School of Engineering and Computing Sciences at NYIT Amman Campus, Jordan. At present, he teaches courses in telecommunications and computer networks, computer architecture, computer organization, logic circuit design, and operating system. His current research is in wired and wireless communication systems and their applications, cloud computing, and virtualization, performance evaluation. He has over 24 years of experience in teaching and conducting research in computer networks fields. He obtained his BSc and MSc in Computer Engineering in September 1985 from Gheorghe Asachi Technical University of Iasi, Romania, and PhD in Computer Networks from Sussex University (UK) in 1996.

**Alfonso Ariza-Quintana** is a PhD on Telecommunication Engineering at the University of Málaga since 2001. Previous to his university career, he worked in a private enterprise focusing on programming embedded systems. In 2001, he became an Associate Professor at the University of Málaga (Spain). His thesis deals with the problem of providing QoS in wired networks. The thesis was recognized as the Best Thesis in Telecommunication Services by the Spanish Association of Telecommunication Engineers in 2002. A significant workload in his thesis relied on the use of simulation tools for telecommunication networks. He is one of the main contributors and manager of the inetmanet framework for OMNeT++. He has been working in network simulation for more than 15 years. This experience has given him the opportunity to act as a member in the Technical Committee Program of Simulation-Based Conferences. He has participated in numerous international conferences about routing in wired and wireless network.

**Adriana Arteaga A.** is a Telematic Engineer graduated from Icesi University, Cali, Colombia in 2010. She is currently in Informatics and Telecommunications Research Group (i2T) of Icesi University as a Research Assistant, and she is also studying Master of Informatics Management and Telecommunication at Icesi University. Her research interests include wireless communications, more specifically, handover vertical and software-defined radio.

**Tatiana Balikhina** received her MSc. in Computer Engineering from Electrical Engineering Institute, St. Petersburg, Russia, 1989, researching Image Processing. Since graduation she has been involved in developing software for business applications. She was a Database Administrator and Main Developer for Finance Department at Petra University (PU) from 1998–2002. She joined the Faculty of Information Technology 2004 as Teacher Assistant. She was awarded a PhD in Computer Science from Oxford Brookes University, UK, in 2005 for her work on Network Architectures for Large Scale Distributed Virtual Environments. Since 2005 she has been an Assistant Professor in the Faculty of Information Technology at PU. She is involved in research relating to network architectures, distributed virtual environments, image processing, network performance, and computer and internet security awareness.

**Amjad Daoud** received his PhD degree from Virginia Tech, VA, in 1993. He joined Oracle Server Technologies and RDB Koda group to work as a Researcher and a Developer for two years on access methods and index organized tables. Later, he worked for EMC and Network Appliance. Currently, he is teaching at WISE University in Jordan. His research interests are algorithms, wireless networks, and access methods.

**Ciprian Dobre** received his PhD in Computer Science at the University Politechnica of Bucharest in 2008. He received his MSc in Computer Science in 2004 and the Engineering degree in Computer Science in 2003, at the same University. His main research interests are Grid computing, monitoring and control of distributed systems, modeling and simulation, advanced networking architectures, and parallel and distributed algorithms. He is a member of the RoGRID consortium and is involved in a number of national projects (CNCSIS, GridMOSI, MedioGRID, PEGAF) and international projects (MonALISA, MONARC, VINCI, VNSim, EGEE, SEE-GRID, EU-NCIT). His research activities were awarded with the Innovations in Networking Award for Experimental Applications in 2008 by the Corporation for Education Network Initiatives (CENIC).

**Khaled El-Zayyat** is a Professor and Director of DePaul University Campus in Jordan, most recently held the post of Chairman of the Computer Sciences Department at Amman University in Jordan. He has also held teaching positions at Al Al-Bayt University, the Arab Academy for Financial and Banking Studies and Jordan University for Women, all in Jordan. Prof. El-Zayyat earned his doctorate in Electrical Engineering from the University of Nevada at Reno. His area of specialization is routing algorithms and network security.

**Lina Escobar P.** is a Systems Engineer graduated from Autonoma de Occidente University, Cali, Colombia, in 2009. She is currently in Applied Informatics and Telematics Research Group (GITI) of Autonoma de Occidente University as a Research Assistant. Her research interests include mobile computing, wireless networks, next generation networks, and system management.

**Alexander Garcia D.** received his degree in Computer Engineering from Moscow State Technical University of Aviation - MGTUGA, Moscow (Russia) in 1995. He received his Master of Computer Science from Instituto Tecnologico de Monterrey - ITESM (Mexico) in 2005. Nowadays, he teaches Mobile Computing and Operating Systems at the Universidad Autonoma de Occidente (Cali, Colombia) and has been working on some research projects with financial support from Colciencias, a Colombian government Office for science, technology, and innovation. His current research topics are wireless networks, ubiquitous computing, and mobile IPTV.

**Fabio G. Guerrero** (M '93) received a B.Eng. degree in Telecommunications Engineering from the Universidad del Cauca, Popayan, Colombia, in 1992 and the M.Sc. degree in Real-Time Electronic Systems from Bradford University, U.K., in 1995. Currently, he works as Assistant Lecturer in the Department of Electrical and Electronics Engineering of the Universidad del Valle, Cali, Colombia, where he is also a member of the Research Group SISTEL-UV on telecommunication systems. His research interests include digital communications, telecommunication systems modeling, and next-generation networks.

**Ali H. Hadi** received the B.S. degree in Computer Science from Philadelphia University in 2002, MSc degree in CIS from Arab Academy for Banking and Financial Sciences in 2004, and Ph.D. degree from University of Banking and Financial Sciences in 2010. He is currently working as an Assistant Professor at Philadelphia University, Jordan. He worked for Arabnix as a Network Security Officer for more than 4 years. He also holds a number of well known technical certificates: CNI, CLP10, CLDA, CLA10, System P Administration, and RHCE. He has published many technical papers in leading Arab websites. His research interests include packet filtering, packet analysis, IDS/IPS systems, and penetration testing.

**Azmi Halasa** received his PhD and M.Sc desgrees in Computer Information Systems from the Arab Academy for Banking and Financial Sciences, Jordan, in 2010 and 2006, respectively. He received his B.Sc degree in Computer Science from the University of Jordan, Jordan, in 1993. He is currently working as a System Analyst and Database Designer. He has an excellent experience in computer network modeling and simulation. He also has a background in setting up, configuring, verifying, and troubleshooting network devices. He has published many papers in numerous leading scholarly and practitioner journals and conference proceedings. His research interests include simulation of computer networks, power conservation in wireless networks, routing protocols, system design and modeling, database systems, and distributed database systems.

**Shakir M. Hussain** received his B.A. degree in statistics from University of Al-Mustansiriyah, Iraq, in 1976, and his M.Sc. degrees in Computing and Information Science from Oklahoma State University, USA, in 1984. In 1997 he received his PhD degree in Computer Science from University of Technology, Iraq. From 1997 to 2008 he was a faculty member at Applied Science University, Jordan. Currently, he is working as an Associate Professor at the Computer Science Department at Petra University, Jordan. His research interest covers block cipher, key generation, authentication, and data compression. He is a member of ACM.

**Ghassan F. Issa** received his B.E.T degree in Electronic Engineering from the University of Toledo, Ohio, USA, in 1983, and B.S.EE in Computer Engineering from Tri-State University, Indiana, USA in 1984. He received his M.S. and Ph.D. in Computer Science from Old Dominion University, Virginia, USA, in 1987 and 1992 respectively. He was a faculty member and department chair of Computer Science at Pennsylvania College of Technology (Penn State) from 1992–1995. He also served as faculty member and the Dean of Computer Science at the Applied Science University in Amman, Jordan, from 1995-2007. Currently he is an Associate Professor and the Dean of Computer Science at Petra University in Amman, Jordan. His research interests cover block cipher and authentication.

**Souheil Khaddaj** is a Reader in the Faculty of Computing, Information Systems, and Mathematics, Kingston University where he leads the Component and Distributed Systems Research Group (CODIS). He completed his PhD at the Centre of Parallel Computing, Queen Mary College. He has been active in the areas of distributed computing, parallel processing, concurrency, applications and modelling of advanced computer architectures and networks since 1990. He has been involved in software development using novel technologies for numerous scientific and business applications, which range from numerical simulation to semantic distributed services. His research interests also include object and component technologies and applications, and meta-quality assurance and management frameworks for QoS use within the software development arena. Khaddaj has been involved, as principal or co-investigator, in a number of national and international research projects and various industrial partnerships, and he has authored/co-authored over 100 technical papers. Khaddaj has chaired/co-chaired a number of international conferences and workshops, and he is serving on many conferences' program committees. He has been a keynote/invited speaker at many national and international conferences and workshops.

**Manzoor Ahmed Khan** received the Bachelors of Engineering degree in Electronic Engineering from the Mehran University of Engineering and Technology (MUET), Pakistan, in 2001, the MS in Computer Science degree from Balochistan University of Engineering, Information Technology and Management Sciences, Pakistan, in 2005. He is pursuing his PhD at DAI Labor, Technical University, Berlin, since 2007. He is the author of several scholarly articles and book chapters. His distinction include a gold medal, silver medal, appreciation certificates, and best paper award during his educational and research career. His research interest includes the resource allocation, network selection algorithms, and representation of user Quality of Experience (QoE).

**Bippin Makoond** received his PhD from Kingston University. Currently he is a Senior Enterprise Architect at Cognizant Technology Solutions who functions as the Global Innovation Lead for the company's Banking and Financial Services practice. He published many papers in journals and conferences. He also holds 3 patents within the domain of wireless distributed systems and is a visiting scholar at Kingston University, London.

**Ali Maqousi** received his PhD in Computer Science from Oxford Brookes University, UK, 2003 for his work on providing Quality of Service (QoS) in packet switched networks. He was a Network Administrator and part-time Teacher Assistant at Petra University (PU) from 1993–1997 and full-time Teacher Assistant from 1999-2003. Since 2003 he is an Assistant Professor at the Faculty of Information Technology at PU, and currently, he is the Head of Computer Science and Networking Department. He is ITSAF Secretary - General (Information Technology Students Activity Fair, ITSAF is a yearly event for University students since 2005). He is the university liaison officer for European Union 7th Framework Program (FP7) and Tempus since 2007. He is involved in research relating to multi-service networking, network performance, security and privacy, and social networks.

**Roger McHaney** is a University Distinguished Teaching Scholar and Professor of Management Information Systems in Kansas State University's College of Business Administration. He currently serves as the Daniel D. Burke Chair for Exceptional Faculty. A K-State faculty member since 1995, McHaney teaches courses in enterprise systems and computing. His research areas include simulation, education technology, virtual worlds, and organizational computing. McHaney holds a doctorate in Computer Information Systems and Quantitative Analysis from the University of Arkansas. He has lectured in many countries including New Zealand, Australia, China, UK, India, Greece, and Italy. McHaney has published in numerous journals, written textbooks, and developed an array of instructional materials including ELATEwiki.org. He is currently working on several projects that investigate how technology and Web 2.0 impact higher education. McHaney spent a year as a Visiting Professor in the School of Computer and Information Sciences at the Auckland University of Technology, New Zealand. He is a member of Decision Sciences, Society for Computer Simulation, and the Informs College on Simulation. He was the co-recipient of the 2006 IRMA International Conference Best Paper Award for a fundamental paper on the modelling and simulation of wireless networks. He recently authored a book, *The New Digital Shoreline: How Web 2.0 and Millennials Are Revolutionizing Higher Education.*

**Andres Navarro C.** obtained the Electronic Engineer degree in 1993 and a Master of Technology Management in 1999, both from Universidad Pontificia Bolivariana in Medellin. He received the Doctor Ingeniero en Telecomunicacion degree from Universidad Politecnica de Valencia, Spain, in 2003. He is Full Professor at Universidad ICESI in Cali, Colombia, and the leader of i2T Research Group. Professor Navarro has been advisor of the National Science and Technology System in Colombia (Colciencias) and has participated in Cost 2100 Action. His research interests are wireless systems, planning and optimization of wireless system, and propagation models in the Andean and rainforest regions.

**Omar Raoof** received his B.Sc. degree in Information and Communication Engineering from Al-Khwarizmi College of Engineering-Baghdad University, Iraq, in 2005, received his M.Sc. in Mobile and Personal Communications from King's College London, UK, in 2007. He was recently granted a PhD degree in Game Theory Application in Cognitive Wireless Networks from Brunel University, Wireless Networks and Communications Centre. His research mainly focused on game theory application in multi-homed wireless nodes and game applications in wireless ad-hoc networks and applications related to spectrum sharing in cognitive wireless networks.

**Abdullah A. Rashed** received his first degree in Computer Science from Applied Science University, Amman, Jordan, in 1997. In 2000, he obtained his Masters in Information System from Arab Academy, Amman, Jordan. In 2004, he got his PhD in Computer Information Systems from Arab Academy, Amman, Jordan. Currently, he is a Researcher in Algoritmi Centre, University of Minho, Azurem Campus, Portugal. His research interests are biometrics and identity management.

**Alia Sabri** received her B.Sc degree in Computer Science from Jordan University of Science and Technology (Jordan) in 2002. She received her M.Sc and PhD in Computer Information Systems from the Arab Academy for Banking and Financial Sciences (Jordan) in 2005 and 2009, respectively. She is currently working as an Assistant Professor at the Applied Science University, Jordan. Her current research interests are in developing efficient dynamic routing protocols for mobile ad hoc networks, wireless networks management and security, and ad hoc networks modeling and simulation.

**Henrique M. Dinis Santos** received his first degree in Electric and Electronic Engineering from the University of Coimbra, Portugal, in 1984. In 1996, he got his PhD in Computer Engineering from the University of the Minho, Portugal. Currently, he is an Associate Professor in the Information Technology and Communications Group at the University of Minho. He is also the President of National Technical Committee (CT 136) for the Information System Security Standards. During the second semester of 1990, under an ERASMUS program, he was teaching in the University of Bristol, United Kingdom, where he was recognized as university academic staff.

**Nurul I. Sarkar** is a Senior Lecturer ATB in the School of Computing and Mathematical Sciences at the Auckland University of Technology, New Zealand. He is the author/co-author of more than 80 refereed technical articles and a book. He is an associate technical editor for the *IEEE Communications Magazine*, and member of various international editorial review boards. He was the recipient of 2009 Academic Staff Doctoral Study Award, and co-recipient of the 2009 IJICTE Editor's award for most outstanding paper for a research article on Miniproject-based learning as an effective tool for teaching advanced computer networks to graduate students. He was the co-recipient of the 2006 IRMA International Conference Best Paper Award for a fundamental paper on the modelling and simulation of wireless networks. Dr Sarkar served as TPC co-chair for mobile and wireless track (IEEE ATNAC 2010) and wireless and communication track (IEEE TENCON 2010). He was a local organising committee member for hosting Asia Pacific Computer Communications Conference 2010 in Auckland. He served as TPC member for various leading networking conferences (e.g. IEEE Globecom, UbiCoNet, ISCC, ICCS, and ICCIT) as well as track and session chairs for several national and international forums.

**Gerald Schaefer** gained his BSc. in Computing from the University of Derby and his PhD in Computer Vision from the University of East Anglia. He worked at the Color and Imaging Institute, University of Derby (1997-1999), in the School of Information Systems, University of East Anglia (2000-2001), in the School of Computing and Informatics at Nottingham Trent University (2001-2006), and in the School of Engineering and Applied Science at Aston University (2006-2009) before joining the Department of Computer Science at Loughborough University. He has published extensively with a total publication count of about 250. He is a member of the editorial board of several international journals, reviews for over 60 journals and served on the program committee of more than 200 conferences. He has been invited as plenary speaker to several conferences, is the organizer of various international workshops and special sessions at conferences, and the editor of several books and special journal issues.

**Miroslav Škorić**, YT7MPB, has been a licensed radio amateur since 1989. During the nineties, he maintained various types of amateur radio bulletin board systems (based on MS DOS™, Windows™ and Linux platforms) with VHF/HF radio frequency and Internet inputs/outputs in the amateur radio union of Vojvodina province and several clubs-societies. He has voluntarily served as the information manager and union's secretary, where he was compiling technical and scientific information for broadcasting via local amateur radio frequencies and repeaters. His teaching experience includes classes in a local high-school amateur radio club, tutorials on the amateur radio in engineering education, and paper presentations during domestic and international conferences. He has also authored several magazine and journal articles related to amateur radio, as well as a dedicated web page http://tldp.org/HOWTO/FBB. html, which includes user manuals for amateur radio e-mail servers. He is an active member of IEEE Computer Society, Communications Society, ACM, and WSEAS.

**Enrique Stevens-Navarro** received the B.Sc. degree in Electronic Engineering with Major in Communications from Universidad Autonoma de San Luis Potosí (UASLP), San Luis Potosi, Mexico, in

2000, the M.Sc. degree in Electronic Engineering with Major in Telecommunications from Instituto Tecnologico y de Estudios Superiores de Monterrey (ITESM), Campus Monterrey, Nuevo Leon, Mexico, in 2002, and the Ph.D. degree in Electrical and Computer Engineering from the University of British Columbia (UBC), British Columbia, Canada, in 2008. He is currently an Assistant Professor with the Faculty of Science of UASLP. His research interests include the design and evaluation of vertical handoff algorithms for heterogeneous wireless networks as well as resource management and protocol design for communication networks. Dr. Stevens-Navarro is member of the IEEE Communications Society since 1999, member of the IEICE Communications Society since 2010, and member of the Mexican National Research System since 2010.

**Umar Toseef** received his Bachelor of Science in Electrical Engineering degree from the University of Engineering and Technology, Lahore, Pakistan, in 2004. In 2007, he received his Master of Science in Communication and Information Technology degree from University of Bremen, Bremen, Germany. Right after completing his master studies he was appointed as a Research Assistant at Center for Computer Science and Information Technology (TZI) at the University of Bremen in the Communication Networks (ComNets) group. From 2006 until 2008, he contributed in research programs under ScaleNet project funded by the German Ministry of Education and Research (BMBF). Since 2009 he has been working in two research projects on LTE (Long Term Evolution) system level studies and LTE transport network dimensioning funded by Nokia Siemens Networks. He is pursuing his PhD at ComNets, University of Bremen. His contributions to research literature include several scholarly articles and patents (pending for approval).

**Alicia Triviño-Cabrera** is a PhD on Telecommunication Engineering. She was granted a scholarship to do her PhD at the University of Málaga (Spain) in 2004. Her thesis focused on Mobile Ad Hoc Networks (MANET) connected to the Internet and how the knowledge of link duration can improve this connection. For this task, she had the opportunity to work at prestigious research centers such as the Samsung Advanced Institute of Technology (South Korea) and the University of Coimbra (Portugal). An important workload of the thesis was dealing with simulation tools for MANETs. After defending her thesis in 2007, she worked for the Spanish government and for France Telecom R&D. Since 2010, she is an Assistant Professor at the University of Málaga (Spain). She has participated in numerous international conferences about multihop wireless networks. She has also an extensive experience on the review of research works on MANETs in international conferences and prestigious journals.

**Shao Ying Zhu** is a Senior Lecturer in the School of Computing and Mathematics at the University of Derby. She received her PhD degree from the Color Imaging Institute at the University of Derby in 2002. She has published a large number of conference papers and journal articles on a range of research areas such as color research, image processing, e-learning, and networking. Her current research interests are in e-learning, network security, mobile computing, and wireless networks.

# Index